TRAINING & REFERENCE

murach's
JavaScript

2ND EDITION

Mary Delamater

MIKE MURACH & ASSOCIATES, INC.
4340 N. Knoll Ave. • Fresno, CA 93722
www.murach.com • murachbooks@murach.com

Editorial team

Authors: Mary Delamater

Editor: Mike Murach

Production: Maria Spera
                       Cyndi Martinez

Books for web developers

Murach's Dreamweaver CC 2014

Murach's HTML5 and CSS3 (3rd Edition)

Murach's JavaScript (2nd Edition)

Murach's jQuery (2nd Edition)

Murach's PHP and MySQL (2nd Edition)

Murach's Java Servlets and JSP (3rd Edition)

Murach's ASP.NET Web Programming with C#

Murach's ASP.NET Web Programming with VB

Books on core Java, C#, and Visual Basic

Murach's Beginning Java with NetBeans

Murach's Beginning Java with Eclipse

Murach's Java Programming (4th Edition)

Murach's Android Programming

Murach's C#

Murach's Visual Basic

Books for database programmers

Murach's MySQL (2nd Edition)

Murach's SQL Server 2012 for Developers

Murach's Oracle SQL and PL/SQL for Developers (2nd Edition)

For more on Murach books, please visit us at www.murach.com

Printed in the United States of America

10 9 8 7 6 5 4 3 2 1
ISBN: 978-1-890774-85-1

Content

Expanded contents

Chapter 6   How to test and debug a JavaScript application

Section 2   JavaScript essentials

Chapter 7   How to work with numbers, strings, and dates

Section 3 Advanced JavaScript skills

Introduction

Today, JavaScript is used on most of the pages of a modern, commercial website. That's why you can think of JavaScript as one of the four technologies that every web developer should master. The first three are HTML5, CSS3, and JavaScript. The fourth is jQuery, but jQuery is a JavaScript library that requires JavaScript skills, so you need to learn JavaScript first.

The problem is that JavaScript is surprisingly difficult to learn, especially if you're coming from an HTML and CSS background. But JavaScript can also be difficult for experienced programmers because it has some quirks that you just don't find in most other languages. That's why we knew we had to do something different if we wanted this book to work for both novices and experienced programmers.

What this book does

This book is divided into three sections that represent the three levels of expertise that you'll develop with this book.

- Section 1 of this book presents a six-chapter course in JavaScript that gets you off to a great start. This section works for programming novices as well as experienced programmers because it lets you set your own pace. If you're a beginner, you'll move slowly and do all the exercises. If you have some experience, you'll move more quickly and do the exercises that you choose. When you finish this section, you'll be able to develop real-world, JavaScript applications of your own.

- Section 2 presents the essential JavaScript skills that every web developer should have. The six chapters in this section not only expand upon what you've learned in section 1, but they also present new skills like how to use arrays, web storage, and JavaScript libraries...how to create object-oriented JavaScript applications...how to handle exceptions...and how to use regular expressions.

- When you're ready to take your skills to the expert level, section 3 presents the advanced skills that you're going to need. These include skills like how to work with images, events, and timers as you build applications like slide shows...how to use closures, callbacks, namespaces, and the module pattern to make your applications bulletproof...and how to use JSON to transmit and store data. This section finishes with an introduction to jQuery that shows you how it can make your JavaScript code even better.

Why you'll learn faster and better with this book

Like all our books, this one has features that you won't find in competing books. That's why we believe you'll learn faster and better with our book than with any other. Here are a few of those features.

- This book is designed to teach you the skills you're going to need on the job without wasting your time on skills that you aren't likely to need. That sounds simple, but most JavaScript books either overwhelm you with information that you'll never need or trivialize the subject by avoiding all of the complications. For instance, this book shows you enough about DOM scripting with JavaScript that you know the basics, but it doesn't go much beyond that since you should use jQuery for most of your DOM scripting.

- If you page through this book, you'll see that all of the information is presented in "paired pages," with the essential syntax, guidelines, and examples on the right page and the perspective and extra explanation on the left page. This helps you learn faster by reading less...and this is the ideal reference format when you need to refresh your memory about how to do something.

- To show you how JavaScript works, this book presents more than 30 complete JavaScript applications that range from the simple to the complex. We believe that studying the program code for complete applications is still the best way to learn a new language. And we think that this is the missing ingredient in most other JavaScript books.

- Of course, this book also presents dozens of short examples, so it's easy to find an example that shows you how to do what you want to do. Even better, our paired pages make it much easier to find the example that you're looking for than it is with traditional books in which the examples are embedded in the text.

- Like all our books, this one has exercises at the end of each chapter that give you hands-on experience by letting you practice what you've learned. These exercises also encourage you to experiment and to apply what you've learned in new ways...just as you'll have to do on the job.

What software you need

To develop JavaScript applications, you can use any text editor. However, a text editor that includes syntax coloring and auto-completion will help you develop applications more quickly and with fewer errors. That's why we recommend Aptana Studio 3 for both Windows and Mac OS users. Although Aptana is free, it provides many powerful features.

Then, to test a web page, we recommend that you do your primary testing with Google's Chrome browser. As you will see, this browser's developer tools have excellent features for testing and debugging your JavaScript applications.

If you decide to use Aptana, chapter 1 presents a short tutorial that will get you started right. And to help you install Aptana and Chrome, appendix A provides the website addresses and procedures that you need for both Windows and Mac systems.

How our downloadable files can help you learn

If you go to our website at www.murach.com, you can download all the files that you need for getting the most from this book. This includes:

- the files for all of the applications in this book
- the files that you will use as the starting points for the exercises
- the files that provide the solutions to the exercises

These files let you test, review, and copy the code. If you have any problems with the exercises, the solutions are there to help you over the learning blocks, an essential part of the learning process. And in some cases, the solutions will show you a more elegant way to handle a problem, even when you've come up with a solution that works. Here again, appendix A shows you how to download and install these files.

Support materials for trainers and instructors

If you're a corporate trainer or a college instructor who would like to use this book for a course, we offer the supporting materials you need: (1) a complete set of PowerPoint slides that you can use to review and reinforce the content of the book; (2) instructional objectives that describe the skills a student should have upon completion of each chapter; (3) test banks that measure mastery of those skills; (4) extra exercises and projects that prove mastery; and (5) solutions to the extra exercises and projects.

To learn more about these materials, please go to our website at www.murachforinstructors.com if you're an instructor. Or if you're a trainer, please go to www.murach.com and click on the *Courseware for Trainers* link, or contact Kelly at 1-800-221-5528 or kelly@murach.com.

Companion books

Because most DOM scripting should be done with jQuery, not with JavaScript, *Murach's jQuery* is the perfect companion to this JavaScript book. It presents all of the jQuery and jQuery UI skills that you'll need on the job, including how to create and use jQuery plugins, how to use Ajax and JSON, how to use the Google Maps API, and much more. It is also a great reference.

Besides JavaScript and jQuery, the best web developers also master HTML5 and CSS3. To that end, you'll find that *Murach's HTML5 and CSS3* is another perfect companion to this JavaScript book. With all three books at your side, you'll be able to develop web pages that use HTML5, CSS3, JavaScript, and jQuery the way the best professionals use them.

To find out more about our new books and latest editions, please go to our website at www.murach.com. There, you'll find the details for all of our books, including complete tables of contents.

Please let us know how this book works for you

From the start of this project, we had three goals. First, we wanted to improve upon the first edition of this book so this new edition will help you learn faster and better than ever. Second, we wanted to make sure that this book presents all of the JavaScript skills that you are likely to need on the job, including expert-level skills. Third, we wanted to make this the best on-the-job reference you've ever used.

Now, we hope we've succeeded. We thank you for buying this book. We wish you all the best with your JavaScript development. And if you have any comments, we would appreciate hearing from you.

Mary Delamater, Author
maryd@techknowsolve.com

Mike Murach
Editor and Publisher

Section 1

Get off to a fast start with JavaScript programming

The chapters in this section are designed to get you off to a fast start with JavaScript programming. First, chapter 1 presents the concepts and terms that you need for developing JavaScript applications. It also shows you how to use the Aptana IDE that we recommend for developing JavaScript applications.

Then, chapter 2 presents a starting subset of the JavaScript language. Chapters 3 and 4 complete that subset. Chapter 5 shows you how to use that subset for DOM scripting, the predominant use of JavaScript. And chapter 6 shows you how to test and debug your JavaScript applications.

At that point, you'll be well on your way to developing JavaScript applications at a professional level. Then, you can expand your skills by reading any of the chapters in section 2 or 3 of this book.

1

Introduction to web development

This chapter presents the background concepts, terms, and skills that you need for developing JavaScript applications. That includes a quick review of the HTML and CSS skills that you need. That also includes a quick tutorial on how to use Aptana Studio 3, which is the IDE that we recommend for developing JavaScript applications.

If you have some web development experience, you should be able to go through this chapter quickly by skimming the topics that you already know. But if you're new to web development, you should take the time to master the concepts and terms of this chapter.

How a web application works

A web application consists of many components that work together as they bring the application to your computer or mobile device. Before you can start developing JavaScript applications, you should have a basic understanding of how these components work together.

The components of a web application

The diagram in figure 1-1 shows that web applications consist of *clients* and a *web server.* The clients are the computers, tablets, and mobile devices that use the web applications. They access the web pages through *web browsers.* The web server holds the files that make up a web application.

A *network* is a system that allows clients and servers to communicate. The *Internet* is a large network that consists of many smaller networks. In a diagram like the one in this figure, the "cloud" represents the network or Internet that connects the clients and servers.

In general, you don't need to know how the cloud works. But you should have a general idea of what's going on.

To start, networks can be categorized by size. A *local area network* (*LAN*) is a small network of computers that are near each other and can communicate with each other over short distances. Computers in a LAN are typically in the same building or adjacent buildings. This type of network is often called an *intranet*, and it can be used to run web applications for use by employees only.

In contrast, a *wide area network* (*WAN*) consists of multiple LANs that have been connected. To pass information from one client to another, a router determines which network is closest to the destination and sends the information over that network. A WAN can be owned privately by one company or it can be shared by multiple companies.

An *Internet service provider* (*ISP*) is a company that owns a WAN that is connected to the Internet. An ISP leases access to its network to companies that need to be connected to the Internet.

The components of a web application

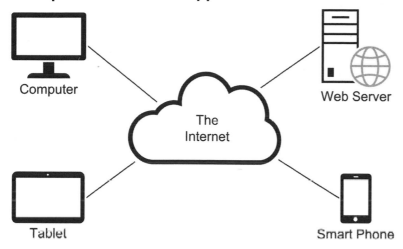

Computer

Web Server

The
Internet

Tablet

Smart Phone

Description

- A web application consists of clients, a web server, and a network.
- The *clients* use programs known as *web browsers* to request web pages from the web server. Today, the clients can be computers, smart phones like the iPhone, or tablets like the iPad.
- The *web server* returns the pages that are requested to the browser.
- A *network* connects the clients to the web server.
- An *intranet* is a *local area network* (or *LAN*) that connects computers that are near each other, usually within the same building.
- The *Internet* is a network that consists of many *wide area networks* (*WANs*), and each of those consists of two or more LANs. Today, the Internet is often referred to as "the Cloud", which implies that you really don't have to understand how it works.
- An *Internet service provider* (*ISP*) owns a WAN that is connected to the Internet.

Figure 1-1   The components of a web application

How static web pages are processed

A *static web page* like the one in figure 1-2 is a web page that doesn't change each time it is requested. This type of web page is sent directly from the web server to the web browser when the browser requests it. You can spot static pages in a web browser by looking at the extension in the address bar. If the extension is .htm or .html, the page is probably a static web page.

The diagram in this figure shows how a web server processes a request for a static web page. This process begins when a client requests a web page in a web browser. To do that, the user can either type the address of the page into the browser's address bar or click a link in the current page that specifies the next page to load.

In either case, the web browser builds a request for the web page and sends it to the web server. This request, known as an *HTTP request*, is formatted using the *HyperText Transfer Protocol* (HTTP), which lets the web server know which file is being requested.

When the web server receives the HTTP request, it retrieves the requested file from the disk drive. This file contains the *HTML* (*HyperText Markup Language*) for the requested page. Then, the web server sends the file back to the browser as part of an *HTTP response*.

When the browser receives the HTTP response, it *renders* (translates) the HTML into a web page that is displayed in the browser. Then, the user can view the content. If the user requests another page, either by clicking a link or typing another web address into the browser's address bar, the process begins again.

A static web page at http://www.modulemedia.com/ourwork/index.html

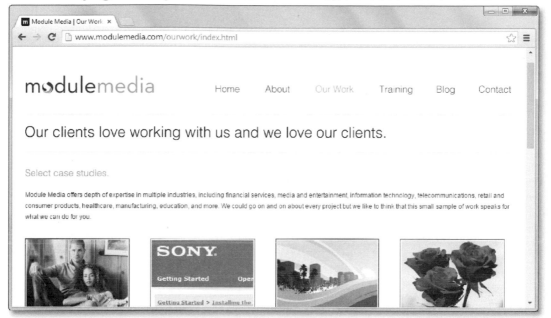

How a web server processes a static web page

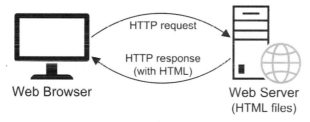

Web Browser

HTTP request

HTTP response
(with HTML)

Web Server
(HTML files)

Description

- *Hypertext Markup Language* (*HTML*) is the language used to define the content for the web pages of an application.

- A *static web page* is an HTML document that's stored on the web server and doesn't change. The filenames for static web pages have .htm or .html extensions.

- When the user requests a static web page, the browser sends an *HTTP request* to the web server that includes the name of the file that's being requested.

- When the web server receives the request, it retrieves the HTML for the web page and sends it back to the browser as part of an *HTTP response*.

- When the browser receives the HTTP response, it *renders* the HTML into a web page that is displayed in the browser.

Figure 1-2   How static web pages are processed

How dynamic web pages are processed

A *dynamic web page* like the one in figure 1-3 is a page that's created by a program or script on the web server each time it is requested. This program or script is executed by an *application server* based on the data that's sent along with the HTTP request. In this example, the HTTP request identified the book that's shown. Then, the program or script retrieved the image and data for that book from a *database server*.

The diagram in this figure shows how a web server processes a dynamic web page. The process begins when the user requests a page in a web browser. To do that, the user can either type the URL of the page into the browser's address bar, click a link that specifies the dynamic page to load, or click a button that submits a form that contains the data that the dynamic page should process.

In each case, the web browser builds an HTTP request and sends it to the web server. This request includes whatever data the application needs for processing the request. If, for example, the user has entered data into a form, that data will be included in the HTTP request.

When the web server receives the HTTP request, the server examines the file extension of the requested web page to identify the application server that should process the request. The web server then forwards the request to the application server that processes that type of web page.

Next, the application server retrieves the appropriate program or script from the hard drive. It also loads any form data that the user submitted. Then, it executes the script. As the script executes, it generates the HTML for the web page. If necessary, the script will request data from a database server and use that data as part of the web page it is generating. The processing that's done on the application server can be referred to as *server-side processing*.

When the script is finished, the application server sends the dynamically generated HTML back to the web server. Then, the web server sends the HTML back to the browser in an HTTP response.

When the web browser receives the HTTP response, it renders the HTML and displays the web page. Note, however, that the web browser has no way to tell whether the HTML in the HTTP response was for a static page or a dynamic page. It just renders the HTML.

When the page is displayed, the user can view the content. Then, when the user requests another page, the process begins again. The process that begins with the user requesting a web page and ends with the server sending a response back to the client is called a *round trip*.

A dynamic web page at amazon.com

How a web server processes a dynamic web page

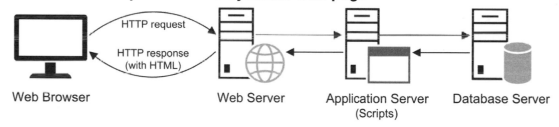

Description

- A *dynamic web page* is a web page that's generated by a program or script that is running on a server.

- When a web server receives a request for a dynamic web page, it looks up the extension of the requested file to find out which *application server* should process the request.

- When the application server receives a request, it runs the specified script. Often, this script uses the data that it gets from the web browser to get the appropriate data from a *database server*. This script can also store the data that it receives in the database.

- When the application server finishes processing the data, it generates the HTML for a web page and returns it to the web server. Then, the web server returns the HTML to the web browser as part of an HTTP response.

Figure 1-3   How dynamic web pages are processed

How JavaScript is used for client-side processing

In contrast to the server-side processing that's done for dynamic web pages, *JavaScript* is a *scripting language* that provides for *client-side processing*. In the web page in figure 1-4, for example, JavaScript is used to change the images that are shown without using server-side processing.

To make this work, all of the required images are loaded into the browser when the page is requested. Then, if the user clicks on one of the color swatches below a shirt, the shirt image is changed to the one with the right color. This is called an *image swap*. Similarly, if the user moves the mouse over a shirt, the image showing the front of the shirt is replaced with an image showing the back of the shirt. This is called an *image rollover*.

The diagram in this figure shows how JavaScript processing works. When a browser requests a web page, both the HTML and the related JavaScript are returned to the browser by the web server. Then, the JavaScript code is executed in the web browser by the browser's *JavaScript engine*. This takes some of the processing burden off the server and makes the application run faster. Often, JavaScript is used in conjunction with dynamic web pages, but it is also commonly used with static web pages.

Besides image swaps and rollovers, there are many other uses for JavaScript. For instance, another common use is to validate the data that the user enters into an HTML form before it is sent to the server for processing. This is called *data validation*, and that saves unnecessary trips to the server. Other common uses of JavaScript are to run slide shows and carousels and to provide information in tabs or accordions.

Over time, programmers have developed JavaScript libraries that contain code that makes it easier to do these and other common functions. The most popular of these libraries is *jQuery*, which you'll learn about in the last chapter of this book. In fact, jQuery is so popular that we've dedicated a whole book to it, called *Murach's jQuery*. But before you can learn jQuery, you need to learn JavaScript.

A web page with image swaps and rollovers

How JavaScript fits into this architecture

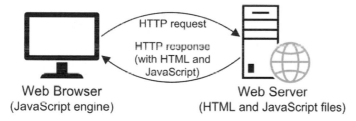

Three of the many uses of JavaScript and jQuery

- Data validation
- Image swaps and rollovers
- Slide shows

Description

- *JavaScript* is a *scripting language* that is run by the *JavaScript engine* of a web browser and controls the operation of the browser.

- When the browser requests an HTML page that contains JavaScript or a link to a JavaScript file, both the HTML and the JavaScript are loaded into the browser.

- Because JavaScript runs on the client, not the server, its functions don't require a trip back to the server. This helps an application run more efficiently.

- *jQuery* is a JavaScript library that makes it easier to do many of the common functions that JavaScript is used for.

Figure 1-4   How JavaScript is used for client-side processing

What you need to know about the ECMAScript specification

JavaScript was invented by NetScape in 1995 and released as part of the Netscape Navigator web browser in early 1996. In response, Microsoft developed a similar language called JScript and released it as part of the Internet Explorer web browser in late 1996.

Since there were differences between the two scripting languages, Netscape gave JavaScript to the *European Computer Manufacturers Association (ECMA)* to develop a standard. The standard is called the *ECMAScript specification*, and the first version was released in June 1997. Since then, there have been several versions. The latest version that's supported by all modern browsers is ECMAScript 5, which was originally released in December 2009 with an update in June 2011.

ECMAScript 5 added several important features to JavaScript, as described in figure 1-5. These features are fully supported by all modern browsers, and you'll learn how to use these features in this book. However, a few of these features won't work in older browsers like Internet Explorer 7, 8, and 9 (which can be referred to as IE7, IE8, and IE9).

If you need to support older browsers, then, you'll need to decide which ECMAScript 5 features to use. Or, you can add workarounds to your code that will make the features work in older browsers. You'll learn more about that in figure 1-17.

As this figure shows, ECMAScript 6 was released in June 2015, right before this book went to press. As result, it will take a while before this version is widely supported. To learn more about it, you can go to the URL that's shown in this figure.

The versions and release dates of the ECMAScript specification

Version	Release date
1	June 1997.
2	June 1998.
3	December 1999.
4	Abandoned, never released.
5	December 2009.
5.1	June 2011.
6	Scheduled for mid 2015.
7	In development.

Some of the important additions in the ECMAScript 5 specification

- Allows you to run in strict mode.
- Adds several methods that make it easier to work with arrays.
- Adds a safer way to create an object and more control over an object's properties.
- Adds a built-in way to work with *JavaScript Object Notation (JSON)*.

The URL for the ECMAScript 6 specification

`http://www.ecma-international.org/ecma-262/6.0/index.html`

Description

- Netscape invented JavaScript in 1995, and turned it over to the *European Computer Manufacturers Association (ECMA)* for standardization in 1996.
- The *ECMAScript specification* details the standards that scripting languages like JavaScript should meet.
- All of the ECMAScript 5 language features are supported by all modern browsers. Most, but not all, will also work on older browsers if you provide for cross-browser compatibility as shown in figure 1-17.
- In this book, you'll learn how to use the most important ECMAScript 5 features and also how to make them work in older browsers. Appendix B summarizes the ECMAScript 5 features that are presented in this book.
- As this book went to press, ECMAScript 6 was officially released. However, it will take a while before its features are widely supported. To learn more about it, you can go to the URL above.

Figure 1-5   What you need to know about the ECMAScript specification

The components
of a JavaScript application

When you develop a JavaScript application, you use HTML to define the content and structure of the page. You use CSS to format that content. And you use JavaScript to do the client-side processing. This is illustrated by the Email List application that is presented in the next three figures.

Figure 1-6 starts with the user interface for the application. It asks the user to make three entries and then click on the Join our List button. The asterisks to the right of the text boxes for the entries indicate that these entries are required.

When the user clicks on the button, JavaScript checks the entries to make sure they're valid. If they are, the entries are sent to the web server for server-side processing. If they aren't, messages are displayed so the user can correct the entries. This is a common use of JavaScript called *data validation* that saves a trip to the server when the entries are invalid.

You might have noticed that the user interface in this figure isn't much to look at. This is what a plain HTML document with no formatting looks like. In the next figure, though, you'll see how applying some CSS can improve its appearance.

The HTML

HyperText Markup Language (*HTML*) is used to define the content and structure of a web page. In figure 1-6, you can see the HTML for the Email List application. In general, this book assumes that you are already familiar with HTML, but here are a few highlights.

First, note that this document starts with a DOCTYPE declaration. This declaration is the one you'll use with HTML5, and you must code it exactly as it's shown here. If you aren't already using HTML5, you can see that this declaration is much simpler than the declaration for earlier versions of HTML. In this book, all of the applications use HTML5.

Second, in the head section of the HTML document, you can see a meta element that specifies that UTF-8 is the character encoding that's used for the page. Then, there is an HTML comment indicating that any link, style, and script elements go here in the head element. In the next figure, you'll see a link element that specifies the CSS file that should be used to format this HTML. And in the figure after that, you'll see a script element that specifies the JavaScript file that should be used to process the user's entries.

Third, in the body section, you can see the use of a main element. That is one of the HTML5 elements that we'll be using throughout this book. Within this element, you can see the use of h1, form, label, input, and span elements.

In this book, as you've just seen, we refer to *HTML elements* like the <link>, <script>, <main>, and <h1> elements as the link, script, main, and h1 elements. However, to prevent confusion when referring to one-letter elements like p and a elements, we enclose the letters in brackets, as in the <p> element or the <a> element.

The HTML file in a browser with no CSS applied to it

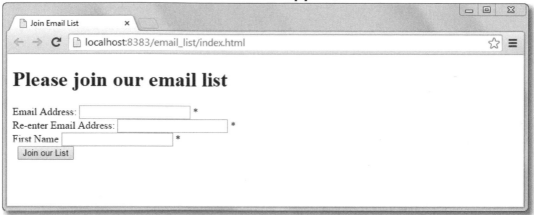

The code for the HTML file named index.html

```
<!DOCTYPE html>
<html>
<head>
    <meta charset="UTF-8">
    <title>Join Email List</title>
    <!-- link, style, and script elements go here -->
</head>
<body>
    <main>
        <h1>Please join our email list</h1>
        <form id="email_form" name="email_form"
              action="join.html" method="get">
            <label for="email_address1">Email Address:</label>
            <input type="text" id="email_address1" name="email_address1">
            <span id="email_address1_error">*</span><br>

            <label for="email_address2">Re-enter Email Address:</label>
            <input type="text" id="email_address2" name="email_address2">
            <span id="email_address2_error">*</span><br>

            <label for="first_name">First Name</label>
            <input type="text" id="first_name" name="first_name">
            <span id="first_name_error">*</span><br>

            <label> </label>
            <input type="button" id="join_list" value="Join our List">
        </form>
    </main>
</body>
</html>
```

Description

- *HTML (HyperText Markup Language)* is used to define the structure and content of a web page.
- To add CSS and JavaScript files to a web page, you code link and script elements in the head element. To embed CSS and JavaScript in a page, you code style and script elements.

Figure 1-6   The HTML for the web page

In practice, you'll often hear *elements* called *tags* so you can think of them as synonyms. In this book, we occasionally use the term *tag*, especially when referring to an opening tag like <h1> or a closing tag like </h1>.

The CSS

Not long ago, HTML documents were coded so the HTML not only defined the content and structure of the web page but also the formatting of that content. However, this mix of structural and formatting elements made it hard to edit, maintain, and reformat the web pages.

Today, *Cascading Style Sheets* (*CSS*) let you separate the formatting from the content and structure of a web page. As a result, the formatting that was once done with HTML should now be done with CSS.

In figure 1-7, then, you can see the link element that links the external CSS file to the HTML. As you saw in figure 1-6, this link element goes in the HTML head element. You can also see how this CSS has changed the appearance of the page in the browser.

After that, you can see the CSS that's used to format the HTML in the last figure. Here again, this book assumes that you are already familiar with CSS, but here is a quick description of what this CSS is doing.

In the rule set for the body element, the font-family property sets the font for the entire document, the margin property centers the body in the browser window, the width property sets the width of the body to 670 pixels, the border property puts a blue border around the body, and the padding property puts space between the contents and the right, left, and bottom borders. This is typical CSS for the applications in the book, just to make them look better.

Similarly, the rule sets for the h1, label, and input elements are intended to make these elements look better. For instance, the rule set for the h1 element sets the font color to blue. And the rule set for the labels floats them left so the text boxes will be to their right. This rule set also sets the width of the labels to 11ems, and it aligns the text for the labels on the right.

Then, the rule set for the input elements sets the left margin so there's space between the labels and the text boxes. It also sets the bottom margin so there's space after each label and text box.

Last, the rule set for the span elements sets the text color to red. When the HTML page is first loaded, these span elements only contain asterisks (*) to indicate that these entries are required. But the JavaScript changes those asterisks to error messages if the related entries are invalid, and it removes the asterisks if the related entries are valid.

The web page in a browser after CSS has been applied to it

The link element in the HTML head element that applies the CSS file

```
<link rel="stylesheet" href="email_list.css">
```

The code for the CSS file named email_list.css

```
body {
    font-family: Arial, Helvetica, sans-serif;
    background-color: white;
    margin: 0 auto;
    width: 670px;
    border: 3px solid blue;
    padding: 0 2em 1em;
}
h1 {
    color: blue;
}
label {
    float: left;
    width: 11em;
    text-align: right;
}
input {
    margin-left: 1em;
    margin-bottom: .5em;
}
span {
    color: red;
}
```

Description

- *Cascading Style Sheets* (*CSS*) are used to control how web pages are displayed by specifying the fonts, colors, borders, spacing, and layout of the pages.

Figure 1-7   The CSS for the web page

The JavaScript

Figure 1-8 shows how this application looks in a browser if the JavaScript finds any invalid data after the user clicks the Join our List button. Here, you can see that error messages are displayed to the right of the user entries for the second and third text boxes. In other words, the JavaScript has actually changed the contents of the span elements.

When JavaScript changes the HTML for a page, it is called *DOM scripting*. That's because the JavaScript is actually changing the *Document Object Model* (or *DOM*) that's generated by the browser when the page is loaded. This DOM represents all of the elements and attributes that are coded in the HTML. Then, when JavaScript changes any aspect of the DOM, the change is immediately made to the browser display too.

After the browser display, this figure shows the script element that links the external JavaScript file to the HTML. This element goes in the HTML head element.

Then, this figure shows the JavaScript for this application. Since you are going to learn how all of this code works in the next four chapters, you may want to skip over this code right now. But if you have any programming experience, it may be worth taking a quick look at it. In that case, here are a few highlights.

To start, this code consists of three functions: a $ function, a joinList function that is executed when the user clicks on the button, and a function that is run after the DOM has been loaded into the browser. Then, in the joinList function, you can see four if-else statements that provide most of the logic for this application.

Here, you can see that the if-else structures are similar to those in any modern programming language like Java, C#, or PHP. You can also see that declaring a variable (var) and assigning a variable is done in a way that's similar to the way that's done in other programming languages.

What's different about JavaScript is that it provides methods and properties that let you modify the DOM. For instance, the $ function uses the getElement-ById method to get the object with the id that's passed to the function. Then, the first statement in the joinList function uses the $ function to get the object that represents the first text box in the HTML. This statement also uses the value property to get the value that the user entered into that text box.

Later, the first if statement checks whether that value is an empty string (""), which means the user didn't make an entry. If it is, the JavaScript replaces the * in the span element for that text box with an error message. To do that, it uses this code:

```
$("email_address1_error").firstChild.nodeValue =
    "This field is required.";
```

Although this code may look daunting right now, you'll see that it's all quite manageable. You'll also come to realize that DOM scripting is where JavaScript get its power.

The web page in a browser with JavaScript used for data validation

The script element in the HTML head element that adds the JavaScript file

```
<script src="email_list.js"></script>
```

The code for the JavaScript file named email_list.js

```javascript
var $ = function(id) {
    return document.getElementById(id);
};
var joinList = function() {
    var emailAddress1 = $("email_address1").value;
    var emailAddress2 = $("email_address2").value;
    var isValid = true;

    if (emailAddress1 == "") {
        $("email_address1_error").firstChild.nodeValue =
            "This field is required.";
        isValid = false;
    } else { $("email_address1_error").firstChild.nodeValue = ""; }

    if (emailAddress1 != emailAddress2) {
        $("email_address2_error").firstChild.nodeValue =
            "This entry must equal first entry.";
        isValid = false;
    } else { $("email_address2_error").firstChild.nodeValue = ""; }

    if ($("first_name").value == "") {
        $("first_name_error").firstChild.nodeValue =
            "This field is required.";
        isValid = false;
    } else { $("first_name_error").firstChild.nodeValue = ""; }

    if (isValid) {
        // submit the form if all entries are valid
        $("email_form").submit(); }
};
window.onload = function() {
    $("join_list").onclick = joinList;
    $("email_address").focus();
};
```

Figure 1-8   The JavaScript for the web page

The HTML skills that you need for this book

Although this book assumes that you are already familiar with HTML, the next three topics present a quick review of the HTML skills that you're going to need for this book. If you don't already have these skills and you can't pick them up from the topics that follow, we recommend that you use *Murach's HTML5 and CSS3* as a reference while you're learning JavaScript.

How to use the HTML5 semantic elements

All of the applications in this book use the *HTML5 semantic elements* whenever they're appropriate. If you aren't already using them or at least familiar with them, figure 1-9 summarizes what you need to know.

In particular, the applications in this book use the main, section, aside, and nav elements. That makes it easier to apply CSS to these elements because you don't have to code id attributes that are used by the CSS. Instead, you can apply the CSS to the elements themselves.

Be aware, however, that older browsers like IE7 and IE8 won't recognize the HTML5 semantic elements, which means that you won't be able to use CSS to apply formatting to them. So, if you want your HTML5 and CSS to work in older browsers, you need to provide a workaround. You'll learn how to do that in figure 1-17.

The primary HTML5 semantic elements

Element	Contents
header	The header for a page.
main	The main content of a page. Can only appear once per page, and cannot be the child of an article, aside, footer, header, or nav element.
section	A generic section of a document that doesn't indicate the type of content.
article	A composition like an article in the paper.
aside	A portion of a page like a sidebar that is related to the content that's near it.
nav	A portion of a page that contains links to other pages or placeholders.
figure	An image, table, or other component that's treated as a figure.
footer	The footer for a page.

A page that's structured with header, main, and footer elements

```
<body>
    <header>
        <h1>San Joaquin Valley Town Hall</h1>
    </header>
    <main>
        <p>Welcome to San Joaquin Valley Town Hall. We have some
            fascinating speakers for you this season!</p>
    </main>
    <footer>
        <p>&copy; San Joaquin Valley Town Hall.</p>
    </footer>
</body>
```

The page displayed in a web browser

San Joaquin Valley Town Hall

Welcome to San Joaquin Valley Town Hall. We have some fascinating speakers for you this season!

© San Joaquin Valley Town Hall.

Description

- HTML5 provides new *semantic elements* that you should use to structure the contents of a web page. Using these elements can be referred to as *HTML5 semantics*.

- All of the HTML5 elements are supported by the modern browsers. They will also work in older browsers if you provide for cross-browser compatibility as shown in figure 1-16.

- This book also uses standard HTML elements like h1 and h2 elements for headings, img elements for images, <a> elements for links, and <p> elements for paragraphs.

Figure 1-9   How to use the HTML5 semantic elements

How to use the div and span elements

If you've been using HTML for a while, you are certainly familiar with the div element. It has traditionally been used to divide an HTML document into divisions that are identified by id attributes. Then, CSS can use the ids to apply formatting to the divisions.

But now that HTML5 is available, div elements shouldn't be used to structure a document. Instead, they should only be used when the HTML5 semantic elements aren't appropriate.

Note, however, that div elements are often used in JavaScript applications. If, for example, a section element contains three h2 elements with each followed by a div element, JavaScript can be used to display or hide a div element whenever the heading that precedes it is clicked. This structure is illustrated by the first example in figure 1-10, and you'll see how this works in chapter 5.

Similarly, span elements have historically been used to identify portions of text that can be formatted by CSS. By today's standards, though, it's better to use elements that indicate the contents of the elements, like the cite, code, and <q> elements.

But here again, span elements are often used in JavaScript applications, as shown by the second example in this figure. In fact, you've just seen this in the Email List application. In that application, JavaScript puts the error messages in the appropriate span elements.

The div and span elements

Element	Description
div	A block element that provides a container for other elements.
span	An inline element that lets you identify text that can be formatted with CSS.

Div elements in the HTML for a JavaScript application

```
<section id="faqs">
    <h1>jQuery FAQs</h1>
    <h2>What is JavaScript?</h2>
    <div>
        // contents
    </div>
    <h2>What is jQuery?</h2>
    <div>
        // contents
    </div>
    <h2>Why is jQuery becoming so popular?</h2>
    <div>
        // contents
    </div>
</section>
```

Span elements in the HTML for a JavaScript application

```
<label for="email_address1">Email Address:</label>
<input type="text" id="email_address1" name="email_address1">
<span id="email_address1_error">*</span><br>

<label for="email_address2">Re-enter Email Address:</label>
<input type="text" id="email_address2" name="email_address2">
<span id="email_address2_error">*</span><br>

<label for="first_name">First Name</label>
<input type="text" id="first_name" name="first_name">
<span id="first_name_error">*</span>
```

Description

- Before HTML5, div elements were used to define the structure within the body of a document. The ids for these div elements were then used by the CSS to apply formatting to the elements.

- Today, the HTML5 semantic elements are replacing div elements. That makes the structure of a page more apparent. However, you will still use div elements to define blocks of code that are used in JavaScript applications.

- Before HTML5, span elements were often used to identify portions of text that you could apply formatting to.

- Today, a better practice is to use specific elements to identify content. However, you will still use span elements for some JavaScript applications, like the Email List application in figures 1-6 through 1-8.

Figure 1-10   How to use the div and span elements

How to use the basic HTML attributes

Figure 1-11 presents the HTML *attributes* that are commonly used in JavaScript applications. You should already be familiar with the *id attribute* that identifies one HTML element and with *class attributes* that can be applied to more than one HTML element. You should also be familiar with the *for attribute* that relates a label to an input element and with the *title attribute* that can be used to provide a tooltip for an element.

When you use JavaScript, you will commonly use the *name attribute* so the server-side code can access the data that is submitted to it. You will sometimes add or remove class attributes to change the formatting of elements. And you will sometimes use title attributes to provide text that's related to elements.

In practice, you usually use the same value for the id and name attributes of an element. For instance, the example in this figure uses "email" as the value of both the id and name attributes for the text box. That makes it easier to remember the attribute values.

The basic HTML attributes

Attribute	Description
id	Specifies a unique identifier for an element that can be referred to by CSS.
class	Specifies one or more class names that can be referred to by CSS, and the same name can be used for more than one element. To code more than one class name, separate the class names with spaces.
name	Specifies a unique name for an element that is commonly used by the server-side code and can also be used by the JavaScript code.
for	In a label element, this attribute specifies the id of the control that it applies to.
title	Specifies additional information about an element. For some elements, the title appears in a tooltip when the user hovers the mouse over the element.

HTML that uses these attributes

```
<body>
    <h1>San Joaquin Valley Town Hall</h1>
    <h2 class="first_h2">Welcome to San Joaquin Valley Town Hall.</h2>
    <p>Please enter your e-mail address to subscribe to our
        newsletter.</p>
    <form id="email_form" name="email_form"
        action="join.html" method="get">
        <label for="email">E-Mail: </label>
        <input type="text" id="email" name="email"
            title="Enter e-mail address here.">
        <input type="button" value="Subscribe">
    </form>
</body>
```

The HTML in a web browser with a tooltip displayed for the text box

Description

- An *attribute* consists of an attribute name, an equals sign, and the value of the attribute enclosed in either single or double quotation marks.

- The *id* and *class attributes* are commonly used to apply CSS formatting,

- The *name attribute* is commonly used by the server-side code to access the data that is sent to it, but this attribute can also be used by the JavaScript code for a page.

- The *for attribute* in a label element is used to identify the control that it applies to.

Figure 1-11   How to use the basic HTML attributes

The CSS skills that you need for this book

Although this book assumes that you are already familiar with CSS, the next three topics present a quick review of the CSS skills that you're going to need for this book. If you don't already have these skills and you can't pick them up from the topics that follow, we recommend that you use *Murach's HTML5 and CSS3* as a reference while you're learning JavaScript.

How to provide the CSS styles for an HTML page

Figure 1-12 shows two ways that you can include CSS styles for an HTML document. First, you can code a link element in the head section of an HTML document that specifies a file that contains the CSS for the page. This is referred to as an *external style sheet*, and this is the method that's used for most of the applications in this book.

Second, you can code a style element in the head section that contains the CSS for the page. This can be referred to as *embedded styles*. In general, it's better to use external style sheets because that makes it easier to use them for more than one page. However, embedded styles can be easier to use for simple applications like the ones in this book because you don't need to create an extra file.

In some cases, you may want to use two or more external style sheets for a single page. You may even want to use both external style sheets and embedded styles for a page. In these cases, the styles are applied from the first external style sheet to the last one and then the embedded styles are applied.

Two ways to provide styles

Use an external style sheet by coding a link element in the head section

```
<link rel="stylesheet" href="styles/main.css">
```

Embed the styles in the head section

```
<style>
    body {
        font-family: Arial, Helvetica, sans-serif;
        font-size: 87.5%; }
    h1 { font-size: 250%; }
</style>
```

The sequence in which styles are applied

- Styles from an external style sheet
- Embedded styles

A head element that includes two external style sheets

```
<head>
    <title>San Joaquin Valley Town Hall</title>
    <link rel="stylesheet" href="../styles/main.css">
    <link rel="stylesheet" href="../styles/speaker.css">
</head>
```

The sequence in which styles are applied

- From the first external style sheet to the last

Description

- When you use *external style sheets*, you separate content (HTML) from formatting (CSS). That makes it easy to use the same styles for two or more pages.

- If you use *embedded styles*, you have to copy the styles to other documents before you can use them in those documents.

- If more than one rule for the same property is applied to the same element, the last rule overrides the earlier rules.

- When you specify a relative URL for an external CSS file, the URL is relative to the current file.

Figure 1-12   How to provide CSS styles for an HTML page

How to code the basic CSS selectors

Figure 1-13 shows how to code the basic *CSS selectors* for applying styles to HTML elements. To start, this figure shows the body of an HTML document that contains a main and a footer element. Here, the two <p> elements in the main element have class attributes with the value "blue". Also, the <p> element in the footer has an id attribute with the value "copyright" and a class attribute with two values: "blue" and "right". This means that this element is assigned to two classes.

The four rule sets in the first group of examples are *type selectors*. To code a type selector, you just code the name of the element. As a result, the first rule set in this group selects the body element. The second rule set selects the main element. The third rule set selects the h1 element. And the fourth rule set selects all <p> elements.

In these examples, the first rule set changes the font for the body, and all of the elements within the body inherit this change. This rule set also sets the width of the body and centers it in the browser. Then, the second rule set puts a border around the main element and puts some padding inside the border. It also makes the main element a block element. This is necessary for IE because it doesn't treat the main element as a block element.

The third rule set that uses a type selector sets the margins for the heading. In this case, all the margins are set to zero except for the bottom margin. Last, the rule set for the paragraphs sets the margins for the top, bottom, and left side of the paragraphs. That's why the paragraphs in the main element are indented.

The rule set in the second group of examples uses an *id selector* to select an element by its id. To do that, the selector is a pound sign (#) followed by the id value that uniquely identifies an element. As a result, this rule set selects the <p> element that has an id of "copyright". Then, its one rule sets the font-size for the paragraph to 90% of the default font size.

The two rule sets in the last group of examples use *class selectors* to select HTML elements by class. To do that, the selector is a period (.) followed by the class name. As a result, the first rule set selects all elements that have been assigned to the "blue" class, which are all three <p> elements. The second rule set selects any elements that have been assigned to the "right" class. That is the paragraph in the footer. Then, the first rule set sets the color of the font to blue and the second rule set aligns the paragraph on the right.

One of the key points here is that a class attribute can have the same value for more than one element on a page. Then, if you code a selector for that class, it will be used to format all the elements in that class. In contrast, since the id for an element must be unique, an id selector can only be used to format a single element.

As you probably know, there are several other selectors that you can use with CSS. But the ones in this figure will get you started. Then, whenever an application in this book requires other selectors, the selectors will be explained in detail.

HTML that can be selected by element type, id, or class

```
<body>
    <main>
        <h1>The Speaker Lineup</h1>
        <p class="blue">October 19: Jeffrey Toobin</p>
        <p class="blue">November 16: Andrew Ross Sorkin</p>
    </main>
    <footer>
        <p id="copyright"class="blue right">Copyright SJV Town Hall</p>
    </footer>
</body>
```

CSS rule sets that select by element type, id, and class

Three elements by type

```
body {
    font-family: Arial, Helvetica, sans-serif;
    width: 400px;
    margin: 1em auto; }
main {
    display: block;
    padding: 1em;
    border: 2px solid black; }
h1 { margin: 0 0 .25em; }
p { margin: .25em 0 .25em 3em; }
```

One element by ID

```
#copyright { font-size: 90%; }
```

Elements by class

```
.blue { color: blue; }
.right { text-align: right; }
```

The elements displayed in a browser

Description

- You code a selector for all elements of a specific type by naming the element. This is referred to as a *type selector*.
- You code a selector for an element with an id attribute by coding a pound sign (#) followed by the id value. This is known as an *id selector*.
- You code a selector for an element with a class attribute by coding a period followed by the class name. Then, the rule set applies to all elements with that class name. This is known as a *class selector*.

Figure 1-13   How to code the basic CSS selectors

How to code CSS rule sets

Figure 1-14 presents the CSS for the Email List application that was presented earlier in this chapter. This is typical of the CSS for the applications in this book. Since the focus of this book is on JavaScript, not CSS, the CSS for the book applications is usually limited. For instance, the CSS in this example doesn't require id or class selectors.

Just to make sure we're using the same terminology, this CSS contains six *rule sets*. Each rule set consists of a selector, a set of braces { }, and one or more *rules* within the braces. Also, each rule consists of a *property name*, a colon, the value or values for the rule, and an ending semicolon.

For instance, the first rule set is for the body element. It consists of six rules that set the font, background color, margins, width, border, and padding for the body. Here, the margin rule sets the top and bottom margins to zero and the right and left margins to "auto", which means the body will be centered in the browser window. And the padding rule sets the padding around the contents to 2 ems on the right and left and 1 em on the bottom. (An *em* is a typesetting term that is approximately equal to the width of a capital letter M.)

The second rule set is for the h1 element, and its one rule sets the color of the font to blue. Then, the third rule set is for the label elements, and the fourth rule set is for the input elements. The third rule set floats the labels to the left of the input elements, sets the labels to a width of 11 ems, and aligns the text in the labels on the right. The fourth rule set sets the left margin of the input elements to 1 em so there's separation between the labels and text boxes, and it sets the bottom margin to .5 em so there's some vertical spacing between the rows of labels and input elements.

The last rule set is for the span elements that follow the input elements. It just sets the color of the text in these elements to red because these elements will display the error messages for the application.

Beyond this brief introduction to CSS, this book will explain any of the CSS that is relevant to the JavaScript for an application. So for now, if you understand the rule sets in this figure, you're ready to continue.

The CSS file for a typical application in this book

```
body {
    font-family: Arial, Helvetica, sans-serif;
    background-color: white;
    margin: 0 auto;
    width: 670px;
    border: 3px solid blue;
    padding: 0 2em 1em;
}
h1 {
    color: blue;
}
label {
    float: left;
    width: 11em;
    text-align: right;
}
input {
    margin-left: 1em;
    margin-bottom: .5em;
}
span {
    color: red;
}
```

Description

- Because the focus of this book is JavaScript, not CSS, the CSS that's used in this book is usually simple. We just apply enough CSS to make each application look okay and work correctly.

- In fact, for most of the applications in this book, you won't have to understand the CSS so it won't even be shown. Whenever the CSS is critical to the understanding of the JavaScript application, though, it will be explained in detail.

- At the least, you should know that the CSS for an HTML document consists of one or more *rule sets*. Each of these rule sets starts with the selector for the rule set followed by a set of braces { }. Within the braces are one or more rules.

- You should also know that each CSS *rule* consists of a *property name*, a colon, the value or values for the property, and a semicolon.

Figure 1-14   How to code CSS rule sets

How to test a JavaScript application

Next, you'll learn how to test a JavaScript application. To do that, you run the HTML for the web page that uses the JavaScript.

How to run a JavaScript application

When you develop a JavaScript application, you're usually working on your own computer or your company's server. Then, to run the application, you use one of the four methods shown in figure 1-15. Of the four, it's easiest to run the HTML page from the IDE that you're using to develop the HTML, CSS, and JavaScript files. You'll learn more about that in a moment.

Otherwise, you can open the HTML file from your browser. To do that, you can press Ctrl+O to start the Open command. Or, you can find the file using the file explorer for your system and double-click on it. If you're using Windows, for example, you can find the file using Windows Explorer. That will open the page in your system's default browser. Of course, you can also run a new page by clicking on the link to it in the current page.

After an application has been uploaded to an Internet web server, you can use the second set of methods in this figure to run the application. The first way is to enter a *Uniform Resource Locator* (*URL*) into the address bar of your browser. The second way is to click on a link in one web page that requests another page.

As the diagram in this figure shows, the URL for an Internet page consists of four components. In most cases, the *protocol* is HTTP. If you omit the protocol, the browser uses HTTP as the default.

The second component is the *domain name* that identifies the web server that the HTTP request will be sent to. The web browser uses this name to look up the address of the web server for the domain. Although you can't omit the domain name, you can often omit the "www." from the domain name.

The third component is the *path* where the file resides on the server. The path lists the folders that contain the file. Forward slashes are used to separate the names in the path and to represent the server's top-level folder at the start of the path. In this example, the path is "/ourwork/".

The last component is the name of the file. In this example, the file is named index.html. If you omit the filename, the web server will search for a default document in the path. Depending on the web server, this file will be named index.html, default.htm, or some variation of the two.

The web page at c:/javascript/book_apps/ch01/email_list/index.html

Four ways to run an HTML page that's on your own server or computer

- From your browser, use the Ctrl+O shortcut key combination to start the Open command. Then, browse to the HTML file for the application and double-click on it.
- Use the file explorer on your system to find the HTML file, and double-click on it.
- Use the features of your text editor or IDE.
- Click on a link in the current web page to load the next web page.

Two ways to run an HTML page that's on the Internet

- Enter the URL of the web page into the browser's address bar.
- Click on a link in the current web page to load the next web page.

The components of an HTTP URL on the Internet

```
http://www.modulemedia.com/ourwork/index.html
```

protocol   domain name   path   filename

What happens if you omit parts of a URL

- If you omit the protocol, the default of http:// will be used.
- If you omit the filename, the default document name for the web server will be used. This is typically index.html, default.htm, or some variation.

Description

- When you are developing JavaScript applications, you usually store them on your own computer instead of the Internet. So when you test the applications, you run them from your own computer.
- Later, after the applications are deployed to your Internet web server, you can run the applications from the Internet.

Figure 1-15   How to run a JavaScript application

How to find errors in your code

As you enter and test even the simplest of applications, you're likely to have errors in your code. When that happens, the JavaScript may not run at all, or it may run for a short while and then stop. That's why figure 1-16 shows you how to find the errors in your code.

As this figure shows, if a JavaScript application doesn't run or stops running, you start by opening the *developer tools*. Although there are several ways to do that, you'll use the F12 key most of the time. That's why the developer tools for Chrome and other browsers are often referred to as the *F12 tools*.

Next, you open the Console panel of the developer tools to see if there's an error message. In this figure, the console shows a message for an error that occurred when the user started the Email List application, clicked on the Join our List button, and nothing happened.

Then, if you click on the link to the right of the error message, the JavaScript source code is displayed with the statement that caused the error highlighted. In this case, the problem is that "email_address" should be "email_address2" since that's the id of the second text box in the HTML.

In chapter 6, you'll learn more about testing and debugging, but this technique will be all that you need until your applications get more complicated.

Chrome with an open Console panel that shows an error

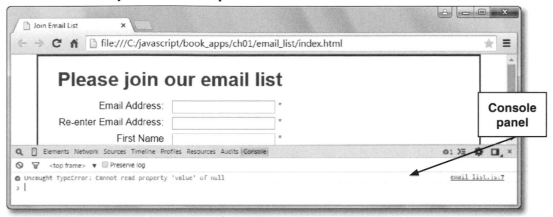

The Sources panel after the link in the Console panel has been clicked

How to open or close Chrome's developer tools

- To open the developer tools, press F12 or Ctrl+Shift+I. Or, click on the Menu button in the upper right corner of the browser, and select More Tools→Developer Tools.

- To close the developer tools, click on the X in the upper right corner of the tools panel or press F12.

How to find the JavaScript statement that caused the error

- Open the Console panel by clicking on the Console tab. You should see an error message like the one above along with the line of code that caused the error.

- Click on the link to the right of the error message that indicates the line of code. That will open the Sources panel with the portion of JavaScript code that contains the statement displayed and the statement highlighted.

Description

- Chrome's *developer tools* provide some excellent debugging features, like identifying the JavaScript statement that caused an error.

- Because you usually start the developer tools by pressing the F12 key, these tools are often referred to as the *F12 tools*.

Figure 1-16   How to find errors in your code

How to provide cross-browser compatibility

If you want your website to be used by as many visitors as possible, you need to make sure that your web pages are compatible with as many browsers as possible. That's known as *cross-browser compatibility*. That means you should test your applications on as many browsers as possible, including the five browsers in the table in figure 1-17. This table shows the variance in the levels of HTML5 compatibility for these browsers, which is significant.

Today, all modern browsers support the HTML5 semantic elements as well as ECMAScript 5 so you shouldn't have any problems with those browsers. It's the older browsers that you may need to be concerned about, especially IE7 and IE8 because they still represent a significant portion of the market. That's why this figure presents four workarounds for making your applications work with these older browsers.

The first workaround is called the *JavaScript shiv*. It ensures that the HTML5 elements will work with older browsers. To implement it, you code the first script element shown in this figure within the head element for a page. This shiv loads a JavaScript file into the web page that provides HTML5 compatibility with older browsers.

The second workaround is the normalize.css style sheet that will fix minor differences in the current browsers. To do that, you download the style sheet and include it as the first style sheet for all of your web pages.

The third workaround is a file named shim.js that provides for ECMAScript 5 compatibility. It is a JavaScript file that makes some (but not all) of the ECMAScript 5 features work with a browser that only supports ECMAScript 3. To implement this workaround, you code the second script element in this figure.

The fourth workaround is a file named sham.js, and it identifies ECMAScript 5 features that can't be implemented with ECMAScript 3. All this file can really do is make it so your application doesn't throw errors when you use the unsupported features. To implement this workaround, you code the third script element in this figure after the one for the shim.js file.

While you're learning, you won't need to test your web pages on old browsers. That's why none of these workarounds is used by any of the applications in this book. For production applications, though, you usually do need to provide for compatibility with older browsers. As you will see in chapter 6, you can test for compatibility with older versions of IE by using the developer tools for the current version of IE.

By the way, IE11 still doesn't support the HTML5 main element. To provide support for this element, though, you just need to use CSS to set its display property to block, as shown in the example in figure 1-13. Or, you can use the JavaScript shiv or the normalize.css style sheet to fix this problem.

The current browsers and their HTML5 ratings (www.html5test.com)

Browser	Release	HTML5 Test Rating
Google Chrome	43	526
Opera	29	519
Mozilla Firefox	38	467
Apple Safari	8	396
Internet Explorer	11	336

The code that includes the JavaScript shiv for HTML5 compatibility

```
<script src="http://html5shiv.googlecode.com/svn/trunk/html5.js"></script>
```

The URL for downloading the normalize.css style sheet

* http://necolas.github.io/normalize.css/

What the normalize.css style sheet does

* Normalize.css is a style sheet that makes adjustments to browser defaults so all browsers render HTML elements the same way. For instance, the normalize.css style sheet sets the margins for the body of the document to zero so there's no space between the body and the edge of the browser window. It also sets the default font family to sans-serif.

The code that includes the shim.js file for ECMAScript 5 compatibility

```
<script
src="https://cdnjs.cloudflare.com/ajax/libs/es5-shim/4.1.10/es5-shim.min.js">
</script>
```

The code that includes the sham.js file for ECMAScript 5 compatibility

```
<script
src="https://cdnjs.cloudflare.com/ajax/libs/es5-shim/4.1.10/es5-sham.min.js">
</script>
```

The difference between the shim.js and sham.js files

* The shim.js file contains ECMAScript 5 features that can be fully implemented using ECMAScript 3. Code that uses these ECMAScript 5 features will run properly in older browsers. The shim.js file can run without the sham.js file.

* The sham.js file contains ECMAScript 5 features that can't be implemented using ECMAScript 3. Code that uses these ECMAScript 5 features won't throw errors in older browsers, but won't run as expected either. The sham.js file requires the shim.js file.

Description

* To provide *cross-browser compatibility* for HTML5 and CSS3, you can use the *JavaScript shiv* and the *normalize.css style sheet*.

* To make sure the ECMAScript 5 features for JavaScript work on older browsers, you can use the shim.js and sham.js files.

* At this writing, you still need to provide workarounds for IE7 and IE8, but you shouldn't need to provide for other old browsers. However, you do need to use CSS to set the display property of the main element to block in all current versions of IE.

Figure 1-17   How to provide cross-browser compatibility

How to use Aptana
to develop JavaScript applications

Because HTML, CSS, and JavaScript are just text, you can use any text editor to create the files for a JavaScript application. However, a better editor or an *Integrated Development Environment* (*IDE*) can speed development time and reduce coding errors. That's why we recommend Aptana Studio 3. It is a free IDE that runs on Windows, Mac OS, and Linux, and it can greatly improve your productivity.

In the appendix for this book, you can learn how to install Aptana. You can also learn how to use Aptana for the common development functions in the topics that follow. If you prefer to use another editor, you can skip these topics. But even then, you may want to browse these topics because they will give you a good idea of what an IDE should be able to do. They may also encourage you to give Aptana a try.

How to create or import a project

In Aptana, a *project* consists of the folders and files for a complete web application. Once you create a project, it's easier to work with its folders and files, to create new files for the project, and so forth.

To create a project, you use the first command in figure 1-18 and complete the dialog boxes. The result is a named project that starts with the top-level folder for the application. Then, you can easily access the folders and files for the application by using the App Explorer window that's shown in the next figure.

To make it easier to work with the applications for this book, we recommend that you import them into one Aptana project that includes all of the book applications. To do that, you can use the second procedure in this figure. The dialog boxes in this figure import the downloaded book applications at this location

`c:/murach/javascript/book_apps`

into a project named JavaScript Book Apps. Once that's done, you can easily access the applications by using the App Explorer window.

The dialog boxes for importing a project in Aptana 3.4 or later

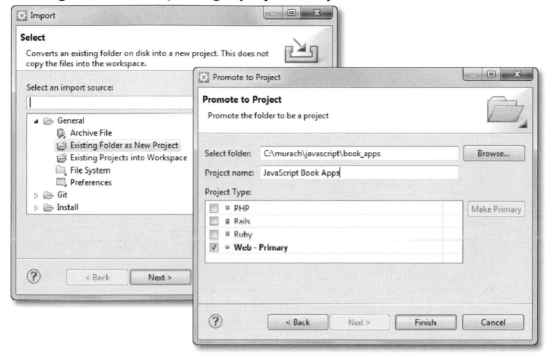

How to create a new project

• Use the File→New→Web Project command.

How to import a project with Aptana 3.4 or later

• Use the File→Import command to display the Import dialog box, click on Existing Folder as New Project, and click Next.

• In the Promote to Project dialog box, browse to the top-level folder for the application, enter a project name, and click the Finish button.

Description

• Aptana works the best when you set up projects for the web applications that you're developing and maintaining.

• In general, each Aptana *project* should contain the folders and files for one web application. For this book, however, you can set up one project for all of the book applications, one project for all exercises, and one project for all exercise solutions.

Figure 1-18   How to create or import a project in Aptana

How to work with files

Figure 1-19 shows how to open or close an HTML, CSS, or JavaScript file after you've created a project. Here, the JavaScript Book Apps project is shown in the App Explorer window on the left side of Aptana. If you have created more than one project, you can switch from one to another by using the drop-down project list that's at the top of the App Explorer window.

Once you have the correct project open, you can drill down to the file that you want to open by clicking on the plus signs for the folders. In this example, the ch01 and email_list folders have been expanded so you can see the four files for the Email List application. Then, to open a file, you just double-click on it.

When you open a file in Aptana, it is opened in a new tab. This means that you can have several files open at the same time and move from one to another by clicking on a tab. This makes it easy to switch back and forth between the HTML, CSS, and JavaScript files for a web page. This also makes it easy to copy code from one file to another.

If you want to open a file that isn't part of a project, you can do that by using one of the methods shown in this figure. First, you can use the Project Explorer window to locate the file on your computer and then double-click on it. Second, you can use the File→Open File command to open a file.

To close one or more files, you can use one of the three methods shown in this figure. This makes it easy to close all of the files except the ones that you're currently working with. And that helps you avoid the mistake of making a change to the wrong file.

This figure ends by showing how to start a new file. Most important is to name the file with the appropriate extension (.html, .css, or .js) depending on whether it is going to be an HTML, CSS, or JavaScript file. Then, Aptana will know what type of file it is, and its editor will be adjusted to the syntax of that type of file when it is opened.

As you work with Aptana, you'll see that it has the same type of interface that you've used with other programs. So if you want to do something that isn't presented in this chapter, try right-clicking on an item to see what menu options are available. Check out the other buttons in the toolbar. See what's available from the drop-down menus. With a little experimentation, you'll find that this program is not only powerful, but also easy to use.

Before you go on, you should notice the two yellow triangles with exclamation marks in them to the left of lines 1 and 5 in the JavaScript file. As you'll learn in the next figure, Aptana uses these markers to indicate warnings.

Aptana with the App Explorer shown and a JavaScript file in the second tab

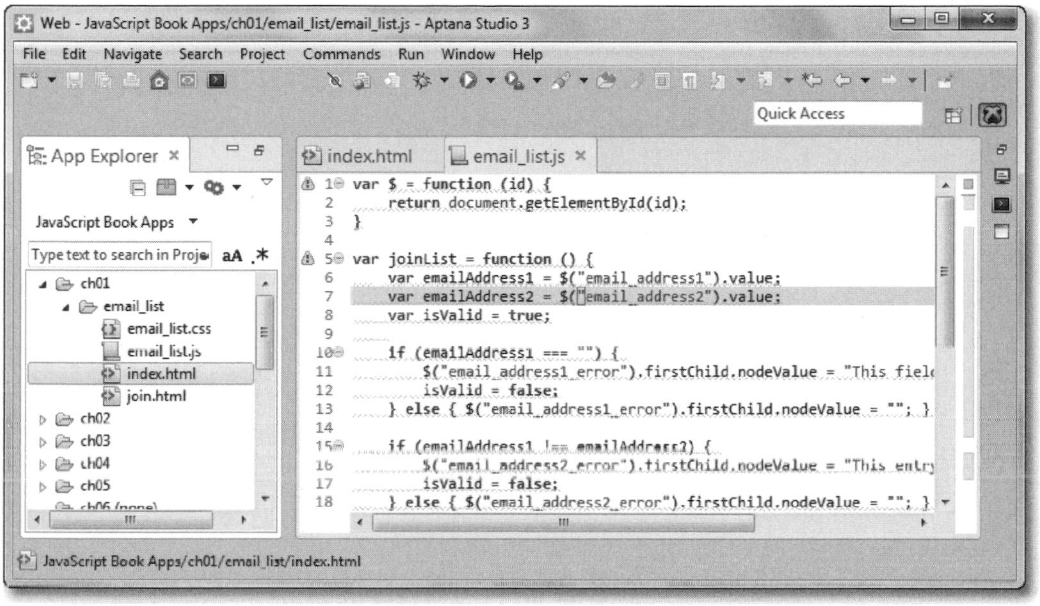

How to open a file within a project

- Use the drop-down list in Aptana's App Explorer to select the project. Then, locate the file in the App Explorer and double-click on it.

Two ways to open a file that isn't in a project

- Use the Project Explorer to locate the file, and double-click on it.
- Use the File→Open File command.

How to close one or more files

- To close one file, click on the X in the tab for the file.
- To close all of the files except one, right click on the tab you don't want to close and select Close Others.
- To close all of the files, right click on any tab and select Close All.

How to start a new file

- To start an HTML, CSS, or JavaScript file, select the File→New→File command. Then, in the New File dialog box, select the folder that the file should be stored in, enter a filename for the new file with an extension (.html, .css, or .js), and click the Finish button.
- To start a new file from another file, use the File→Save As command to save the file with a new name.

Figure 1-19   How to work with files in Aptana

How to edit a file

Figure 1-20 shows how to edit a JavaScript file with Aptana, but editing works the same for HTML and CSS files. When you open a file with an html, css, or js extension, Aptana knows what type of file you're working with so it can use color to highlight the syntax components. The good news is that color coding is also used for CSS that's in a style element of an HTML document or JavaScript that's in a script element of an HTML document.

As you enter a new line of code, the auto-completion feature presents lists of words that start with the letters that you've entered. This type of list is illustrated by this figure. Here, the list shows the JavaScript choices after the letter *t* has been entered. Then, you can select a word and press the Tab key to insert it into your code.

This also works with HTML and CSS entries. If, for example, you type <s in an HTML document, Aptana presents a list of the elements that start with s. Then, if you select one of the elements, Aptana finishes the opening tag and adds the ending tag. This feature also works when you start an attribute.

Similarly, if you enter # to start a CSS rule set, Aptana presents a list of the ids that can be used in an id selector. If you enter *b* to start a rule, Aptana presents a list of the properties that start with b. And if you start an entry for a property value, Aptana will present a list of values. In short, this is a powerful feature that can help you avoid many entry errors.

Beyond that, Aptana provides error markers and warning markers that help you find and correct errors. In this figure, for example, you can see two error markers and a warning marker. Then, to get the description for a marker, you can hover the mouse over the marker.

As you're editing, you may want to enlarge the editing area by closing the side pane and restoring that pane later on. Or you may want to close the Project Explorer, as shown in this figure, because you don't use it often. To work with the panes and the Explorers, you can use the third set of procedures in this figure.

Last, if you want to change the colors that are used by the editor, you can use the fourth procedure in this figure. In this book, we use the Dreamweaver theme, but you can experiment with other themes until you find one that you like. If you click the Apply button after you select a theme, you can see the colors that are used in the window behind the dialog box. Then, if you like the colors, you can click the OK button to close the dialog box.

Aptana with an auto-completion list for a JavaScript entry

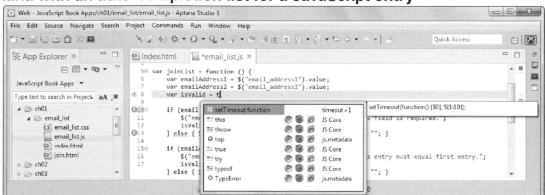

How to use the auto-completion feature

- The auto-completion feature displays a list of items that start with what you've typed. To insert one of those items, double-click on it or use the arrow keys to highlight it and press the Tab key.

- For some JavaScript statements, like an if-else statement, the editor will insert a snippet that contains the starting code including parentheses and braces.

How to identify the errors that are marked by the Aptana editor

- An error marker is a red circle that contains a white X at the start of a line. A warning marker is a yellow triangle that contains an exclamation mark. These markers are displayed as you enter and edit code.

- To get the description for an error or warning marker, hover the mouse over the marker.

How to hide and restore the Project and App Explorers

- To hide the Project or App Explorer, click on the X in its tab. To display the Project or App Explorer, use the Window→Show View→App Explorer or Project Explorer command.

- To hide the pane on the left side of the window, click on its minimize button. To restore the pane, click on the Restore icon at the top of the vertical bar that's to the left or right of the editing window.

How to set the colors that are used to highlight the syntax

- Use the Window→Preferences command to open the Preferences dialog box.

- Click on Aptana Studio, and then click on Themes to display the Themes dialog box.

- Choose a theme from the Editor Theme list. (This book uses the Dreamweaver theme.)

Description

- Aptana provides many features that make it easier to enter and edit JavaScript code.

- Aptana provides many ways to display the panes for its many features.

Figure 1-20   How to edit a file in Aptana

How to run a JavaScript application

Figure 1-21 shows how to run a JavaScript application from Aptana. To do that, you open the HTML file for the application. Or, if the HTML file is already open, you click on its tab to select it as shown in this figure. Then, you click on the Run button. This opens the default browser and runs the file in that browser. You can also run an HTML file in another browser using the drop-down list to the right of the Run button.

Before you run a JavaScript application, you need to save any changes to the HTML file and its related files. To do that, you can click on the Save or Save All button in the toolbar. If you don't save the files before you click the Run button, though, you'll get a warning message with an option that will save the files for you.

When you run a JavaScript application this way, a new browser or browser tab is opened each time you click the Run button. So, if you click on the Run button 10 times for an application, 10 browsers or tabs will be opened.

Another way to do this, though, is to run an application the first time by clicking on the Run button. Then, after you find and fix the errors in Aptana, you can click on the Save All button in Aptana to save the changes, switch to the browser, and click on the Reload or Refresh button in the browser to reload the application with the changes. That way, you use the same tab or Browser instance each time you test the application.

Aptana's Run button

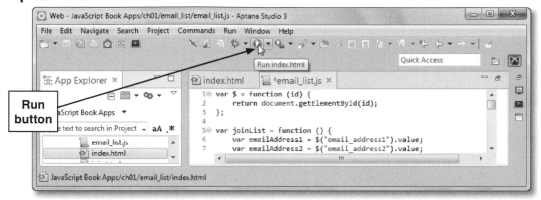

The web page in Chrome

How to run a JavaScript application from Aptana

- Before you run a file, you should save any changes that you've made to it or any of its related files. To do that, you can click on the Save or Save All button in the toolbar.

- To run a JavaScript application in the default browser, open the HTML file for the application, select its tab, and click on the Run button. (The Run button won't work if the HTML file isn't the one that's selected.)

- To run a JavaScript application in another browser, select the tab for its HTML file, click the down-arrow to the right of the Run button, and select the browser.

Description

- When you test an application, you run its HTML page. Then, you can note the errors, fix the errors in Aptana, save the changes, and run the page again.

- Every time you run a page from Aptana, another browser instance or browser tab is opened. Another alternative is to save the corrected files in Aptana, switch to the browser, and click its Reload or Refresh button. That way, another browser or tab isn't opened.

Figure 1-21   How to run a JavaScript application from Aptana

Perspective

This chapter has presented the background concepts and terms that you need for developing JavaScript applications. Now, if you're comfortable with everything that you've learned, you're ready for chapter 2.

But what if you aren't comfortable with your HTML and CSS skills? First, we recommend that you keep going in this book because you don't have to be an HTML or CSS expert to develop JavaScript applications. Second, we recommend that you get a copy of *Murach's HTML5 and CSS3*, because every web developer should eventually master HTML5 and CSS3.

Terms you should know

client	tag
web browser	CSS (Cascading Style Sheets)
web server	DOM scripting
network	Document Object Model (DOM)
intranet	HTML5 semantic elements
local area network (LAN)	HTML5 semantics
Internet	attribute
wide area network (WAN)	id attribute
Internet service provider (ISP)	class attribute
HTML (HyperText Markup	name attribute
Language)	for attribute
static web page	title attribute
HTTP request	external style sheet
HTTP (HyperText Transfer Protocol)	embedded styles
HTTP response	CSS selector
render a web page	type selector
dynamic web page	id selector
application server	class selector
database server	rule set
server-side processing	rule
round trip	property name
JavaScript	URL (Uniform Resource Locator)
JavaScript engine	protocol
scripting language	domain name
client-side processing	path
image swap	developer tools
image rollover	cross-browser compatibility
data validation	JavaScript shiv
jQuery	IDE (Integrated Development
ECMAScript specification	Environment)
HTML element	Aptana project

Summary

- A web application consists of clients, a web server, and a network. *Clients* use *web browsers* to request web pages from the web server. The *web server* returns the requested pages.

- A *local area network* (*LAN*) connects computers that are near to each other. This is often called an *intranet*. In contrast, the *Internet* consists of many *wide area networks* (*WANs*).

- To request a web page, the web browser sends an *HTTP request* to the web server. Then, the web server gets the HTML for the requested page and sends it back to the browser in an *HTTP response*. Last, the browser *renders* the HTML into a web page.

- A *static web page* is a page that is the same each time it's retrieved. In contrast, the HTML for a *dynamic web page* is generated by a server-side program or script, so its HTML can change from one request to another.

- *JavaScript* is a *scripting language* that is run by the *JavaScript engine* of a web browser. It provides for *client-side processing*. *jQuery* is a JavaScript library that makes it easier to code many common functions.

- JavaScript is commonly used to modify the *Document Object Model* (*DOM*) that's built for each web page when it is loaded. This is referred to as *DOM scripting*. When the DOM is changed, the browser immediately changes its display so it reflects those changes.

- The ECMAScript specification provides the standards that JavaScript implements. ECMAScript 5 is the version that's in common use today.

- *HTML* (*HyperText Markup Language*) is the language that defines the structure and contents of a web page. *CSS* (*Cascading Style Sheets*) is used to control how the web pages are formatted.

- You can view a web page that's on your own computer or server or on an Internet server. To view a web page on an Internet server, you can enter the *URL* (*Uniform Resource Locator*) that consists of the *protocol*, *domain name*, *path*, and filename into a browser's address bar.

- To help find errors when you test a JavaScript application, you can use the Console panel in Chrome's *developer tools*.

- When you develop a JavaScript application, you need to provide for *cross-browser compatibility*. That means you have to test your applications on all modern browsers as well as older versions of those browsers.

- To provide compatibility with older browsers like IE7 and IE8, you can use the *JavaScript shiv* for the HTML5 semantic elements and the shim.js and sham.js files for ECMAScript 5.

- To develop JavaScript applications, you can use a text editor or an *Integrated Development Environment* (*IDE*) like Aptana Studio 3.

Before you do the exercises for this book...

Before you do the exercises for this book, you should download and install the Chrome browser as well as the applications for this book. If you're going to use Aptana, you should also download and install that product too. The procedures for installing the software and applications for this book are in appendix A.

Exercise 1-1   Run the Email List application

In this exercise, you'll run the Email List application that's presented in figures 1-6 through 1-8.

Open the application in Chrome

1. Start Chrome if it isn't already open. Then, use the Ctrl+O key combination to open this HTML file:

   `c:\murach\javascript\book_apps\ch01\email_list\index.html`

2. To test what happens when you don't enter any data, just click the Join our List button without entering any data.

3. Enter an email address in the first text box and invalid data in the second text box and click the Join our List button to see what error messages are displayed.

4. Enter valid data for all three text boxes and click on the button. Then, the data is submitted for processing and a new web page is displayed.

Preview the developer tools

5. To rerun the application, click the Back button. Then, click on the Reload button. This should reset the entries.

6. Enter an email address in the first text box and leave the other text boxes empty. Then, press F12 to open Chrome's developer tools, and note that the Console tab doesn't contain any error messages.

7. Click on the Sources tab to see the JavaScript code for the page. Then, click on the index.html tab to see the HTML for the page.

8. Click on the Elements tab, and drill down to see the HTML elements within the form element for the page. In the span elements, you can see the error messages that are displayed, not the starting values in the HTML. That's because the Elements tab represents the Document Object Model for the page, and JavaScript has changed that model.

9. Do more experimenting if you want. These are powerful debugging tools that you'll use a lot as you go through this book so it's good to become familiar with them. When you're through, press the F12 button to close the tools.

Exercise 1-2   Run other section 1 applications

This exercise has you run two of the applications presented in chapters 4 and 5. That will give you some idea of what you'll able to do when you complete this section.

Run the Miles Per Gallon application of chapter 4

1. Open this file in the Chrome browser:

        c:\murach\javascript\book_apps\ch04\mpg\index.html

2. Enter invalid data into the text boxes and see the results. Then, enter valid data into the text boxes and see the results.

Run the FAQs application of chapter 5

3. Open this file in the Chrome browser:

        c:\murach\javascript\book_apps\ch05\faqs\index.html

4. Click on the first heading to display the text for it, and click the heading again to hide the text.

5. Tab to the next heading and press the Enter key to display the text for it, and press the Enter key again to hide the text.

Exercise 1-3   Get started with Aptana

This exercise is for readers who are going to use Aptana with this book. It guides you through the process of creating projects that provide easy access to the book applications and exercises that you've downloaded.

Create the projects

1. Start Aptana, and use the procedure in figure 1-18 to create a project for the book applications that are stored in this folder:

        c:\murach\javascript\book_apps

    This project should be named JavaScript Book Apps, and the entries for the last dialog box should be just like those in this figure.

2. Use the same procedure to create a project named JavaScript Exercises for the exercises that are stored in this folder:

        c:\javascript\exercises

3. Use the same procedure to again create a project named JavaScript Solutions for the exercise solutions that are stored in this folder:

        c:\murach\javascript\solutions

Test the Email List application

4. Use the drop-down list in the App Explorer to select the JavaScript Exercises project. This provides access to all of the exercises that are in this book.

5. In the App Explorer, click on the plus sign before ch01 to display the email_list folder, and click on the plus sign for the email_list folder to display the files for the Email List application.

6. Double-click on the file named index.html to open that file. Then, click the Run button in the toolbar to run the application in the default browser. That will automatically switch you to that browser.

7. Switch back to Aptana, and click on the down arrow to the right of the Run button. If the drop-down list offers Internet Explorer, click on it to run the application in that browser. Then, return to Aptana.

Edit the JavaScript code

8. In the App Explorer, double click on the file named email_list.js to open that file, and note the colors that are used for syntax highlighting.

9. If you don't like the colors that are used, use the procedure in figure 1-20 to change them.

10. In the JavaScript file, delete the right parenthesis in the first line of code. This should display two error markers. Then, hover the mouse over the markers to display the error descriptions. This illustrates Aptana's error-checking feature. Now, undo the change that you made. (To undo a change with the keyboard, press Ctrl+Z.)

11. In the JavaScript file, after the third statement that starts with var, start a statement on a new line with these characters:

    ```
    if (e
    ```

    This should display a list of the possible entries that start with the letter *e*. Here, you can see that emailAddress1 and emailAddress2 are included in the list. These are the variables that are created by the first two var statements, and this illustrates Aptana's auto-completion feature. Now, undo this change.

12. Enter this statement on a new line that comes right before the last line of the JavaScript code, which consists of just a right brace (}):

    ```
    alert("The DOM has now been built");
    ```

    In other words, this statement will become the second last line in the file.

13. To test the statement that you've added, click on the Save All button in the toolbar to save your changes. Then, switch to your browser and click on the Reload or Refresh button to run the application with this change. This should display a dialog box that you can close by clicking on its OK button. After that, the application should work the same as it did before.

14. If you're curious, do more experimenting on your own. Then, close the files and exit from Aptana.

2

Getting started
with JavaScript

The goal of this chapter is to get you off to a good start with JavaScript, especially if you're new to programming. If you have programming experience with another language, you should be able to move rapidly through this chapter. Otherwise, take it easy and do the exercises at the end of this chapter.

How to include JavaScript in an HTML document

In chapter 1, you saw how the JavaScript for an application can be coded in a separate file. But there are actually three different ways to include JavaScript in an HTML document. You'll learn all three now.

Two ways to include JavaScript in the head of an HTML document

Figure 2-1 presents two of the three ways to include JavaScript in an HTML document. As you saw in the last chapter, one way is to code the JavaScript in a separate *external file*. Then, you code a script element in the head section of the HTML document to include that file.

In the script element, the src attribute is used to refer to the external file. For this element, you can also code a type attribute with the value "text/javascript" to tell the browser what kind of content the file contains. But with HTML5, that attribute is no longer needed because the assumption is that all files that are referred to in script elements contain JavaScript.

In the example in this figure, the src attribute refers to a file named calculate_mpg.js. The assumption here is that this file is in the same folder as the HTML file. Otherwise, you need to code a relative URL that provides the right path for the file. If, for example, the JavaScript file is in a folder named javascript and that folder is in the same folder as the HTML file, the src attribute would be coded this way:

```
<script src="javascript/calculate_mpg.js"></script>
```

This works the same as it does for any other file reference in an HTML document.

The second way to include JavaScript in an HTML document is to code the JavaScript within the script element in the head section. This can be referred to as *embedded JavaScript*. Note, however, that the application will work the same whether the JavaScript is embedded in the head section or loaded into the head section from an external file.

The benefit of using an external file is that it separates the JavaScript from the HTML. Another benefit is that it makes it easier to re-use the code in other pages or applications.

The benefit of using embedded JavaScript is that you don't have to switch between the HTML and JavaScript files as you develop the application. In the examples in this book, you'll see both uses of JavaScript.

As you'll see in the next figure, script elements can be in the body section of the document, too. In fact, some developers prefer to place their script elements just before the closing body tag. This can make the page appear to load faster because the HTML will render before the JavaScript loads. But if you need JavaScript functionality as the HTML renders, scripts at the bottom won't work. Ultimately, you'll make this decision based on your application's needs.

Two attributes of the script element

Attribute	Description
`src`	Specifies the location (source) of an external JavaScript file.
`type`	With HTML5, this attribute can be omitted. If you code it, use "text/javascript" for JavaScript code.

A script element in the head section that loads an external JavaScript file

```
<script src="calculate_mpg.js"></script>
```

A script element that embeds JavaScript in the head section

```
<head>
    . . .
    <script>
        alert("The Calculate MPG application");
        var miles = prompt("Enter miles driven");
        miles = parseFloat(miles);
        var gallons = prompt("Enter gallons of gas used");
        gallons = parseFloat(gallons);
        var mpg = miles/gallons;
        mpg = parseInt(mpg);
        alert("Miles per gallon = " + mpg);
    </script>
</head>
```

Description

- A script element in the head section of an HTML document is commonly used to identify an *external JavaScript file* that should be included with the page.

- A script element in the head section can also contain the JavaScript statements that are included with the page. This can be referred to as *embedded JavaScript*.

- If you code more than one script element in the head section, the JavaScript is included in the sequence in which the script statements appear.

- When a script element in the head section includes an external JavaScript file, the JavaScript in the file runs as if it were coded in the script element.

- Some programmers prefer to place their script elements at the bottom of the page, just before the closing body tag. This can make a page seem to load faster, but the JavaScript won't run until after the page is loaded.

Figure 2-1   Two ways to include JavaScript in the head of an HTML document

How to include JavaScript in the body of an HTML document

Figure 2-2 shows a third way to include JavaScript in an HTML document. This time, the two script elements in the first example are coded in the body of the HTML document.

If you want to provide for browsers that don't have JavaScript enabled, you can code a noscript element after a script element as shown in the second example. Then, if JavaScript is disabled, the content of the noscript element will be displayed. But if JavaScript is enabled, the code in the script element runs, and the noscript element is ignored. This way, some output will be displayed whether or not JavaScript is enabled.

In the second example, the noscript element is coded right after a script element, so 2015 will replace the output of the script element if JavaScript isn't enabled in the browser. This means that the result will be the same in the year 2015 whether or not JavaScript is enabled. But after 2015, the year will be updated by the JavaScript if it is enabled.

You can also code a noscript element that doesn't follow a script element. For instance, you can code a noscript element at the top of a page that warns the user that the page won't work right if JavaScript is disabled. This is illustrated by the third example. In this case, nothing is displayed if JavaScript is enabled and the message is displayed if JavaScript is disabled.

In most of the applications in this book, the JavaScript is either embedded in the head section of the HTML or in an external file that's identified in the head section of the HTML. However, you shouldn't have any trouble including the JavaScript in the body of an HTML document whenever you want to do that.

JavaScript in the body of an HTML document

```
<p>
    <script>
        var today = new Date();
        document.write("Current date: ");
        document.write(today.toDateString());
    </script>
</p>
<p>&copy; 
    <script>
        var today = new Date();
        document.write( today.getFullYear() );
    </script>
, San Joaquin Valley Town Hall
</p>
```

The result of the JavaScript in a web browser

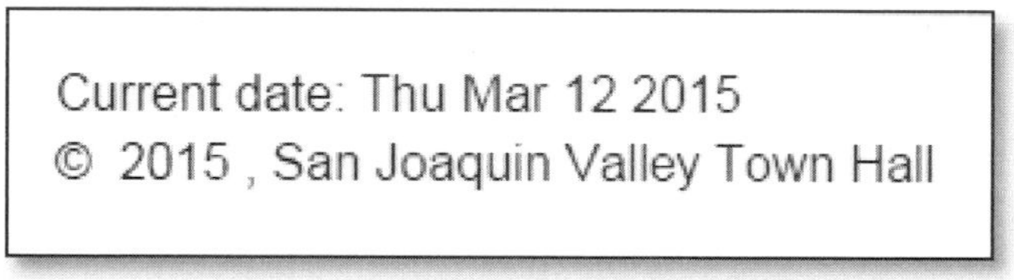

```
Current date: Thu Mar 12 2015
© 2015 , San Joaquin Valley Town Hall
```

A noscript element in the body of an HTML document

```
<p>&copy; 
    <script>
        var today = new Date();
        document.write( today.getFullYear() );
    </script>
    <noscript>2015</noscript>
, San Joaquin Valley Town Hall
</p>
```

A noscript element at the start of an HTML document

```
<h2><noscript>To get the most from this web site,
    please enable JavaScript.</noscript></h2>
```

Description

- The JavaScript code in a script element in the body of a document is run when the page is loaded.
- The noscript element can be used to display content when JavaScript is disabled in a user's browser.

Figure 2-2   How to include JavaScript in the body of an HTML document

The JavaScript syntax

The *syntax* of JavaScript refers to the rules that you must follow as you code statements. If you don't adhere to these rules, your web browser won't be able to interpret and execute your statements.

How to code JavaScript statements

Figure 2-3 summarizes the rules for coding *JavaScript statements*. The first rule is that JavaScript is case-sensitive. This means that uppercase and lowercase letters are treated as different letters. For example, *salestax* and *salesTax* are treated as different names.

The second rule is that JavaScript statements must end with a semicolon. If you don't end each statement with a semicolon, JavaScript won't be able to tell where one statement ends and the next one begins.

The third rule is that JavaScript ignores extra whitespace in statements. Since *whitespace* includes spaces, tabs, and new line characters, this lets you break long statements into multiple lines so they're easier to read.

Be careful, though, to follow the guidelines in this figure about where to split a statement. If you don't split a statement at a good spot, JavaScript will sometimes try to help you out by adding a semicolon for you, and that can lead to errors.

A block of JavaScript code

```
var joinList = function() {
    var emailAddress1 = $("email_address1").value;
    var emailAddress2 = $("email_address2").value;

    if (emailAddress1 == "") {
        alert("Email Address is required.");
    } else if (emailAddress2 == "") {
        alert("Second Email Address is required.");
    } else if (emailAddress1 != emailAddress2) {
        alert("Second Email entry must equal first entry.");
    } else if ($("first_name").value == "") {
        alert("First Name is required.");
    } else {
        $("email_form").submit();
    }
};
```

The basic syntax rules

- JavaScript is case-sensitive.
- Each JavaScript statement ends with a semicolon.
- JavaScript ignores extra whitespace within statements.

How to split a statement over two or more lines

- Split a statement after:
  an arithmetic or relational operator such as +, -, *, /, =, ==, >, or <
  an opening brace ({), bracket ([ ), or parenthesis
  a closing brace (})
- Do not split a statement after:
  an identifier, a value, or the *return* keyword
  a closing bracket ( ]) or closing parenthesis

Description

- A JavaScript *statement* has a syntax that's similar to the syntax of Java.
- *Whitespace* refers to the spaces, tab characters, and return characters in the code, and it is ignored by the compiler. As a result, you can use spaces, tab characters, and return characters to format your code so it's easier to read.
- In some cases, JavaScript will try to correct what it thinks is a missing semicolon by adding a semicolon at the end of a split line. To prevent this, follow the guidelines above for splitting a statement.

Figure 2-3   How to code JavaScript statements

How to create identifiers

Variables, functions, objects, properties, methods, and events must all have names so you can refer to them in your JavaScript code. An *identifier* is the name given to one of these components.

Figure 2-4 shows the rules for creating identifiers in JavaScript. Besides the first four rules, you can't use any of the JavaScript *reserved words* (also known as *keywords*) as an identifier. These are words that are reserved for use within the JavaScript language. You should also avoid using any of the JavaScript global properties or methods as identifiers, which you'll learn more about as you progress through this book.

Besides the rules, you should give your identifiers meaningful names. That means that it should be easy to tell what an identifier refers to and easy to remember how to spell the name. To create names like that, you should avoid abbreviations. If, for example, you abbreviate the name for monthly investment as mon_inv, it will be hard to tell what it refers to and hard to remember how you spelled it. But if you spell it out as monthly_investment, both problems are solved.

Similarly, you should avoid abbreviations that are specific to one industry or field of study unless you are sure the abbreviation will be widely understood. For example, mpg is a common abbreviation for miles per gallon, but cpm could stand for a number of different things and should be spelled out.

To create an identifier that has more than one word in it, many JavaScript programmers use a convention called *camel casing*. With this convention, the first letter of each word is uppercase except for the first word. For example, monthlyInvestment and taxRate are identifiers that use camel casing.

The alternative is to use underscore characters to separate the words in an identifier. For example, monthly_investment and tax_rate use this convention. If the standards in your shop specify one of these conventions, by all means use it. Otherwise, you can use whichever convention you prefer...but be consistent.

In this book, underscore notation is used for the ids and class names in the HTML, and camel casing is used for all JavaScript identifiers. That way, it will be easier for you to tell where the names originated.

Rules for creating identifiers

- Identifiers can only contain letters, numbers, the underscore, and the dollar sign.
- Identifiers can't start with a number.
- Identifiers are case-sensitive.
- Identifiers can be any length.
- Identifiers can't be the same as *reserved words*.
- Avoid using global properties and methods as identifiers. If you use one of them, you won't be able to use the global property or method with the same name.

Valid identifiers in JavaScript

```
subtotal        index_1              $
taxRate         calculate_click      $log
```

Camel casing versus underscore notation

```
taxRate              tax_rate
calculateClick       calculate_click
emailAddress         email_address
firstName            first_name
futureValue          future_value
```

Naming recommendations

- Use meaningful names for identifiers. That way, your identifiers aren't likely to be reserved words or global properties.
- Be consistent: Either use camel casing (taxRate) or underscores (tax_rate) to identify the words within the variables in your scripts.
- If you're using underscore notation, use lowercase for all letters.

Reserved words in JavaScript

```
abstract      else          instanceof    switch
boolean       enum          int           synchronized
break         export        interface     this
byte          extends       long          throw
case          false         native        throws
catch         final         new           transient
char          finally       null          true
class         float         package       try
const         for           private       typeof
continue      function      protected     var
debugger      goto          public        void
default       if            return        volatile
delete        implements    short         while
do            import        static        with
double        in            super
```

Description

- *Identifiers* are the names given to variables, functions, objects, properties, and methods.
- In *camel casing*, all of the words within an identifier except the first word start with capital letters.

Figure 2-4   How to create identifiers

How to use comments

Comments let you add descriptive notes to your code that are ignored by the JavaScript engine. Later on, these comments can help you or someone else understand the code whenever it needs to be modified.

The example in figure 2-5 shows how comments can be used to describe or explain portions of code. At the start, a *block comment* describes what the application does. This kind of comment starts with /* and ends with */. Everything that's coded between the start and the end is ignored by the JavaScript engine when the application is run.

The other kind of comment is a *single-line comment* that starts with //. In the example, the first single-line comment describes what the JavaScript that comes before it on the same line does. In contrast, the second single-line comment takes up a line by itself. It describes what the two statements that come after it do.

In addition to describing JavaScript code, comments can be useful when testing an application. If, for example, you want to disable a portion of the JavaScript code, you can enclose it in a block comment. Then, it will be ignored when the application is run. This can be referred to as *commenting out* a portion of code. Later, after you test the rest of the code, you can enable the commented out code by removing the markers for the start and end of the block comment. This can be referred to *uncommenting*.

Comments are also useful when you want to experiment with changes in code. For instance, you can make a copy of a portion of code, comment out the original code, and then paste the copy just above the original code that is now commented out. Then, you can make changes in the copy. But if the changes don't work, you can restore your old code by deleting the new code and uncommenting the old code.

When should you use comments to describe or explain code? Certainly, when the code is so complicated that you may not remember how it works if you have to maintain it later on. This kind of comment is especially useful if someone else is going to have to maintain the code.

On the other hand, you shouldn't use comments to explain code that any professional programmer should understand. That means that you have to strike some sort of balance between too much and too little. One of the worst problems with comments is changing the way the code works without changing the related comments. Then, the comments mislead the person who is trying to maintain the code, which makes the job even more difficult.

A portion of JavaScript code that includes comments

```
/* this application validates a user's entries for joining
   our email list
*/
var $ = function(id) {                          // the standard $ function
    return document.getElementById(id);
}
// this function gets and validates the user entries
var joinList = function() {
    var emailAddress1 = $("email_address1").value;
    var emailAddress2 = $("email_address2").value;
    var firstName = $("first_name").value;
    var isValid = true;

    // validate the first entry
    if (emailAddress1 == "") {
        $("email_address1_error").firstChild.nodeValue =
            "This field is required.";
        isValid = false;                        // set valid switch to off
    } else {
        $("email_address1_error").firstChild.nodeValue = "";
    }

    // validate the second entry
    ...
    ...
```

The basic syntax rules for JavaScript comments

- Block comments begin with /* and end with */
- Single-line comments begin with two forward slashes and continue to the end of the line.

Guidelines for using comments

- Use comments to describe portions of code that are hard to understand.
- Use comments to disable portions of code that you don't want to test.
- Don't use comments unnecessarily.

Description

- JavaScript provides two forms of *comments*, *block comments* and *single-line comments*.
- Comments are ignored when the JavaScript is executed.
- During testing, comments can be used to *comment out* (disable) portions of code that you don't want tested. Then, you can remove the comments when you're ready to test those portions.
- You can also use comments to save a portion of code in its original state while you make changes to a copy of that code.

Figure 2-5   How to use comments

How to use objects, methods, and properties

In simple terms, an *object* is a collection of methods and properties. A *method* performs a function or does an action. A *property* is a data item that relates to the object. When you develop JavaScript applications, you will often work with objects, methods, and properties.

To get you started with that, figure 2-6 shows how to use the methods and properties of the window object, which is a common JavaScript object. To *call* (execute) a method of an object, you use the syntax in the summary after the tables. That is, you code the object name, a *dot operator* (period), the method name, and any *parameters* that the method requires within parentheses.

In the syntax summaries in this book, some words are italicized and some aren't. The words that aren't italicized are keywords that always stay the same, like *alert*. You can see this in the first table, where the syntax for the alert method shows that you code the word *alert* just as it is in the summary. In contrast, the italicized words are the ones that you need to supply, like the string parameter you supply to the alert method.

In the first example after the syntax summary, you can see how the alert method of the *window object* is called:

```
window.alert("This is a test of the alert method");
```

In this case, the one parameter that's passed to it is "This is a test of the alert method". So that message is displayed when the alert dialog box is displayed.

In the second example, you can see how the prompt method of the window object is called. This time, though, the object name is omitted. For the window object (but only the window object), that's okay because the window object is the *global object* for JavaScript applications.

As you can see, the prompt method accepts two parameters. The first one is a message, and the second one is an optional default value for a user entry. When the prompt method is executed, it displays a dialog box like the one in this figure. Here, you can see the message and the default value that were passed to the method as parameters. At this point, the user can change the default value or leave it as is, and then click on the OK button to store the entry in the variable named userEntry. Or, the user can click on the Cancel button to cancel the entry, which returns a null value.

The third method in the table doesn't require any parameters. It is the print method. When it is executed, it issues a request to the browser for printing the current web page. Then, the browser starts its print function, usually by displaying a dialog box that lets the user set some print options.

To access a property of an object, you use a similar syntax. However, you code the property name after the dot operator as illustrated by the second syntax summary. Unlike methods, properties don't require parameters in parentheses. This is illustrated by the statement that follows the syntax. This statement uses the alert method of the window object to display the location property of the window object.

As you progress through this book, you'll learn how to use the methods and properties of many objects.

Common methods of the window object

Method	Description
`alert(string)`	Displays a dialog box that contains the string that's passed to it by the parameter along with an OK button.
`prompt(string, default)`	Displays a dialog box that contains the string in the first parameter, the default value in the second parameter, an OK button, and a Cancel button. If the user enters a value and clicks OK, that value is returned as a string. If the user clicks Cancel, null is returned to indicate that the value is unknown.
`print()`	Issues a print request for the current web page.

One property of the window object

Property	Description
`location`	The URL of the current web page.

The syntax for calling a method of an object

`objectName.methodName(parameters)`

A statement that calls the alert method of the window object

`window.alert("This is a test of the alert method");`

A statement that calls the prompt method with the object name omitted

`var userEntry = prompt("This is a test of the prompt method", 100);`

The prompt dialog box that's displayed

The syntax for accessing a property of an object

`objectName.propertyName`

A statement that displays the location property of the window object

`alert(window.location);          // Displays the URL of the current page`

Description

- An *object* has *methods* that perform functions that are related to the object as well as *properties* that represent the data or attributes that are associated with the object.

- When you *call* a method, you may need to pass one or more *parameters* to it by coding them within the parentheses after the method name, separated by commas.

- The *window object* is the *global object* for JavaScript, and JavaScript lets you omit the object name and *dot operator* (period) when referring to the window object.

Figure 2-6   How to use objects, methods, and properties

How to use the write and writeln methods of the document object

Figure 2-7 shows how to use the write and writeln methods of the *document object*. These methods write their data into the body of the document so it's displayed in the browser window.

As the table shows, the only difference between these methods is that the writeln method ends with a new line character. However, the new line character is ignored by the browser unless it's coded in a pre element. As a result, there's usually no difference in the way these methods work.

This is illustrated by the examples in this figure. Note that you can include HTML tags within the parentheses of these methods. For instance, the first write method writes the heading at the top of the page because h1 tags were coded around the text. Similarly, the fourth method in that group writes a <br> tag into the document, which is the HTML tag that moves to the next line.

These examples also show that the writeln method doesn't skip to the next line unless it is coded within a pre element in the HTML. For instance, the first two writeln methods in the body of the document display the data with no skipping to a new line. However, when pre tags are added before and after the output, the writeln method does skip to a new line.

Please note that you wouldn't normally use these methods in the head section or an external file to write HTML in the body of the document. Instead, you would code these statements within elements in the body.

Two methods of the document object

Method	Description
`write(string)`	Writes the string that's passed to it into the document.
`writeln(string)`	Writes the string that's passed to it into the document ending with a new line character (see figure 2-11). However, the new line character isn't recognized by HTML except within the HTML pre element.

Examples of write and writeln methods

```
<head>
    <title>Write Testing</title>
    <script>
        var today = new Date();
        document.write("<h1>Welcome to our site!</h1>");
        document.write("Today is ");
        document.write(today.toDateString());
        document.write("<br>");
        document.writeln("Today is ");
        document.writeln(today.toDateString());
        document.write("<br>");
    </script>
</head>
<body>
    <script>
        document.writeln("Welcome to our site!");
        document.writeln("Today is Monday.");
    </script>
    <script>
        document.writeln("<pre>Welcome to our site!");
        document.writeln("Today is Monday.</pre>");
    </script>
</body>
```

The output in a browser

Welcome to our site!

Today is Thu Apr 02 2015
Today is Thu Apr 02 2015
Welcome to our site! Today is Monday.

```
Welcome to our site!
Today is Monday.
```

Description

- The *document object* is the object that lets you work with the Document Object Model (DOM) that represents all of the HTML elements of the page.

- The write and writeln methods are normally used in the body of a document.

- The writeln method doesn't skip to the next line unless it is coded within a pre element. However, you can code <br> tags within the output to provide for line spacing.

Figure 2-7   How to use the write and writeln methods of the document object

How to work with JavaScript data

When you develop JavaScript applications, you frequently work with data, especially the data that users enter into the controls of a form. In the topics that follow, you'll learn how to work with the three types of JavaScript data.

The primitive data types

JavaScript provides for three *primitive data types*. The *number data type* is used to represent numerical data. The *string data type* is used to store character data. And the *Boolean data type* is used to store true and false values. This is summarized in figure 2-8.

The number data type can be used to represent either integers or decimal values. *Integers* are whole numbers, and *decimal values* are numbers that can have one or more decimal digits. The value of either data type can be coded with a preceding plus or minus sign. If the sign is omitted, the value is treated as a positive value. A decimal value can also include a decimal point and one or more digits to the right of the decimal point.

As the last example of the number types shows, you can also include an exponent when you code a decimal value. If you aren't familiar with this notation, you probably won't need to use it because you won't be working with very large or very small numbers. On the other hand, if you're familiar with scientific notation, you already know that this exponent indicates how many places the decimal point should be moved to the left or right. Numbers that use this notation are called *floating-point numbers.*

To represent string data, you code the *string* within single or double quotation marks (quotes). Note, however, that you must close the string with the same type of quotation mark that you used to start it. If you code two quotation marks in a row without even a space between them, the result is called an *empty string*, which can be used to represent a string with no data in it.

To represent Boolean data, you code either the word *true* or *false* with no quotation marks. This data type can be used to represent one of two states.

Examples of number values

```
15                  // an integer
-21                 // a negative integer
21.5                // a decimal value
-124.82             // a negative decimal value
-3.7e-9             // floating-point notation for -0.0000000037
```

Examples of string values

```
"JavaScript"        // a string with double quotes
'String Data'       // a string with single quotes
""                  // an empty string
```

The two Boolean values

```
true                // equivalent to true, yes, or on
false               // equivalent to false, no, or off
```

The number data type

- The *number data type* is used to represent an integer or a decimal value that can start with a positive or negative sign.

- An *integer* is a whole number. A *decimal value* can have one or more decimal positions to the right of the decimal point.

- If a result is stored in a number data type that is larger or smaller than the data type can store, it will be stored as the value Infinity or –Infinity.

What you need to know about floating-point numbers

- In JavaScript, decimal values are stored as *floating-point numbers*. In that format, a number consists of a positive or negative sign, one or more significant digits, an optional decimal point, optional decimal digits, and an optional exponent.

- Unless you're developing an application that requires the use of very large or very small numbers, you won't have to use floating-point notation to express numbers. If you need to use this notation, however, it is illustrated by the last example of number values above.

The string data type

- The *string data type* represents character (*string*) data. A string is surrounded by double quotes or single quotes. The string must start and end with the same type of quotation mark.

- An *empty string* is a string that contains no characters. It is entered by typing two quotation marks with nothing between them.

The Boolean data type

- The *Boolean data type* is used to represent a *Boolean value*. A Boolean value can be used to represent data that has two possible states: true or false.

Figure 2-8   The primitive data types

How to code numeric expressions

A *numeric expression* can be as simple as a single value or it can be a series of operations that result in a single value. In figure 2-9, you can see the operators for coding numeric expressions. If you've programmed in another language, these are probably similar to what you've been using. In particular, the first four *arithmetic operators* are common to most programming languages.

Most modern languages also have a *modulus operator* that calculates the remainder when the left value is divided by the right value. In the example for this operator, 13 % 4 means the remainder of 13 / 4. Then, since 13 / 4 is 3 with a remainder of 1, 1 is the result of the expression.

In contrast to the first five operators in this figure, the increment and decrement operators add or subtract one from a variable. To complicate matters, though, these operators can be coded before or after a variable name, and that can affect the result. To avoid confusion, then, it's best to only code these operators after the variable names and only in simple expressions like the one that you'll see in the next figure.

When an expression includes two or more operators, the *order of precedence* determines which operators are applied first. This order is summarized in the table in this figure. For instance, all multiplication and division operations are done from left to right before any addition and subtraction operations are done.

To override this order, though, you can use parentheses. Then, the expressions in the innermost sets of parentheses are done first, followed by the expressions in the next sets of parentheses, and so on. This is typical of all programming languages, as well as basic algebra, and the examples in this figure show how this works.

Common arithmetic operators

Operator	Description	Example	Result
+	Addition	`5 + 7`	`12`
−	Subtraction	`5 - 12`	`-7`
*	Multiplication	`6 * 7`	`42`
/	Division	`13 / 4`	`3.25`
%	Modulus	`13 % 4`	`1`
++	Increment	`counter++`	adds 1 to counter
--	Decrement	`counter--`	subtracts 1 from counter

The order of precedence for arithmetic expressions

Order	Operators	Direction	Description
1	++	Left to right	Increment operator
2	--	Left to right	Decrement operator
3	* / %	Left to right	Multiplication, division, modulus
4	+ −	Left to right	Addition, subtraction

Examples of precedence and the use of parentheses

```
3 + 4 * 5         // Result is 23 since the multiplication is done first
(3 + 4) * 5       // Result is 35 since the addition is done first

13 % 4 + 9        // Result is 10 since the modulus is done first
13 % (4 + 9)      // Result is 0  since the addition is done first

100 + 100 * 2     // Result is 300 since the multiplication is done first
100 + (100 * 2)   // Result is still 300 since the multiplication is first
```

Description

- To code a *numeric expression*, you can use the *arithmetic operators* to operate on two or more values.
- The *modulus operator* returns the remainder of a division operation.
- An arithmetic expression is evaluated based on the *order of precedence* of the operators.
- To override the order of precedence, you can use parentheses.
- Because the use of increment and decrement operators can be confusing, it's best to only use these operators in expressions that consist of just a variable name followed by the operator, as shown in the next figure.

Figure 2-9   How to code numeric expressions

How to work with numeric variables

A *variable* stores a value that can change as the program executes. When you code a JavaScript application, you frequently declare variables and assign values to them. Figure 2-10 shows how to do both of these tasks with numeric variables.

To *declare* a numeric variable in JavaScript, code the *var* (for variable) keyword followed by the identifier (or name) that you want to use for the variable. To declare more than one variable in a single statement, code *var* followed by the variable names separated by commas. This is illustrated by the first group of examples in this figure.

To assign a value to a variable, you code an *assignment statement*. This type of statement consists of a variable name, an *assignment operator* like =, and an expression. Here, the expression can be a *numeric literal* like 74.95, a variable name like subtotal, or an arithmetic expression. When the equals sign is the operator, the value of the expression on the right of the equals sign is stored in the variable on the left and replaces any previous value in the variable. The use of this operator is illustrated by the second group of examples.

The second operator in the table in this figure is the += operator, which is a *compound assignment operator*. It modifies the variable on the left of the operator by adding the value of the expression on the right to the value of the variable on the left. When you use this operator, the variable must already exist and have a value assigned to it. The use of this operator is illustrated by the third group of examples.

The fourth group of examples shows three different ways to increment a variable by adding one to it. As you will see throughout this book, this is a common JavaScript requirement. In this group, the first statement assigns a value of 1 to a variable named counter.

Then, the second statement in this group uses an arithmetic expression to add 1 to the value of the counter, which shows that a variable name can be used on both sides of the equals sign. The third statement adds one to the counter by using the += operator.

The last statement in this group uses the increment operator shown in the previous figure to add one to the counter. This illustrates the best way to use increment and decrement operators. Here, the numeric expression consists only of a variable name followed by the increment operator, and it doesn't include an assignment operator.

The last group of examples illustrates a potential problem that you should be aware of. Because decimal values are stored internally as floating-point numbers, the results of arithmetic operations aren't always precise. In this example, the salesTax result, which should be 7.495, is 7.495000000000001. Although this result is extremely close to 7.495, it isn't equal to 7.495, which could lead to a programming problem if you expect a comparison of the two values to be equal. The solution is to round the result, which you'll learn how to do in the next chapter.

The most useful assignment operators

Operator	Description
=	Assigns the result of the expression to the variable.
+=	Adds the result of the expression to the variable.

How to declare numeric variables without assigning values to them

```
var subtotal;                       // declares one variable
var investment, interestRate, years;   // declares three variables
```

How to declare variables and assign values to them

```
var subtotal = 74.00;        // subtotal = 74.00
var salesTax = subtotal * .1;   // salesTax = 7.4
```

How to code compound assignment statements

```
var subtotal = 74.95;        // subtotal = 74.95
subtotal += 20.00;           // subtotal = 94.95
```

Three ways to increment a variable named counter by 1

```
var counter = 1;             // counter = 1
counter = counter + 1;       // counter now = 2
counter += 1;                // counter now = 3
counter++;                   // counter now = 4
```

A floating-point result that isn't precise

```
var subtotal = 74.95;        // subtotal = 74.95
var salesTax = subtotal * .1;   // salesTax = 7.495000000000001
```

Description

- A *variable* stores a value that can change as the program executes.
- To *declare* a variable, code the keyword *var* and a variable name. To declare more than one variable in a single statement, code *var* and the variable names separated by commas.
- To assign a value to a variable, you use an *assignment statement* that consists of the variable name, an *assignment operator*, and an expression. When appropriate, you can declare a variable and assign a value to it in a single statement.
- Within an expression, a *numeric literal* is a valid integer or decimal number that isn't enclosed in quotation marks.
- If you use a plus sign in an expression and both values are numbers, JavaScript adds them. If both values are strings, JavaScript concatenates them as shown in the next figure. And if one value is a number and one is a string, JavaScript converts the number to a string and concatenates.
- When you do some types of arithmetic operations with decimal values, the results aren't always precise, although they are extremely close. That's because decimal values are stored internally as floating-point numbers. The only problem with this is that an equality comparison may not return true.

Figure 2-10   How to work with numeric variables

How to work with string and Boolean variables

To declare a string or Boolean variable, you use techniques that are similar to those you use for declaring a numeric variable. The main difference is that a *string literal* is a value enclosed in quotation marks, while a numeric literal isn't. Besides that, the + sign is treated as a *concatenation operator* when working with strings. This means that one string is added to the end of another string.

This is illustrated by the first two groups of examples in figure 2-11. In the second group, the first statement assigns string literals to the variables named firstName and lastName. Then, the next statement concatenates lastName, a string literal that consists of a comma and a space, and firstName. The result of this concatenation is

`Hopper, Grace`

which is stored in a new variable named fullName.

In the third group of examples, you can see how the += operator can be used to get the same results. When the expressions that you're working with are strings, this operator does a simple concatenation.

In the fourth group of examples, though, you can see what happens if the += operator is used with a string and a numeric value. In that case, the number is converted to a string and then the strings are concatenated.

The fifth group of examples shows how you can use *escape sequences* in a string. Three of the many escape sequences that you can use are summarized in the second table in this figure. These sequences let you put characters in a string that you can't put in just by pressing the appropriate key on the keyboard. For instance, the \n escape sequence is equivalent to pressing the Enter key in the middle of a string. And the \' sequence is equivalent to pressing the key for a single quotation mark.

Escape sequences are needed so the JavaScript engine can interpret code correctly. For instance, since single and double quotations marks are used to identify strings in JavaScript statements, coding them within the strings would cause syntax errors. But when the quotation marks are preceded by escape characters, the JavaScript engine can interpret them correctly.

The last example in this figure shows how to create and assign values to Boolean variables. Here, a variable named isValid is created and a value of false is assigned to it.

The concatenation operator for strings

Operator	Example	Result
+	`"Grace " + "Hopper"`	`"Grace Hopper"`
	`"Months: " + 120`	`"Months: 120"`

Escape sequences that can be used in strings

Operator	Description
`\n`	Starts a new line in a string.
`\"`	Puts a double quotation mark in a string.
`\'`	Puts a single quotation mark in a string.

How to declare string variables without assigning values to them

```
var zipCode;                            // declares one variable
var lastName, state, zipCode;           // declares three variables
```

How to declare string variables and assign values to them

```
var firstName = "Grace", lastName = "Hopper"; // assigns two string values
var fullName = lastName + ", " + firstName;   // fullName is "Hopper, Grace"
```

How to code compound assignment statements with string data

```
var firstName = "Grace", lastName = "Hopper";
var fullName = lastName;            // fullName is "Hopper"
fullName += ", ";                   // fullName is "Hopper, "
fullName += firstName;              // fullName is "Hopper, Grace"
```

How to code compound assignment statements with mixed data

```
var months = 120;
message = "Months: ";
message += months;                  // message is "Months: 120"
```

How escape sequences can be used in a string

```
var message = "A valid variable name\ncannot start with a number.";
var message = "This isn\'t the right way to do this.";
```

How to declare Boolean variables and assign values to them

```
var isValid = false;                // Boolean value is false
```

Description

- To assign values to string variables, you can use the + and += operators, just as you use them with numeric variables.

- To *concatenate* two or more strings, you can use the + operator.

- Within an expression, a *string literal* is enclosed in quotation marks.

- *Escape sequences* can be used to insert special characters within a string like a return character that starts a new line or a quotation mark.

- If you use a plus sign in an expression and both values are strings, JavaScript concatenates them. But if one value is a number and one is a string, JavaScript converts the number to a string and concatenates the strings.

Figure 2-11   How to work with string and Boolean variables

How to use the parseInt and parseFloat methods

The parseInt and parseFloat methods are used to convert strings to numbers. The parseInt method converts a string to an integer, and the parseFloat method converts a string to a decimal value. If the string can't be converted to a number, the value *NaN* is returned. NaN means "Not a Number".

These methods are needed because the values that are returned by the prompt method and the values that the user enters into text boxes are treated as strings. The is illustrated by the first group of examples in figure 2-12. For this group, assume that the default value in the prompt method isn't changed by the user. As a result, the first statement in this group stores 12345.6789 as a string in a variable named entryA. Then, the third statement in this group converts the string to an integer value of 12345.

Note that the object name isn't coded before the method name in these examples. That's okay because window is the global object of JavaScript. Note too that the parseInt method doesn't round the value. It just removes, or truncates, any decimal portion of the string value.

The last four statements in the first group of examples show what happens when the parseInt or parseFloat method is used to convert a value that isn't a number. In that case, both of these methods return the value NaN.

Note, however, that these methods can convert values that consist of one or more numeric characters followed by one or more nonnumeric characters. In that case, these methods simply drop the nonnumeric characters. For example, if a string contains the value 72.5%, the parseFloat method will convert it to a decimal value of 72.5.

The second group of examples in this figure shows how to get the same results by coding the parse methods as the parameters of the alert methods. For instance, the third statement in this group uses the parseInt method as the parameter of the alert method.

Note in the first set of examples that the values of the entryA, entryB, and entryC variables are all changed by the parse methods. For instance, entryA becomes the number 12345 and entryC becomes NaN. In contrast, the entries aren't changed by the statements in the second set of examples. That's because the parsed values aren't assigned to the variables; they're just displayed by the alert statements.

The parseInt and parseFloat methods of the window object

Method	Description
`parseInt(string)`	Converts the string that's passed to it to an integer data type and returns that value. If it can't convert the string to an integer, it returns NaN.
`parseFloat(string)`	Converts the string that's passed to it to a decimal data type and returns that value. If it can't convert the string to a decimal value, it returns NaN.

Examples that use the parseInt and parseFloat methods

```
var entryA = prompt("Enter any value", 12345.6789);
alert(entryA);                          // displays 12345.6789
entryA = parseInt(entryA);
alert(entryA);                          // displays 12345

var entryB = prompt("Enter any value", 12345.6789);
alert(entryB);                          // displays 12345.6789
entryB = parseFloat(entryB);
alert(entryB);                          // displays 12345.6789

var entryC = prompt("Enter any value", "Hello");
alert(entryC);                          // displays Hello
entryC = parseInt(entryC);
alert(entryC);                          // displays NaN
```

The same examples with the parse methods embedded in the alert method

```
var entryA = prompt("Enter any value", 12345.6789);
alert(entryA);                          // displays 12345.6789
alert(parseInt(entryA));                // displays 12345

var entryB = prompt("Enter any value", 12345.6789);
alert(entryB);                          // displays 12345.6789
alert(parseFloat(entryB));              // displays 12345.6789

var entryC = prompt("Enter any value", "Hello");
alert(entryC);                          // displays Hello
alert(parseInt(entryC));                // displays NaN
```

Description

- The window object provides parseInt and parseFloat methods that let you convert string values to integer or decimal numbers.

- When you use the prompt method or a text box to get numeric data that you're going to use in calculations, you need to use either the parseInt or parseFloat method to convert the string data to numeric data.

- *NaN* is a value that means "Not a Number". It is returned by the parseInt and parseFloat methods when the value that's being parsed isn't a number.

- When working with methods, you can embed one method in the parameter of another. In the second group of examples above, the parse methods are coded as the parameters for the alert methods.

Figure 2-12   How to use the parseInt and parseFloat methods

Two illustrative applications

This chapter ends by presenting two applications that illustrate the skills that you've just learned. These aren't realistic applications because they get the user entries from prompt statements instead of from controls on a form. However, these applications will get you started with JavaScript.

The Miles Per Gallon application

Figure 2-13 presents a simple application that issues two prompt statements that let the user enter the number of miles driven and the number of gallons of gasoline used. Then, the application calculates miles per gallon and issues an alert statement to display the result in a third dialog box.

Because this application uses prompt methods to get the input and an alert method to display the output, the HTML for this application is trivial. It contains one h1 element that is displayed after the JavaScript finishes executing.

In the JavaScript, you can see how the user's entries are stored in variables named miles and gallons and then parsed into decimal values. After that, miles is divided by gallons, and the result is saved in a variable named mpg. Then, the value in that variable is parsed into an integer so any decimal places are removed. Last, an alert statement displays the result that's shown in the third dialog box. When the user clicks on the OK button in that box, the JavaScript ends and the page with its one heading is displayed in the browser.

Can you guess what will happen if the user enters invalid data in one of the prompt dialog boxes? Then, the parse method will return NaN instead of a number, and the calculation won't work. Instead, the last alert statement will display:

```
Miles per gallon = NaN
```

Unlike other languages, though, the JavaScript will run to completion instead of crashing when the calculation can't be done, so the web page will be displayed.

When you look at the second and third dialog boxes in this figure, you can see that they contain checkboxes with messages that say "Prevent this page from creating additional dialogs." After an application has popped up one dialog box, most modern browsers will include this message on any more dialog boxes. This is a security feature designed to prevent endless loops of dialog boxes from locking the browser, and this can't be disabled.

Incidentally, the dialog boxes in this figure are the ones for a Chrome browser. When you use other browsers, the dialog boxes will work the same but have slightly different appearances.

The dialog boxes for the Calculate MPG application

The first prompt dialog box

```
Enter miles driven

273

                              OK        Cancel
```

The second prompt dialog box

```
Enter gallons of gas used

12.5

☐ Prevent this page from creating additional dialogs.

                              OK        Cancel
```

The alert dialog box that displays the result

```
Miles per gallon = 21

☐ Prevent this page from creating additional dialogs.

                                        OK
```

The HTML and JavaScript for the application

```html
<html>
<head>
    <title>The Calculate MPG Application</title>
    <script>
        var miles = prompt("Enter miles driven");
        miles = parseFloat(miles);
        var gallons = prompt("Enter gallons of gas used");
        gallons = parseFloat(gallons);
        var mpg = miles/gallons;
        mpg = parseInt(mpg);
        alert("Miles per gallon = " + mpg);
    </script>
</head>
<body>
    <!-- Will show after the JavaScript has run -->
    <h1>Thanks for using the Miles Per Gallon application!</h1>
</body>
</html>
```

Description

- If an application pops up more than one dialog box, most browsers will give you the option to prevent the page from creating any more. This is a built in security measure that can't be disabled.

Figure 2-13   The Miles Per Gallon application

The Test Scores application

Figure 2-14 presents a simple application that uses prompt methods to let the user enter three test scores. After the third one is entered, this application calculates the average test score. That ends the JavaScript that's embedded in the head element of the HTML document.

Then, the JavaScript that's coded in the body element is executed. It uses one write method to write an h1 element at the top of the page. Then, it uses another write method to write the three test scores and the average score into the body of the document so it is displayed in the browser window. This shows that the variables that were created by the JavaScript in the head element are available to the JavaScript in the body element.

If you take another look at the JavaScript in the head element, you can see that it starts by declaring the variables that are needed to get and process the entries. The entry and average variables are declared but not assigned a value. The entry variable will be used to receive the user entries, and the average variable will receive the calculated average of the scores entered by the user.

In contrast, the total variable is assigned a starting value of zero. Then, each entry is added to this total value, and it is divided by 3 to calculate the average score. In addition, the score1, score2, and score3 variables are declared and assigned values after each score has been entered and parsed.

The results displayed in the browser

The Test Scores App

Score 1 = 72
Score 2 = 78
Score 3 = 85

Average score = 78

Thanks for using the Test Scores application!

The HTML and JavaScript for the application

```
<html>
<head>
    <title>Average Test Scores</title>
    <script>
        var entry;
        var average;
        var total = 0;

        //get 3 scores from user and add them together
        entry = prompt("Enter test score");
        entry = parseInt(entry);
        var score1 = entry;
        total = total + score1;

        entry = prompt("Enter test score");
        entry = parseInt(entry);
        var score2 = entry;
        total = total + score2;

        entry = prompt("Enter test score");
        entry = parseInt(entry);
        var score3 = entry;
        total = total + score3;

        //calculate the average
        average = parseInt(total/3);
    </script>
</head>
<body>
    <script>
        document.write("<h1>The Test Scores App</h1>");
        document.write("Score 1 = " + score1 + "<br>" +
            "Score 2 = " + score2 + "<br>" +
            "Score 3 = " + score3 + "<br><br>" +
            "Average score = " + average + "<br><br>");
    </script>
    Thanks for using the Test Scores application!
</body>
</html>
```

Figure 2-14   The Test Scores application

Perspective

If you have programming experience, you can now see that JavaScript syntax is similar to other languages like Java and C#. As a result, you should have breezed through this chapter. You may also want to skip the exercises.

On the other hand, if you're new to programming and you understand all of the code in both of the applications in this chapter, you're off to a good start. Otherwise, you need to study the applications until you understand every line of code in each application. You should also do the exercises that follow.

Terms

external JavaScript file	number data type
embedded JavaScript	integer
JavaScript statement	decimal value
syntax	floating-point number
whitespace	string data type
identifier	string
reserved word	empty string
keyword	Boolean data type
camel casing	Boolean value
comment	numeric expression
block comment	arithmetic operator
in-line comment	modulus operator
comment out	order of precedence
uncomment	variable
object	declare a variable
method	assignment statement
property	assignment operator
call a method	compound assignment operator
dot operator (dot)	numeric literal
parameter	concatenate
window object	concatenation operator
global object	string literal
document object	escape sequence
primitive data type	NaN

Summary

- The JavaScript for an HTML document page is commonly coded in an *external JavaScript file* that's identified by a script element. However, the JavaScript can also be *embedded* in a script element in the head or body of a document.

- A JavaScript *statement* has a *syntax* that's similar to Java's. Its *identifiers* are case-sensitive and usually coded with either *camel casing* or underscore notation. Its c*omments* can be block or in-line.

- JavaScript provides many *objects* that provide *methods* and *properties* that you can *call* or refer to in your applications. Since the *window object* is the *global object* for JavaScript, you can omit it when referring to its methods or properties.

- The *document object* provides some commonly used methods like the write and writeln methods.

- JavaScript provides three *primitive data types*. The *number data type* provides for both *integers* and *decimal values*. The *string data type* provides for character (*string*) data. And the *Boolean data type* provides for true and false values.

- To assign a value to a *variable*, you use an *assignment operator*.

- When you assign a value to a number *variable*, you can use *numeric expressions* that include *arithmetic operators*, variable names, and *numeric literals*.

- When you assign a value to a string variable, you can use *string expressions* that include *concatenation operators*, variable names, and *string literals*. Within a string literal, you can use *escape sequences* to provide special characters.

Before you do the exercises for this book...

If you haven't already done so, you should install the Chrome browser and install the downloads for this book as described in appendix A.

Exercise 2-1   Modify the Miles Per Gallon application

In this application, you'll modify the code for the MPG application so the results are displayed in the browser window instead of an alert dialog box. The browser window should look something like this:

The Miles Per Gallon Application

Miles driven = 125
Gallons of gas = 12

Miles per gallon = 10

Thanks for using our MPG application.

---

1. Open your text editor or IDE. Then, open this HTML file:
   `c:\javascript\exercises\ch02\mpg.html`

2. Run the application with valid entries, and note the result. Then, run it with invalid entries like zeros or spaces, and note the result.

3. Modify this application so the result is displayed in the browser instead of an alert statement. This result should include the user's entries for miles and gallons as shown above.

4. If you have any problems when you test your exercises, please use Chrome's developer tools as shown in figure 1-16 of the last chapter.

Exercise 2-2   Modify the Test Scores application

In this exercise, you'll modify the Test Scores application so it works the same but uses less code. The output of the application will still be displayed in the browser as it is in figure 2-14.

1. Open your text editor or IDE. Then, open this HTML file:
    ```
    c:\javascript\exercises\ch02\scores.html
    ```

2. Run the application with valid entries, and note the result.

3. Modify this application so the variable declarations for the three scores parse the entries before storing their values. In other words, the two lines of code for each variable
    ```
    entry = parseInt(entry);
    var score1 = entry;
    ```
    should be combined into one.

4. Change the statements that accumulate the score total so they use the += assignment operator shown in figure 2-10 instead of the equals operator.

Exercise 2-3   Create a simple application

Copying and modifying an existing application is often a good way to start a new application. So in this exercise, you'll modify the Miles Per Gallon application so it gets the length and width of a rectangle from the user, calculates the area and the perimeter of the rectangle, and displays the results in the browser like this:

The Area and Perimeter App

Length = 25
Width = 10

Area = 250
Perimeter = 70

Thanks for using the Area and Perimeter application!

1. Open your text editor or IDE. Then, open this HTML file:
    ```
    c:\javascript\exercises\ch02\rectangle.html
    ```
    As you can see, this file contains the code for the Miles Per Gallon application.

2. Modify the code for this application so it works for the new application. (The area of a rectangle is just length times width. The perimeter is 2 times length plus 2 times width.)

3

The essential JavaScript statements

In the last chapter, you were introduced to the basics of JavaScript coding. Now, you'll learn how to code the JavaScript statements that drive the logic of an application.

How to code the basic control statements

Like all programming languages, JavaScript provides *control statements* that let you control how information is processed in an application. These statements include if statements as well as looping statements. Before you can learn how to use these statements, though, you need to learn how to code conditional expressions.

How to code conditional expressions

Figure 3-1 shows you how to code *conditional expressions* that use the six *relational operators*. A conditional expression returns a value of true or false based on the result of a comparison between two expressions. If, for example, the value of lastName in the first expression in the first table is "Harrison", the expression will return false. Or, if the value of rate in the last expression is 10, the expression will return true (because 10 / 100 is .1 and .1 is greater than or equal to 0.1).

In addition to using the relational operators to code a conditional expression, you can use the global isNaN method. This method determines whether a string value is a valid numeric value, as illustrated by the next set of examples. To use this method, you pass a parameter that represents the string value that should be tested. Then, this method returns true if the value can't be converted to a number or false if it can be converted.

To code a *compound conditional expression*, you use the *logical operators* shown in the second table in this figure to combine two conditional expressions. If you use the AND operator, the compound expression returns true if both expressions are true. If you use the OR operator, the compound expression returns true if either expression is true. If you use the NOT operator, the value returned by the expression is reversed. For instance, !isNaN returns true if the parameter is a number, so isNaN(10) returns false, but !isNaN(10) returns true.

Note that the logical operators in this figure are shown in their order of precedence. That is the order in which the operators are evaluated if more than one logical operator is used in a compound expression. This means that NOT operators are evaluated before AND operators, which are evaluated before OR operators. Although this is normally what you want, you can override this order by using parentheses.

In most cases, the conditional expressions that you use are relatively simple so coding them isn't much of a problem. In the rest of this chapter, you'll see some of the types of conditional expressions that are commonly used.

The relational operators

Operator	Description	Example
==	Equal	`lastName == "Hopper"` `testScore == 10`
!=	Not equal	`firstName != "Grace"` `months != 0`
<	Less than	`age < 18`
<=	Less than or equal	`investment <= 0`
>	Greater than	`testScore > 100`
>=	Greater than or equal	`rate / 100 >= 0.1`

The syntax of the global isNaN method

```
isNaN(expression)
```

Examples of the isNaN method

```
isNaN("Hopper") // Returns true since "Hopper" is not a number
isNaN("123.45") // Returns false since "123.45" can be converted to a number
```

The logical operators in order of precedence

Operator	Description	Example
!	NOT	`!isNaN(age)`
&&	AND	`age > 17 && score < 70`
||	OR	`isNaN(rate) || rate < 0`

How the logical operators work

- Both tests with the AND operator must be true for the overall test to be true.
- At least one test with the OR operator must be true for the overall test to be true.
- The NOT operator switches the result of the expression to the other Boolean value. For example, if an expression is true, the NOT operator converts it to false.
- To override the order of precedence when two or more logical operators are used in a conditional expression, you can use parentheses.

Description

- A *conditional expression* uses the *relational operators* to compare the results of two expressions.
- A *compound conditional expression* joins two or more conditional expressions using the *logical operators*.
- The isNaN method tests whether a string can be converted to a number. It returns true if the string is not a number and false if the string is a number.

Note

- Confusing the assignment operator (=) with the equality operator (==) is a common programming error.

Figure 3-1   How to code conditional expressions

How to code if statements

If you've programmed in other languages, you won't have any trouble using JavaScript if statements. Just study figure 3-2 to get the syntax and see how the conditions are coded. But if you're new to programming, let's take it slower.

An *if statement* lets you control the execution of statements based on the results of conditional expressions. In a syntax summary like the one in this figure, the brackets [ ] indicate a portion of the syntax that is optional. As a result, this summary means that each if statement must start with an *if clause*. Then, it can have one or more *else if clauses*, but they are optional. Last, it can have an *else clause*, but that clause is also optional.

To code the if clause, you code the keyword *if* followed by a conditional expression in parentheses and a block of one or more statements inside braces. If the conditional expression is true, this block of code will be executed and any remaining clauses in the if statement will be skipped over. If the conditional expression is false, the next clause that follows will be executed.

To code an else if clause, you code the keywords *else if* followed by a conditional expression in parentheses and a block of one or more statements inside braces. If the conditional expression is true, its block of code will be executed and any remaining clauses in the if statement will be skipped over. This will continue until one of the else if expressions is true or they all are false.

To code an else clause, you code the keyword *else* followed by a block of one or more statements inside braces. This code will only be executed if all the conditional expressions in the if and else if clauses are false. If those expressions are false and there isn't an else clause, the if statement won't execute any code.

The first example in this figure shows an if statement with an else clause. If the value of the age variable is greater than or equal to 18, the first message will be displayed. Otherwise, the second message will be displayed.

The second example shows an if statement with two else if clauses and an else clause. If the rate is not a number, the first message is displayed. If the rate is less than zero, the second message is displayed. If the rate is greater than 12, the third message is displayed. Otherwise, the message in the else clause is displayed.

The third example shows an if statement with a compound conditional expression that tests whether the value of the userEntry variable is not a number or whether the value is less than or equal to zero. If either expression is true, a message is displayed. If both expressions are false, nothing is done because this if statement doesn't have else if clauses or an else clause.

The fourth set of examples shows two ways to test whether a Boolean variable is true. Here, both statements are evaluated the same way. That's because a condition that is coded as just a Boolean variable is tested to see whether the variable is equal to true. In practice, this condition is usually coded the way it is in the second statement, with just the name of the variable.

The fifth set of examples is similar. It shows three ways to test whether a Boolean variable is false. Here again, the last statement illustrates the way this condition is usually coded: !isValid.

The syntax of the if statement

```
if ( condition-1 ) { statements }
[ else if ( condition-2 ) { statements }
  ...
  else if ( condition-n ) { statements } ]
[ else { statements } ]
```

An if statement with an else clause

```
if ( age >= 18 ) {
    alert ("You may vote.");
} else {
    alert ("You are not old enough to vote.");
}
```

An if statement with else if and else clauses

```
if ( isNaN(rate) ) {
    alert ("You did not provide a number for the rate.");
} else if ( rate < 0 ) {
    alert ("The rate may not be less than zero.");
} else if ( rate > 12 ) {
    alert ("The rate may not be greater than 12.");
} else {
    alert ("The rate is: " + rate + ".");
}
```

An if statement with a compound conditional expression

```
if ( isNaN(userEntry) || userEntry <= 0 ) {
    alert ("Please enter a valid number greater than zero.");
}
```

Two ways to test whether a Boolean variable is true

```
if ( isValid == true ) { }
if ( isValid ) { }                 // same as isValid == true
```

Three ways to test whether a Boolean variable is false

```
if ( isValid == false ) { }
if ( !isValid == true ) { }
if ( !isValid ) { }                // same as !isValid == true
```

Description

- An *if statement* always has one *if clause*. It can also have one or more *else if clauses* and one *else clause* at the end.

- The statements in a clause are executed when its condition is true. Otherwise, control passes to the next clause. If none of the conditions in the preceding clauses are true, the statements in the else clause are executed.

- If necessary, you can code one if statement within the if, else if, or else clause of another if statement. This is referred to as *nesting if statements*.

Figure 3-2   How to code if statements

How to code while and do-while loops

Figure 3-3 starts by presenting the syntax of the *while statement* that is used to create *while loops*. This statement executes the block of code that's in the loop while its conditional expression is true.

The example that follows this syntax shows how a while loop can be used to add the numbers 1 through 5. Before the while statement starts, a variable named sumOfNumbers is set to zero, a variable named numberOfLoops is set to 5, and a variable named counter is set to 1. Then, the condition for the while statement says that the while loop should be repeated as long as the counter value is less than or equal to the numberOfLoops value.

Within the while loop, the first statement adds the counter value to the sumOfNumbers variable. Then, the counter is increased by 1. As a result, this loop is executed five times, one time each for the counter values 1, 2, 3, 4, and 5. The loop ends when the counter is no longer less than or equal to 5, which is when the counter value equals 6.

This example is followed by the syntax for the *do-while statement* that is used to create *do-while loops*. This is like the while statement, but its condition is tested at the end of the loop instead of at the start. As a result, the statements in the loop are always executed at least once. This statement is illustrated by the example that follows the syntax, which gets the same result as the while statement.

In general, you use the do-while statement when you want to execute the statements in the loop at least once, and you use the while statement for other types of loops. Coded correctly, though, you can get the same results with both statements.

The last example in this figure shows another example of a do-while loop. This loop keeps going while the user's entry isn't a number (isNaN). Within the loop, a prompt statement gets the user's entry, the entry is parsed, and an if statement displays an error message if the entry isn't a number. This loop continues until the user enters a number.

The syntax of a while loop

```
while ( condition ) { statements }
```

A while loop that adds the numbers from 1 through 5

```
var sumOfNumbers = 0;
var numberOfLoops = 5;
var counter = 1;
while (counter <= numberOfLoops) {
    sumOfNumbers += counter;     // adds counter to sumOfNumbers
    counter++;                   // adds 1 to counter
}
alert(sumOfNumbers);             // displays 15
```

The syntax of a do-while loop

```
do { statements } while ( condition );
```

A do-while loop that adds the numbers from 1 through 5

```
var sumOfNumbers = 0;
var numberOfLoops = 5;
var counter = 1;
do {
    sumOfNumbers += counter;     // adds counter to sumOfNumbers
    counter++;                   // adds 1 to counter
}
while (counter <= numberOfLoops);
alert(sumOfNumbers);             // displays 15
```

A do-while loop that gets a user entry until it is a number

```
do {
    var investment = prompt("Enter investment amount as xxxxx.xx", 10000);
    investment = parseFloat(investment);
    if ( isNaN(investment) ) {
        alert("Investment must be a number");
    }
}
while ( isNaN(investment) );
```

Description

- The *while statement* creates a *while loop* that contains a block of code that is executed while its condition is true. This condition is tested at the beginning of the loop, and the loop is skipped if the condition is false.

- The *do-while statement* creates a *do-while* loop that contains a block of code that is executed while its condition is true. However, its condition is tested at the end of the loop instead of the beginning, so the code in the loop will always be executed at least once.

Figure 3-3   How to code while and do-while loops

How to code for loops

Figure 3-4 shows how to use the *for statement* to create *for loops*. Within the parentheses of a for statement, you initialize a *counter* (or *index*) variable that will be used within the loop. Then, you code a condition that determines when the loop will end. Last, you code an expression that specifies how the counter should be incremented.

The first example in this figure shows how this works. Here, the first statement in the parentheses of the for statement declares a variable named counter and initializes it to 1. Then, the condition in the parentheses determines that the loop will continue as long as counter is less than or equal to the value in numberOfLoops, and the expression that follows increments the counter by 1 each time through the loop. Within the loop, the value of the counter variable is added to the variable named sumOfNumbers.

If you compare this example to the first two examples in figure 3-3, you can see that all three get the same results. But with the for statement, you don't have to initialize the counter before the statement, and you don't have to increment the counter within the statement.

The next example shows a more realistic use of a for loop. This loop calculates the future value of an investment amount ($10,000) at a specific interest rate (7.0%) for a specific number of years (10). This time, *i* is used as the name for the counter variable, which is a common coding practice, and the loop continues as long as this index is less than or equal to the number of years. In other words, the statement in the loop is executed once for each of the 10 years.

Within the loop, this expression is used to calculate the interest for the year

```
futureValue * annualRate / 100
```

Then, the += operator adds the interest to the futureValue variable. Note here that the annualRate needs to be divided by 100 for this calculation to work right (7.0 / 100 = .07). Note too in the statements after this example, that this statement could be coded in more than one way and still get the same results.

In both of the examples in this figure, the counter is incremented by 1 each time through the loop, which is usually the way this statement is coded. However, you can also increment or decrement the counter by other amounts. That just depends on what you're trying to do. To increment by 2, for example, you could code the increment expression as:

```
i = i + 2
```

The syntax of a for statement

```
for ( counterInitialization; condition; incrementExpression ) {
    statements
}
```

A for loop that adds the numbers from 1 through 5

```
var sumOfNumbers = 0;
var numberOfLoops = 5;
for ( var counter = 1; counter <= numberOfLoops; counter++ ) {
    sumOfNumbers += counter;     // adds counter to sumOfNumbers
}
alert(sumOfNumbers);              // displays 15
```

A for loop that calculates the future value of an investment

```
var investment = 10000;
var annualRate = 7.0;
var years = 10;
var futureValue = investment;
for ( var i = 1; i <= years; i++ ) {
    futureValue += futureValue * annualRate / 100;
}
alert (futureValue);                  // displays 19672
```

Other ways that the future value calculation could be coded

```
futureValue = futureValue + (futureValue * annualRate / 100);
futureValue = futureValue * (1 + (annualRate / 100))
```

Description

- The *for statement* is used when you need to increment or decrement a counter that determines how many times the *for loop* is executed.

- Within the parentheses of a for statement, you code an expression that initializes a *counter* (or *index*) variable, a conditional expression that determines when the loop ends, and an increment expression that indicates how the counter should be incremented or decremented each time through the loop.

- The variable name *i* is commonly used for the counter in a for loop.

Figure 3-4   How to code for loops

Three illustrative applications

The three applications that follow illustrate the use of the control statements that you just learned about. These still aren't realistic applications because they get the user entries from prompt statements instead of from controls on a form. But these applications should give you a better understanding of how the control statements work.

The enhanced Miles Per Gallon application

Figure 3-5 presents an enhanced version of the Miles Per Gallon application that you reviewed in chapter 2. This application just gets user entries for miles driven and gallons of gas used and then displays the miles per gallon in an alert dialog box.

This time, though, this application lets the user do the calculation for more than one set of entries. It also checks the entries to make sure that both are valid, and displays an error message if one or both aren't valid.

In the JavaScript, you can see how a do-while loop is used to let the user repeat the calculation. Before entering this loop, a variable named "again" is set to a value of "y". Then, the do-while loop is repeated until that value is changed by the user. The user can do that when the last statement in the loop displays the second prompt dialog box shown in this figure.

Within the do-while loop, you can see how an if-else statement is used to provide the data validation. Here, the condition for the if clause uses the and (&&) operator to check whether the value entered for miles is a number (!isNaN) and greater than zero and also whether the value entered for gallons is a number and greater than zero. If all four conditions are true, the application calculates miles per gallon and displays the result in an alert dialog box. If any one of the conditions isn't true, the application displays an error message in an alert dialog box.

In other words, this if-else statement tests to see whether both entries are valid. If so, it does the calculation and displays the result. If not, it displays an error message. Note, however, that you could reverse this by testing to see whether one of the entries is invalid by using or (||) operators. If so, you display the error message. If not, you do the calculation and display the result. This can simplify the coding because you don't have to use the not operator with the isNaN method (!isNaN).

Two of the dialog boxes for the Miles Per Gallon application

The alert dialog box that displays an invalid data message

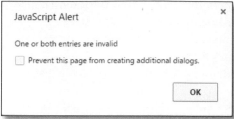

The prompt dialog box for continuing the application

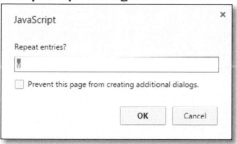

The HTML and JavaScript for the application

```
<head>
    <title>Calculate Miles Per Gallon</title>
    <script>
        var again = "y";
        do {
            var miles = prompt("Enter miles driven");
            miles = parseFloat(miles);
            var gallons = prompt("Enter gallons of gas used");
            gallons = parseFloat(gallons);
            if (!isNaN(miles) && miles > 0
                    && !isNaN(gallons) && gallons > 0)
            {
                var mpg = miles/gallons;
                mpg = parseInt(mpg);
                alert("Miles per gallon = " + mpg);
            }
            else
            {
                alert("One or both entries are invalid");
            }
            again = prompt("Repeat entries?", "y");
        }
        while (again == "y");
    </script>
</head>
<body>
    <main>
        <!-- Will show after JavaScript has run -->
        Thanks for using the Miles Per Gallon application!
    </main>
</body>
```

Figure 3-5   The enhanced Miles Per Gallon application

The Future Value application

Figure 3-6 presents a Future Value application that shows how a for loop can be used to calculate the future value of an investment amount. If you study the code for this application, you can see that prompt statements are used to get the investment amount, interest rate, and number of years.

Then, a for loop uses these entries to calculate the future value of the investment. To do that, it uses i as the name of the index and increments it by 1 each time through the loop. It does that as long as the index is less than or equal to the number of years entered by the user. This means that the loop will be run once for each year. If, for example, the user enters 10 for the number of years, the loop will be run 10 times.

Within the loop, the future value is calculated. To do that, the expression in the parentheses calculates the interest for the year. Then, the interest is added to the current value of the futureValue variable, and the result is stored in the futureValue variable. As figure 3-4 shows, this calculation could also be coded in other ways.

After the for loop finishes, this application just parses the future value to an integer so the decimal places will be dropped. Then, the JavaScript in the body of the HTML document displays the results in the browser.

The first of three prompt dialog boxes for the Future Value application

The results in a browser

Investment amount = 10000 Interest rate = 7.5 Years = 10 Future Value is 20610

Thanks for using the Future Value application.

The HTML and JavaScript for the application

```
<head>
    <meta charset="UTF-8">
    <title>Future Value Application</title>
    <script>
        var futureValue;

        // get user entries
        var investment =
            prompt("Enter investment amount as xxxxx.xx", 10000);
        investment = parseFloat(investment);
        var rate = prompt("Enter interest rate as xx.x", 7.5);
        rate = parseFloat(rate);
        var years = prompt("Enter number of years", 10);
        years = parseInt(years);

        // calulate future value
        futureValue = investment;
        for (var i = 1; i <= years; i++ ) {
            futureValue = futureValue + (futureValue * rate / 100);
        }
        futureValue = parseInt(futureValue);
    </script>
</head>
<body>
    <main>
        <script>
            document.write("Investment amount = " + investment);
            document.write(" Interest rate = " + rate);
            document.write(" Years = " + years);
            document.write(" Future Value is " + futureValue + "<br><br>");
        </script>
        Thanks for using the Future Value application.
    </main>
</body>
```

Figure 3-6   The Future Value application

The enhanced Test Scores application

Figure 3-7 presents an enhanced version of the Test Scores application that you reviewed in chapter 2. This time, the application uses a do-while loop to let the users enter as many scores as they want. Then, when a user enters 999 to end the entries, the application displays the average test score.

This version of the application also tests to make sure that each entry is a valid number from 0 through 100 before it is added to the test score total. If an entry isn't valid, the application displays an error message and issues another prompt statement so the user can either enter another score or 999 to end the entries.

If you look at the JavaScript in the script element of the head section of the HTML, you can see that it starts by declaring the three variables that are needed. The total variable has a starting value of zero, and it will be used to sum the valid test scores. The entryCount variable has a starting value of 0, and it will be used to count the number of valid test scores. The third variable is named entry, and it doesn't have a starting value assigned to it because it will be used to receive the user entries.

After the variables are declared, a do-while loop is used to get the user entries. Because this application has to get at least one user entry, it makes sense to use a do-while loop instead of a while loop.

Within the do-while loop, the prompt method is used to get each user entry. Note that the second parameter is set to 999 so the user can just press the Enter key to end the entries.

After a user makes an entry, the entry is parsed into an integer and an if clause checks to make sure the entry is between 0 and 100. If it is, the entry is valid so the entry value is added to the total variable and 1 is added to the entryCount variable.

If the entry isn't between 0 and 100, the else if clause that follows checks to see whether the entry is not equal to 999. If it isn't, an alert method displays an error message and the entry isn't processed. If the entry is 999, nothing is done.

When the statements in the loop are finished, the condition for the loop is tested. Then, if the entry value is 999, the loop ends. Otherwise, the loop is repeated for the next entry.

When the loop ends, the average test score is calculated by dividing the total variable by the entryCount variable. Then, the parseInt method is used to convert the decimal value to an integer, and an alert statement displays the average score.

The dialog boxes for the Test Scores application

The prompt dialog box for the next test score

Enter test score
Or enter 999 to end entries

999

OK   Cancel

The alert dialog box for an entry error

Entry must by a valid number from 0 through 100
Or enter 999 to end entries

☐ Prevent this page from creating additional dialogs.

OK

The alert dialog box that displays the result

Average score is 79

☐ Prevent this page from creating additional dialogs.

OK

The JavaScript in the head section of the HTML file

```
<script>
    var total = 0;
    var entryCount = 0;
    var entry;
    do {
        entry = prompt("Enter test score\n" +
                       "Or enter 999 to end entries", 999);
        entry = parseInt(entry);
        if (entry >= 0 && entry <= 100) {
            total = total + entry;
            entryCount++; }
        else if (entry != 999){
            alert("Entry must by a valid number from 0 through 100\n" +
                  "Or enter 999 to end entries"); }
    }
    while (entry != 999);
    var average = total/entryCount;
    average = parseInt(average);
    alert("Average score is " + average);
</script>
```

Figure 3-7   The enhanced Test Scores application

How to work with arrays

The next two figures present the basic skills for working with arrays. As you will see, arrays are commonly used in JavaScript applications.

How to create and use arrays

An *array* is an object that contains one or more items called *elements*. Each of these elements can be a primitive data type or an object. The *length* of an array indicates the number of elements that it contains.

Figure 3-8 shows two ways to create an array. When you use the first method, you use the *new* keyword followed by the Array object name to create an array with the number of elements that is indicated by the length parameter. This length must be a whole number that is greater than or equal to zero. If you don't specify the length, the array will be empty.

When you use the second method, you just code a set of brackets. This gives you the same result that you get with the first method and no parameter, an empty array.

To refer to the elements in an array, you use an *index* that ranges from zero to one less than the number of elements in an array. In an array with 12 elements, for example, the index values range from 0 to 11.

To use an index, you code it within brackets after the name of the array. In this figure, all of the examples use literal values for the indexes, but an index can also be a variable that contains an index value, as you'll see shortly. If you try to access an element that hasn't been assigned a value, the value of undefined will be returned.

The last two examples in this figure show how to work with the array's length property. The length property returns the number of elements in an array. In the first example, the length property is stored in a variable for later use.

In the second example, the length property is used as the index of a new element. Since this property will always be 1 more than the highest index used in the array, this adds the new element at the end of the array.

The syntax for creating an array

Using the new keyword with the Array object name
```
var arrayName = new Array(length);
```

Using an array literal
```
var arrayName = [];
```

The syntax for referring to an element of an array
```
arrayName[index]
```

The syntax for getting the length property of an array
```
arrayName.length
```

How to add values to an array
```
var totals = [];
totals[0] = 141.95;
totals[1] = 212.25;
totals[2] = 411;
```

How to refer to the elements in an array
```
totals[2]          // Refers to the third element - 411
totals[1]          // Refers to the second element - 212.25
```

How to determine how many elements are in an array
```
var count = totals.length;        //3
```

How to add a value to the end of an array
```
totals[totals.length] = 135.75;    //adds a fourth element at index = 3
```

Description

- An *array* can store one or more *elements*. The *length* of an array is the number of elements in the array.

- One way to create an array is to use the new keyword, the name of the object (Array), and an optional length parameter.

- The other way to create an array is to code a set of brackets.

- To refer to the elements in an array, you use an *index* where 0 is the first element, 1 is the second element, and so on.

- One way to add an element to the end of an array is to use the length property as the index.

Figure 3-8   How to create and use an array

How to use for loops to work with arrays

For loops are commonly used to process one array element at a time by incrementing an index variable. Figure 3-9 shows how this works.

The first example in this figure shows how to create an array and fill it with the numbers 1 through 10. First, this code creates an empty array named numbers. Then, it uses a for loop to add the numbers 1 through 10 to the array. In the body of this loop, one is added to the value in i and the result is stored in the array element. As a result, the element at index 0 stores a 1, the element at index 1 stores a 2, and so on.

Next, this example displays the values in the array. First, this code creates an empty string named numbersString. Then, it uses a for loop to access the elements in the array. In the for loop, the length property of the array is used to control how many times the loop executes. This allows the same code to work with arrays of different lengths. Inside the for loop, the value in the element and a space are concatenated to the end of numbersString. Finally, numbersString is displayed, which shows the ten numbers that were stored in the array.

The next example in this figure shows how to use for loops to add the totals in an array and to display those totals. First, the code puts four values into an array named totals. Then, a for loop adds the four totals in the array to a variable named sum. Last, a for loop concatenates the four totals in the array to a string variable that is displayed when the loop ends.

Code that puts the numbers 1 through 10 into an array

```
var numbers = [];
for (var i = 0; i < 10; i++) {
    numbers[i] = i + 1;
}
```

Code that displays the numbers in the array

```
var numbersString = "";
for (var i = 0; i < numbers.length; i++) {
    numbersString += numbers[i] + " ";
}
alert (numbersString);
```

The message that's displayed

Code that puts four totals in an array

```
var totals = [];
totals[0] = 141.95;
totals[1] = 212.25;
totals[2] = 411;
totals[3] = 135.75;
```

Code that sums the totals in the array

```
var sum = 0;
for (var i = 0; i < totals.length; i++) {
    sum += totals[i];
}
```

Code that displays the totals and the sum

```
var totalsString = "";
for (var i = 0; i < totals.length; i++) {
    totalsString += totals[i] + "\n";
}
alert ("The totals are:\n" + totalsString + "\n" + "Sum: " + sum);
```

The message that's displayed

Description

- When you use a for loop to work with an array, you can use the counter for the loop as the index for the array.

Figure 3-9   How to use for loops to work with arrays

The Test Scores application with an array

Figure 3-10 presents an enhanced version of the Test Scores application that stores the valid entries in an array. This will give you a better idea of how arrays and for loops can be used.

The user interface

The user interface for this application works the same as the one in figure 3-7. It lets the users enter as many test scores as they want. Then, when a user enters 999 to end the series of entries, the application displays the average score.

The JavaScript

If you look at the JavaScript for this application, you can see that it starts by declaring the variables that are needed to get and process the entries. Here, entry and average variables are declared but not assigned values. The scores variable is declared as an empty array. The total variable is given a starting value of zero. And the show variable is given a starting value of a string that ends with a new line escape sequence. This variable will be used to build the alert message that displays the results at the end of the application.

After the variables are declared, a do-while loop is used to get the user entries. This is like the do-while loop in figure 3-7. The only difference is that the highlighted statement adds each valid entry to the scores array. It doesn't add each value to total variable.

When the do-while loop ends, a for loop processes the scores in the array. This loop uses the length property of the scores array to determine how many times to execute the loop, and the loop's index variable (i) is used to retrieve the elements from the scores array. Each time through the loop, the array element is added to the total variable and concatenated to the show variable.

When the for loop ends, the average test score is calculated and stored in the variable named average. This calculation simply divides the total variable by the length of the scores array, which is the number of scores in the array. This calculation is embedded within the parseInt method to convert the result to an integer. Last, an alert method displays the concatenated values of the show variable and the average variable.

The alert dialog box that displays the result

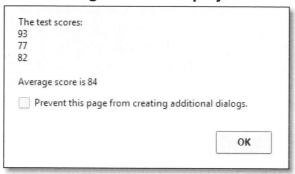

The test scores:
93
77
82

Average score is 84

☐ Prevent this page from creating additional dialogs.

OK

The JavaScript for the enhanced Test Scores application

```
<script>
    var entry;
    var average;
    var scores = [];
    var total = 0;
    var show = "The test scores:\n";

    //first use a do-while loop to put the scores in an array
    do {
        entry = prompt("Enter test score\n" +
                       "Or enter 999 to end entries", 999);
        entry = parseInt(entry);
        if (entry >= 0 && entry <= 100) {
            scores[scores.length] = entry;
        }
        else if (entry != 999){
            alert("Entry must by a valid number from 0 through 100\n" +
                  "Or enter 999 to end entries");
        }
    }
    while (entry != 999);

    //next use a for loop to process the scores
    for (var i = 0; i < scores.length; i++) {
        total = total + scores[i];        //both are numbers so adds
        show = show + scores[i] + "\n";   //strings & numbers so concatenates
    }

    //then calculate the average and display
    average = parseInt(total/scores.length);
    alert(show + "\nAverage score is " + average);
</script>
```

Figure 3-10   The Test Scores application with an array

Perspective

If you have programming experience, you can now see that the JavaScript control statements are similar to those in other languages like Java and C#. As a result, you probably skimmed your way through this chapter. You may also want to skip the exercises.

On the other hand, if you're new to programming and you understand all of the code in the applications in this chapter, you're off to a good start. Otherwise, you need to study the applications until you understand every line of code in each application. You should also do the exercises that follow.

Terms

control statement	while loop
conditional expression	do-while statement
relational operator	do-while loop
compound conditional expression	for statement
logical operator	for loop
if statement	loop counter
if clause	loop index
else if clause	array
else clause	array element
nested if statements	array length
while statement	

Summary

- When you code a *conditional expression*, you can use *relational operators*, the global isNaN method, and *logical operators*.

- An *if statement* always starts with an *if clause*. It can also have one or more *else if clauses* and a concluding *else clause*, but those clauses are optional.

- The *while* and *do-while* statements can be used to loop through a series of statements while a condition is true.

- The *for statement* can be used to loop through a series of statements once for each time a *counter* or *index* is incremented or decremented.

- An *array* can store one or more *elements* that you can refer to by the *indexes* of the elements. The *length* property of the array holds the number of elements in the array. To process the elements in an array, you can use a for loop.

Exercise 3-1   Enhance the Future Value application

This exercise will give you a chance to use if statements, do loops, and for loops as you enhance the Future Value application in figure 3-6. The eventual output of this application will be displayed in the browser and should look something like this:

```
Investment amount = 10000 Interest rate = 7.5 Years = 5
Year=1 Interest=750 Value=10750
Year=2 Interest=806.25 Value=11556
Year=3 Interest=866.71875 Value=12422
Year=4 Interest=931.72265625 Value=13354
Year=5 Interest=1001.60185546875 Value=14356

Investment amount = 10000 Interest rate = 8.5 Years = 6
Year=1 Interest=850 Value=10850
Year=2 Interest=922.25 Value=11772
Year=3 Interest=1000.64125 Value=12772
Year=4 Interest=1085.69575625 Value=13858
Year=5 Interest=1177.97989553125 Value=15036
Year=6 Interest=1278.10818665514062 Value=16314

Thanks for using the Future Value application.
```

If you have any problems when you're testing, remember to use Chrome's developer tools as shown in figure 1-16 of chapter 1.

Test the Future Value application

1. Open your text editor or IDE. Then, open this HTML file:

    `c:\javascript\exercises\ch03\future_value.html`

2. Test the application with valid entries, and note the result. Then, test it with invalid entries, and note the result.

Add a do-while statement for continuing the entries

3. Add a do-while statement to the application like the one in figure 3-5 so the user can repeat the calculation for another series of entries.

Add validation for the investment and rate entries

4. Add a do-while statement like the one in the third example of figure 3-3 so the user will have to enter a valid investment amount before the application will continue with the next entry.

5. Add a similar do-while statement for the interest rate entry. This time, the application shouldn't continue until the user enters a value that's greater than zero and less than 15.

Enhance the display of the results as shown above

6. Modify the for loop that calculates the future value so it displays the interest rate and future value for each year, as shown above. Note that you'll also have to change the location of the existing write methods to get the display the way it is above.

Exercise 3-2   Enhance the Test Scores application

In this exercise, you'll make an enhancement to the Test Scores application in figure 3-10 that uses an array. What you'll do is add a for loop that gets the highest score in the array and displays it below the average score in the alert dialog box:

```
The test scores:
85
96
72
98

Average score is 87
Highest score is 98

☐ Prevent this page from creating additional dialogs.

                                              OK
```

If you have any problems when you're testing, remember to use Chrome's developer tools as shown in figure 1-16 of chapter 1.

1. Open your text editor or IDE. Then, open this HTML file and review its code:

   `c:\javascript\exercises\ch03\scores_array.html`

2. Test the application with valid entries, and note the result. Then, test it with invalid entries, and note the result.

3. Declare a variable named highestScore at the start of the script that will be used to store the highest score. Its starting value should be zero.

4. Add a second for loop right before the alert statement at the end of the script. This for loop should be executed once for each score in the array. Within the loop, an if statement should replace the value in the highestScore variable with the current score if that score is greater than the value in highestScore. That way, the highestScore variable will eventually store the highest score in the array.

5. Modify the alert statement that follows the for loop so it displays both the average score and highest score as shown above.

6. When you've got that working, comment out the second for loop. Then, modify the first for loop so it not only sums the scores but also puts the highest score in the highestScore variable. After this change, the application should work the same as it did after step 5.

4

How to work with JavaScript objects, functions, and events

In the last two chapters, you learned how to code some simple, but unrealistic, applications using the prompt and alert methods. Now, in this chapter, you'll learn how to work with objects, functions, and events. When you finish this chapter, you'll be able to start developing useful applications of your own.

How to use objects to work with data

In the last chapter, you learned the syntax for using the methods and properties of objects. You were also introduced to some of the methods and properties of the window object and document objects. Now, you'll learn how to use the objects, methods, and properties that you need for working with data, starting with a partial review of the methods of the window and document objects.

How to use the window and document objects

In chapter 2, you were introduced to the prompt and alert methods of the *window object*. Now, the first table in figure 4-1 presents another method of the window object that can be used to confirm an action.

Then, the second table in this figure summarizes the parseInt and parseFloat methods that you learned about in chapter 2. They are also methods of the window object. These methods are needed because the values that are returned by the prompt method and the values that the user enters into text boxes are treated as strings.

The use of these methods is illustrated by the first group of examples, starting with an example of the confirm method. For the statements after that, assume that the default values in the prompt methods aren't changed by the user. As a result, the second statement in this group stores 12345.6789 as a string in a variable named entryA, and the third statement converts the string to an integer value of 12345. Similarly, the fourth statement stores 12345.6789 as a string in a variable named entryB, and the fifth statement converts the string to a decimal value of 12345.6789.

Note that the object name isn't coded before the method name in these examples. That's okay because window is the *global object* of JavaScript. Note too that the parseInt method doesn't round the value. It just removes, or truncates, any decimal portion of the string.

In contrast to the window object, the *document object* is the highest object in the DOM structure. It represents the document, and you do need to code the object name (document) and the dot when you use one of its methods.

The second group of examples in this figure shows how to use three of the methods of the document object. The first is the getElementById method. It requires one parameter, which is the id for an element in the HTML document. When it is executed, it returns an object that represents that HTML element. In this example, this object is stored in a variable named rateBox.

The other two methods in this group are the write and writeln methods that you learned how to use in figure 2-7 of chapter 2. You saw how these methods work in some of the applications in the last two chapters.

Another method of the window object that displays a dialog box

Method	Description
confirm(*string*)	Displays a dialog box that contains the string in the parameter, an OK button, and a Cancel button. If the user clicks OK, true is returned. If the user clicks Cancel, false is returned.

Two methods of the window object for working with numbers

Method	Description
parseInt(*string*)	Converts the string that's passed to it to an integer data type and returns that value. If it can't convert the string to an integer, it returns NaN.
parseFloat(*string*)	Converts the string that's passed to it to a decimal data type and returns that value. If it can't convert the string to a decimal value, it returns NaN.

Examples of window methods

```
confirm("Are you sure you want to delete it?");

var entryA = prompt("Enter any value", 12345.6789);
entryA = parseInt(entryA);                    // entryA = 12345

var entryB = prompt("Enter any value", 12345.6789);
entryB = parseFloat(entryB);                  // entryB = 12345.6789
```

Three methods of the document object

Method	Description
getElementById(*id*)	Gets the HTML element that has the id that's passed to it and returns that element.
write(*string*)	Writes the string that's passed to it into the document.
writeln(*string*)	Writes the string ending with a new line character.

Examples of document methods

```
// returns the object for the HTML element
var rateBox = document.getElementById("rate");

// writes a line into the document
document.write("Today is " + today.toDateString());
```

Description

- The *window object* is the *global object*, and JavaScript lets you omit the object name and dot operator when referring to the window object.

- The *document object* is the object that lets you work with the Document Object Model (DOM) that represents all of the HTML elements of the page.

- Data in a text box is treated as a string. Before you can use it in a calculation, you need to use either the parseInt or parseFloat method to convert it to numeric data.

- *NaN* is a value that means "Not a Number". It is returned by the parseInt and parseFloat methods when the value that's being parsed isn't a number.

- The getElementById method is commonly used to get the object for an HTML element.

Figure 4-1   How to use the window and document objects

How to use Textbox and Number objects

The Textbox object is one of the DOM objects. It represents a text box in the web page that is used to get input from the user or display output to the user. The first two tables in figure 4-2 summarize one of its methods and two of its properties. Then, this figure shows the HTML code for two text boxes that have "first_name" and "sales_amount" as their ids. These text boxes will be used by the examples that follow.

The first group of examples in this figure shows two ways to get the value from the text box with "first_name" as its id. To do that with two statements, the first statement uses the getElementById method of the document object to get the Textbox object for that text box. Then, the second statement uses the value property of the Textbox object to get the value that the user entered into the text box.

In practice, though, you would do that with just one statement by using *method chaining*, or just *chaining*. In that case, a single statement first uses the getElementById method to get the Textbox object, and then uses the value property of the Textbox object to get the value from the text box. In other words, you combine the use of the two methods into a single statement.

The second group of examples takes chaining to a third level. Without chaining, it takes three statements to get a valid number from a text box. First, the getDocumentById method gets the Textbox object for the text box with sales_amount as its id. Second, the value property of the Textbox object gets the value that the user entered into the text box. Third, the parseFloat method of the window object converts the string value to a decimal number. If the user entry is a valid number, this stores the number in the salesAmount variable, so it becomes a Number object.

With chaining, though, this requires only one statement. Code like this is sometimes called *fluent,* because it's more like a sentence and thus more readable to a human eye. It can also make your code shorter, and shorter code is usually easier to understand. You'll want to be careful with this, though. Like a run-on sentence in a book, if you get to the end of the statement and can't remember what the beginning was doing, you might have chained too much.

The third table in this figure summarizes the toFixed method of a Number object. When a user enters a valid number in a text box and the parseInt or parseFloat method is used to parse it before it is stored in a variable, the variable becomes a Number object. Then, you can use the toFixed method of that Number object to round the number to a specific number of decimal places.

This is illustrated by the first statement in the third group of examples. This statement takes chaining to a fourth level by adding the toFixed method to the chain. As a result, the number that's stored in the salesAmount variable is rounded to two decimal places. Some might consider this an example of chaining taken too far.

The last two statements in this group present two more examples of chaining. The first one shows how to assign a value to a text box. In this case, the value is an empty string, which in effect clears the text box of any data. The second statement shows how to move the focus to a text box.

One method of the Textbox object

Method	Description
`focus()`	Moves the cursor into the text box, but doesn't return anything.

Two properties of the Textbox object

Property	Description
`value`	A string that represents the contents of the text box.
`disabled`	A Boolean value that controls whether the text box is disabled.

One method of the Number object

Method	Description
`toFixed(digits)`	Returns a string representation of the number after it has been rounded to the number of decimal places in the parameter.

HTML tags that define two text boxes

```
<input type="text" id="first_name">
<input type="text" id="sales_amount">
```

How to use the value property to get the value from a text box

Without chaining

```
var firstName = document.getElementById("first_name");
firstName = firstName.value;
```

With chaining

```
var firstName = document.getElementById("first_name").value;
```

How to use the parseFloat method to get a number value from a text box

Without chaining

```
var salesAmount = document.getElementById("sales_amount");
salesAmount = salesAmount.value;
salesAmount = parseFloat(salesAmount);
```

With chaining

```
var salesAmount = parseFloat(document.getElementById("sales_amount").value);
```

Other examples of chaining

```
var salesAmount =
    parseFloat(document.getElementById("sales_amount").value).toFixed(2);
document.getElementById("first_name").value = "";    // clear a text box
document.getElementById("first_name").focus();       // move focus to a text box
```

Description

- When you use the getElementById method to get a text box, the method returns a Textbox object. Then, you can use its value property to get the value in the box.
- When you assign a numeric value to a variable, a Number object is created. Then, you can use the Number methods with the variable.

Figure 4-2   How to use Textbox and Number objects

How to use Date and String objects

When you store a numeric or string value in a variable, it is automatically converted to a Number or String object. This lets you use the properties and methods of the Number and String objects without having to explicitly create the objects.

However, there isn't a primitive data type for dates. As a result, you need to create a Date object before you can use its methods. To do that, you can use the syntax shown in figure 4-3. When you create a Date object, it is initialized with the current date and time, which is the date and time on the user's computer.

After you create a Date object, you can use the methods in this figure to work with it. These methods are illustrated by the first group of examples, assuming that the date is March 9, 2015. Here, the toDateString method converts the date to a string. The getFullYear method gets the four-digit year from the date. The getDate method gets the day of the month. And the getMonth method gets the month, counting from 0, not 1. As a result, the getMonth method returns 2 for March, not 3.

This figure also presents one property and five methods of a String object. Then, the last group of examples presents some statements that show how these properties work. For example, the second statement uses the toUpperCase method to convert a string to uppercase, and the third statement uses the length property to get the number of characters in a string.

The last two statements show how the indexOf and substr methods of a String object can be used to extract a substring from a string. Here, the indexOf method is used to get the position (index) of the first space in the string, counting from zero. Since the space is in the sixth position, this method returns 5. Then, the substr method gets the substring that starts at the first position and has a length of 5. As a result, this method returns "Grace".

It's important to note the difference between the substr and substring methods. If you start from the first position, as in the example, there is no difference. In that case, both methods will return "Grace". However, if you start anywhere else, you'll get different results depending on which method you use.

For example, if you start at the third position (with an index of 2), the substr method will still return five characters, and you'll get the string "ace H". The substring method, on the other hand, will stop at the sixth position (with an index of 5). This means it will only return 3 characters, the string "ace".

Incidentally, JavaScript provides many more methods and properties for Date and String objects, but these will get you started. You can learn about the others in chapter 7.

The syntax for creating a JavaScript object and assigning it to a variable

```
var variableName = new ObjectType();
```

A statement that creates a Date object

```
var today = new Date();
```

A few of the methods of a Date object

Method	Description
toDateString()	Returns a string with the formatted date.
getFullYear()	Returns the four-digit year from the date.
getDate()	Returns the day of the month from the date.
getMonth()	Returns the month number from the date. The months are numbered starting with zero. January is 0 and December is 11.

Examples that use a Date object

```
var today = new Date();           // creates Date object with current date
alert ( today.toDateString() );   // displays Mon Mar 09 2015 on 3/9/2015
alert ( today.getFullYear() );    // displays 2015
alert ( today.getDate() );        // displays 9
alert ( today.getMonth() );       // displays 2, not 3 for March
```

One property of a String object

Method	Description
length	Returns the number of characters in the string.

A few of the methods of a String object

Method	Description
indexOf(search,position)	Searches for the first occurrence of the search string starting at the position specified or zero if position is omitted. If found, it returns the position of the first character, counting from 0. If not found, it returns -1.
substr(start,length)	Returns the substring that starts at the specified position (counting from zero) and contains the specified number of characters.
substring(start,stop)	Returns the substring that starts at the specified position (counting from zero) and stops at the specified position (counting from zero).
toLowerCase()	Returns a new string with the letters converted to lowercase.
toUpperCase()	Returns a new string with the letters converted to uppercase.

Examples that use a String object

```
var name = "Grace Hopper";
var nameUpper = name.toUpperCase();     // nameUpper = GRACE HOPPER
var nameLength = name.length;           // nameLength = 12
var index = name.indexOf(" ");          // index = 5
var firstName = name.substr(0, index);  // firstName = Grace
```

Description

- To create a Date object and assign it to a variable, use the syntax shown above.
- When you assign a string value to a variable, a String object is automatically created.

Figure 4-3   How to use Date and String objects

How to use the DOM to change the text for an element

As a browser loads an HTML page, it builds a *Document Object Model* (*DOM*) that contains *nodes* that represent all of the HTML elements and attributes for the page. This is illustrated by the HTML page and diagram in figure 4-4.

The DOM starts with one node for the html element and follows the nesting down to the lowest levels. In this example, those are the nodes for the label, input, and span elements. Besides the *element nodes* that are represented by ovals in this diagram, the DOM includes *text nodes* that hold the data for the HTML elements. In this diagram, these text nodes are rectangles. For instance, the first text node contains the text for the title element in the head section: "Join Email List". The one to the right of that contains the text for the h1 element in the body: "Please join our email list". And so on.

The DOM also contains other types of nodes like *attribute nodes* and *comment nodes*. For simplicity, though, these nodes aren't included in the diagram in this figure.

To modify the contents of a text node with JavaScript, you can use the syntax shown in the summary in this figure. This syntax is illustrated by the example that follows it:

```
document.getElementById(
    "email_address_error").firstChild.nodeValue = "New contents";
```

Here, the getElementById method is used to get the object for the HTML element with email_address_error as the value of its id attribute. Then, the firstChild property gets the first dependent node of the HTML element (the text node), and the nodeValue property refers to the value of the text node. Last, the statement assigns a new value to that node.

You should know, though, that there are a few HTML elements that don't have closing tags, like input and image elements. These elements are sometimes called *void* or *singleton elements*, and they don't have any child nodes. This means that firstChild.nodeValue won't work on a void element like a textbox.

If this is confusing, just accept the fact that firstChild.nodeValue represents the value of the text for an HTML element that has a closing tag. You'll see this illustrated more fully in the application at the end of this chapter.

The code for a web page

```
<!DOCTYPE html>
<html>
<head>
    <title>Join Email List</title>
</head>
<body>
    <h1>Please join our email list</h1>
    <form id="email_form" name="email_form"
          action="join.html" method="get">
        <label for="email_address">Email Address:</label>
        <input type="text" id="email_address">
        <span id="email_address_error">*</span><br>
        <label> </label>
        <input type="button" id="join_list" value="Join our List">
    </form>
</body>
</html>
```

The DOM for the web page

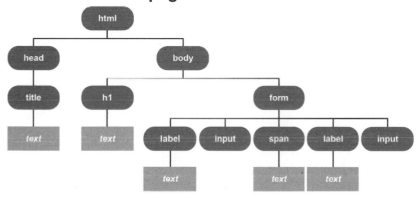

The syntax for changing the text node for an element

```
elementObject.firstChild.nodeValue = "The text for the element";
```

An example that puts a message in the span element

```
document.getElementById("email_address_error").firstChild.nodeValue =
    "This entry is required";
```

Description

- The *DOM* (*Document Object Model*) is a hierarchical collection of *nodes* in the web browser's memory that represents the current web page.

- The DOM for a web page is built as the page is loaded by the web browser.

- JavaScript can modify the web page in the browser by modifying the DOM. Whenever the DOM is changed, the web browser displays the results of the change.

- To modify the text for an HTML element like an h1, label, or span element, you can use the firstChild property to get the first descendent node for the element and then the nodeValue property to access the text for that node. For this to work, the node must contain some text to start with, even if it's just a space.

Figure 4-4   How to use the DOM to change the text for an element

How to use functions

When you develop JavaScript applications, you need to handle events like a user clicking on a button. To do that, you need to code and call functions that handle the events. As you will see, you can also use functions in other ways.

How to create and call a function expression

A *function* is a block of statements that performs an action. It can receive *parameters* and return a value by issuing a *return statement*. Once you've defined a function, you can call it from other portions of your JavaScript code. In figure 4-5, you can see how to create and call a *function expression*.

To start a function expression, you code the keyword *var* followed by the name of the variable that will store the function. Then, you code an assignment operator, the keyword *function*, a list of parameters in parentheses, and a block of code in braces. Functions coded this way are called function expressions because they're assigned to a variable.

Note in the syntax summary that there's a semicolon in braces [ ] after the closing brace, which means the semicolon is optional. Nevertheless, some IDEs like Aptana and NetBeans issue a warning if you omit the semicolon. That makes sense because you have to code a semicolon after other types of assignment statements. In this book, semicolons are coded at the end of all function expressions, but remember that they are optional.

To *call* a function expression, you code the name of the variable that the function is stored in, followed by the parameters in parentheses. Then, the function uses the data that's passed to it in the parameters as it executes its block of code. Here again, the parentheses are required even if there are no parameters.

The first example in this figure creates a function that's stored in a variable named showYear. This function doesn't require any parameters and doesn't return a value. When called, this function displays a dialog box that shows the current year.

The second example creates a function that's stored in a variable named $. This function takes one parameter, which is the value of the id attribute of an HTML element. This function returns an object that represents the HTML element. In this example, the call statement gets the object for the HTML text box with "email_address1" as its id, and then uses the value property of that object to get the value that the user entered.

The third example in this figure creates a function named calculateTax that requires two parameters and returns a value. It calculates sales tax, rounds it to two decimal places, and returns that rounded value to the statement that called it.

To call this function, the statement passes two variables named subtotal and taxRate. In this case, the variable names for these values are the same as the parameter names in the function, but that isn't necessary. What is required is that the calling statement must pass parameters with the same data types and in the same sequence as the parameters in the function.

The syntax for a function expression

```
var variableName = function(parameters) {
    // statements that run when the function is executed
}[;]
```

A function expression with no parameters that doesn't return a value

```
var showYear = function() {
    var today = new Date();
    alert( "The year is " + today.getFullYear() );
};
```

How to call the function

```
showYear();
```

A function expression with one parameter that returns a DOM element

```
var $ = function(id) {
    return document.getElementById(id);
};
```

How to call the function

```
var emailAddress1 = $("email_address1").value;
```

A function expression with two parameters that returns a value

```
var calculateTax = function( subtotal, taxRate ) {
    var tax = subtotal * taxRate;
    tax = tax.toFixed(2);
    return tax;
};
```

How to call the function

```
var subtotal = 85.00;
var taxRate = 0.05;
var salesTax = calculateTax( subtotal, taxRate );    // calls the function
alert(salesTax);                                     // displays 4.25
```

Description

- A *function* is a block of code that can be *called* (or *invoked*) by other statements in the program. When the function ends, the program continues with the statement that comes after the statement that called the function.

- A function can require that one or more *parameters* be passed to it when the function is called. In the calling statement, these parameters can also be referred to as *arguments*.

- To return a value to the statement that called it, a function uses a *return statement*. When the return statement is executed, the function returns the specified value and ends.

- A *function expression* is assigned to a variable and is referred to by the variable name. Although the semicolon at the end of a function isn't required, some IDEs warn you if it's omitted. That's why the function expressions in this book end with semicolons.

- Function expressions are sometimes called *anonymous functions* because they don't have names. Technically, function expressions can have names, but usually they don't.

- In the JavaScript for an application, a function expression must be coded before any statements that call it. Otherwise, an error will occur.

Figure 4-5   How to create and call a function expression

Incidentally, some programmers treat *parameter* and *argument* as synonyms. Others use *parameter* to refer to a parameter in a function and *argument* to refer to the value that is passed to the function. In this section of the book, we use *parameter* for both purposes.

How to create and call a function declaration

Since function expressions are commonly used to handle the events that occur in JavaScript applications, you'll use them most of the time. However, you should know that JavaScript also lets you code *function declarations*.

Figure 4-6 shows you how to create and call a function declaration. It uses the same examples as the previous figure but with function declarations instead of function expressions. As the syntax shows, a function declaration isn't stored in a variable, and its name is coded after the keyword *function* and before the parameters.

As in the previous figure, the showYear function doesn't have any parameters and doesn't return a value. Also, the calculateTax function requires two parameters and returns the sales tax value rounded to two decimal places. In these examples, using function declarations is just another way to get the same results as function expressions.

The one benefit of using function declarations is that they can be coded after any statements that call them. In contrast, function expressions must be coded before any statements that call them. Nevertheless, most programmers use function expressions. And some programmers think that coding function declarations after they are called is a confusing practice that should be avoided.

The syntax for a function declaration

```
function functionName (parameters) {
    // statements that run when the function is executed
}
```

A function declaration with no parameters that doesn't return a value

```
function() showYear {
    var today = new Date();
    alert( "The year is " + today.getFullYear() );
}
```

How to call the function

```
showYear();
```

A function declaration with two parameters that returns a value

```
function calculateTax ( subtotal, taxRate ) {
    var tax = subtotal * taxRate;
    tax = tax.toFixed(2);
    return tax;
}
```

How to call the function

```
var subtotal = 85.00;
var taxRate = 0.05;
var salesTax = calculateTax( subtotal, taxRate );   // calls the function
alert(salesTax);                                     // displays 4.25
```

Description

- A *function declaration* is one that is coded as shown above. This is just another way to code functions.

- In contrast to a function expression, a function declaration doesn't have to be coded before any statements that call it.

Figure 4-6   How to create and call a function declaration

When and how to use local and global variables

Scope in a programming language refers to the visibility of variables and functions. That is, it tells you where in your program you are allowed to use the variables and functions that you've defined.

When you use JavaScript, *local variables* are variables that are defined within functions. They have *local scope*, which means that they can only be used within the functions that define them.

In contrast, *global variables* are variables that are defined outside of functions. These variables have *global scope*, so they can be used by any function without passing them to the function as parameters.

The first example in figure 4-7 illustrates the use of a local variable. Here, the calculateTax function creates a variable named tax and returns that variable to the calling statement. Then, that statement can store the variable in another variable. Note, however, that a statement outside of the function can't refer to the variable named tax without causing an error. That's because it has local scope.

In contrast, the second example first creates a global variable named tax. Then, the function calculates the sales tax and stores the result in that global variable. As a result, the function doesn't have to return the tax variable. Instead, a statement outside of the function can refer to the variable because it is global.

Although it may seem easier to use global variables than to pass data to a function and return data from it, global variables often create problems. That's because any function can modify a global variable, and it's all too easy to misspell a variable name or modify the wrong variable, especially in large applications. That in turn can create debugging problems.

In contrast, the use of local variables reduces the likelihood of naming conflicts. For instance, two different functions can use the same names for local variables without causing conflicts. That of course means fewer errors and debugging problems. With just a few exceptions, then, all of the code in your applications should be in functions so all of the variables are local.

To complicate the use of variables, the JavaScript engine assumes that a variable is global if you accidentally omit the var keyword when you declare it. This is illustrated by the third example in this figure. Here, the var keyword is missing before the first assignment statement so tax is assumed to be a global variable.

This is a weakness of JavaScript that you need to be aware of because it can lead to coding errors. If, for example, you misspell the name of a variable that you've already declared when you code an assignment statement, it will be treated as a new global variable. With this in mind, be sure to include the var keyword when you declare new variables and always declare a variable before you refer to it in your code. Besides that, EMCAScript 5 addresses this weakness as explained in the next figure.

A function that uses a local variable named tax

```
var calculateTax = function( subtotal, taxRate ) {
    var tax = subtotal * taxRate;      // tax is a local variable
    tax = tax.toFixed(2);
    return tax;
};
```

Referring to a local variable from outside the function causes an error

```
alert("Tax is " + tax);                // causes error
```

A function that uses a global variable named tax

```
var tax;                               // tax is a global variable
var calculateTax = function( subtotal, taxRate ) {
    tax = subtotal * taxRate;
    tax = tax.toFixed(2);
};
```

Referring to a global variable from outside the function doesn't cause an error

```
alert("Tax is " + tax);                // will not cause error
```

A function that inadvertently uses a global variable named tax

```
var calculateTax = function( subtotal, taxRate ) {
    tax = subtotal * taxRate;   // no var keyword so tax is treated as global
    tax = tax.toFixed(2);
};
```

Referring to the tax variable from outside the function doesn't cause an error...but it should!

```
alert("Tax is " + tax);                // will not cause error
```

Discussion

- The *scope* of a variable or function determines what code has access to it.
- Variables that are created inside a function are *local variables*, and local variables can only be referred to by the code within the function.
- Variables created outside of functions are *global variables*, and the code in all functions has access to all global variables.
- If you forget to code the var keyword in a variable declaration, the JavaScript engine assumes that the variable is global. This can cause debugging problems.
- In general, it's better to pass local variables from one function to another as parameters than it is to use global variables. That will make your code easier to understand with less chance for errors.

Figure 4-7   When and how to use local and global variables

When and how to use strict mode

To address the problem of JavaScript creating unwanted variables when you misspell an identifier or omit the var keyword, ECMAScript 5 provides a new mode of operation called *strict mode*. To use strict mode, you code the strict mode directive shown in figure 4-8 at the start of your JavaScript code. Then, the JavaScript engine in a modern browser will throw an error if a variable name is used before it has been declared in a statement that uses the var keyword.

This is illustrated by the first two examples. In the first example, strict mode isn't used so omitting the var keyword will cause a debugging problem, but the application will continue running. In the second example, strict mode is used so the same omission will cause the JavaScript engine to throw an error and stop running the JavaScript code. That alerts you to the problem and forces you to fix it.

Note, however, that this feature of ECMAScript 5 isn't supported by older browsers like IE7, IE8, and IE9. In this case, that's okay, because if you fix the problems in a modern browser, the problems won't be there for older browsers either.

With that in mind, this figure summarizes the best coding practices for working with local and global variables. First, use local variables whenever possible. Second, use the var keyword to declare all variables. Third, always use strict mode. Fourth, declare the variables that are used by a function at the start of the function, before you use them.

You'll see these practices illustrated in the applications at the end of this chapter and throughout this book. If our code doesn't always show the strict mode declaration or declare all of the variables at the start of a function, it's just to fit the coding onto a single page.

The strict mode directive

```
"use strict";   // goes at the top of a file or function
```

A function that inadvertently uses a global variable named tax

```
var calculateTax = function( subtotal, taxRate ) {
    tax = subtotal * taxRate;   // no var keyword so tax is treated as global
    tax = tax.toFixed(2);
};
```

Referring to the tax variable from outside the function doesn't cause an error...but it should!

```
alert("Tax is " + tax);        // will not cause error
```

The same function in strict mode

```
"use strict";
var calculateTax = function( subtotal, taxRate ) {
    tax = subtotal * taxRate;   // in strict mode so error is thrown
    tax = tax.toFixed(2);
};
```

Referring to the tax variable causes a JavaScript error

```
alert("Tax is " + tax);        // causes error
```

Best coding practices

- Use local variables whenever possible.
- Use the var keyword to declare all variables.
- Use strict mode.
- Declare the variables that are used in a function at the start of the function.

Discussion

- The strict mode directive goes at the top of a file or function, before any other code.
- When you're coding in strict mode, if you forget to code the var keyword in a variable declaration or if you misspell a variable name that has been declared, the JavaScript engine will throw an error.
- Because strict mode became available with ECMAScript 5, it won't work with IE7, IE8, and IE9. However, if you test your applications in strict mode in a modern browser, you'll catch all of your omissions of the var keyword so they won't cause debugging problems in older browsers.

Figure 4-8   When and how to use strict mode

How to handle events

JavaScript applications commonly respond to user actions like clicking on a button. These actions are called *events*, and the function expressions that handle the events are called *event handlers*. To make that happen, you have to *attach* the functions to the events.

How to attach an event handler to an event

The table in figure 4-9 summarizes some of the events that are commonly handled by JavaScript applications. For instance, the load event of the window object occurs when the browser finishes loading the HTML for a page. The click event of a button object occurs when the user clicks on the button. And the mouseover action of an element like a heading or link occurs when the user hovers the mouse over the element.

After this table, you can see the syntax for attaching a function to an event. To do that, you code the object name, a dot, and the event name preceded by the word on. Then, you code an equals sign followed by the name of the variable for the function expression that's going to handle the event.

In the group of examples that follows the syntax summary, the first example starts with a function expression that can be used as an event handler. This function is stored in a variable named joinList, and all it does is display a message. In an actual application, of course, this function would perform the actions needed for handling the event.

The second example in this first group shows a JavaScript statement that attaches the joinList function to the click event of a button that has "submit_button" as its id. To do that, this statement first uses the $ function that uses the getElementById method to get the object for the button. This is followed by the dot operator and the event name preceded by *on* (onclick). Then, an equal sign is followed by joinList, which is the variable name for the function that will handle the click event.

Note here that you don't code the parentheses after the name of the variable that's used for the function, as in figure 4-5. That's because you're *attaching* the event handler, not *calling* it. That's why the function won't be called until the click event is fired. In contrast, if you were to put parentheses after joinList, the function would be called right away, and the function wouldn't be attached to the event.

The next statement in this group attaches the joinList event handler to the double-click event of a text box that has text_box_1 as its id. This means that the same event handler will be used for two different events. Here again, you don't code the parentheses when you attach the function.

The last example in this figure illustrates how to create an event handler and attach it to the window.onload event in one step. This is a common way to attach an onload event handler.

Common events

Object	Event	Occurs when...
`window`	`load`	The document has been loaded into the browser.
`button`	`click`	The button is clicked.
`control or link`	`focus`	The control or link receives the focus.
	`blur`	The control or link loses the focus.
`control`	`change`	The user changes the value in the control.
	`select`	The user selects text in a text box or text area.
`element`	`click`	The user clicks on the element.
	`dblclick`	The user double-clicks on the element.
	`mouseover`	The user moves the mouse over the element.
	`mousein`	The user moves the mouse into the element.
	`mouseout`	The user moves the mouse out of the element.

The syntax for attaching an event handler

```
objectVariable.oneventName = eventHandlerName;
```

An event handler named joinList

```
var joinList = function() {
    alert("The statements for the function go here");
};
```

How to attach the event handler to the click event of a button

```
$("submit_button").onclick = joinList;
```

How to attach the event handler to the double-click event of a text box

```
$("text_box_1").ondblclick = joinList;
```

How to create and attach an event handler in one step

```
window.onload = function() {
    alert("This is the window onload event handler function.");
};
```

Description

- An *event handler* is a function that's executed when an *event* occurs, so it "handles" the event. As a result, you code an event handler just like any other function.

- To *attach* an event handler to an event, you must first specify the object and the event that triggers the event handler. Then, you assign the event handler function to that event.

- When you code the event for an event handler, you precede the event name with *on*. So, for example, onclick is used for the click event.

- You can create a function expression as an event handler and then attach it to an event. This is useful when you want to use the same function for more than one event, as shown above. When you do it this way, you don't code the parentheses after the variable name.

- You can also create and attach an event handler function in one step, as in the last example above. This is commonly done for the load event as you'll see in the next figure.

Figure 4-9   How to attach an event handler to an event

How to use an onload event handler to attach other event handlers

When do you attach an event handler like the one in the previous figure? You attach it after all the HTML has been loaded into a user's browser and the DOM has been built. To do that, you code an event handler for the load event of the window object as shown in figure 4-10.

In the HTML for this example, you can see a label, a text box, a label that contains one space, and a button. This simple application is supposed to display a message when the button is clicked or when the user changes the value in the text box.

In the JavaScript code, you can see three function expressions. The first one is stored in a variable named $. This function uses the getElementById method of the document object to get an element object when the id of an HTML element is passed to it. This function makes it easy to get an element object without coding the document.getElementById method every time. As a result, you'll see it throughout this book.

The second function is the event handler for the click event of the button, and the third function is the event handler for the change event of the text box. Both of these functions just display a message.

The fourth function is the event handler for the load event. It is used to attach the other event handlers to the click and change events. Note that this function starts with

```
window.onload
```

so it is attached to the load event of the window object. As a result, this event handler is executed after the page is loaded and the DOM has been built.

Within this event handler are the two statements that attach the other event handlers. The first one attaches the joinList handler to the click event of the button. The second one attaches the changeValue handler to the change event of the text box. Both of these statements use the $ function to get the object that the event applies to, which makes the code easier to read and understand.

Incidentally, the event handler for the window.onload event can do more than assign functions to events. In fact, it can do whatever needs to be done after the DOM is loaded. You'll see this illustrated throughout this book.

The web browser after the Email Address has been changed

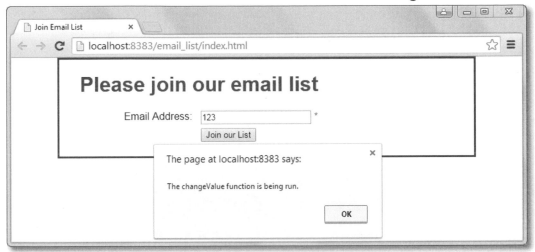

The HTML

```
<h1>Please join our email list</h1>
<label for="email_address">Email Address:</label>
<input type="text" id="email_address" name="email_address"><br>
<label> </label>
<input type="button" id="join_list" value="Join our List"><br>
```

The JavaScript

```
// the $ function
var $ = function(id) {
    return document.getElementById(id);
};
// the event handler for the click event of the button
var joinList = function() {
    alert("The joinList function is being run.");
};
// the event handler for the change event of the text box
var changeValue = function() {
    alert("The changeValue function is being run.");
};
// the event handler for the load event that attaches two event handlers
window.onload = function() {
    $("join_list").onclick = joinList;          // attaches 1st handler
    $("email_address").onchange = changeValue;  // attaches 2nd handler
};
```

Description

- The event handler for the onload event of the window object can be used to attach the event handlers for other events after the DOM has been built.

Figure 4-10   How to use an onload event handler to attach other event handlers

Two illustrative applications

To show you how the JavaScript you've just learned can be used to build applications, this chapter ends by presenting two of them.

The Miles Per Gallon application

Figure 4-11 presents the Miles Per Gallon application from chapter 2, but this time it uses text boxes and a button, rather than prompt and alert dialogs boxes. This version gets the user entries for miles and gallons. Then, it calculates miles per gallon, rounds it to one decimal place, and displays it on the page.

In the HTML, the disabled attribute is set for the third text box. This disables and shades this text box so the user can't enter data into it. In this figure, the CSS isn't shown, but you can see it when you review this downloaded application.

In the JavaScript, you can see that all of the code is within four functions. As a result, all the variables have local scope. Also, the variables for each function are declared at the start of the function, and strict mode is used. These are all best coding practices.

You should also note the sequence of the functions. Here, the first function is the $ function. The second function is the calculateMpg function, which calculates the miles per gallon. The third function is the processEntries function, which calls both the $ function and the calculateMpg function. And the fourth function is the event handler for the load event, which attaches the processEntries function and moves the focus to the first text box.

In short, each function only calls functions that precede it in the code. This is a logical sequence that makes your code easier to read and understand.

In the processEntries function, the user entries are retrieved using the $ function and then parsed into the miles and gallons variables. Then, an if statement tests whether either entry is invalid because it isn't numeric. If so, an error message is displayed. If both entries are valid, the one statement in the else clause calls the calculateMpg function and passes it the valid entries.

The calculateMpg function calculates the miles per gallon by dividing miles by gallons. Then, it rounds the result to one decimal place and returns the result to the calling statement, which stores it in the value property of the text box with "mpg" as its id.

When the web page with is loaded, the onload event handler is executed first, even though it comes last in the script. It attaches the event handler for the click event of the Calculate MPG button. After that, the browser waits until the user clicks on that button. Then, the procssEntries function validates the entries, calls the calculateMpg function if the entries are valid, and displays the rounded result when it is returned.

In this application, the calculateMpg function illustrates the use of a function that isn't an event handler. Because this function consists of just three statements, you could easily delete this function and put the two statements that calculate and round the result into the else clause of the processEntries function. But when a calculation is more complicated, moving its code into a function like this can simplify the code in the calling function.

The Miles Per Gallon application in a browser

Calculate Miles Per Gallon

Miles Driven:	2021
Gallons of Gas Used:	55.3
Miles Per Gallon	36.5
	Calculate MPG

The HTML and JavaScript for the application

```
<head>
    <title>Calculate MPG</title>
    <link rel="stylesheet" href="mpg.css">
    <script>
        "use strict";
        var $ = function(id) {
            return document.getElementById(id);
        };
        var calculateMpg = function(miles, gallons) {
            var mpg = (miles / gallons);
            mpg = mpg.toFixed(1);
            return mpg;
        };
        var processEntries = function() {
            var miles = parseFloat($("miles").value);
            var gallons = parseFloat($("gallons").value);
            if (isNaN(miles) || isNaN(gallons)) {
                alert("Both entries must be numeric");
            } else {
                $("mpg").value = calculateMpg(miles, gallons);
            }
        };
        window.onload = function() {
            $("calculate").onclick = processEntries;
            $("miles").focus();
        };
    </script>
</head>
<body>
    <main>
        <h1>Calculate Miles Per Gallon</h1>
        <label for="miles">Miles Driven:</label>
        <input type="text" id="miles"><br>
        <label for="gallons">Gallons of Gas Used:</label>
        <input type="text" id="gallons"><br>
        <label for="mpg">Miles Per Gallon</label>
        <input type="text" id="mpg" disabled><br>
        <label> </label>
        <input type="button" id="calculate" value="Calculate MPG"><br>
    </main>
</body>
```

Figure 4-11   The Miles Per Gallon application

The Email List application

Figure 4-12 presents an Email List application like the one that you were introduced to in chapter 1. In this application, the user enters the data for three text boxes and clicks the Join our List button. Then, the JavaScript application checks the data for validity. If any entry is invalid, this application displays an error message to the right of the entry. If all entries are valid, the data is submitted to the server for server-side processing.

The data validation that's done in this application is typical of the client-side validation that's done for any form before its data is submitted to the server for processing. This application also illustrates DOM scripting because it changes the text that's displayed by the span elements of the HTML.

In the head section of the HTML, you can see that a link element is used to include a CSS file for this page. You can also see a script element that includes an external JavaScript file for this page. Here again, the CSS isn't shown because it's irrelevant to the operation of the application.

In the body of the HTML, you can see the form, label, and input elements for this page. You can also see that the first three input elements are followed by span elements that include asterisks. Since the CSS for this page applies the color red to the text in span elements, the asterisks are red when the page is displayed. Then, since the JavaScript stores the error messages in the span elements, the error messages are also red.

You might also notice the id attributes for the form, text boxes, and span elements. The id for the form is email_form. The ids for the text boxes are email_address1, email_address2, and first_name. And the ids for the span elements are email_address1_error, email_address2_error, and first_name_error. These are the ids that will be passed to the $ function in the JavaScript.

Note too that the values for the name attributes of the form and text boxes are the same as the values for their id attributes. The name attributes for the text boxes are used by the server-side code to get the user entries that are passed to it when the form data is submitted to the server.

The Email List application in a web browser

Please join our email list

Email Address: `grace@yahoo.com`

Re-enter Email Address: `grace@yahoo`   This entry must equal first entry.

First Name   This field is required.

`Join our List`

The HTML file for the page

```html
<!DOCTYPE html>
<html>
<head>
    <title>Join Email List</title>
    <link rel="stylesheet" href="email_list.css">
    <script src="email_list.js"></script>
</head>
<body>
    <main>
        <h1>Please join our email list</h1>
        <form id="email_form" name="email_form"
              action="join.html" method="get">
            <label for="email_address1">Email Address:</label>
            <input type="text" id="email_address1 name="email_address1">
            <span id="email_address1_error">*</span><br>

            <label for="email_address2">Re-enter Email Address:</label>
            <input type="text" id="email_address2" name="email_address2">
            <span id="email_address2_error">*</span><br>

            <label for="first_name">First Name</label>
            <input type="text" id="first_name" name="first_name">
            <span id="first_name_error">*</span><br>

            <label> </label>
            <input type="button" id="join_list" value="Join our List">
        </form>
    </main>
</body>
</html>
```

Figure 4-12   The HTML for the Email List application

Figure 4-13 shows one way that the JavaScript for this application can be coded. Here again, the functions are coded in a sequence that's easy to read because the called functions always precede the function calls. And here again, the best practices for declaring variables are used. As a result, all of the variables used by the joinList function are declared at the start of the function, strict mode is used, and there are no global variables.

In this application, the onload event handler attaches the joinList function to the click event of the button with join_list as its id. The onload event handler also moves the focus to the first text box.

When the joinList function is called, its first three statements use the $ function to store the user's textbox entries in variables named emailAddress1, emailAddress2, and firstName. Then, the next statement sets a Boolean variable named isValid to true. The three if statements that follow will change this variable to false if any entries are invalid.

Each of the three if statements that follow checks one user entry for validity. If an error is detected, the statement sets the text in the span element for the field to an appropriate error message. To do that, it uses the firstChild and nodeValue properties of the span element, as shown in figure 4-4. An if statement that detects an invalid entry also sets the isValid variable to false. However, if the entry is valid, the else clause of the statement sets the text in the span element to an empty string so nothing is displayed.

After the three entries are checked for validity, a fourth if statement tests the isValid variable to see whether it's true or false. If it's true, that means that none of the preceding if statements have set it to false, which means that all of the entries are valid. As a result, the if clause uses the submit method of the form object to send the data to the server. Although this method hasn't been presented yet, you'll learn more about it in the next chapter.

On the other hand, if isValid is false, nothing is done because the if statement doesn't have an else clause. Instead, the application waits for the user to correct the entries and click again on the Join our List button.

If you study this code, you can see that the second if statement checks the second entry for two types of validity. First, it checks to make sure an entry has been made. Second, if an entry has been made, it checks to make sure that the first email address entry is equal to the second email address entry.

You might notice, though, that the code for this application doesn't provide all of the validity checking that you might want. In particular, it doesn't test whether the entries in the first two text boxes are valid email addresses. In the chapter on regular expressions, though, you'll learn how to provide that type of data validation.

The JavaScript for the Email List application

```javascript
"use strict";
var $ = function(id) {
    return document.getElementById(id);
};
var joinList = function() {
    var emailAddress1 = $("email_address1").value;
    var emailAddress2 = $("email_address2").value;
    var firstName = $("first_name").value;
    var isValid = true;

    // validate the first entry
    if (emailAddress1 == "") {
        $("email_address1_error").firstChild.nodeValue =
            "This field is required.";
        isValid = false;
    } else {
        $("email_address1_error").firstChild.nodeValue = "";
    }

    // validate the second entry
    if (emailAddress2 == "") {
        $("email_address2_error").firstChild.nodeValue =
            "This field is required.";
        isValid = false;
    } else if (emailAddress1 != emailAddress2) {
        $("email_address2_error").firstChild.nodeValue =
            "This entry must equal first entry.";
        isValid = false;
    } else {
        $("email_address2_error").firstChild.nodeValue = "";
    }

    // validate the third entry
    if (firstName === "") {
        $("first_name_error").firstChild.nodeValue =
            "This field is required.";
        isValid = false;
    } else {
        $("first_name_error").firstChild.nodeValue = "";
    }

    if (isValid) {
        // use the submit method of the form object to submit the form
        $("email_form").submit();
    }
};
window.onload = function() {
    $("join_list").onclick = joinList;
    $("email_address1").focus();
};
```

Figure 4-13   The JavaScript for the Email List application

Perspective

In this chapter, you've seen the way real-world JavaScript applications use objects and respond to events. Now, if you understand everything in this chapter, you should be ready to start developing useful applications of your own.

Terms

window object	call a function
global object	return statement
document object	parameter
NaN	argument
method chaining	function declaration
chaining	scope
fluent coding	local variable
DOM (Document Object Model)	local scope
DOM node	global variable
element node	global scope
text node	strict mode
void element	event
singleton element	event handler
function	attach an event handler
function expression	

Summary

- The *document object* provides methods and properties that let you work with the *Document Object Model*, or *DOM*.

- The Textbox, Number, Date, and String objects provide methods and properties for text boxes, number data types, dates, and string data types. When working with the methods and properties of these objects, you often use *method chaining*.

- The DOM is built when a page is loaded into a browser. It includes *element nodes* that represent the elements in an HTML document and *text nodes* that represent the text within those elements. To access the text for an element, you can refer to the nodeValue property of the firstChild property of the element.

- A *function* consists of a block of code that is executed when the function is *called* (or *invoked*). The function can require one or more *parameters* that are passed to it by the calling statement.

- A *function expression* is stored in a variable, and a *function declaration* is given a name but not stored in a variable.

- *Local variables* are defined within a function and can only be accessed by statements within the function. *Global variables* are defined outside of all functions and can be accessed by any of the other code.

- *Strict mode* is an ECMAScript 5 feature that causes the JavaScript engine to throw an error if a variable name is used before it has been declared.

- An *event handler* is a function that is called when an *event* like clicking on a button occurs. To make this work, the function must be *attached* to the event.

Exercise 4-1   Enhance the MPG application

In this exercise, you'll enhance the MPG application in two ways. One will be to provide better data validation with error messages to the right of the entries:

Calculate Miles Per Gallon

Miles Driven:		Miles must be numeric
Gallons of Gas Used:	0	Gallons must be greater than zero.
Miles Per Gallon		

Calculate MPG

Clear Entries

If you have any problems when you're testing, remember to use Chrome's developer tools as shown in figure 1-16 of chapter 1.

Test the application

1. Open your text editor or IDE, and open this HTML file:

   `c:\javascript\exercises\ch04\mpg\index.html`

   Then, review the JavaScript code to see that it's the same as in figure 4-11.

2. Test this application with valid data to see how it works. When you click the Calculate MPG button, the correct result should be displayed.

3. Test the data validation routine. Note that one error message is displayed in an alert dialog box no matter which entry is invalid.

Enhance the data validation

4. Review the HTML and notice that span elements that contain asterisks have been added right after the first two input controls. When you enhance the data validation, these elements should receive your error messages.

5. Enhance the data validation so it displays the error messages in the span elements and so a different error message is displayed for each type of error:

   Miles must be numeric
   Miles must be greater than zero
   Gallons must be numeric
   Gallons must be greater than zero

   Do this with one if statement that consists of one if clause that tests the first condition, three else if clauses that test the next three conditions, and an else clause that calls the calculationMpg function.

Add other enhancements

6. Change the calculateMpg function from a function expression to a function declaration.

7. Add a Clear Entries button below the Calculate MPG button. To do that, copy the HTML for the label and input elements for the Calculate button, and paste it after the input element for the Calculate button. Then, modify the HTML for the Clear Entries button so it has a unique id and an appropriate value attribute.

8. Add a function expression named clearEntries that clears the entries in the four text boxes and puts asterisks into the span elements for the first three. Then, add a statement in the onload event handler that attaches the clearEntries function to the click event of the Clear Entries button.

9. Add a statement to the onload event handler that attaches the clearEntries function to the double-click event of the miles text box. Then, test this change.

See what happens when the span elements in the HTML are empty

10. In the HTML, delete the asterisk from the first span element. Then, test the application in Chrome by clicking on the Calculate MPG button before making an entry. Nothing will happen.

11. Press the F12 key to display the developer tools, click on the Console tab, and see this error message: Cannot set property 'nodeValue' of null. This shows that the text node of the first span element hasn't been added to the DOM because it didn't have a starting value.

12. Restore the asterisk in the span element, and test again to make sure the application is working.

See what can happens when you remove strict mode

13. Change the second statement in the calculateMpg function as follows so the variable name is misspelled as *Mpg* instead of *mpg*.

```
var mpg = (miles / gallons);
Mpg = mpg.toFixed(1);
return mpg;
```

14. Test this application with valid entries, and note that it doesn't work. Then, press F12 to display the developer tools, click on the Console tab, and see this error message: Mpg is not defined. This shows that strict mode prevents the declaration of a variable without using the var keyword.

15. Delete the strict mode declaration, and test again with the 1000 for miles and 33 for gallons. This time, the application works, but the result isn't rounded. That's because the JavaScript engine treated Mpg as a new variable.

16. Restore the strict mode declaration and return the variable name to mpg. Then, test again to make sure the application is working.

Exercise 4-2 Build a new Future Value application

In this exercise, you will build a new version of the Future Value application of chapter 3. Its user interface will look like this:

If you have any problems when you're testing, remember to use Chrome's developer tools as shown in figure 1-16 of chapter 1.

Open and review the starting files

1. Open your text editor or IDE, and open the HTML and JavaScript files in this folder:

   `c:\javascript\exercises\ch04\future_value\`

2. Run the HTML file to see that it provides the user interface, but nothing works. Then, review the HTML code, and note that the span elements contain non-breaking spaces ( ). That way, the text nodes for these elements will be added to the DOM.

3. Review the JavaScript file. Note that it contains just the $ function.

Create a function for the Future Value calculation

4. Create a new function named calculateFV. It should have three parameters that receive the user's entries: investment amount, interest rate, and number of years. It should calculate the future value based on these parameter values, round the result to two decimal places, and return the rounded result. If you need help with this calculation, you can refer back to the Future Value application in figure 3-6.

Create the event handler for the click event of the Calculate button

5. Create a function expression named processEntries that gets the user entries with no data validation. Use strict mode, and start by declaring the variables that will hold the user's entries and assigning the user's entries to these variables.

6. Code a statement that calls the calculateFV function and stores the result that's returned in the fourth text box.

7. Create an event handler for the onload event that attaches the processEntries function to the click event of the Calculate button. This handler should also move the focus to the first text box.

8. Test this application with valid entries, and debug until this works correctly.

Add data validation with error messages to the right of the entries

9. Declare any variables that you are going to need for data validation right after the other declarations. For instance, you may want to use an isValid variable, although that depends on how you code the validation routines.

10. Add data validation that tests whether the first entry is a valid number that's greater than zero and less than or equal to 100,000, and display an appropriate error message in the span element after the investment text box if it isn't.

11. If the entry is valid, the else clause should issue the statement that you coded in step 6. But it should also set the contents of the span element for the entry to an empty string (""). Now, test this change.

12. If you have the time, add similar data validation for the next two entries. The interest entry should be greater than zero and less than or equal to 15. The years entry should be greater than zero and less than or equal to 50.

5

How to script the DOM with JavaScript

At this point, you have all of the JavaScript skills that you need for some serious DOM scripting. You just need to learn how to use some of the properties and methods that are provided by the DOM specifications, as well as some special skills for working with forms, controls, and tables.

DOM scripting properties and methods

In chapter 4, you were introduced to DOM scripting by using two properties to put a message into a span element. Now, you'll learn other properties and methods that you can use for DOM scripting. These properties and methods are defined by the *DOM Core specification* that is implemented by all current browsers as well as the *DOM HTML specification*.

DOM scripting concepts

Before you learn the properties and methods of the *DOM Core specification*, figure 5-1 presents the DOM scripting concepts that you should understand before using them. First, as you may recall from chapter 3, the *Document Object Model*, or *DOM*, is built as an HTML page is loaded into the browser. It contains *nodes* that represent all of the HTML elements and attributes for the page. This is illustrated by the HTML and diagram in this figure.

Besides the *element nodes* that are represented by ovals in this diagram, the DOM includes *text nodes* that hold the data for the HTML elements. In this diagram, these text nodes are rectangles. For instance, the first text node contains the text for the title element in the head section: "Join Email List". The one to the right of that contains the text for the h1 element in the body: "Please join our email list". And so on.

For simplicity, this diagram only includes the element and text nodes, but the DOM also contains *attribute nodes*, and each attribute node can have a text node that holds the attribute value. Also, if the HTML includes comments, the DOM will include *comment nodes*.

If you study the table in this figure, you can see that an element node can have element, text, and comment nodes as child nodes. An attribute node can have a text node as a child node. And a text node can't have a child node. Even though an attribute node is attached to an element node, it isn't considered to be a child node of the element node.

The properties and methods for working with DOM nodes are defined by a specification called an *interface*. In the topics that follow, you'll learn how to work with the properties and methods of the Node, Document, and Element interfaces.

As you work with these interfaces, you'll come across terms like *parent*, *child*, *sibling*, and *descendant*. These terms are used just as they are in a family tree. In the diagram in this figure, for example, the form element is the parent of the label, input, and span elements, and the label, input, and span elements are children of the form element. The label, input, and span elements are also siblings because they have the same parent. Similarly, the h1 and form elements are children of the body element, and the h1, form, label, input, and span elements are all descendants of the body element.

You should also be able to see these relationships in the HTML for a web page. In the HTML in this figure, for example, the indentation clearly shows the children and descendants for each element.

The code for a web page

```
<!DOCTYPE html>
<html>
<head>
    <title>Join Email List</title>
</head>
<body>
    <h1>Please join our email list</h1>
    <form id="email_form" name="email_form" action="join.html" method="get">
        <label for="email_address">Email Address:</label>
        <input type="text" id="email_address" name="email_address">
        <span id="email_error">*</span><br>
    </form>
</body>
</html>
```

The DOM for the web page

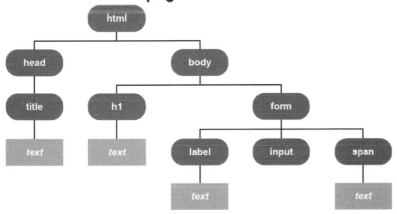

The DOM nodes that you commonly use

Type	Description
Document	Root node of the DOM. It can only have one Element node as a child node.
Element	An element in the web page. It can have Element, Text, and Comment nodes as child nodes.
Attr	An attribute of an element. Although it is attached to an Element node, it isn't considered a child node. It can have a Text node as a child node.
Text	The text for an element or attribute. It can't have a child node.

Description

- The *DOM* (*Document Object Model*) is a hierarchical collection of *nodes* in the web browser's memory that represents the current web page.

- The DOM for a web page is built as the page is loaded by the web browser.

- JavaScript can modify the web page in the browser by modifying the DOM. Whenever the DOM is changed, the web browser displays the results of the change.

- To modify the DOM, you can use the properties and methods that are defined by the *DOM Core specification.*

Figure 5-1   DOM scripting concepts

The properties of the Node interface

Figure 5-2 describes six properties that you can use for working with nodes. These properties are defined by the Node interface. All the examples in this figure assume the use of the $ function that gets an element by id.

The first example shows how to use the firstChild and nodeValue properties to get the text of an HTML element. In this case, this statement will store an asterisk (*) in the variable named errorText if the statement is run before the node is changed. That's because this node is set to the asterisk by the HTML.

If you refer back to the diagram in the previous figure, you can see that the firstChild property is needed to get the text node for the span element. Then, the nodeValue property gets the text from that text node.

The second example shows how to use the firstChild and nodeValue properties to put text into the text node of an HTML element. This is how the Email List application of the last chapter put the error messages in the span elements that follow the text boxes.

The third example shows how to use three properties of the input element with "email_address" as its id to set the text for the span element that follows it to an empty string. First, the nextElementSibling property gets the span element that is the next sibling of the input element. Then, the firstChild and nodeValue properties get the text.

You should know that, in all of these examples, you'll need to make sure that the text node contains a text value when it initially loads. Otherwise, the element won't have a firstChild property. You'll learn more about this in figure 5-13.

Some of the properties of the Node interface

Property	Description
nodeValue	For a Text, Comment, or Attribute node, this property returns the text that's stored in the node. Otherwise, it returns a null value.
parentNode	Returns the parent node of the current node if one exists. Otherwise, this property returns a null value.
childNodes	Returns an array of Node objects representing the child nodes of the current node. If this node doesn't have child nodes, the array contains no elements.
firstChild	Returns a Node object for the first child node. If this node doesn't have child nodes, this property returns a null value.
lastChild	Returns a Node object for the last child node. If this node doesn't have child nodes, this property returns a null value.
nextElementSibling	Returns a Node object for the next sibling. If this node doesn't have a sibling element that follows it, this property returns a null value.

HTML that contains element and text nodes

```
<body>
    <h1>Please join our email list</h1>
    <form id="email_form" name="email_form" action="join.html" method="get">
        <label for="email_address">Email Address:</label>
        <input type="text" id="email_address" name="email_address">
        <span id="email_error">*</span><br>
        <label> </label>
        <input type="button" id="join_list" value="Join our List">
    </form>
</body>
```

How to get the text of an HTML element with "email_error" as its id

```
var errorText = $("email_error").firstChild.nodeValue;
```

How to set the text of an HTML element with "email_error" as its id

```
$("email_error").firstChild.nodeValue = "Entry is invalid.";
```

How to set the text of an HTML element without using its id

```
$("email_address").nextElementSibling.firstChild.nodeValue = "";
```

Description

- An *interface* describes the properties and methods for an object.
- When DOM scripting, you often use the properties of the Node interface. Some of the most useful ones are summarized in the table above.
- In the examples above, the $ sign calls the function that gets the element that has the id that's passed to it as the parameter.

Figure 5-2   The properties of the Node interface

The methods of the Document and Element interfaces

The first table in figure 5-3 summarizes three methods that are in both the Document and Element interfaces. All three of these methods return arrays. For instance, the getElementsByTagName method returns an array that contains all of the Element nodes with the specified tag name.

If these methods are used with the document object, they get all of the elements in the document. This is illustrated by the first example that gets all of the <a> elements in the document and puts them in an array named links.

If these methods are used with an element as the object, they get all of the elements that are descendants of that element. For instance, the first statement in the second example gets the element with "image_list" as its id. Then, the second statement gets an array of all of the li elements that are descendants of the image_list element.

The second table in this figure summarizes some of the methods of the Element interface that work with attributes. For instance, the third example in this figure uses the hasAttribute method to find out whether an element has a class attribute. If it does, it uses the getAttribute method to get the value of that attribute.

The fourth example shows how to use the setAttribute method to set an attribute. Here, the second statement sets the class attribute to "open". When this method is used, if the class attribute doesn't already exist, the method adds it to the element before setting its value. Then, the last example in this figure uses the removeAttribute method to remove the class attribute from an element.

Common methods of the Document and Element interfaces

Method	Description
getElementsByTagName(*tagName*)	Returns an array of all Element objects descended from the document or element that have a tag that matches the specified tag.
getElementsByName(*name*)	Returns an array of all Element objects descended from the document or element that have a name attribute that matches the specified name.
getElementsByClassName(*classNames*)	Returns an array of all Element objects descended from the document or element that have a class attribute with a name or names that match the parameter. The classNames parameter can be a single name or a space-separated list of class names.

Common methods of the Element interface

Method	Description
hasAttribute(*name*)	Returns true if the Element has the attribute specified in name.
getAttribute(*name*)	Returns the value of the attribute specified in name or an empty string if an attribute of that name isn't set.
setAttribute(*name, value*)	Sets the attribute specified in name to the specified value. If the attribute doesn't already exist, it creates the attribute too.
removeAttribute(*name*)	Removes the attribute specified in name.

How to create an array of all <a> tags in a document
```
var links = document.getElementsByTagName("a");
```

How to create an array of all li tags within a ul element (image_list)
```
var list = document.getElementById("image_list");
var items = list.getElementsByTagName("li");
```

How to test for and get an attribute
```
var list = document.getElementById("image_list");
if ( list.hasAttribute("class") ) {
    var classAttribute = list.getAttribute("class"));
}
```

How to set an attribute
```
var list = document.getElementById("image_list");
list.setAttribute("class", "open");
```

How to remove an attribute
```
var list = document.getElementById("image_list");
list.removeAttribute("class");
```

Description
• The methods of the Document and Element interfaces let you get arrays of elements.
• The methods of the Element interface also let you work with attributes.

Figure 5-3   The methods of the Document and Element interfaces

The properties of the DOM HTML specification

The properties and methods that you've seen so far are part of the DOM Core specification. But there's also a *DOM HTML specification* that provides properties that make it easier to work with HTML elements. Figure 5-4 summarizes some of these properties and shows you how to use them.

When you work with the DOM HTML specification, you should remember that its properties don't provide new functionality. Instead, they provide shortcuts that make it easier to work with the DOM nodes of an HTML document.

The differences are illustrated by the first set of examples in this figure, which get and set the src attribute for an img element. With the DOM core specification, the getAttribute and setAttribute methods are used. With the DOM HTML specification, the src property is used, which shortens and simplifies the code.

The other examples in this figure show how to use some of the other properties of the DOM HTML specification. You'll also see some other properties used in the applications in this book. Usually, the property name is the same as the attribute name, but sometimes the property name is different. For instance, as one of the examples shows, the className property is used to get and set the class attribute.

If you want to use the online documentation for the DOM HTML specification, it helps to know that this specification is composed of several *interfaces* that describe the properties and methods of an object type. The base interface is HTMLElement, which describes a base HTML element. In addition, the HTMLElement interface *inherits* properties and methods from the DOM Core Element interface, which in turn inherits from the DOM Core Node interface. This means that all the Node, Element, and HTMLElement properties and methods are available to you when you work with HTML elements in JavaScript.

Beyond that, specific HTML elements use specific DOM HTML interfaces that inherit from the base HTMLElement interface. For example, an img element uses the HTMLImageElement interface, and an input element uses the HTMLInputElement interface.

Most of the time, you won't need to know which interface an element uses. Usually, you'll be able to use the element's attribute name as the DOM HTML property name in your code. But if that doesn't work, you can use the URL at the top of this figure to look up the correct property name. In the table of contents that you'll find there, you can find subheadings for the base HTMLElement interface, and for the more specific interfaces that inherit from HTMLElement, like HTMLLinkElement, HTMLImageElement, and HTMLInputElement.

The URL for the DOM HTML specification

`www.w3.org/TR/DOM-Level-2-HTML/html.html`

Typical properties available with the DOM HTML specification

Element	Property	Attribute
all	id	The id attribute
	title	The title attribute
	className	The class attribute. To set multiple class names, separate the names with spaces.
	tagName	The name of the tag, like div, h1, h2, a, or img.
<a>	href	The href attribute
img	src	The src attribute
	alt	The alt attribute
input	disabled	The disabled attribute

How the DOM HTML specification can simplify your code

How to get and set an img tag src attribute with the DOM core specification

```
var imageElement = $("image");
alert(imageElement.getAttribute(src);        // displays the src attribute
imageElement.setAttribute(src, "lures.jpg"); // sets the src attribute
```

How to get and set the same attribute with the DOM HTML specification

```
alert(imageElement.src);                      // displays the src attribute
imageElement.src = "lures.jpg";               // sets the src attribute
```

Other examples of using the DOM HTML specification

How to get the id attribute of the first element in an array

```
links = document.getElementsByTagName("a");
var firstLinkId = links[0].id);
```

How to get the href attribute of an <a> element

```
var target = $("first_link").href;
```

How to set and get the class attribute of an element with two class names

```
$("div").className = "open plus";
var classNames = $("div").className;          // classNames = "open plus"
```

How to get the tag attribute of the first element in an array

```
links = document.getElementsByTagName("a");
var tagName = links[0].tagName);              // tagName = "a"
```

How to disable and enable an element

```
$("btnPlay").disabled = true;
$("btnPlay").disabled = false;
```

Description

- The HTML specification provides shortcuts that make it easier to work with DOM nodes.

- The HTML specification is composed of *interfaces* that *inherit* properties and methods from other interfaces. The HTMLElement interface represents a base HTML element.

Figure 5-4   The properties and methods of the DOM HTML specification

The FAQs application

Now, you'll see how the properties and methods of the Node, Document, and Element interfaces are used in a typical DOM scripting application. We call this the FAQs (Frequently Asked Questions) application, and you can see its user interface in figure 5-5.

Quite simply, if the user clicks on a heading with a plus sign before it, the text below it is displayed and the plus sign is changed to a minus sign. Similarly, if the user clicks on a heading with a minus sign before it, the text below it is hidden and the minus sign is changed to a plus sign. The user can display the text below all three headings at the same time, and the user can hide the text below all three headings at the same time.

The HTML and CSS

In the HTML in this figure, you can see that each of the questions is coded in an <a> element within an h2 element, and each h2 element is followed by a div element that contains the answer. Note that the href attributes in these elements are coded as # signs so these links don't go anywhere.

Because <a> elements are coded within the h2 elements, a user can tab from one heading to the next. Then, when a user tabs to a heading and presses the Enter key, the effect is the same as clicking on the heading. This makes this app easier to use for motor-impaired users who can't handle a mouse.

In the CSS, you can see that both the focus and hover pseudo-classes are set to the color blue. That way, the <a> elements will look the same whether the user hovers the mouse over a link or tabs to the link.

Next, look at the two rule sets for the h2 elements. The first one applies to all h2 elements, and it sets the cursor to a pointer when the user hovers the mouse over an h2 element. It also applies a background property that includes an image named plus.png. This image is displayed just once (no-repeat) to the left of the element and it is vertically centered.

The second rule set for the h2 elements applies to elements that have a class property set to "minus". This rule set applies a background property like the one for all h2 elements, but this time it uses an image named minus.png. That's the image that's used when the text below a heading is displayed.

Now, look at the two rule sets for the div elements. The first one sets the display property, which hides the contents of the div element. In contrast, the second rule set applies to div elements that have a class attribute set to "open". It sets the display property to block, which means that the contents of the div element are displayed.

With the HTML and CSS set up this way, all the JavaScript has to do is turn these classes on and off as the user clicks on a heading. If, for example, the user clicks on the middle h2 heading when the application starts and its text is hidden, the JavaScript needs to set the class attribute for the clicked h2 element to "minus" and the class attribute for its sibling div element to "open".

The FAQs application in a browser

> ### JavaScript FAQs
> ##### − What is JavaScript?
> JavaScript is a browser-based programming language that makes web pages more responsive and saves round trips to the server.
> ##### + What is jQuery?
> ##### + Why is jQuery becoming so popular?

The HTML

```html
<body>
    <main id="faqs">
        <h1>JavaScript FAQs</h1>
        <h2><a href="#">What is JavaScript?</a></h2>
        <div>
            <p>JavaScript is a browser-based programming language that
                makes web pages more responsive and saves round trips
                to the server.</p>
        </div>
        <h2><a href="#">What is jQuery?</a></h2>
        <div>
            <p>jQuery is a library of the JavaScript functions that you're
                most likely to need as you develop web sites.</p>
        </div>
        <h2><a href="#">Why is jQuery becoming so popular?</a></h2>
        <div>
            <p>Three reasons:</p>
            <ul>
                <li>It's free.</li>
                <li>It lets you get more done in less time.</li>
                <li>All of its functions are cross-browser compatible.</li>
            </ul>
        </div>
    </main>
</body>
```

The CSS

```css
a {
    color: black;
    text-decoration: none; }
a:focus, a:hover {
    color: blue; }
h2 {
    cursor: pointer;
    background: url(images/plus.png) no-repeat left center; }
h2.minus {
    background: url(images/minus.png) no-repeat left center; }
div {
    display: none; }
div.open {
    display: block; }
```

Figure 5-5   The HTML and CSS for the FAQs application

The JavaScript

Figure 5-6 shows the JavaScript for this application. Here, the event handler for the onload event attaches the event handlers for each of the h2 elements. To do that, its first statement gets the object for the element that has "faqs" as its id. That's the main element in the HTML code. Then, the second statement uses the getElementsByTagName method to get an array of the h2 elements within that section. This array is stored in a variable named h2Elements.

This is followed by a for statement that attaches the event handler for each h2 element. Its loop is executed once for each element in the h2Elements array. The only statement in this loop attaches the event handler named "toggle" to the current h2 element in the array.

The onload event handler ends by setting the focus to the <a> element in the first h2 element in the array of h2 elements. It does that with this code:

```
h2Elements[0].firstChild.focus();
```

This refers to the first child of the first h2 element in the array (index zero), which is its <a> element.

Now, look at the toggle function that is the event handler for the click event of each h2 element. Remember that it is assigned to each h2 element in the h2 array.

The first statement within this function declares a new variable named h2 and assigns the *this* keyword to it. This is the critical statement in this function, because the this keyword refers to that specific h2 object in the DOM. As a result, one event handler is created for each h2 element in the DOM.

Without this statement, the loop would create just one event handler and attach it to each h2 element. That's because the statements in the event handler would be replaced each time through the loop, ending up with the statements for the last heading. As a result, clicking on any h2 heading would only toggle the last heading.

The second statement in the toggle function gets the div element below the current h2 element by using the nextElementSibling method. Then, the if statement that follows tests whether the h2 element has a class attribute. If it does, it removes that attribute. If it doesn't, it adds a class attribute with a value of "minus". That means that the CSS will change the background image from a plus sign to a minus sign, or vice versa.

Then, the second if statement uses similar coding to add an "open" class if the div element doesn't have one and to remove the class if it does have one. And that means that the CSS will change the display property from none to block, or vice versa.

Now that you've reviewed this code, you should note that it will work for any number of h2 and division elements that are defined by the HTML. You should also note that the div elements can contain whatever HTML elements the application requires, including img, <a>, and list elements.

This application should also give you some idea of what JavaScript and DOM scripting can do. For the remainder of this chapter, though, you'll learn the DOM scripting skills for working with forms and controls.

The JavaScript for the FAQs application

```
"use strict";
var $ = function(id) { return document.getElementById(id); };

// the event handler for the click event of each h2 element
var toggle = function() {
    var h2 = this;                         // this refers to the clicked h2 tag
    var div = h2.nextElementSibling;    // div = h2's sibling div

    // toggle + and - image in h2 elements by adding or removing a class
    if (h2.hasAttribute("class")) {
        h2.removeAttribute("class");
    } else {
        h2.setAttribute("class", "minus");
    }

    // toggle div visibility by adding or removing a class
    if (div.hasAttribute("class")) {
        div.removeAttribute("class");
    } else {
        div.setAttribute("class", "open");
    }
};


window.onload = function() {
    // get the h2 tags
    var faqs = $("faqs");
    var h2Elements = faqs.getElementsByTagName("h2");

    // attach event handler for each h2 tag
    for (var i = 0; i < h2Elements.length; i++ ) {
        h2Elements[i].onclick = toggle;
    }
    // set focus on first h2 tag's <a> tag
    h2Elements[0].firstChild.focus();
};
```

Notes

- The first two statements in the onload event handler create an array of the h2 elements in the section with "faqs" as its id.

- The for loop in the onload event handler is executed once for each of the h2 elements. It attaches the toggle event handler to the onclick event of each h2 element.

- In the code for the toggle event handler, the *this* keyword refers to the h2 element that has been clicked. You'll learn more about this keyword in chapter 10.

Figure 5-6   The JavaScript for the FAQs application

How to script forms and controls

A *form* contains one or more *controls* such as text boxes and buttons. The controls that accept user entries are also known as *fields*. In the topics that follow, you'll learn how to work with forms and controls.

How forms work

Figure 5-7 shows how to create a form that contains three controls: two text boxes and a button. To start, you code the form element. On the opening tag for this element, you code the action and method attributes. The action attribute specifies the file on the web server that will be used to process the data when the form is submitted. The method attribute specifies the HTTP method that will be used for sending the form to the web server.

In the example in this figure, the form will be submitted to the server using the HTTP "get" method when the user clicks the Join our List button. Then, the data in the form will be processed on the server by the code that's in the file named join.php. That file will use PHP as the scripting language.

When you use the get method, the form data is sent as part of the URL for the HTTP request. That means that the data is visible in the address bar of the browser. This is illustrated by the URL in this figure. Here, the URL is followed by a question mark and name/value pairs separated by ampersands that present the name attributes and field values. In this case, two values are submitted: the email address and first name entries.

When you use the post method, by contrast, the form data is packaged as part of an HTTP request and isn't visible in the browser. Because of that, the submission is more secure than it is when you use the "get" method.

Within the opening and closing tags of the form element, you code the controls for the form. In this example, the first two input elements are for text boxes that will receive the user's email address and first name. The third input element has "submit" as the value for its type attribute, which means it is a *submit button*. When it is clicked, the data in the form will automatically be submitted to the server.

If the type attribute of an input element is "reset", the button is a *reset button*. When that type of button is clicked, all of the values in the controls of the form will be reset to their starting HTML values.

When a form is submitted to the server, the data in the form should be completely validated on the server before the data is processed. Then, if any of the data isn't valid, the form is sent back to the browser with appropriate error messages so the entries can be corrected. This is referred to as *data validation*.

Usually, the form data is validated by the browser too before it is submitted to the server. Note, however, that the browser validation doesn't have to be as thorough as the server-side validation. If the browser validation catches 80 to 90% of the entry errors, it will save many round trips to the server.

A form in a web browser

Email Address:	grace@yahoo.com
First Name:	Grace
	Join our List

The HTML for the form

```
<form id="email_form" name="email_form" action="join.php" method="get">
    <label for="email_address">Email Address:</label>
    <input type="text" id="email_address" name="email_address"><br>
    <label for="first_name">First Name:</label>
    <input type="text" id="first_name" name="first_name"><br>
    <label> </label>
    <input type="submit" id="join_list" value="Join our List"><br>
</form>
```

The URL that's sent when the form is submitted with the get method

```
join.php?email_address=grace%40yahoo.com&first_name=Grace
```

Attributes of the form element

Attribute	Description
name	A name that can be referred to by client-side or server-side code.
action	The URL of the file that will process the data in the form.
method	The HTTP method for submitting the form data. It can be set to either "get" or "post". The default value is "get".

Description

- A *form* contains one or more *controls* (or *fields*) like text boxes, radio buttons, lists, or check boxes that can receive data.

- When you click on a *submit button* for a form (type is "submit"), the form data is sent to the server as part of an HTTP request. When you click on a *reset button* for a form (type is "reset"), the form data is reset to its default values.

- When a form is submitted to the server for processing, the data in the controls is sent along with the HTTP request.

- When you use the get method to submit a form, the URL that requests the file is followed by a question mark and name/value pairs that are separated by ampersands. These pairs contain the name attributes and values of the data that is submitted. When you use the post method, the data is hidden.

- *Data validation* refers to checking the data collected by a form to make sure it is valid, and complete data validation is always done on the server. Then, if any invalid data is detected, the form is returned to the client so the user can correct the entries.

- To save round trips to the server when the data is invalid, some validation is usually done on the client before the data is sent to the server. However, this validation doesn't have to be as thorough as the validation that's done on the server.

Figure 5-7   How forms work

How to script Textbox, Textarea, and Select objects

Text boxes, text areas, and select lists are common controls that you should be familiar with. A Textbox object provides a single line for an entry, a Textarea object provides multiple lines for an entry, and a Select object provides a list of options that the user can select from, usually in a drop-down list.

The table in figure 5-8 shows the value property common to all three of these HTML objects. It returns a string containing either the entry that the user made or the option that the user selected from the list.

The HTML code in this figure uses these controls to get a user's name, comments, and country. Note that the select control's initial option has no display string and a value of an empty string. This is a common way to make the control appear as if no selection has been made when the page first loads. Another way to do this is to have the display string say something like "Select One" instead of being blank. If, however, you want to make sure that the user makes a selection, you can remove this blank option. This forces the user to either accept the default option or select a different one.

The first JavaScript example in this figure shows how to use the value property of these controls to get the values the user entered or selected. The first two statements use the $ function to store the text box and text area values in variables named name and comment. Then, because the value property returns strings, the next two lines use the length property of the value string to make sure the user entered a value.

When doing this kind of check for a text area, though, you'll need to think about line returns. For instance, if the user presses just the Enter key, a *hard return* is entered and becomes a character in the value property, even though the user didn't type any other text. In contrast, *soft returns* are the automatic returns that occur when the line the user is entering overflows to the next line. These returns don't become characters in the value property.

The last portion of code in this example works with the select element. First, it uses the value property to retrieve the user's selection and store it in a variable called country. Then, it checks the value of the variable and performs different processing depending on which country was chosen, or it notifies the user if no country was chosen.

In addition to using the value property to retrieve the content of these controls, you can use it to set the content of the controls. The second JavaScript example in this figure shows how this works. In this case, each of the controls on the form has its value property set to an empty string. This is a common way to clear a form, but you can set the value property to any string.

When you set the value property for a Textbox or Textarea object, the value will replace the contents of the value property. But when you set the value of a Select object, it selects the option in the list with that value. For example, setting the value property of the select object to "can" will make the Canada option show in the list. If you set the value property to a value that isn't in the option list, nothing is selected, not even the select object's default value.

Properties of a Textbox, Textarea, or Select object

Property	Description
`value`	The content of the value attribute for the entered text or selected option. Returns a string.

HTML code for a text box, text area, and select list

```
<label for="name">First Name:</label>
<input type="text" name="name" id="name"><br>
<label for="comment">Comment:</label>
<textarea name="comment" id="comment" rows="5" cols="40"></textarea><br>
<label for="country">Country:</label>
<select name="country" id="country">
    <option value=""></option>
    <option value="usa">USA</option>
    <option value="can">Canada</option>
    <option value="mex">Mexico</option>
</select>
```

JavaScript code to get the text box, text area, and select list values

```
var name = $("name").value;
var comment = $("comment").value;

if (name.length == 0) { alert("Please enter a name."); }
if (comment.length == 0) { alert("Please enter a comment."); }

var country = $("country").value;
if ( country == "usa" ) { /* USA processing */ }
else if ( country == "can" ) { /* Canada processing */ }
else if ( country == "mex" ) { /* Mexico processing */ }
else { alert("Please select a country."); }
```

JavaScript code to set the text box, text area, and select list values

```
$("country").value = "";
$("name").value = "";
$("comment").value = "";
```

Description

- The name and id attributes of these controls should be set to the same value.

- After you use the value property of one of these objects to get the value string, you can use the length property of the String object to get the number of characters in the string.

- Setting the value property of a Textbox or Textarea object replaces the text contents.

- Setting the value property of a Select object selects the option with the corresponding value.

- When the user presses the Enter key while typing in a text area, a *hard return* is entered into the text. Hard returns appear as characters in the value property.

- When the user types past the end of a line in a text area and a new line is automatically started, a *soft return* occurs. Soft returns do not appear as characters in the value property.

Figure 5-8   How to script Textbox, Textarea, and Select objects

How to script Radio and Checkbox objects

Two other types of controls that you should be familiar with are radio buttons and check boxes. Both of these controls let a user select an option. A group of radio buttons in a web page lets a user select one of several options. When the user clicks one button in a group, the other buttons in the group are deselected. By contrast, each check box on a page is independent. Selecting one check box has no effect on any other check box.

The table in figure 5-9 shows two of the properties common to these HTML objects. The value property returns a string containing the contents of the control's value attribute. The checked property returns a Boolean value indicating whether or not the button or check box is checked.

The HTML example in this figure contains two radio buttons and a check box. When you create a group of radio buttons, they must have the same name so the web browser knows they are in the same group. However, they must have different id values. In the example, both radio buttons have the name *contact*, but one has an id of *text* and a value of *text* while the other has an id of *email* and a value of *email*. Note that the id and value attributes don't have to be the same, but they often are.

Unlike radio buttons, when you create a check box, it must have a unique name and the name and id attributes must be set to the same value. In the example, the check box has a name and id of *accept*.

The first JavaScript example in this figure shows how to get the user's choices from radio buttons and check boxes. First, it declares a variable called contact. Then, it checks to see to see if the radio button with an id of *text* is checked. If it is, it gets the contents of the radio button's value property and stores it in the contact variable.

Next, the code checks to see if the radio button with an id of *email* is checked. If it is, it gets the contents of the radio button's value property and stores it in the contact variable. Remember, though, that only one member of a radio button group can be checked. This means that only one of these radio buttons is going to have its checked property set to true.

Then, the code checks the value of the contact variable and does either text or email processing based on that value. If no radio button was selected, the code notifies the user to make a selection.

Finally, the code gets the value of the check box's checked property and stores it in a variable called accept. Then, the code checks to see if the value of the accept variable is true. If it is, the code processes the acceptance. If it isn't, the code notifies the user that the box needs to be checked.

The second JavaScript example in this figure shows how to set the checked property of radio buttons and check boxes. In this example, the radio buttons are unchecked and the check box is checked.

Two properties of a Radio or Checkbox object

Property	Description
`value`	The contents of the value attribute for the button or check box. Returns a string.
`checked`	If set to true, the button or check box is selected. If set to false, it isn't selected.

HTML code for two radio buttons and a check box

```
<label>Contact me by:</label>
<input type="radio" name="contact" id="text" value="text" checked>Text
<input type="radio" name="contact" id="email" value="email">Email<br>
<label>Terms of Service:</label>
<input type="checkbox" name="accept" id="accept" value="accept">I accept<br>
```

JavaScript code to get the radio button and check box values

```
var contact;
if ( $("text").checked ) { contact = $("text").value; }
if ( $("email").checked ) { contact = $("email").value; }

if ( contact == "text" ) { /*text processing*/ }
else if ( contact == "email" ) { /*email processing*/ }
else { alert("You must select a contact method"); }

var accept = $("accept").checked;
if ( accept ) {
    /*accept processing*/
} else { alert("You cannot use the web store at this time."); }
```

JavaScript code to set the radio button and check box values

```
$("text").checked = false;
$("email").checked = false;
$("accept").checked = true;
```

Description

- All radio buttons in a group must have the same name, but different ids. Only one button in a group may be checked at a time, but none of the buttons has to be checked.

- Each check box is independent of the other check boxes on the page. They aren't treated as a group. The name and id attributes of a check box should be set to the same value.

- To set a radio button, set its checked property to true. When you set a radio button, any other checked button in the same group will be cleared.

- To clear a radio button, set its checked property to false. When you clear a radio button, no other button will become checked.

- To set a check box, set its checked property to true. To clear a check box, set its checked property to false.

Figure 5-9   How to script Radio and Checkbox objects

How to use the methods and events for forms and controls

Figure 5-10 presents some of the common methods and events that you are likely to use with forms and controls. The first table summarizes two methods that are commonly used with forms.

The first method is to submit the form to the web server for processing. That's usually done after the user clicks a button to submit the form and all of the data is valid. The second method is to reset the data in the controls. That's usually done when the user clicks a button.

If you're familiar with HTML buttons, you know that input elements with their type attributes set to "submit" or "reset" call the submit and reset methods automatically with no JavaScript. If you want to validate the data in a form before you submit it to the server, though, you don't want that. As a result, you should use a regular input button.

The same is true for reset buttons. You'll often want to use a regular button as the reset button and issue the reset method from your JavaScript. You'll see this illustrated for both submit and reset buttons in the application that follows.

The second table in this figure summaries two methods that are commonly used with controls. In chapter 4, you learned how to use the focus method to move the focus to a control. But you can also use the blur method to remove the focus from a control.

The third table summaries six events that are commonly used with controls. In chapter 4, you learned how to use the onclick and ondblclick events to start event handlers. But you can also use other events to work with controls like text boxes, select lists, text areas, and links. For instance, you can write an event handler for the onchange event of a text box or the onblur event of an <a> element.

The examples in this figure illustrate how these methods and events can be used. You code the reset and submit methods for forms, not controls. You write the event handlers for controls before you attach events to them. And you use the event handler for the window.onload event to attach event handlers.

Two methods that are commonly used with forms

Method	Description
`submit`	Submits the form and its data to the server.
`reset`	Resets the controls in the form to their starting values.

Two methods that are commonly used with controls

Method	Description
`focus`	Moves the focus to the control.
`blur`	Removes the focus from the control.

Common control events

Event	Description
`onfocus`	The control receives the focus.
`onblur`	The control loses the focus.
`onclick`	The user clicks the control.
`ondblclick`	The user double-clicks the control.
`onchange`	The value of the control changes.
`onselect`	The user selects text in a text box or text area.

Statements that use the reset and submit methods

```
$("registration_form").reset();
$("registration_form").submit();
```

An event handler for the onchange event of a select list

```
var investmentChange = function() {
    calculateClick();           // call the calculateClick function
    $("investment").blur();     // remove the focus from the select list
};
```

An event handler for the dblclick event of a text box

```
var yearsDblclick = function() {
    $("years").value = "";      // clear text box when double clicked
};
```

An onload event handler that assigns event handlers to events

```
window.onload = function() {
    $("investment").onchange = investmentChange;
    $("years").ondblclick = yearsDblclick;
    $("years").focus();
};
```

Description

- Input elements with the type attribute set to "submit" or "reset" automatically submit or reset a form. When validating data, though, regular buttons are often used and the form is submitted or reset by using the JavaScript submit or reset method.

Figure 5-10   How to use the methods and events for forms and controls

The Register application

Figure 5-11 presents a Register application that consists of several controls on a form. If an entry is required, a red asterisk is displayed to the right of the control. Then, when the user clicks the Register button, the application checks the entries to make sure they're valid. If any of them aren't valid, the application displays error messages to the right of the fields. If all are valid, the application submits the form.

If the user clicks the Reset button somewhere along the way, the application resets the controls on the form to their starting values. That's done by issuing the reset method for the form. But this application also clears any error messages and restores the starting asterisks, which isn't done by the reset method.

The HTML and CSS

In the HTML, you can see a form named registration_form. This form uses the get method to submit the values of the controls to register_account.html. In real life, though, a registration page would use the post method because it's more secure.

Inside the form, there are two text boxes named email_address and phone, a select element named country, a radio button group named contact, and a check box named terms. Within the radio button group are three radio buttons with ids of text, email, and none. Below these controls are two button elements named register and reset_form.

After some of the controls, you can see span elements. The starting values of these controls are asterisks (*) to indicate that these entries are required.

Below the HTML in this figure, you can see the CSS for these span elements. This rule set selects the span elements that are within the form that has "registration_form" as its id attribute. It sets the color for the asterisks and any subsequent error messages in the span elements to red.

The Register application in a browser

> ### Register for an Account
>
> E-Mail: `ben@yahoo`
>
> Mobile Phone: This field is required.
>
> Country: Select an option ▼ | Please select a country.
>
> Contact me by: ◉ Text   ○ Email   ○ Don't contact me
>
> Terms of Service: ☐ I accept This box must be checked.
>
> | Register | Reset |

The HTML

```
<main>
    <h1>Register for an Account</h1>
    <form action="register_account.html" method="get"
        name="registration_form" id="registration_form">
        <label for="email_address">E-Mail:</label>
            <input type="text" name="email_address" id="email_address">
            <span>*</span><br>
        <label for="phone">Mobile Phone:</label>
            <input type="text" name="phone" id="phone">
            <span>*</span><br>
        <label for="country">Country:</label>
            <select name="country" id="country">
                <option value="">Please select a country</option>
                <option>USA</option>
                <option>Canada</option>
                <option>Mexico</option>
            </select>
            <span>*</span><br>
        <label>Contact me by:</label>
            <input type="radio" name="contact" id="text"
                value="text" checked>Text
            <input type="radio" name="contact" id="email"
                value="email">Email
            <input type="radio" name="contact" id="none"
                value="none">Don't contact me<br>
        <label>Terms of Service:</label>
            <input type="checkbox" name="terms" id="terms"
                value="yes">I accept
            <span>*</span><br>
        <input type="button" id="register" value="Register">
        <input type="button" id="reset_form" value="Reset"><br>
    </form>
</main>
```

The CSS for the span elements in the registration form

```
#registration_form span {
    color: red;
}
```

Figure 5-11   The HTML and CSS for the Register application

The JavaScript

Figure 5-12 presents the JavaScript for this application, which consists of four functions starting with the $ function. Then, the second function is an event handler named processEntries that does the data validation for the controls and submits the form when all of the controls are valid. The third function is an event handler named resetForm that resets the form. And the fourth function is the event handler for the onload event that attaches the processEntries and resetForm event handlers to the click events of the Register and Reset buttons.

The processEntries function is executed when the user clicks the Register button. It starts by declaring a Boolean variable named isValid that is assigned a starting value of true. Then, the next statements declare the variables that are assigned the values for the email, phone, country, contact, and terms controls. Note that the contact value is set to either Text, Email, or None, based on which radio button is checked.

After the user's data has been stored in the variables, one long if statement checks each of the entries for validity. If any of the variables is invalid, an error message is moved into the span element that follows the related control. It does that by using code like this:

```
$("email_address").nextElementSibling.firstChild.nodeValue
    = "This field is required.";
```

This puts the message into first child element (the text node) of the next sibling element after the control (the span element). If the entry is valid, the code puts an empty string into the span element, which removes the asterisk. If an entry is invalid, the code also sets the isValid variable to false.

After the data validation, another if statement checks whether the isValid variable is true. If so, it submits the form to the server for processing by issuing the submit method of the form. If the isValid variable is false, the form isn't submitted so the user can correct the entries.

The resetForm function is executed when the user clicks the Reset button. It starts by calling the form's reset method, which resets all of the values in the controls to their starting HTML values. But more needs to be done. So the next four statements reset the values in the span elements to asterisks, and the last statement sets the focus on the first text box.

The last function is the event handler for the onload event. It just attaches the two event handlers to the Register and Reset buttons. Then, it sets the focus on the first text box element.

Now take a moment to look at the naming conventions used for the event handlers for the click events of the Register and Reset buttons. Here again, they consist of verbs and nouns that indicate what type of processing they're going to do.

The JavaScript for the Register application

```javascript
"use strict";
var $ = function(id) { return document.getElementById(id); };


var processEntries = function() {
    var isValid = true;

    // get values for user entries
    var email = $("email_address").value;
    var phone = $("phone").value;
    var country = $("country").value;
    var contact = "Text";
    if ($("email").checked) { contact = "Email"; }
    if ($("none").checked) { contact = "None"; }
    var terms = $("terms").checked;

    // check user entries for validity
    if (email == "") {
        $("email_address").nextElementSibling.firstChild.nodeValue
            = "This field is required.";
        isValid = false; }
    else {
        $("email_address").nextElementSibling.firstChild.nodeValue = ""; }
    if (phone == "") {
        $("phone").nextElementSibling.firstChild.nodeValue
            = "This field is required.";
        isValid = false; }
    else { $("phone").nextElementSibling.firstChild.nodeValue = ""; }
    if (country == "") {
        $("country").nextElementSibling.firstChild.nodeValue
            = "Please select a country.";
        isValid = false; }
    else { $("country").nextElementSibling.firstChild.nodeValue = ""; }
    if (terms == false) {
        $("terms").nextElementSibling.firstChild.nodeValue
            = "This box must be checked.";
        isValid = false; }
    else { $("terms").nextElementSibling.firstChild.nodeValue = ""; }


    // submit the form if all fields are valid
    if (isValid == true) {
        $("registration_form").submit(); }
};
var resetForm = function() {
    $("registration_form").reset();
    $("email_address").nextElementSibling.firstChild.nodeValue = "*";
    $("phone").nextElementSibling.firstChild.nodeValue = "*";
    $("country").nextElementSibling.firstChild.nodeValue = "*";
    $("terms").nextElementSibling.firstChild.nodeValue = "*";
    $("email_address").focus();
};
window.onload = function() {
    $("register").onclick = processEntries;
    $("reset_form").onclick = resetForm;
    $("email_address").focus();
};
```

Figure 5-12   The JavaScript for the Register application

How to add new nodes to the DOM

Besides working with existing nodes, JavaScript lets you add new nodes to the DOM. The next two figures show how.

How to create nodes and add them to the DOM

The first table in figure 15-13 summarizes two of the methods of the document object that you can use for creating new DOM nodes. The createText-Node method lets you create a Text node by coding the text for the node in the parameter. The createElement method lets you create an Element node by coding the element type in the parameter.

This is illustrated by the first set of examples that follow the table. The first statement creates a text node that contains "Waders". The second statement creates an element node for an li element.

The next set of examples shows how to modify the attributes of a new node. Here, the first statement creates an img element node. The second statement sets its src attribute to "lures.jpg".

The second table in this figure summarizes two methods of the document object that you can use to add an existing node to the DOM. The appendChild method adds the node that's specified in the parameter as the last child in the childNode array for the element that's specified. In contrast, the insertBefore method adds the node as the first child for the element that's specified.

This is illustrated by the examples after the second table. Here, the first statement appends a text node to an li element node. The second statement inserts the li node as the first child in the array for a ul node. Note that these are the statements that actually add new nodes to the DOM. But until they're added to the DOM, the new nodes won't be displayed by the browser.

Two methods of the document object for creating new nodes

Method	Description
`createTextNode(text)`	Creates a new Text node that has the specified text in its nodeValue property.
`createElement(tagName)`	Creates a new Element node for the specified type of tag.

How to create new nodes

How to create a Text node
```
var textNode = document.createTextNode("Waders");
```

How to create an Element node
```
var liNode = document.createElement("li");
```

How to modify the attributes of a new node
```
var imgNode = document.createElement("img");
imgNode.src = "lures.jpg";
```

Two methods of the document object for adding nodes to the DOM

Method	Description
`appendChild(newNode)`	Adds the new node as the last child in the childNode array.
`insertBefore(newNode, childNode)`	Inserts the new node just before the child node in the childNode array. If childNode is the first child, the new node will be added at the start of the childNode array.

How to make one node a child of another node

How to add a node as the last child node
```
liNode.appendChild( textNode );
```

How to add a node as the first child node
```
ulNode.insertBefore( liNode, ulNode.firstChild );
```

Description

- A newly created node isn't displayed in the browser until it is added to the DOM tree. To add a node to the DOM tree, you can use one of the methods in the second table above.
- When you add nodes to the DOM, you must follow the rules of the document type. For example, you can't add one <a> tag node as the child of another <a> tag node.

Figure 5-13   How to create nodes and add them to the DOM

How to add rows and cells to a DOM table

Figure 5-14 shows how to add rows and cells to a table. Keep in mind, though, that you can't add a row directly to a table element. Instead, you must add the row to a table's tbody element, which is a child element of the table element.

This figure starts with the HTML for a table element. Then, the first JavaScript example shows how to use the tBodies property of the table node to retrieve the tbody element. It does this by referring to the first tbody node in the array. Then it checks it to make sure a tbody node was returned. If not, it uses the createElement method to create one.

The last statement in this example shows how to add a new row to the table. It uses the insertRow method of the tbody node with a parameter that specifies where you want to add the row. For example, a value of 0 adds the new row at the beginning of the table. To add the row to the end of the table, you use the value -1.

It's important to note that the insertRow method returns a reference to the newly created row node. This is useful because it provides a way to add cells to the row that's created by this method.

The second code example in this figure adds a cell to the row created in the first example. First, it uses the createTextNode method to create a new text node that contains the string value "$9.95". Then, it uses the insertCell method, which works like the insertRow method. Specifically, this example uses the insertCell method to add a cell to the end of a row. Then, it uses the appendChild method to add the text node to the cell.

Although it's easy enough to use the methods described above to add content to a table, they can become cumbersome. That's why many developers prefer to use the innerHTML property of a node instead. This is illustrated by the last set of examples. As you can see, you first code the HTML as a string, and then set the string as the innerHTML value.

Two methods of the document object for working with tables

Method	Description
`insertRow(index)`	Adds a row to a table at the location specified by the parameter: 0 refers to the first row in the table, -1 to the end of the table.
`insertCell(index)`	Adds a cell to a row at the location specified by the parameter: 0 refers to the first cell in the row, -1 to the end of the row.

The HTML for an empty table (no rows)

```
<table id="tbl"></table>
```

How to add a row to a table

```
var table = $("tbl");
var tBody = table.tBodies[0];
if (tBody == undefined) {
    tBody = document.createElement("tbody");
    table.appendChild(tBody);
}
var row = tBody.insertRow(-1);
```

How to add a cell to a row

```
var textNode = document.createTextNode("$9.95");
var cellNode = row.insertCell(-1);
cellNode.appendChild(textNode);
```

One property of the document object for working with DOM content

Property	Description
`innerHTML`	Represents the contents for any node in the DOM.

How to use the innerHTML property to set the content of any node

How to add text to a cell
```
cellNode.innerHTML = "<i>$10.95</i>";
```

How to add cells to a row
```
rowNode.innerHTML = "<td>MBT-2843</td><td>Aqua Case</td><td>$10.95</td>";
```

Description

- You can't add rows directly to a table element. Instead, you must add rows to the tbody element for the table, which the browser creates when it builds the DOM.

- You can use the tBodies property of a table element to return an array of the tbody elements for the table, but most tables only have one tbody element in the array.

- You can use the appendChild method to add rows and cells to a table, but you must add rows to a tbody element.

- You can use the insertRow and insertCell methods to add rows and cells to a table, but you must add rows to a tbody element.

- You can use the innerHTML property to set the HTML content of any node. That's usually easier than adding content to the DOM by using the other methods.

Figure 5-14   How to add rows and cells to a DOM table

The Register application with a table

Figure 5-15 illustrates a Register application that has controls on a form. When the user clicks the Register button, the application performs data validation to make sure all the fields are filled out correctly. If they are, the application submits the form. If they aren't, the application displays a table that shows what values have been entered and what values didn't pass validation. When the user clicks the Reset button, the application resets the controls on the form and clears the table of information.

The HTML and CSS

The HTML for this application is the same as the HTML in figure 5-11, but with two exceptions. First, the h2 and table elements shown in figure 5-15 are added to the end of the HTML in the main element.

Second, the span elements after the controls have been deleted because they aren't used in this application. Instead, the validation results and messages are shown in the table below the form. Please note, however, that the HTML for table has no rows. That's because the rows will be added by the JavaScript.

In the CSS in this figure, you can see one change to the CSS for the earlier Register application. Instead of setting the font color for the span elements in the form to red, it sets the font color for the span elements in the table to red. You'll see that these span elements are added to the table by the JavaScript in the next figure.

The Register application with a table that's created for the user's entries

Register for an Account

E-Mail: `ben@yahoo`

Mobile Phone:

Country: `Select an option ▼`

Contact me by: ● Text   ○ Email   ○ Don't contact me

Terms of Service: ☐ I accept

[Register]   [Reset]

Please review your entries and complete all required fields

Email: ben@yahoo
Phone: Required field
Country: Required field
Contact: Text
Terms: Required field

The HTML for the two elements below the form

```
        </form>
        <h2 id="registration_header"> </h2>
        <table id="registration_info"></table>
    </main>
```

The CSS for the span elements in the table

```
#registration_info span {
    color: red;
}
```

Description

- When the user clicks the Register button, this application displays a table below the form that displays the data for valid entries and error messages for invalid entries. If all of the entries are valid, this application calls the submit method to submit the form to the server.

- When the user clicks the Reset button, this application calls the reset method to reset the values in the controls. But this application also removes the table below the form.

- Besides the two elements shown above that have been added to the HTML, the span elements after the controls have been removed because the asterisks and error messages aren't displayed to the right of the controls.

- In the CSS, the selector for the rule set that sets the color of the error messages to red has been changed to the one shown above. It selects all span elements in the table, which has an id of "registration_info".

Figure 5-15   The Register application with a table that shows the user's entries

The JavaScript

Figure 5-16 presents the JavaScript for this application. It illustrates some interesting code that shows another way to apply some of the skills that you learned in this chapter.

Here, as a best practice, the processEntries function starts by declaring the variables that will be used by the function. In this case, the first two statements declare variables named "header" and "html" and assigns empty strings to them. The header variable will be used to store the header for the table that is displayed below the form. The html variable will be used to store the content for the innerHTML property that will fill the table element with the user's entries.

The next two statements declare variables named "required" and "msg". The required variable is set to a span element with "Required field" as its content. It will be placed in the table when the user doesn't enter a required field. Because this is a span element, the CSS will set the color for the message to red. The msg variable contains the header that will be printed before the table if one or more errors are detected.

The next seven statements are just like those in the earlier version of this application. They get the user's entries from the form and store them in variables.

This is followed by four if statements that check the validity of four of the entries to make sure they aren't empty strings. If an entry is an empty string, the related variable is changed to the value of the required variable. So instead of an entry, the variable will be set to a span element that contains "Required field". Then, the value of the header variable is replaced with the text in the msg variable. That will become the heading that's displayed before the table.

After the data validation, the nodeValue property of the firstChild property of the h2 element with "registration_header" as its id is set to the value of the header variable. This will either be an empty string or the starting value of the msg variable. If it's the value of the msg variable, the heading will be displayed after the form.

This is followed by an if statement that checks whether the header variable is equal to the msg variable. If it is, that means one or more fields are invalid because the header variable was changed from its starting value of an empty string. In that case, the next five statements add the HTML for five rows to the html variable. Then, the sixth statement puts the value of the html variable into the innerHTML property of the table. As soon as that's done, the table is displayed

On the other hand, if none of the entries is invalid, the else clause of the if statement clears any previous values from the table element by setting its innerHTML property to an empty string. Then, it submits the form by issuing the submit method of the form.

After that explanation, you shouldn't have any trouble understanding the code for the resetForm and the onload event handlers. The resetForm function uses the reset method to reset the controls on the form, sets the h2 element and table that are after the form to empty strings, and sets the focus to the first control on the form. The onload event handler just attaches the event handlers to the right events and sets the focus to the first control on the form.

The JavaScript for the Register application

```
"use strict";
var $ = function(id) { return document.getElementById(id); };

var processEntries = function() {
    var header = "";
    var html = "";
    var required = "<span>Required field</span>";
    var msg = "Please review your entries and complete all required fields";

    var email = $("email_address").value;
    var phone = $("phone").value;
    var country = $("country").value;
    var contact = "Text";
    if ($("email").checked) { contact = "Email"; }
    if ($("none").checked) { contact = "None"; }
    var terms = $("terms").checked;

    if (email == "") {
        email = required;
        header = msg; }
    if (phone == "") {
        phone = required;
        header = msg; }
    if (country == "") {
        country = required;
        header = msg; }
    if (terms == false) {
        terms = required;
        header = msg; }

    $("registration_header").firstChild.nodeValue = header;
    if (header == msg) {
        html = html + "<tr><td>Email:</td><td>" + email + "</td></tr>";
        html = html + "<tr><td>Phone:</td><td>" + phone + "</td></tr>";
        html = html + "<tr><td>Country:</td><td>" + country + "</td></tr>";
        html = html + "<tr><td>Contact:</td><td>" + contact + "</td></tr>";
        html = html + "<tr><td>Terms:</td><td>" + terms + "</td></tr>";
        $("registration_info").innerHTML = html;
    } else {
        $("registration_info").innerHTML = "";
        $("registration_form").submit();
    }
};
var resetForm = function() {
    $("registration_form").reset();
    $("registration_header").firstChild.nodeValue = "";
    $("registration_info").innerHTML = "";
    $("email_address").focus();
};
window.onload = function() {
    $("register").onclick = processEntries;
    $("reset_form").onclick = resetForm;
    $("email_address").focus();
};
```

Figure 5-16   The JavaScript for the Register application with a table

Perspective

This goal of this chapter has been to introduce you to some of the capabilities of DOM scripting with JavaScript. As a result, three different types of applications were presented. The FAQs application showed how you can create special features like accordions. The Register application showed how JavaScript is commonly used for data validation. And the Register application with the table showed how HTML elements like a table can be added to the DOM.

Before you continue, you should know that there's a limit to how much DOM scripting you should do with JavaScript. That's because jQuery is a JavaScript library that is designed to make DOM scripting easier. As a result, most DOM scripting is done with a combination of JavaScript and jQuery.

With that in mind, chapter 17 introduces you to jQuery and shows you how to get started with it. At that time, you'll have all of the JavaScript skills you need, and you can get *Murach's jQuery* when you're ready to add jQuery to your skillset.

Terms

DOM Core specification	form
DOM (Document Object Model)	control
DOM node	field
element node	submit button
text node	reset button
attribute node	data validation
comment node	hard return
interface	soft return

Summary

- The *Document Object Model*, or *DOM*, is built when a page is loaded into a browser. It consists of various types of *nodes*.

- In the DOM, *element nodes* represent the elements in an HTML document and *text nodes* represent the text within those elements. The DOM can also contain *comment nodes*, and it can contain *attribute nodes* that have text nodes that store the attribute values.

- JavaScript provides properties and methods for the objects of the DOM that are described in the *DOM Core Specification*. These include the properties and methods that are described by the Node, Document, and Element *interfaces*.

- JavaScript also provides properties for the objects of the DOM that are described in the *DOM HTML Specification*. Although these properties don't provide new functionality, they do provide shortcuts that make it easier to work with the DOM nodes of an HTML document.

- A *form* contains one or more *controls* such as text boxes and buttons. The controls that accept user entries are also known as *fields*. Some common controls are text boxes, text areas, select lists, radio buttons, and check boxes.

- When you work with controls, you use properties like value and checked, methods like focus and blur, and events like onfocus, onclick, and onblur.

- When you work with forms, you can use the submit method to submit a form and the reset method to reset the values in the controls of the form.

- To add nodes to the DOM, you can use methods of the document object like the createTextNode, createElement, appendChild, insertRow, and insert-Cell methods. You can also use the innerHTML property to set the HTML content for any node in the DOM.

Exercise 5-1   Experiment with the FAQs application

This exercise will give you a chance to better understand the FAQs application by forcing you to work with its code. It will also give you a chance to use one of the properties of the DOM HTML specification.

If you have any problems when you're testing, remember to use Chrome's developer tools as shown in figure 1-16 of chapter 1.

Test and review the application

1. Use your text editor or IDE to open the HTML and JavaScript files in this folder:

    `c:\javascript\exercises\ch05\faqs`

2. Then, test this application to see how it works, and review its code.

Attach the event handlers to the <a> elements instead of the h2 elements

3. Change this application so the toggle event handlers are attached to the <a> elements within the h2 elements instead of to the h2 elements themselves.

4. Test this change. When you do that, clicking on the headings should work, but clicking on the plus or minus signs before them shouldn't work.

Use the className property of the DOM HTML specification

5. Comment out the statements in the toggle event handler that use the removeAttribute and setAttribute methods.

6. Below each commented out statement, code a statement that gets the same result by using the className property. For instance, you can remove a class attribute by setting the className property equal to an empty string ("").

7. Test this change.

Exercise 5-2   Add controls to the Register application

In this exercise, you'll add another radio button and a comments control to the form for the Register with table application, so the form looks like this:

Register for an Account

E-Mail:	
Mobile Phone:	
Country:	Select an option ▾
Contact me by:	○ Text ○ Email ◉ Mobile phone ○ Don't contact me
Terms of Service:	☑ I accept
Comments:	These are the times that try men's souls.

Register	Reset

If you have any problems when you're testing, remember to use Chrome's developer tools as shown in figure 1-16 of chapter 1.

1. Use your text editor or IDE to open the index.html and register.js files that are in this folder:

    `c:\javascript\exercises\ch05\register_table`

2. Test this application with both invalid and valid data.

3. In the HTML file, add a radio button for Mobile phone and a text area for Comments, but watch out for duplicate id attributes. For the text area, you can use the example in figure 5-8 as your guide, but note that the width of the area will be set by the CSS.

4. In the JavaScript file, add the code that gets the data entered by the user. Then, modify the code that builds the html table rows by adding a row for the comments entry. Note, however, that this entry is optional so no validation is required.

5. Test the application to see how a comment is displayed in the table below the form. Remember, though, that if all the entries are valid, the application will go to a new page and not display the table. So at least leave the Terms box unchecked.

6. Test the application again, but enter just two hard returns in the comments area by pressing the Enter key twice. Then, note that the table shows no entry.

7. Change the code in the JavaScript file so instead of displaying the comments in the table, the length of the comments entry is displayed, like this: Entry length = 41. You can use the length property of the entry to get the length. Then, test this change with hard return entries, text entries, and no entry.

8. Test the Reset button for the new fields. If changes are required, make them.

9. Enter all valid data, and click the Register button to submit the form. Because the "get" method is used, the entries are added to the URL for the next page.

6

How to test and debug a JavaScript application

As you build a JavaScript application, you need to test it to make sure that it performs as expected. Then, if there are any problems, you need to debug your application to correct those problems. This chapter shows you how to do both.

An introduction to testing and debugging

When you *test* an application, you run it to make sure that it works correctly. As you test the application, you try every possible combination of input data and user actions to be certain that the application works in every case. In other words, the goal of testing is to make an application fail.

When you *debug* an application, you fix the errors (*bugs*) that you discover during testing. Each time you fix a bug, you test again to make sure that the change you made didn't affect any other aspect of the application.

Typical test phases for a JavaScript application

When you test an application, you typically do so in phases, like the three that are summarized in figure 6-1.

In the first phase, you test the application with valid data. To start, you can enter the data that you would expect a user to enter. Before you're done, though, you should enter valid data that tests the limits of the entries.

In the second phase, you test the application with invalid data. That way, you can make sure that all of the error messages are displayed correctly, and that the application doesn't fail due to invalid data entries.

In the third phase, you go all out to make the application fail by testing every combination of data and user action that you can think of. That should include random actions like pressing the Enter key or clicking the mouse at the wrong time or place.

The three types of errors that can occur

As you test an application, three types of errors can occur. *Syntax errors* violate the rules for coding JavaScript statements. These errors are detected by the JavaScript engine as a page is loaded into the browser. As you learned in chapter 1, some syntax errors are also detected by IDEs like Aptana. Syntax errors are the easiest to fix, because web browsers and IDEs provide error messages that help you do that.

A *runtime error* occurs after a page has been loaded and the application is running. Then, when a statement can't be executed, the JavaScript engine *throws an exception* (or *error*) that stops the execution of the application.

Logic errors are errors in the logic of the coding: an arithmetic expression that delivers the wrong result, using the wrong relational operator in a comparison, and so on. To illustrate, the Miles Per Gallon application in this figure has a logic error. Here, you can see that the second entry is empty and the result of the calculation is NaN, but the calculation shouldn't be done at all if one of the entries is empty. Could it be a problem with the if statement?

The Calculate MPG application with a logic error

The goal of testing

- To find all errors before the application is put into production.

The goal of debugging

- To fix all errors before the application is put into production.

Typical test phases

- Test the application with valid input data to make sure the results are correct.
- Test the application with invalid data to make sure that the proper error messages are displayed and that the application doesn't fail.
- Try everything you can think of to make the application fail, like unusual or unexpected combinations of user actions.

The three types of errors that can occur

- *Syntax errors* violate the rules for how JavaScript statements must be written. These errors are caught by the JavaScript engine as a page is loaded into the web browser.
- *Runtime errors* occur after a page is loaded and the application is being run. When a runtime error occurs, the JavaScript engine throws an error that stops the execution of the application.
- *Logic errors* are statements that don't cause syntax or runtime errors, but produce the wrong results.

Description

- To *test* a JavaScript application, you run it to make sure that it works properly no matter what data you enter or what events you initiate.
- When you *debug* an application, you find and fix all of the errors (*bugs*) that you find when you test the application.

Figure 6-1   An introduction to testing and debugging

Common JavaScript errors

Figure 6-2 presents some of the coding errors that are commonly made as you write a JavaScript application. If you've been doing the exercises, you most likely have encountered several of these errors already. Now, if you study this figure, you'll have a better idea of what to watch out for.

If you're using a good text editor or IDE, you can avoid most of these errors by noting the error markers and warnings that are displayed as you enter the code. For instance, Aptana will help you avoid most of the errors in the first two groups in this figure. However, it won't help you avoid the errors in the third group.

The fourth group in this figure addresses the problem with floating-point arithmetic that was mentioned in chapter 2. In brief, JavaScript uses the IEEE 754 standard for floating-point numbers, and this standard can introduce inexact results, even for simple calculations. Although these results are extremely close to the exact results, they can cause problems, especially in comparisons. For instance, the number 7.495 is not equal to 7.495000000000001.

To get around this problem, you can round the result as shown by the examples. Here, the first statement rounds the salesTax value to two decimal places by using the toFixed method of the number. In this case, the result is stored as a string because the toFixed method returns a string.

In contrast, the second statement gets the rounded result and then uses the parseFloat method to store it as a number. Which approach you use depends on whether you need the result to be a string or a number.

The last group in this figure illustrates the type of problem that can occur when JavaScript assumes that a variable is global. In this example, the salesTax variable is declared properly by using the var keyword. But the next statement misspells salesTax as salestax when it tries to assign a rounded and parsed value to salesTax. As a result, salestax is treated as a global variable, and the rounded and parsed value goes into salestax, not salesTax, which of course causes a bug.

As you learned in chapter 4, though, you can avoid that type of error by declaring strict mode for all of your JavaScript files. Then, the JavaScript engine will throw an error if you use a variable before it's declared so you'll have to fix the error. Otherwise, an error like this will go undetected, which may lead to a difficult debugging problem.

Common syntax errors

- Misspelling keywords, like coding getElementByID instead of getElementById.
- Omitting required parentheses, quotation marks, or braces.
- Not using the same opening and closing quotation mark.
- Omitting the semicolon at the end of a statement.
- Misspelling or incorrectly capitalizing an identifier, like defining a variable named salesTax and referring to it later as salestax.

Problems with HTML references

- Referring to an attribute value or other HTML component incorrectly, like referring to an id as salesTax when the id is sales_tax.

Problems with data and comparisons

- Not testing to make sure that a user entry is the right data type before processing it.
- Not using the parseInt or parseFloat method to convert a user entry into a numeric value before processing it.
- Using one equal sign instead of two when testing for equality.

Problems with floating-point arithmetic

- The number data type in JavaScript uses floating-point numbers, and that can lead to arithmetic results that are imprecise. For example,

```
var salesAmount = 74.95;
salesTax = salesAmount * .1;                // result is 7.495000000000001
```

- One way to fix this potential problem is to round the result to the right number of decimal places. If necessary, you can also convert it back to a floating-point number:

```
salesTax = salesTax.toFixed(2)              // result is 7.50 as a string
salesTax = parseFloat(salesTax.toFixed(2)); // result is 7.50 as a number
```

Problems with undeclared variables that are treated as global variables

- If you don't declare strict mode and you assign a value to a variable that hasn't been declared, the JavaScript engine treats it as a global variable, as in this example:

```
var calculateTax = function(subtotal, taxRate) {
    var salesTax = subtotal * taxRate;          // salesTax is local
    salestax = parseFloat(salesTax.toFixed(2)); // salestax is global
    return salesTax;        // salesTax isn't rounded but salestax is
};
```

- The solution to this type of problem is to always declare strict mode.

Description

- When the JavaScript engine in a browser comes to a JavaScript statement that it can't execute, it *throws an exception* (or *error*) and skips the rest of the JavaScript statements.

Figure 6-2   Common JavaScript errors

How top-down coding and testing can simplify debugging

One way to simplify debugging is to code and test just a small portion of code at a time. This can be referred to as *top-down coding and testing* or just *top-down testing*. The implication is that you test the most important operations first and work your way down to the least important operations and the finishing touches.

This is illustrated by the example in figure 6-3. Here, the first testing phase consists of 15 lines of code that provide an event handler for the click event of the Calculate button. However, that event handler doesn't do any data validation. It just calculates the future value of the investment amount, which is the essence of this application.

Then, phase 2 adds to this code by doing the data validation for just the first entry. Phase 3 adds the data validation for the other two entries. And phase 4 adds finishing touches like moving the focus to the first text box when the application starts.

The result is that you're testing a small amount of code at a time. That makes debugging easy because you know that any errors were introduced by the lines of code that you've just added. This also makes developing an application more enjoyable because you're making continuous progress without the frustration of complex debugging problems.

The user interface for a Future Value application

Future Value Calculator

Investment Amount: `1375000`

Annual Interest Rate: `5.5`

Number of Years: `7`

Future Value: `2000184`

[Calculate]

Testing phase 1: No data validation

```
var $ = function(id) {
    return document.getElementById(id);
};
var calculateClick = function() {
    var investment = parseFloat( $("investment").value );
    var annualRate = parseFloat( $("rate").value );
    var years = parseInt( $("years").value );
    for ( var i = 1; i <= years; i++ ) {
        investment += investment * annualRate / 100;
    }
    $("future_value").value = investment.toFixed();
};
window.onload = function() {
    $("calculate").onclick = calculateClick;
};
```

Testing phase 2: Add data validation for just the first entry

```
if (isNaN(investment) || investment <= 0) {
    alert("Investment must be a number and greater than zero.");
}
else {
    // the future value calculation from phase 1
}
```

Testing phase 3: Add data validation for the other entries

```
// Add data validation for the other entries
```

Testing phase 4: Add the finishing touches

```
// Add finishing touches like moving the focus to the first text box
```

Discussion

- When you use *top-down coding and testing*, you start by coding and testing a small portion of code. Then, you build on that base by adding the code for an operation or two at a time and testing after each addition.

- Top-down testing simplifies debugging because you know that the errors are caused by the code that you've just added. As a result, it's relatively easy to find the errors.

Figure 6-3 How top-down coding and testing can simplify debugging

How to debug with Chrome's developer tools

In chapter 1, you were introduced to the Console panel of Chrome's *developer tools* as a way to find errors. Besides that, though, Chrome offers some excellent debugging features for more complicated problems.

Since Chrome's developer tools are relatively easy to use, the topics that follow don't present the procedures for using all of its features. Instead, they present the skills that you're going to use the most. Then, if you decide that you want to use some of the other features, you can experiment with them on your own.

How to use Chrome to find errors

As figure 6-4 shows, there are several ways to open and close the developer tools, but most of the time you'll use the F12 key. That's why the developer tools for Chrome and other browsers are often referred to as the *F12 tools*.

One of the primary uses of Chrome's developer tools is to get error messages when a JavaScript application throws an error and stops running. To get the error message, you open the developer tools and click on the Console tab to display the Console panel, which will show the error message. Then, you can click on the link to the right of the message to switch to the Sources panel with the JavaScript code for the error statement highlighted.

In the example in this figure, the problem is that the first *isNaN* in the statement is spelled wrong. It is *isNan* when it should be *isNaN*. This shows how easy it can be to find an error. Often, the statement that's highlighted isn't the one that caused the error, but at least you have a clue that should help you find the actual error.

Incidentally, the error message that's displayed is for the first error that's detected, but there can be other errors in the code. To catch them, you have to correct the first error and run the application again. Then, if there are other errors, you repeat the process until they're all fixed and the application runs to completion.

Chrome with an open Console panel that shows an error

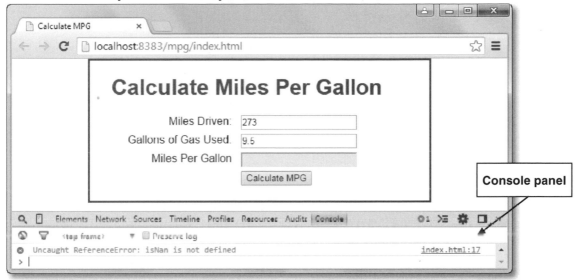

The Sources panel after the link in the Console panel has been clicked

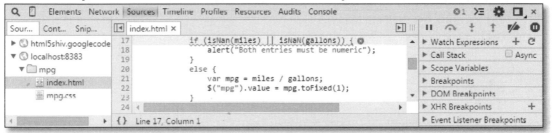

How to open or close Chrome's developer tools

* To open the developer tools, press F12 or Ctrl+Shift+I. Or, click on the Menu button in the upper right corner of the browser, and select More Tools→Developer Tools.

* To close the developer tools, click on the X in the upper right corner of the tools panel or press F12.

How to find the JavaScript statement that caused the error

* Open the Console panel by clicking on the Console tab. You should see an error message like the one above along with the line of code that caused the error.

* Click on the link to the right of the error message that indicates the line of code. That will open the Sources panel with the portion of JavaScript code that contains the statement displayed and the statement highlighted.

Description

* Chrome's *developer tools* provide some excellent debugging features, like identifying the JavaScript statement that caused an error.

* Because you usually start the developer tools by pressing the F12 key, these tools are often referred to as the *F12 tools*.

Figure 6-4   How to use Chrome's developer tools to find errors

How to use breakpoints and step through your code

A *breakpoint* is a point in your code at which the execution of your application will be stopped. Then, you can examine the contents of variables to see if your code is executing as expected. You can also *step through* the execution of the code from that point on. These techniques can help you solve diffícult debugging problems.

Figure 6-5 shows you how to set breakpoints, step through the code, and view the contents of variables. In this example, you can see that a breakpoint has been set on line 6 of the Email List application.

When you run your application, it will stop at the first breakpoint that it encounters and highlight the line of code next to the breakpoint. While your code is stopped, you can hover your mouse over an object's name in the center pane of the Sources panel to display the current value of that object.

At a breakpoint, you can also view the current variables in the Scope Variables pane on the right side of the panel. That pane has two sections, Local and Global. The Local section contains the variables that are used by the function that is being executed. You can also see the values of other variables and expressions by clicking the plus sign to the right of Watch Expressions at the top of the pane and typing the variable name or expression that you want to watch.

To step through the execution of an application after a breakpoint is reached, you can use the Step Into, Step Over, and Step Out buttons. These buttons are just above the Watch Expressions pane. Or, you can press the key associated with these operations, as shown in the table in this figure.

If you repeatedly click or press Step Into, you will execute the code one line at a time and the next line to be executed will be highlighted. After each line of code is executed, you can use the Local or Watch Expressions pane to observe any changes in the variables.

As you step through an application, you can use Step Over if you want to execute a called function without taking the time to step through it. Or, you can use Step Out to step out of a function that you don't want to step all the way through. When you want to return to normal execution, you can use Resume. Then, the application will run until the next breakpoint is reached.

These are powerful debugging features that can help you find the causes of serious debugging problems. Stepping through an application is also a good way to understand how the code in an existing application works. If, for example, you step through the if statements in the Email List application, you'll get a better idea of how they work.

A breakpoint in the Sources panel

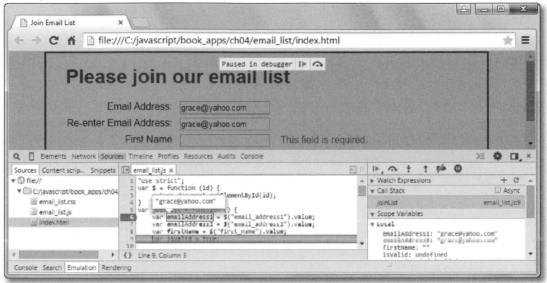

How to set or remove a breakpoint in the Sources panel

- Click on the Sources tab to display the Sources panel. Then, click on the JavaScript file in the left pane that you want to debug.

- In the center pane, click on a line number in the bar to the left of a statement. This will either add a breakpoint or remove an existing one.

The buttons and keys for stepping through the JavaScript code

Button	Key	Description
Step Into	F11	Step through the code one line at a time.
Step Over	F10	Run any called functions without stepping through them.
Step Out	SHIFT+F11	Execute the rest of a function without stepping through it.
Resume	F8	Resume normal execution.

How to view the current data values at each step

- Hover the mouse pointer over a variable name in the center pane of the Sources panel.

- View the current variables in the Scope Variables→Local section of the right-hand pane.

- Click the plus sign in the Watch Expressions section of the right-hand pane and type the variable name or expression that you want to watch.

Description

- You can set a *breakpoint* on any line except a blank line. When the JavaScript engine encounters a breakpoint, it stops before executing the statement with the breakpoint.

- A dark blue arrow around the line number marks a breakpoint, and a light blue highlight marks the next statement to be executed as you *step through* your code.

Figure 6-5   How to use breakpoints and step through your code

Other debugging methods

Because Chrome has excellent developer tools, you should use them for most of your debugging. Here, though, are other debugging methods that you should be aware of.

How to debug in Internet Explorer

Sometimes things that work fine in the other major browsers won't work in Internet Explorer, especially in the older IE versions. As a result, you should always test your applications in a standard browser like Chrome as well as in IE. Then, if you have problems with IE, you can use its developer tools to help you debug them.

That's why figure 6-6 shows how to use the developer tools for the current version of IE. If you experiment with them, you'll see that when an error occurs, the Debugger panel is displayed with the statement in error highlighted and an error message displayed.

You can also set breakpoints and step through statements using techniques similar to those you use in Chrome. In this figure, for example, a breakpoint has been set on line 6 and the next statement to be executed is the one on line 8.

One of the unique features of the IE developer tools is that they let you emulate earlier versions of IE, like IE7, 8, 9, and 10. To do that, you use the Emulation tab as described in this figure. Then, you can test your applications in these versions of the browsers, which should give you a strong indication of what (if any) compatibility problems you're going to encounter.

Remember, though, that these versions are only emulators. They are not the actual browsers. As a result, if you need to make sure that your applications are going to work on these older browsers, you need to test your applications on the actual browsers.

Internet Explorer in debugging mode

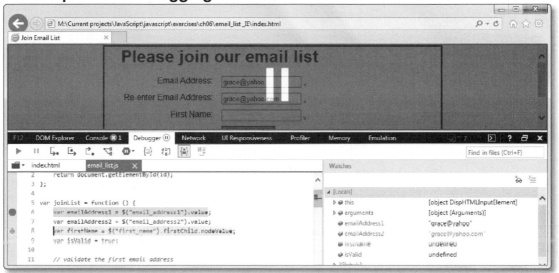

How to display or hide the developer tools

- Press F12. Or, click on the Settings icon (the gear) in the upper right corner of the browser, and then click on F12 Developer Tools.

How to find a JavaScript error

- Open the developer tools and run the application. When an error occurs, the Debugger panel is displayed, the statement in error is highlighted, and an error message is displayed.

How to set breakpoints and step through an application

- To set a breakpoint, click in the space to the left of a statement in the Debugger panel.

- To step through the statements, use the buttons below the tabs or press the keys shown in figure 6-5.

How to test applications in older versions of IE

- Click on the Emulation tab in the developer tools. Then, select the version that you want to use from the Documents Mode list. When the session ends, IE returns to its default mode.

Description

- IE along with its older versions is most likely to cause compatibility problems. That's why you always need to test your applications in IE.

- If you have problems when testing with IE, you can use its developer tools for debugging, which are similar to Chrome's.

- One of the features of the IE developer tools is that they let you emulate older versions of IE, like IE7, 8, 9, and 10. This makes it easy to test your applications in the older browsers, although these are only approximations to the actual browsers.

Figure 6-6   How to debug in Internet Explorer

How to trace the execution of your JavaScript code

When you *trace* the execution of an application, you determine the sequence in which the statements in the application are executed. An easy way to do that is to add statements to your code that log messages or variable values at key points in the code. You can then view this information in the Console panel of Chrome's developer tools.

This is illustrated by the example in figure 6-7. Here, the first log statement that's highlighted lets you know that the calculateMpg function has been started. The second and third log statements display the user entries for miles and gallons to make sure the two statements that precede it have worked correctly. The fourth log statement lets you know that the else clause of the if statement has been started. And the fifth log statement lets you know the value of the mpg calculation, both to be sure that the statement that preceded it worked correctly, and to see the calculated value before the toFixed method is run.

When you use this technique, you usually start by adding just a few log statements to the code. Then, if that doesn't help you solve the problem, you can add more. Often, this is all you need for solving simple debugging problems, and this is quicker than setting breakpoints and stepping through the code.

One way that tracing is better than stepping through code is when you're dealing with code that is executed many times. Say, for example, you've got an error that occurs somewhere inside a loop that performs a calculation on each element of an array with 1000 elements. Then, it would be daunting to step through the entire array to find the calculation that fails. With the console.log method, though, you can send the loop's index and the element's value to the console on each iteration, and then look at the complete log when the script has stopped running.

You can also use the alert method to trace the execution of an application. This has the benefit of displaying the trace data directly in the browser, rather than having to open the Console panel. But it has the drawback of being intrusive.

In the example in this figure, for instance, you would need to close an alert dialog box 5 times each time you ran the calculateMpg function. That may not seem like much, but that can quickly become annoying, especially if you're tracing something extensive. Imagine tracing the loop that I just described with alert statements! Of course, if you just want to check one or two values, the alert method might be all that you need.

JavaScript with five log statements that trace the execution of the code

```
var calculateMpg = function() {
    console.log("calculateMpg function has started");
    var miles = parseFloat($("miles").value);
    var gallons = parseFloat($("gallons").value);
    console.log("miles = " + miles);
    console.log("gallons = " + gallons);

    if (isNaN(miles) || isNaN(gallons)) {
        alert("Both entries must be numeric");
    }
    else {
        console.log("The data is valid and the calculation is next");
        var mpg = miles / gallons;
        console.log("mpg = " + mpg);
        $("mpg").value = mpg.toFixed(1);
    }
};
```

The messages in the Console panel of Chrome's developer tools

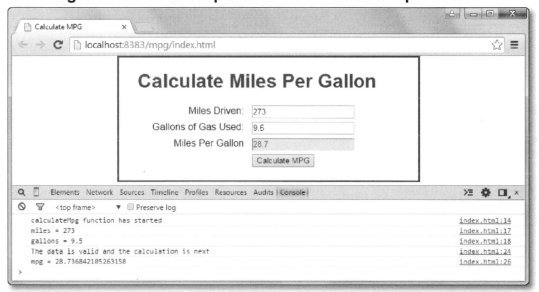

Description

- A simple way to *trace* the execution of a JavaScript application is to insert console.log method calls at key points in the code. Then, the messages specified in these method calls are displayed in the Console panel.

- The log statements can display messages that indicate what portion of the code is being executed or display the values of variables.

- You can also use the alert method for tracing, but the resulting popups can be intrusive, especially if you're tracing something extensive like a loop.

Figure 6-7   How to trace the execution of your JavaScript code

How to view the source code

Occasionally, when nothing seems to be working right as you test an application, you may want to view the source code for the application. That will at least confirm that you're testing the right files.

To view the HTML source code, you can use one of the techniques in figure 6-8. Be aware, however, that the HTML source code is the code that is initially loaded into the browser, so it doesn't reflect any changes made to the DOM by the JavaScript.

In this figure, for example, the JavaScript code has changed the text in the span elements after the text boxes. If you were to look at the HTML source code, though, you would see that the span elements still contain asterisks. In other words, the HTML source code doesn't reflect any changes made to the DOM by DOM scripting.

Luckily, you can use the Elements panel in Chrome's developer tools to see the changes that JavaScript has made to the DOM. By using the techniques described in this figure, you can drill down into the document's elements. In this figure, for example, the Elements panel is open and the span element with the id "email_address2_error" is selected. You can tell it's selected because the line is highlighted in blue. Within the highlighted line, you can see that the span's text has changed from an asterisk to "This field is required."

In the Styles pane to the right of the Elements pane, you can also see the CSS that has been applied to the selected element. This pane shows all of the styles that have been applied from all of the style sheets that are attached to the web page. If a style in this pane has a line through it, that means it has been overridden by another style. This pane can be invaluable when you're trying to solve complicated formatting problems with cascading style sheets.

The Elements panel after JavaScript has changed the DOM

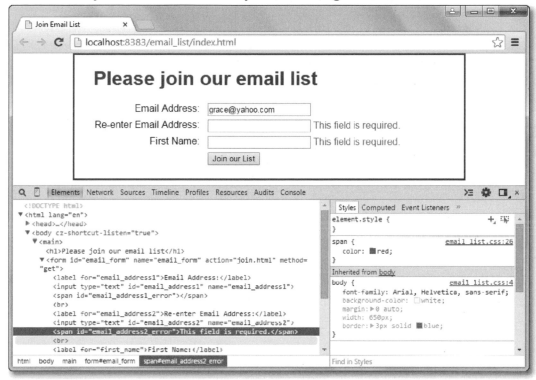

How to view the source code for a web page in any browser

- If it's available, use a menu command like View→Source or View→Page Source.
- You can also right-click on the page and select a command like Source, View Source, or View Page Source.

How to view DOM changes in the Elements panel in Chrome

- Press F12 and then click on Elements to open the Elements panel.
- Expand the HTML nodes until you get to the node you're interested in.
- Click on the node to select it. You'll see any changes made to the DOM by JavaScript, and you'll see the CSS that's applied to the element in the Styles pane to the right.

Description

- When you're debugging, it can be useful to view the page's HTML. You can do so easily in any browser, but that will only show the HTML that has been loaded into the browser and not any subsequent changes to the DOM.
- If you're using Chrome, you can use the Elements panel to see the changes to the DOM that your JavaScript has made.

Figure 6-8   How to view the source code for a web page

When and how to validate the HTML

In some cases, an HTML error will cause a JavaScript error. Then, if you suspect that might be happening, it's worth taking the time to *validate* the HTML code. To do that, you can use the technique in figure 6-9.

Suppose, for example, that you accidentally use the same id attribute for more than one element in an HTML document. Then, when the JavaScript refers to that id, it won't run correctly...although it may not throw an error. If you validate the HTML, though, the problem with duplicate ids will be identified, so you can fix the ids in the HTML as well as the JavaScript that refers to those ids.

In fact, we recommend that you validate the HTML for all of the pages in an application. Of course, this isn't necessary when you're doing exercises or developing applications for a class, but this may help you fix a problem that is affecting your JavaScript.

The home page for the W3C validator

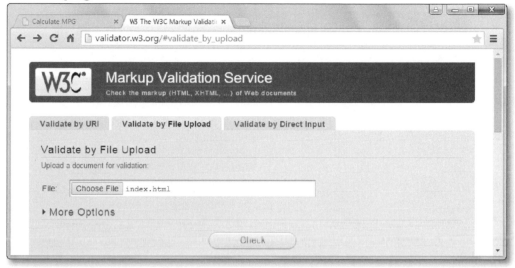

The validation results with one error

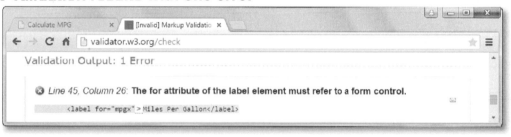

How to use the W3C Markup Validation Service

- Go to the URL that follows, identify the file to be validated, and click the Check button:
  `http://validator.w3.org/`

How to validate an HTML file from Aptana

- Select the file. Then, select the Commands→HTML→Validate Syntax (W3C) command.

Description

- Occasionally, an error in the HTML for a page will affect the operation of the JavaScript for that page. If you suspect that could be happening, *validating* the HTML for the page will sometimes expose the error.

- To validate the HTML for a page, you can use a program or web site for that purpose. One of the most popular web sites is the W3C Markup Validation Service.

- When you use the W3C Markup Validation Service, if the file you want to validate has already been uploaded to a web server, you can validate it by entering its URL on the Validate by URI tab. If the file you want to validate hasn't been uploaded to a web server, you can validate it by locating it on the Validate by File Upload tab.

- If you're using Aptana, you can validate an HTML file by using the command above.

Figure 6-9   When and how to validate an HTML file

Perspective

All too often, JavaScript applications are put into production before they have been thoroughly tested and debugged. In the early days of JavaScript programming, that was understandable because the tools for testing and debugging were limited. Today, however, you have all the tools that you need for thoroughly debugging an application before you put it into production.

Terms

test	top-down coding and testing
debug	top-down testing
bug	developer tools
syntax error	F12 tools
runtime error	breakpoint
throw an exception	step through code
throw an error	trace
logic error	validate the HTML

Summary

- When you *test* an application, you try to make it fail. When you *debug* an application, you fix all of the problems that you discover during testing.

- When you write the code for a JavaScript application, you are likely to introduce three types of errors: *syntax errors*, *runtime errors*, and *logic errors*.

- *Top-down coding and testing* simplifies debugging because you build an application by coding and testing a small number of statements at a time.

- Chrome's *developer tools* (or *F12 tools*) can help you debug an application when it stops running. First, the Console panel displays an error message. Then, the link in the message goes to the error statement in the Sources panel.

- In the Sources panel of Chrome's developer tools, you can set *breakpoints* that stop the execution of code. Then, you can *step through* the code starting from a breakpoint and view the changes in the variables at each step.

- You can use Internet Explorer's developer tools to find errors in a way that's similar to Chrome's. IE's developer tools also let you emulate older versions of IE, like IE 7 through IE10.

- An easy way to *trace* the execution of an application is to call the console.log method at key points in the JavaScript code. This method logs the specified data in Chrome's Console panel. You can also use alert methods for tracing.

- As you debug, you may occasionally want to view the HTML that has been loaded into the browser. You can also use Chrome's Elements panel to view any changes in the HTML that have been made by scripting the DOM.

- *Validating* the HTML for a page will occasionally help you debug an application.

Exercise 6-1   Use Chrome's developer tools

In this exercise, you'll use Chrome's developer tools to find a syntax error, set a breakpoint, and step through the Email List application.

1. Open the HTML and JavaScript files for the Email List application in this folder:

    `c:\javascript\exercises\ch06\email_list`

2. Run the application in Chrome, enter valid values in just the first two text boxes, and click on the Join our List button. Then, note that nothing happens.

3. Open the developer tools and use the Console panel to display the error that caused the problem, as shown in figure 6-4. Then, click the link for the error to find the statement that caused the error.

4. Switch to your text editor or IDE and fix the code. The correction should be fairly obvious. Then, test the application again with valid values in the first two text boxes.

5. In Chrome's developer tools, switch to the Elements panel. Then, drill down to the span elements to see that their values have been changed by the JavaScript.

6. Still in the developer tools, switch to the Sources panel. Then, if necessary, click on the email_list.js file in the Sources pane on the left to display the JavaScript code in the email_list.js file.

7. Set a breakpoint on the first statement in the joinList function, as shown in figure 6-5. Then, with valid values in just the first two text boxes, click the Join our List button. The application should stop at the breakpoint.

8. Use the Step Into button or F11 key to step through the application. At each step, notice the values that are displayed in the local variables pane. Also, hover the mouse over a variable in the JavaScript code to see what its value is.

9. Experiment with the Step Over and Step Out buttons as you step through the application. When you're done, remove the breakpoint and continue.

Exercise 6-2   Use IE's developer tools

In this exercise, you'll use Internet Explorer's developer tools.

1. Open the HTML and JavaScript files for the Email List application in this folder:

    `c:\javascript\exercises\ch06\email_list_IE`

2. Run the application in IE, and open the developer tools so you can use them to debug the application.

3. Enter valid values in just the first two text boxes, click on the Join our List button, and notice the error message in the Debugger panel.

4. Switch to your text editor or IDE, fix the error, and test again. The correction should be fairly obvious.

Exercise 6-3   Use other debugging methods

In this exercise, you'll use the other debugging methods that you learned in this chapter.

1. Open this HTML file, and notice that it includes calls to console.log methods for tracing the execution of this application, as shown in figure 6-7:

    `c:\javascript\exercises\ch06\mpg\index.html`

2. Run this application in Chrome, don't enter anything into the text boxes, and click on the Calculate button. Note that an error message is displayed below the button.

3. Use one of the methods in figure 6-8 to display the source code for the page. Then, use Chrome's Elements panel to see that the content of the <p> element has been changed to the error message by DOM scripting.

4. Switch to the Console panel, and review the information in the log.

5. Enter valid values in the two text boxes, and click on the Calculate button. Then, go to the Console panel to review the new information.

6. In the JavaScript for this application, replace each console.log method with the alert method. Then, run the application to see how this works.

7. In the HTML, change the name in the for attribute for the Miles Per Gallon label from *mpg* to *mpgx*. This may not be identified as an error by your text editor or IDE. Then, use one of the methods in figure 6-9 to validate the HTML for the page, which should identify this error.

Section 2

JavaScript essentials

The first four chapters in this section expand upon what you learned in section 1. In chapter 7, you'll learn more about working with numbers, strings, and dates. In chapter 8, you'll learn more about working with control structures, including the switch statement. In chapter 9, you'll learn more about working with arrays as well as how to use web storage for storing arrays. And in chapter 10, you'll learn more about creating and using functions.

Then, the next two chapters present entirely new information. In chapter 11, you'll learn how to create and use your own objects. And in chapter 12, you'll learn how to use regular expressions and handle exceptions as you validate the data in a form before it is submitted to the server.

With one exception, you can read these chapters in whatever sequence you prefer and whenever you feel that you need them. The one exception is that you should read chapter 10 on functions before you read chapter 11 on objects because functions and objects are so closely related.

When you finish this section, you'll know the JavaScript language. Then, section 3 presents the advanced skills that will help take you to the expert level. At that point, you'll be able to develop extensive JavaScript applications that can be used by others and can't be broken.

7

How to work with numbers, strings, and dates

In chapter 2, you learned some basic skills for working with numbers, strings, and dates. Now, you'll learn the other essential skills for working with data in your JavaScript applications.

How to work with numbers

In chapter 2, you learned how to declare numeric variables, perform common arithmetic operations, and convert a decimal value to a fixed number of decimal places. Now, you'll build on those skills.

How to use the properties and methods of the Number object

Figure 7-1 starts with a table that summarizes five properties of the Number object that you can use to represent special values. For instance, Number. MAX_VALUE represents the largest positive value that can be represented by JavaScript. Curiously, each language has a maximum value that it can represent and JavaScript's is approximately 1798 followed by 305 zeros (an extremely large number). Similarly, MIN_VALUE is an extremely small number, POSITIVE_INFINITY is any number greater than the maximum value, and NEGATIVE_INFINITY is any number smaller than the minimum value.

The last property in this table stands for "not a number", which represents any non-numeric value. Because NaN can represent around 9 quadrillion different values, the equality test NaN == NaN will always return false. That's why you must use the isNaN method to test whether a value is not a number.

When you code these properties, you always use Number as the object name as shown in the table. That's because these are static properties. However, you can also refer to the last three values in this table by using their shortcut names. For instance, the first example in this figure shows how to test a result for Infinity, -Infinity, or NaN and display an appropriate message.

When you divide 0 by 0 with JavaScript, the result is NaN. However, when you divide a non-zero number by zero, the result is either Infinity or -Infinity, depending on the sign of the non-zero number. This is different than the way most languages handle this. In other languages, division by zero usually results in a runtime error because there is no way to represent Infinity.

These examples are followed by a table that presents two methods of a Number object. Remember that a Number object is created when a numeric value is stored in a variable. Then, you can use the methods of the Number object to work with the values in these objects.

For instance, the first example after this table shows how to use the toFixed method. Here, the third statement rounds the number 1.49925 to two decimal places, or 1.50. However, because the toFixed method returns a string, this statement also uses the parseFloat method to store the rounded value as a number in the tax variable, which converts it to 1.5. Then, the last statement in this example uses the toFixed method again to ensure that any number that was rounded to 0 in the hundreds place is correctly displayed with two digits. As a result, 1.5 is converted to 1.50 before it is displayed by the alert method.

The second example shows how the toString method is used implicitly by JavaScript. Here, the integer value in age is automatically converted to a string

Properties of the Number object

Property	Shortcut	Description
`Number.MAX_VALUE`		The largest positive value that can be represented.
`Number.MIN_VALUE`		The smallest positive value that can be represented.
`Number.POSITIVE_INFINITY`	Infinity	Represents positive infinity.
`Number.NEGATIVE_INFINITY`	-Infinity	Represents negative infinity.
`Number.NaN`	NaN	Represents a value that isn't a number.

Example 1: Testing for Infinity, -Infinity, and NaN

```
if ( result == Infinity ) {
    alert( "The result exceeds " + Number.MAX_VALUE ); }
else if ( result == -Infinity ) {
    alert( "The result is below -" + Number.MAX_VALUE ); }
else if ( isNaN(result) ) {
    alert( "The result is not a number" );
else { alert( "The result is " + result ); }
```

Example 2: Division by zero

```
alert(  0 / 0 );    // Displays NaN
alert( 10 / 0 );    // Displays Infinity
```

Methods of the Number object

Method	Description
`toFixed(digits)`	Returns a string with the number rounded to the specified decimal digits.
`toString(base)`	Returns a string with the number in the given base. If base is omitted, 10 is used.

Example 1: Using the toFixed method

```
var subtotal = 19.99, rate = 0.075;
var tax = subtotal * rate;          // tax is 1.49925
tax = parseFloat( tax.toFixed(2) ); // tax is 1.5
alert ( tax.toFixed(2) );           // displays 1.50
```

Example 2: Implicit use of the toString method for base 10 conversions

```
var age = parseInt( prompt("Please enter your age.") );
alert( "Your age is " + age );
```

Description

- Any numerical operation that results in a number greater than Number.
  MAX_VALUE will return the value Infinity, and any operation that results in a
  number less than Number.MIN_VALUE will return the value -Infinity.

- Any numerical operation with a non-numeric operand will return NaN.

- You cannot test for equality with the value NaN. You must use the global method
  isNaN() to test if a value is NaN.

- Division of zero by zero results in NaN, but division of a non-zero number by zero
  results in either Infinity or -Infinity.

- The toString method with no parameters is used implicitly whenever JavaScript
  needs to convert a number to a string.

Figure 7-1   How to work with the properties and methods of the Number object

by the toString method when age is concatenated with a string literal. This implicit conversion is done whenever a number is used in an expression that mixes string and number values. Occasionally, though, you may want to use the toString method explicitly.

How to use the methods of the Math object

Figure 7-2 shows how to use some of the common methods of the Math object. When you use these methods, you always start by coding Math with a capital letter. Here again, that's because these methods are static methods.

The first example shows you how to use the abs, or absolute value, method. When given a negative number, it returns that number as a positive value.

The second example show you how to use the round method. Note that in the third statement, -3.5 rounds up to -3. It does not round down to -4.

The third example shows you how to use the ceil (ceiling) and floor methods. The ceil method always rounds a fractional value towards positive infinity. The floor method always rounds a fractional value towards negative infinity. You can think of the floor method as truncating or removing the fractional portion.

The fourth example shows you how to use the pow and sqrt methods. The power parameter of the pow method can be a fractional value. In the second statement, 125 is raised to the 1/3rd power. This is the equivalent of taking the cube root of 125.

The fifth example shows you how to use the min and max methods. These methods are not limited to two parameters so you can supply as many parameters as needed. Then, these methods will find the minimum or maximum value in the list of parameters.

The Math object also provides many trigonometric and logarithmic methods. If you have the appropriate mathematical background, you should be able to use these methods with no problem. If you use them, though, one point to remember is that the trigonometric methods use radians to measure angles, not degrees.

Common methods of the Math object

Method	Description
`Math.abs( x )`	Returns the absolute value of x.
`Math.round( x )`	Returns the value of x rounded to the closest integer value. If the decimal part is .5, x is rounded up to the next higher integer value.
`Math.ceil( x )`	Returns the value of x rounded to the next higher integer value.
`Math.floor( x )`	Returns the value of x rounded to the next lower integer value.
`Math.pow(x, power)`	Returns the value of x raised to the power specified. The power may be a decimal number.
`Math.sqrt( x )`	Returns the square root of x.
`Math.max( x1, x2, … )`	Returns the largest value from its parameters.
`Math.min( x1, x2, … )`	Returns the smallest value from its parameters.

Example 1: The abs method
```
var result_1a = Math.abs(-3.4);        // result_1a is 3.4
```

Example 2: The round method
```
var result_2a = Math.round(12.5);      // result_2a is 13
var result_2b = Math.round(-3.4);      // result_2b is -3
var result_2c = Math.round(-3.5);      // result_2c is -3
var result_2d = Math.round(-3.51);     // result_2d is -4
```

Example 3: The floor and ceil methods
```
var result_3a = Math.floor(12.5);      // result_3a is 12
var result_3b = Math.ceil(12.5);       // result_3b is 13
var result_3c = Math.floor(-3.4);      // result_3c is -4
var result_3d = Math.ceil(-3.4);       // result_3d is -3
```

Example 4: The pow and sqrt methods
```
var result_4a = Math.pow(2,3);         // result_4a is 8 (the cube of 2)
var result_4b = Math.pow(125, 1/3);    // result_4b is 5 (cube root of 125)
var result_4c = Math.sqrt(16);         // result_4c is 4
```

Example 5: The min and max methods
```
var x = 12.5, y = -3.4;
var max = Math.max(x, y);              // max is 12.5
var min = Math.min(x, y);              // min is -3.4
```

Description

*   The max and min methods can take one or more parameters. If there are no parameters, the max method returns -Infinity and the min method returns Infinity.

Figure 7-2   How to use the methods of the Math object

How to generate a random number

The random method of the Math object generates a random number that is equal to or greater than zero but less than one. This is illustrated by the first example in figure 7-3. Often, though, you want a random number that is in a range other than from zero to one.

The second example presents a function that will generate a random number in a range between 1 and a specified maximum. The getRandomNumber function takes a single parameter, which is the maximum value for the range of random numbers that the function should generate.

This function first declares a variable named random. This variable will hold the random number generated by the function. Next, the function validates the max parameter to ensure it is a number. If it fails the isNaN test, the function simply returns the random variable declared at the beginning of the function. This variable has not been assigned a value yet, so that means if the max parameter is not a number, the getRandomNumber function returns undefined.

If the max parameter is a number, the function computes a whole number between 1 and max. To do this, the function takes a value from the random method and multiplies it by the value of max. It then takes the floor of this intermediate result to remove any fractional part. Finally, the function adds 1 to the result of the floor method.

For example, if max is 6, then 6 times a random number from 0 to just under 1 returns a value in the range of 0 to just less than 6. Next, using the floor method to truncate the fractional part returns a whole number from 0 to 5. Last, adding 1 to any number in this range returns a number in the range 1 to 6, which is the range requested.

The random number generator function in this figure is a simple one, but you could easily improve it by making it so you can pass in the minimum value for the range, or have a range of decimals in addition to a range of whole numbers. There are many online examples of random number generation that you can use as examples.

The random method of the Math object

Method	Description
`Math.random()`	Returns a random decimal number >= 0.0 but < 1.0.

Example 1: Generating a random number

```
var result = Math.random();
```

Example 2: A function that generates a random number

```
var getRandomNumber = function(max) {
    var random;
    if (!isNaN(max)) {
        //value >= 0.0 and < 1.0
        random = Math.random();

        //value is an integer between 0 and max - 1
        random = Math.floor(random * max);

        //value is an integer between 1 and max
        random = random + 1;
    }
    //if max is not a number, will return undefined
    return random;
};

// Returns an integer that ranges from 1 through 100
var randomNumber = getRandomNumber(100);
```

Description

- You can use the getRandomNumber function in this figure to generate a random number between 1 and the specified maximum value.

- Random numbers can be used for testing and are often used in games or applications that provide animation.

- There are many ways to use the Math.random function to create a random number generator. If you do an internet search, you will find many examples, some with more extensive functionality than the simple generator shown above.

Figure 7-3   How to generate a random number

The PIG application

Figure 7-4 shows the user interface for a dice game called PIG. This application requires the use of just one die and illustrates the use of a random number generator.

When the application starts, the two bottom rows of the game are hidden. Then, the players enter their names into the Player 1 and Player 2 text boxes, and they click the New Game button to start the game. This displays the bottom two rows of the interface with the first player's name shown.

From that point on, the players take turns until one of them reaches 100 and wins. For each turn, the player has the option of clicking the Roll button to try for more points or clicking the Hold button to keep the points that have been earned during that turn. But if the player rolls a 1, the turn ends and the player gets zero points.

The HTML

As this figure shows, the HTML for this application consists primarily of labels, text boxes, and buttons. Most important, of course, are the id attributes because these are the ones that are used in the JavaScript. That's why they're highlighted in this figure.

As you can see, the section at the bottom of the HTML has the id of "turn" and doesn't have a class attribute. This section is hidden when the application starts because the CSS sets its display property to "none". To display it, the JavaScript adds a class named "open" to this element, and the CSS for this class sets the display attribute to "block". If you want to see the CSS for this application, you can of course review it in the downloaded application.

The user interface for the PIG application

The HTML for the application

```
<h1>Let's Play PIG!</h1>
<fieldset>
    <legend>Rules</legend>
    <ul>
        <li>First player to 100 wins.</li>
        <li>Players take turns rolling the die.</li>
        <li>Turn ends when player rolls a 1 or chooses to hold.</li>
        <li>If player rolls a 1, they lose all points earned ...</li>
        <li>If player holds, points earned during the turn ...</li>
    </ul>
</fieldset>
<label for="player1">Player 1</label>
    <input type="text" id="player1" >
<label for="score1">Score</label>
    <input type="text" id="score1" value="0" disabled><br>
<label for="player2">Player 2</label>
    <input type="text" id="player2">
<label for="score2">Score</label>
    <input type="text" id="score2" value="0" disabled>
<input type="button" id="new_game" value="New Game"><br>
<section id="turn">
    <p><span id="current"> </span>'s turn</p>
    <input type="button" id="roll" value="Roll">
    <input type="button" id="hold" value="Hold">
    <label for="die">Die</label>
    <input type="text" id="die" disabled>
    <label for="total">Total</label>
    <input type="text" id="total" disabled>
</section>
```

Figure 7-4   The HTML for the PIG application

The JavaScript

Figure 7-5 presents the JavaScript for this application. It consists of seven functions, starting with the $ function. This is followed by the getRandomNumber function that you reviewed in the last figure.

The third function is changePlayer, and it is called when the turn for one player ends. Its if statement changes the name in the "current" span element to the name that's in that text box for the other player. Then, it sets the values of the "die" and "total" text boxes to zero and the focus to the Roll button.

The newGame function is the event handler for the click event of the New Game button. It resets the scores for the players to zero. Then, its if statement checks whether the name in the text box for either player is an empty space (blank). If either is, this function removes the class attribute for the "turn" section, which hides the last two rows in the user interface, and it displays a message that says the players must enter their names. Otherwise, the else clause of the if statement sets the class attribute for the section to "open", and calls the changePlayer function.

The rollDice function is the event handler for the click event of the Roll button. It starts by getting the total value for that turn from the "total" text box. Then, it calls the getRandomNumber function to get the result of one roll of the die. If the result is 1, the total is reset to zero and the changePlayer function is called. Otherwise, the result of the roll is added to the total value, and the die and total values are displayed in their text boxes so the player can roll again.

The holdTurn function is the event handler for the click event of the Hold button. It starts by declaring a variable named score and getting the total value from the "total" text box. Next, an if statement tests whether the current player is player 1. If so, the code gets the score1 Textbox object and stores it in the score variable. Otherwise, it gets the score2 Textbox object, and stores it in the score variable. Then, it sets the new value of the score Textbox object to the value of the score Textbox object plus the total value. Last, if the score value is greater than or equal to 100, an alert dialog box is displayed that declares the winner and the newGame function is called. If it isn't greater than or equal to 100, the changePlayer function is called.

The last function for this application is the window.onload event handler. It attaches the newGame, rollDice, and holdTurn event handlers to the click events of the New Game, Roll, and Hold buttons.

The JavaScript for the application

```javascript
var $ = function(id) { return document.getElementById(id); };
var getRandomNumber = function(max) {
    var random;
    if (!isNaN(max)) {
        random = Math.random();              //value >= 0.0 and < 1.0
        random = Math.floor(random * max);   //integer between 0 and max - 1
        random = random + 1;                 //integer between 1 and max }
    return random;
};
var changePlayer = function() {
    if ($("current").firstChild.nodeValue == $("player1").value) {
        $("current").firstChild.nodeValue = $("player2").value; }
    else {
        $("current").firstChild.nodeValue = $("player1").value; }
    $("die").value = "0";
    $("total").value = "0";
    $("roll").focus();
};
var newGame = function() {
    $("score1").value = "0";
    $("score2").value = "0";
    if ($("player1").value == "" || $("player2").value == "") {
        $("turn").removeAttribute("class");
        alert("Please enter two player names."); }
    else {
        $("turn").setAttribute("class", "open");
        changePlayer(); }
};
var rollDice = function() {
    var total = parseInt($("total").value);
    var die = getRandomNumber(6);
    if (die == 1) {
        total = 0;
        changePlayer(); }
    else { total = total + die; }
    $("die").value = die;
    $("total").value = total;
};
var holdTurn = function() {
    var score;
    var total = parseInt($("total").value);
    if ( $("current").firstChild.nodeValue == $("player1").value) {
        score = $("score1"); }
    else { score = $("score2"); }
    score.value = parseInt(score.value) + total;
    if (score.value >= 100) {
        alert($("current").firstChild.nodeValue + " WINS!");
        newGame(); }
    else { changePlayer(); }
};
window.onload = function() {
    $("new_game").onclick = newGame;
    $("roll").onclick = rollDice;
    $("hold").onclick = holdTurn;
};
```

Figure 7-5   The JavaScript for the PIG application

How to work with strings

In chapter 2, you learned how to create and work with simple strings. Now, you'll learn more about using escape sequences in your strings. You'll also learn how to use the methods of the String object.

How to use escape sequences in strings

Figure 7-6 shows you how to use *escape sequences* in your strings. These sequences let you include special characters in a string. To start all escape sequences, you code the backslash. For instance, \n starts a new line when a string is displayed, and \t represents a tab character. Similarly, \" adds a double quotation mark to a string, and \\ adds a single backslash to a string.

You can also include any Unicode character in a JavaScript string by using the \u escape sequence. Unicode is a standard set of 17-bit codes that allows more than 65,000 characters to be identified in a text string. These 17-bit values are entered as four-digit hexadecimal (hex) values that aren't case sensitive. For example, \u00a2 is the escape sequence for the cents character, where 00a2 is the hex value.

As the third table in this figure shows, you can also include Unicode characters with hex values that start with 00 by using the \x escape sequence. In this case, you don't code the 00, so \u00a2 and \xa2 are equivalent.

For a complete list of Unicode characters, you can go to the web site specified in this figure. Be aware, however, that not all fonts provide representations for all Unicode characters. If you specify a Unicode character that isn't available in the font used in the web browser, a filler character (often just an empty box or a question mark) will be used instead.

Basic escape sequences

Sequence	Description
\b	Backspace
\t	Tab
\n	New line
\r	Carriage return
\f	Form feed
\v	Vertical tab
\"	Double quote
\'	Single quote
\\	Backslash

Examples of strings using the basic escape sequences

```
var quote = "He said \"Goodbye.\"";
var message = "Error\t123\nText\tInvalid Operation";
var info = "The file is in C:\\murach";
```

Escape sequences for some of the Unicode characters

Sequence	Character	Sequence	Character
\u00a2	¢	\u00bc	¼
\u00a9	©	\u00bd	½
\u00ae	®	\u00d7	×
\u00b0	°	\u00f7	÷
\u00b1	±	\u2026	...
\u00b5	µ		

Two ways to code Unicode escape sequences

Sequence	Description
\udddd	Character whose Unicode value (UTF-16) is given by a four-digit hexadecimal number.
\xdd	Equivalent to \u00*dd*. This is in the Latin-1 range of the Unicode characters.

Examples of strings using the Unicode escape sequences

```
alert( "99\u00a2" );     // Displays 99¢
alert( "\xa9 2008" );    // Displays © 2008
```

Description

- *Escape sequences* let you insert characters that aren't on the keyboard.
- For a complete list of Unicode characters, go to http://www.unicode.org/charts/.
- Be aware that not all fonts provide all of the Unicode characters. If you use a Unicode character that isn't in the user's font, a filler character will be used instead.

Figure 7-6   How to use escape sequences in strings

How to use the methods of the String object

Figure 7-7 describes one property and several methods of String objects. The length property lets you find out how many characters are in a string. This is illustrated by the first example. Because the positions in a string are numbered from zero, not 1, the last character in a string is at the position identified by the length minus 1.

Example 2 in this figure shows you how to use the charAt method. Here, the J in JavaScript is the character at position 0, and the character at position 4 is S.

Example 3 shows you how to use the concat method. If you specify more than one parameter, the strings are concatenated in order. This is the same operation performed by the + operator when one of the two operands is a string. Although there was a performance difference between using + and the concat method in earlier implementations of JavaScript, there is little difference today. As a result, you can usually use whichever coding method you prefer. You'll see the use of both methods in this book.

Example 4 shows the use of the indexOf method. If you omit the position parameter, the search is performed from the start of the string. If the search string isn't found, the method returns -1.

Example 5 shows the use of the substr and substring methods. Note that the character specified in the end parameter for the substring method is *not* included in the result. If start is greater than end, the two values are swapped. If either value is less than 0, it is replaced with 0. If either value is greater than the length of the string, it is replaced with the length of the string.

Example 6 shows you how to use the toUpperCase and toLowerCase methods. These methods have no parameters, but don't forget to include the empty set of parentheses after the method name.

If you're familiar with the string methods for other languages, you may be wondering whether there are useful methods that aren't shown in this figure. In particular, you may be looking for methods that make it easier to format numbers and dates. For instance, both Java and C# provide string methods that make it easy to insert commas into numbers and to format dates and times.

The answer is that this figure summarizes all of the useful string methods that JavaScript provides, except for the ones that use arrays and regular expressions, which you'll learn how to use in chapters 9 and 12. What this means is that JavaScript doesn't have as rich a set of string methods as some languages. Although this means more coding for some tasks, this isn't a serious limitation.

One property of String objects

Property	Description
length	The number of characters in the string.

Example 1: Displaying the length of a string

```
var message_1 = "JavaScript";
var result_1 = message_1.length;                    // result_1 is 10
```

Methods of String objects

Method	Description
charAt (position)	Returns the character at the specified position in the string.
concat(string1, string2, …)	Returns a new string that is the concatenation of this string with each of the strings specified in the parameter list.
indexOf(search, start)	Searches the string for the first occurrence of the search string starting at the position specified or the beginning if the position is omitted. If the search string is found, it returns the position in the string. If not found, it returns -1.
substr(start, length)	Returns the substring from the start position through the number of characters specified by the length parameter.
substring(start)	Returns the substring from the start position to the end of the string.
substring(start, end)	Returns the substring from the start position to, but not including, the end position.
toLowerCase()	Returns the string with all uppercase letters converted to lowercase.
toUpperCase()	Returns the string with all lowercase letters converted to uppercase.

Example 2: The charAt method

```
var message_2 = "JavaScript";
var letter = message_2.charAt(4);                   // letter is "S"
```

Example 3: The concat method

```
var message_3 = "Java";
var result_3 = message_3.concat("Script");          // result_3 is "JavaScript"
```

Example 4: The indexOf method

```
var result_4a = message_2.indexOf("a");             // result_4a is 1
var result_4b = message_2.indexOf("a", 2);          // result_4b is 3
var result_4c = message_2.indexOf("s");             // result_4c is -1
```

Example 5: The substr and substring methods

```
var result_5a = message_2.substr(4, 5);             // result_5a is "Scrip"
var result_5b = message_2.substring(4);             // result_5b is "Script"
var result_5c = message_2.substring(0,4);           // result_5c is "Java"
```

Example 6: The toLowerCase and toUpperCase methods

```
var result_6a = message_2.toLowerCase();            // result_6a is "javascript"
var result_6b = message_2.toUpperCase();            // result_6b is "JAVASCRIPT"
```

Figure 7-7   How to use the methods of the String object

Examples of working with strings

In the previous figure, you saw simple examples that used the string methods. Now, figure 7-8 shows you how to perform more complex manipulations by using combinations of string methods and loops. This should give you some ideas for how you can apply these methods in your own applications.

Example 1 shows how to trim the spaces off the beginning of a string by using a function named ltrim that takes the string to be trimmed as its only parameter. This function first initializes the start variable to 0. Then, a while loop tests the character at the start position. As long as it is a space, the start position is moved forward one character and the loop continues. The loop exits when it finds a non-space character, and the function returns the substring from the current value of the start position to the end.

Example 2 shows you how to use a function named rtrim to trim spaces off the end of a string. This is like the ltrim function, but the end variable is set to the last position in the string (length - 1). Then, the while loop tests the character at the end position. As long as it is a space, the end position is moved backward one character. The loop exits when it finds a non-space character, and the function then returns the substring from the beginning to the current value of the end position + 1. Here, end + 1 is used because the substring method doesn't return the character specified by the end position.

Example 3 shows you how to trim spaces off both ends of a string by combining the ltrim and rtrim functions of examples 2 and 3. This type of trimming is often done when working with user entries.

Example 4 shows how to perform a case insensitive test for equality between two strings. This is useful because the == operator is case sensitive when used with strings. This example just uses the toLowerCase function to convert each string to lowercase before doing the comparison.

Example 5 shows you how to use a function named equalIgnoreCase to perform a case insensitive test for equality between two strings. Like example 4, this function tests the equality of the two parameters that are passed to it after it converts them both to lowercase.

Example 1: How to trim spaces off the beginning of a string

```
var ltrim = function( text ) {
    var start = 0;
    while ( text.charAt(start) == " " ) {
        start++;
    }
    return text.substring(start);
}
var result = ltrim("  JavaScript");      // result is "JavaScript"
```

Example 2: How to trim spaces off the end of a string

```
var rtrim = function( text ) {
    var end = text.length - 1;
    while ( text.charAt(end) == " " ) {
        end--;
    }
    return text.substring(0, end + 1);
}
var result = rtrim("JavaScript   ");      // result is "JavaScript"
```

Example 3: How to combine ltrim and rtrim to trim all spaces

```
var trim = function( text ) {
    return ltrim( rtrim(text) );
}
var result = trim("  JavaScript   ");      // result is "JavaScript"
```

Example 4: How to compare two strings ignoring case

```
var text1 = "JavaScript";
var text2 = "javascript";) {
if ( text1.toLowerCase() == text2.toLowerCase() ) {
    alert("The strings are the same.");
}
```

Example 5: A function for comparing two strings while ignoring case

```
var equalIgnoreCase = function( text1, text2 ) {
    return text1.toLowerCase() == text2.toLowerCase();
};

if ( equalIgnoreCase("JavaScript", "javascript") ) {
    alert("The strings are the same.");
}
```

Figure 7-8   Examples of working with strings

How to work with dates and times

In chapter 4, you learned how to create Date objects and how to use four methods for working with them. In this topic, you'll learn more about creating Date objects and using the methods of those objects.

In JavaScript, dates are represented by the number of milliseconds since Midnight, January 1, 1970. Positive values come after this date while negative values come before. Internally, the dates are stored in universal time, or Greenwich Mean Time (GMT). However, JavaScript has access to the time zone on the client's computer and adjusts the dates to the local time.

How to create Date objects

Figure 7-9 presents four ways to create Date objects with JavaScript. The first example shows how to create a Date object that represents the local time on the user's computer. This is done by specifying the Date constructor with no parameters. This is the method that you learned in chapter 4.

The second example shows how to create a Date object by specifying a date and time in a string parameter. In this case, the year must be four digits, and the hours must be specified in 24-hour (or military) time. For example, 3:15pm is 15:15 on a 24-hour clock. If you omit the time, midnight is used.

The third example shows how to create a Date object by specifying the parts of the date. Here, year and month are required. Then, if day is omitted, 1 is used. And if any of the remaining date parts are omitted, 0 is used.

When you use this method, remember that the months are numbered from 0 through 11 where 0 is January and 11 is December. As a result, 3 is April and 10 is November. This makes it easier to use the month numbers with arrays, which are also numbered starting with 0.

The fourth example shows you how to create a Date object by copying another Date object. This lets you manipulate the copy without affecting the original. You'll learn more about that in the next two figures.

The last example shows you some unexpected results you might get if you use a string parameter with dashes or with a 2-digit year. Not all browsers produce these results, but some do, so you should keep this in mind when working with the Date object. If, for example, you're accepting dates from users, you'll want to validate them to make sure they're in a correct format before passing them as an argument to the Date object.

How to create a Date object that represents the current date and time

```
var now = new Date();
```

How to create a Date object by specifying a date string

```
var electionDay = new Date("11/8/2016");
var grandOpening = new Date("2/16/2015 8:00");
var departureTime = new Date("4/6/2015 18:30:00");
```

How to create a Date object by specifying date parts

Syntax of the constructor

```
new Date( year, month, day, hours, minutes, seconds, milliseconds)
```

Examples

```
var electionDay = new Date(2016, 10, 8);            // 10 is November
var grandOpening = new Date(2015, 1, 16, 8);        // 1 is February
var departureTime = new Date(2015, 3, 6, 18, 30);   // 3 is April
```

How to create a Date object by copying another date object

```
var invoiceDate = new Date("8/8/2015");
var dueDate = new Date(invoiceDate);
// You can then add a number of days to due_date. See figure 7-11.
```

Some unexpected results when specifying a date string

```
var electionDay = new Date("11-8-2016");            // Invalid Date
var electionDay = new Date("11/8/16");              // 11/8/1916
```

How the constructor for the Date object works

- If you call the Date constructor with no parameters, it creates a new Date object and sets it to the current date and time.

- If you call the Date constructor with a string as the parameter, the constructor parses the string as a date or a date and time and uses it to create a new date object. However, you may get unexpected results if you don't use slashes and a 4-digit year in the parameter.

- If you call the Date constructor with two or more numbers as parameters, the numbers are used in the order shown above to create a new date object. In this case, year and month are required, but the remaining parameters are optional.

- If you call the Date constructor with another date object as the parameter, it creates a new Date object that is a copy of the other date object.

- If you call the Date constructor with parameters that aren't a valid date, it creates a new Date object that contains "Invalid Date".

Description

- In JavaScript, dates are represented by the number of milliseconds since Midnight, January 1, 1970.

- When you create a Date object, the date and times are specified as local time. Local time is in the time zone specified on the computer that's running the user's web browser.

- Month numbers start with 0, so January is 0 and December is 11. This allows these values to be used with arrays.

Figure 7-9   How to create Date objects

The methods of the Date object

Figure 7-10 describes several methods that are provided by the Date object. The first group of methods creates a formatted string from a date. However, as the examples show, you can't control the format used by these methods. In the next figure, though, you'll learn how to create your own formats for date and time strings.

The methods in the second group are used to extract the parts from a Date object. Here, all of the methods except the getTime method return the date part from the local time. In contrast, the getTime method uses universal time. There is also a getYear method that returns a two-digit year, but its use is not recommended.

The methods in the third group are used to set new values for the parts in a Date object. These methods let you use values that are outside the allowed range. Then, any value over or under the allowed range will cause the next most significant date part to roll over.

For example, if you set the hours of a date to 25, the time will be set to 1 and one day will be added to the day of the month. Or, if you set the date to -1, the month will be rolled back one and the day set to one day prior to the end of the new month. By letting you use values that are out of the normal range, JavaScript provides a mechanism to perform date math using any of the parts of the date or time. You'll see examples of this in the next figure.

The formatting methods of a Date object

Method	Description
toString()	Returns a string containing the date and time in local time using the client's time zone.
toDateString()	Returns a string representing just the date in local time.
toTimeString()	Returns a string representing just the time in local time.

Examples of the formatting methods
```
var birthday = new Date( 2015, 0, 4, 8, 25);     // Jan 4, 2015 8:25am
alert( birthday.toString() );          // "Sat Jan 04 2015 08:25:00 GMT-0500"
alert( birthday.toDateString() );      // "Sat Jan 04 2015"
alert( birthday.toTimeString() );      // "08:25:00 GMT-0500"
```

The get methods of a Date object

Method	Description
getTime()	Returns the number of milliseconds since Midnight, January 1, 1970 in universal time (GMT).
getFullYear()	Returns the four-digit year in local time.
getMonth()	Returns the month in local time, starting with 0 for January.
getDate()	Returns the day of the month in local time.
getHours()	Returns the hour in 24-hour format in local time.
getMinutes()	Returns the minutes in local time.
getSeconds()	Returns the seconds in local time.
getMilliseconds()	Returns the milliseconds in local time.

The set methods of a Date object

Method	Description
setFullYear(year)	Sets the four-digit year in local time.
setMonth(month)	Sets the month in local time.
setDate(day)	Sets the day of the month in local time.
setHours(hour)	Sets the hour in 24-hour format in local time.
setMinutes(minute)	Sets the minutes in local time.
setSeconds(second)	Sets the seconds in local time.
setMilliseconds(ms)	Sets the milliseconds in local time.

Description
- Except for the getTime method, the get and set methods use the time zone specified on the user's computer to work with local time.
- There are complementary get and set methods that start with getUTC and setUTC that work with the Date object in universal time (GMT). For example, the getUTCHours method returns the hour in 24-hour format in universal time.

Figure 7-10   The methods of the Date object

Examples of working with dates

Figure 7-11 shows how you can apply the methods of the last figure. The first example shows you how to format a date. The last three examples show you how to perform calculations with dates. This should give you some ideas for how you can use Date objects in your own applications.

Example 1 shows you how to format a date. To do that, the JavaScript code first creates a new Date object that contains a date and time. Next, it extracts the year, month, and date parts, and it adds 1 to the month number. Then, it builds a text string using these values. As the string is built, the month and date numbers are padded with a leading zero if they are less than ten.

Example 2 shows you how to calculate the number of days from the current date until the New Year. First, the current date is retrieved in a Date object and a copy of this object is made. Then, the month and day in the copy are set to January 1ˢᵗ, and 1 is added to the year. At this point, the now variable contains the current date and the newYear variable contains the January 1ˢᵗ date.

Next, the number of milliseconds between the two dates is calculated by subtracting the dates that are extracted by the getTime method. Then, the number of days is calculated by dividing the number of milliseconds by the number of milliseconds in one day (86,400,000) and rounding that value up using the ceil method. Last, a message is displayed that indicates the number of days remaining. To do that, a conditional operator is used to alter the message when there is only one day left.

Example 3 shows you how to calculate a due date. Here, the invoiceDate variable contains a Date object with the current date. Then, a dueDate variable is created that contains a Date object with the same date as the one in the invoiceDate variable. Last, 21 is added to the date in the dueDate object so the due date is 21 days after the invoice date.

Example 4 shows you how to determine the last day of the current month. Here, the endOfMonth variable starts at today's date. Then, 1 is added to the month, and the date is set to zero. This rolls the date back one day, which causes 1 to be subtracted from the month and the day of the month to be set to the last day of the month. If, for example, the current date is December 2, adding 1 to the month number rolls it over to month 0, or January. Then, when the date is set to zero, the date and month roll back to December 31.

Example 1: How to display the date in your own format

```
var departTime = new Date(2015, 3, 6, 18, 30);        // Apr. 6, 2015 6:30pm
var year = departTime.getFullYear();
var month = departTime.getMonth() + 1;     // Add 1 since months start at 0
var date = departTime.getDate();

var dateText = year + "-";
dateText += ((month < 10) ? "0" + month : month) + "-";     // Pad month
dateText += (date < 10) ? "0" + date : date;                // Pad date
// Final dateText is "2015-04-06"
```

Example 2: How to calculate the days until the New Year

```
var now = new Date();           // Get the current time
var newYear = new Date(now);    // Copy the current time
newYear.setMonth(0);            // Set the month to January
newYear.setDate(1);             // Set the day to the 1st
newYear.setFullYear( newYear.getFullYear() + 1 );   // Add 1 to the year

var time_left = newYear.getTime() - now.getTime();  // Time in milliseconds
var days_left = Math.ceil( time_left / 86400000);   // Convert ms to days

var message = "There ";
message += (days_left == 1) ? "is one day" : "are " + days_left + " days";
message += " left until the New Year.";

// If today is April 6, 2015, message is
// "There are 271 days left until the New Year."
```

Example 3: How to calculate a due date

```
var invoiceDate = new Date();
var dueDate = new Date( invoiceDate );
dueDate.setDate( dueDate.getDate() + 21 );      // Due date is 3 weeks later
```

Example 4: How to find the end of the month

```
var endOfMonth = new Date();

// Set the month to next month
endOfMonth.setMonth( endOfMonth.getMonth() + 1 );

// Set the date to one day before the start of the month
endOfMonth.setDate( 0 );
```

Figure 7-11   Examples of working with dates

The Count Down application

To illustrate the use of strings and dates, the next two figures present a Count Down application. This web application accepts an event name and event date from a user and calculates the number of days until that event. To do that, this application uses a Date object for the calculation and a String object to create the message that's displayed.

The HTML and CSS

In figure 7-12, you can see the HTML and CSS for this application. The HTML consists of two text boxes and a button. When the user enters data into the text boxes and clicks the Countdown! button, the number of days until the event is displayed in the <p> element below the button. Note that the id attributes for these elements are "event", "date", "countdown", and "message", because those are the ids used by the JavaScript.

In the CSS in this figure, you can see the rule set for the <p> element that has "message" as its id attribute. This sets the font color to red and the font weight to bold.

The user interface of the Count Down application

Countdown To...

Event Name: `My birthday`

Event Date: `12/22/2015`

[Countdown!]

231 day(s) until my birthday! (Tue Dec 22 2015)

The HTML for the application

```
<!DOCTYPE html>
<html>
<head>
    <title>Countdown To...</title>
    <link type="text/css" rel="stylesheet" href="countdown.css">
    <script type="text/javascript" src="countdown.js"></script>
</head>
<body>
    <main>
        <h1>Countdown To...</h1>

        <label for="event">Event Name:</label>
        <input type="text" name="event" id="event"><br>

        <label for="date">Event Date:</label>
        <input type="text" name="date" id="date"><br>

        <input type="button" name="countdown" id="countdown"
            value="Countdown!">

        <p id="message"> </p>
    </main>
</body>
</html>
```

The CSS rule set for the <p> element

```
#message {
    font-weight: bold;
    color: red;
}
```

Figure 7-12   The HTML and CSS for the Count Down application

The JavaScript

The JavaScript in figure 7-13 has the same structure that you've seen in the applications for section 1. First, it creates the $ function. Then, it creates the calculateDays function that will be executed when the user clicks the Countdown button. Last, it creates the onload event handler that assigns the calculateDays function to the calculate button's onclick event.

The calculateDays function starts by using the $ function to get the event name and date that the user entered. Then, it uses the $ function to the get the text node for the <p> element with "message" as its id. This is the element that will display messages to the user.

After that, this function starts a series of data validation checks using if statements. First, it uses the length property of the String object to make sure that the user entered something for the event and the event date. Second, it uses the indexOf method of the String object to make sure the date has been entered with slashes. Third, it uses the substring method of the String object to get the last four characters of the date string, and then uses the isNaN method to make sure those characters are a number. Fourth, it uses the date string entered by the user to create a new Date object, and then checks to see if the object contains "Invalid Date".

If any of these data validation checks fail, they set the nodeValue property of the text node to an appropriate error message and then return. This means that as soon as a check fails, the message is displayed and the function stops running.

If all the data validation checks pass, the code calculates the number of days until the event. To do that, it creates a new Date object with the current date and stores it in the today variable. It calculates the number of milliseconds in a day and stores it in the oneDay variable. It uses the getTime method of the Date object to subtract the today value from the event date value, which are both in milliseconds, and divides the result by the oneDay value, which is in milliseconds. The result of this calculation is then rounded up using the Math. ceil method and stored in the days variable, which now represents the number of days until the event.

Next, this function checks to see if the date entered by the user is in the future, in the past, or is today's date. If the number of days is zero, the date entered by the user is today. If the number of days is less than zero, the date is in the past. And if the number of days is greater than zero, the date is in the future. For each result, this function constructs a different message and uses the nodeValue property of the text node of the <p> element to display that message.

To build these messages, the concat method of the String object is used. Notice that you can call this method whether you are working with a string variable like event or days.toString() or with a string literal like "Hooray! Today is ". Depending on the message, the event name is either made all lower case by using the toLowerCase method or capitalized by using the substring and toUpperCase methods. And in each message, the date entered by the user is displayed using the toDateString method of the Date object.

The JavaScript for the Countdown application

```
var $ = function(id) { return document.getElementById(id); };

var calculateDays = function() {
    var event = $("event").value;
    var dt = $("date").value;
    var message = $("message").firstChild;

    //make sure task and due date are entered
    if (event.length == 0 || dt.length == 0) {
        message.nodeValue = "Please enter both a name and a date.";
        return;
    }
    //make sure due date string has slashes and a 4-digit year
    if (dt.indexOf("/") == -1) {
        message.nodeValue = "Please enter the date in MM/DD/YYYY format.";
        return;
    }
    var year = dt.substring(dt.length - 4);
    if (isNaN(year)) {
        message.nodeValue = "Please enter the date in MM/DD/YYYY format.";
        return;
    }
    //convert due date string to Date object and make sure date is valid
    var date = new Date(dt);
    if (date == "Invalid Date") {
        message.nodeValue = "Please enter the date in MM/DD/YYYY format.";
        return;
    }

    //calculate days
    var today = new Date();
    var oneDay = 24*60*60*1000; // hours * minutes * seconds * milliseconds
    var days = ( date.getTime() - today.getTime() ) / oneDay;
    days = Math.ceil(days);

    //create and display message
    if (days == 0) {
        message.nodeValue = "Hooray! Today is ".concat(event.toLowerCase(),
            "!\n(", date.toDateString(), ")");
    }
    if (days < 0) {
        //capitalize event
        event = event.substring(0,1).toUpperCase() + event.substring(1);
        message.nodeValue = event.concat(" happened ", Math.abs(days),
            " day(s) ago. \n (", date.toDateString(), ")");
    }
    if (days > 0) {
        message.nodeValue = days.toString().concat(" day(s) until ",
            event.toLowerCase(), "!\n(", date.toDateString(), ")");
    }
};
window.onload = function() {
    $("countdown").onclick = calculateDays;
    $("event").focus();
};
```

Figure 7-13   The JavaScript for the Count Down application

Perspective

This chapter has presented the essential skills for working with numbers, strings, and dates. To add to this skillset, you can read chapters 9 and 12, which show how to use the string methods for working with arrays and regular expressions.

Unlike some languages, though, JavaScript doesn't provide methods that make it easy to format numbers and dates. As a result, you need to write your own code for that type of formatting. If you do the exercise that follows, you'll get a chance to do that.

Terms

escape sequence

Summary

- To work with numeric data, you can use the properties and methods of the Number and Math objects, including the random method of the Math object, which generates a random number between 0 and 1.

- *Escape sequences* let you use characters that aren't on the keyboard. That includes all of the Unicode characters, although all of them may not be included in a specific font.

- The length property of a String object returns the number of characters in the string, and the methods of a String object let you work with the characters in the string.

- In JavaScript, dates are stored in Date objects, and they are represented by the number of milliseconds since Midnight, January 1, 1970.

- The constructors of the Date object let you create a Date object in four different ways. Then you can use the methods of the Date object to work with the date in the object.

Exercise 7-1   Enhance the Future Value application

In this exercise, you'll enhance a Future Value application that looks like the one that follows. Along the way, you'll work with large numbers, use a random number generator, work with dates, and work with strings.

Open, review, and test the application

1. Use your text editor or IDE to open the index.html and future_value.js files for the Future Value application, which can be found in this folder:

   ```
   c:\javascript\exercises\ch07\future_value\
   ```

   Then, test this application with valid values to see how it works.

2. Review the JavaScript code for this application. There you can see that the getRandomNumber function of figure 7-3 has been copied into the file so you can use it later on.

Work with large numbers

3. Test this application with these values: 10000 for investment amount, 15 for interest rate, and 1000 for number of years. Notice that this returns the future value with e notation and as many significant digits as JavaScript provides for.

4. Change the entry for the number of years to 10000 and test the application again. This time, it returns Infinity for the future value amount. Runaway loops like this are a common error that causes an application to produce values of Infinity and -Infinity.

5. Modify the JavaScript by adding an if statement to the for loop that calculates the future value. This if statement should test whether future value is equal to infinity. If it is, the if statement should use the alert method to display a message like this, where i is the counter for the loop:

   ```
   Future value = Infinity
   i = 5342
   ```

   This if statement should also set the value of i to the value of years so the loop will end.

6. Add an alert statement that displays the maximum value of a JavaScript number after the for loop finishes since this has nothing to do with the calculation.

Use a random number generator

7. Comment out the three statements that get investment, rate, and years from the text boxes. Then, use the getRandomNumber function to get random values for investment, rate, and years. The maximum values for these variables should be 50000; 15, and 50. The application should get these random values each time the user clicks the Calculate button, these values should be displayed in the first three text boxes, and future value should be calculated using these values.

8. Test this application by clicking on the Calculate button several times to see how the values are varied. This illustrates how a random number generator can be used to quickly test an application with a wide range of values.

Format the future value with a dollar sign and commas

9. Create a new function named formatFV that gets the future value after it has been calculated and returns a formatted version of that value like the one shown above.

   To do this, you need to use the indexOf method to get the location of the decimal point and the substring methods to extract the cents, hundreds, thousands, and millions digits from the future value. Then, you can concatenate the parts with a dollar sign, commas, and decimal point. The trick is that some future values won't have millions digits so you need to provide for that with if statements.

10. Modify the processEntries function so it calls this method to format the future value after it has been calculated and then displays it in the future value text box.

Add the current date to the <p> element below the button

11. Start by creating a new function named getDate that gets the current date and formats it as shown above:

    `Today is 12/04/2015 at 14:29.`

    To do that, you need to get a Date object that contains the current date. Then, you need to use the Date methods to extract the appropriate date and time parts so you can format them as shown above. Note that 24-hour format is used.

12. Modify the event handler for the onload function so it calls the getDate method to get the formatted date and then displays it in the <p> element below the button in the HTML.

8

How to code control statements

In chapter 3, you were introduced to conditional expressions and if, while, do-while, and for statements. Now, you'll learn more about coding these expressions and statements. You'll also learn how to use the conditional operator and the switch, break, and continue statements.

How to code conditional expressions

In chapter 3, you learned the basics of coding conditional expressions. In this topic, you'll learn more about using the equality, relational, and logical operators.

How to use the equality and identity operators

Figure 8-1 summarizes the use of the equality and identity operators in conditional expressions. For simple comparisons, the two *equality operators* are sufficient. If, for example, you want to test whether a numeric variable contains a certain number, the equal operator (==) works just fine.

When the tests are more complex, however, unexpected results may occur when you use the equality operators. To illustrate, this figure lists several equality expressions that don't produce the results you might expect.

The problems that you get when you use the equality operators come from two sources. The first is that the equality operators perform *type coercion*. This means that if different types of data are being compared, the values will be converted to the same data type before the comparison takes place. For example, in the test 3 == "3", the string "3" is converted to the number 3 and then the comparison is done so the result is true. Although the rules for doing the type coercion are complex, they tend to convert values of different data types into numerical values before performing the comparison.

The other problem with the use of equality operators is that the type conversion that's done for type coercion is different than the type conversion that's done by the parseInt and ParseFloat methods. For instance, an empty string is converted to 0 during type coercion, but the parseFloat method converts an empty string to NaN.

These problems can be avoided by using the *identity operators*, because the identity operators don't perform type coercion. Then, if two values of different types are compared, the result will always be false. In fact, if you were to replace all of the equality operators in the table of unusual results with identity operators, all of the results would be false. For this reason, some IDE's warn you when you use an equality operator instead of an identity operator.

When you use the identity operators, it's usually best to use the parseInt or parseFloat methods to do your own data conversions before you do the comparisons. That way, you're sure that you're comparing values of the same type.

The equality operators

Operator	Description	Example
==	Equal	`lastName == "Hopper"`
!=	Not equal	`months != 0`

Unusual results with the equality operator

Expression	Result	Description
`null == undefined`	true	Null and undefined are treated as equivalent.
`3.5 == " \t3.5\n "`	true	Whitespace around a number is ignored.
`"" == 0`	true	The empty string is converted to 0.
`" \t\n " == 0`	true	A string of all whitespace is converted to 0.
`false == 0`	true	False is converted to 0.
`false == "0"`	true	False and "0" are converted to 0.
`false == "false"`	false	False is converted to 0 but "false" is converted to NaN.
`true == 1`	true	True is converted to 1.
`true == "1"`	true	True and "1" are converted to 1.
`true == "true"`	false	True is converted to 1 but "true" is converted to NaN.
`Infinity == "Infinity"`	true	The string "Infinity" is converted to the value Infinity.
`NaN == NaN`	false	You must use the isNaN method to test for NaN.
`NaN == "NaN"`	false	The string "NaN" is converted to NaN, but two NaNs still return false.

The identity operators

Operator	Description	Example
===	Equal	`lastName === "Hopper"`
!==	Not equal	`months !== 0`

Description

- The *equality operators* perform *type coercion*. Type coercion converts data from one type to another. For example, it often converts strings to numbers.
- The type conversion that's done by the equality operators is different from that done by the parseInt or parseFloat methods.
- The *identity operators* do not perform type coercion. If the two operands are of different types, the result will always be false. As a result, all of the expressions listed above for the equality operator would return false for the identity operator.
- When comparing different data types, it is often best to use parseInt or parseFloat to perform your own type conversion and then use the identity operator to perform the comparison.

Figure 8-1   How to use the equality and identity operators

How to use the relational operators

In chapter 3, you learned how to use the four relational operators with examples that showed two values of the same type being compared. Those operators are summarized in the first table in figure 8-2.

Like the equality operators, the relational operators perform type coercion when the two values are of different types. For instance, when you compare strings and numbers, the string value is converted to a numerical value before the comparison takes place. This is illustrated by the second table in this figure. As a result, you often need to make sure that you're comparing two values of the same type before you use these operators.

When you use these operators to compare two strings, the strings are compared character by character from the start of the strings based on the Unicode value of each character. However, the Unicode values of all of upper-case letters are less than (come before) the Unicode values of all of the lower-case letters. This is illustrated by the examples in the third table in this figure.

In many cases, this isn't the way you would like the comparison of two strings to be evaluated. To get around that, though, you can use the toLowerCase method that you learned about in the last chapter to convert the strings to lower-case characters before they are compared:

```
string1.toLowerCase() < string2.toLowerCase()
```

Here, if string1 is "Orange" and string2 is "apple", the result of the expression is false.

Finally, this figure shows some unusual results that you get when you use the relational operators. Here again, the results are unusual because the type conversions that are done by type coercion are different from those that are done by the parseInt and parseFloat methods.

The last example is probably the most unusual. Given that null == undefined is true, as shown in the previous figure, you would think that null <= undefined would also be true. However, although the equality test explicitly says that null is equal to undefined, the relational test ignores this and lets null and undefined be converted to numbers before being compared. Then, since they are both converted to NaN and any comparison involving NaN is false, the result is false.

The relational operators

Operator	Description	Example
<	Less than	`age < 18`
<=	Less than or equal	`investment <= 0`
>	Greater than	`testScore > 100`
>=	Greater than or equal	`rate / 100 >= 0.1`

Comparing strings to numbers with the relational operators

Expression	Result	Description
`1 < "3"`	true	The string "3" is converted to the number 3.
`"10" < 3`	false	The string "10" is converted to the number 10.

Comparing strings with the relational operators

Expression	Result	Description
`"apple" < "orange"`	true	An earlier letter is less than a later letter.
`"apple" < "appletree"`	true	Shorter strings are less than longer strings.
`"Orange" < "apple"`	true	Any capital letter is less than any lowercase letter.
`"@" < "$"`	false	Characters are compared using their Unicode values.

Unusual results with the relational operators

Expression	Result	Description
`0 < NaN`	false	A value of NaN as an operand will always return false.
`0 < "test"`	false	The string "test" is converted to NaN and the result is false.
`"" < 5`	true	The empty string is converted to 0.
`"2000" < "3"`	true	Two strings are not converted to numbers.
`false < true`	true	False is converted to 0 and true is converted to 1.
`null <= undefined`	false	Given that null == undefined is true, this should be true. However, null and undefined are both converted to NaN and the result is false.

Description

- When you use the relational operators, the operands are converted to numbers, except when both operands are strings.
- Whenever one of the operators is NaN or converted to NaN, the result will be false.
- When both operands are strings, they are compared character by character from the start of the strings based on the Unicode value of each character.
- If one string is shorter than the other but contains the same characters as the start of the longer string, the shorter string is the lesser of the two.

Figure 8-2   How to use the relational operators

How to use the logical operators

The first table in figure 8-3 lists the three logical operators that you learned about in chapter 3. This is followed by three examples that use these operators in *conditional expressions*.

In the first example, the NOT operator is used to reverse the Boolean value that's returned by the isNaN method so this expression is true when the value of the variable named number is a number. In the second example, the AND operator is used to return true only when age is 18 or higher and credit score is 680 or higher.

In the third example, the OR operator is used to return true if the state variable is either CA or NC. Note that you need to repeat the entire equality test on both sides of the OR.

The second table in this figure shows the order of precedence for conditional expressions. For instance, this table shows that relational operations are done before equality and identity operations, and AND operations are done before OR operations. This table is followed by three examples that use these operators in complex conditional expressions. These expressions mix two or more of the logical operators. That makes these expressions more difficult to evaluate.

In example 4, the AND and OR operators are used in the conditional expression. Because the AND operator is evaluated first, this expression will return true if the age is 18 or more *and* the score is 680 or more. This expression will also return true if the state is NC.

In example 5, the AND, OR, and NOT operators are used in one expression. This expression will return true if oldCustomer is false. It will also return true if the loan amount is greater than or equal to 10000 *and* the score is less than the minimum score plus 200. Note that this expression uses an arithmetic operator, which is evaluated before the relational operators.

In example 6, you can see how parentheses affect the evaluation of the code that's in example 5. This time, the OR operation is inside a set of parentheses. As a result, this expression will return true if oldCustomer is false *and* the score is less than the minimum score plus 200. It will also return true if the loan amount is greater than or equal to 10000 *and* the score is less than the minimum score plus 200.

As these examples illustrate, complex conditional expressions are hard to evaluate. That's why you should use parentheses to clarify the order of evaluation. But even then, you need to carefully test these expressions with all of the possible combinations of data to make sure they work correctly.

Another thing you need to know about the OR and AND operators is that they use *short-circuit evaluation*. This means that if the first operand is enough to determine the value of the expression, then the second one is ignored. If, for example, the first operand in example 2 is false (age is less than 18), the expression is going to return false so the second operand isn't evaluated. Similarly, if the first operand in example 3 is true (state is "CA"), the expression is going to return true so the second operand isn't evaluated. You'll see why this is useful in figure 8-7.

The logical operators

Operator	Name	Description
!	NOT	Returns the opposite Boolean value of its expression.
&&	AND	Returns true only when the expressions on both sides are true.
||	OR	Returns true when the expression on either side or both sides is true.

The logical operators in compound conditional expressions

Example 1: The NOT operator
```
!isNaN(number)
```

Example 2: The AND operator
```
age >= 18 && score >= 680
```

Example 3: The OR operator
```
state == "CA" || state == "NC"
```

The order of precedence for conditional expressions

Order	Operators	Direction	Description
1	!	Left to right	The NOT operator
2	<, <=, >, >=	Left to right	Relational operators
3	==, !=, ===, !==	Left to right	Equality and identity operators
4	&&	Left to right	The AND operator
5	||	Left to right	The OR operator

The logical operators in complex conditional expressions

Example 4: AND and OR operators
```
age >= 18 && score >= 680 || state == "NC"
```

Example 5: AND, OR, and NOT operators
```
!oldCustomer || loanAmount >= 10000 && score < minScore + 200
```

Example 6: How parentheses can change the evaluation
```
(!oldCustomer || loanAmount >= 10000) && score < minScore + 200
```

Description

- You can always use parentheses to clarify the sequence of operations. Then, the operations within parentheses are done first, working from the innermost sets of parentheses to the outermost sets.
- JavaScript uses *short-circuit evaluation* for the AND and OR operators. For the AND operator, that means the second operand isn't evaluated if the first one is false. For the OR operator, that means the second operand isn't evaluated if the first one is true.
- If you use arithmetic expressions within conditional expressions, they are evaluated after the NOT operator but before the relational operators.

Figure 8-3   How to use the logical operators

How to code the selection structures

In chapter 3, you were introduced to the if statement. Now, this topic will expand upon what you learned. It will also present the switch statement. These statements implement structures that are often referred to as the *selection structures*.

Then, this topic shows you how to use the conditional operator, which in some cases can be used instead of an if statement. Finally, this topic shows how you can use the AND and OR operators for selections that aren't within if and switch statements.

How to code if statements

Figure 8-4 presents some new information about the if and else clauses of an if statement. To start, you don't have to use braces to enclose the statements in these clauses if each clause consists of just one statement. This is illustrated by the first example. When you omit the braces, it's best to place each clause on one line to make it clear that the clause executes only one statement.

The second example shows an if statement without braces that is followed by another statement. As the indentation shows, the intent is to have the last statement be executed as part of the else clause. But when you don't use braces for the else clause, only the first statement is part of that clause, no matter how it's indented. As a result, the last statement in this example will always be executed.

The third example shows the use of multiple else if clauses. This code is testing the value of the variable named average in order to set the value of the variable named grade. Note here that the values must be tested from the high end of the range to the low. If, for example, the first test was >= 69.5, the code wouldn't work for the A and B ranges.

Of course, the first test could be coded as

```
average >= 69.5 && average < 79.5
```

but that would mean extra code. Also, testing the ranges out of order would make the code harder to read and maintain. In general, then, it's best to test for a range of values in sequence.

The last example illustrates an if statement that's *nested* three layers deep. Here, the use of braces and indentation help make the code easier to read. To understand this code, though, you need to know that a leap year isn't just a year that is divisible by 4. If a year is divisible by 100, it must also be divisible by 400 to be a leap year. That's why 2000 was a leap year but 2100 won't be.

Another thing to note about this example is that nesting can make your code confusing. Braces and indentation can help, but code that's nested too deep can be hard to understand, debug, and maintain.

Example 1: An if statement without braces for the clauses

```
if ( age < 18 ) alert("You're too young for a loan.");
else if ( score < 680 ) alert("Your credit score is too low for a loan.");
else alert("You're approved for your loan.");
```

Example 2: Why you should always use braces with else clauses

```
if ( age >= 18 )
    alert("You may vote.");
else
    alert("You may not vote.");
    may_vote = false;     // This statement isn't a part of the else clause.
```

Example 3: An if statement to determine a student's letter grade

```
if ( average >= 89.5 ) {
    grade = "A";
} else if ( average >= 79.5 ) {
    grade = "B";
} else if ( average >= 69.5 ) {
    grade = "C";
} else if ( average >= 64.5 ) {
    grade = "D";
} else {
    grade = "F";
}
```

Example 4: A nested if statement to determine if a year is a leap year

```
var isLeapYear;
if ( year % 4 == 0 ) {
    if ( year % 100 == 0 ) {
        if ( year % 400 == 0) {
            isLeapYear = true;       // divisible by 4, 100, and 400
        } else {
            isLeapYear = false;      // divisible by 4 and 100, but not 400
        }
    } else {
        isLeapYear = true;           // divisible by 4, but not 100
    }
} else {
    isLeapYear = false;              // not divisible by 4
}
```

Description

- If you only have one statement after an if statement or an else clause, you don't have to put braces around that statement.

- Using braces around single statements in if or else clauses makes your code easier to read, modify, and enhance. Combining braces with indentation is helpful, too.

- If necessary, you can nest an if statement within a clause of another if statement, as in example 4.

Figure 8-4   How to code if statements

How to code switch statements

A *switch statement* is a convenient way to express a certain form of if statement. Specifically, it can be used in place of an if statement with multiple else if clauses in which one expression is tested for equality with several values. This is illustrated by the statements in figure 8-5. The switch statement implements a control structure that is often referred to as the *case structure*.

The switch statement starts with the word switch followed by a switch expression inside of parentheses. This expression is not a conditional expression. It is an expression that returns a single value that will be used to determine which *case* to execute. The expression is often as simple as a single variable as shown in the examples in this figure.

Once the value for the expression is found, the switch statement checks each of the values in the *case labels*. Then, it begins executing the code that follows the first case label that is equal to the result of the expression. It continues executing until it reaches either a break statement or the end of the switch statement.

If no case labels match the value in the switch expression, the switch statement starts executing the code that follows the default label. But this default case is optional. If it is omitted and no case labels match the expression, the switch statement won't execute any code.

In the first example in this figure, the expression is just a variable named letterGrade that should contain a letter. Then, each case label is checked against the value of this variable. If, for example, letterGrade is "B", the switch statement starts executing the code after the label for that case and sets the message variable to "above average". It then encounters a break statement and no further code is executed by the switch statement. If letterGrade had been "Z", however, the code after the default label would have been executed and the message would have been set to "invalid grade".

In the second example, the case labels are coded in a way that provides *fall through*. This occurs when code starts executing at one case label but doesn't encounter a break statement, so it passes another case label and keeps executing. Although this is often discouraged because it can be confusing, this example shows one case where fall through is useful.

In this example, the same code should be executed when letterGrade is "A" or "B". Instead of repeating the code, two case labels are placed before the code. Then, if letterGrade is "A", the switch statement will fall through and execute the code after the case for "B". Likewise, if letterGrade is "D", the switch statement will fall through and execute the code after the case for "F". Except for cases like this, though, you should avoid using fall through in your switch statements because that can lead to unexpected errors and be hard to debug.

When you use a switch statement, you can nest if statements within the cases. You can also nest switch statements within the cases of another switch statement. As always, you need to use caution with nesting since it can make your code confusing and hard to maintain.

A switch statement with a default case

```
switch ( letterGrade ) {
    case "A":
        message = "well above average";
        break;
    case "B":
        message = "above average";
        break;
    case "C":
        message = "average";
        break;
    case "D":
        message = "below average";
        break;
    case "F":
        message = "failing";
        break;
    default:
        message = "invalid grade";
        break;
}
```

A switch statement with fall through

```
switch ( letterGrade ) {
    case "A":
    case "B":
        message = "Scholarship approved.";
        break;
    case "C":
        message = "Application requires review.";
        break;
    case "D":
    case "F":
        message = "Scholarship not approved.";
        break;
}
```

Description

- The *switch statement* starts by evaluating the *switch expression* in the parentheses.

- After evaluating the expression, the switch statement transfers control to the *case label* that has the value that matches the value of the expression. Then, it executes the statements for that *case*. It stops executing when it reaches a break statement or the end of the switch statement.

- The default case is optional and may be omitted. If included, you can only have one default case. It is usually the last case in the switch statement, but it can be anywhere.

- The values in the case label may be literal values or they may be expressions.

- If a case doesn't contain a break statement, execution will *fall through* to the next label.

- You can nest if statements or other switch statements within the cases of a switch statement. Again, you'll want to be careful with this.

Figure 8-5   How to code switch statements

How to use the conditional operator

Figure 8-6 shows how to use JavaScript's *conditional operator*. This is JavaScript's only *ternary operator*, which means it has three operands. In contrast, a *unary operator*, such as ++, has one operand and a *binary operator*, such as *, has two operands.

Since the conditional operator has three operands, it needs two symbols to separate them. As the syntax at the top of this figure shows, the question mark and colon are used as the separators.

When executed, the conditional operator first evaluates the conditional expression to get a true or false result. Then, if the conditional expression is true, the result of the expression in the middle operand is used as the result of the conditional operator. If the conditional expression is false, the result of the expression in the last operand is used as the result of the conditional operator.

The first example in this figure shows how to use the conditional operator to set a variable to one of two values based on the comparison. If the age is 18 or more, message will contain "Can vote". If the age is less than 18, message will contain "Cannot vote".

The second example shows how to use an expression in one of the operands. If hours is over 40, overtime will contain 1.5 times the pay rate for the hours over 40. If hours is not over 40, overtime will be zero.

The third example shows how to select between a singular or plural ending for use in a message to the user. If error_count is 1, the ending will be empty. Otherwise, "s" will be used for the ending.

The fourth example shows how to add one to a value or set it back to 1 depending on whether the value is at its maximum. For example, if max_value is 10 and value is 6, the test will be false and value will become the value plus 1. However, when value reaches 10, it will be set to 1.

If you need to perform this kind of rollover of a variable, but the starting value is 0 instead of 1, you don't have to use the conditional operator. Instead, you can use the % operator. For example, if you execute this statement repeatedly with a starting value of 9

```
value = (value + 1) % 10
```

the values will range from 0 to 9 and then back to 0.

The fifth example shows how to combine the conditional operator with the return keyword so the result is returned by a function. Here, if number is greater than highest, highest is returned. Otherwise, the number is returned.

For clarity, it is often better to use if statements than conditional operators. This is illustrated by the last two examples in this figure. Nevertheless, many JavaScript programmers like to use conditional operators because it means less coding.

Syntax of the conditional operator

```
( conditional_expression ) ? value_if_true : value_if_false
```

Examples of using the conditional operator

Example 1: Setting a string based on a comparison
```
var message = ( age >= 18 ) ? "Can vote" : "Cannot vote";
```

Example 2: Calculating overtime pay
```
var overtime = ( hours > 40 ) ? ( hours - 40 ) * rate * 1.5 : 0;
```

Example 3: Selecting a singular or plural ending based on a value
```
var ending = ( errorCount == 1 ) ? "" : "s".
var message = "Found " + error_count + " error" + ending + ".";
```

Example 4: Setting a value to 1 if it's at a maximum value when adding 1
```
var value = ( value == maxValue ) ? 1 : value + 1;
```

Example 5: Returning one of two values based on a comparison
```
return ( number > highest ) ? highest : number;
```

How conditional operators can be rewritten with if statements

Example 1 rewritten with an if statement
```
var message;
if ( age >= 18 ) {
    message = "Can vote";
} else {
    message = "Cannot vote";
}
```

Example 4 rewritten with an if statement
```
if ( value == maxValue ) {
    value = 1;
}
else {
    value = value + 1;
}
```

Description

- The conditional operator first evaluates the conditional expression. Then, if the expression is true, the value that results from the middle operand is returned. But if the expression is false, the value that results from the third operand is returned.

- Although the use of the conditional operator can lead to cryptic code, JavaScript programmers commonly use this operator. For clarity, though, conditional operators can be rewritten with if statements.

Figure 8-6   How to use the conditional operator

How to use the AND and OR operators for selections

In figure 8-3, you learned how to use the logical operators AND and OR in conditional expressions. You might have thought from those examples that the AND and OR operators return Boolean values. Actually, though, they return the value of the last operand they evaluate. This and the short-circuit evaluation you learned about in figure 8-3 means you can use these operators in selection structures. The examples in figure 8-7 show how this works.

In the first example, both the operands are equality statements that return a Boolean value. This means the OR operator returns a Boolean value, because both of its operands return true or false.

In contrast, the second example could return several different data types, depending on the values of the operands. If the first operand is null or undefined, it's evaluated as false and the AND operator short-circuits. This means the second operand isn't evaluated, and the AND operator returns the value of the first operand, which is null or undefined. Otherwise, the second operand is evaluated, and the result of calling the toString method is returned. If the toString method doesn't exist, the result of calling it is undefined. If it does exist, it returns a String.

The third example could also return several data types depending on the values of its operands, but it won't return null or undefined. If the first operand isn't null or undefined, it's evaluated as true and the OR operator short-circuits. This means the second operand isn't evaluated, and the OR operator returns whatever value the first operand contains. Otherwise, the second operand is evaluated, and it returns a string.

The remaining examples show how you can use this behavior of the AND and OR operators to make your code better. Example 4 shows how to use the OR operator to provide a default value. It assigns either the value of the dt variable or a new Date object to the selected variable. Specifically, if the value of the dt variable isn't null or undefined, its value is assigned to the selected variable. But if it is null or undefined, it evaluates as false and the second operand is evaluated. As a result, a new Date object is assigned to the selected variable.

The next set of examples shows how to use the AND operator to make sure an object exists before using it. First, example 5 shows that if you try to use a method on an object that doesn't exist, you'll get an error. Then, example 6 shows how to use the AND operator to check that the object exists before using it. Here, the first operand returns the value of the obj variable. Since it's undefined, it evaluates to false and the second operand isn't evaluated. As a result, the code that would throw an error never runs.

Example 7 shows how you can combine the AND and OR operators to create complex selection structures. The one line of code in this example first uses the AND operator to check that the node object exists before getting its value property. Since this AND expression is the first operand of the first OR expression, if the AND expression returns a value, the rest of the code won't run.

But if the AND expression returns null or undefined, the evaluation of the first OR operator moves to its second operand and tries to return the node object.

How to use the AND and OR operators to select values

Example 1: An OR selection that returns a Boolean value of true or false

```
var selected = (state == "CA" || state == "NC");
```

Example 2: An AND selection that returns a null, undefined, or String value

```
var selected = state && state.toString()
```

Example 3: An OR selection that won't return null or undefined values

```
var selected = state || "CA";      // state value or "CA"
```

How to use the OR operator to provide a default value

Example 4: Provide today's date as a default value if dt is null or undefined

```
var selected = dt || new Date();
```

How to use the AND operator to make sure an object exists before using it

Example 5: Using a method of an object that doesn't exist

```
var obj = undefined;
obj.none();            // TypeError: Cannot read property 'none' of undefined
```

Example 6: How to use the AND operator to check whether an object exists

```
var obj = undefined;
obj && obj.none();   // No error: first operand is false so second is ignored
```

How to use the AND and OR operators in a complex selection

Example 7: Returns the node value, the node object, or an empty space

```
var v = node && node.value || node || "";
```

How selections can be rewritten with if statements

Example 6 rewritten with an if statement

```
if ( obj ) {                    // if obj exists
    obj.none();                 // call its none method
}
```

Example 7 rewritten with an if statement

```
var v;
if ( node ) {                   // if node exists
    if ( node.value ) {         // if the node.value property exists
        v = node.value;         // set variable v to the node value
    } else {
        v = node;               // set variable v to the node object
    }
} else {                        // if node doesn't exist
    v = "";                     // set variable v to an empty space
}
```

Description

- The AND and OR operators return the value of the last operand they evaluate. Thus, you can use them in selection structures and store the value they return in a variable.

- This works due to the short-circuit evaluation of the logical operators that's described in figure 8-3.

Figure 8-7   How to use the AND and OR operators for selections

If this node object exists, the first OR operator evaluates as true, the node object is stored in the variable, and the rest of the code won't run. But if it doesn't exist, the second OR operator returns its second operand, which is the default value of an empty string.

The last group of examples in this figure shows how you can rewrite examples 6 and 7 with if statements. This illustrates that using AND and OR operators in selection structures can actually simplify your code and make it easier to read. You'll see this illustrated in some of the book applications in the chapters that follow.

The Invoice application

The two figures that follow show a web application that calculates a discount amount and total for an invoice. This application uses some of the conditional expressions and selection structures described in this chapter to determine the discount percent.

Figure 8-8 shows the user interface for the Invoice application. It consists of a drop-down list, four text boxes, and a button. The drop-down list is used to select the type of customer: Regular, Loyalty Program, or Honored Citizen. The first text box accepts an invoice subtotal amount from the user. And the next three text boxes are used to display the results of this application.

The HTML

In the HTML, you can see that a select element is used for the drop-down list, and the values that it returns are "r" for Regular, "l" for Loyalty Program, and "h" for Honored Citizen. You'll see these values used by the JavaScript code in the next figure.

Otherwise, this code is similar to what you've been seeing. Of interest are the id attributes because they're used by the JavaScript code. Also, note that the last three text boxes have their disabled attributes turned on. This means that the user can't enter data into them and their backgrounds are shaded.

The user interface of the Invoice application

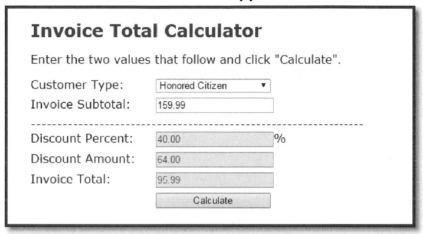

Some of the HTML for the application

```
<main>
    <h1>Invoice Total Calculator</h1>
    <p>Enter the two values that follow and click "Calculate".</p>

    <label for="type">Customer Type:</label>
    <select id="type">
        <option value="r">Regular</option>
        <option value="l">Loyalty Program</option>
        <option value="h">Honored Citizen</option>
    </select><br>

    <label for="subtotal">Invoice Subtotal:</label>
    <input type="text" id="subtotal"><br>

    <label for="percent">Discount Percent:</label>
    <input type="text" id="percent" disabled>%<br>
    <label for="discount">Discount Amount:</label>
    <input type="text" id="discount" disabled><br>
    <label for="total">Invoice Total:</label>
    <input type="text" id="total" disabled><br>

    <label> </label>
    <input type="button" id="calculate" value="Calculate">
</main>
```

Figure 8-8   The HTML for the Invoice application

The JavaScript

The JavaScript code in figure 8-9 follows a structure that should be familiar to you by now. First, it declares the $ function. Second, it declares a function that will be used to calculate the discount percent for the invoice. Third, it declares a processEntries function that will be run when the user clicks the Calculate button. Last, the event handler for the onload event attaches the processEntries function to the click event of the Calculate button. It also sets the focus on the drop-down list.

Of most interest is the calculateDiscountPercent function. It receives the value of the customer type and the amount of the invoice subtotal. Then, it uses an if statement with two else if clauses to check the customer type. Nested within the if clause and one of the else if clauses are more if statements. These inner and outer if statements use the values of the customer type and subtotal variables to determine the discount percent. For example, a Regular customer gets no discount for a subtotal under 100, a 10% discount for a subtotal between 100 and 250, a 25% discount for a subtotal between 250 and 500, and a 30% discount for a subtotal over 500.

Note that this function uses the identity equals operator to check the type values. Note too that you could code this function with a switch statement. In fact, if you do exercise 8-1 at the end of this chapter, you'll get a chance to do that.

Otherwise, this JavaScript should be easy to follow. The processEntries function starts by declaring three variables that will be used by the function as it does its processing. It then uses the $ function and the value property to get the values that the user entered for customer type and invoice subtotal. It also calls the parseFloat method to convert the subtotal amount to a decimal, and then reloads it in the subtotal textbox using the $ function and the toFixed method of the Number object. This means that when a user clicks the Calculate button, the subtotal entry will be displayed with two decimal digits. If the user enters a non-numeric value, the subtotal text box will display "NaN".

Next, the calculateDiscountPercent function is called to return the discount percent. Then, the processEntries function multiplies the invoice subtotal by the discount percent to get the discount amount. It calculates the invoice total by subtracting the discount amount from the invoice subtotal. And it stores the results of these calculations in the variables it declared at the top of the function.

Once these values are calculated, the processEntries function uses the $ function to display discount percent, discount amount, and invoice total in the related text boxes. Then, it sets the focus back on the drop-down list for customer type so the user can start another invoice calculation.

The JavaScript for the Invoice application

```javascript
"use strict";
var $ = function(id) { return document.getElementById(id); };

var calculateDiscountPercent = function(customerType, invoiceSubtotal) {
    var discountPercent = 0;
    if (customerType === "r") {
        if (invoiceSubtotal < 100) {
            discountPercent = .0;
        } else if (invoiceSubtotal >= 100 && invoiceSubtotal < 250) {
            discountPercent = .1;
        } else if (invoiceSubtotal >= 250 && invoiceSubtotal < 500) {
            discountPercent = .25;
        } else if (invoiceSubtotal >= 500) {
            discountPercent = .3;
        }
    } else if (customerType === "l") {
        discountPercent = .3;
    } else if (customerType === "h") {
        if (invoiceSubtotal < 500) {
            discountPercent = .4;
        } else if (invoiceSubtotal >= 500) {
            discountPercent = .5;
        }
    }
    return discountPercent;
};
var processEntries = function() {
    var discountAmount;
    var invoiceTotal;
    var discountPercent;

    //get values from page, reset subtotal to 2 decimals
    var customerType = $("type").value;
    var invoiceSubtotal = parseFloat( $("subtotal").value );
    $("subtotal").value = invoiceSubtotal.toFixed(2);

    //call function to get discount percent
    discountPercent = calculateDiscountPercent(customerType,
                         invoiceSubtotal);

    //calculate and display discount percent, amount, and new total
    discountAmount = invoiceSubtotal * discountPercent;
    invoiceTotal = invoiceSubtotal - discountAmount;

    $("percent").value = (discountPercent * 100).toFixed(2) ;
    $("discount").value = discountAmount.toFixed(2);
    $("total").value = invoiceTotal.toFixed(2);

    $("type").focus;
};
window.onload = function() {
    $("calculate").onclick = processEntries;
    $("type").focus();
};
```

Figure 8-9   The JavaScript for the Invoice application

How to code the iteration structures

In chapter 3, you learned how to use while, do-while, and for statements. Now, you'll learn more about coding those statements, and you'll learn how to code the break and continue statements. These statements implement structures that are often referred to as the *iteration structures*.

How to code while and do-while loops

As you learned in chapter 3, a *while loop* executes a block of code as long as its conditional expression is true. A *do-while loop* is similar to the while loop except that the conditional expression is tested at the end of the loop. The result is that the code inside a do-while loop will always be executed at least once. Figure 8-10 presents three examples that will give you some ideas for what you can do with while and do-while loops.

In the first example, one die is rolled until a 6 appears and the loop counts the number of times the die needed to be rolled to get that 6. This code assumes that the getRandomNumber function from figure 7-3 has been included at the beginning of the code. Since the first roll of the die takes place in the while loop's expression, the increment statement in the loop won't be executed if the first roll is a 6. That's why the value for rolls is initially set to 1.

In the second example, the while loop from the first example is nested inside another while loop that is executed 10,000 times. Each time the inner loop rolls a 6, the number of rolls to get that 6 is added to the variable named total. In addition, the value of the variable named max is changed if the number of rolls is greater than the current value of max. Since the value of max starts at −Infinity, any number of rolls the first time through the inner loop will be greater than that and the starting value of max will be changed. Then, when the outer loop finishes, the average number of tries to get a 6 is calculated and the average and maximum values are displayed.

The third example uses a do-while loop to prompt the user for a series of numbers. It then displays the minimum and maximum values that the user entered. Here, the Boolean valueEntered variable is used to indicate whether at least one number was entered, and the Boolean stop variable is used to indicate that a non-numeric value was entered so the do-while loop should stop.

The do-while loop in this example starts by prompting the user for a number. If the user enters a number, valueEntered is set to true and the value is compared to the min and max variables. If the user enters a non-numeric value, stop is set to true. This loop continues as long as stop is false.

After the do-while loop, the code checks the valueEntered variable. If it's true, the maximum and minimum values are displayed. If it's false, it means that the user entered a non-numeric value at the first prompt and an appropriate message is displayed.

Example 1: A while loop that counts dice rolls until a six is rolled

```
var rolls = 1;
while ( getRandomNumber(6) !== 6 ) {
    rolls++;
}
alert("Number of times to roll a six: " + rolls);
```

Example 2: Nested while loops that get the average and max to roll a six

```
var total = 0, count = 0, max = -Infinity;
var rolls;

while ( count < 10000 ) {
    rolls = 1;
    while ( getRandomNumber(6) !== 6 ) {
        rolls++;
    }
    total += rolls;
    count++;
    if ( rolls > max ) max = rolls;
}
var average = total / count;
alert ("Average rolls: " + average.toFixed(2) + "\n\nMax rolls: " + max);
```

Example 3: A do-while loop that finds the maximum and minimum values

```
var max = -Infinity;
var min = Infinity;
var number;
var valueEntered = false;
var stop = false;
alert("Enter values to find the max and min. " +
      "Enter any non-number to stop.");

do {
    number = parseFloat( prompt("Enter a number") );
    if ( isNaN(number) ) {
        stop = true;
    } else {
        valueEntered = true;
        if ( number > max ) max = number;
        if ( number < min ) min = number;
    }
} while ( !stop );

if (valueEntered) {
    alert("Max: " + max + ", Min: " + min);
} else {
    alert("No numbers entered.");
}
```

Description

- The *while statement* executes the block of statements within its braces as long as its conditional expression is true. So does the *do-while statement*, but the condition is tested after the first execution of the statements in the block.

Figure 8-10   How to code while and do-while loops

How to code for loops

Figure 8-11 starts by showing the differences between a *for loop* and a while loop. Here, the first line of the for statement declares the counter variable, provides the condition that will end the loop, and provides the code for incrementing the counter variable. In contrast, these tasks have to be done separately for a while loop.

This comparison is followed by four examples that will give you some ideas for what you can do with for loops. The first example shows that you can start and increment the counter variable with values other than 1. Here, the statement initializes the counter to 2 and increments the counter by 2. As a result, the loop displays the numbers from 2 through 10.

The second example shows that you can increment the counter by negative values (which decrements the value). Here, the counter named position is initialized to one less than the length of a string. Then, the counter is decremented by 1 after each iteration of the loop, and the loop executes as long as position is greater than or equal to zero. Inside the loop, the character from the current position in the original string is added to the end of the variable named reverse. Since this loop runs backwards, the characters from the message variable are added to the reverse variable in reverse order.

The third example displays all the factors of a number. A *factor* is any number that can be divided into the number with a remainder of zero, so 1, 2, 3, 6, and 9 are factors of 18. This time, the counter starts at 1 and is incremented by 1, and the loop continues as long as the counter is less than the original number. Inside the loop, a message is displayed if the original number divided by the current value of the counter has a remainder of zero.

The fourth example determines whether a number is prime. A *prime number* has no factors other than one and itself. This code starts by assuming that the number is prime so it sets the Boolean variable named prime to true. Then, the number is tested against each of the possible factors that is less than the value of the number starting with 2. If any factor is found, the prime variable is set to false. After the for loop, a message is displayed based on the value in the prime variable.

Incidentally, the third and fourth examples use i as the variable name for the counter. This is a common practice. And when one loop is nested within another loop, j is often used as the counter name for the inner loop.

The for statement compared to the while statement

The for statement

```
for ( var count = 1; count <= 10; count++ ) {
    alert ( count );
}
```

The while statement

```
var count = 1;
while ( count <= 10 ) {
    alert ( count );
    count++;
}
```

Example 1: A for loop to display even numbers from 2 to 10

```
for ( var number = 2; number <= 10; number += 2 ) {
    alert( number );
}
```

Example 2: A for loop to reverse a string

```
var message = "JavaScript", reverse = "";
for (var position = message.length - 1; position >= 0; position-- ) {
    reverse += message.charAt(position);
}
alert(reverse);   // Displays "tpircSavaJ"
```

Example 3: A for loop to display all the factors of a number

```
var number = 18, factors = "";
for ( var i = 1; i < number; i++ ) {
    if ( number % i === 0 ) {
        factors +=  i + " ";
    }
}
alert("Factors of ".concat(number, ": ", factors));
```

Example 4: A for loop to determine if a number is prime

```
var number = 31, prime = true;
for ( var i = 2; i < number; i++ ) {
    if ( number % i === 0 ) prime = false;
}
if (prime) {
    alert( number + " is prime.");
} else {
    alert( number + " is not prime.");
}
```

Description

- Within the parentheses of a *for statement*, you code an expression that declares a counter variable and assigns a starting value to it, a conditional expression that determines when the loop ends, and an increment expression that indicates how the counter should be incremented or decremented each time through the loop.

Figure 8-11   How to code for loops

How to use the break and continue statements

The break and continue statements give you additional control over loops. The *break statement* causes the loop to end immediately. The *continue statement* causes the loop to skip to the start of the loop.

The first example in figure 8-12 shows the break statement inside a while loop. Here, the condition in the while loop is intentionally coded as true, which would normally cause a runaway or infinite loop. However, when the conditional expression in the if statement becomes false, the break statement ends the while loop. This will occur when the number that the user enters is valid.

The second example shows the break statement used inside a for loop. Here, the loop determines whether the value in the number variable is prime. Once one factor is found, though, the number isn't prime so the code sets the value of the prime variable to false and issues the break statement. If, for example, the value of number is 42, the loop will end as soon as 2 is found to be a factor so the loop won't check the values from 3 to 41.

The third example shows the continue statement used in a for loop. Here, when the number to be displayed is a multiple of 3, the continue statement skips the remainder of the loop and starts the loop again after the counter is incremented. As a result, only numbers that are not multiples of 3 will be displayed by the loop.

The fourth example shows the use of the continue statement in a while loop. Here, the while loop is supposed to do what the for loop in the previous example does. So, the number++ statement has been added as part of the if statement and before the continue statement. Had this increment statement not been added to the if statement, the loop would have become an infinite loop as soon as the number variable became 3. After that, the continue statement would repeat the loop but the number variable would never be incremented so the loop would never end. This would continue until the browser stopped the script because it was taking too long to execute or the user closed the browser.

When you use break and continue statements within nested loops, you need to know that the break or continue statement applies only to the loop that it's in. If, for example, you code the break statement within an inner loop, it skips to the end of that loop, not the end of the outer loop.

Example 1: The break statement in a while loop

```
var number;
while (true) {
    number = parseInt( prompt("Enter a number from 1 to 10.") );
    if ( isNaN(number) || number < 1 || number > 10 ) {
        alert("Invalid entry. Try again.");
    } else {
        break;
    }
}
```

Example 2: The break statement in a for loop

```
var number = 31, prime = true;
for ( var i = 2; i < number; i++ ) {
    if ( number % i == 0 ) {
        prime = false;
        break;
    }
}

if (prime) {
    alert(number + " is prime.");
} else {
    alert(number + " is not prime.");
}
```

Example 3: The continue statement in a for loop

```
for ( var number = 1; number <= 10; number++ ) {
    if ( number % 3 == 0 ) continue;
    alert(number);
}
// Only displays 1, 2, 4, 5, 7, 8, and 10
```

Example 4: The continue statement in a while loop

```
var number = 1;
while ( number <= 10 ) {
    if ( number % 3 == 0 ) {
        number++;
        continue;
    }
    alert(number);
    number++;
}
// Only displays 1, 2, 4, 5, 7, 8, and 10
```

Description

- The *break statement* ends a loop. In other words, it jumps out of the loop.
- The *continue statement* ends the current iteration of a for or while loop, but allows the next iteration to proceed. In other words, it jumps to the start of the loop.
- When you're working with nested loops, the break and continue statements apply only to the loop that they're in.

Figure 8-12   How to use the break and continue statements

Perspective

Now that you've finished this chapter, you should know how to code if statements, switch statements, while statements, do-while statements, and for statements. These are the JavaScript statements that implement the selection, case, and iteration structures. You should also know how to use the conditional operator as well as how to use the short-circuit evaluation of the AND and OR operators in assignment statements. You'll see many examples of these structures in the chapters that follow that will help you master their use.

Terms

equality operator	while statement
type coercion	while loop
identity operator	do-while statement
short-circuit evaluation	do-while loop
selection structure	for statement
switch statement	for loop
case structure	factor
case	prime number
case label	break statement
conditional operator	continue statement
iteration structure	

Summary

- Unlike the *equality operators*, the *identity operators* don't use *type coercion* in their comparisons. If an identity operator is used to compares two variables that aren't of the same type, the result is always false.

- The *relational* and *logical operators* in a condition have an order of precedence, but you can override that order by using parentheses.

- *Short-circuit evaluation* means that the second operand in an AND or OR expression won't be evaluated if the first operand determines the result. When these operators are used in assignment statements, the value of the last operand that is evaluated is stored in the variable.

- The *switch statement* is JavaScript's implementation of the *case structure*. It evaluates the expression at the start of the statement and then executes the case indicated by the expression.

- The *conditional operator* returns one value if a condition is true and another if it is false. This is an alternative to a simple if/else statement.

- *While*, *do-while*, and *for statements* are used to create *loops* that are executed until a condition becomes true.

- The *break statement* jumps out of a loop and ends the loop. The *continue statement* jumps to the start of the loop but lets the loop continue.

Exercise 8-1   Work with loops and prime numbers

This exercise will give you a chance to work with loops and prime numbers. Remember that a prime number is a number that can only be divided by one and itself. The interface that follows lists the prime numbers from 1 through 100:

Find Prime Numbers

Enter any a number to find out how many prime numbers there are up to and including that value.

Enter Number: `100`

Prime count: `25`

Prime numbers: `2 3 5 7 11 13 17 19 23 29 31 37 41 43 47 53 59 61 67 71 73 79 83 89 97`

`Calculate`

Open, review, and test

1. Use your text editor or IDE to open the HTML and JavaScript files in this folder:

   `c:\javascript\exercises\ch08\loops\`

2. Review the code in the JavaScript file to see that it includes some of the examples from figures 8-10 and 8-11, and each has been placed in a function.

3. Test this application by clicking on the Calculate button, and see that the results are displayed in alert dialog boxes. Then, comment out the call to the displayFactors function from the processEntries function.

Modify the function for average rolls

4. Modify the averageRolls function so it uses a for loop for the outer loop.

5. Modify the function again so it uses a do-while loop instead of a do loop for the inner loop. When you've got that working, comment out the call to the averageRolls function from the processEntries function.

Modify the function for finding prime numbers

6. Modify the determineIfPrime method so it displays its messages in the text area for Prime Numbers, not with alert methods.

7. Create a function called isPrime that receives a number and returns the number if it is prime or 0 if it isn't. You can get most of the coding for this function from the determineIfPrime method.

8. Modify the determineIfPrime method so it calls the isPrime method to find out whether a number is prime. Then, test these changes.

9. If you didn't code it this way, modify the isPrime method so it uses a conditional operator like example 5 in figure 8-6 to return either the prime number or 0.

10. If you didn't code it this way, use a break statement in the isPrime function to exit from the loop as soon as the loop determines that a number isn't prime.

Add a function for displaying all of the prime numbers

11. Create a function named getPrimeNumbers that will get all the prime numbers between 1 and the number that the user enters. It should use a for loop to call the isPrime method for each value. Within the loop, each prime number should be added to a string that will later be displayed in the text area and 1 should be added to a count of the prime numbers. After the for loop finishes, the count of prime numbers should be displayed in the second text box and the list of numbers should be displayed in the text area.

12. Change the processEntries function so it calls the getPrimeNumbers function instead of the determineIfPrime function. Then, test and debug.

Exercise 8-2 Use if and switch statements

In this exercise, you'll enhance the Invoice application of figures 8-8 and 8-9 and also replace the if statement for calculating the discount with a switch statement.

Open, review, and test

1. Use your text editor or IDE to open the HTML and JavaScript files in this folder:

   `c:\javascript\exercises\ch08\invoice_total\`

2. Review the code to see that's it the same as the code in the book. Then, test this application with valid values to see how it works.

Change the code that determines the discount percent

3. In the JavaScript file, find the if statement that determines the discount percent for customers of type "r". Then, change the discount percentages for the first two categories from 0 and 10 percent to 10 and 20 percent. Then, add another category for subtotals greater than or equal to 1000 that gets a 40 percent discount. Then, test these changes.

4. In the HTML file, find the select element, and add an Employee option with its value set to "e". Then, modify the if statement so customers of type "e" get a 50% discount for all subtotals. Then, test these changes.

Use a switch statement with nested if statements to get the same results

5. Code a switch statement right before the if statement. This statement should provide the structure for handling the four cases for customer types. Then, within each of these cases, you can copy the related code from the if statement to provide for the discounts that are based on subtotal variations. In other words, the if statements will be nested within the switch cases.

6. Comment out the entire if statement that's below the switch statement. Then, test to make sure the switch statement works correctly.

9

How to work with arrays and web storage

In chapter 3, you were introduced to arrays. Now, in this chapter, you'll learn more about working with arrays, which are an important part of many JavaScript applications. For example, you can use an array to hold a list of tasks that you can update and display.

You'll also learn how to work with web storage, which is a way to store information in the browser for later use. As you'll see, you can store information for the duration of the time that the application is running, or you can store information indefinitely.

How to create and use an array

To start, you'll review the skills you learned in chapter 3 and learn the other skills for creating and using arrays.

How to create an array

An *array* is an object that contains one or more items called *elements*. Each of these elements can be a primitive data type or an object. For instance, you can store numbers, strings, and Date objects in the same array.

The *length* of an array indicates the number of elements that it contains. Because JavaScript arrays are dynamic, you can change the length of an array by adding or removing elements from the array.

Figure 9-1 shows two ways to create an array. When you use the first method, you use the new keyword with the Array constructor to create an array with the number of elements that is indicated by the length parameter. This length must be a whole number that is greater than or equal to zero. If you don't specify the length, the array will be empty.

When you use the second method, you just code a set of brackets. This gives you the same result that you get with the first method and no parameter, an empty array.

Next, this figure shows you how to create a new array and assign values to its elements in a single statement. In this case, you code the values in a list that's separated by commas. For instance, the first group of examples shows a statement that creates an array named rates that contains four numeric values and a statement that creates an array named names that contains three strings.

Note, however, that when you create an array with the new keyword, the array list must not be a single number. Otherwise, it will be treated as the length of the array, not a value in the array.

To refer to the elements in an array, you use an *index* that ranges from zero to one less than the number of elements in an array. In an array with 12 elements, for example, the index values range from 0 to 11. This is the reason the getMonth method of a Date object numbers the months from 0 to 11 instead of 1 to 12. Then, the return value of the getMonth method can be used as an index for an array of month names.

To use an index, you code it within brackets after the name of the array. In this figure, all of the examples use literal values for the indexes, but an index can also be a variable that contains an index value. If you try to access an element that hasn't been assigned a value, the value of undefined will be returned.

The last group of examples in this figure shows how to assign values to an empty array. To do that, you refer to the elements by using indexes, and you assign values to those elements.

The syntax for creating an array

Using the new keyword with the Array object name
```
var arrayName = new Array(length);
```

Using an array literal
```
var arrayName = [];
```

The syntax for creating an array and assigning values in one statement

Using the new keyword with the Array object name
```
var arrayName = new Array(arrayList);
```

Using an array literal
```
var arrayName = [arrayList];
```

How to create an array and assign values in one statement
```
var rates = new Array(14.95, 12.95, 11.95, 9.95);
var names = ["Grace", "Charles", "Ada"];
```

The syntax for referring to an element of an array
```
arrayName[index]
```

Code that refers to the elements in an array
```
rates[2]        // Refers to the third element in the rates array
names[1]        // Refers to the second element in the names array
```

How to assign values to an array by accessing each element

How to assign rates to an array that starts with four undefined elements
```
var rates = new Array(4);
rates[0] = 14.95;
rates[1] = 12.95;
rates[2] = 11.95;
rates[3] = 9.95;
```

How to assign strings to an array that starts with no elements
```
var names = [];
names[0] = "Grace";
names[1] = "Charles";
names[2] = "Ada";
```

Description

- An *array* can store one or more *elements*. The *length* of an array is the number of elements in the array.

- If you create an array without specifying the length, the array doesn't contain any elements.

- When you create an array of one or more elements without assigning values to them, each element is set to undefined.

- To refer to the elements in an array, you use an *index* where 0 is the first element, 1 is the second element, and so on.

Figure 9-1   How to create an array

How to add and delete array elements

There is one property and one operator that can help you modify arrays. They are described in figure 9-2.

To add an element to the end of an array, you can use the length property of the array as the index of the new element. This is illustrated by the first example in this figure. Since this property will always be 1 more than the highest index used in the array, this adds the new element at the end of the array.

To add an element at a specific index, you use its index to refer to the element and assign a value to it. This is illustrated by the second example. If you use an index that's greater than the length of the array, the elements that you skipped over will be created and assigned the value of undefined.

To delete an element from an array, you can use the delete operator. This is illustrated by the third example. When you do this, the deleted element is left in the array with an undefined value. In other words, the elements that are above the element that you deleted are not shifted down to fill in this gap. Later in this chapter, though, you'll learn how to use the splice method of an array to delete elements without leaving a gap in the array.

To remove all the elements in an array, you set the length property of the array to zero. This is illustrated by the fourth example. Note that this is different than using the delete operator, because the elements are not left in the array with an undefined value. Rather, the elements are completely removed, leaving the array with no elements.

In JavaScript, a *sparse array* is an array with a large number of elements but few assigned elements. This is illustrated by the fifth example in this figure. Here, the array has 1001 elements, but only two of these elements have assigned values. With some programming languages, space would be reserved for all 1001 elements in the computer's memory. With JavaScript, though, space is only reserved for the elements that have assigned values.

One property and one operator for an array

Property	Description
`length`	The number of elements in an array.
Operator	**Description**
`delete`	Deletes the contents of an element and sets the element to undefined, but doesn't remove the element from the array.

How to add an element to the end of an array

```
var numbers = [1, 2, 3, 4];     // array is 1, 2, 3, 4
numbers[numbers.length] = 5;    // array is 1, 2, 3, 4, 5
```

How to add an element at a specific index

```
var numbers = [1, 2, 3, 4];     // array is 1, 2, 3, 4
numbers[6] = 7;                 // array is 1, 2, 3, 4, undefined, undefined, 7
```

How to delete a number at a specific index

```
var numbers = [1, 2, 3, 4];     // array is 1, 2, 3, 4
delete numbers[2];              // array is 1, 2, undefined, 4
```

How to remove all elements

```
var numbers = [1, 2, 3, 4];     // array contains four elements
numbers.length = 0;             // removes all elements from array
```

A sparse array that contains 999 undefined elements

```
var numbers = [1];              // array is 1
numbers[1000] = 1001;           // array contains 1 and 1001 with 999
                                // undefined elements in between
```

Description

- One way to add an element to the end of an array is to use the length property as the index.

- If you add an element at a specific index that isn't the next one in sequence, undefined elements are added to the array between the new element and the end of the original array.

- When you use the delete operator, the element's value is deleted but the element stays in the array with an undefined value.

- To remove all the elements from an array, you can set the array's length property to zero. Unlike the delete operator, this removes all the elements, not just the elements' values.

- A *sparse array* is a large array with few defined elements. For efficiency, though, JavaScript only reserves space for the elements that are assigned values.

- You can also add items to an array by using the methods of an Array object as shown in figure 9-5.

Figure 9-2   How to add and delete array elements

How to use for loops to work with arrays

For loops are commonly used to process one array element at a time by incrementing an index variable. Figure 9-3 shows how this works.

The first example in this figure shows how to create an array and fill it with the numbers 1 through 10. First, the code creates an empty array named numbers. Then, an index variable named i is used to loop through the first ten elements of the array by using values that range from 0 to 9. In the body of this loop, one is added to the value in i and the result is stored in the element. As a result, the element at index 0 stores a 1, the element at index 1 stores a 2, and so on.

Next, this example displays the values in the array. First, it creates an empty string named numbersString. Then, it uses a for loop to access the elements in the array. In the for loop, the length property of the array is used to control how many times the loop executes. This allows the same code to work with arrays of different lengths. Inside the for loop, the value in the element and a space are concatenated to the end of numbersString. Finally, numbersString is displayed, which shows the ten numbers that were stored in the array.

The second example in this figure shows how you can calculate the sum and average of an array of totals. First, the code creates an array named totals that stores four total values. Then, it creates a variable named sum that is initialized to zero. Next, it uses a for loop to access each of the elements in the totals array and add it to the sum. Finally, it calculates the average by dividing the sum by the length of the array.

Next, this example displays the totals, the sum, and the average. First, it creates an empty string named totalsString. Then, it uses a for loop to concatenate the value of each element and a new line character to totalsString. Finally, it displays a message containing totalsString, the sum, and the average.

Code that puts the numbers 1 through 10 into an array

```
var numbers = [];
for (var i = 0; i < 10; i++) {
    numbers[i] = i + 1;
}
```

Code that displays the numbers array

```
var numbersString = "";
for (var i = 0; i < numbers.length; i++) {
    numbersString += numbers[i] + " ";
}
alert (numbersString);
```

The message that's displayed

Code that computes the sum and average of an array of totals

```
var totals = [141.95, 212.95, 411, 10.95];
var sum = 0;
for (var i = 0; i < totals.length; i++) {
    sum += totals[i];
}
var average = sum / totals.length;
```

Code that displays the totals array, the sum, and the average

```
var totalsString = "";
for (var i = 0; i < totals.length; i++) {
    totalsString += totals[i] + "\n";
}
alert ("The totals are:\n" + totalsString + "\n" +
        "Sum: " + sum.toFixed(2) + "\n" + "Average: " + average.toFixed(2));
```

The message that's displayed

Description

- When you use a *for loop* to work with an array, you can use the counter for the loop as the index for the array.

Figure 9-3   How to use for loops to work with arrays

How to use for-in loops to work with arrays

In contrast to a for loop, a *for-in loop* makes it easier to work with an array. Figure 9-4 shows how this type of loop works.

As the syntax at the top of this figure shows, the for-in loop doesn't require separate expressions that initialize, test, and increment an index counter like a for loop does. Instead, you declare a variable that will be used to refer to the index of each element in the array. Then, within the loop, you can use this variable to access each element in the array.

The first example in this figure stores the numbers 1 through 10 in an array and creates an empty string named numbersString. Then, it uses a for-in loop to concatenate each of the numbers in the array and a space to the string. Last, it displays the numbers in a message box.

The second example shows the differences in the ways that for loops and for-in loops handle the undefined elements in an array. In short, a for loop processes the undefined elements, but a for-in loop skips over them. You can see these differences in the messages that are displayed for each of the loops in this example.

You should know, though, that two types of undefined elements can be in an array. The first type is an element that doesn't have a value assigned to it so it is undefined. The second type is an element that has a value of "undefined" assigned to it. Although the for-in loop skips the first type of undefined element, it processes the second type of undefined element.

To illustrate, the fourth line in the second example in this figure

```
delete names[1]
```

creates the first type of undefined element. But the fifth line

```
names[names.length] = undefined
```

creates the second type of undefined element. As you can see in this figure, the for-in loop processes the undefined value created in the fifth line and displays "undefined" as the last value in the array. The message for the for loop, by contrast, shows both types of undefined values.

The syntax of a for-in loop

```
for (var elementIndex in arrayName) {
    // statements that access the elements
}
```

A for-in loop that displays the numbers array in a message box

```
var numbers = [1, 2, 3, 4, 5, 6, 7, 8, 9, 10];
var numbersString = "";
for (var index in numbers) {            // The start of the for-in loop
    numbersString += numbers[index] + " ";
}
alert(numbersString);
```

The message that's displayed

Code that shows the difference between for and for-in loops

```
var names = ["Grace", "Charles", "Ada"];
names[4] = "Alan";                  // Grace, Charles, Ada, undefined, Alan
names[names.length] = "Linus";      // Linus is added to the end of the array
delete names[1];                    // Charles is deleted from the array
names[names.length] = undefined;    // value of "undefined" added to the array

var namesString1 = "The elements displayed by the for loop:\n\n";
for (var i = 0; i < names.length; i++) {    // The start of the for loop
    namesString1 += names[i] + "\n"; }      // Includes undefined elements

var namesString2 = "The elements displayed by the for-in loop:\n\n";
for (var i in names) {                      // The start of the for-in loop
    namesString2 += names[i] + "\n"; }      // Omits undefined elements

alert (namesString1);
alert (namesString2);
```

The messages that are created by the for and the for-In loops

Description

- You can use a *for-in statement* to create a *for-in loop* that accesses only those elements in an array that are specifically assigned. This includes undefined values if the undefined value was specifically assigned.

Figure 9-4   How to use for-in loops to work with arrays

How to use the methods of an Array object

To help you work with arrays, JavaScript provides many methods. That includes a set of methods that became available with ECMAScript 5.

The methods of an Array object

Figure 9-5 summarizes the most useful methods for working with arrays. All of these methods, except for the last five, modify the original array.

The first two methods, push and pop, are used to add elements to and remove elements from the end of an array. This lets you use an array as a stack in which the last element added to it is the first element removed (last-in, first-out). In this case, the oldest element is at the start of the array.

The next two methods, unshift and shift, are used to add elements to and remove elements from the start of an array. These methods also let you use an array as a stack in which the last element added to it is the first element removed. In this case, though, the oldest element is at the end of the array.

If you combine the unshift and pop methods, you can use an array as a queue in which the first element added it is the first element removed (first-in, first out). In this case, the oldest element is at the end of the array. You can also use push and shift to use an array as a first-in, first-out queue. In this case, though, the oldest element is at the start of the array.

The reverse and sort methods of an Array object let you change the order of the elements in an array. By default, the sort method treats all of the elements as strings. This means that the numbers 5, 10, 101, and 250 are sorted as 10, 101, 250, and 5. If you need to sort the array in numeric order, though, you can pass a function to the sort method that compares two values at a time. You'll see how this works in the next figure.

The splice method lets you remove, replace, and add elements anywhere in an array. To remove elements, you call the splice method with the index of the first element to remove and the number of elements to remove. To replace elements, you call the splice method with the index of the first element to replace, the number of elements to be replaced, and a list of the replacement values. To add elements, you call the splice method with the index of the element just after the insertion point in the array, a zero, and a list of the values to add to the array.

The slice and concat methods let you create a new array from part or all of an array, and the original array isn't modified. If you want the original array to be replaced by the new array, you can set the old array equal to the new array.

The join, toString, and toLocaleString methods let you create a single string that contains the elements in the array. They differ mainly in how they handle the separator string. These methods use an empty string for any undefined elements, both those that aren't defined and those that were set equal to undefined.

The methods of an Array object

Methods	Description
`push(elements_list)`	Adds one or more elements to the end of the array, and returns the new length of the array.
`pop()`	Removes the last element in the array, decrements the length, and returns the element that it removed.
`unshift(elements_list)`	Adds one or more elements to the beginning of the array, and returns the new length of the array.
`shift()`	Removes the first element in the array, decrements the array length, and returns the element that it removed.
`reverse()`	Reverses the order of the elements in the array.
`sort()`	When no parameter is passed, this method sorts the elements in an array into ascending alphanumeric sequence. If necessary, it converts numeric elements to strings for this sort.
`sort(comparison_function)`	To change the default order of the sort method, you can pass the name of a comparison function to the method. This function should receive two parameters and return a positive value if the first parameter is greater than the second, zero if the two parameters are equal, and a negative value if the first parameter is less than the second parameter.
`splice(start, number)`	Removes the number of elements given by the second parameter starting with the index given by the first parameter. It returns the elements that were removed.
`splice(start, number, elements_list)`	Removes the number of elements given by the second parameter starting with the index given by the first parameter, and replaces those elements with the ones given by the third parameter. It returns the elements that were removed.
`slice(start, number)`	Returns a new array that starts with the index given by the first parameter and continuing for the number of elements given by the second parameter.
`concat(array_list)`	Returns a new array that consists of the original array concatenated with the arrays in the array list.
`join(separator)`	When no parameter is passed, this method converts all the elements of the array to strings and concatenates them separated by commas. To change the separator, you can pass this method a string literal.
`toString()`	Same as the join method without any parameter passed to it.
`toLocaleString()`	Same as the toString method but using a locale-specific separator.

Description

- The push and pop methods are used to add elements to and remove elements from the end of an array.
- The unshift and shift methods are used to add elements to and remove elements from the beginning of an array.

Figure 9-5   The methods of an Array object

Examples of the Array methods

Figure 9-6 shows you how to use the methods that are summarized in the last figure. If you study the summary, the examples, and the comments in the code, you shouldn't have much trouble understanding how these methods work.

For instance, the first example uses the push and pop methods to add and remove elements. The second example uses the unshift and shift methods to do the same. And the third example uses the splice method to delete, replace, and add an element.

In the fourth example, the slice method is used to create a new array that consists of two elements taken from an array named names. Then, the concat method is used to combine the two arrays in another new array. When all of the statements are finished, there are three arrays named names, namesSlice, and namesConcat, and the names array hasn't changed.

The fifth example shows how to use the sort method without and with a parameter. Without a parameter, the elements are sorted as strings. This means that alphabetic elements are sorted in alphabetic order, but numbers aren't sorted in numeric order.

If you want to sort the elements in an array numerically, though, you can pass a function to the sort method. As the summary in the last figure states, this function should receive two parameters, and it should return a positive, zero, or negative value based on a comparison of the two parameter values. The returned value should be positive if the first parameter is greater than the second, zero if they're equal, and negative if the first parameter is less than the second.

In this example, this function is named comparison, and it returns x − y. As a result, it returns the proper positive, zero, or negative value. Then, when this function is used as the parameter for the sort method, the function definition (not the result of calling the function) is passed to the method.

The sixth example shows how to use the reverse method to reverse the order of the elements in an array. This method can be used after you use the sort method if you want the elements in descending order.

The last example shows how to use the join and toString methods. The difference is that the join method lets you supply a parameter that is used as the separator for the list of elements. Otherwise, the comma is used.

How to use the push and pop methods to add and remove elements

```
var names = ["Grace", "Charles", "Ada"];
names.push("Alan", "Linus");    // names is Grace, Charles, Ada, Alan, Linus
var removedName = names.pop();  // removedName is Linus
alert (names.join());           // displays Grace,Charles,Ada,Alan
```

How to use the unshift and shift methods to add and remove elements

```
var names = ["Grace", "Charles", "Ada"];
names.unshift("Alan", "Linus");  // names is Alan, Linus, Grace, Charles, Ada
var removedName = names.shift(); // removedName is Alan
alert (names.toString());        // displays Linus,Grace,Charles,Ada
```

How to use the splice method

```
var names = ["Grace", "Ada", "Charles", "Alan"];
names.splice(2, 1);             // names is Grace, Ada, Alan
names.splice(2, 1, "Linus");    // names is Grace, Ada, Linus
names.splice(2, 0, "Bill");     // names is Grace, Ada, Bill, Linus
```

How to use the slice and concat methods

```
var names = ["Grace", "Charles", "Ada", "Alan"];
var namesSlice = names.slice(0, 2);    // namesSlice is Grace, Charles
alert (names.join(", "));              // displays Grace, Charles, Ada, Alan

var namesConcat = names.concat(namesSlice);
alert (namesConcat.join()); // displays Grace,Charles,Ada,Alan,Grace,Charles
```

How to use the sort method

For alphanumeric sorting

```
var names = ["Grace", "Charles", "Ada", "Alan", "Linus"];
names.sort();                   // names is Ada, Alan, Charles, Grace, Linus
```

For numeric sorting

```
// The function used for the parameter of the sort method
var comparison = function(x, y) {
    return x - y;
};
var numbers = [520, 33, 9, 199];
numbers.sort(comparison);       // numbers is 9, 33, 199, 520
```

How to use the reverse method

```
var names = ["Grace", "Ada", "Charles", "Alan", "Linus"];
names.reverse();                // names is Linus, Alan, Charles, Ada, Grace
```

How to use the join and toString methods

```
var names = ["Grace", "Charles", "Ada", "Linus"];
alert (names.join());           // displays Grace,Charles,Ada,Linus
alert (names.join(", "));       // displays Grace, Charles, Ada, Linus
alert (names.toString());       // displays Grace,Charles,Ada,Linus
```

Figure 9-6   Examples of the Array methods

The ECMAScript 5 methods

Besides the array methods you've just learned, the ECMAScript 5 specification provides another set of array methods. They are summarized in figure 9-7. All of these methods are in the shim.js file, which means that you can use these methods with older browsers as long as you include the shim.js file.

The methods in the first table work like the methods you've just learned about. For example, the isArray method accepts an object and returns a Boolean value. As its name suggests, it returns true if the object passed to it is an array, and false if it isn't.

The next two methods, indexOf and lastIndexOf, are similar to the String methods of the same name. But instead of returning the position of a character in a string, they return the index of an element in an array. Also, like the String methods, they return -1 if the element isn't found. The indexOf method starts its search from the beginning of the array, while the lastIndexOf method starts its search from the end. Both have an optional start parameter, so you can specify the index to start searching from.

The methods in the second table all accept a function as a parameter. These methods work by calling the function that's passed to the method for every element in the array. This is similar to the way the sort method in the last figure works. For all these methods, the function won't be called for undefined elements.

The syntax of the function parameter for the first five methods in this table is shown in the first syntax summary below the table. Here, the first parameter is the value of the current element being processed, and it is required. The next parameter is the index of the current element, and the third is the array itself. You'll see how these parameters are used in the next figure.

The forEach method accepts a function that will be executed once for each item in the array. It returns a value of undefined. In contrast, the every and some methods accept a function that tests each item in the array to see if it meets a condition, and then returns a Boolean value that indicates how many of the items passed the test. As their names suggest, the every method returns true if all the array elements pass the test, and the some method returns true if some pass.

The map and filter methods both return new arrays, leaving the initial array unchanged. The map method returns an array that contains the result of calling the function on each element. The filter method, meanwhile, returns an array with that contains only those elements that meet the specified condition of the function.

The last two methods in the second table, reduce and reduceRight, accept a function and return all the elements in the array reduced to a single value. The functions that are passed to these methods use the syntax in the second syntax summary after the table. The first parameter for these methods is the value returned by the last function call. This is how these methods keep track of the single value that the array elements will be reduced to. The only difference between the methods is the order in which the elements are processed.

ECMAScript 5 methods with simple parameters

Methods	Description
isArray(*object*)	Checks whether the object passed to it is an array. Returns true if it is, false if it isn't.
indexOf(*value, start*)	Returns the first index at which the first parameter is found, or -1 if the value isn't found. The second parameter specifies the index to start searching from, and is optional.
lastIndexOf(*value, start*)	Returns the last index at which the first parameter is found, or -1 if the value isn't found. The second parameter specifies the index to start searching from, and is optional.

ECMAScript 5 methods with functions as parameters

Methods	Description
forEach(*function, this*)	Accepts a function that is executed once for each element. Returns a value of undefined.
every(*function, this*)	Accepts a function that tests each element in the array to see if it meets a specified condition. Returns true if all elements in the array pass the test, false otherwise.
some(*function, this*)	Accepts a function that tests each element in the array to see if it meets a specified condition. Returns true if at least one element in the array passes the test, false otherwise.
map(*function, this*)	Accepts a function that is executed once for each element, and returns a new array containing the results of each function call.
filter(*function, this*)	Accepts a function that is executed once for each element, and returns a new array containing the elements that meet the specified condition of the function.
reduce(*function, init*)	Accepts a function that returns all the elements reduced to one value, processed in ascending order.
reduceRight(*function, init*)	Accepts a function that returns all the elements reduced to one value, processed in descending order.

The syntax of the function for most of the methods
```
function(currentValue, currentIndex, array);
```

The syntax of the function for the reduce and reduceRight methods
```
function(previousValue, currentValue, currentIndex, array);
```

Description
- The functions passed to the methods above can have up to 4 parameters. These functions won't be called for undefined elements.
- The methods that accept a function also accept an optional second parameter. For reduce and reduceRight, this parameter is the initial value for the previousValue parameter. For the rest, it's the value of the *this* keyword, which you'll learn about in the next chapter.
- All of these methods are in the shim.js file so they will work correctly in older browsers if you include that file.

Figure 9-7   The ECMAScript 5 methods of an Array object

Examples of the ECMAScript 5 methods

To give you a better idea of how the methods that receive functions as parameters work, figure 9-8 presents some examples. Here, the first example shows how to use the every and some methods. First, this example creates a function that will test the elements of the array to see if they meet a certain condition, in this case whether they start with the letter "a". This function accepts a single parameter named value. Remember from the last figure that this is the value of the current element in the array.

Then, this example creates a names array, and calls the every and some methods of the names array. The every method returns a value of false, because every name in the array doesn't begin with the letter "a". But the some method returns a value of true, because some of the names do.

The second example shows how to use the forEach method to total all of the numbers in an array. First, the example creates an array of numbers. Next, it declares a variable named total1 and sets its value to 0. Then, it defines a function called sum, which adds the value parameter to the total1 variable. Finally, it calls the forEach method of the numbers array, passing it the sum argument, to get the sum of the elements in the array.

The third example shows how to use the reduce method of the array to produce the same result. Unlike the forEach method, the reduce method returns a value. Also, it internally keeps track of the results of the function calls by using the previousValue parameter of the function argument. Thus, a variable to store the total value isn't needed, like it was before. Instead, the total value is returned by the reduce method. This example also shows how to use the optional initial value parameter, which is passed after the function is passed.

The fourth example shows how to use the map method to create a new array that contains the results of calling the function argument on each item of the original array. As before, the example starts by creating an array to work with. Then, it calls the map method, passes it a function that multiplies the value by itself, and stores the result in a variable called squared. In this example, the function parameter is declared at the same time it is passed, which is a common coding pattern.

Next, the map method is called again, but this time it passes the sqrt method of the Math object to get the square roots of the numbers in the array. Since the original array isn't affected by calls to the map method, the numbers array is unchanged after the two calls for it. However, the squared array contains the squares of the numbers array elements, and the root array contains the square roots of the numbers array elements.

The fifth example shows how to use the filter method. Like the map method, the filter method creates a new array, and the function argument is called on each array element. However, instead of returning the result of every function call, filter only returns an element in the array if the function call returns true. In this example, the checkPrime function is passed to the filter method so all the prime numbers in an array of numbers are returned by the method.

How to use the every and some methods

```
var startsWithA = function(value) {
    return value.substring(0,1).toLowerCase() === "a";
};
var names = ["Grace", "Charles", "Ada", "Alan", "Linus"];
var all = names.every(startsWithA);        // all is false
var some = names.some(startsWithA);        // some is true
```

How to use the forEach method

```
var numbers = [520, 33, 9, 199];
var total1 = 0;
var sum = function( value ) { total1 = total1 + value; };
numbers.forEach( sum );
alert(total1);                             // displays 761
```

How to use the reduce method

```
var numbers = [520, 33, 9, 199];
var sum = function(previousValue,value) { return previousValue + value; };
var total2 = numbers.reduce( sum );
alert(total2);                             // displays 761

total2 = numbers.reduce( sum, -200 );      // pass an initial value
alert(total2);                             // displays 561
```

How to use the map method

```
var numbers = [1,4,9,16];
// define and pass function argument in one step
var squared = numbers.map(function( value ) {
    return value * value;
});                                        // squared is 1,16,81,256
// pass an object's method as the function argument
var root = numbers.map( Math.sqrt );       // root is 1,2,3,4
```

How to use the filter method

```
var numbers = [1,2,3,4,5,6,7,8,9,10,11,12,13,14,15,16,17,18,19,20];
var checkPrime = function( value ){
    var isPrime = true;
    for ( var i = 2; i < value; i++ ) {
        if ( value % i === 0 ) {
            isPrime = false;
            break;
        }
    }
    return isPrime;
};
var prime = numbers.filter(checkPrime);    // prime is 1,2,3,5,7,11,13,17,19
```

Description

- When passing a function as an argument, you can define the function first and then pass it, or you can define and pass the function in one step. You can also pass functions that already exist, like the sqrt method of the Math object.

Figure 9-8   Examples of the ECMAScript 5 methods

Other skills for working with arrays

Now that you've learned the basic skills for creating and working with arrays, you're ready to learn some other skills for working with arrays. Keep an eye out, too, for some of the skills from the last figures in the examples coming up.

How to use a String method to create an array

Figure 9-9 presents the split method of a String object. This method can be used to divide a string into multiple substrings based on a separator character that's coded as the first parameter. It then creates a new array with each of the substrings as elements. If you code a second parameter, it is used to limit the number of elements that can be included in the new array.

The first example in this figure shows how to split a string that's separated by spaces into an array named nameParts. Next, it displays the length of the new array and the elements in the array. Then, it moves the element at the last index in the array (length − 1) into a variable named lastName and displays the contents of that variable.

Similarly, the second example shows how to split a string that's separated by hyphens into an array. Then, the third example shows how to split a string into individual characters. This happens when you call the split method with an empty string as its parameter.

Note the ways that the examples so far use the join and toString methods of the array. The second example calls the join method and specifies the string literal "/" as the separator, which produces the string "1/2/2016". The third example, by contrast, doesn't specify a separator when it calls join, so the default separator of "," is used. And the first example calls the toString method, which works the same way as the third example's call of the join method.

The fourth example shows what happens if the separator character isn't in the string. Here, a date string is created that has hyphens, but the split method is called with a slash as the separator. In this case, the resulting array only has one element and it is a copy of the original date string.

The fifth example shows how to limit the number of substrings copied into the new array. Here, the split method uses a space as the separator, but it limits the number of substrings to one. The result is an array that contains just the first name in one element.

Note in this example that the last statement uses the alert method to display this one-element array. Since the alert method expects a string, it automatically calls the toString method for any parameter that isn't a string. Then, since there is only one element in the array, the toString method of the array returns that element without using a separator.

A String method that creates an array

Method	Description
split(*separator*, *limit*)	Splits a string into an array based on the value of the separator parameter and returns the array. The optional limit parameter specifies the maximum number of elements in the new array.

How to split a string that's separated by spaces into an array

```
var fullName = "Grace M Hopper";
var nameParts = fullName.split(" ");        // creates an array
alert (nameParts.length);                   // displays 3
alert (nameParts.toString());               // displays Grace,M,Hopper
var lastName = nameParts[nameParts.length - 1];
alert (lastName);                           // displays Hopper
```

How to split a string that's separated by hyphens into an array

```
var date = "1-2-2016";
var dateParts = date.split("-");            // creates an array
alert (dateParts.length);                   // displays 3
alert (dateParts.join("/"));                // displays 1/2/2016
```

How to split a string into an array of characters

```
var fullName = "Grace Hopper";
var nameCharacters = fullName.split("");
alert (nameCharacters.length);              // displays 12
alert (nameCharacters.join());              // displays G,r,a,c,e, ,H,o,p,p,e,r
```

What happens if the string doesn't contain the separator

```
var date = "1-2-2016";
var dateParts2 = date.split("/");
alert (dateParts2.length);                  // displays 1
alert (dateParts2.join());                  // displays 1-2-2016
```

How to get just one element from a string

```
var fullName = "Grace M Hopper";
var firstName = fullName.split(" ", 1);
alert (firstName.length);                   // displays 1
alert (firstName);                          // displays Grace
```

Description

- The split method of a String object is used to convert the components of a string into the elements of an array.

- If a string doesn't include the separator that's specified in the parameter of the split method, the entire string is returned as the first element in a one-element array.

- If the separator that's specified by the parameter is an empty string, each character in the string becomes an element in the array that's returned by the method.

Figure 9-9   How to use a String method to create an array

How to create and use an associative array

So far, the arrays you've worked with have used whole numbers as the indexes. In contrast, an *associative array* is an array that uses strings as the indexes. In figure 9-10, you can learn how to create and work with associative arrays.

The first example in this figure creates an associate array with four elements. First, it creates an empty array. Then, it stores four values in the array using strings for the indexes. Finally, it displays the length of the associative array. However, because the length property of an array only counts elements with numeric indexes, the length is zero.

The second example adds an element to the array with another string index. The new value is the result of a calculation that uses two existing elements of the array, and the toFixed method is used to round the result.

The third example displays a formatted string that's built from the elements in the array. In the dialog box that follows, you can see that the array now contains five elements.

The fourth example shows how to use the for-in loop with an associative array. This for-in loop builds a formatted string that contains the element indexes and values. The comments after the last statement show the string that would be displayed by the alert statement.

Although you can mix numeric and string indexes within a single array, you usually should avoid doing that because mixed arrays present some unnecessary complications. If you do mix them, the length property indicates only the number of elements with numeric indexes. If you process a mixed array with a for loop, the associative elements aren't included in the processing. And if you process a mixed array with a for-in loop, all of the elements are processed.

This happens because an associative array isn't really an array. Instead, it's a JavaScript Object object. You'll learn more about that in chapter 11.

For now, you may want to know that you can use the keys method of the Object object to return an array that contains the names of the associative array's string indexes. Then, you can use that array's length property to get the length of the associative array. Since the keys method is in the shim.js file, you can use this method with older browsers as long as you include the shim.js file.

How to create an associative array with four elements

```
var item = [];
item["itemCode"] = 123;
item["itemName"] = "HTML5";
item["itemCost"] = 54.5;
item["itemQuantity"] = 5;
alert( item.length );                     // Displays 0
alert( Object.keys(item).length );        // Displays 4
```

How to add an element to the associative array

```
item["lineCost"] = (item["itemCost"] * item["itemQuantity"]).toFixed(2);
```

How to retrieve and display the elements in the associative array

```
alert ("Item elements:\n\nCode = " + item["itemCode"] +
        "\nName = " + item["itemName"] +
        "\nCost - " + item["itemCost"] +
        "\nQuantity = " + item["itemQuantity"] +
        "\nLine Cost = " + item["lineCost"]);
```

The message displayed by the alert statement

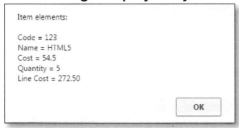

```
Item elements:

Code = 123
Name = HTML5
Cost = 54.5
Quantity = 5
Line Cost = 272.50

                    OK
```

How to use a for-in loop with the associative array

```
var result = "";
for ( var i in item ) {
    result += i + " = " + item[i] + "\n";
}
alert(result);
// "itemCode = 123\nitemName = HTML5\nitemCost = 54.5\n" +
// "itemQuantity = 5\nlineCost = 272.50"
```

Description

- When you create an *associative array*, you use strings as the indexes instead of numbers.

- If you mix numeric and string indexes in an array, the length will indicate only the number of elements with numeric indexes, a for loop will only process the elements with numeric indexes, and a for-in loop will process all the elements.

- An associative array is actually an Object object (see chapter 11), not an Array object, so some of the array properties and methods don't work as expected. For instance, the length property returns 0 and the pop method returns undefined.

Figure 9-10   How to create and use an associative array

How to create and use an array of arrays

Although JavaScript doesn't let you create multi-dimensional arrays, you can get the same effect by creating an *array of arrays*. To do that, you store arrays in each element of another array. These arrays don't have to be the same length, and you will often see an associative array nested inside a numerically indexed array. In figure 9-11, you can learn how to create and use an array of arrays.

The first example in this figure shows how to create and use an array of arrays. First, it creates an empty array called testScores. Then, it stores arrays of test scores in the first four elements of the outer testScores array.

The next two statements in the first example shows how to access the elements in this array. Here, the first statement displays the value in the element at index 1 of the array that's in the element at index 0 of the testScores array. The second statement displays the value in the element at index 3 of the array that's in the element at index 2 of the testScores array.

The second example in this figure shows how to nest associative arrays in a numerically indexed array. Here, the first statement creates an array named invoice that will be numerically indexed.

The second group of statements stores an empty array as the first element in the invoice array. After that, it adds four elements to the empty array, using strings as indexes. This creates an associative array nested within a numeric array.

The third group of statements illustrates another way to add an associative array as an element of a numeric array. In this case, a new array called item is created, and four elements with string indexes are added to it. Then, the item array is passed to the push method of the invoice array. This adds the item array to the end of the invoice array.

Note that if you're going to add arrays this way, you can't re-use the item array for the next array you want to add. That's because the push method puts a reference to the item array, rather than a copy of it, in the element of the invoice array. So you'll need to declare a separate array variable for each array you want to add. You'll learn more about references in the next chapter.

The fourth group of statements accesses the elements of the nested arrays. Here, the first statement uses the alert method to display the value of the itemCode element that's in the first element (index 0) of the invoice array. This displays 123. Then, the second statement uses the alert method to display the value of the itemName element that's in the second element (index 1) of the invoice array. This displays jQuery.

How to create and use an array of arrays

Code that creates an array of arrays

```
var testScores = [];
testScores[0] = [80, 82, 90, 87, 85];
testScores[1] = [79, 80, 74];
testScores[2] = [93, 95, 89, 100];
testScores[3] = [60, 72, 65, 71];
```

Code that refers to elements in the array of arrays

```
alert (testScores[0][1]);        // displays 82
alert (testScores[2][3]);        // displays 100
```

How to create and use an array of associative arrays

Code that creates an array

```
var invoice = [];                          // create an empty invoice array
```

Code that adds an associative array to the invoice array directly

```
invoice[0] = [];
invoice[0]["itemCode"] = 123;
invoice[0]["itemName"] = "HTML5";
invoice[0]["itemCost"] = 54.5;
invoice[0]["itemQuantity"] = 5;
```

Code that creates an associative array and then adds it to the invoice array

```
var item = [];
item["itemCode"] = 456;
item["itemName"] = "jQuery";
item["itemCost"] = 52.5;
item["itemQuantity"] = 2;
invoice.push(item);   // add the item array to the end of the invoice array
```

Code that refers to the elements in the array of associative arrays

```
alert (invoice[0]["itemCode"]);     // displays 123
alert (invoice[1]["itemName"]);     // displays jQuery
```

Description

- Although JavaScript doesn't provide for multi-dimensional arrays, you can get the same effect by creating an *array of arrays*. In an array of arrays, each element in the first array is another array.

- The arrays within an array can be regular arrays or associative arrays.

- To refer to the elements in an array of arrays, you use two index values for each element. The first value is for an element in the primary array. The second value is for an element in the array that's in the element of the primary array.

- If necessary, you can nest arrays beyond the two dimensions that are illustrated here. In other words, you can create an array of arrays of arrays. As usual, be careful with this as your code can become hard to read and maintain if it's too complex.

Figure 9-11   How to create and use an array of arrays

How to use web storage

In the past, you had to use cookies to store data on the user's system. But that meant that the data had to be processed by server-side code. That also meant that the data was passed to the browser with every HTTP request. Beyond that, the storage in a cookie is limited to about 4,000 bytes.

But modern browsers now offer *web storage* that can be processed by JavaScript on the browser. Then, the data isn't passed to the server with every HTTP request. In addition, web storage can be used to store approximately 5MB of data.

When you use web storage, you can use either *local storage* or *session storage*. The difference is that items in local storage persist between browser sessions, but items in session storage are removed when the browser session ends. This happens when the users close their browsers.

How to use local and session storage

Figure 9-12 shows how to work with local and session storage. To do that, you use the localStorage and sessionStorage objects, which store their items in *name/value pairs*. Then, you use the setItem, getItem, removeItem, and clear methods of the objects to work with the items.

For instance, the setItem method requires two parameters that provide the name of an item and the value for the item. So you can use code like this to add items named "email" and "phone" that store the email address and phone number for a user:

```
localStorage.setItem("email", "grace@gmail.com");
localStorage.setItem("phone", "555-555-1212");
```

Then, you can use the getItem method with the item name as the parameter to retrieve the data for the phone item with a statement like this:

```
var phone = localStorage.getItem("phone");
```

To simplify, you can use the shortcut syntax in this figure. For instance, you can use this code to save the email and phone items:

```
localStorage.email = "grace@gmail.com";
localStorage.phone = "555-555-1212";
```

And this code to retrieve the items:

```
var phone = localStorage.phone;
```

The shortcut syntax is used in the example in this figure. Here, if statements test to see whether the "hits" item in local storage and session storage exists. If it does, it converts the value in that name/value pair to a number and adds 1 to it. If it doesn't, it saves a new item named "hits" with a value of 1 in it. After that, the alert method is used to display the value of the "hits" item in both local and session storage. This assumes that the user closed the browser after the first 8 page hits and then reopened the page for two more hits.

The syntax for working with local or session storage

```
localStorage.setItem("itemname", "value")    // saves the data in the item
localStorage.getItem("itemname")             // gets the data in the item
localStorage.removeItem("itemname")          // removes the item
localStorage.clear()                         // removes all items

sessionStorage.setItem("itemname", "value")  // saves the data in the item
sessionStorage.getItem("itemname")           // gets the data in the item
sessionStorage.removeItem("itemname")        // removes the item
sessionStorage.clear()                       // removes all items
```

The shortcut syntax for getting or saving an item

```
localStorage.itemname                        // saves or gets the data in the item
sessionStorage.itemname                      // saves or gets the data in the item
```

JavaScript that uses local and session storage for hit counters

```
window.onload = function() {
    if (localStorage.hits) {
        localStorage.hits = parseInt(localStorage.hits) + 1;
    } else { localStorage.hits = 1; }

    if (sessionStorage.hits) {
        sessionStorage.hits = parseInt(sessionStorage.hits) + 1;
    } else { sessionStorage.hits = 1; }

    alert("Number of hits this browser: " + localStorage.hits + "\n\n" +
          "Number of hits this session: " + sessionStorage.hits)
};
```

A message box that shows the current value of both hits fields

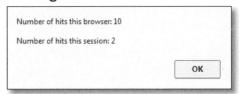

Description

- *Web storage* lets the web page use JavaScript to store data in *key/value pairs*. This feature is currently supported by every modern browser.

- One type of web storage is *local storage*, which is retained indefinitely. The other type storage is *session storage*, which is lost when the user ends the session by closing the browser or tab for the page.

- Unlike cookies, web storage is meant to be accessed by JavaScript, not server-side code. This means that web storage isn't passed to the server along with each HTTP request.

- You can also store more data in web storage than you can in cookies. In fact, the HTML5 specification recommends a storage limit of 5MB.

- To refer to web storage from JavaScript, you use the localStorage or sessionStorage objects.

Figure 9-12   How to use web storage

How to use Chrome to view and edit items in web storage

Sometimes as you test an application that uses local or session storage, it can be helpful to see what values are currently stored. To do that, you can use the technique described in figure 9-13.

The Resources panel of the Chrome browser's developer tools will show you the name/value pairs stored in local storage and session storage, as well as the values stored in cookies and in the application's cache. It will also show you what's in the browser-based databases that most modern browsers support.

This can be useful not only for testing your own applications, but for seeing what other websites are storing in your browser. For example, you can navigate to google.com and then open the Resources panel to see what Google is storing on your computer, which can be an interesting exercise.

In addition to letting you see what a website has stored on your computer, the Resources panel lets you delete items from local or session storage. This can be useful when testing and debugging your own applications. You'll want to be careful about doing this for other websites, though, since you might delete something that the website needs to run properly.

The Resources panel of Chrome's developer tools

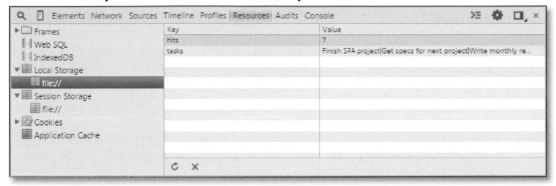

How to use the Resources panel to view local and session storage

- Press F12 to open the developer tools, and click on the Resources tab.
- Click the arrow beside Local Storage or Session Storage to expand that section, and then click on the website URL. That will display the name/value pairs for that type of storage in the grid.

How to use the Resources panel to delete a storage item

- Select the item you want to delete, and then click the X at the bottom left of the grid. The item will be removed when you refresh the page.

Description

- You can use the Resources panel in Chrome's developer tools to view and delete items in local and session storage.

Figure 9-13   How to use Chrome to view and edit web storage

The Task Manager application

To show you how some of the skills you've just learned can be used in an application, the next two figures present a Task Manager application. This application displays the tasks that the user adds to the task list in a text area on the right side of the page. To add a task, the user enters the task in the first text box and clicks on the Add Task button. To clear all the tasks, the user clicks on the Clear Tasks button.

To make this application more useful, the task list is stored in local storage. This means that the task list is saved when the user closes the browser tab or window. Then, when the user reopens the page, the task list is restored.

The HTML and CSS

Figure 9-14 presents the HTML and CSS for this application. Note here that a div element is used for the label and text area that's used for the task list. Then, the CSS floats this div element to the right of the text box and buttons. Note also the ids used for the controls in the HTML since they are the ones that are used in the JavaScript.

This figure also shows the format for the tasks that are stored in a single key/value pair in local storage. Here, the tasks are separated by pipes. You'll see how this works in the JavaScript code.

The Task Manager application

Task Manager

Task

[   ]

Add Task

Clear Tasks

Task List

Finish current project
Get specs for new project
Meet with Mike

The HTML for the application

```
<head>
    <title>Ch09 Task Manager</title>
    <link type="text/css" rel="stylesheet" href="task_list.css">
    <script type="text/javascript" src="task_list.js"></script>
</head>
<body>
  <main>
    <h1>Task Manager</h1>
    <div id="tasks">
        <label for="tasks">Task List</label><br>
        <textarea id="task_list" rows="6" cols="50"></textarea>
    </div>

    <label for="task">Task:</label><br>
    <input type="text" name="task" id="task"><br>

    <input type="button" name="add task" id="add_task" value="Add Task"><br>
    <input type="button" name="clear_tasks" id="clear_tasks"
        value="Clear Tasks">
  </main>
</body>
```

The CSS for the "tasks" id

```
#tasks {
    margin-top: 0;
    float: right;
}
```

The string that's stored in local storage

```
Finish current project|Get specs for new project|Meet with Mike
```

Description

- The Task Manager application lets the user build a list of tasks to be done, stores them in local storage, and displays the list of tasks in the text area.
- The user can add new tasks to the list or clear all of the tasks.
- The tasks are stored in local storage in one name/value pair with "tasks" as the name and the value as the tasks in one string with pipes (|) used as separators.

Figure 9-14   The HTML and CSS for the Task Manager application

The JavaScript

Figure 9-15 presents the JavaScript for this application. As usual, it starts with the $ function. After that, it creates a global variable called tasks, and initializes it as an empty array. This is the array that will store the tasks that the user adds. Then, the JavaScript creates the functions that work with those tasks.

The displayTaskList function updates the text area to display the current tasks. It starts by initializing a variable named list to an empty string. Then, it checks to see whether the tasks array variable has any elements. If it doesn't, it checks to see if there are any items in local storage. It does this by using the getItem method of the localStorage object to retrieve an item named "tasks" and store it in a variable named storage. But if there is no item named "tasks" in local storage, this code uses the OR operator to provide a default value of an empty string. This use of the OR operator is explained in figure 8-7 of the chapter 8.

This function then checks the storage variable. If it isn't an empty string, it will contain task strings separated by the pipe character. So, the function uses the split method of the String object to split the string at the pipe separator, and stores the resulting array in the global tasks variable.

This function then checks again to see whether the tasks array has any elements. If it does, this function calls the array's sort method, and then calls the array's join method to convert the array back to a single string. This time, however, the string will have a separator of the newline character rather than the pipe character. This function then sets the value of the task area element to the string of tasks, or to an empty string if there are no elements in the array. Last, it sets the focus on the task text box.

The addToTask function first retrieves the text box element containing the task entered by the user. Then, it checks the text box's value to make sure the user entered something. If not, this function notifies the user.

If the user did enter a task, this function updates both the global tasks array and the local storage item. It updates the tasks array by using the array's push method. This adds the new task to the end of the tasks array. It updates local storage by setting its task property to the result of a call to the task array's join method. This converts the elements of the array to a single string separated by pipe characters.

After local storage has been updated with the new task, this function clears the task text box and calls the displayTaskList function to update the text area with the new task data.

The clearTaskList function sets the length property of the tasks array to zero. This removes all the elements from the array. Then, it sets the tasks property in local storage to an empty string. Note that it uses the shortcut syntax this time. Last, it clears the text area element and sets the focus on the task text box.

The last function in this figure is the event handler for the onload event. First, this function assigns the addToTaskList and clearTaskList functions to the click events of the add_task and clear_task buttons. Then, it calls the displayTaskList function to update the task list text area. This makes sure that anything already in local storage is displayed to the user when the application starts.

The JavaScript for the Task Manager application

```
var $ = function(id) { return document.getElementById(id); };
var tasks = [];

var displayTaskList = function() {
    var list = "";
    // if there are no tasks in tasks array, check storage
    if (tasks.length === 0) {
        // get tasks from storage or empty string if nothing in storage
        var storage = localStorage.getItem("tasks") || "";

        // if not empty, convert to array and store in global tasks variable
        if (storage.length > 0) { tasks = storage.split("|"); }
    }
    // if there are tasks in array, sort and create tasks string
    if (tasks.length > 0) {
        tasks.sort();
        list = tasks.join("\n");
    }
    // display tasks string and set focus on task text box
    $("task_list").value = list;
    $("task").focus();
};
var addToTaskList = function() {
    var task = $("task");
    if (task.value === "") {
        alert("Please enter a task.");
    } else {
        // add task to array and local storage
        tasks.push(task.value);
        localStorage.tasks = tasks.join("|");

        // clear task text box and re-display tasks
        task.value = "";
        displayTaskList();
    }
};
var clearTaskList = function() {
    tasks.length = 0;
    localStorage.tasks = "";
    $("task_list").value = "";
    $("task").focus();
};
window.onload = function() {
    $("add_task").onclick = addToTaskList;
    $("clear_tasks").onclick = clearTaskList;
    displayTaskList();
};
```

Description

- This application keeps tasks in local storage in a string separated by pipes ("|").

- To display the tasks, it retrieves the tasks string from local storage and uses its split method to create an array of tasks. To store the string for the tasks in local storage, the application uses the array's join method.

Figure 9-15   The JavaScript for the Task Manager application

The JavaScript with an ECMAScript 5 enhancement

Figure 9-16 presents the JavaScript for a slightly enhanced version of this application. The difference is that the application capitalizes the first letter in each task in case the user doesn't do that. To do the capitalization, this application uses the ECMAScript 5 map method of an array.

The main difference in the enhanced version is in the displayTaskList function that updates the text area to display the current tasks. It starts the same way as before by either getting the items in the task list from local storage and storing them in an array named storage or by storing an empty string in that variable.

This function then checks to see whether the tasks array has any elements. If it does, this function first calls the array's sort method. Since the sort method returns a sorted array, the code can then call the array's map method to capitalize the items in the tasks array. It does this by defining and passing a function that gets the first letter of the task and capitalizes it. The new capitalized array is stored in a variable called capitalized.

Finally, this function uses the AND and OR operators to either call the array's join method with the newline character to convert the array back to a single string or to return an empty string. The resulting string is set as the value of the task area element so it is displayed in the browser. Last, this method sets the focus on the task text box. Here again, the use of the AND and OR operators is explained in figure 8-7 of chapter 8.

The only other difference between this code and the code in the last figure is the highlighted line in the clearTaskList event handler. After the tasks array and the tasks item in local storage are cleared, the displayTaskList function is called. In contrast, the code in the previous page sets the value in the text area to an empty space and sets the focus on the task text box. Both versions get the same result, of course, because the displayTaskList function in this figure ends by setting the value of the text area and setting the focus on the task text box.

The JavaScript for the enhanced Task Manager application

```javascript
var $ = function(id) { return document.getElementById(id); };
var tasks = [];

var displayTaskList = function() {
    // if there are no tasks in array, get from storage and add to array
    if (tasks.length === 0) {
        var storage = localStorage.getItem("tasks") || "";
        if (storage.length > 0) { tasks = storage.split("|"); }
    }
    // if there are tasks in array, sort and create capitalized tasks
    if (tasks.length > 0) {
        var capitalized = tasks.sort().map(function(value){
            var first = value.substring(0,1);       // get first letter
            var remaining = value.substring(1);      // get remaining letters
            return first.toUpperCase() + remaining;   // capitalize
        });
    }
    // display capitalized tasks or empty string, set focus on task text box
    $("task_list").value = capitalized && capitalized.join("\n") || "";
    $("task").focus();
};

var addToTaskList = function() {
    var task = $("task");
    if (task.value === "") {
        alert("Please enter a task.");
    } else {
        // add task to array and local storage
        tasks.push(task.value);
        localStorage.tasks = tasks.join("|");

        // clear task text box and re-display tasks
        task.value = "";
        displayTaskList();
    }
};
var clearTaskList = function() {
    tasks.length = 0;
    localStorage.tasks = "";
    displayTaskList();
};
window.onload = function() {
    $("add_task").onclick = addToTaskList;
    $("clear_tasks").onclick = clearTaskList;
    displayTaskList();
};
```

Description

- This version of the application capitalizes the first letter of each task before displaying it in the browser. To do that, it uses the ECMAScript 5 map method of an array.

Figure 9-16   The JavaScript with an ECMAScript 5 enhancement

Perspective

Arrays are an important part of many JavaScript applications, and JavaScript provides some excellent methods for working with arrays. In the chapters that follow, you'll see other uses of arrays and other ways to work with them.

Terms

array	for-in loop
element	associative array
length	array of arrays
index	web storage
sparse array	local storage
for statement	session storage
for loop	name/value pair
for-in statement	

Summary

- An *array* can store one or more *elements*. The *length* of an array is the number of elements in the array. To refer to the elements in an array, you use an *index* where 0 is the index of the first element in the array.

- Both *for loops* and *for-in loops* can be used to work with the elements in an array. In contrast to a for loop, though, a for-in loop only accesses the elements in the array that are specifically assigned.

- JavaScript provides many methods for working with Array objects, including a set of methods that became available with ECMAScript 5.

- You can use the split method of a String object to create an array from substrings within a string.

- An *associative array* uses strings for the indexes instead of numbers.

- In an *array of arrays*, each element in one array is another array.

- Web storage comes in two types. *Local storage* remains indefinitely, while *session storage* is lost when the browser session ends. In either case, the data items are stored in *name/value pairs*.

- You can use Chrome's developer tools to view and edit the items that are in local and session storage.

Exercise 9-1   Enhance the Task Manager application

This exercise will give you a chance to work with arrays and web storage as you enhance the first version of the Task Manager application in this chapter. The enhanced version of the user interface has four new buttons and looks like this.

Open, test, and review this application

1. Use your text editor or IDE to open the HTML and JavaScript files in this folder:

   `c:\javascript\exercises\ch09\task_list\`

2. Test this application in Chrome by using the Add Task button to add tasks to the list and the Clear Tasks button to clear the list. Then, click on the other four buttons to learn that they don't do anything.

3. Press the F12 key to display the developer tools, and review the local storage items as shown in figure 9-13.

4. Review the JavaScript file for this application to see that there are several changes to the chapter application. First, there's another global variable named sortDirection with an initial value of "ASC". Second, there are four empty function expressions called deleteTask, toggleSort, setName, and filterTasks. Last, the onload event handler attaches these functions as the event handlers for the click events of the four new buttons.

Code the Delete Task event handler

5. Code the deleteTask function so it uses the prompt method to ask the user for the index number of the task to delete. Assume the entry is valid, and use the splice method of the tasks array to delete the element at the specified index. Then, use the join method and the pipe separator ("|") to create a string from the tasks array, update the localStorage value with the string, and call the displayTaskList function to re-display the tasks. Now, test this function.

6. Add data validation to this function so the user's entry has to be a number, but don't display a message if it isn't. Then, test this change to make sure that nothing is done if you enter an index value that isn't in the array or a value that isn't a number.

Code for the Toggle Sort event handler

7. Code the toggleSort function so it sets the value of the global sortDirection variable based its current value. So, if the current value is "ASC", change it to "DESC", and vice versa. You can do this using a conditional operator as described in chapter 8. Then, call the displayTaskList function to re-display the tasks in the page.

8. In the displayTaskList function, find the line of code that calls the tasks array's sort method, and comment it out. Below this line, add an if statement that checks the value of the sortDirection variable. If the value is "ASC", call the tasks array's sort method. Otherwise, call the tasks array's reverse method. Then, test this change.

Code the Set Name event handler

9. Code the setName function so it uses the prompt method to ask the user for a name. It should then store the name in session storage and call the display-TaskList function to re-display the tasks in the page.

10. In the displayTaskList function, add code that gets the name value from session storage or an empty string if there's nothing in session storage. Then, set the value of the span element with "name" as its id to either the name from session storage or an empty string if there's nothing in storage. If you're feeling fancy, add an apostrophe and s after the name as shown above.

11. Test this change by using the Set Name button. Then, press the F5 button to refresh the browser. Notice that the name you stored still shows above the task list. Now, close the browser, re-start the application, and note that the name you stored is gone because you used session storage.

Extra: Code the Filter Tasks event handler

12. This event handler is supposed to filter the items in the task list so only the items that contain "important!" or "Important!" are listed. To do that, start by coding a function called importantTasks that accepts a parameter called element. This function should (1) call the element's toLowerCase method and store the result in a variable called lower; (2) call lower's indexOf method and pass it the value "important!"; (3) store the result in a variable called index, and (4) return true or false based on whether the index is greater than -1.

13. In the filterTasks function, call the filter method of the tasks array, pass it the importantTasks function you just coded, and store the array that's returned in a variable called filtered. Then, use the join method of the filtered array and the newline character ("\n") to create a string, and set this string as the value of the task_list text area.

14. Test this change by adding one or more tasks that contain "Important!" or "important!". Then, click the Filter Tasks button to display only those tasks that contain one of those words. Now, click the Toggle Sort button again and notice that the tasks that were filtered out re-appear.

10

How to create and use functions

In chapter 4, you learned how to write simple functions and you've been using functions ever since. Now, this chapter reviews some of the skills you already know and presents additional skills that you need to know. As you will see, JavaScript treats all functions as objects, and you're going to learn how to use one of the properties and three of the methods of a function object.

As you read this chapter, keep in mind three of the reasons for using functions. First, functions provide a way to divide the code of an application into manageable blocks. Second, functions let you re-use code by writing it once and then using it in multiple places. Third, functions make it easier to update code because you'll only need to change it in one place.

Basic skills for working with functions

This topic reviews the basic skills that you've already learned for working with functions. Then, it adds some new perspective and skills to those basics.

How to create and call a function

Figure 10-1 shows two ways to create a function. The first way is the one that you've been using. It assigns a *function expression* to a variable. This kind of function is sometimes called an *anonymous function* because usually a function expression doesn't have a name. It is possible, though, to name a function expression. In this example, the function is stored in a variable named displayError and that name is used to call the function.

When you declare a function expression, you can pass the declaration as a parameter to another function without having to store it. As you will learn in the next chapter, you can also store a function expression as a property of an object so it is treated as a method. The one restriction on the use of function expressions is that you must declare them in your code before you can call them, as illustrated in figure 10-3.

The second way to create a function is to code a *function declaration*, which creates a *named function* without assigning it to a variable. The one advantage of this is that you can place your function declaration anywhere in the code. For instance, you can call the function at the start of the code, but place the declaration at the end of the code. Otherwise, this method works the same as storing a function expression in a variable.

The *parameter* list in a function lets you specify variable names for the arguments that will be passed to the function. In this figure, the coinToss function expects no parameters, so its list is empty, but the avgOf3 function expects three parameters named x, y, and z.

When you *call* (or *invoke*)a function, you code the name of the function and a set of parentheses that contains a list of the parameters that you're passing to the function. If no parameters are required, you code an empty set of parentheses.

If a function returns a value, you can use the function call as if it were the value it returns. But if the function doesn't return a value or your code is going to ignore the return value, you can place the function call on a line by itself.

Please note that when you call a function, the parameters are commonly referred to as *arguments* instead of parameters. In other words, you code a parameter list when you declare a function, but you code an argument list when you call a function. From this point forward, then, you'll see these terms used in this way. In practice, though, *parameter* and *argument* are commonly treated as synonyms.

Two ways to create a function

How to create a function expression

```
var displayError = function( message ) {
    alert("Error: " + message);
};
```

How to create a function declaration

```
function isEven ( value ) {
    return value % 2 == 0;
}
```

How to specify parameters in a function

A function with no parameters

```
var coinToss = function() {
    return ( Math.random() > 0.5 ) ? "Heads" : "Tails";
};
```

A function with three parameters

```
var avgOf3 = function( x, y, z ) {
    return ( x + y + z ) / 3;
};
```

How to call a function

Calling a function that returns a value

```
var average = avgOf3( 5, 2, 8 );       // average is equal to 5
alert( coinToss() );                   // displays "Heads" or "Tails"
```

Calling a function that doesn't explicitly return a value

```
displayError("Value out of range");
```

Description

- A *function expression* is a function that's assigned to a variable as part of a statement. When the function in a function expression doesn't have a name, it is sometimes called an *anonymous function*.

- A *function declaration* is a function that is declared and given a name.

- If a function requires that one or more values be passed to it, a list of *parameters* is coded within the parentheses for the function.

- When you *call* (or *invoke*) a function, you code a list of the parameters that will be passed to the function. When they're passed, parameters are commonly referred to as *arguments*.

- All functions return a value. If a function isn't ended by a return statement, the function returns a value of undefined.

- A function call may be used anywhere its return value could be used. Typically, it will be stored in a variable, used in an expression, or passed as a parameter to another function.

- In non-strict mode, you can use duplicate names in the parameter list. If you do, when you refer to the parameter name in the function body, it will use the last one.

- In strict mode, you will get a syntax error if you use duplicate names in the parameter list, which tells you that you shouldn't do that.

Figure 10-1   How to create and call a function

How values are passed to functions

When you pass a number, string, or Boolean value to a function, it is *passed by value*. This means that a copy of the value is sent to the function, not the value itself. As a result, the function can't change the original value.

This is illustrated by the first example in figure 10-2. Here, a string named message is passed by value to the addTimestamp function. Then, this function concatenates a date and time to the string and displays the entire string, which shows that the argument has been changed. However, as the last statement in this example shows, the original message string was never changed because a copy of the string was passed to the function.

In contrast to the primitive types, when you pass an object to a function, it is *passed by reference*. This means that a reference to the object is sent to the function instead of a copy of the object. Then, the function changes the object that the reference identifies. As a result, those changes will persist after the function has finished.

This is illustrated by the second example in this figure. Here, an array is passed by reference to the uppercaseFirst function. Then, this function converts the letters in the first element of the array to uppercase by using the toUpperCase function of a string. In this example, the last statement displays the first element of the original array, which shows that the original array has been changed.

A primitive type is passed to a function by value

A function that receives a string, adds a timestamp to it, and displays it

```
var addTimestamp = function( text ) {
    var now = new Date();
    text = text + " " + now.toString();
    alert(text);
};
```

Code that calls the function and passes a string argument

```
var message = "Error: Value out of range.";
addTimestamp(message);     // displays message and timestamp
```

Code that displays the value that was passed to the function

```
alert(message);              // message hasn't been changed
```

An object is passed to a function by reference

A function that receives an array and changes its first element

```
var uppercaseFirst = function( x ) {
    x[0] = x[0].toUpperCase();
};
```

Code that calls the function and passes an array argument

```
var fruits = [ "apple", "orange" ];
uppercaseFirst(fruits);
```

Code that displays the first element in the array that's passed to the function

```
alert( fruits[0] );        // displays "APPLE" so the array has been changed
```

Description

- The *primitive types* are numbers, strings, and Booleans.

- When a primitive type is passed to a function, it is *passed by value*. This means that a copy of the value is sent to the function. As a result, the function changes the copy, not the original value.

- When an object is passed to a function, it is *passed by reference*. This means that a reference to the object, not the object itself, is sent to the function. As a result, when the function changes the object, it is actually changing the original object.

Figure 10-2   How values are passed to functions

How lexical scope works

Scope in a programming language refers to the visibility of variables and functions. That is, it tells you where in your program you are allowed to use the variables and functions that you've defined. JavaScript uses *lexical scoping* to determine where you can access variables and functions.

Lexical scope is sometimes referred to as *static scope*, because it doesn't change when the program runs. This means that you can tell a variable's scope by looking at where it is in the code. Conversely, *dynamic scope* can change when the program runs.

With JavaScript's lexical scope, *global variables* are variables that are defined outside of functions. These variables have *global scope* so they can be used by any function without passing them to that function. In contrast, *local variables* are variables that are defined within functions. They have *local scope*, which means that they can only be used within the functions that define them.

The first example in figure 10-3 illustrates the use of global and local variables. Here, the displayMessage function displays the contents of a global variable named message. But if that variable hasn't been defined, it creates a local variable named message1 and then displays that variable.

The code that follows first calls the displayMessage function. But since the message variable hasn't been defined, the function creates the local variable named message1 and displays that. Next, the code creates a global variable named message and calls the displayMessage function to display it. This shows that a function has access to all global variables. Last, the code tries to display the message1 variable from outside the function. This, however, causes a runtime error, which shows that local variables aren't available outside of the function that defines them.

Another feature of JavaScript is that function declarations can be called before they are defined. That's because the JavaScript engine scans your code before it executes it and creates the function declarations first. Then, it goes back and starts executing your code from the beginning. This is illustrated by the second example in this figure.

In contrast, function expressions can't be called before they are defined. Instead, they are treated by the JavaScript engine just like any other expression. This is illustrated by the third example in this figure. In this case, the code will cause a runtime error because the function hasn't been created yet.

If you've programmed in other languages, you may be familiar with *block scope*. In block scope, variables that are created within blocks of code aren't available outside the blocks. With JavaScript, though, this isn't true, as shown by the fourth example in this figure. Here, the canVote variable that's defined within the block of code in the if clause is available outside of that block.

Global and local scope

A function that creates a local variable and displays a global variable

```
var displayMessage = function() {
    if ( message == undefined ) {
        var message1 = "Unknown message.";   // message1 has local scope
        alert ( message1 ); }
    else { alert(message); }                 // displays a global variable
};
```

All functions have access to global variables

```
displayMessage();           // Displays "Unknown message."
var message = "Index out of range.";         // message has global scope
displayMessage();           // Displays "Index out of range."
```

Local variables are only available to the function that defines them

```
alert ( message1 );         // Runtime error: message1 isn't defined
```

Function declarations are created before any code is executed

```
alert( coinToss() );        // Displays Heads or Tails
function coinToss() {
    return (Math.random() > 0.5) ? "Heads" : "Tails";
};
```

Function expressions are created in sequence when the code is executed

```
alert( coinToss() );        // Runtime error: coinToss is not a function
var coinToss = function() {
    return (Math.random() > 0.5) ? "Heads" : "Tails";
};
```

Variables created inside a block of code can be used outside the block

```
if ( age >= 18 ) {
    var canVote = "Yes";
    alert ( canVote );
}
alert( "Voting status: " + canVote );        // canVote is available
```

Description

- The *scope* of a variable or function determines what code has access to it. JavaScript uses *lexical scope*, as opposed to *dynamic scope*. This means that you can determine the scope of a variable or function by looking at where it is in the code.

- Any variable created outside of a function has *global scope*, and the code inside a function has access to these *global variables*.

- Any variable created inside a function has *local scope*, and the code outside a function doesn't have access to these *local variables*.

- Because all function declarations are created before any code runs, you can call a function declaration before it is defined.

- Because function expressions are created when the code is executed, a runtime error occurs if the call to a function expression comes before the function is created.

- Variables that are created within blocks of code are available outside the blocks.

Figure 10-3   How lexical scope works

How to create and use JavaScript libraries

One of the main benefits of functions is code re-use. This is because you can write a function once and then call that function from several different places in your code. But what if you want to use the function in other applications as well? Or, what if you have a lot of functions doing a lot of things, and you find it confusing?

This is where JavaScript *libraries* come in. A library is a just a group of related functions, objects, or both that you keep in an external file. Often, you will write your own libraries, but you can also use third-party libraries like the ones in the table in figure 10-4.

When you create a library, you help keep your JavaScript files smaller, which makes them easier to understand and easier to re-use. For example, you can write a library that provides the functions for working with web storage. Since that's all it does, it will be small. Then, you can include that file with any applications that need to use web storage. In fact, you'll see such a library shortly.

The example below the table in this figure shows how to include JavaScript libraries for an application. Since a JavaScript library is just a JavaScript file, you use the same script tags that you've been using throughout this book. The first script tag in this example refers to a custom library that works with web storage, and the one after that refers to a custom library that works with the tasks in a task list. The last script tag is for the JavaScript file that uses the libraries and drives the way the application works.

When you include JavaScript library files in this way, you need to think about the order in which you include them. Specifically, if one library depends on the functionality in another library, you need to include the libraries in the proper order. For example, the jQuery UI library uses the functionality in the jQuery library. So when you use jQuery UI, you not only need to make sure that you include jQuery, but also that the script tag for jQuery UI comes after the script tag for jQuery. The same goes for working with your own libraries.

Some popular JavaScript libraries

Library	Purpose
jQuery	General-purpose, cross-browser functionality for DOM scripting.
jQuery UI	User interface functionality like tabs and accordions. It requires the jQuery library.
AngularJS	Framework for Single-Page Applications (SPAs).
Underscore	Utility functions for common programming tasks.
Backbone	Framework for SPAs based on the Model View Presenter design pattern.
shim.js, sham.js	ECMAScript 5 compatibility for older browsers.

How to include JavaScript libraries in your application

```
<head>
    <title>Ch10 Task Manager</title>
    <link type="text/css" rel="stylesheet" href="task_list.css">
    <script type="text/javascript" src="library_storage.js"></script>
    <script type="text/javascript" src="library_tasklist.js"></script>
    <script type="text/javascript" src="task_list.js"></script>
</head>
```

The benefits of JavaScript libraries

- Allows you to group similar functionality in a single file.
- Makes code easier to understand, maintain, and reuse.

Description

- A JavaScript *library* is an external file that contains related functions, objects, or both.
- JavaScript libraries range from simple collections of functions that you write yourself to extensive third-party tools like jQuery.
- Organizing your code in libraries encourages *separation of concerns*, which makes it easier to maintain and reuse code.
- A JavaScript library is normal JavaScript, so you create a library by grouping related functions and objects in a single file. You should also name your JavaScript libraries so it's clear what they do.
- You include JavaScript libraries in your applications by using script tags. If a library depends on another library, you must make sure that the script tag for the needed library precedes the one for the library that uses it.

Figure 10-4   How to create and use JavaScript libraries

The Task Manager application

The Task Manager application is similar to the one you saw in the last chapter. It accepts tasks from the user and displays them in a list. It also stores the tasks in local storage so they will persist after the user closes their browser.

This Task Manager application has two main differences, though. First, it adds the ability to delete individual tasks. Second, it uses functions and function libraries to organize its code.

The HTML and CSS

Figure 10-5 presents the user interface for the Task Manager application. This application lets the user add a task, delete a task, and clear all tasks. It also saves the tasks to local storage, so they persist between browser sessions.

The HTML for this application is similar to what you've seen throughout this book, but there are a few points of interest. First, the head section has script tags for three JavaScript files instead of one. The first file is for a library that works with web storage. The second is for a library that works with the task list. The third is for the main JavaScript file that uses the functions in these libraries

When the page is loaded into the browser, the JavaScript in these files is loaded into the browser in the sequence in which the files are listed. The result is the same as if all of the JavaScript was stored in a single file.

Second, the main section contains a div element with an id attribute of "tasks". This is where the JavaScript code will load the tasks in the task list, and this element will be floated to the right of the text box and buttons that follow. Then, after the buttons, there is another div element with no id attribute but a class attribute of "clear". The CSS for this element will stop the floating of the first div element.

The CSS snippet below the HTML in this figure shows the rule sets for the "tasks" id and the "clear" class. Here, you can see that the tasks rule set floats the tasks div to the right. It also sets its width, margins, and padding, and it puts a border around it.

This is followed by a CSS rule set for the <a> elements within the tasks div. This rule set contains only one rule, which adds some space to the right of the <a> element. You can see this in the user interface in this figure. Note, however, that there aren't any <a> elements in the HTML for the tasks div element. These are added by the JavaScript code along with the tasks in the task list.

Last, the rule set for the "clear" class sets the CSS clear property to "both". This clears the floating of the elements that precede it. If you omit this rule set, the border of the main element won't expand as tasks are added to the task list.

The user interface for the Task Manager application

Task Manager

Task:

[   ]

[Add Task   ]

[Clear Tasks   ]

Delete Finish current project

Delete Meet with Mike

Delete Write project summary

The HTML for the application

```
<!DOCTYPE html>
<html>
<head>
    <title>Ch10 Task Manager</title>
    <link type="text/css" rel="stylesheet" href="task_list.css">
    <script type="text/javascript" src="library_storage.js"></script>
    <script type="text/javascript" src="library_tasklist.js"></script>
    <script type="text/javascript" src="task_list.js"></script>
</head>
<body>
    <main>
        <h1>Task Manager</h1>
        <div id="tasks"></div>
        <label for="task">Task:</label><br>
            <input type="text" name="task" id="task"><br>
        <input type="button" name="add_task" id="add_task"
            value="Add Task"><br>
        <input type="button" name="clear_tasks" id="clear_tasks"
            value="Clear Tasks">
        <div class="clear"></div>
    </main>
</body>
</html>
```

Some of the CSS for the application

```
#tasks {
    float: right;
    width: 25em;
    margin: 0 0 .5em;
    padding: 1em;
    border: 2px solid black;
}
#tasks a {
    margin-right: 0.5em;
}
.clear {
    clear: both;
}
```

Description

- Like the chapter 9 application, this application lets you store tasks in local storage and manage a task list. This application also lets you delete individual tasks.

Figure 10-5   The HTML and CSS for the Task Manager application

The storage library

Figure 10-6 shows the JavaScript library file that contains functions for working with items in local storage. Most of the code in these functions should look familiar to you, since it is similar to the code in the Task Manager application of the last chapter.

The first function, getStorage, accepts a key parameter and returns an array. It uses the key parameter to retrieve the associated item from local storage and store it in a variable named storage. Note that it uses the OR operator to return a default value of an empty string if the item isn't in local storage.

After retrieving the value from local storage, the function checks the storage variable. If it contains an empty string, the function returns an empty array object. Otherwise, it uses the split method of the String object and the pipe separator to create an array and then returns that array.

The second function, setStorage, accepts a key parameter and an array parameter. It uses the isArray method of the Array object to make sure that the second parameter is an array. If it isn't, the function does nothing. If it is, the function uses the join method of the Array object and the pipe separator to create a string. Then, it uses the setItem method of the localStorage object to add the string to local storage. Since this function doesn't use the return keyword, it returns a value of undefined, but that value isn't used by this application.

The third function, clearStorage, accepts a key parameter. It uses the setItem method of the localStorage object to set the string in local storage to an empty string. Since this function doesn't use the return keyword either, it returns a value of undefined that isn't used by this application.

Note that all the functions are general in that they don't know what they're storing. They're just focused on getting items to and from local storage, and on transforming local storage items from strings to arrays and back again. A general library like this is sometimes called a *utility* library, and could easily be used for any application that needs to store strings in local storage.

The library_storage.js file

```
var getStorage = function(key) {
    //get string from storage or an empty string if nothing in storage
    var storage = localStorage.getItem(key) || "";
    if (storage === "") {
        return [];
    } else {
        return storage.split("|");
    }
};

var setStorage = function(key, arr) {
    if (Array.isArray(arr)) {
        var storageString = arr.join("|");
        localStorage.setItem(key, storageString);
    }
};

var clearStorage = function(key) {
    localStorage.setItem(key, "");
};
```

Description

- The functions in this library focus on getting values into and out of local storage.

- Because the functions are general, you could re-use this library for any application that needs to access local storage. A general-purpose library like this is sometimes called a *utility* library.

Figure 10-6   The storage library used by the Task Manager application

The task list library

Figure 10-7 shows the task list library that contains the functions for working with and displaying tasks in the task list. Here, the first function, sortTaskList, accepts an array parameter named tasks. Then, it uses the isArray method of the Array object to make sure that the tasks argument that's passed to it is an array. If it is, this function calls the sort method of the array. Last, this function returns the value from the isArray method call, which is a true or false value.

The second function, displaySortedTaskList, accepts an array parameter, a div parameter, and an event handler parameter. It starts by declaring a variable called html and setting it to an empty string. Then, it passes the tasks array to the sortTaskList function to sort the tasks. Remember that this function returns a Boolean value that indicates whether the object that's passed to it is an array. The displaySortedTaskList function uses this return value to determine how to proceed.

If the tasks argument that was passed to it is an array, the function loops through it and constructs an HTML string that puts each task in the array in a <p> element. It also puts an <a> element within each <p> element. The href attribute for each <a> element has a placeholder value of "#", and the id attribute is given the value of the index of the task item in the array. As you'll see in the next figure, this is how the application knows which task to delete. After creating the HTML string, this function uses the innerHTML property of the element in the div parameter to display the tasks in the browser.

Next, this function adds event handlers to the <a> tags it just created. To do that, it first uses the div's getElementsByTagName method to get all the <a> tags in the div. Then, it loops through the <a> tags and assigns the function in the handler parameter of this function as the link's click event handler. In the next figure, you'll see how these div and handler arguments are passed.

The third function, deleteTask, accepts an array parameter and an index parameter. It also starts by using the sortTaskList function to sort the tasks and then using the return value of that function to determine how to proceed. If the tasks argument is an array, it removes the element at the specified index using the splice method of the array.

The fourth function, capitalizeTask, accepts a string parameter and returns a string. This function starts by using the substring method to get the first letter of the task string. Then, in the return statement, it uses the toUpperCase method of a string to capitalize the first letter, the substring method to get the remaining letters, and the plus operator to concatenate the two.

Note that these functions aren't as general as the ones in the storage library. Instead, they are specific to the Task Manager application. This means that you probably wouldn't re-use this library with other applications. Still, it's good to group the task list functions together like this, because that makes the application easier to modify.

When working with a project-specific library like this one, though, you sometimes find that you can re-use some of its functions. For example, you might want to re-use the capitalize or sort method in this library. In that case, you may want to move the functions to a utility library so it's easier to re-use them.

The library_tasklist.js file

```
var sortTaskList = function(tasks) {
    var isArray = Array.isArray(tasks);
    if (isArray) {
        tasks.sort();
    }
    return isArray;
};

var displaySortedTaskList = function(tasks, div, handler) {
    var html = "";
    var isArray = sortTaskList(tasks);

    if (isArray) {
        //create and load html string from sorted array
        for (var i in tasks) {
            html = html.concat("<p>");
            html = html.concat("<a href='#' id='", i, "'>Delete</a>");
            html = html.concat(tasks[i]);
            html = html.concat("</p>");
        }
        div.innerHTML = html;

        // get links, loop and add onclick event handler
        var links = div.getElementsByTagName("a");
        for (var i = 0; i < links.length; i++) {
            links[i].onclick = handler;
        }
    }
};

var deleteTask = function(tasks, i) {
    var isArray = sortTaskList(tasks);
    if (isArray) { tasks.splice(i, 1); }
};

var capitalizeTask = function(task) {
    var first = task.substring(0,1);
    return first.toUpperCase() + task.substring(1);
};
```

Description

- The functions in this library focus on working with the tasks the user enters in the Task Manager application.

- Unlike the storage library, which is more general, this library is specific to the Task Manager application and probably wouldn't be re-used in other applications.

- However, the capitalizeTask function is a more general function, so you might want to move it from this specific library to a utility library.

Figure 10-7   The task list library for the Task Manager application

The main JavaScript file

Figure 10-8 shows the main JavaScript file for this application As usual, it starts with the $ function. Then, it creates a global tasks variable and initializes it as an empty array. This is followed by five functions.

The displayTaskList function updates the tasks div to display the current tasks. It is called by the other functions in this page. First, it checks whether the tasks array has any elements. If it doesn't, the function calls the getStorage function in the storage library to get an array of tasks. Here, the key that's used is "tasks_10" to distinguish it from the keys that later versions of this application use.

Then, this function passes three arguments to the displaySortedTaskList function of the tasklist library to load the tasks. First, it passes the array of tasks. Next, it passes the div element with an id of "tasks". Finally, it passes the function named deleteFromTaskList, which is the event handler that will be attached to the Delete links. This might look funny to you, but functions are objects, and that means they can be passed as arguments to other functions. The displayTaskList function ends by setting the focus on the task text box.

The addToTaskList function gets the task entered by the user and adds it to both the global tasks array and to local storage. First, it retrieves the text box element for the task entered by the user and checks it to make sure the user has entered something into it. If not, the function notifies the user.

If the user did enter a task, the function calls the capitalizeTask function in the tasklist library to capitalize the task entered by the user, and then calls the task array's push method to add the capitalized task to the array. Next, it calls the setStorage function from the storage library, and passes it a key value and the tasks array. Finally, it clears the task text box and calls the displayTaskList function described above.

The deleteFromTaskList function is the one you just saw passed as an argument to the displaySortedTaskList function of the task list library. This deleteFromTaskList function deletes a task from local storage, and it's called when the user clicks on the Delete link described in the last figure.

First, this function passes the tasks array and the index of the task to delete to the deleteTask function of the task list library. Note that it gets the index of the task to delete from the function's this keyword, which in this case is the link that was clicked. Then, it calls the setStorage function of the storage library to save the updated task list, and it calls the displayTaskList function to display the updated task list. In a moment, you'll learn more about using the this keyword.

The clearTaskList function clears the tasks from the tasks array and local storage. It is called when the user clicks the Clear button. First, it sets the tasks array's length property to zero. Then, it calls the clearStorage function of the storage library. Finally, it clears the innerHTML property of the tasks div element and sets the focus on the task text box.

The last function is the event handler for the onload event. First, this function assigns the addToTaskList and clearTaskList functions to the click events of the add_task and clear_task buttons. Then, it calls the displayTaskList function. This makes sure that anything in local storage is displayed when the application starts.

The task_list.js file

```javascript
var $ = function(id) { return document.getElementById(id); };
var tasks = [];

var displayTaskList = function() {
    // get tasks from storage
    if (tasks.length === 0) {
        tasks = getStorage("tasks_10");
    }
    // display sorted tasks with delete links
    displaySortedTaskList(tasks, $("tasks"), deleteFromTaskList);

    // set focus on task text box
    $("task").focus();
};

var addToTaskList = function() {
    var task = $("task");
    if (task.value === "") {
        alert("Please enter a task.");
    } else {
        tasks.push(capitalizeTask(task.value));
        setStorage("tasks_10", tasks);

        task.value = "";
        displayTaskList();
    }
};

var deleteFromTaskList = function() {
    deleteTask(tasks, this.id); // 'this' = clicked link
    setStorage("tasks_10", tasks);
    displayTaskList();
};

var clearTaskList = function() {
    tasks.length = 0;
    clearStorage("tasks_10");
    $("tasks").innerHTML = "";
    $("task").focus();
};

window.onload = function() {
    $("add_task").onclick = addToTaskList;
    $("clear_tasks").onclick = clearTaskList;
    displayTaskList();
};
```

Description

- The main JavaScript file for this application calls many of the functions defined in the storage and task list libraries. This makes the code easier to read and understand.

- Another benefit of this structure is that it's easier to make changes. For example, if you decide you want to store tasks in session storage or one of the HTML5 web databases, you won't have to change anything here. You'll only need to adjust the storage library.

Figure 10-8   The main JavaScript file for the Task Manager application

Object-oriented skills for working with functions

In JavaScript, all functions are objects. This means that functions have properties and methods, just like other objects. In this topic, you'll learn how to use one property and three methods of a function object. Note, however, that much of this applies to functions that are used as object methods, so you'll have a better perspective on these skills after you read the next chapter.

How to use the arguments property of a function

When you call a function in JavaScript, the arguments are stored in the parameter list of the function. This is similar to other programming languages. What sets JavaScript apart, however, is that the parameters are also stored in the arguments property of the function object.

This arguments property is similar to an array. Within this property, each of the arguments that was passed to the function is stored in an element starting with index 0. Then, you can access these elements by using indexes.

Note, however, that the arguments property isn't a true array object, so you can't use the properties and methods of an array that you learned about in the last chapter. The good news is that you're going to learn a way around this.

The first example in figure 10-9 shows how to use the arguments property to access an argument that's passed to a function. Here, the element at index 0 in the arguments property is used in an expression that returns true if the argument is divisible by 2 with no remainder.

The second example shows how to use the length property of the arguments property to determine the number of arguments passed to a function. Here, the countArgs function just displays the number of arguments that are passed to it.

One of the benefits that you get from using the arguments property is that you can create functions that can receive fewer arguments than the parameter list calls for. This lets you create functions with optional parameters.

This is illustrated by the third example. Here, the padLeft function lists three parameters, but the last parameter is optional. To provide for that, the function first checks to make sure that at least two arguments are passed to it. If not, an empty string is returned. Next, if the function received only two arguments, the third parameter (pad) is set to a space character. Last, the function uses a while loop to add the pad character to the text argument while the length of that string is less than the width argument. Then, the function returns the padded text.

By using the arguments property, a function can also process more arguments than the parameter list calls for. This is illustrated by the fourth example. Here, the function has no parameters in its list, but it will calculate the average of all of the arguments that are passed to it.

A function that uses the arguments property to get an argument

```
var isEven = function() {
    return arguments[0] % 2 === 0;
};
```

How to determine the number of arguments that have been passed

```
var countArgs = function() {
    alert( "Number of arguments: " + arguments.length );
};

countArgs( 1, "Text", true );          // Displays "Number of arguments: 3"
```

Calling a function with fewer arguments than the named parameters

```
var padLeft = function(text, width, pad) {
    if ( arguments.length <  2 ) return "";
    if ( arguments.length == 2 ) pad = " ";
    while( text.length < width ) {
        text = pad + text;
    }
    return text;
};

alert( "Welcome to " + padLeft("JavaScript", 15) );
// Displays "Welcome to     JavaScript"
```

Calling a function with more arguments than the named parameters

```
var average = function() {
    if ( arguments.length == 0 ) return 0;
    var sum = 0;
    for ( var i = 0; i < arguments.length; i++) {
        sum += arguments[i];
    }
    return sum / arguments.length;
};

alert ( average(8, 15, 5, 10) );        // Displays 9.5
```

Description

- In JavaScript, all functions are objects, and all of the arguments passed to a function are stored in the arguments property of the function object.

- The arguments property is similar to an array, so you can use an index to access its elements. However, the arguments property isn't a true array, so you can't use the array methods of chapter 9 with it.

- If a function uses the arguments property to get the arguments that are passed to it, the calling statement can pass more or fewer arguments than the parameter list specifies.

Figure 10-9   How to use the arguments property of a function

How to use the this keyword and the call and apply methods

When a function is invoked, it has an internal parameter that can be referred to by the *this* keyword. As the second table in figure 10-10 shows, the value of the this keyword depends on how the function is invoked. In an event handler, for example, the this keyword refers to the object that raised the event, like an \<a> element that has been clicked.

When you invoke a function by its call or apply method, though, you can use the first argument to specify the object that you want to use for the this keyword. To illustrate, the first example in this figure is a thisTest function. Its if statement checks whether the function was invoked normally, and displays a message if it was. Otherwise, the else clause displays the value of the this keyword.

The second example in this figure consists of statements that use the call and apply methods to invoke the thisTest function. Here, the first statement calls the thisTest function in the normal way so the this keyword is equivalent to the window object or undefined. But the second statement uses the call method of the thisTest function to invoke it with a first parameter that sets the this parameter to a string. As a result, the thisTest function displays the string, which is "Test String".

Similarly, the third statement uses the apply method of the thisTest function to invoke the function with a first parameter that changes the this parameter to a number. As a result, the function displays 456.72.

With both the call and the apply methods, you use the first argument to specify the object for the this keyword. And with both methods, you can pass any other arguments the function might need. The difference is in how the other arguments are passed. With the call method, you pass the arguments in a comma separated list, but with the apply method, you pass them in an array.

One use of the call and apply methods is to borrow functionality from other objects. For instance, recall from the last figure that the arguments property of a function isn't a true array, so it doesn't have many of the useful array methods. But you can borrow these methods by using their call and apply methods.

The last example in this figure shows how this is done. Here, the code presents a function called sortAndDisplay, which accepts a variable number of arguments, sorts them, and then displays them as a comma-separated string. To do this, it borrows the Array object's sort and join methods by using the Array object's prototype object. You'll learn more about object prototypes in the next chapter, but the point here is the use of the call methods.

Specifically, the code invokes the array methods by using their call methods and passing the function's arguments property, plus any other arguments the borrowed function needs. Since the arguments property is the first argument passed to the call method, it will be the value of the borrowed method's this keyword. Then, since the arguments property is an array-like object that has a length property, the borrowed array methods will function correctly with it.

The this keyword

Keyword	Description
`this`	Refers to an internal parameter of a function. Its value depends on how it's invoked.

The value of the this keyword

How function is invoked	Value of this
Normal function	Global object (window) in non-strict mode; undefined in strict mode.
As a method of an object	The object that contains the function (e.g., the Array object).
As an event handler	The object that raised the event (e.g, the button that was clicked).
By the call or apply method	The first argument sent to the call or apply method.

A function that uses the this keyword

```
var thisTest = function() {
    if (this === window || this === undefined) {
        alert( "Called normally." );
    } else { alert( this ); }
};
```

How to invoke the thisTest function using the call and apply methods

```
thisTest();                      // Displays "Called normally."
thisTest.call("Test String");    // Displays "Test String"
thisTest.apply(456.72);          // Displays 456.72
```

How to use the call method to borrow methods from another object

```
var sortAndDisplay = function() {
    Array.prototype.sort.call(arguments);
    return Array.prototype.join.call(arguments, ", ");
};
sortAndDisplay("Charles", "Grace", "Alan", "Ada");
// Ada, Alan, Charles, Grace
```

Description

- All functions have a *this* keyword, but its value depends on how the function is invoked.

- The call and apply methods of a function let you invoke the function and also set the value of the function's this keyword by sending it as the first argument.

- The call and apply methods also have optional parameters for sending other arguments to the function. The difference is that the call method sends these arguments as a comma-separated string, and the apply method sends them in an array. To help you remember the difference, you can think of each method's first letter: "c" for comma, "a" for array.

Figure 10-10   How to use the this keyword and the call and apply methods

How to use the bind method to set the this keyword

The call and apply methods of a function let you specify the value of the this keyword when you invoke the function. Sometimes, though, you want to specify the value of the this keyword when you code or assign the function. To do this, you can use a function's bind method to create a *bound function.*

The first group of examples in figure 10-11 shows how to specify the value of the this keyword when you code a function. It presents the thisTest function from the last figure, but it's re-written with the bind method of the function setting the value of the this keyword.

Once the function is bound in this way, you can't change the value of the this keyword when you invoke it. You can see this in the three statements that call the thisTest function, which are just like those in the last figure. This time, though, the value of the this keyword for the function remains the object that's passed in the bind method. The values sent in with the call and apply methods are ignored.

This use of the bind method is often used when working with closures, which you'll learn about in section 3. But another common use of the bind method is when you're assigning a method of an object as an event handler. The next group of examples illustrate this.

Recall from the last figure that the value of the this keyword depends on how a function is invoked. For instance, when a function is used as an event handler, the value of the this keyword is the object that raised the event, such as the button that was clicked. Sometimes, though, that isn't what you want.

To illustrate, the next group of examples starts with the code for a circle object. You won't learn how to create an object like this until the next chapter, but accept for now that this object has pi and radius properties, a getRadius method that gets a new radius value, and a calculateArea method that calculates the circle's area. Each of these methods uses the this keyword to refer to the properties of the circle object.

Now, if you assign the circle object's methods as event handlers for buttons, as shown in the next example, the methods won't work properly. That's because the value of the this keyword will be the clicked button, which doesn't have either a pi or a radius property. As a result, the getRadius method adds a radius property to the button that raised the event, and the calculateArea method displays NaN.

However, if you use the bind method and pass the circle object as the argument, as in the next example, you can use the object's methods as event handlers. That's because, when you call each method's bind method, you're telling it to use the circle object as the value of this, rather than the clicked button. Thus, the getRadius method correctly updates the circle object's radius property, and the calculateArea method correctly displays the circle's area.

How to use the bind method to set the this keyword for a function

```
var thisTest = function() {
    if (this === window || this === undefined) {
        alert( "Called normally." );
    } else { alert( this ); }
}.bind("Can't change this");
```

What happens when you call a bound function using call and apply

```
thisTest();                          // Displays: Can't change this
thisTest.call("Test String");        // Displays: Can't change this
thisTest.apply(456.72);              // Displays: Can't change this
```

How to use the bind method to set the this keyword for an event handler

A circle object with properties and methods

```
var circle = {
    pi: 3.1415926535,
    radius: 1.0, //default radius
    getRadius: function() {
        this.radius = parseFloat(prompt("Enter radius"));
    },
    calculateArea: function() {
        alert (this.radius * this.radius * this.pi);
    }
};
```

Without the bind method, 'this' refers to the button that was clicked

```
// getRadius will add a radius property to the radius button
// calculateArea will return NaN because the calc button doesn't have radius
// or pi properties
window.onload = function() {
    $("radius").onclick = circle.getRadius;
    $("calc").onclick = circle.calculateArea;
};
```

With the bind method, 'this' refers to the circle object

```
// getRadius will correctly update the value of the radius property
// calculateArea will correctly calculate the circle's area
window.onload = function() {
    $("radius").onclick = circle.getRadius.bind(circle);
    $("calc").onclick = circle.calculateArea.bind(circle);
};
```

Description

- The bind method lets you specify the value of the this keyword at the time you code or assign the function. A function coded or assigned in this way is called a *bound function*.

- The first parameter in the bind method is the value of the this keyword for the function, and it is required. After that, you can include an optional parameter list.

- The value of the this keyword in a bound function can't be changed later, even when you invoke the function using the call or apply methods described in the last figure.

- The bind method is in the shim.js file described in figure 1-17. This means that you can use this method with older browsers as long as you include the shim.js file.

Figure 10-11   How to use the bind method to set the this keyword

Perspective

Now that you have completed this chapter, you should have the basic skills that you need for using functions. For instance, you should understand how primitive variables and objects are passed to a function and how lexical scope works. And you should understand how libraries can be used to group related functions and organize your code.

Beyond that, though, you've learned some advanced skills that play a central role in JavaScript's object-oriented architecture. In fact, it is through functions that JavaScript creates new types of objects. And you'll learn all about that in the next chapter.

Terms

function expression	static scope
anonymous function	dynamic scope
function declaration	global scope
named function	global variable
parameter	local scope
call a function	local variable
invoke a function	block scope
argument	library file
primitive type	third-party library
passed by value	separation of concerns
passed by reference	utility library
scope	this keyword
lexical scope	bound function

Summary

- A *function expression* is a function that's assigned to a variable. A function expression has to be coded before any statements that call it.

- A *function declaration* is a function that is declared and given a name. A function declaration doesn't have to be coded before statements that call it.

- If a function requires that one or more values be passed to it, you code a list of *parameters* for the function. Then, when you *call* (or *invoke*) the function, you code a list of the parameters that will be passed to the function. In a calling statement, the parameters are commonly referred to as *arguments*.

- When a primitive type is passed to a function, it is *passed by value*. When an object is passed to a function, it is *passed by reference*.

- Any variables created outside of a function have *global scope*, and all functions can access these *global variables*. Any variables created inside a function have *local scope*, and code outside the function can't access these *local variables*.

- A JavaScript *library* is an external file that contains related functions, objects, or both. You include a library in a page by coding a script element for it. If one library depends on another library, you must make sure that the script element for the needed library precedes the one for the library that uses it.

- In JavaScript, all functions are objects, and all of the arguments passed to a function are stored in the arguments property of the function object. Since the arguments property is similar to an array, you can use an index to access its elements.

- All functions have a *this* keyword, but its value depends on how the function is invoked. The call and apply methods of a function let you invoke a function and also set the value of the function's this keyword by sending the value as the first argument.

- The bind method lets you specify the value of the this keyword at the time you code a function or the time you assign the function. A function coded or assigned in this way is called a *bound function*.

Exercise 10-1   Enhance the Task Manager application

This exercise asks you to enhance the Task Manager application by adding links that let the user edit the tasks in the list. This exercise will also give you a chance to experiment with functions and function calls.

Open, test, and review the application

1. Use your text editor or IDE to open the JavaScript files in this folder:
   `c:\javascript\exercises\ch10\task_manager\`

2. Test this application in Chrome by adding three tasks and deleting one. Then, review the code in the three JavaScript files for this application. In particular, note how the code in the task_list.js file calls the functions contained in the two library files.

Add an Edit function to the application

3. In the library_tasklist.js file, find the displaySortedTaskList function. Within this function, find the line of code that creates the Delete link. Then, after this line, add the code that creates an Edit link like the one shown above. This code should be similar to the code for creating the Delete link, but use the title attribute instead of the id attribute to store the index for the task. That's because using the id attribute for both <a> elements would mean duplicate ids.

4. Also in the library_tasklist.js file, find the function stub called editTask. Note that it accepts three parameters: a tasks parameter that contains an array, an i parameter that contains the index of the task to be edited, and a newText parameter that contains the new text.

5. In the body of this function, use the isArray method of the Array object to make sure the tasks argument is an array. If it is, use the i index argument to set the value of the element at that position in the array to the value of the newText argument.

6. In the task_list.js file, find the function stub called editTaskListItem. Note that it uses the prompt function to display the text of the old task and get new text for the task from the user. It then checks to make sure the user didn't click cancel.

7. In the if clause, add a call to the editTask function that you coded in steps 4 and 5. Pass it the tasks array, the index parameter, and the new text from the user. Then, call the setStorage function and the displayTaskList function to store and re-display the updated tasks array (see the deleteFromTaskList function for an example of how to do that).

8. Test this new Edit function.

Use the arguments property and call method of a function

9. In the library_tasklist.js file, find the deleteTask function. Note how it accepts two parameters and calls another function.

10. Modify the deleteTask function so it doesn't have any parameters, but instead uses its arguments property to get the two arguments that are passed to it (see figure 10-9). Then, test the application to make sure the delete function still works as expected.

11. Modify the deleteTask function so it calls the sortTaskList function by using the call method of that function (see figure 10-10). In this case, you don't need to change the object that's used for the this keyword, but you do need to pass in the function's arguments, so you'll need to pass something for the this keyword too. For that, you can pass this, null, or undefined, followed by the array that contains the arguments. Then, test the application to make sure the delete function still works as expected.

11

How to create and use objects

In earlier chapters, you learned how to use native JavaScript object types such as the String, Number, Date, and Array object types. Now, you'll learn how to create and use your own objects and object types. You'll learn how JavaScript creates objects and how that affects the code you write. And along the way, you'll see how the use of your own objects can help you improve the code within a JavaScript application.

Basic skills for working with objects

This topic will show you how to create and use objects in JavaScript. That will include both native objects and your own objects.

How to create and use the native object types

In contrast to other languages, JavaScript has the flat hierarchy of native *object types* that's shown by the chart in figure 11-1. At the top level is the Object object type. At the next level are the other native object types like the String, Number, Boolean, Date, Array, and Function object types that you've already learned about.

This hierarchy means that all of the object types at the second level *inherit* the properties and methods of the Object type. This also means that every object type can use the properties and methods of the Object type. For instance, the Object type has a toString method that converts an object to a string. However, because this toString method is so general, most of the other object types override this toString method with a specific method that converts the object type to a string.

After the hierarchy chart, this figure shows the syntax for creating a new object with the *new* keyword. This figure then shows an example of creating a new Date object.

You can also create a new object of a native object type by declaring a variable with a literal value. When you do that, JavaScript automatically converts the value to the corresponding native object. You can see this in the examples, where String, Number, Boolean, Array, and Object types are created by storing literal values in a variable. It's a best practice to use literal values like this to create native objects, rather than the new keyword. However, JavaScript doesn't have a literal date value, so you need to use the new keyword to create Date objects.

Last, this figure shows the two ways that you can access properties and methods. First, you can code the object name, the dot operator, and the property or method name. Second, you can code the object name followed by the property or method name within parentheses. Note, however, that when you use brackets, the property or method name must be in quotes. Otherwise, JavaScript will interpret the identifier as a variable name rather than a property name.

Note too that if you're invoking a method, you must follow it with a set of parentheses that lists the arguments. This is required whether you use the dot operator or brackets to identify the method, even if the method doesn't require any arguments. If you omit the parentheses, you'll get a reference to the method rather than invoking the method.

The JavaScript hierarchy of some of the native object types

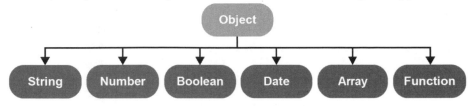

The syntax for creating a new object of a native type

```
var variableName = new ObjectType(arguments);
```

How to create a new object of the Date type

```
var today = new Date();
```

How to create a new object of a native type with literal values

How to create a new object of the String type

```
var lastName = "Hopper";       // Same as = new String("Hopper");
```

How to create a new object of the Number type

```
var taxRate = .0875;           // Same as = new Number(.0875);
```

How to create a new object of the Boolean type

```
var validFlag = true;          // Same as = new Boolean(true);
```

How to create a new object of the Array type

```
var tasks = [];                // Same as = new Array();
```

How to create a new object of the Object type

```
var invoice = {};              // Same as = new Object();
```

How to use the properties and methods of the native object types

How to use the length property of a String object

```
length = lastName.length;                  // Same as lastName["length"];
```

How to use the toFixed method of a Number object

```
formattedRate = taxRate.toFixed(4);   // Same as taxRate["toFixed"](4);
```

Description

- JavaScript provides a two-level hierarchy of *object types*. The top-level consists of the Object object type. The next level consists of types like String, Number, Date, and Array.

- All object types at the second level *inherit* the properties and methods of the Object object type, and also provide properties and methods specific to those objects.

- When you create a variable with a literal value, JavaScript converts it to the corresponding native object type. It's a best practice to create native objects this way, rather than with the new keyword. However, JavaScript doesn't have a literal date value, so you need to use the new keyword with Date objects.

- To access a property or method, you can use the dot operator or brackets.

Figure 11-1   How to create and use the native object types

How to create your own objects with object literals

The simplest way to create your own object is by storing an *object literal* in a variable. To do that, you declare a variable that's equal to a pair of braces. Then, within the braces, you can code properties and methods for the object, as shown in figure 11-2.

In example 1, an object named invoice is initialized with one property named taxRate that has a value of 0.0875. As you can see, the property name and value must be separated by a colon.

In example 2, the invoice object is initialized with one method named getTotal. Here, the method name is followed by a colon and a function expression that does the task of the method. What's happening here is that a function is stored as a property of the object, which turns it into a method of the object.

In example 3, the invoice object is initialized with a property and two methods. Here, the property and methods must be separated by commas. Note also that the getSalesTax method of the object uses the this keyword to get the value of the taxRate property. That's because the this keyword in the method of an object usually refers to the object itself. There are some exceptions to this, though, depending on how the method is invoked. You can refer to figure 10-10 for more information on how the this keyword works in JavaScript.

After you create the properties and methods for an object, you can use them just as you use the properties and methods of native objects. That means you can use either the dot operator or brackets to refer to the properties and methods. In practice, though, the dot operator is commonly used because it's easier to code and easier to understand.

The last set of examples in this figure shows that you can also *nest* one object within another. In this case, a terms object is nested within an invoice object. To do that, the invoice object is initialized with one property named terms, and the terms property is itself an object that is initialized with two properties named taxRate and dueDays.

To access the properties and methods of a nested object, you chain the property names with dot operators or brackets. But here again, dot operators are easier to understand.

How to initialize a new object with properties and methods

Example 1: How to initialize a new object with one property

```
var invoice = { taxRate: 0.0875 };
```

Example 2: How to initialize a new object with one method

```
var invoice = {
    getTotal: function( subtotal, salesTax ) {
        return subtotal + salesTax;
    }
};
```

Example 3: How to initialize a new object with properties and methods

```
var invoice = {
    taxRate: 0.0875,
    getSalesTax: function( subtotal ) {
        return ( subtotal * this.taxRate );
    },
    getTotal: function( subtotal, salesTax ) {
        return subtotal + salesTax;
    }
};
```

How to refer to the properties and methods of an object

```
alert( invoice.taxRate );                    // Displays 0.0875
var salesTax = invoice.getSalesTax(100)      // salesTax = 8.75
```

How to nest objects and refer to the nested properties and methods

How to nest one object within another

```
var invoice = {
    terms: {
        taxRate: 0.0875,
        dueDays: 30
    }
};
```

How to refer to the properties and methods of a nested object

```
alert( invoice.terms.taxRate );              // Displays 0.0875
alert( invoice["terms"]["dueDays"] );        // Displays 30
```

Description

- When you create an object with a literal value (known as an *object literal*), you can add properties by coding pairs of property names and values that are separated by colons.

- When a property name is paired with a function, it's called a method. In strict mode, you can't have duplicate property or method names.

- Inside a method, the value of the this keyword is usually the object itself. Two exceptions, though, are when the method is an event handler or when it's invoked via its call method. You can refer to figure 10-10 for more information on the this keyword.

- If necessary, you can *nest* one object inside another by making the inner object a property of the outer object.

Figure 11-2   How to create your own objects with object literals

How to extend, modify, or delete an object

After you create an object, you can extend the object by adding new properties and methods to it. This is illustrated by the first set of examples in figure 11-3. To add a property, you assign a new property to an object and give it a value. To add a method, you assign a new property and code a function expression as its value.

Once a property has been created, you can modify it by assigning a new value to it. This is illustrated by the second example in this figure. You can also change a method by assigning a new function expression to it.

To remove a property from an object, you can use the *delete operator* as shown in the third example. Here, the delete operator is used to remove the taxRate property from the invoice object. Once deleted, the property has a value of undefined, just as though it had never been created.

When you create an object and store it in a variable, you need to realize that JavaScript actually stores a *reference* to the object in the variable. This is illustrated by the diagram in this figure. In this case, both the today and now variables refer to the same Date object.

This means that if you change the Date object that the today variable refers to, the change will also be seen through the now variable. If, for example, you use the setFullYear method of the today variable to set the year to 2016, the get-FullYear method of the now variable will get 2016. This is the same mechanism that is used when you pass an argument by reference.

After you're through with an object in your code, you can free up the memory it used by deleting the object. To do that, you use the delete operator followed by the object name. For instance, the next example in this figure shows how to delete the object named today.

If more than one variable refers to the object, though, the object isn't deleted until all of the other references to it have been deleted. This is illustrated by the last example in this figure. Here, the today and now variables both refer to the same Date object. As a result, when the delete operator is used with the today variable, only the today reference is deleted. The now variable still refers to the Date object.

How to add properties and methods to an object

```
invoice.taxRate = 0.0875;                    // Adds the taxRate property
invoice.getSalesTax = function(subtotal) {   // Adds the getSalesTax method
    return ( subtotal * this.taxRate );
};
```

How to modify the properties of an object

```
invoice.taxRate = 0.095;
```

How to remove a property from an object

```
delete invoice.taxRate;
alert( invoice.taxRate );          // Displays undefined
```

Two variables that refer to the same object

```
var today = new Date();
var now = today;
```

A diagram that illustrates these references

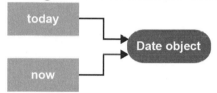

How to delete an object

```
var today = new Date();
delete today;
alert(today);                      // Displays undefined
```

How to delete a reference to an object

```
var today = new Date();
var now = today;
delete today;
alert( today );                    // Displays undefined
alert( now.getFullYear() );        // Displays the year
```

Description

- Once an object is created, you can add new properties and methods to it. You can also change the value of an existing property by assigning it a new value.

- To remove a property or method from an object, you can use the *delete operator*.

- A variable holds a *reference* to an object, not the object itself. When you pass an object to a function as an argument, you are passing a reference to the object.

- You can also use the delete operator to delete an object or a reference to an object. If two or more variables refer to an object, the delete operator deletes the reference to the object. But if there are no references to the object, the object itself is deleted.

Figure 11-3   How to extend, modify, or delete an object

How to create your own object types with constructor functions

When you use JavaScript, you can also create your own object types with *constructor functions* (or just *constructors*). This lets you create multiple *instances* of an object. This is illustrated in figure 11-4.

Here, the first group of examples shows how to create a constructor for an Invoice object type. Here, the first constructor creates an instance of the Invoice object that contains an array variable named items and a numeric variable named taxRate that has an initial value of .07. Within the body of the constructor, the this keyword is used to refer to the new object that the function will create.

Usually, though, you won't want to hard code an object's properties like that. Instead, the constructor will receive parameters that it uses to set the initial values of the properties for each object that's initialized. For example, the second constructor in the first group in this figure accepts a taxRate parameter, and uses it to set the value of the taxRate property. Although the parameter and property names don't have to be the same, they often are because that's a good coding practice.

To add a method to an object type, you add the method to the object type's *prototype object*, as shown by the next example. Here, the deleteItem method is added to the prototype object of the Invoice type. This prototype object is stored in the prototype property of the constructor function, and you'll learn more about prototypes in the next topic.

The third group of examples shows how to create and use object types. To create an instance of an object type, you call its constructor with the new keyword. This automatically returns a new instance of the object type, just as though the last statement in the constructor was "return this". Here, two Invoice objects are created from the constructor, each with its own tax rate value, and they are assigned to variables named invoice1 and invoice2.

After the objects have been created, you can refer to their properties and methods just as you refer to the properties and methods of any other object. This is illustrated by the last two examples in this figure. Here, the taxRate properties of invoice1 and invoice2 are retrieved and multiplied by the number 125. Because each object has its own tax rate value, they produce different results. Then, the deleteItem method of one of the invoice objects is called to delete an item in its items array.

When you create an instance of an object type, you need to be sure to code the new keyword. If you omit it, the constructor will still create an object, but the object might behave strangely. By convention, then, the names of constructor functions start with a capital letter, to help remind programmers to use the new keyword.

How to code constructors that create instances of object types

How to code a constructor with no parameters

```
// A constructor that creates an Invoice object type
var Invoice = function() {
    this.items = [];
    this.taxRate = 0.07;
};
```

How to code a constructor with a parameter

```
var Invoice = function(taxRate) {
    this.items = [];
    this.taxRate = taxRate;
};
```

How to add a method to an object type

```
// The delete item method is added to the Invoice object type
Invoice.prototype.deleteItem = function(itemCode) {
    if ( itemCode in this.items ) {
        delete this.items[itemCode];
    }
};
```

How to create and use object types

How to create new instances of an object type

```
var invoice1 = new Invoice(0.075);
var invoice2 = new Invoice(0.07);
```

How to access a new object's properties

```
alert (125 * invoice1.taxRate);      // Displays 9.375
alert (125 * invoice2.taxRate);      // Displays 8.75
```

How to use a new object's methods

```
invoice1.deleteItem(itemCode);       // Deletes an item
```

Description

- If you want to be able create multiple *instances* of your own object types, you can code a *constructor function* (or just *constructor*) for the objects to be created. Then, to create an object from the constructor, you call the constructor with the *new* keyword.

- If the constructor function has parameters, you pass the data for the object that's going to be created (or *initialized*) to the constructor.

- If you forget to use the new keyword when you call a constructor, the object is still created, but it may behave strangely. By convention, then, constructor names are capitalized to help programmers remember that they need to use the new keyword.

- Methods that are added to the *prototype object* of an object type are the same for all objects that are initialized by the constructor. You'll learn more about prototypes next.

Figure 11-4   How to create your own object types with constructor functions

What you need to know about JavaScript prototypes

As you saw in the last figure, you put the methods of a constructor on the object's prototype. But what's a prototype, and why would you put methods there?

How prototypes work

If you've worked in other programming languages, you're probably familiar with *classes*. A class is a description of the features of an object, but it isn't itself an object. Languages that use classes to define and create objects are *class-based* or *classical*.

In contrast, JavaScript uses *prototypes* to create objects. Unlike a class, a prototype is an object, and it's cloned to create a new object. This is called *prototype inheritance*. When you create a new object with an object literal, it inherits the methods of the Object object. Three of those methods are summarized in the table in figure 11-5.

The methods on a prototype object are available to every object that uses the prototype. You've already seen this in the constructors of the last figure. For example, every instance of the Invoice object has access to the deleteItem method. This is also true of the native JavaScript objects. If, for example, you add a method to Date.prototype, it will be available to all instances of the Date object.

Once you've created an instance of an object, any property you add to it will be added directly to that object, not to the object's prototype. In that case, it will be that object's *own property*, and it will only be available to that instance of the object. If, for example, you add a method named test to the invoice1 object in the last figure, the invoice2 object won't have access to it.

This is illustrated by the examples in this figure. The first one uses an object literal to create an object named obj with one property named prop that has a string literal as its value. Then, the next group of examples shows how the hasOwnProperty and toString methods work with this object.

Here, the first statement uses the hasOwnProperty method to check whether the toString method is an own property of the object. But it isn't because it is defined on the object's prototype. The second statement checks whether the prop property is an own property, which it is. And the third statement shows the output of the toString method of the object.

The next group of examples shows that you can override the methods on an object's prototype by coding a method of the same name directly on the object instance. Here, the first statement overrides the toString method and returns a string literal value. The second statement shows that the overridden toString method is now an own method of the object. And the third statement shows the results of the new toString method.

Some of the methods of a new object's prototype object

Method	Description
`toString`	Returns a string that represents the object.
`valueOf`	Returns the primitive value of the object.
`hasOwnProperty(prop)`	Returns a Boolean value indicating whether the specified property is defined directly on the object, rather than on the object's prototype.

Examples of calling and overriding the methods of an object's prototype

Creating an object with one property

```
var obj = { prop: "This is a property" };
```

Calling methods of the object's prototype

```
// 'toString' is a method defined on the object's prototype
alert( obj.hasOwnProperty("toString") );     // false

// 'prop' is a property defined directly on the object
alert( obj.hasOwnProperty("prop") );          // true

// the default string representation of the object
alert( obj.toString() );    // "[object Object]"
```

Overriding the toString method

```
obj.toString = function() {
    return "This is the best object ever!";
};
// 'toString' is now defined directly on the object
alert( obj.hasOwnProperty("toString") );     // true

// the custom string representation of the object
alert( obj.toString() );    // "This is the best object ever!"
```

Description

- Many programming languages use *classes* to create objects. A class is a description of the object that the class will create. This kind of language is called *class-based* or *classical*.

- JavaScript, by contrast, uses *prototype objects* that are cloned to create new objects. This kind of language is called *classless* or *prototypal*.

- When you create a new object with an object literal, it's cloned from an object named Object.prototype.

- When you add a property to an existing object, it's created directly on the object, not on the object's prototype. This kind of property is called an object's *own property*.

- You can override properties on an object's prototype by coding a property of the same name directly on the object. When you do so, the property becomes an own property of that object.

Figure 11-5   How prototypes work

When and how to create custom prototypes

Now that you have a general idea of how prototypes work, you're ready to learn how to use custom prototypes with your own objects. But the first question is, why would you want to do that? Why not just create object literals with properties and methods instead? The answer has to do with how JavaScript allocates memory. This is best demonstrated with an example.

So, imagine that you have invoice data in an array, as in the first example in figure 11-6. Imagine too that you want to loop through that array, load each nested array in an object with a getTotal method, and store the resulting object in an array called invoices. Last, imagine that there are over a million nested arrays in your data array.

The second example shows how you could do this with an object literal for each nested array. But that would create a new getTotal function for each iteration of the loop. So when the loop ends, you'll have over a million getTotal functions stored in memory, all of them exactly the same.

You'll also have over a million invoiceID, subtotal, and taxRate properties stored in memory, but that's OK, because each nested array will have different values for those properties. Put another way, it makes sense for those to be each object's *own properties*, because they'll change from one object to another. But each object's version of the getTotal method will be exactly the same.

The third example shows how to do this with just one version of the getTotal function that all the objects can refer to. This is what happens when you add a method to an object's prototype instead of to the object itself. In this example, the constructor named Invoice has parameters and properties for the three invoice variables. Then, it adds a getTotal method to the Invoice's prototype object. As a result, this method exists in just this one place, and it will be the same for every instance of the Invoice object type.

Then, in the loop that creates the instances of the Invoice object, new versions of the getTotal method aren't being created. Instead, references are created that point to the single version of the getTotal method that exists on the object prototype.

This illustrates the main reason that you would want to customize an object's prototype object. In short, if you're going to need multiple instances of an object, and the object has methods, you'll want to put the methods for the object on its prototype. One way to do that is with a constructor. You'll learn about the other way in the next figure.

The arrays used in the examples that follow

```
// data array contains one million records
// each nested array contains an invoice number, an amount, and a tax rate
var data = [
    [1001, 560.50, 0.07], [1002, 1425.50, 0.085], [1003, 325, 0], ...
];
var invoices = [];
```

Code that creates a new object for every invoice in the array

```
// this example creates one million identical getTotal methods in memory
for (var i = 0; i < data.length; i++) {
    invoices[i] = {
        invoiceID: data[i][0],
        subtotal: data[i][1],
        taxRate: data[i][2],
        getTotal: function() {
            return this.subtotal + (this.subtotal * this.taxRate);
        }
    };
}
```

Code that uses a constructor for every invoice in the array

```
// this example creates a single getTotal method in memory, and one million
// objects that have a reference to it
var Invoice = function(id, subtotal, taxRate) {
    this.invoiceID = id;
    this.subtotal = subtotal;
    this.taxRate = taxRate;
};
Invoice.prototype.getTotal = function() {
    return this.subtotal + (this.subtotal * this.taxRate);
};
for (var i = 0; i < data.length; i++) {
    invoices[i] = new Invoice(data[i][0],data[i][1],data[i][2]);
}
```

Description

- If you're going to create multiple instances of an object that has methods, you should create the methods on the object's prototype, not directly on the object.

- This saves memory since each instance of an object refers to a prototype method rather than creating a duplicate method of its own.

- To add methods to an object's prototype, you can use constructors or the create method of the Object object. You'll learn about the create method next.

Figure 11-6   When and how to create custom prototypes for your objects

How to use the create method of the Object object

Constructor functions in JavaScript let you create an object type and customize its prototype. They also provide a familiar syntax to programmers who are used to working with classical languages.

But JavaScript isn't a classical language. Because of this, constructor functions don't always behave the way programmers with a classical background expect them to. For example, in classical languages, the this keyword always refers to the object that contains it, but in JavaScript it can refer to various things. Also, it can be hard to remember to code methods on the object type's prototype or to use the new keyword when you create an instance of an object. Even worse, JavaScript doesn't throw errors if you forget these things.

To address these issues and make the prototypal nature of JavaScript more clear, ECMAScript 5 added a create method to the Object object. This create method lets you directly specify what object to use as an object's prototype. This means that you can create a prototype object that contains the methods you need, and then pass this custom prototype object to the create method.

The table at the top of figure 11-7 shows the syntax of the create method. The first parameter is the prototype object that you want to use for the new object. The second parameter is an optional object that describes the properties the new object should have. You'll learn more about this second parameter in chapter 15.

The first example in this figure shows how to use the create method. Here, the prototype of the Object object is used as the prototype for the new object. This is the same as creating a new object with an object literal.

Usually, though, you'll use the create method with a custom prototype object. The second example shows how to do that. Here, a custom prototype object is created with a single method, the getTotal method from the last figure. Then, the third example uses the custom prototype and the create method to rewrite the loop that's in the last figure. Like the use of the constructor in the last figure, the getTotal method is only created once on the prototype object, and the objects returned by the create method refer to it.

The last example in this figure shows how to use a *factory function* to create a custom prototype object. Factory functions are functions that create, initialize, and return objects. They look similar to constructor functions in that you can add properties to the object and initialize those properties with the values passed to the function. But you don't need to use the new keyword with a factory function, and you do need to specifically return the object that the function creates.

The code that follows the factory function shows how it can be used. It calls this function to create an object for each nested array and add it to the invoices array. Note that this doesn't require the use of the new keyword or the create method, which is what makes a factory function easy to use.

Because the create method is in the sham.js file described in figure 1-17, it won't work correctly in older browsers. But it's the second parameter, not the first, that doesn't always work.

The create method of the Object object

Method	Description
create(*prototype*, *properties*)	Creates a new object. The first parameter is the prototype used to create the object. The optional second parameter sets the object's properties. See chapter 15 for information on the second parameter.

How to use the create method to create a new object

```
var obj = Object.create(Object.prototype);     // the same as = {};
```

A custom prototype object with one method

```
var invoicePrototype = {
    getTotal: function() {
        return this.subtotal + (this.subtotal * this.taxRate);
    }
};
```

Code that uses the custom prototype object with the create method

```
// this example uses the arrays described in the last figure
for (var i = 0; i < data.length; i++) {
    invoices[i] = Object.create(invoicePrototype);
    invoices[i].invoiceID = data[i][0];
    invoices[i].subtotal = data[i][1];
    invoices[i].taxRate = data[i][2];
}
```

A factory function that creates a custom prototype object

```
var getInvoice = function(id, subtotal, taxRate) {    // factory function
    var invoice = Object.create(invoicePrototype);
    invoice.invoiceID = id;
    invoice.subtotal = subtotal;
    invoice.taxRate = taxRate;
    return invoice;
};
```

Code the uses the factory function

```
for (var i = 0; i < data.length; i++) {
    invoices[i] = getInvoice(data[i][0],data[i][1],data[i][2]);;
}
```

Description

- The create method of the Object object lets you specify an object's prototype. Then, you can use the techniques of figure 11-3 to add properties to the object returned by the method. In particular, you should add any properties that the prototype expects.

- *Factory functions* can be used to create custom prototype objects. These functions are similar to constructor functions, but they don't require the use of the new keyword.

- The create method is in the sham.js file described in figure 1-17. This means that it may not work correctly with older browsers. Although everything in this figure will work, the second parameter that works with properties may not.

Figure 11-7   How to use the create method of the Object object

The Task Manager application

The Task Manager application in figure 11-8 is another version of the one you saw in chapter 10. The difference is that this version uses objects instead of functions. As you will see, it illustrates most of the concepts and techniques that you've just learned.

The HTML and CSS

The script elements in the head section identify the three libraries that are used by this application: a storage library, a task library, and a task list library. The last script element is for the main JavaScript file that uses these libraries.

The HTML in the body element is the same as it was for the application in the last chapter. Here, the tasks are listed in the div element with "tasks" as its id, and the text for a new task is entered into the text box with "task" as its id.

The CSS for this application is also the same as it was in the last chapter. It floats the div element that contains the task list to the right of the text box and buttons.

The Task Manager application

Task Manager

Task:
[   ]

[Add Task   ]

[Clear Tasks   ]

Delete Finish current project
Delete Meet with Mike
Delete Write project summary

The HTML

```
<head>
    <title>Ch11 Task Manager</title>
    <link type="text/css" rel="stylesheet" href="task_list.css">
    <script type="text/javascript" src="library_storage.js"></script>
    <script type="text/javascript" src="library_task.js"></script>
    <script type="text/javascript" src="library_tasklist.js"></script>
    <script type="text/javascript" src="task_list.js"></script>
</head>
<body>
    <main>
        <h1>Task Manager</h1>
        <div id="tasks"></div>
        <label for="task">Task:</label><br>
        <input type="text" name="task" id="task"><br>
        <input type="button" name="add_task" id="add_task"
            value="Add Task"><br>
        <input type="button" name="clear_tasks" id="clear_tasks"
            value="Clear Tasks"><br>
        <div class="clear"></div>
    </main>
</body>
```

Description

- The Task Manager application for this chapter is an object version of the application in chapter 10 that was built with function libraries.

- Specifically, this application converts the storage and task list libraries from function libraries to object libraries. It also adds a task library for working with individual tasks.

Figure 11-8   The user interface and HTML for the Task Manager application

The storage library

Figure 11-9 presents the library for working with local storage. It starts by creating an object called storagePrototype. As the name implies, this object will be used as a prototype to create another object. Although you aren't required to include the word "prototype" in a prototype object's name, it can help make it clear what the object is for.

The prototype object contains three methods named get, set, and clear. The get method retrieves a string from local storage, converts it to an array with one task in each element, and returns the array. The set method accepts an array, converts it to a string, and stores it in local storage. The clear method sets the string in local storage to an empty string. All three methods use the object's key property to know which string to get, set, or clear.

After the prototype object, the code creates a factory function called getTaskStorage. This function accepts a parameter named key. Within the function, it uses the prototype object and the create method of the Object object to create a new storage object. Then, it creates a property named key and sets its value to the value of the key parameter that it received. This property will be used by the three prototype methods that are available to the object that's created. Finally, the factory function returns the new object.

The task library

Figure 11-9 shows the task library for working with individual tasks. It contains a constructor function named Task, which accepts a parameter named task. Within the constructor, a property named text is created, and assigned the value in the task parameter.

After the constructor function, the code adds two methods to the prototype object. The isValid method tests the value of the text property and returns a Boolean value. If the text property is an empty string, it returns false. Otherwise, it returns true.

The toString method overrides the base Object's toString method and returns a string. It starts by using the substring method to get the first letter of the text property and store it in a variable named first. Then, it has a return statement that uses the toUpperCase method to capitalize the letter in the first variable, uses the substring method to get the remaining letters in the text property, and concatenates the remaining letters with the capitalized first letter. Thus, it returns the string value in the text property with its first letter capitalized.

This Task constructor illustrates an important use of objects, which is to encapsulate the code that's specific to the object. For example, the isValid method provides a way to check whether a task is valid, and the toString method provides a way to capitalize the first letter of each task. This makes it easier to work with tasks and stops the unnecessary duplication of code.

The library_storage.js file

```
var storagePrototype = {
    get: function() {
        var str = localStorage.getItem(this.key) || "";
        return (str === "")? []: str.split("|");
    },
    set: function(arr) {
        if (Array.isArray(arr)) {
            var str = arr.join("|");
            localStorage.setItem(this.key, str);
        }
    },
    clear: function() { localStorage.setItem(this.key, ""); }
};
var getTaskStorage = function(key) {
    var storage = Object.create(storagePrototype);
    storage.key = key;
    return storage;
};
```

The library_task.js file

```
var Task = function(task) {
    this.text = task;
};
Task.prototype.isValid = function() {
    if (this.text === "") { return false; }
    else { return true; }
};
Task.prototype.toString = function() {
    // capitalize the first letter of the task text
    var first = this.text.substring(0,1);
    return first.toUpperCase() + this.text.substring(1);
};
```

Description

- The storage library creates a prototype object with methods for getting tasks out of local storage, putting tasks into local storage, and clearing local storage.

- The storage library uses a factory function to create a storage object by using the Object.create method with the prototype object. This factory function adds a key as an own property of each object, sets the key's value, and returns the object.

- The task library uses a constructor to create an object for working with individual tasks. It adds text as an own property of the object, and sets the value of the text property to the value that's passed to it.

- The task library also adds two methods to the Task object's prototype. The first checks to make sure the text for the task is valid, and the second overrides the toString method by capitalizing the first letter of the text.

- You could build the storage and task libraries with either factory functions or constructor functions. Which you choose is mostly a matter of preference, but using the Object.create method in a factory function offers more flexibility, as you'll see in chapter 15.

Figure 11-9   The storage and task libraries for the Task Manager application

The task list library

Figure 11-10 shows the library for working with the task list. It contains an object named tasklist that holds, edits, and displays tasks. Because only one instance of this object is needed, it is coded as an object literal that has four properties and seven methods.

The tasks property contains an array that holds the tasks in the task list. The storage property contains an instance of the storage object that it gets by calling the factory function in the storage library. The displayDiv and deleteClickHandler properties are initially set to null, but the main JavaScript file will set their values.

The load method checks whether the tasks array has any elements. If it doesn't, it calls the get method of the storage object to retrieve the tasks from local storage. The save method calls the set method of the storage object to store the tasks in the array in local storage.

The sort method calls the sort method of the array. Since that's all it does, you could dispense with this method and call the array sort method directly. This way, though, if you ever want to change the sort criteria by passing a function to the array sort method, you'll only have to make the change here.

The add method accepts an instance of the Task object. It uses the push method of the tasks array to add the task description to the array. Inside the push method, it calls the toString method of the Task object to get the capitalized description.

The delete method accepts an index parameter. It starts by calling the sort method to sort the tasks. Then, it removes the element at the specified index using the splice method of the array.

The clear method sets the length property of the array to zero, which empties the array. Then, it calls the clear method of the storage object to remove the string in local storage. Finally, it sets the innerHTML property of the element in the displayDiv property to an empty string to clear the tasks in the div.

The last method is the display method. It starts by calling the sort method to sort the tasks. Then, it loops through the tasks and constructs an HTML string.

As in the chapter 10 application, the HTML string has a Delete link for each task, and the href attribute of each Delete <a> tag has a placeholder value of "#". Then, the title attribute is given the value of the index of the task item in the array. This is how the application knows which task to delete. After creating the HTML string, the method uses the innerHTML property of the element in the displayDiv property to display the tasks.

Next, the method adds event handlers to the <a> tags that it just added to the element in the displayDiv property. First, it uses the getElementsByTagName method to get all the <a> tags. Then, it loops through the <a> tags and assigns the function in the deleteClickHandler property as the link's click handler. In the next figure, you'll see how the values of the displayDiv and deleteClickHandler properties are passed to the tasklist object.

The library_tasklist.js file

```javascript
var tasklist = {
    tasks: [],                              // array to hold Task objects
    storage: getTaskStorage("tasks_11"),    // storage object
    displayDiv: null,                       // div that displays tasks
    deleteClickHandler: null,               // delete click event handler
    load: function() {
        if (this.tasks.length === 0) {
            tasklist.tasks = this.storage.get();
        }
    },
    save: function() {
        this.storage.set(this.tasks);
    },
    sort: function() {
        this.tasks.sort();
    },
    add: function(task) {
        this.tasks.push(task.toString());   // call the custom toString
    },                                       // method of the Task object
    delete: function(i) {
        this.sort();
        this.tasks.splice(i, 1);
    },
    clear: function() {
        this.tasks.length = 0;
        this.storage.clear();
        this.displayDiv.innerHTML = "";
    },
    display: function() {
        var html = "";
        this.sort();

        //create and load html string from sorted array
        for (var i in this.tasks) {
            html = html.concat("<p>");
            html = html.concat("<a href='#' title='", i, "'>Delete</a>");
            html = html.concat(this.tasks[i]);
            html = html.concat("</p>");
        }
        this.displayDiv.innerHTML = html;

        // get links and add click event handlers
        var links = this.displayDiv.getElementsByTagName("a");
        for (var i = 0; i < links.length; i++) {
            links[i].onclick = this.deleteClickHandler;
        }
    }
};
```

Description

- The tasks property contains an array for Task objects, and the storage property contains an object returned by the getTaskStorage function. The values of the displayDiv and deleteClickHandler properties will be set by code in the main JavaScript file.

Figure 11-10   The task list library for the Task Manager application

The main JavaScript file

Figure 11-11 shows the main JavaScript file for this application. After the $ function, the code creates three more functions, which will be used as event handlers. Then, it uses the onload event hander to attach these event handlers.

You should note that all three of these functions call methods on the tasklist object. This is possible because the tasklist object is coded as an object literal outside of a function, so it has global scope. Note, however, that the script tag for the tasklist library file needs to come before the script tag for the main JavaScript file. Otherwise, this code won't have access to the tasklist object in the tasklist library.

The addToTask function is called when the user clicks the Add button. First, it uses the $ function to retrieve the text box that holds the task entered by the user. Next, it creates a new Task object by using the new keyword and passing it the value in the task text box. Then, it calls the Task object's isValid method to make sure the user entered a valid task. If so, the function calls three methods of the tasklist object to add the new task, save the updated tasks array to local storage, and display the task list. After that, the function clears the task text box.

However, if the task isn't valid, the function notifies the user. And valid or not, the function ends by setting the focus on the task text box.

The clearTaskList function is called when the user clicks the Clear button. It calls the clear method of the tasklist object and sets the focus on the task text box.

The deleteFromTaskList function is called when the user clicks one of the Delete links that are created by the display method of the tasklist object. This function starts by getting the index of the task to delete from the title attribute of the link that has been clicked. Here, the this keyword refers to the link that was clicked. Then, this function calls three methods of the tasklist object to delete the task at the specified index, save the updated tasks array to local storage, and display the task list again. After that, it sets the focus on the task text box.

The last function in this figure is the event handler for the onload event. First, it assigns the addToTaskList and clearTaskList functions to the click events of the add_task and clear_task buttons. Then, it assigns the deleteFromTask function to the tasklist object's deleteClickHandler property, and it assigns the tasks div to the displayDiv property of the tasklist object. This is how the tasklist object gets the div element and click handler function it uses in its display method.

Finally, the onload event handler calls two methods of the tasklist object to retrieve the tasks array and display the tasks when the page is loaded, and it sets the focus on the task text box.

The main JavaScript for the Task Manager application

```
var $ = function(id) { return document.getElementById(id); };

var addToTaskList = function() {
    var taskTextbox = $("task");
    var newTask = new Task(taskTextbox.value);
    if (newTask.isValid()) {
        tasklist.add(newTask);
        tasklist.save();
        tasklist.display();
        taskTextbox.value = "";
    } else {
        alert("Please enter a task.");
    }
    taskTextbox.focus();
};
var clearTaskList = function() {
    tasklist.clear();
    $("task").focus();
};
var deleteFromTaskList = function() {
    tasklist.delete(this.title); // 'this' = clicked link
    tasklist.save();
    tasklist.display();
    $("task").focus();
};

window.onload = function() {
    $("add_task").onclick = addToTaskList;
    $("clear_tasks").onclick = clearTaskList;

    tasklist.deleteClickHandler = deleteFromTaskList;
    tasklist.displayDiv = $("tasks");

    tasklist.load();
    tasklist.display();
    $("task").focus();
};
```

Description

- The JavaScript code for the Task Manager application creates three event handlers. All of them call methods of the tasklist object in the last figure.

- The onload event handler attaches these event handlers. The first two functions are attached to the click events of the add_task and clear_tasks buttons.

- The deleteFromTaskList function is passed to the tasklist object in its deleteClick-Handler property. This is the function that's attached to the click events of the Delete links created by the tasklist object's display method.

- The display method also needs the div element for the tasks, which is passed to the object in its displayDiv property.

- The last three statements in the onload event handler call the load and display methods of the tasklist object and set the focus on the text box with "task" as its id.

Figure 11-11   The main JavaScript file for the Task Manager application

Advanced skills for working with objects

This topic presents some advanced skills for working with objects. Although you won't use these skills in every application, you should at least be aware of them so you can use them when they're appropriate.

How to inherit methods from another object with Object.create methods

When you create objects, you can *inherit* methods from other objects. This lets you create a base object with common methods and then extend it with more specialized methods. Figure 11-12 shows how this works when you're using the create method of an Object object.

The first example creates a prototype object called percentPrototype that contains a single method called getPercent. This method accepts a subtotal parameter and returns the result of multiplying the subtotal amount by the object's rate property.

Note, however, that the rate property doesn't exist on the prototype. If it did, it would be the same for every object that used the prototype. That is, if one object set its rate to 0.07, it would change the rate for all other instances to 0.07. Then, if another object set its rate to 0.075, that would change the rate for all other instances to 0.075. So remember that only properties that should be the same for all instances should be on the prototype. Usually, this means that only methods will be on the prototype.

The second example creates a prototype object called commissionPrototype. It passes the percentPrototype object to the create method that creates the new object. As a result, the commissionPrototype object inherits the getPercent method.

This example then defines a new method on the commissionPrototype object called calculateCommission, which calculates a commission using the getPercent method of the object it inherited. This method also checks the isSplit property to see if it should return the value returned by the getPercent method or divide it by two.

The examples in the third group use these prototypes. In the first example, the percentPrototype object is used to create a new object called salesTax, and its getPercent method is invoked. In the second example, the commissionPrototype object is used to create a new object called commission, and its getPercent and calculateCommission methods are invoked. In both examples, the properties that the prototypes need are added to the objects before their methods are called.

As you learned in figure 11-5, you can override methods on the prototype that an object inherits. When you do that, the new method replaces the overridden one. Sometimes, though, you want to use the functionality of the method you're overriding in the new method. To do that, you can use the call method of the overridden method, as in the last example.

A percentPrototype object

```
var percentPrototype = {
    getPercent: function(subtotal) { return subtotal * this.rate; }
};
```

A commissionPrototype object that inherits the percentPrototype object

```
var commissionPrototype = Object.create(percentPrototype);
commissionPrototype.calculateCommission = function(subtotal) {
    var percent = this.getPercent(subtotal);
    return (this.isSplit)? percent / 2 : percent;
};
```

Some objects that use the prototypes

```
var salesTax = Object.create(percentPrototype);        // inherit
salesTax.rate = 0.0825;                                // add own property
alert( salesTax.getPercent(100) );                     // 8.25


var commission = Object.create(commissionPrototype);   // inherit
commission.rate = 0.07;                                // add own property
commission.isSplit = true;                             // add own property
alert( commission.getPercent(100) );                   // 7.0
alert( commission.calculateCommission(100) );          // 3.5
```

How to override a prototype's method while still using its functionality

```
var commissionPrototype = Object.create(percentPrototype);
commissionPrototype.getPercent = function(subtotal) {
    var percent = percentPrototype.getPercent.call(this, subtotal);
    return (this.isSplit)? percent / 2 : percent;
};

var commission = Object.create(commissionPrototype);
commission.rate = 0.07;
commission.isSplit = false;
alert( commission.getPercent(100) );                   // 7.0
```

Description

- *Inheritance* lets you share base functionality among several objects.
- When you override a method on a prototype object, the new method replaces the old one.
- If you want to override a prototype method but still use its functionality, you can use the call method of the overridden method (see figure 10-10).

Figure 11-12   How to inherit methods from another object with Object.create methods

How to inherit methods from another object with constructors

You can also inherit methods from another object when you use constructors. This is illustrated by the examples in figure 11-13.

The first example creates a constructor called Percent with a property called rate. Then, it adds a single method called getPercent to the Percent prototype object. As before, the getPercent method accepts a subtotal parameter and returns the result of multiplying the subtotal amount by the object's rate property.

The second example creates another constructor called Commission with properties called rate and isSplit. It then sets the prototype object of the Commission object type to a new instance of the Percent object. You can think of this as setting the prototype object of the child object to an instance of the parent object. As a result, the Commission object type inherits the methods of the Percent object type.

Then, this example adds a calculateCommission method to the Commission prototype object. As before, this method calculates a commission by using the getPercent method of the object it inherited and its own isSplit property.

Note that the rate property has to be defined again in the Commission constructor, even though it's defined in the Percent constructor. That's because it isn't defined on the Percent prototype object, so it isn't inherited.

The next group of examples shows the use of these constructor functions. In the first example, the Percent constructor is used to create a new object called salesTax, and its getPercent method is invoked. In the second example, the Commission constructor is used to create a new object called commission, and its getPercent and calculateCommission methods are invoked.

Just like the last figure, you can override methods on the prototype that an object inherits but still use the functionality of the overridden method. To do that, you can use the call method of the overridden method, as in the last example.

A constructor function that creates a Percent object

```
var Percent = function() {
    this.rate;
};
Percent.prototype.getPercent = function(subtotal) {
    return subtotal * this.rate;
};
```

A constructor for a Commission object that inherits the Percent object

```
var Commission = function() {
    this.rate;
    this.isSplit;
};
Commission.prototype = new Percent();                    // inherit
Commission.prototype.calculateCommission = function(subtotal) {
    var percent = this.getPercent(subtotal);
    return (this.isSplit)? percent / 2 : percent;
};
```

Some objects that use the constructor objects

```
var salesTax = new Percent();
salesTax.rate = 0.0825;
alert( salesTax.getPercent(100) );                       // 8.25

var commission = new Commission();
commission.rate = 0.07;
commission.isSplit = true;
alert( commission.calculateCommission(100) );            // 3.5
```

How to override a prototype's method while still using its functionality

```
Commission.prototype = new Percent();
Commission.prototype.getPercent = function(subtotal) {
    var percent = Percent.prototype.getPercent.call(this, subtotal);
    return (this.isSplit)? percent / 2 : percent;
};

var salesTax = new Percent();
salesTax.rate = 0.0825;
alert( salesTax.getPercent(100) );                       // 8.25

var commission = new Commission();
commission.rate = 0.07;
commission.isSplit = true;
alert( commission.getPercent(100) );                     // 3.5
```

Description

- To inherit the methods of an object created by a constructor, set the prototype object of the child object to an instance of the parent object.

- As you learned in the last figure, you can use the call method of a prototype method if you want to override it but still use its functionality.

Figure 11-13   How to inherit methods from another object with constructors

How to add methods to the native object types

JavaScript's prototype inheritance makes it so you can extend the functionality of any object type. This includes the native JavaScript objects, the DOM objects, and the browser objects.

To extend a native JavaScript object, you simply add a new method to the prototype object of that object type. In fact, many JavaScript libraries start by extending the functionality of the existing object types.

To illustrate, figure 11-14 shows how to add new methods to the String and Date object types. In the first example, the capitalize method is added to the String.prototype object. This method returns a new string with the first character of the original string capitalized. Because the object that is referred to by the this keyword is never modified, the new method doesn't change the original string.

In the second example, the isLeapYear method is added to the Date.prototype object. This method first retrieves the full year from the Date object by using the this keyword to call the getFullYear method of the object. The method then uses a nested if statement to return true or false depending on whether the year is a leap year. If a year is divisible by 4, it is a leap year if it isn't divisible by 100 or if it is divisible by 400.

The third example in this figure shows how to add a function to the Math object. The Math object is different because it isn't an object type created by a constructor function, so it doesn't have a prototype object that can be customized. Instead, you add new methods directly to the Math object. In this case, an add method is added to the Math object. This method converts the parameters that are passed to it to numbers and returns their sum, ignoring any parameter that isn't a number.

You should know that many books and online sources recommend against adding methods to native objects. The biggest reason is that, if a method with the same name is added to the native object in a future version, your custom method will override it. To protect against this, you can check if the method exists, as shown in the last example in this figure.

Even then, if only some browsers implement the new feature, and the new implementation is different than your custom method, you can have unexpected results. Thus, you should be judicious in your use of this feature.

How to add a method to the String object type

```
String.prototype.capitalize = function() {
    var first = this.substring(0,1);
    return first.toUpperCase() + this.substring(1);
};

var message = "javaScript";
alert( message.capitalize() );         // Displays "JavaScript"
```

How to add a method to the Date object type

```
Date.prototype.isLeapYear = function() {
    var year = this.getFullYear();
    if ( year % 4 == 0 ) {
        if ( year % 100 == 0 ) {
            if ( year % 400 == 0) {
                return true;
            } else { return false; }
        } else { return true; }
    } else { return false; }
};

var opening = new Date( 2016, 1, 1 );   // Feb 1, 2016
alert( opening.isLeapYear() );          // Displays true
```

How to add a method to the Math object

```
Math.add = function() {
    var arg;
    var sum = 0;
    for (var i = 0; i < arguments.length; i++) {
        arg = parseFloat(arguments[i]);
        if (!isNaN(arg)) { sum = sum + arg; }
    }
    return sum;
};

alert( "3" + "-" + 5 );          // Displays 3-5
alert( Math.add("3", "-", 5) );  // Displays 8
```

How to check if the method exists before adding it

```
String.prototype.capitalize = String.prototype.capitalize || function() {
    // code to capitalize a string goes here
};
```

Description

- To add a method to a native object type, you add the new method to its prototype object. Then, all objects of that type, including existing objects, will inherit the new method.

- You can use the this keyword to refer to the object that's created by the object type.

- Because the Math object isn't an object type, it doesn't have a prototype object. As a result, you add new methods directly to the Math object.

- It's a good practice to check if the method exists before adding it to a native object in case a method with the same name is added to the native object later on.

Figure 11-14   How to add methods to the native object types

How to create cascading methods

A *cascading method* is a method of an object that can be chained with other methods. To do that, the method must return a reference to the original object by using the this keyword. This is illustrated by figure 11-15.

In the first example, a method named add is added to the Array object type. However, this method doesn't return a reference to the object so it can't be chained with other Array methods. If you do try to chain the methods, a runtime error will occur.

In the second example, the add method ends with a "return this" statement. This returns a reference to the original object so this method can be chained. This example then shows two add calls that are chained.

Since chaining is commonly used with method calls, it's a good practice to provide for chaining by ending your methods with a return this statement. Of course, if you're returning something else, like a Boolean value or a string, then you can't return the this keyword too. But whenever you can return the this keyword, you should.

The last example shows how this works with a custom Vehicle property. Since some of its methods return this, you can chain them. This style of coding is sometimes called *fluent* because a line of code like

```
myCar.drive(2000).changeOil().drive(4000)
```

reads like a sentence.

A method that modifies an object but doesn't return the object

An add method that's added to the Array object type

```
Array.prototype.add = function(key, value) {
    this[key] = value;
};
```

Chaining the add method calls won't work

```
var pinCodes = [];
pinCodes.add("Grace", "1234").add("Charles", "9876");    // TypeError
```

The add methods must be called one at a time

```
var pinCodes = [];
pinCodes.add("Grace", "1234");
pinCodes.add("Charles", "9876");
```

A method that modifies an object and then returns the object

An add method that's added to the Array object type

```
Array.prototype.add = function(key, value) {
    this[key] = value;
    return this;
};
```

Chaining the add method calls does work

```
var pinCodes = [];
pinCodes.add("Grace", "1234").add("Charles", "9876");
```

Chaining method calls on a custom object

```
var Vehicle = function() {
    this.miles = 0;
    this.lastOilChange = 0;
};
Vehicle.prototype.drive = function(miles) {
    this.miles = this.miles + miles;
    return this;
};
Vehicle.prototype.changeOil = function() {
    this.lastOilChange = this.miles;
    return this;
};
Vehicle.prototype.needsOilChange = function() {
    return (this.miles - this.lastOilChange > 3000);
};
var myCar = new Vehicle();
myCar.drive(2000).changeOil().drive(4000);
alert(myCar.needsOilChange());    // Displays true
```

Description

- A *cascading method* is a method of an object that can be chained with other methods. This style of coding is sometimes called *fluent* because of the way it reads.

- A method must return the object represented by the this keyword if it is going to be chained with other methods.

Figure 11-15   How to create cascading methods

How to use the in, instanceof, and typeof operators

To help you get information about an object or variable, JavaScript provides the in, instanceof, and typeof operators. These operators can be used within a method to ensure that the right type of object or variable has been passed as an argument. The use of these operators is illustrated in figure 11-16.

The *in operator* is used to determine if an object has a specific property. It returns true if the property has been assigned a value. In the examples, the rate property of the application object has been defined so the operator returns true. But the month property hasn't been defined so the operator returns false. Similarly, both the items and taxRate properties of the invoice object have been defined by the constructor so the in operator returns true. And the calc object has inherited the square method of the proto object, so the in operator returns true.

The *instanceof operator* is used to determine the type of an object. If an object is an instance of the specified object type, the instanceof operator returns true. That includes instances of inherited object types. If an object isn't an instance of the specified object type, the instanceof operator returns false.

In the examples, the today object is obviously an instance of the Date object type. But it is also an instance of the Object object type because Date inherits from that type. Similarly, the application object is an instance of the Object object type because all objects inherit from that type. Clearly, though, the application object isn't an instance of the Date object type. Then, the examples show that the invoice object, which was built by the Invoice constructor, is an instance of both the Object and the Invoice type.

The last examples illustrate that the instanceof operator only checks for instances of constructors. This is because only constructor functions create new object types. The objects created by object literals and the create method are always of type Object. Thus, if you check whether calc is an instance of Object, it returns true. But if you try to check whether calc is an instance of proto, it throws an exception because proto isn't an object type. Rather, it's an actual object.

The *typeof operator* lets you determine whether a variable is a number, string, Boolean, object, or function. This is illustrated by the third set of examples. Notice here that the type of the Invoice constructor is "function", while the type of the proto prototype object is "object".

The objects and variables used by the operators that follow

```
var application = { rate: 0.04, years: 10 };

var Invoice = function() {
    this.items = [];
    this.taxRate = 0.07;
};
var invoice = new Invoice();

var proto = { square: function(a) { return a * a; } };
var calc = Object.create(proto);

var today = new Date();
var testArray = [];
var testString = "123";
var testNumber = 123;
```

How to use the in operator

```
alert( "rate" in application );        // Displays true
alert( "month" in application );       // Displays false
alert( "items" in invoice );           // Displays true
alert( "taxRate" in invoice );         // Displays true
alert( "square" in calc );             // Displays true
```

How to use the instanceof operator

```
alert( today instanceof Object );          // Displays true
alert( today instanceof Date );            // Displays true
alert( application instanceof Object );    // Displays true
alert( application instanceof Date );      // Displays false
alert( invoice instanceof Object );        // Displays true
alert( invoice instanceof Invoice );       // Displays true
alert( calc instanceof Object );           // Displays true
alert( calc instanceof proto );            // proto not a constructor
// TypeError: Expecting a function in instanceof check, but got #<Object>
```

How to use the typeof operator

```
alert( typeof application );           // Displays object
alert( typeof testArray );             // Displays object
alert( typeof testString );            // Displays string
alert( typeof testNumber );            // Displays number
alert( typeof application.rate );      // Displays number
alert( typeof invoice );               // Displays object
alert( typeof Invoice );               // Displays function
alert( typeof proto );                 // Displays object
```

Description

- The *in operator* returns true if an object has the named property.

- The *instanceof operator* returns true if an object is an instance of the specified object type. That includes the object type of the object as well as an inherited object type.

- The *typeof operator* lets you determine the type of a variable. It evaluates to "number", "string", or "Boolean" for the primitive values; to "object" for objects and nulls; to "function" for functions and constructors; and to "undefined" if the operand is undefined.

Figure 11-16   How to use the in, instanceof, and typeof operators with objects

The enhanced Task Manager application

This topic uses some of the advanced skills you've just learned to enhance the Task Manager application that you saw earlier in this chapter.

The new native objects library

The first example in figure 11-17 shows a library file for working with native JavaScript objects. It contains a single function that adds a capitalize method to the native String object.

The change to the task library

When you add a method to a native object's prototype object, the new method is available to all instances of the native object. You can see how that works in the second example in this figure. Here, the toString method of the Task object in the task library is rewritten so it uses the capitalize method that is now available on its text property, which is a string.

The enhanced storage library

Figure 11-17 shows the enhanced storage library. Instead of the one storage-Prototype object that it used before, the enhanced library uses two prototype objects.

The first one, localStoragePrototype, focuses only on getting strings to and from local storage. Because it's so basic, it could be inherited by any object that needs to work with local storage, regardless of what the object needs to do with the strings.

The second one, stringArrayStoragePrototype, inherits the localStorage-Prototype object. It then extends it by overriding the get and set methods. The new get method converts the storage string to an array of strings, and the new set method accepts an array of strings and converts it to a string. In both cases, the new methods use the functionality of the methods they are overriding by invoking the call method.

This library ends with the same factory function you saw before. This time, though, the factory function uses the new stringArrayStoragePrototype to create the storage object.

The structure of this library gives you a lot of coding flexibility. For example, you could write another prototype object that inherits the base localStoragePrototype and then converts the storage strings to an array of arrays, and another that converts the storage string to an array of objects. Or, you could write another object that inherits the stringArrayStoragePrototype object, and then further transforms the strings in the array.

The library_native_objects.js file

```
String.prototype.capitalize = String.prototype.capitalize || function() {
    var first = this.substring(0,1);
    return first.toUpperCase() + this.substring(1);
};
```

The toString method of the Task object that now uses the capitalize method of the native String object

```
Task.prototype.toString = function() {
    return this.text.capitalize();
};
```

The enhanced library_storage.js file

```
var localStoragePrototype = {
    get: function() { return localStorage.getItem(this.key); },
    set: function(str) { localStorage.setItem(this.key, str); },
    clear: function() { localStorage.setItem(this.key, ""); }
};

var stringArrayStoragePrototype = Object.create(localStoragePrototype);

// the get and set methods use functionality of the overridden methods
stringArrayStoragePrototype.get = function() {
    var str = localStoragePrototype.get.call(this) || "";
    return (str === "")? []: str.split("|");
};
stringArrayStoragePrototype.set = function(arr) {
    if (Array.isArray(arr)) {
        var str = arr.join("|");
        localStoragePrototype.set.call(this, str);
    }
};

var getTaskStorage = function(key) {
    var storage = Object.create(stringArrayStoragePrototype);
    storage.key = key;
    return storage;
};
```

Description

- The native objects library file adds a capitalize method to the native String object. Then, the Task object uses the capitalize method in its toString method.

- The storage library file has been enhanced to separate the functionality that gets strings in and out of local storage from the functionality that converts the tasks to and from arrays of strings. This way, any object that needs to store strings in local storage can inherit the base localStoragePrototype object, no matter what form the strings will be converted to.

- The getTaskStorage factory function accepts a key value and uses the create method to create a new object with the stringArrayStoragePrototype object. It then adds an own property named key, and it returns a storage object.

Figure 11-17   Three library enhancements for the Task Manager application

The enhanced task list library

Figure 11-18 shows the enhanced task list library. Most of the code is the same as what you saw in figure 11-10, so it isn't shown again here.

What's different is that each of the methods in the tasklist object is enhanced so it returns the this keyword. This means that the methods can now be chained. In the next figure, you'll see how chaining the method calls can make your code better.

The enhanced library_tasklist.js file

```
var tasklist = {
    tasks: [],
    storage: getTaskStorage("tasks_11"),
    displayDiv: null,
    deleteClickHandler: null,
    load: function() {
        /* same as figure 11-10 */
        return this;
    },
    save: function() {
        /* same as figure 11-10 */
        return this;
    },
    sort: function() {
        /* same as figure 11-10 */
        return this;
    },
    add: function(task) {
        /* same as figure 11-10 */
        return this;
    },
    delete: function(i) {
        /* same as figure 11-10 */
        return this;
    },
    clear: function() {
        /* same as figure 11-10 */
        return this;
    },
    display: function() {
        /* same as figure 11-10 */
        return this;
    }
};
```

Description

- The properties of the enhanced Task Manager application are the same as in figure 11-10, and the methods have the same functionality.

- What's different is that all the methods now return the this keyword, which makes them cascading methods that can be chained.

Figure 11-18   The enhanced task list library for the Task Manager application

The enhanced main JavaScript file

Figure 11-19 shows the main JavaScript code of Task Manager application. As in the last figure, nothing has changed except that now the method calls can be chained.

In the addToTaskList function, for instance, code that used to look like this:

```
tasklist.add(newTask);
tasklist.save();
tasklist.display();
```

now looks like this:

```
tasklist.add(newTask).save().display();
```

The deleteFromTaskList function also reduces three lines of code to one by chaining methods, and the onload event handler reduces two lines of code to one.

In addition to reducing the number of lines of code, this fluent style of method chaining makes the code easier to read. For example, the line of code above reads like a sentence that says "Add a new task to the tasks array, save the array in web storage, and then display the new task list."

The enhanced main JavaScript for the Task Manager application

```
var $ = function(id) { return document.getElementById(id); };

var addToTaskList = function() {
    var taskTextbox = $("task");
    var newTask = new Task(taskTextbox.value);
    if (newTask.isValid()) {
        tasklist.add(newTask).save().display();
        taskTextbox.value = "";
    } else {
        alert("Please enter a task.");
    }
    taskTextbox.focus();
};

var clearTaskList = function() {
    tasklist.clear();
    $("task").focus();
};

var deleteFromTaskList = function() {
    tasklist.delete(this.title).save().display(); // 'this' = clicked link
    $("task").focus();
};

window.onload = function() {
    $("add_task").onclick = addToTaskList;
    $("clear_tasks").onclick = clearTaskList;

    tasklist.displayDiv = $("tasks");
    tasklist.deleteClickHandler = deleteFromTaskList;

    tasklist.load().display();
    $("task").focus();
};
```

Description

- The main JavaScript file for the enhanced Task Manager application is the same it was in figure 11-11, except now it can chain the methods of the tasklist object. Thus, the tasklist method calls use fewer lines of code and are more readable.

Figure 11-19   The enhanced main JavaScript file for the Task Manager application

Perspective

Now that you've finished this chapter, you should be able to develop applications that are built around your own objects, methods, and properties. That in turn should make your applications easier to code, test, and debug. That's especially true for applications that are large or complex, and that's why object-oriented techniques are used in most of the applications that are presented in the rest of this book.

Terms

object type	prototype inheritance
inheritance	prototypal language
object literal	own property
nested object	factory function
delete operator	cascading method
reference	chaining
constructor function	fluent
constructor	in operator
prototype object	instanceof operator
class	typeof operator
classical language	

Summary

- JavaScript provides a two-level hierarchy of native *object types*. All object types at the second level *inherit* the properties and methods of the Object object type. They also provide properties and methods specific to those objects.

- When you create an object by coding an *object literal*, you can add properties and methods to it by coding pairs of property names and values that are separated by colons. You can also *nest* one object inside another. Within a method, the this keyword usually refers to the object itself.

- Once an object is created, you can add new properties and methods to it, change the value of existing properties and methods, and delete properties and methods with the *delete operator*.

- A variable holds a *reference* to an object, not the object itself. If more than one variable refers to an object, the delete operator will only delete the reference. But if there are no other references, the delete operator deletes the object itself.

- You can use a *constructor* to create your own object type, and you can add methods to the object type's *prototype object*. When a constructor is called with the new keyword, an *instance* of that object type is created so you can have multiple instances of the same object type.

- You can use the create method of the Object object to create a new object that's based on a custom prototype object. This is another way to create multiple instances of an object.

- You can also use the create method of the Object object to create a *factory function* that creates instances of an object that's based on a custom prototype.

- You can *inherit* the methods of another object by passing its prototype object to the Object.create method. You can also use constructors to inherit the methods of another object by setting a constructor's prototype object to a new instance of the object to be inherited.

- You can add a method to a native object like a string by adding the method to the prototype object for the native object.

- *Cascading methods* are created by returning the this keyword. This creates methods that can be *chained*. This way of coding is sometimes called *fluent*.

- The *in operator* returns true if an object has the named property. The *instanceof operator* returns true if an object is an instance of the specified object type. The *typeof operator* lets you determine the type of a variable.

Exercise 11-1   Enhance the Task Manager application

This exercise asks you to enhance the Task Manager application by adding links that let the user edit the tasks in the list.

Task Manager

Task:

Add Task

Clear Tasks

Delete Edit Finish current project
Delete Edit Meet with Mike
Delete Edit Write project summary

Open, test, and review the application

1. Use your text editor or IDE to open the JavaScript files in this folder:
   `c:\javascript\exercises\ch11\task_manager\`

2. Test this application in Chrome by adding three tasks and deleting one. Then, review the code in the JavaScript files for this application. These are the files that are shown in figures 11-9, 11-10, and 11-11.

Add an Edit function to the application

The steps that follow guide you through the process of adding an Edit link to each task as show above. You may want to start by trying to make this enhancement without the guidance.

3. In the task list library, find the display method, and find the line of code that creates the Delete link. Then, after this line, add code that creates an Edit link like the one shown above. This code should be similar to the code for creating the Delete link.

4. Still in the display method of the task list library, note the if statement that has been added to the second for loop. This statement adds one event handler if the innerHTML property for the link is "Delete" and another event handler if it isn't. Now, add a variable to the task list object that will hold the click event handler for the Edit links.

5. Still in the task list library, add an edit method that receives the index of the task that's being edited and the Task object that will replace the current task at that index. This method should save the task in the tasks array at the specified index, but it should use the toString method of the task to capitalize the first letter before it's saved.

6. In the main JavaScript file, add a function named editTaskListItem. It should uses the prompt method to display the text of the old task and get the text for the edited task from the user. Then, it should create a new Task object with the new text as the task description, and use the isValid method of that object to test whether the text is valid. If it isn't, an error message should be displayed by the alert method. If it is valid, the function should call the edit method of the tasklist object to save the edited task in the tasks array. After that, it should call the save and display methods to save the tasks array and redisplay the task list. Last, it should set the focus on the task text box.

7. In the onload event handler, add a statement that sets the variable for the click event handler for the Edit links to the function that you just created. Now, test the new Edit function.

Use chaining with the methods in the task list library

8. Add a return this statement to each of the methods in the task list library. Then, modify your editTaskListItem function in the main JavaScript file so it chains the calls to the edit, save, and display methods of the task list library.

Use a factory function to create the Task objects

9. In the task library, comment out everything but the "use strict" directive. Then, rewrite this library so it uses a factory function and the Object.create method to create task objects with isValid and toString methods.

   Start by creating a prototype object for the task objects. Then, code a factory function named getTask that creates a task object and sets its text property to the task description. You can use figure 11-7 as a guide for writing this code, but be sure to use a name for the parameter that will work with the rest of the code. Remember that the parameter is the text for a task, not the task object.

10. In the main JavaScript file, comment out the two lines of code that create new Task objects. Below these statements, code the statements that use the factory function to create the task objects. Then, test these changes. This illustrates the two ways that you can work with multiple instances of an object.

12

How to use regular expressions, handle exceptions, and validate data

In this chapter, you'll learn how to use regular expressions and how to handle any exceptions that might be thrown by an application. Then, you'll study a Register application that uses regular expressions and exception handling to do data validation. When you complete this chapter, you'll be able to develop bulletproof JavaScript applications.

How to use regular expressions

Regular expressions are coded patterns that can be used to search for matching patterns in strings. These expressions are commonly used to validate the data that is entered by users.

How to create and use regular expressions

Figure 12-1 shows how regular expressions work. To start, you create a *regular expression object* that contains the *pattern* that will be used. To do that, you can use either of the techniques that are shown in this figure.

With the first technique, you code the pattern in quotation marks as the parameter of the RegExp constructor. With the second technique, you code a *regular expression literal*, which consists of the pattern between slashes. In either case, you create a new RegExp object that contains the pattern. In the first two examples, that pattern is simply "Babbage".

Once you've created a regular expression object, you can use it to find pattern matches in a string. To do that, you can use the test method of the regular expression object. This is illustrated by the two examples.

In the first example, the test method searches for the pattern "Babbage" in the variable named inventor. Since that variable contains "Charles Babbage", the pattern is found and the method returns true. In the second example, the variable contains "Ada Lovelace" so the pattern isn't found, and the method returns false.

By default, the search that's done is case-sensitive. However, you can change that to case-insensitive as shown in the next set of examples. What you're actually doing is changing the ignoreCase property of the regular expression object to true. Then, the last example shows that a pattern of "lovelace" will match "Lovelace" when this property is set to true.

Two ways to create a regular expression object that will find "Babbage"

By using the RegExp constructor function

```
var pattern = new RegExp("Babbage");   // Creates a regular expression object
```

By coding a regular expression literal

```
var pattern = /Babbage/;               // This creates the same object
```

One method of a regular expression

Method	Description
test(*string*)	Searches for the regular expression in the string. It returns true if the pattern is found and false if it's not found.

How to use the test method of a regular expression

Two strings to test

```
var inventor = "Charles Babbage";
var programmer = "Ada Lovelace";
```

How to use the test method to search for the pattern

```
alert ( pattern.test(inventor) );     // Displays true
alert ( pattern.test(programmer) );   // Displays false
```

How to create a case-insensitive regular expression

When using the RegExp constructor function

```
var pattern = new RegExp("lovelace", "i");
```

When coding a regular expression literal

```
var pattern = /lovelace/i;
```

How to use a case-insensitive regular expression

```
alert ( pattern.test(programmer) );   // Displays true
```

Description

- A *regular expression* defines a *pattern* that can be searched for in a string. This pattern is stored in a *regular expression object*.

- To create a regular expression object, you can use the RegExp constructor function. Then, the pattern is coded within quotation marks as the only parameter.

- Another way to create a regular expression object is to code a *regular expression literal*. To do that, you code a pattern within two forward slashes.

- You can use the test method of a regular expression object to search for the pattern in the string parameter.

- By default, a regular expression pattern is case-sensitive, but you can change that by setting the ignoreCase property of the regular expression object to true.

Figure 12-1   How to create and use regular expressions

How to create regular expression patterns

The trick to using regular expressions is coding the patterns, and that can get complicated. That's why the two parts of figure 12-2 move from the simple to the complex as they show you how to create patterns. To start, though, remember that all letters and numbers represent themselves in a pattern.

The first table in this figure shows you how to include special characters in a pattern. To do that, you start with the *escape character*, which is the backslash. For instance, \\ is equivalent to one backslash; \/ is equivalent to one forward slash; and \xA9 is equivalent to \u00A9, which is equivalent to the copyright symbol.

Note, however, that this table doesn't include all of the special characters that you need to precede with backslashes. For instance, the second table points out that you need to use \. to represent a period, and the third table on the next figure page points out that you need to use \$ to match a dollar sign.

The examples after the first table show how these special characters can be used in regular expression patterns. Here, the second and third statements use a regular expression literal followed by .test to call the test method for that expression object. The second statement looks for one slash in the variable named string and finds it. The third statement looks for the copyright symbol and finds it.

Then, the fourth statement uses the first technique in figure 12-1 to create a RegExp object. But when you use the RegExp constructor to create a regular expression object, you have to code two backslashes in the pattern for every one that you use in a regular expression literal. That's because the RegExp constructor takes a string parameter, and the backslash is also the escape character for strings. For this reason, it's easier to use regular expression literals. In this example, the pattern is equivalent to one backslash, but the fifth statement doesn't find it because the string variable contains the escape sequence for a new line (\n), not a backslash.

The second table shows how to match types of characters instead of specific characters. If, for example, the literal is /MB\d/, the pattern will match the letters MB followed by any digit. Or, if the literal is /MB.../, the pattern will match MB followed by any three characters.

The examples after this table show how this works. Here, the second statement looks for MB followed by any character and finds it. The third statement looks for MB followed by either T or F and finds it. And the fourth statement looks for MBT- followed by any character that's not a letter, number or the underscore. It doesn't find a match, though, because the string contains MBT-3.

How to match special characters

Pattern	Matches
\\	Backslash character
\/	Forward slash
\t	Tab
\n	Newline
\r	Carriage return
\f	Form feed
\v	Vertical tab
[\b]	Backspace (the only special character that must be inside brackets)
\udddd	The Unicode character whose value is the four hexadecimal digits.
\xdd	The Latin-1 character whose value is the two hexadecimal digits. Equivalent to \u00*dd*.

Examples

```
var string = "©2015 MMA Inc.\nAll rights reserved (5/2015).";
alert( /\//.test(string) );          // Matches / and displays true
alert( /\xA9/.test(string) );        // Matches © and displays true

var pattern = new RegExp("\\\\");    // Same as /\\/
alert( pattern.test(string) );       // Displays false since there's no \
```

How to match types of characters

Pattern	Matches
.	Any character except a newline (use \. to match a period)
[ ]	Any character in the brackets (use \[or \] to match a bracket)
[^]	Any character not in the brackets
[a-z]	Any character in the range of characters when used inside brackets
\w	Any letter, number, or the underscore
\W	Any character that's not a letter, number, or the underscore
\d	Any digit
\D	Any character that's not a digit
\s	Any whitespace character (space, tab, newline, carriage return, form feed, or vertical tab)
\S	Any character that's not whitespace

Examples

```
var string = "The product code is MBT-3461.";
alert( /MB./.test(string) );         // Displays true
alert( /MB[TF]/.test(string) );      // Displays true
alert( /MBT-\W/.test(string) );      // Displays false
```

Description

- The backslash is used as the *escape character* in regular expressions.

- When you use the RegExp constructor, any backslash in your pattern must be preceded by another backslash. That's because the backslash is also the escape character in strings.

Figure 12-2   How to create regular expression patterns (part 1 of 2)

The first table in part 2 of this figure shows how to match characters at specific positions in a string. For instance, the pattern /^com/ will find the letters "com" at the start of a string. And the pattern /com$/ will find the letters "com" at the end of a string. This is illustrated by the examples after this table.

Here, the last example displays false because "Ad" is followed by another word character. To say that another way, "Ad" is found at the beginning of a word but not at the end of a word (the first word in the string is "Ada"). One use of the \b pattern is to find whole words.

The second table shows how to group and match a *subpattern* that is coded in parentheses. This is illustrated by the examples after this table. Here, the second statement will match a subpattern of either "Rob" or "Bob".

If you code more than one subpattern in a pattern, the patterns are numbered from left to right. Then, if you want to repeat the subpattern in the pattern, you can specify the number of the pattern that you want to repeat. This is illustrated by the third statement after the table. Here, the \1 indicates that the first pattern, which matches any three letters, numbers, or underscores, should be used again. This returns true because that pattern is repeated. It would also return true if the pattern were /(Rob) \1/ because "Rob" is repeated.

The third table shows how to use a *quantifier* that's coded in braces to match a repeating pattern. For instance, /\d{3}/ will match any three digits in succession, and /\${1,3}/ will match from one to three occurrences of a dollar sign. Here again, this is illustrated by the examples that follow the table. The third statement matches three digits at the start of a string, a hyphen, three more digits, another hyphen, and four digits at the end of the string. And the fourth statement matches a left parenthesis at the start of the string, three digits, a right parenthesis, zero or one space (as indicated by the question mark quantifier after the space), and four digits at the end of the string.

Then, the pattern in the fifth statement combines the patterns of the third and fourth statements so a phone number can start with either three digits in parentheses or three digits followed by a hyphen. Here again, the question mark after the space means that zero or one space can be used after an area code in parentheses, so this pattern will find telephone numbers like 559-555-1234, (559)555-1234, and (559) 555-1234.

These tables and examples should get you started coding patterns of your own. And you'll get more proficient with them as you study the examples in the rest of this chapter. Before you take on a complex pattern, though, you might want to do an Internet search for "regular expressions" or "regular expression library" first. You'll probably find that someone else has already written the pattern you need.

How to match string positions

Pattern	Matches
^	The beginning of the string (use \^ to match a caret)
$	The end of the string (use \$ to match a dollar sign)
\b	Word characters that aren't followed or preceded by a word character
\B	Word characters that are followed or preceded by a word character

Examples

```
var inventor = "Charles Babbage";
alert( /^Charles/.test(inventor) );         // Displays true
alert( /Babbage$/.test(inventor) );         // Displays true
alert( /^Babbage/.test(inventor) );         // Displays false
var programmer = "Ada Lovelace";
alert( /Ad/.test(programmer) );             // Displays true
alert( /Ad\b/.test(programmer) );           // Displays false
```

How to group and match subpatterns

Pattern	Matches
(*subpattern*)	Creates a numbered subpattern (use \(and \) to match a parenthesis)
(?:*subpattern*)	Creates an unnumbered subpattern
|	Matches either the left or right subpattern (use \\| to match a vertical bar)
\n	Matches a numbered subpattern

Examples

```
var name = "Rob Robertson";
alert( /^(Rob)|(Bob)\b/.test(name) );       // Displays true
alert( /^(\w\w\w) \1/.test(name) );         // Displays true
```

How to match a repeating pattern

Pattern	Matches
{*n*}	Pattern must repeat exactly *n* times (use \{ and \} to match a brace)
{*n*,}	Pattern must repeat *n* or more times
{*n*,*m*}	Subpattern must repeat from *n* to *m* times
?	Zero or one of the previous subpattern (same as {0,1})
+	One or more of the previous subpattern (same as {1,})
*	Zero or more of the previous subpattern (same as {0,})

Examples

```
var phone = "559-555-6627";
var fax   = "(559) 555-6635";
alert( /^\d{3}-\d{3}-\d{4}$/.test(phone) );       // Displays true
alert( /^\(\d{3}\) ?\d{3}-\d{4}$/.test(fax) );    // Displays true

var phonePattern = /^(\d{3}-)|(\(\d{3}\) ?)\d{3}-\d{4}$/;
alert( phonePattern.test(phone) );                // Displays true
alert( phonePattern.test(fax) );                  // Displays true
```

Figure 12-2   How to create regular expression patterns (part 2 of 2)

How to use the global and multiline flags

In figure 12-1, you saw how you could set the ignoreCase property of a regular expression object to true to make a match case-insensitive. Now, figure 12-3 shows you how to use the global and multiline properties of a regular expression object.

To turn these properties on, you can use one of the techniques in this figure. If, for example, you use the RegExp constructor, you code "g" or "m" as the second parameter. If you use a regular expression literal, you code "g" or "m" after the literal. This works the same as it does for the ignoreCase property.

When you use "g" or "m" to turn the property on, the "g" or "m" is commonly called a *flag*. So you can refer to the g flag, the m flag, or the i flag (for the case-insensitive flag). When you set these flags, they cause the corresponding property to be set to true.

When the global property is on, you can use the test method to find more than one match in a string. To do that, the test method uses the lastIndex property of the regular expression object to determine where the next search should start. This property starts with a value of zero, but is reset to the starting position for the next search after each match.

This is illustrated by the global example in this figure. Here, the test method is used four times in a row with the same string. The first time, it finds a match for the pattern "MBT" in the first three characters of the string so it returns true and sets the lastIndex property to 3. The second time, it finds another match so it returns true and sets the lastIndex property to 12. The third time, it doesn't find a match so it returns false and sets the lastIndex property back to zero. And the fourth time, the results are the same as the first time.

When the multiline property is off, the ^ and $ characters look for matches at the start and end of the string. But when this property is on, those characters look for matches at the start and end of each line in the string. This is illustrated by the multiline example. Here, the string contains two lines with "G. Hopper" on the first line and "Programmer" on the second line. As a result, the pattern /Hopper$/ returns false if the multiline flag isn't on, but true if the flag is on.

How to create a global regular expression

By using the RegExp constructor function
```
var pattern = new RegExp("Hopper", "g");
```

By coding a regular expression literal
```
var pattern = /Hopper/g;
```

One property of a regular expression

Property	Description
lastIndex	The position in the string at which the search is started. This property is initially set to zero. But if a match is found, this property is reset to one more than the position of the last character matched by the pattern, even if this position is past the end of the string. If a match isn't found, this property is reset to zero.

How to use a global regular expression
```
var pattern = /MBT/g;
var string  = "MBT-6745 MBT-5712";
alert( pattern.test(string) + ", " + pattern.lastIndex );   // true, 3
alert( pattern.test(string) + ", " + pattern.lastIndex );   // true, 12
alert( pattern.test(string) + ", " + pattern.lastIndex );   // false, 0
alert( pattern.test(string) + ", " + pattern.lastIndex );   // true, 3
```

How to create a multiline regular expression

By using the RegExp constructor function
```
var pattern = new RegExp("Hopper$", "m");
```

By coding a regular expression literal
```
var pattern = /Hopper$/m;
```

How to use a multiline regular expression
```
var pattern1 = /Hopper$/;            // A non-multiline regular expression
var pattern2 = /Hopper$/m;           // A multiline regular expression
var string = "G. Hopper\nProgrammer"; // A multiline string
alert( pattern1.test(string) );      // Displays false
alert( pattern2.test(string) );      // Displays true
```

Description

- If the global property is set to true, you can use the test method to look for more than one match in a string.

- If the multiline property is set to true, the ^ pattern looks for matches at the beginning of each line and the $ pattern looks for matches at the end of each line.

Figure 12-3   How to use the global and multiline flags

String methods that use regular expressions

Besides the test method of a regular expression object, you can use three string methods to work with regular expressions. These expressions are summarized in figure 12-4. Note that all three take the regular expression object as the first parameter.

The search method of a string searches for a match in the string. If it finds one, it returns the index of the first character of the match within the string. Otherwise, it returns -1. The first set of examples in this figure shows how this works.

The match method of a string is often used with the global flag turned on. Then, it returns an array of all the matches. This is illustrated by the second set of examples. If no matches are found, this method returns null.

If you use the match method without the global flag turned on, it returns an array with the first match in element 0 and any subpatterns in the pattern in the subsequent elements. This is illustrated by the third set of examples in which "MBT-6745" is the first match, and "6745" is the only subpattern that was used in the pattern. Here again, if a match isn't found, this method returns null.

The replace method is like the search method, but it replaces a match with the value of the second parameter. If the global flag is set, it replaces all matches with the value. If the global flag isn't set, it replaces just the first match. This is illustrated by the last two sets of examples.

All three of these methods are often used in combination with the string methods that you learned about in chapter 7. Together, they give you all of the capabilities that you'll need for working with the characters in a string.

Three string methods that you can use with regular expressions

Method	Description
`search(regexp)`	Searches for the regular expression in the string. If not found, it returns -1. If found, it returns the index of the first character in the match within the string.
`match(regexp)`	Searches for the regular expression in the string. If the global flag is set, it returns an array of all matching substrings. If the global flag isn't set, it returns an array with the matched characters in element 0, numbered substrings in subsequent elements, and the index property set to the index of the first character in the match. If a match isn't found, this method always returns null.
`replace(regexp, value)`	Searches for the regular expression in the string. When found, the matched string is replaced by the string in the value parameter. If the global flag is set, all matches are replaced. If the global flag isn't set, only the first match is replaced.

How to use the search and match methods with a regular expression

How to use the search method

```
var email = "grace@yahoo.com";
alert ( email.search( /\.com$/ ) );      // displays 11
alert ( email.search( /\.net$/ ) );      // displays -1
if ( email.search( /\.edu$/ ) === -1 ) {
    alert ("Not an .edu address");       // displays the message
}
```

How to use the match method with a global regular expression

```
var items = "Items: MBT-6745 MBT-572";
var result = items.match( /MBT-(\d{1,4})/g );
// result is the array [ "MBT-6745", "MBT-572" ]
```

How to use the match method with a non-global regular expression

```
var items = "Items: MBT-6745 MBT-572";
var result = items.match( /MBT-(\d{1,4})/ );
// result is the array [ "MBT-6745", "6745" ]
// result.index is 7, the offset of the first match
```

How to use the replace method with a regular expression

How to replace text

```
var items = "MBT-6745 MBT-572";
alert( items.replace(/MBT/,  "ITEM") );  // Displays ITEM-6745 MBT-572
alert( items.replace(/MBT/g, "ITEM") );  // Displays ITEM-6745 ITEM-572
```

How to trim whitespace from a string

```
var message = "   JavaScript   ";
string = message.replace(/^\s+/,"");     // Trim start of string
string = message.replace(/\s+$/,"");     // Trim end of string
alert( "(" + message + ")" );            // Displays (JavaScript)
```

Figure 12-4   String methods that use regular expressions

Regular expressions for data validation

Figure 12-5 starts with some patterns that are commonly used for data validation. For instance, the first pattern is for phone numbers so it matches 3 digits at the start of the string, a hyphen, 3 more digits, another hyphen, and 4 digits at the end of the string. Similarly, the second one is for credit card numbers so it matches four groups of 4 digits separated by hyphens.

The third pattern is for 5- or 9-digit zip codes. It requires 5 digits at the start of the string. Then, it uses the ? quantifier with a subpattern that contains a hyphen followed by four digits. As a result, this subpattern is optional.

The fourth pattern is for dates in the mm/dd/yy format, but it also accepts a date in the m/yy/dd format. To start, this pattern uses the ? quantifier to show that the string can start with zero or one occurrences of 0 or 1. This means that the month in the date can be coded like 03/19/1940 or 3/19/1940. But if two digits are used for the month, the first digit has to be either 0 or 1.

Then, the pattern calls for one digit, a slash, either 0, 1, 2, or 3, another digit, another slash, and four more digits. As a result, this pattern doesn't match a string if its first month digit is greater than 1 or if its first day digit is greater than 3. But this will still match invalid dates like 19/21/2015 or 9/39/2016 so additional data validation is required. You'll see the additional validation later.

The examples that follow these patterns show how they can be used in your code. The first example uses the phone number pattern with the match method and displays an error message if a match isn't found. Here, the if statement works because the match method returns a null if a match isn't found. The second example works the same, but it uses the date pattern. Remember, though, that this pattern will match some invalid date formats.

This figure ends by presenting a function named isEmail that is based on the SMTP specification for how an email address may be formed. This specification calls the part before the @ symbol the "local part", and the part after the @ symbol the "domain part". Then, it gives the requirements for each part.

In brief, this isEmail function splits the address into the parts before and after the @ symbol and returns false if there aren't two parts. Next, this function builds a regular expression pattern named localPart by combining two subpatterns with the | character, which means that the string can match either subpattern. Then, it looks for a match in the part of the address before the @ symbol. If it doesn't find one, it returns false.

Similarly, the last part of this function builds a regular expression pattern named domainPart by combining two subpatterns. Then, it looks for a match in the part of the address after the @ symbol. If it doesn't find one, it returns false. Otherwise, this function returns true because the email address is valid.

Of course, it is the patterns in this function that are the most difficult to understand. For instance, [^\\\\\\"] matches any character that isn't a backslash or a quotation mark. The good news is that you don't need to understand this pattern to use it. In fact, many programmers find complex patterns like this online and use them without completely understanding them.

Regular expressions for testing validity

A pattern for testing phone numbers in this format: 999-999-9999
```
/^\d{3}-\d{3}-\d{4}$/
```

A pattern for testing credit card numbers in this format: 9999-9999-9999-9999
```
/^\d{4}-\d{4}-\d{4}-\d{4}$/
```

A pattern for testing zip codes in either of these formats: 99999 or 99999-9999
```
/^\d{5}(-\d{4})?$/
```

A pattern for testing dates in this format: mm/dd/yyyy
```
/^[01]?\d\/[0-3]\d\/\d{4}$/
```

Examples that use these expressions

Testing a phone number for validity
```
var phone = "559-555-6624";                    // valid phone number
var phonePattern = /^\d{3}-\d{3}-\d{4}$/;
if ( !phone.match(phonePattern) ) {
    alert("Invalid phone number");             // Not displayed
}
```

Testing a date for a valid format, but not for a valid month, day, and year
```
var startDate = "8/10/215";                    // Invalid date
var datePattern = /^[01]?\d\/[0-3]\d\/\d{4}$/;
// This pattern will match dates like 19/21/2015 and 9/39/2016
if ( !startDate.match(datePattern) ) {
    alert("Invalid start date");               // Displays error message
}
```

A function that does complete validation of an email address
```
var isEmail = function(email) {
    if (email.length === 0) return false;
    var parts = email.split("@");
    if (parts.length !== 2) return false;
    if (parts[0].length > 64) return false;
    if (parts[1].length > 255) return false;

    var address =
        "(^[\\w!#$%&'*+/=?^`{|}~-]+(\\.[\\w!#$%&'*+/=?^`{|}~-]+)*$)";
    var quotedText = "(^\"(([^\\\\\\"])|(\\\\[\\\\\\"]))+\"$)";
    var localPart = new RegExp( address + "|" + quotedText );
    if ( !parts[0].match(localPart) ) return false;

    var hostnames =
        "(([a-zA-Z0-9]\\.)|([a-zA-Z0-9][-a-zA-Z0-9]{0,62}[a-zA-Z0-9]\\.))+";
    var tld = "[a-zA-Z0-9]{2,6}";
    var domainPart = new RegExp("^" + hostnames + tld + "$");
    if ( !parts[1].match(domainPart) ) return false;

    return true;
};

alert (isEmail("grace@yahoo.com"));             // Displays true
alert (isEmail("grace@yahoocom"));              // Displays false
```

Figure 12-5   Regular expressions for data validation

How to handle exceptions

To prevent your applications from crashing due to runtime errors, you can write code that handles any *exceptions*. These are runtime errors that occur due to unexpected error conditions. You can also "throw" your own exceptions and then write code that handles them.

How to create and throw Error objects

In some applications, like the one that's illustrated at the end of this chapter, you will want to *throw* your own exceptions. To do that, you can create a new Error object and use the *throw statement* to throw it. This is illustrated by figure 12-6.

To create a new Error object, you call the Error constructor and pass one parameter to it that contains a message. This message is then stored in the Error object's message property.

After you create an Error object, you can throw it. This is illustrated by the first example in this figure. Here, a function that calculates future value throws an exception if one of the values that is passed to it is invalid. When the exception is thrown, the function ends and control is passed to the function that called it. Then, that function can catch the exception and display its message property as shown in the next figure.

Besides Error objects, JavaScript throws other types of error objects that inherit from the Error object. These are summarized in the second table in this figure. For instance, a RangeError object is thrown when a numeric value has exceeded an allowable range. In the examples after this table, the first statement throws this type of error because the parameter of the toFixed method is out of range.

Similarly, a SyntaxError object is thrown when the syntax of a statement is invalid. In the third statement in the examples, this occurs because "x" is an invalid second parameter for the RegExp constructor.

You can also create and throw objects of these other Error types in your applications. This is illustrated by the last example in this figure. Here, the throw statement is used to throw a RangeError object with a message that says a user entry is invalid.

To determine what type of error has been thrown, you can use the name property of the error object. If, for example, an Error object has been thrown, this property is set to "Error". But if a RangeError object has been thrown, this property is set to "RangeError".

The syntax for creating a new Error object

```
new Error(message)
```

The syntax for the throw statement

```
throw errorObject;
```

A calculateFutureValue method that throws a new Error object

```
var calculateFutureValue = function( investment, annualRate, years ) {
    if ( investment <= 0 || annualRate <= 0 || years <= 0 ) {
        throw new Error("Please check your entries for validity.");
    }

    var monthlyRate = annualRate / 12 / 100;
    var months = years * 12;
    var futureValue = 0;

    for ( var i = 1; i <= months; i++ ) {
        futureValue = (futureValue + investment) * (1 + monthlyRate);
    }
    return futureValue.toFixed(2);
};
```

Two properties of Error objects

Property	Description
message	The message used when the Error object was created
name	The type of error ("Error" for Error objects)

Other types of error objects that inherit from the Error type

Type	Thrown when
RangeError	A numeric value has exceeded the allowable range
ReferenceError	A variable is read that hasn't been defined
SyntaxError	A runtime syntax error is encountered
TypeError	The type of a value is different from what was expected
URIError	A URI handling function was used incorrectly

Example of statements that generate these errors

```
alert( (3.275).toFixed(101) );              // Throws RangeError
alert( firstName );                         // Throws ReferenceError
var pattern = new RegExp("Hopper", "x");    // Throws SyntaxError
```

A statement that throws a RangeError object

```
throw new RangeError("Annual rate is invalid.");   // Throws RangeError
```

Description

- To create a new Error object, you use its constructor with a string as the parameter. If the parameter isn't a string, it is converted to one.

- To trigger a runtime error, you use the *throw statement*. It can throw a new or existing Error object.

Figure 12-6   How to create and throw Error objects

How to use the try-catch statement
to handle exceptions

When Error objects are thrown, your application needs to "catch" and handle them. Otherwise, your application will end with a runtime error.

To catch errors, you use a *try-catch statement* as shown in figure 12-7. First, you code a *try block* around the statement or statements that may throw an exception. Then, you code a *catch block* that contains the statements that will be executed if an exception is thrown by any statement in the try block. This is known as *exception handling*.

The first example in this figure shows how you can use a try-catch statement to catch any exceptions that are thrown by the four statements in the try block. Here, the fourth statement calls the calculate_future_value function in the previous figure. Then, if that function throws an exception, control immediately jumps to the first statement in the catch block. In addition, the Error object is passed to the catch block.

In the parentheses after the catch keyword, you code a name that you can use to refer to this Error object. Then, you can use the message property of this object to access the message that's associated with the object. You can also use the name property to find out what type of Error object has been thrown. In this example, the catch block uses the alert method to display the value of the message property.

If an exception is thrown within a try block, the exception is caught by the catch block. But if a catch block isn't coded, the exception is passed to the calling function. This passing of the exception continues until the exception is caught or the application ends with a runtime error.

In some cases, you may want use a catch block to rethrow an error to the calling function. This is illustrated by the second example in this figure. Here, the throw statement throws the variable that the Error object was stored in. Then, this error can be handled by the next function in the call stack.

Often, you only need to code the try and catch blocks for a try-catch statement. But as the syntax at the top of this figure shows, you can also code a *finally block*. Then, the code in the finally block is executed after the statements in the try block if no exception occurs or after the statements in the catch block if an exception occurs. The finally block is useful if you need to clean up resources or restore a page to its original state.

The syntax for a try-catch statement

```
try { statements }
catch(errorName) { statements }
finally { statements }          // The finally block is optional
```

A try-catch statement that contains a throw statement

```
var calculate = function() {
    try {
        var investment = parseFloat( $("investment").value );
        var annualRate = parseFloat( $("rate").value );
        var years = parseInt( $("years").value );

        $("futureValue").value =
            calculateFutureValue(investment, annualRate, years);
    } catch(error) {
        alert (error.message);
    }
};
```

The dialog box that displays the message property of the error object

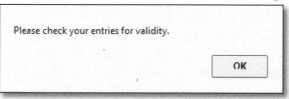

A try-catch statement that rethrows an Error object to its calling function

```
try {
    $("futureValue").value =
        calculateFutureValue(investment, annualRate, years);
} catch(error) {
    // If needed, do something before rethrowing error
    throw error;
}
```

Description

- You can use a *try-catch statement* to process any errors that are thrown by an application. These errors are often referred to as *exceptions*.

- In a try-catch statement, you code a *try block* that contains the statements that may throw exceptions. Then, you code a *catch block* that contains the statements that are executed when an exception is thrown in the try block.

- In the catch block, the Error object is available for use in the *errorName* variable. When execution leaves this block, the Error object is no longer available.

- JavaScript syntax requires that you code either a catch block, a *finally block*, or both. The finally block is executed whether or not the statements in the catch block are executed, and is used for things like cleaning up resources or restoring a page to its original state.

Figure 12-7   How to use the try-catch statement to handle exceptions

The Register application

Now, to show you how exception handling and data validation are used in a real-world JavaScript application, this chapter presents a Register application. This application validates the data that the user enters into the form before submitting the form to the server for processing.

Although you could use functions to do the validation for this application, this application takes an object-oriented approach. That will help solidify what you learned in the last chapter. It will also demonstrate the value of creating and using objects.

The user interface

Figure 12-8 presents the user interface for this application when it first loads, and then after a user has entered some invalid data. When the application loads, the JavaScript code adds informational messages to the right of some text boxes that show how the data should be entered. After the user enters data and clicks the Register button, the JavaScript code checks the data for validity.

If the data is valid, the application submits the data to the server for processing. It also displays a confirmation page. If the data isn't valid, it displays error messages to mark the invalid entries so the user can correct them. In the second screen shot in this figure, you can see error messages to the right of five fields, and these messages are displayed in red.

The Register form when it's first displayed

The Register form with error messages

Figure 12-8   The Register application

The HTML and CSS

Figure 12-9 presents some of the HTML for this application. First, you can see the script elements in the head section. They show that this application uses five JavaScript files: four library files and the main JavaScript file.

Then, you can see that the main element consists of an h1 element, a form, and a section. The form has an id of registration_form, and a class attribute with a value of "show". This is the form shown in the last figure. The section has an id of registration_result, and a class attribute with a value of "hide". This is the section that is displayed when a registration is successful. As you might guess, the class values determine whether the form or section is displayed.

The HTML for the form consists of several input elements of type text and password. After each of these input elements is a span element. These span elements are where the informational messages show when the page loads, and where error messages show after data validation. Both types of messages are added by JavaScript code.

You'll notice that the id value of each of these span elements is identical to the input element it follows, except that the span element's id adds the string "_error". This is how the JavaScript code associates a span element with the related input element.

At the end of the form are two buttons with ids of "register" and "reset". They will be used to initiate the validation of the data in the form and to reset the data and messages in the form.

The HTML in the section contains some information for the user in <p> elements, and an input element for a button with the id of "back". This is displayed when all entries are valid and the form is submitted to the server.

After the HTML in this figure, you can see three of the CSS rule sets for this application. The first one applies the color red to the error class. However, if you look through the HTML, you won't find an error class. Instead, as you will see in a moment, this class name is assigned to the span elements if the message it contains is an error message. As a result, error messages are displayed in red.

The next two rule sets apply values for the CSS display property. The value for the show class is block, and the value for the hide class is none. This determines the visibility for the elements that have these classes assigned. In the HTML in this figure, for example, the form element is assigned the class show, so it is visible when the page loads. Conversely, the section element is assigned the class hide, so it isn't visible when the page loads.

Then, when the data validation succeeds and the registration is successful, the JavaScript code switches these class names. When that happens, the form element is hidden and the section shows. Then, when the user clicks the Back button, the class names are switched again, so that the page goes back to showing the form element and hiding the section.

The script elements in the head section that identify the libraries

```
<script src="library_navigate.js"></script>
<script src="library_fields.js"></script>
<script src="library_validate.js"></script>
<script src="library_validate_form.js"></script>
<script src="register.js"></script>
```

The HTML for the main element of the document

```
<main>
    <h1>Register for an Account</h1>
    <form id="registration_form" action="register_account.php" method="get"
        name="registration_form" class="show">
        <label for="email">E-Mail:</label>
            <input type="text" name="email" id="email">
            <span id="email_error"> </span><br>
        <label for="password">Password:</label>
            <input type="password" name="password" id="password">
            <span id="password_error"> </span><br>
        <label for="verify">Verify Password:</label>
            <input type="password" name="verify" id="verify">
            <span id="verify_error"> </span><br>
        <label for="first_name">First Name:</label>
            <input type="text" name="first_name" id="first_name">
            <span id="first_name_error"> </span><br>
        <label for="last_name">Last Name:</label>
            <input type="text" name="last_name" id="last_name">
            <span id="last_name_error"> </span><br>
        <label for="zip">ZIP Code:</label>
            <input type="text" name="zip" id="zip">
            <span id="zip_error"> </span><br>
        <label for="card_type">Card Type:</label>
            <select name="card_type" id="card_type">
                <option value="v">Visa</option>
                <option value="m">MasterCard</option>
                <option value="d">Discover</option>
            </select><br>
        <label for="card_number">Card Number:</label>
            <input type="text" name="card_number" id="card_number">
            <span id="card_number_error"> </span><br>
        <label for="exp_date">Expiration Date:</label>
            <input type="text" name="exp_date" id="exp_date">
            <span id="exp_date_error"> </span><br>
        <input type="button" id="register" value="Register">
        <input type="button" id="reset" value="Reset">
    </form>
    <section id="registration_result" class="hide">
        <p>Congratulations! Your account registration has been submitted.</p>
        <p>You'll receive an email shortly with more information. Welcome!</p>
        <input type="button" id="back" value="Back">
    </section>
</main>
```

Some of the CSS for the application

```
.error { color: red; }
.show { display: block; }
.hide { display: none; }
```

Figure 12-9   The HTML and CSS for the Register application

The navigate and fields libraries

Figure 12-10 shows two JavaScript library files. The library_navigate file starts with the $ function for retrieving objects from the page. Because many of the JavaScript files will need to use this function, it is in the first JavaScript file listed in the head section of the HTML document. That way, it can be used by all the JavaScript files that follow.

Next is an object literal named navigate, which contains two methods, showForm and showResults. These methods use the $ function to assign the CSS show and hide classes you just learned about. This object is called navigate because showing and hiding the elements creates the impression of navigating between pages.

The library_fields file contains another object literal called fields, which contains eight properties called email, password, verify, first_name, last_name, zip, card_number, and exp_date. Notice that these property names match the names of the input elements, or fields, in the HTML shown in the last figure. Each of these properties in turn contains an object that contains the text for the informational and error messages that get displayed in the field's span element.

It's important to note that the objects created in these files are not created by constructors. Rather, they are objects created with object literals, as described in figure 11-2. They also have global scope so they can be used throughout the Register application.

The library_navigate.js file

```
var $ = function(id) { return document.getElementById(id); };

var navigate = {
    showForm: function() {
        $("registration_form").setAttribute("class","show");
        $("registration_result").setAttribute("class","hide");
    },
    showResults: function() {
        $("registration_form").setAttribute("class","hide");
        $("registration_result").setAttribute("class","show");
    }
};
```

The library_fields.js file

```
var fields = {
    email: {
        message: "Must be a valid email address.",
        required: "Email is required.",
        isEmail: "Email is invalid."
    },
    password: {
        required: "Password is required."
    },
    verify: {
        required: "Please retype your password.",
        noMatch: ["Passwords do not match.", "password"]
    },
    first_name: {
        required: "First name is required."
    },
    last_name: {
        required: "Last name is required."
    },
    zip: {
        message: "Use 5 or 9 digit ZIP code.",
        required: "ZIP Code is required.",
        isZip: "ZIP Code is invalid."
    },
    card_number: {
        message: "Use 1111-2222-3333-4444 format.",
        required: "Card number is required.",
        isCC: "Card number is invalid."
    },
    exp_date : {
        message: "Use mm/yyyy format.",
        required: "Expiration date is required.",
        isDate: "Expiration date is invalid.",
        expired: "Card has expired."
    }
};
```

Description

- The navigate library provides methods for navigating between the form and the section. The fields library creates an object that contains fields and messages for data validation.

Figure 12-10   The navigate and fields libraries for the Register application

The validate library

Figure 12-11 shows the validate library. It starts with a constructor for a Validate object. This constructor declares two properties, month and year, and sets their initial values to zero. As you will see in the next figure, this object 's methods are inherited by the RegisterForm object, so they can be used by that object.

The methods of the Validate object validate specific fields. Most accept one parameter named text, which is the value to be checked. For instance, the isEmail method validates an email entry, and the isBlank method validates whether an entry has a value. However, the isMatch method accepts two text parameters instead of one, because it validates whether two entries match.

These methods return true if the text that is passed to them is valid, and false if it isn't. Note here that many of the method names match the names in the properties of the fields object shown in the last figure. For example, fields.email has a property called isEmail, and fields.card_number has a property called isCC.

Most of the methods in the Validate object use the regular expression patterns that you were introduced to in figure 12-5. Two of them, however, you haven't seen before.

The isDate method tests whether a date is valid. The hasExpired method tests whether a date is in the past. Here again, both of these methods return true if the date is valid, false if it isn't.

If you look at the isDate method, you can see that it uses a regular expression pattern like the one in figure 12-5 to check the format of the date. But this time, it just checks for month and year, and it also checks to see whether the month is less than 1 or greater than 12. This makes it so a date like "19/2015"returns false.

The hasExpired method checks to see whether the current date is greater than the date that's passed to it. First, it calls the isDate method described above to make sure the text is a date. This also ensures that the object's month and year properties have values. This is because those property values are assigned in the isDate method. Then, the hasExpired method tests the expiration date, but it does so in an interesting way.

Typically, you would subtract one from the expiration month before using it in JavaScript. But here, because credit cards are valid until the end of the month, you can test the current date against the month after the card expires so you don't have to subtract one from the expiration month.

The library_validate.js file

```javascript
var Validate = function() {
    this.month = 0;
    this.year = 0;
};
Validate.prototype.isBlank = function(text) {
    return (text === "");
};
Validate.prototype.isMatch = function(text1, text2) {
    return (text1 === text2);
};
Validate.prototype.isEmail = function(text) {
    if (text.length === 0) return false;
    var parts = text.split("@");
    if (parts.length !== 2) return false;
    if (parts[0].length > 64) return false;
    if (parts[1].length > 255) return false;
    var address =
        "(^[\\w!#$%&'*+/=?^`{|}~-]+(\\.[\\w!#$%&'*+/=?^`{|}~-]+)*$)";
    var quotedText = "(^\"(([^\\\\\"])|(\\\\[\\\\\"]))+\"$)";
    var localPart = new RegExp( address + "|" + quotedText );
    if ( !parts[0].match(localPart) ) return false;
    var hostnames =
        "(([a-zA-Z0-9]\\.)|([a-zA-Z0-9][-a-zA-Z0-9]{0,62}[a-zA-Z0-9]\\.))+";
    var tld = "[a-zA-Z0-9]{2,6}";
    var domainPart = new RegExp("^" + hostnames + tld + "$");
    if ( !parts[1].match(domainPart) ) return false;
    return true;
};
Validate.prototype.isZip = function(text) {
    return /^\d{5}(-\d{4})?$/.test(text);
};
Validate.prototype.isCC = function(text) {
    return /^\d{4}-\d{4}-\d{4}-\d{4}$/.test(text);
};
Validate.prototype.isDate = function(text) {
    if ( ! /^[01]\d\/\d{4}$/.test(text) ) return false;
    var dateParts = text.split("/");
    this.month = parseInt(dateParts[0]);
    this.year = parseInt(dateParts[1]);
    if ( this.month < 1 || this.month > 12 ) return false;
    return true;
};
Validate.prototype.hasExpired = function(text) {
    if (this.isDate(text)) {
        var now = new Date();
        var exp = new Date( this.year, this.month);
        return ( now > exp );
    } else { return false; }
};
```

Description

- The validate library creates an object with methods for validating user entries.

Figure 12-11   The validate library for the Register application

The validate_form library

Figure 12-12 shows the validate_form library. This file starts with a constructor for an object named RegisterForm. Next, this object inherits the methods of the Validate object in the last figure. This means that the RegisterForm object can use those methods. Then, the code adds five more methods to the RegisterForm object.

The first method, validateField, is the top-level method that is used to validate a field on the form. It receives two parameters. The first one is the name of the field. The second one is the text that the user enters.

First, this method stores the field object with the specified field name in a variable named field. Thus, "exp_date" gets and stores the fields.exp_date object. Then, the if statements that follow use that object's properties to determine what methods should be called to validate the text that's passed to it.

For instance, if the object has a required property, the nested if statement calls the isBlank method to determine whether the text has a length of at least 1. If not, it throws an Error object with the message that's in the object's required property. For "exp_date", the error message is "Expiration date is required."

Please note that only the noMatch method requires two parameters. The second parameter is the value property of the field that's named by element 0 in the field's noMatch property. And it throws an Error object with a message property that contains element 0.

The next two methods, setError and clearError, take two parameters, field-name and message. They each concatenate "_error" to the field name and use the $ function to get the span element with that name. Then, setError sets the span's class attribute to "error", so the message will be in red, and it sets the span's text to the value in the message parameter. Conversely, clearError removes the "error" class from the span, and sets the text to the default informational message or to an empty string.

The next method, resetForm, loops through the properties in the fields object, which match the field names in the HTML. Each field name is used to get the informational message for the field. Then, the field name and message are sent to the clearError method to reset the span message, and the $ function is used to clear the associated text box.

The last method, validateForm, first declares a Boolean flag named isOK and sets it to true. Then, it loops through each field in the fields array. For each field, it calls the clearError method to clear any previous error messages.

Next, within a try block within the loop, this method calls the validateField method to validate the field. As you have seen, this method will call all of the validation methods that are appropriate for the field. If one of these methods determines that the field is invalid, the validateField method will throw an error that will be caught by the catch block. So within the catch block, the isOK variable is set to false, and the setError method is called to set the class name for the related span element to "error", and to display the message property in the Error object in the span element. When this loop ends and all of the fields have been processed, this method returns the isOK variable.

The library_validate_form.js file

```javascript
var RegisterForm = function() { };
RegisterForm.prototype = new Validate();       //inherit

RegisterForm.prototype.validateField = function(fieldName, text) {
    var field = fields[fieldName];
    if (field.required) {
        if ( this.isBlank(text) ) { throw new Error(field.required); }
    }
    if (field.noMatch) {
        if ( ! this.isMatch(text, $(field.noMatch[1]).value ) ) {
            throw new Error(field.noMatch[0]);
        }
    }
    if (field.isEmail) {
        if ( ! this.isEmail(text) ) { throw new Error(field.isEmail); }
    }
    if (field.isZip) {
        if ( ! this.isZip(text) ) { throw new Error(field.isZip); }
    }
    if (field.isCC) {
        if ( ! this.isCC(text) ) { throw new Error(field.isCC); }
    }
    if (field.isDate) {
        if ( ! this.isDate(text) ) { throw new Error(field.isDate); }
    }
    if (field.expired) {
        if ( this.hasExpired(text) ) { throw new Error(field.expired); }
    }
};
RegisterForm.prototype.setError = function( fieldName, message ) {
    $(fieldName + "_error").setAttribute("class", "error");
    $(fieldName + "_error").firstChild.nodeValue = message;
};
RegisterForm.prototype.clearError = function( fieldName, message ) {
    $(fieldName + "_error").setAttribute("class", "");
    $(fieldName + "_error").firstChild.nodeValue = message || "";
};
RegisterForm.prototype.resetForm = function() {
    for ( var fieldName in fields ) {
        this.clearError(fieldName, fields[fieldName].message);
        $(fieldName).value = "";     //clear textbox
    }
};
RegisterForm.prototype.validateForm = function() {
    var isOK = true;
    for ( var fieldName in fields ) {
        this.clearError(fieldName);
        try { this.validateField(fieldName, $(fieldName).value ); }
        catch (error) {
            isOK = false;
            this.setError( fieldName, error.message);
        }
    }
    return isOK;
};
```

Figure 12-12   The validate_form library for the Register application

The main JavaScript code

Figure 12-13 presents the JavaScript code in the register.js file. To start, this file declares a variable that will be used for the RegisterForm object. Then, it defines the onload event handler, which starts by using the new keyword to call the constructor for the RegisterForm object and create the object. This is followed by a statement that calls the resetForm method of that object to put all of the starting messages in the span elements for the fields.

You should notice, though, that the rest of this onload event handler looks a little different from what you've seen so far. That's because the event handlers for the click events of the Register, Reset, and Back buttons are coded within the onload event handler instead of as separate functions that are attached to the events by the onload event handler. This is another common coding pattern.

In the click event handler for the Register button, the conditional expression in an if statement calls the validateForm method of the RegisterForm object. If this method returns false, which means the form has errors, nothing is done because the validateForm method has already provided for the display of the appropriate error messages. If the method returns true, the submit method of the form submits the form to the server for processing. Then, the showResults method of the navigate object is called to "navigate" to the results page.

In the click event handler for the Reset button, the resetForm method of the RegisterForm object is called. This method clears all of the fields on the form and resets the default informational messages.

In the click event handler for the Back button in the section, the showForm method of the navigate object is called to "navigate" back to the form. Then, the resetForm method of the RegisterForm object is called to reset the fields and informational messages.

The register.js file

```javascript
var registerForm;

window.onload = function() {
    // create validation object and set field messages
    registerForm = new RegisterForm();
    registerForm.resetForm();

    // create and attach the event handlers
    $("register").onclick = function() {
        if ( registerForm.validateForm() ) {
            $("registration_form").submit();
            navigate.showResults();
        }
    };
    $("reset").onclick = function() {
        registerForm.resetForm();
    };
    $("back") = function() {
        navigate.showForm();
        registerForm.resetForm();
    };
};
```

Description

- The JavaScript code for the Register application creates a RegisterForm object and calls its resetForm method to set the initial messages for the application.

- Unlike previous examples, the event handlers for the click events of the Register, Reset, and Back buttons are coded in the load event handler.

Figure 12-13   The main JavaScript file for the Register application

Perspective

Although you can code a data validation application in many different ways, the Register application in this chapter is worth studying because it presents a highly structured approach to data validation. If at first it seems complicated, this structure actually makes it easier to test, debug, and enhance an application like this.

Another benefit to using an approach like this is that it can be easily modified for use with the data on any form. To customize the approach, you just change the field objects, starting messages, error messages, and validation methods so they're appropriate for the form that you're developing.

Now, if you understand the code in the Register application, that's a good indication that you have a solid grounding in the use of objects, methods, and properties, and that you've mastered the skills in section 2 of this book.

Terms

regular expression	exception
regular expression object	throw an exception
pattern	throw statement
regular expression literal	try-catch statement
escape character	try block
subpattern	catch block
quantifier	exception handling
flag	finally block

Summary

- A *regular expression* defines a *pattern* that can be searched for in a string. This pattern is stored in a *regular expression object*.

- The test method of a regular expression object is commonly used to test the validity of user entries.

- Regular expressions can also be used with three methods of a String object to search for, match, and replace the pattern of a regular expression.

- An *exception* is a runtime error that is *thrown* automatically when an error conditions occurs. However, you can also create and throw your own exceptions in the form of Error objects.

- To catch an exception when it is thrown, you use a *try-catch statement*, which consists of a *try block*, a *catch block*, and an optional *finally block*.

Exercise 12-1   Add exception handling to a Future Value application

This exercise will give you a chance to use try-catch and throw statements and to display error messages that show the message and name of the Error object:

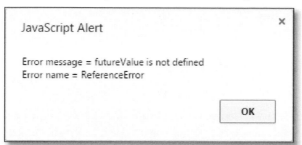

1. Use your text editor or IDE to open the JavaScript file in this folder:

   `c:\javascript\exercises\ch12\future_value\`

2. Enclose all of the statements for the calculateFV function in a try block, and code a catch block that displays the message and name properties of any Error object that's thrown, as shown above.

3. Test the application, and note that the application doesn't throw an exception, no matter what combinations of invalid data you use.

4. Remove the var keyword in the first statement in the try block, and test again with valid data. This time, it should throw an error and your dialog box should be displayed.

5. Put back the var keyword, but add a throw statement before the return statement that throws a RangeError object with this message "Error in Future Value calculation". Then, test to make sure that this error is caught and displayed by the catch block.

6. Comment out the statements in the catch block, and add a statement that throws the error object that's caught. Then, code a try block around the statement in the processEntries function that calls the calculateFV function, and code a catch block that displays the message and name properties of the error object. Now, test this change.

Exercise 12-2   Enhance the Register application

This exercise asks you to enhance the Register application for this chapter by adding a phone number field. That will show how easy it is to modify the data validation functions when you use an object-oriented approach.

Open and test the application

1. Use your text editor or IDE to open the HTML and JavaScript files in this folder:

    `c:\javascript\exercises\ch12\register\`

    In the HTML, notice the new phone number field.

2. Test the application to see how it works. Notice that there's a new phone number field, but no messages are displayed for it. Then, click the Reset button to reset the form.

Validate the phone number field

3. In the library_fields.js file, add an object for the new phone number field to the fields object. Remember that to work properly, the name of the object must match the name of the input element for the phone number.

4. Add three properties to the object named message, required, and isPhone. Set the message property to "Use 555-123-4567 format", the required property to "Phone number is required", and the isPhone property to "Phone number is not valid".

5. In the library_validate.js file, add a Validate.prototype.isPhone method that accepts a parameter named text. In the body of the method, use the regular expression for phone numbers in figure 12-5 and the test method of the regular expression object to make sure the text argument contains a valid phone number.

6. Run the application and see that the default message for the phone number field shows. Then, click the Register button without entering any data, and see that the required message for the phone number shows. This is because the code that handles the default and required messages is already in the Register-Form object.

7. Still in the browser, enter an invalid phone number and click the Register button. This time, no error message shows, because the isPhone method hasn't yet been hooked up in the RegisterForm object.

8. In the library_validate_form file, add an if statement to the validateField method of the RegisterForm object. The if statement should check the fields. isPhone property, and throw the appropriate error if the check fails.

9. Run the application, enter an invalid phone number, and click the Register button. The error message for the phone number should now be displayed.

Section 3

Advanced JavaScript skills

Now that you've completed section 2, you should have a solid set of
JavaScript skills. But to get the most from JavaScript, you need to add the
advanced skills of this section to your skillset. That will not only help you
become a better JavaScript programmer, but also move you toward the
expert level of JavaScript programming.

So, in chapter 13, you'll learn how to work with events, images, and
timers. In chapter 14, you'll learn how to work with closures, callback
functions, and recursion. In chapter 15, you'll learn how to work with
namespaces and the module pattern, including some of the newer
ECMAScript 5 techniques for customizing the properties of an object. In
chapter 16, you'll learn how to use JavaScript Object Notation (JSON) for
data transfer and storage. And in chapter 17, you'll learn when and how to
use jQuery instead of JavaScript for your DOM scripting.

How to work with events, images, and timers

In previous chapters, you've done some basic DOM scripting as part of building JavaScript applications. But now, you'll learn some advanced DOM scripting techniques. Specifically, you'll learn how to use cross-browser techniques for working with event objects, how to work with images, and how to use timers.

How to work with events

When an event occurs, the event is dispatched to the target element. This event dispatch starts at the document object, and travels down the DOM tree to the target element, where the event is handled. In the next few topics, you'll learn more about events and event handling.

You should know, however, that working with events is often complicated, and you always to need make sure your event code works correctly across browsers. Because the jQuery library can simplify this for you, you'll use jQuery most of the time when working with events. Nevertheless, it's good to have a basic understanding of events before you start using jQuery.

An overview of event types

You can think of all events as being one of three types, as shown in the first table in figure 13-1. First, *HTML events* are triggered by a change to the HTML page. For example, when the browser loads an HTML page, it triggers the HTML load event.

Second, *mouse events* are triggered by the user's mouse. For example, when a user clicks on an element, a click event is triggered.

Third, *keyboard events* are triggered by the user's keyboard. For example, when a user presses a key, a keypress event is triggered. The rest of the tables in this figure give an overview of the HTML, mouse, and keyboard events.

As you've seen throughout this book, you can attach event handlers to these events. These handlers run when the events occur.

There are just a few other things you should know about this. First, the contextclick mouse event, which occurs when you right-click on an element, causes a context menu to be displayed by default. As a result, if you want your application to handle this event, you typically want to cancel its default action, which you'll soon learn about. Also, not all browsers support this event, so you'll need to test it carefully if you choose to use it.

Second, the mouse events are valid for all HTML elements, not just elements like links and buttons. For example, you can handle the click event for an <h2> element, as you saw in the FAQs application of chapter 5.

Common types of events

Event type	Description
HTML event	An event that's triggered by the HTML page.
Mouse event	An event that's triggered by the user's mouse.
Keyboard event	An event that's triggered by the user's keyboard.

HTML events

Event	Triggers when
load	The browser loads all content in a document. Same as the window.onload event.
unload	The browser removes a document from the window.
submit	A form is submitted.
reset	A form is reset.
select	The user selects text in a field.
change	The content of an element has changed.
focus	An element gains focus.
blur	An element loses focus.

Mouse events

Event	Triggers when
mousedown	A mouse button is pressed down.
mouseup	A mouse button is released.
click	A mouse button is pressed and released over the same spot.
dblclick	A mouse button is pressed and released twice over the same spot.
contextclick	The right mouse button is pressed and released over the same spot.
mouseover	The mouse moves into an element.
mouseout	The mouse moves out of an element.
mousemove	The mouse moves over an element without leaving it.

Keyboard events

Event	Triggers when
keydown	A key has been pressed down.
keypress	A key has generated text input.
textInput	A key has generated text input.
keyup	A key has been released.

Description

- Events are triggered when the user does something with the mouse or keyboard or when an HTML action occurs on the page.
- Event handlers can be attached to these events so the handlers run when the events are triggered.

Figure 13-1   An overview of event types

How to attach and detach event handlers

Up until now, you've attached *event handlers* using JavaScript properties, like this:

```
$("button").onclick = eventHandlerName;
```

But now, you'll learn how to use methods to attach event handlers.

One benefit of using methods is that you can attach multiple event handlers to an element or event. Another benefit is that you can also detach event handlers.

The drawback is that you need to make some adjustments for *cross-browser compatibility*. That's because the modern browsers use the DOM-compliant addEventListener and removeEventListener methods, but older versions of Internet Explorer use the attachEvent and detachEvent methods.

Figure 13-2 shows the syntax for these methods. As you can see, each method takes a string that specifies the event type, and the name of the event handler to be attached or removed.

As the table shows, the main difference between these methods is that for the addEventListener and removeEventListener methods, you don't include "on" before the name of the event, but with the attachEvent and detachEvent methods, you do. For example, to attach a handler for a click event with the addEvent-Handler method, the first argument is "click". By contrast, the first argument for the attachEvent method is "onclick".

To resolve these differences, the examples below the table in this figure present functions for attaching and detaching events that are cross-browser compatible. Each of these functions accepts three parameters. The first is the node or element whose event will be handled. The second is the event to be handled, without the prefix "on". And the third is the event handler.

Within the body of each function, the code checks to see if the node object has the addEventListener or removeEventListener method. If it does, the code calls that method, passing it the eventName and handler arguments. If it doesn't, the code checks to see if the node object has the attachEvent or detachEvent method. If it does, the code calls that method, passing it the eventName and handler arguments. Note that for the attachEvent and detachEvent methods, the code adds the prefix "on" to the eventName value.

As this shows, it takes some effort to make a function that works with events cross-browser compatible. That's why, for all but the simplest actions, you'll want to use jQuery for event handling. However, if this is all you need to do, the functions in this figure are easy to use, as shown by the last example. Here, event handlers named hover and click are created. Then, in the onload event handler, the attachEvent function is used to attach both a click event handler and a mouseover event handler to a button.

The DOM addEventListener and removeEventListener methods

```
element.addEventListener( eventType, handler );
element.removeEventListener( eventType, handler );
```

The IE attachEvent and detachEvent methods

```
element.attachEvent( eventType, handler );
element.detachEvent( eventType, handler );
```

The parameters for these methods

Parameter	Description
`eventType`	A string that specifies the type of event.
	For the DOM methods, you don't include "on" before the name of the event.
	For the IE methods, you do include "on" before the name of the event.
`handler`	The event handler to be attached or removed.

A cross-browser compatible function for attaching event handlers

```
var attachEvent = function(node, eventName, handler) {
    if (node.addEventListener) {
        node.addEventListener(eventName, handler);
    } else if (node.attachEvent) {
        node.attachEvent("on" + eventName, handler);
    }
};
```

A cross-browser compatible function for removing event handlers

```
var detachEvent = function(node, eventName, handler) {
    if (node.removeEventListener) {
        node.removeEventListener(eventName, handler);
    } else if (node.detachEvent) {
        node.detachEvent("on" + eventName, handler);
    }
};
```

How to add multiple event handlers to a single button

Two event handler functions

```
var hover = function() { console.log(this.id + " was hovered over!"); };
var click = function() { console.log(this.id + " was clicked!"); };
```

How to attach the event handlers

```
window.onload = function() {
    var btnPlay = $("btnPlay");
    attachEvent(btnPlay, "click", click);
    attachEvent(btnPlay, "mouseover", hover);
};
```

Description

- Modern browsers have addEventListener and removeEventListener methods for adding and removing event handlers. But older versions of IE use the attachEvent and detachEvent methods instead.

- Using these methods lets you attach more than one event handler to an element. To ensure *cross-browser compatibility*, though, you need to handle both sets of methods.

Figure 13-2   How to attach and detach event handlers

How to cancel the default action of an event

Most of the time, when a user clicks on an element, nothing happens unless a JavaScript event handler has been attached to that element. In other words, there is no default action for most elements. However, when a user clicks on some elements of a web page, the browser performs a *default action*.

Figure 13-3 lists the default action for several elements. If, for example, a user clicks on a link, the browser loads the URL specified by the link. Similarly, if a user clicks on a button of the submit type, the browser submits the form to the server.

Although these default actions usually work the way you want, you may occasionally need to cancel a default action. If, for example, the user clicks on a link with an href attribute that points to an image, the browser by default loads the specified image, which displays the image and exits from the application. But if the application is running a slide show, for example, you don't want that. As a result, you need to cancel the default action for this event.

When an event occurs, an *event object* is created. This object contains information about the event that occurred and provides methods that let you control the behavior of the event. To cancel the default action of an event, for example, you need to create an event handler that accesses the event object and uses one of its methods to cancel the default action.

As the first example in this figure shows, most web browsers are DOM-compliant so they pass the event object as the first parameter to the event handler. In addition, this event object has a method named preventDefault that you can use to prevent the default action from occurring.

Unfortunately, older versions of Internet Explorer weren't completely DOM-compliant. So, as the second example shows, you get the event object by using the global window.event property. In addition, you set the returnValue property of this event object to false to prevent the default action from occurring.

To make your applications compatible with all browsers, you can use the code in the third example. Here, the first statement stores the event parameter in the e variable if the browser is DOM-compliant, but it stores the window.event property if the event parameter is null.

Then, the if statement tests the e variable to see if it provides a preventDefault method. If so, it calls the preventDefault method. If not, the else clause sets the returnValue property to false.

Common HTML elements that have default actions for the click event

Element	Default action for the click event
`<a>`	Load the page in the href attribute.
`<input>`	Submit the form if the type attribute is set to submit.
`<input>`	Reset the form if the type attribute is set to reset.
`<button>`	Submit the form if the type attribute is set to submit.
`<button>`	Reset the form if the type attribute is set to reset.

DOM-compliant code that cancels the default action

```
var event_handler = function(e) {
    e.preventDefault();
};
```

Older IE code that cancels the default action

```
var event_handler = function() {
    var e = window.event;
    e.returnValue = false;
};
```

Cross-browser compatible code that cancels the default action

```
var eventHandler = function(e) {
    // The event object sent to the event handler, or window.event
    e = e || window.event;

    // Cancel the default action
    if (e.preventDefault) {
        e.preventDefault();        // for most browsers
    }
    else {
        e.returnValue = false;     // for older versions of IE
    }
};
```

Description

- Modern browsers send an *event object* to the event handler that's handling the event. They also provide a DOM-compliant preventDefault method for the event object. When called, this method prevents the *default action* of the event from occurring.

- Older versions of IE store the event object in the global window.event property, and provide a property named returnValue in the event object. When set to false, this property prevents the default action of the event from occurring.

- To ensure cross-browser compatibility, you need to provide for both ways of cancelling a default action.

Figure 13-3   How to cancel the default action of an event

The FAQs application

In chapter 5, you reviewed a FAQs application that displayed or hid the answers to some frequently asked questions about JavaScript and jQuery. This chapter updates that application by using the techniques of the preceding topics to attach events and prevent the default action of its links.

The user interface

As figure 13-4 shows, the user interface for the FAQs application in this chapter is the same as the one in chapter 5. But the application in this chapter prevents the default action of the <a> elements that are coded within the h2 elements that are clicked.

Since the value in the href properties of the <a> tags is "#", the browser reloads the same page when it is clicked if the default action isn't prevented. So in this case, no harm is done, except for the time it takes for the unnecessary page load. But for some actions, default actions can cause problems.

You can tell this page load occurs in the chapter 5 application because the URL address is "index.html" when the page first loads. But after clicking on a question, the URL is changed to "index.html#". In contrast, this figure shows that the URL for the FAQs application in this chapter hasn't been changed even though a heading and therefore an <a> element has been clicked.

This figure also shows the Chrome developer tools open to the Console panel, with a lot of information displayed in that panel. That's because the FAQs application for this chapter is modified to send information about the event object to the Console panel. This is partly to demonstrate attaching multiple events, but also to demonstrate a way to get more information about an object.

Basically, whenever you're curious about an object, you can send it to the Console panel. Then, you can use the features of the Console panel to explore the object's properties and methods.

The user interface of the FAQs application with the Console panel open

Description

- The FAQs application in this chapter is a modified version of the one in chapter 5. One of modifications is a log feature that sends information about the event objects for the event handlers to the Console panel, as shown above. Another modification is cancelling the default action of the <a> elements that contain the FAQs.

- The information sent to the Console panel lets you see some of the different types of event objects, and the properties of those objects. For example, both the click event and the mouseover event send a MouseEvent object to the event handler. But if you scroll down through the properties list to the type property, you'll see that the click event has a type value of 'click', while the mouseover event has a type value of 'mouseover'.

- Sending objects to the Console panel like this is a good way to learn about them. You can also do an Internet search for specific information about event objects and their properties.

Figure 13-4   The user interface for the FAQs application

The event library

Figure 13-5 presents the event library that the FAQs application uses. This library uses the techniques you learned in figure 11-2 to create an object literal named evt. This object has a method to attach an event handler, a method to remove an event handler, and a method to prevent the default action of an event. All three methods are cross-browser compatible and use the code you've seen in the previous figures.

The library_event.js file

```
var evt = {
    attach: function(node, eventName, func) {
        if (node.addEventListener) {
            node.addEventListener(eventName, func);
        } else if (node.attachEvent) {
            node.attachEvent("on" + eventName, func);
        }
    },
    detach: function(node, eventName, func) {
        if (node.removeEventListener) {
            node.removeEventListener(eventName, func);
        } else if (node.detachEvent) {
            node.detachEvent("on" + eventName, func);
        }
    },
    preventDefault: function(e) {
        e = e || window.event;
        if ( e.preventDefault ) { e.preventDefault(); }
        else { e.returnValue = false; }
    }
};
```

Description

- This event library provides cross-browser compatible methods for attaching and detaching events and for canceling the default action of an event.

- This library creates an object literal named evt with methods named attach, detach, and preventDefault.

- For any event handling requirements that go beyond these, you should probably use jQuery.

Figure 13-5   The event library for the FAQs application

The main JavaScript file

Figure 13-6 presents the main JavaScript file of the FAQs application. Much of this code is the same as in the chapter 5 application. For instance, the toggle event handler is the same. The main differences are the addition of a log function, and changes in how the event handlers are attached.

The log function is an event handler that takes the event object argument it receives, and passes it to the console.log method. That displays the event object in the Console panel.

Here, the log function doesn't check to make sure the event object exists before passing it to console.log method. That's because this application assumes that you are working with a modern browser, specifically Chrome. However, if you want to make the log function able to handle an older version of Internet Explorer, you can add the check that appears in the first line of the preventDefault method in the last figure.

The onload event handler appears next, and it is similar to what you saw before. As in the earlier application, it uses the getElementsByTagName method to get all the h2 tags. Then, it loops through the h2 tags to attach event handlers. It ends by setting the focus on the child <a> tag of the first h2 tag.

However, how it attaches the event handlers is different. First, for each h2 tag it stores a reference to both the h2 tag and that tag's child <a> tag. Then, it uses the attach method of the evt object to attach several events. It attaches the toggle event handler to the h2 tag's click event, but it also attaches the evt object's preventDefault method to the <a> tag's click event. This will prevent the page from reloading when a frequently asked question is clicked.

Next, the code attaches the log function to the click, focus, and mouseover events of the <a> tag. This sends the event object for those events to the log function so those event objects can be seen in the Console panel of the developer tools in the browser.

Note that using these methods to attach event handlers lets you attach multiple handlers to the same element or event. For example, the <a> tag has event handlers attached to three different events, and the <a> tag's click event has two different handlers attached to it.

The faqs.js file

```
var $ = function(id) { return document.getElementById(id); };

var toggle = function() {
    var h2 = this;                      // clicked h2 tag
    var div = h2.nextElementSibling;    // h2 tag's sibling div tag

    // toggle plus/minus image
    if (h2.hasAttribute('class')) { h2.removeAttribute('class');
    } else { h2.setAttribute('class', 'minus'); }

    // toggle div visibility
    if (div.hasAttribute('class')) { div.removeAttribute('class');
    } else { div.setAttribute('class', 'open'); }
};

var log = function(e) {
    console.log( e );
};

window.onload = function() {
    // get the h2 tags
    var faqs = $("faqs");
    var elements = faqs.getElementsByTagName('h2');

    // attach event handlers
    for (var i = 0; i < elements.length; i++) {
        var h2 = elements[i];            //h2 tag
        var a = h2.firstChild;           //h2 tag's child <a> tag
        //attach h2 click event
        evt.attach(h2, "click", toggle);
        //cancel the default action of the <a> tag
        evt.attach(a, "click", evt.preventDefault);
        //log various events of the <a> tag
        evt.attach(a, "click", log);
        evt.attach(a, "focus", log);
        evt.attach(a, "mouseover", log);
    }
    // set focus on first h2 tag's <a> tag
    elements[0].firstChild.focus();
};
```

Description

- The event handler named toggle is the same as in the chapter 5 FAQs application.
- The event handler named log sends the event object it receives to the Console panel. You can see the results of these calls to the log event handler in the last figure.
- The onload event handler attaches several event handlers. This shows that you can attach more than one event handler to an element, and you can attach more than one event handler to a single event. For example, two different handlers are attached to the <a> tag's click event.
- Since the <a> tag's click event is handled by the preventDefault method, the page won't load the page for the URL in the tag's href property when the link is clicked.

Figure 13-6   The main JavaScript file for the FAQs application

How to work with images

Two common tasks when working with images are creating image rollovers and preloading images. In the following topics, you'll learn both skills.

How to create image rollovers

An *image rollover* occurs when the user positions the mouse over an image and the image changes to another image. Then, when the user moves the mouse out of the image, the image changes back to the first image. To achieve this effect, you change the value of an image tag's src attribute when certain mouse events are triggered. These events are presented in the table in figure 13-7.

Below the table are two event handlers named showFirstImage and showSecondImage. These functions will be attached to an image tag's mouseover and mouseout events. Now, remember that when a function is used as an event handler, the value of the this keyword is the object that triggered the event. As a result, the value of this in each function is the image tag that triggered the event. Then, each function uses the this keyword to change the image that the tag's src attribute points to.

Next, you can see how these event handlers are used to create an image rollover. Here, the HTML is for an image tag with an id attribute of "rollover" and with a src attribute that points to the same image as the one in the showFirstImage function.

Then, the onload event handler gets the image tag and stores it in a variable named image. After that, it makes two calls to the attach method of the evt object that's in the event library in figure 13-5. In the first call, it attaches the showSecondImage function to the image tag's mouseover event. In the second call, it attaches the showFirstImage function to the image tag's mouseout event.

Later, when the user positions the mouse over the original image, the onmouseover event will occur, its event handler will be executed, and the old image will be replaced with the new image. Then, when the user moves the mouse out of the new image, the onmouseout event will occur, its event handler will be executed, and the old image will be restored.

Two mouse events

Event	Triggers when...
`mouseover`	The mouse is moved inside an element.
`mouseout`	The mouse is moved outside an element.

Event handlers for the two mouse events

```
var showFirstImage = function() {
    // 'this' = image that triggered the event
    this.src = "images/image1.jpg";
};

var showSecondImage = function() {
    // 'this' = image that triggered the event
    this.src = "images/image2.jpg";
};
```

How to create an image rollover

The HTML code for the image

```
<img id="rollover" src="images/image1.jpg" alt="">
```

The JavaScript code to create the rollover

```
window.onload = function() {
    //get the img tag
    var image = document.getElementById("rollover");

    //attach the event handlers
    evt.attach(image, "mouseover", showSecondImage);
    evt.attach(image, "mouseout", showFirstImage);
};
```

Description

- An *image rollover* occurs when the user positions the mouse over an image and the image is changed.
- To create an image rollover, you change the src attribute of an <img> tag in response to the mouseover and mouseout events.
- Rollovers work best when the two images are the same size. Otherwise, the layout of the page changes in response to the rollover.

Figure 13-7   How to create image rollovers

How to preload images

In JavaScript applications that load an image in response to a user event, the image isn't loaded into the browser until the JavaScript code changes the src attribute of the <img> tag. For large images or slow connections, this can cause a delay of a few seconds before the browser is able to display the image.

To solve this problem, an application can download the images before the user event occurs. This is known as *preloading images*. Then, the browser can display the images without noticeable delays. Although this may result in a longer delay when the page is initially loaded, the user won't encounter any delays when using the application.

Figure 13-8 shows how to preload images. To start, the first line of code creates a new Image object and stores it in a variable named image. This creates a new image node that's empty. Then, the second line of code sets the src property to the URL of the image to be preloaded. This causes the web browser to preload the image. Note here that you don't need to use the Image object after you've set the src property. The act of setting the src property is what causes the browser to preload the image.

The second example shows two lines of code for preloading the second image of the last figure. Note here that you don't need to preload the original image. Since the src attribute of the image tag specifies that image, the browser downloads it and displays it when it loads the page.

How to preload an image with the Image object

How to create an Image object

```
var image = new Image();
```

How to load an image in an Image object

```
image.src = "image_name.jpg";
```

How to preload the second image in the rollover example

```
window.onload = function() {
    //get the img tag
    var image = document.getElementById("rollover");

    //preload the rollover's second image
    var secondImage = new Image();
    secondImage.src = "images/image2.jpg";

    //attach the event handlers
    evt.attach(image, "mouseover", showSecondImage);
    evt.attach(image, "mouseout", showFirstImage);
};
```

Description

- When an application *preloads images*, it loads all of the images that it's going to need when the page loads, and it stores these images in the web browser's cache for future use.

- When the images are preloaded, the browser can display them whenever they're needed without any noticeable delay.

- To preload an image, you start by creating a new Image object, which creates a new, empty image node. Then, setting the src attribute of this image node to the URL for an image causes the web browser to preload the image.

- The example in this figure uses the methods of the event library in figure 13-5 to attach the event handlers.

Figure 13-8   How to preload images

The Rollover application

Figure 13-9 shows a Rollover application that illustrates the use of the skills you've just learned. Here, both of the starting images are rolled over when the user moves the mouse pointer over them. In this example, you can see the mouse pointer on the image on the left so that's the one that has been rolled over. This application not only shows how to create multiple rollovers for a page, but also how to improve accessibility by using the alt attributes for the images.

The HTML

This figure shows the HTML for this application. In the head section, you can see two script elements. The first is for the event library in figure 13-5. The second is for the main JavaScript file.

Next, you can see the HTML for the main element of the application. It starts with heading and paragraph tags that provide information about the application. This is followed by another paragraph tag that contains two image tags.

The image tags are where the rollovers will be. They contain information about the first image in each rollover in their src and alt attributes. When the page initially loads, these image tags display those images. Then, when the user hovers over one of the images, the Rollover application displays the rollover image.

The Rollover application while the image on the left is rolled over

The head element of the HTML file

```
<head>
    <title>Image Rollover</title>
    <link rel="stylesheet" type="text/css" href="rollover.css">
    <script type="text/javascript" src="library_event.js"></script>
    <script type="text/javascript" src="rollover.js"></script>
</head>
```

The main element of the HTML file

```
<main>
    <h1>Fishing Images</h1>
    <p>Move the mouse over the image to view the rollover image.</p>
    <p><img src="images/release.jpg" id="img1" alt="Catch and release">
        <img src="images/bison.jpg" id="img2" alt="Bison in meadow"></p>
</main>
```

Description

- This page displays two images that are defined within a <p> element.
- When the user moves the mouse pointer over either image, the image is rolled over and replaced by another image.
- When the user moves the mouse pointer off an image, the original image is displayed.

Figure 13-9   The user interface and HTML for the Rollover application

The main JavaScript file

Figure 13-10 presents the main JavaScript file for this application. Here, the createRollover function has three parameters. The first one specifies the image tag where the rollover will take place. The second one specifies the url for the second image in the rollover. And the third one specifies the alt attribute value for the second image in the rollover.

Within this function, the first statement creates variables named firstUrl and firstAlt and assigns them the src and alt values from the first image in the rollover. This information is in the HTML attributes of the img tag.

Then, this function preloads the second image in the rollover. It does this by creating a new Image object, and then assigning the URL in the secondURL parameter to the Image object's src property. Remember that you don't need to do anything further with the Image object because just setting the src property preloads the image. Also, you don't need to preload the first image because it's assigned to the image tag and thus loaded with the page.

Next, this function creates two event handlers named mouseover and mouseout, which handle the events of the same names. The function for the mouseover event sets the image tag's src and alt attributes to the values of the secondUrl and secondAlt parameters. The function for the mouseout event restores the image tag's src and alt attributes to the values of the first image.

Finally, this createRollover function uses the attach method in the event library to attach these event handlers to the image tag's events. Specifically, it attaches the mouseover event handler to the mouseover event, and the mouseout event handler to the mouseout event.

Because the createRollover function uses variables for the image tag and its attributes, it can be called repeatedly. This lets you create more than one image rollover in a page without having to repeat the same rollover code.

You can see this in the onload event handler that comes next. This event handler calls the createRollover function twice. Each time it passes the image tag for the rollover and the url and alt values for the second image.

The rollover.js file

```
var $ = function(id) { return document.getElementById(id); };

var createRollover = function(imgTag, secondUrl, secondAlt) {
    //store first image info
    var firstUrl = imgTag.src;
    var firstAlt = imgTag.alt;

    //preload second image
    var image = new Image();
    image.src = secondUrl;

    //create event handlers
    var mouseover = function() {
        imgTag.src = secondUrl;
        imgTag.alt = secondAlt;
    };
    var mouseout = function() {
        imgTag.src = firstUrl;
        imgTag.alt = firstAlt;
    };

    //attach event handlers
    evt.attach(imgTag, "mouseover", mouseover);
    evt.attach(imgTag, "mouseout", mouseout);
};

window.onload = function() {
    createRollover($("img1"), "images/hero.jpg", "Hero photo");
    createRollover($("img2"), "images/deer.jpg", "Deer near lodge");
};
```

Description

- The Rollover application uses a function called createRollover to set up each rollover. That way, you can create several image rollovers without having to repeat the rollover code.

- The createRollover function accepts three parameters: an image element, the URL for the second image, and the text for the Alt attribute of the second image.

- The createRollover function preloads the second image, creates event handlers for the mouseover and mouseout events, and attaches those event handlers to the image tag that is passed to it.

- The onload event handler calls the createRollover function for each image that is going to be rolled over. There, you can see the three parameters that are passed to this function.

Figure 13-10   The main JavaScript file for the Rollover application

How to use timers

Timers let you execute a function after specified periods of time. However, timers aren't a part of the DOM or ECMAScript standards. Instead, they're provided by the web browser. As you will soon see, timers are often useful in DOM scripting applications, and you'll learn about the two types of timers in this topic.

You should know that the jQuery library has some similar functionality, but it's more limited. So, even if you're using jQuery in your applications, you might need to work with the native JavaScript timers.

How to use a one-time timer

The first type of timer calls its function only once. To create this type of timer, you use the global setTimeout method that's shown in figure 13-11. Its first parameter is the function that the timer calls. Its second parameter is the number of milliseconds to wait before calling the function.

When you use the setTimeout method to create a timer, this method returns a reference to the timer that's created. Then, if necessary, you can use this reference to cancel the timer. To do that, you pass this reference to the clearTimeout method.

Since this timer only runs once, you might be wondering why you'd need to cancel it. Usually you'd do that to prevent a one-time action, like a download or a redirection to another page.

For instance, the examples in this figure use a one-time timer to start the download and installation of an upgrade after a delay of five seconds. The HTML in this example adds a fieldset element to the FAQs application. Inside the fieldset are a legend tag and <p> tag that explain what's going to happen, a button to cancel the upgrade, and a span element where messages will show. Also, a CSS class named closed has been added to the CSS file. It will be used to hide an element by setting its display property to none.

In the JavaScript code, a variable for the timer is declared. This variable is global so all the functions in the code can access it. This is followed by functions named startUpgrade and cancelUpgrade. The startUpgrade function starts the upgrade and then sets the value of the message span to notify the user of the progress of the upgrade.

The cancelUpgrade function uses the clearTimeout method to stop the timer started by the setTimeout method. If this function is called before the timer calls the startUpgrade function, it will keep the code in the startUpgrade function from running. Then, this function hides the fieldset element by setting its class attribute to "closed".

This is followed by the onload event hander. It uses the setTimeout method to set the global timer variable to a timer that calls the startUpgrade function after a delay of 5 seconds (5000 milliseconds). Then, it attaches the cancelUpgrade function to the Cancel Upgrade button so the upgrade can be cancelled before those 5 seconds elapse.

Two methods for working with a timer that calls a function once

```
setTimeout( function, delayTime )     // creates a timer
clearTimeout ( timer )                // cancels a timer
```

The FAQs application with an upgrade that starts after 5 seconds

JavaScript FAQs

A new version is available!

Upgrade will start in 5 seconds! Cancel Upgrade

⊕ What is JavaScript?

The HTML for the upgrade section

```
<fieldset id="upgrade">
    <legend>A new version is available!</legend>
    <p>Upgrade will start in 5 seconds!
        <input type="button" id="cancel" value="Cancel Upgrade">
        <span id="message"> </span></p>
</fieldset>
```

The CSS for the closed class

```
.closed { display: none; }
```

How to use the setTimeout method to start or cancel the upgrade

```
// create a variable to hold the reference to the timer; make it
// global so all the functions can access it
var timer;

var startUpgrade = function() {
    /* code to start the upgrade goes here */
    $("message").firstChild.nodeValue = "Download starting...";
};
var cancelUpgrade = function() {
    clearTimeout( timer );
    $("upgrade").setAttribute("class", "closed");
};

window.onload = function() {
    timer = setTimeout( startUpgrade, 5000 );
    $("cancel").onclick = cancelUpgrade;
};
```

Description

- The setTimeout method creates a timer that calls the specified function once after the specified delay in milliseconds. This method returns a reference to the new timer that can be used to cancel the timer.

- The clearTimeout method cancels the timer that was created with the setTimeout method.

Figure 13-11   How to use a one-time timer

How to use an interval timer

The second type of timer calls its function repeatedly. To create this type of timer, you use the global setInterval method shown in figure 13-12. Its first parameter is the function to be called. Its second parameter is the time interval between function calls. To cancel this type of timer, you pass the timer to the clearInterval method.

The example in this figure shows how to use an interval timer to create a counter that is incremented every second. This counter value is displayed in a span element within an h3 element at the bottom of the page.

The first JavaScript example in this figure shows one way to create and use the timer. Here, global timer and counter variables are declared with the counter set to a starting value of zero. Then, the updateCounter function increases this counter by 1 and displays the new value in the span element. Last, the onload event handler creates the timer by using the updateCounter function as the function parameter of the setTimeout method and 1000 (one second) as the interval time.

If you want to cancel an interval timer that's stored in a global variable, you can use the clearInterval method that's right after this example. This is useful when you want to modify a timer. To do that, you need to cancel the old timer and create a new one that works the way you want it to.

The second JavaScript example shows another way you can code the setInterval method. Here, the function that the setInterval method will call is coded at the same time that it's passed to the method. This is called an *anonymous* function, and coding it this way means that you don't have to code a variable to hold it. This is a common way to code both the setInterval method and the setTimeout method of the last figure.

When you use the setInterval method to create a timer, the timer waits for the specified interval to pass before calling the function the first time. So, if you want the function to be called immediately, you need to call the function before you create the timer.

Two methods for working with a timer that calls a function repeatedly

```
setInterval( function, intervalTime )      // creates a timer
clearInterval ( timer )                     // cancels a timer
```

The FAQs application with a counter at the bottom

jQuery FAQs

⨁ What is jQuery?

⨁ Why is jQuery becoming so popular?

⨁ Which is harder to learn: jQuery or JavaScript?

Number of seconds on page: 8

The HTML for the counter

```
<h3>Number of seconds on page: <span id="counter">0</span></h3>
```

How to use the setInterval method to add a counter to a page

```
// create global variables to hold the timer and the current count
var timer;
var counter = 0;

// create the function that the timer calls
var updateCounter = function() {
    counter++;
    $("counter").firstChild.nodeValue = counter;
};
// create a timer that calls the updateCounter function repeatedly
window.onload = function() {
    timer = setInterval( updateCounter, 1000 );
};
```

How to cancel the timer

```
clearInterval( timer );
```

How to use an anonymous function with the setInterval method

```
var timer;
var counter = 0;
window.onload = function() {
    timer = setInterval( function() {     // the function parameter
        counter++;
        $("counter").firstChild.nodeValue = counter;
    },
    1000 );                               // the time interval parameter
};
```

Description

- The setInterval method creates a timer that calls a function each time the specified interval in milliseconds has passed. This method returns a reference to the new timer that can be used by the clearInterval method to cancel the timer.

- Although you can't modify an interval timer, you can cancel it and create a new one.

Figure 13-12   How to use an interval timer

The Slide Show application

Now that you know how to use timers, you're ready to learn how to create a Slide Show application like the one in figure 13-13. When the user starts this application, it displays the images and captions for the slide show, one at a time, using the time interval that's set for the timer.

If the user clicks Pause while the slideshow is running, the slide show stops on the image currently in the browser, and the link's text changes from "Pause" to "Resume". If the user clicks Resume, the slide show starts up again, and the link's text changes back to "Pause".

The HTML

For this application, the script elements in the head section link to three JavaScript files: the event library in figure 13-5, a slide show library, and the main JavaScript file.

The main element of the body section contains a heading tag and three paragraph tags. The first paragraph tag is an <a> tag with an id of play_pause. The second paragraph tag contains a single image tag with an id of "image". This is where the images in the slide show will be displayed, and the URL of the first image in the slide show is coded in the tag's src attribute. The third paragraph tag contains the span tag in which the image's caption will be displayed, and the caption for the first image in the slide show is coded in this span tag.

To keep things simple, this application doesn't adjust the image tag's alt attribute. But in a real-world application, you would probably do that for accessibility reasons.

The Slide Show application in the browser

The HTML for the application

```
<head>
    <title>Chapter 13 Slide Show</title>
    <link rel="stylesheet" type="text/css" href="slide_show.css"/>
    <script type="text/javascript" src="library_event.js"></script>
    <script type="text/javascript" src="library_slide_show.js"></script>
    <script type="text/javascript" src="slide_show.js"></script>
</head>
<body>
    <main>
        <h1>Fishing Slide Show</h1>
        <p><a href="#" id="play_pause">Pause</a></p>
        <p><img src="images/gear.jpg" id="image" alt=""></p>
        <p><span id="caption">Fishing Gear</span></p>
    </main>
</body>
```

Figure 13-13   The user interface and HTML for the Slide Show application

The slideshow library

The slideshow library creates an object literal called slideshow that provides the properties and methods for the slide show. The timer property will hold a reference to the timer. The nodes property contains an object with properties named image and caption that will hold references to the image and span tags. The img property contains an object with two properties: an array named cache and a number named counter.

The last two properties are play and speed. The play property indicates whether the slide show is playing or paused, while the speed property sets the slide show's speed in milliseconds.

After the properties are six methods. Note that most of these methods return the this keyword, which means they can be chained.

The loadImages method accepts an array of slide objects that is passed to it from the onload event handler in the next figure. It loops through the slides and preloads each image by creating a new Image object and setting its src property. Then, the code sets the Image object's title property and stores the Image object in the img.cache property of the object literal.

The startSlideShow method uses its arguments property to get its parameters. If two arguments are sent in, it stores them in the nodes.image and nodes.caption properties of the object literal. Next, this method calls the setInterval method with the displayNextImage method and the speed property as its arguments. Then, it stores a reference to this timer in the timer property. This timer will execute the displayNextImage method repeatedly at the interval set by the speed property.

Note here that the bind method is used to pass the displayNextImage method to the setInterval method. Since *this* is used as the argument of the bind method, the slideshow object is the value of the this keyword in the displayNextImage method. Otherwise, it would be the Window object or undefined. To refresh your memory on the bind method, you can refer back to figure 10-11 in chapter 10.

The stopSlideShow method follows. It passes the timer property to the clearInterval function to stop the timer.

The displayNextImage method is next. It increments the img.counter property by one, and it uses the modulus operator (%) to get the remainder when the img.counter property is divided by the length of the img.cache array. This ensures that the img.counter property stays within the bounds of the array. Then, it uses the img.counter value to get an Image object from the img.cache array, and uses its properties to set the image tag's src attribute and the span tag's value. Remember that the bind method was used when this method was passed to make sure that its this keyword refers to the slideshow object.

The next method is setPlayText, which accepts an <a> tag. It sets the text of this tag based on the value of the play property. To do that, it uses the conditional operator (see figure 8-6 in chapter 8 to refresh your memory).

The last method is togglePlay, which pauses and resumes the slide show. Here, because this method is an event handler, the value of the this keyword is the element that triggered the event. This method starts by checking whether

The library_slide_show.js file

```javascript
var slideshow = {
    timer: null,
    nodes: { image: null, caption: null },
    img: { cache: [], counter: 0 },
    play: true,
    speed: 2000,
    loadImages: function(slides) {
        var image;
        for ( var i in slides ) {
            // Preload image, copy title property, and save in array
            image = new Image();
            image.src = slides[i].href;
            image.title = slides[i].title;
            this.img.cache.push( image );
        }
        return this;
    },
    startSlideShow: function() {
        if (arguments.length === 2) {
            this.nodes.image = arguments[0];
            this.nodes.caption = arguments[1];
        }
        // Use bind to ensure 'this' is the slideshow object.
        this.timer = setInterval(this.displayNextImage.bind(this),
            this.speed);
        return this;
    },
    stopSlideShow: function() {
        clearInterval( this.timer );
        return this;
    },
    displayNextImage: function() {
        this.img.counter = ++this.img.counter % this.img.cache.length;
        var image = this.img.cache[this.img.counter];
        this.nodes.image.src = image.src;
        this.nodes.caption.firstChild.nodeValue = image.title;
    },
    setPlayText: function(a) {
        a.text = (this.play)? "Resume" : "Pause";
        return this;
    },
    togglePlay: function(e) {
        if ( slideshow.play ) {
            slideshow.stopSlideShow().setPlayText(this);
        } else {
            slideshow.startSlideShow().setPlayText(this);
        }
        slideshow.play = ! slideshow.play;     //toggle play flag
        evt.preventDefault(e);
    }
};
```

Figure 13-14   The slideshow library for the Slide Show application

the slideshow is playing. Based on that, it chains either the stopSlideShow or startSlideShow method with the setPlayText method. Then, it toggles the value of the play property between true and false, and it cancels the default action of the link by using the preventDefault method of the event library.

The main JavaScript file

Figure 13-15 shows the main JavaScript file for the Slide Show application. Here, the onload event handler starts by loading a variable named slides with an array of objects that contain information about the images in the slideshow. This application hard codes this information, but you could also get this kind of information from a database.

Then, the code chains the loadImages and startSlideShow methods of the slideshow object to start the slide show. There are four points of interest about this statement.

First, the slideshow object in the last figure is a global object literal, which means that you don't have to create it or declare it before you can use it. Second, this statement passes the slides object that was just created to the loadImages method. This is how the slideshow object knows what images to work with.

Third, this statement passes the image tag and span tag to the startSlideShow method. Recall from the last figure that the startSlideShow method checks to see whether it receives these arguments. If it does, it stores them for later use. This is how the slideshow object knows which image and span tags to work with.

Fourth, because the slideshow object receives the information it needs in this way, it is reuseable. Thus, you can use it whenever you want to add a slide show to an application.

The last statement in the onload event handler attaches the slideshow's togglePlay method to the click event of the <a> tag with "play_pause" as its id. As a result, clicking this <a> tag stops and starts the slide show. Also, because the slideshow's togglePlay method is used as the event handler, the value of its this keyword will be the play_pause link, not the slideshow object. As you saw in the last figure, the togglePlay method depends on this.

The slide_show.js file

```
var $ = function(id) { return document.getElementById(id); };

window.onload = function() {
    var slides = [
        {href:"images/gear.jpg", title:"Fishing Gear"},
        {href:"images/plane.jpg", title:"Bush Plane"},
        {href:"images/release.jpg", title:"Catch and Release"},
        {href:"images/lunch.jpg", title:"Streamside Lunch"},
        {href:"images/dusk.jpg", title:"Day's End"}
    ];
    slideshow.loadImages(slides).startSlideShow($("image"), $("caption"));

    evt.attach($("play_pause"), "click", slideshow.togglePlay);
};
```

What the onload event handler does

1. Creates an array of objects that contain information about the images in the slideshow.

2. Passes this array to the slideshow object's loadImages method.

3. Passes the img element with the id of "image" and the span element with the id of "caption" to the startSlideShow method, which starts the slide show on page load.

4. Attaches the slideshow object's togglePlay method as the event handler for the click event of the <a> element with the id of play_pause.

Description

- Since the slideshow object in the last figure is a global object literal, the main JavaScript file doesn't need to create it before using it.

- Since the slideshow object in the last figure has cascading methods, the onload event handler is able to chain the loadImages and startSlideShow methods.

- Because the togglePlay method is invoked as an event handler, the value of its this keyword will be the <a> element, not the slideshow object. This is what the toggle-Play method expects.

- If you needed the this keyword in the togglePlay method to be the slideshow object, you could call the togglePlay method's bind method and pass it the slideshow object.

Figure 13-15   The main JavaScript file for the Slide Show application

Perspective

Now that you're through with this chapter, you should have a better grasp on working with events, images, and timers. When your DOM scripting applications get more complicated than the ones in this chapter, though, you should probably use jQuery for the DOM scripting. The one exception is the use of timers, because they don't have an equivalent in jQuery.

Terms

HTML event	event object
mouse event	image rollover
keyboard event	preload an image
cross-browser compatibility	timer
default action	

Summary

- The events that are used in JavaScript applications can be divided into three types: *HTML events*, *mouse events*, and *keyboard events*.

- When you use JavaScript methods to attach and detach event handlers, you need to provide for *cross-browser compatibility*. That's because DOM-compliant browsers use different methods for this than the older IE browsers.

- Modern browsers send an *event object* to the event handler. That object provides a method for cancelling the *default action* of the event. Because older versions of IE provide for this in a different way, you need to cancel default actions in a way that is cross-browser compatible.

- An *image rollover* occurs when the user positions the mouse over an image and the image is changed.

- To preload an image, you create a new Image object and set its src attribute to the URL for the image.

- Browsers provide two types of *timers*. A one-time timer executes a function just once after the specified interval of time. An interval timer executes a function each time the specified time interval passes.

Exercise 13-1   Test the FAQs application

In this exercise, you'll test the FAQs applications of this chapter, and you'll use the Console panel to explore event objects.

Open, test, and review the application

1. Use your text editor or IDE to open and review the files in this folder:

   `c:\javascript\exercises\ch13\faqs\`

2. Use the Chrome browser to test this application. Note that the URL in the address bar ends with "index.html" when the page is loaded. Then, click on a question, and note that the URL has changed to "index.html#", which means the page has been reloaded. That's because the statement that prevents the default action event of an <a> tag has been commented out.

3. Find the statement that has been commented out in the onload event handler and uncomment it. Then, restart the application and repeat step 2. Now, the URL in the address bar ends with "index.html" when you click on a heading, so the default action of the click event of the <a> tag has been cancelled.

4. Click the browser's Reload button or press F5 to reload the page. Then, press F12 to open Chrome's developer tools, and click on the Console tab to display the Console panel. Note that a single FocusEvent object shows in the Console panel. That's because this application sets the focus on the first <a> tag when the page loads, and the <a> tag's focus event has a handler attached to it.

5. Use your mouse to click on one of the question in the FAQs application. Note that this adds at least three new event objects to the Console panel: a MouseEvent, a FocusEvent, and another Mouse Event. Expand each one and scroll down to its "type" property. Note that the values are "mouseover", "focus", and "click".

Exercise 13-2   Enhance the Slide Show application

In this exercise, you'll enhance the Slide Show application by adding the JavaScript code for a Change Speed link that has been added to the user interface.

Open and test the application

1. Use your text editor or IDE to open and review the files in this folder:

   `c:\javascript\exercises\ch13\slide_show\`

2. Use Chrome to test this application, and experiment with the Pause/Resume link. Then, click the Change Speed link and note that it reloads the page but doesn't otherwise do anything.

Modify the application so the Change Speed link works

3. In the slide_show.js file for this application, note that an event handler named changeSpeed has been added. This handler accepts an event object and contains one comment and a prompt statement.

4. In the onload event handler, add the code for attaching this event handler to the click event of the Change Speed link. Then, test this change. It should display the prompt dialog box and accept a user entry, but not do anything else.

5. In the changeSpeed function, set the slideshow's speed property to the value entered by the user. Then, call the slideshow object's startSlideShow method with no parameters. Test this application with a valid speed entry, and notice that it behaves strangely after you change the speed.

6. Remember from figure 13-12 that you can't modify a timer once it's started. Instead, you need to cancel the timer and then create a new timer with the changed speed. To do that, change the code in the changeSpeed function so it first calls the stopSlideShow method and then calls the startSlideShow method. Because both of these methods return the this keyword, you can chain them. Now, test this application with a valid speed entry.

7. Even after you get the Change Speed link working correctly, the page is being reloaded every time the link is clicked. To fix that, modify the changeSpeed function so it cancels the default action of the link by using the preventDefault method of the event library.

Add the refinements

8. Modify the changeSpeed function in the slideshow.js file so the prompt statement displays a message like this:

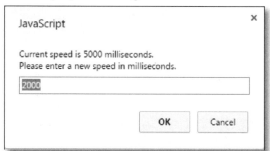

Here, the current speed is displayed in the message above the text box. To put that speed in the message, you need to get the current speed from the speed property.

9. Add data validation that displays an alert dialog box with an error message if the entry isn't a valid number and also if the user clicks on the Cancel button, which returns a null value.

Move the changeSpeed function to the slideshow object

10. Comment out the changeSpeed function in the slide_show.js file. Then, copy it to the slide show library and make whatever modifications are necessary for it to become a method of the slideshow object. Last, change the onload event handler in the slide_show.js file so it uses this method as the event handler for the click event of the Change Speed link.

14

How to work with closures, callbacks, and recursion

Throughout this book, you have been creating and working with basic functions. Now, in this chapter, you'll learn some advanced techniques for working with functions. First, you'll learn how to use closures to protect your code and solve a specific problem with loops. Then, you'll learn how to use callback functions to make your code more flexible. And finally, you'll learn how to use recursive functions for iterating hierarchical structures or large arrays. These are critical skills that will take your JavaScript programming to a new level.

Introduction to closures

Closures are a powerful feature of the JavaScript language, but they can also be hard to understand. In the figures that follow, you'll learn what closures are and some of the many ways you can use them. But before you can learn about closures, you need to learn about JavaScript's *scope chain*.

How the scope chain works

Back in figure 4-7, you learned about *scope*, which refers to the visibility of JavaScript objects. In brief, objects coded outside a function have *global scope*, so they can be seen and used by any other JavaScript object. In contrast, an object that's coded inside a function has *local scope*, so it can only be seen and used inside the function that it's in.

Although discussions about scope often focus on variables, these rules apply to functions, too. That is, a function written outside any other function has global scope, while a function written inside another function has local scope.

The other important feature of scope in JavaScript is that objects have access to their own scope, and to the scope of the objects that contain them. This is what creates *scope chains*.

This is easiest to understand by looking at code. The example in figure 14-1 creates a global variable named g and a global function named outerFunction. Then, within outerFunction, it creates a local variable named o and a local function named innerFunction. And finally, within innerFunction, it creates a local variable named i.

Then, at various points in this code, the log method of the console object is called and passed the g, o, and i variables. When the log statements are in the global scope, only the g variable is visible, or *in scope*. In other words, the code can't move down the scope chain and see the variables in either of the functions.

When the log statements are in the local scope of outerFunction, the g and o variables are visible. This shows that the code can see its own scope, and move up the scope chain to see the global scope. But it still can't move down, so it can't see the i variable inside innerFunction.

When the log statements are in the local scope of innerFunction, all three variables are visible. This shows that the code can see its own scope, and it can move up to see the scope of the object that contains it (outerFunction), and then up to the see the global scope.

The one other scope concept that you should be aware of is this. If an object in the scope chain has something referring to it, it will stay in scope even if the object that contains it is *out of scope*. If, for example, an object refers to the o variable inside outerFunction, then the o variable will stay "alive" and available to that object, even after outerFunction is done. This is the essence of a closure, and you'll see how that works next.

An example that illustrates the scope chain

```
var g = "I am global";                    // Contained by global context
console.log(g);  // I am global
console.log(o);  // Reference error - o is not defined
console.log(i);  // Reference error - i is not defined

var outerFunction = function() {          // Contained by global context
    var o = "I am outer";                 // Contained by outerFunction
    console.log(g);  // I am global
    console.log(o);  // I am outer
    console.log(i);  // Reference error - i is not defined

    var innerFunction = function() {      // Contained by outerFunction
        var i = "I am inner";             // Contained by innerFunction
        console.log(g);  // I am global
        console.log(o);  // I am outer
        console.log(i);  // I am inner
    };
};
```

You can move up the scope chain but not down

- The global scope has access to its own g variable, but can't move down to access the o variable within outerFunction.

- outerFunction can move up to access the g variable in the global scope, and has access to its own o variable, but can't move down to access the i variable within innerFunction.

- innerFunction can move up to access the g variable in the global scope, and the o variable in outerFunction, and has access to its own i variable.

Description

- The *scope chain* in JavaScript refers to what is *in scope*, or what can be seen and used by other objects. The scope chain starts with global scope and moves down.

- Objects that are created within other objects have access to their own scope, and the scope of the object that contains them.

- Object visibility moves up the scope chain, not down.

- An object in the scope chain will be available, or "alive", as long as something is referring to it. This is true even if the object that contains it has finished and is *out of scope*.

Figure 14-1   How the scope chain works

How closures work

You just learned that an object in the scope chain stays in scope as long as there is a reference to it. But how do you create the reference? The most common way is for an outer function to return an inner function that refers to something in the outer function's scope. This is called a *closure.*

You can see this in the example in figure 14-2. Here, the function named createClickCounter contains a variable named count that is set to zero, and an inner function named clickCounter that increments the count variable by one. This inner function also logs the id of the element that was clicked and the current value of the count variable. Finally, the createClickCounter function returns the inner clickCounter function.

The critical thing to note about this code is that the count variable is in the outer function, not the inner function. This means that when the clickCounter function is returned by the outer function, the count variable will stay alive, even though the outer function is finished. This is because the inner clickCounter function has a reference to it.

Next is an event handler function for the window's onload event, which attaches event handlers for two buttons. Up until now, the event handlers you've seen have been attached by assigning a function definition as the value of the handler. In this case, however, the createClickCounter function isn't assigned. Rather, it's invoked by including parentheses after it.

When the createClickCounter function is invoked, its count variable is created and set to zero, the inner clickCounter function definition is returned and assigned as the button's event handler, and then the createClickCounter function finishes and goes out of scope. Remember, though, that the inner function refers to the outer function's count variable, and the button refers to the inner function. These references mean that the count variable is still in scope, even though the createClickCounter function that contains it is out of scope.

This also means that each button has a separate version of the count variable in its scope. That's because the createClickCounter function is invoked twice, once for each button. Thus, each button has access to an internal count variable that will keep track of how many times it's been clicked.

Last, this means that the count variable is available in the scope chain of the button it's attached to, but nowhere else. If you try to access it directly, as in the last line of code in the onload event handler, you'll get an exception. This protects the internal count variable from being changed or deleted by other code.

This example is followed by a screen shot that shows Chrome's console panel after the two buttons named first_button and second_button have been clicked a few times each. Notice that clicking either button doesn't affect the click count of the other button. This is because each has access to a separate internal count variable.

When you work with closures, keep in mind that they work by keeping extra scope in memory. So, you'll want to be judicious about what you decide to keep alive. If you have too many closures with too much stored in memory, you can have performance problems.

What a closure is

- A *closure* is an inner function that has access to an outer function's variables.

- Closures are created when a reference is made to a variable, object, or function that is defined within another function.

An example that illustrates a closure

```
var createClickCounter = function() {
    var count = 0;

    // inner function that refers to the outer function's local variable
    var clickCounter = function() {
        count++;
        // the value of 'this' is the clicked element
        console.log(this.id + " count is " + count);
    };

    // returning the inner function, or closure, keeps the variables it
    // refers to "alive", even after the outer function is out of scope
    return clickCounter;
};

window.onload = function() {
    // each call to createClickCounter creates a closure that is assigned
    // as the button's event handler with its own count variable
    $("first_button").onclick = createClickCounter();
    $("second_button").onclick = createClickCounter();

    console.log(count);    // ReferenceError: count is not defined
};
```

The Console panel after clicking the two buttons several times

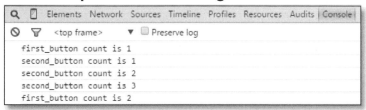

```
first_button count is 1
second_button count is 1
second_button count is 2
second_button count is 3
first_button count is 2
```

Description

- One common way to create a closure is for an outer function to return the inner function.

- Closures keep extra scope in memory, which can cause performance problems if they are overused.

Figure 14-2   How closures work

Closures in the Rollover application

Now that you know what a closure is and how it works, you may be surprised to learn that you've used one before. In fact, the Rollover application of the last chapter included closures.

Figure 14-3 shows this Rollover application. Recall that it works by showing a new image when you move your mouse pointer over an image, and by restoring the old one when you move your mouse pointer out of the image.

In the code for this application, the createRollover function has three parameters named imgTag, secondURL, and secondAlt. It then creates two variables named firstUrl and firstAlt, where it stores the values of the src and alt attributes of the img tag specified by the imgTag parameter.

After that, it creates two functions called mouseover and mouseout. These are inner functions that refer to variables that exist in the outer function's scope. Specifically, mouseover refers to imgTag, secondUrl, and secondAlt, while mouseout refers to imgTag, firstUrl, and firstAlt.

Note, however, that the inner functions aren't returned to create the closures. Instead, they're assigned as the event handlers for the mouseover and mouseout events of the image tag. That's what creates the closures.

Here's how it works. When the createRollover function is called in the onload event handler, it uses the attach method of the evt library (see figure 13-5) to attach the inner mouseover and mouseout functions as event handlers to the img tag it receives. This img tag then refers to the mouseover and mouseout functions, which keeps them in scope. The functions, in turn, refer to the variables and parameters in the outer function, which keeps them in scope.

As a result, all the variables are in the image's scope chain, and they are used to keep track of the images used by the rollover, even after the createRollover function finishes and goes out of scope. Also, these variables can't be accessed outside the image's scope chain, so they can't be overwritten or changed by outside code.

The Rollover application from chapter 13

Fishing Images

Move the mouse over the image to view the rollover image.

The JavaScript code for the Rollover application

```
var createRollover = function(imgTag, secondUrl, secondAlt) {
    //store first image info
    var firstUrl = imgTag.src;
    var firstAlt = imgTag.alt;

    //create event handlers
    var mouseover = function() {
        imgTag.src = secondUrl;
        imgTag.alt = secondAlt;
    };
    var mouseout = function() {
        imgTag.src = firstUrl;
        imgTag.alt = firstAlt;
    };

    //attach event handlers
    evt.attach(imgTag, "mouseover", mouseover);
    evt.attach(imgTag, "mouseout", mouseout);
};
window.onload = function() {
    createRollover($("img1"), "images/hero.jpg", "Hero photo");
    createRollover($("img2"), "images/deer.jpg", "Deer near lodge");
};
```

Description

- The createRollover function contains two inner functions called mouseover and mouseout. Each of these inner functions refers to the local variables of the outer function.

- Since the inner functions are attached as event handlers, any references to them stay "alive". This, in turn, means that references to the local variables of the outer function also stay "alive", even after the outer function has completed and is out of scope.

- Thus, each call to the createRollover function creates a closure that has its own variables. This is how each rollover stores the image information that's sent to the outer function.

Figure 14-3   Closures in the Rollover application

How to use closures

Now that you have the general idea of how closures work, you're going to see some practical applications of the use of closures.

How to use closures to create private state

In the last chapter, you saw an application that worked with images and timers to create a slide show. The essence of that application was the slide show library, which consisted of an object literal named slideshow that had all the properties and methods needed for the slide show. In figure 14-4, the first table lists those properties and methods.

The next table in this figure shows how many of those properties and methods are needed by code outside of the slideshow object. In fact, no properties and only three methods are called by outside code. This means that all the properties and most of the methods of the slideshow object are only used by the slideshow object itself. The trouble is that these properties and methods are also available to outside code, which means they can be accidently overwritten by programmers who use this library.

With many programming languages, you can code *public* and *private* keywords that let you designate which properties and methods should be available to outside code and which should only be available to the object itself. But JavaScript doesn't offer those keywords right now, although they might be added in some future release. Until then, however, you can use closures to create *private state* in your objects.

To illustrate, the example in this figure shows how to rewrite the object literal for the slide show of chapter 13 with three public methods and the rest of the object's properties and methods in private state. Although the code in the functions and methods isn't shown here, what's important is where the variables, functions, and methods are placed in the code. (You can see all the code for this library in figure 14-9.)

First, instead of creating an object literal, this code starts by creating a function called getSlideshow. Then, this function declares several variables that correspond to the properties of the chapter 13 slideshow object. After that, the function creates several functions that correspond to the methods of the chapter 13 slideshow object that aren't used by outside code. Because these variables and functions are coded inside the outer function, they have local scope. This makes them private.

Finally, this function creates and returns an object that contains the three methods of the chapter 13 slideshow object that are used by outside code. These methods are inner functions that refer to the variables and functions of the outer function. Thus, they are closures. Returning an object with methods is a common way to return more than one inner function from an outer function.

This means that as long as the returned object exists, it has access to the objects in its private state. But no other code has access to the objects in its private state, so they can't be changed by outside code.

The properties and methods of the slideshow object from chapter 13

Object Name	Description
`timer`	A property that holds a reference to a timer object.
`nodes`	A property that contains an object that holds references to image and span tags.
`img`	A property that contains an object that holds an array of Image objects and a numeric value.
`play`	A Boolean property that indicates whether the slide show is playing.
`speed`	A number property that indicates the speed of the slide show in milliseconds.
`stopSlideShow`	A method that stops the timer.
`displayNextImage`	A method that gets and displays the next image.
`setPlayText`	A method that toggles the text of the Pause/Resume link.
`loadImages`	A method that accepts an array of slide objects, preloads images, and stores Image objects in the img.cache array.
`startSlideShow`	A method that accepts and stores references to image and span tags, starts the timer, and stores a reference to the timer object.
`togglePlay`	A method used to start and stop the slide show.

The methods called by code outside the slideshow object

Object Name	Used by
`loadImages`	The onload event handler.
`startSlideShow`	The onload event handler.
`togglePlay`	The play_pause link's event handler.

How to use a closure to create private state in the slideshow object

```
var getSlideshow = function() {
    //private variables and functions
    var timer, play = true, speed = 2000;
    var nodes = { image: null, caption: null };
    var img = { cache: [], counter: 0 };
    var stopSlideShow = function() { ... };
    var displayNextImage = function() { ... };
    var setPlayText = function() { ... };
    //public methods that have access to private variables and functions
    return {
        loadImages: function(slides) { ... },
        startSlideShow: function() { ... },
        togglePlay: function(e) { ... }
    };
};
```

Description

- All the properties and methods of a JavaScript object are publically available. That means that an object's critical properties and methods can be overwritten.

- To protect an object's properties and methods, you can use closures to create *private state*.

Figure 14-4   How to use closures to create private state in objects

How to code an immediately invoked function expression (IIFE)

Normally, you first define a function and then invoke it, as in the first example in figure 14-5. However, you can also define and invoke a function expression in one step by adding parentheses at the end, as in the second example. This is called an *immediately invoked function expression (IIFE)*. Since the function is immediately invoked, it doesn't need to be stored in a variable.

If you don't store a function expression in a variable, though, it starts with the *function* keyword. But when the JavaScript engine sees a line of code that starts with the *function* keyword, it interprets it as a function declaration, so the parentheses will cause a syntax error. To fix this, you need to put the function definition inside parentheses, as this second example shows.

You should also know that there are two ways to code the parentheses of an IIFE, as shown in the third group of examples. You'll see both coding styles in books and online examples. Although some programmers have strong opinions about which one is best, they both work, so you can choose whichever one is easiest for you to understand and use. This book uses the first style.

You should also know that if an IIFE comes after the start of a line of code, the JavaScript engine doesn't require the outside parentheses. Nevertheless, you should still use the parentheses since it's a programming convention that helps other programmers recognize that you're using an IIFE.

How to use an IIFE to create block scope

With many programming languages, *block scope* refers to variables that are declared inside a block of code, like an if statement or a loop. Then, a variable declared inside the block isn't visible outside the block. Although JavaScript doesn't provide for block scope, you can simulate block scope by using an IIFE.

The last two examples in figure 14-5 show how this works. The first is a function that contains a normal loop. Here, the i variable declared in the loop is available inside the function after the loop completes. That shows that JavaScript doesn't have block scope.

In the next example, however, the loop is inside an IIFE. Then, the IIFE runs immediately, and its scope is destroyed as soon as it's done. That means that as long as it doesn't return a reference to anything in its local scope, its scope is destroyed when the function completes. Thus, the i variable isn't available outside the loop.

This example also has three other points of interest. First, because the IIFE is an inner function, it has access to the outer function's variables. Thus, it can use the arr variable. Second, because it's a function within a function, it's a closure. But instead of keeping scope alive, it makes the i variable of the loop go out of scope. Third, the IIFE doesn't accept any parameters or return anything, but it could do both. You'll see how that works later on.

A function expression that is defined and then invoked

```
var sayHello = function() {        // define function
    console.log("Hello");
};
sayHello();                        // invoke function
```

An immediately invoked function expression (IIFE)

```
(function() {                      // define and invoke function
    console.log("Hello");
})();
```

Two ways to code the parentheses of an IIFE

```
(function() { console.log ("Hello"); } ) ();
(function() { console.log ("Hello"); } () );
```

A function with a normal for loop: i is available throughout the function

```
var regularLoop = function() {
    var arr = [];
    for (var i = 0; i < 5; i++) {
        arr.push(i);
    }
    console.log(arr.join());        // Displays 0,1,2,3,4
    arr.push(i);
    console.log(arr.join());        // Displays 0,1,2,3,4,5
};
```

A function with a for loop in an IIFE: i is only available in the loop

```
var blockScopeLoop = function() {
    var arr = [];
    (function() {
        for (var i = 0; i < 5; i++) {
            arr.push(i);
        }
    })();
    console.log(arr.join());        // Displays 0,1,2,3,4
    arr.push(i);                    // Reference error: i is not defined
};
```

Description

- An *immediately invoked function expression (IIFE)* is a function that is defined and invoked all at once.

- An IIFE should be always coded within parentheses, so the JavaScript engine as well as other programmers will interpret it as an IIFE.

- Like a regular function call, an IIFE ends with opening and closing parentheses, which can accept arguments. In the next figure, you'll see how to send arguments to an IIFE.

- Unlike some languages, JavaScript doesn't have *block scope* to protect the variables in an if statement or for loop. However, you can use an IIFE to simulate block scope.

- As long as no reference to the IIFE remains when it's done running, its scope is destroyed, even though the function that contains it is still in scope.

Figure 14-5   How to use an IIFE to create block scope

How to solve the closure loop problem

If you're working with closures in a loop, you can have a problem if you don't understand the two points at the start of figure 14-6. First, a closure has access to the values in its scope chain by reference. This means that if the value of an outer variable changes, then its value will change inside the inner function as well. Second, the values of the variables in a function are determined when the function is invoked, not when the function is defined.

The first example in this figure illustrates the loop problem. In it, an onload event handler starts by creating an array of website names and storing them in an array variable named topSites. Then, it uses the getElementsByTagName method to get all the <a> tags in an HTML element named top_sites, and it stores the resulting array in a variable named links.

Next, the code loops through the topSites array. Within the loop, it uses the value of the i variable to get the <a> tag with the corresponding index from the links array. Then, it uses the value of the current element in the topSites array to set the tag's text attribute to the current site name. Last, it attaches an event handler to the tag's onclick event. This event handler should display a message indicating which link the user clicked on.

After this example is a screen shot showing how the <a> tags look in the page, and the result of clicking on the middle link. As expected, the three tags display the names of the three sites in the topSites array. But unexpectedly, they all say "You clicked on Twitter" when clicked.

Why is this? The onclick event handler is within the onload event handler. Thus, it's a function within a function, or a closure. That's why it has access to the i variable and the topSites array, which are defined in the outer onload function. But it has access to them by reference. That means that each time through the loop, the value of i changes, both in the outer onload function and in the inner onclick function. So, when the link is clicked in the page, the onclick function takes the current value of i, which is the last index in the array, and uses it to retrieve and display the site name.

One way to fix this is to rewrite the code so it uses a function that returns a function. The next example shows how this is done. First, it shows a function called createHandler, which accepts a name parameter and returns a function. Then, in the loop, the createHandler function is called, and passed the current value of the topSites array. Because the createHandler function is being invoked, the value of name is set to the current site name. Then, the function that createHandler returns, with the correct site name, is set as the <a> tag's event handler.

Another way to fix this is to rewrite the code so it uses an IIFE as in the last example. Since an IIFE is a regular function, you can pass arguments to it in the parentheses that invoke the function. In this case, the current value of the topSites array is passed to the IIFE. It will become the name parameter in the function.

What else you need to know about closures

- A closure has access to the values in its scope chain by reference. This means that if an outer variable changes, it will change for the closure, too.

- The variables in a function are set when the function is invoked, not when it's defined.

How this affects closures in a loop

Assigning click event handlers in a loop

```
window.onload = function() {
    var topSites = ["Google", "Facebook", "Twitter"];
    var links = $("top_sites").getElementsByTagName("a");
    for (var i in topSites) {
        links[i].text = topSites[i];
        // This is a closure so value of i is by reference and can change.
        // When the function is invoked, value of i will be its last value.
        links[i].onclick = function() {
            alert("You clicked on " + topSites[i]);
        };
    }
};
```

Result of loop – all links display the last value

Google
Facebook
Twitter   You clicked on Twitter

How to fix the loop problem by calling a function that returns a function

```
window.onload = function() {
    /* topSites and links variables go here */
    var createHandler = function(name) {
        return function() { alert("You clicked on " + name); };
    };
    for (var i in topSites) {
        links[i].text = topSites[i];
        links[i].onclick = createHandler(topSites[i]);       // i won't change
    }
};
```

How to fix the loop problem by using an IIFE

```
window.onload = function() {
    /* topSites and links variables go here */
    for (var i in topSites) {
        links[i].text = topSites[i];
        links[i].onclick = (function(name) {
            return function() {
                alert("You clicked on " + name);
            };
        })(topSites[i]);     // value for 'name' parameter passed to the IIFE
    }
};
```

Figure 14-6   How to solve the closure loop problem

How to work with the this keyword in closures

Earlier you learned that an inner function has access to the scope of the object that contains it. You might think, then, that you could use the this keyword in a function inside a method to access the object that contains the method. However, you would be wrong, as the first example in figure 14-7 demonstrates.

Remember from figure 10-10 that every function has a this keyword. This means that the function within the displayFullPrice method in the first example has its own this keyword. Then, since the inner function is invoked normally, its this keyword is undefined in strict mode or the Window object in non-strict mode. And if this inner function is invoked as an event handler, the element that raised the event is the value of the this keyword. In either case, the object that's the value of the this keyword in this example doesn't have a calc method, so an exception is thrown.

Remember, though, that you can use the bind method of the inner function to set the value of its this keyword. This is shown in the second example. This is the same as the first example, except that after the closing brace of the inner function, the bind method is called. This makes the value of the inner function's this keyword the object that contains the displayFullPrice method. Thus, the code works correctly.

Most of the time, using the bind method will handle a problem like this. Sometimes, though, you'll need to access both the outer function's this keyword and the inner function's this keyword. If, for example, the inner function is attached as a link's event handler, the value of its this keyword is the link that was clicked, and you might want to use some of the link's properties in your code, like the id or the href property.

In that case, you can store the value of the outer function's this keyword in a variable, as in the third example. Then, because the inner function has access to the outer function's scope, it will have access to both the variable containing the outer this keyword and its own this keyword.

This is illustrated by the third example. Here, the outer function's this keyword is stored in a variable named "that". This adheres to a programming convention that says that when you store the value of the this keyword in a variable, the name of the variable should be "that", "self", or "me". Be aware, though, that the Window object also has a global property named self, so it's better to use "that" or "me".

You should also know that the arguments property of a function works similarly. That is, each function has its own arguments property, so you can't access the outer function's arguments property from within the inner function. However, you can store the outer arguments property in a variable if the inner function needs to use it.

An object with a method that returns a closure that throws an error

```
var tax = {
    rate: 0.075,
    calc: function(sub) { return (sub + (sub * this.rate)).toFixed(2); },
    displayFullPrice: function(subtotal) {
        return function() {
            alert(this.calc(subtotal));
        };
    }
};
```

Invoking the closure throws an exception

```
var calc = tax.displayFullPrice(100);
calc();         // TypeError: this.calc is not a function
```

How to use the bind method to set the value of the closure's this keyword

```
var tax = { /* rate and calc are the same as before */,
    displayFullPrice: function(subtotal) {
        return function() {
            alert(this.calc(subtotal));
        }.bind(this);
    }
};
```

Invoking the closure works correctly

```
var calc = tax.displayFullPrice(100);                    // 107.50
```

How to use a variable to store the outer function's this keyword value

```
var tax = { /* rate and calc are the same as before */,
    displayFullPrice: function(subtotal) {
        var that = this;
        return function() {
            // 'this' is the clicked link; 'that' is the tax object
            alert(this.id + ": " + that.calc(subtotal));
        };
    }
};
```

Attaching the closure as an event handler

```
$("camera").onclick = tax.displayFullPrice(100);      // camera: 107.50
```

Description

- Although a closure has access to the variables higher up in its scope chain, each function has its own this keyword. That can cause problems when working with closures.

- If a closure needs access to the outer function's this keyword, the outer function can pass it to the closure using the bind method. This sets the inner function's this keyword.

- If a closure needs access to both the outer function's this keyword and its own, the outer function can store the value of its this keyword in a new variable that by convention is named "that", "self", or "me". Then, the closure has access to the new variable.

- Each function also has its own arguments property. Thus, if the closure needs access to the outer function's arguments property, the outer function should store it in a variable.

Figure 14-7   How to work with the this keyword in closures

The Slide Show application

Now that you know how closures work, you'll see the Slide Show application of the last chapter rewritten so it uses closures. This will protect the variables and functions the application needs for its internal operations.

The HTML

Figure 14-8 shows the HTML for the rewritten Slide Show application. In the head element, you can see that this version only requires a slide show library and the main JavaScript file.

In the main element, the only difference from the chapter 13 application is that this HTML uses an input tag of type "button" instead of an <a> tag for the Pause/Resume toggle function. Since a button element doesn't have a default action, the application no longer needs to cancel the default action when the slide show is paused or resumed.

The Slide Show application in the browser

The head element in the HTML file

```
<head>
    <title>Chapter 14 Slide Show</title>
    <link rel="stylesheet" type="text/css" href="slide_show.css"/>
    <script type="text/javascript" src="library_slide_show.js"></script>
    <script type="text/javascript" src="slide_show.js"></script>
</head>
```

The main element in the HTML file

```
<main>
    <h1>Fishing Slide Show</h1>
    <p><input type="button" id="play_pause" value="Pause"></p>
    <p><img src="images/gear.jpg" id="image" alt=""></p>
    <p><span id="caption">Fishing Gear</span></p>
</main>
```

Description

- The Slide Show application works the same as the one in the last chapter.
- One trivial difference is that it uses a button instead of a link for the Pause/Resume function, which means that it doesn't need to cancel a default action.
- The main difference is that the slide show library has been rewritten to use closures. This protects its internal variables and functions from being overwritten by outside code.

Figure 14-8   The Slide Show application

The slide show library

Figure 14-9 shows the JavaScript code in the slide show library. This code is similar to the code you saw in the last chapter, but what's important is how it's arranged.

First, instead of an object literal, this code starts with a function called createSlideshow. This function declares a timer variable, a Boolean play variable, a numeric speed variable, a nodes variable that's an object literal, and an img variable that's an object literal. These variables are similar to the object properties from chapter 13. However, because they're variables inside a function, they have local scope. This means they can't be accessed by code outside the function, so they can't be changed or deleted by outside code.

After that, the stopSlideShow, displayNextImage, and setPlayText functions are similar to three of the object methods from chapter 13. But because they're now functions inside a function, they have local scope and can't be accessed by outside code. Also, because they're functions inside a function, they have access to the outer function's scope, so they can use all the private variables.

After creating the private variables and functions it needs for its internal operations, the function creates and returns an object literal that has three methods: loadImages, startSlideShow, and createToggleHandler. These correspond to the methods called by the outside code in chapter 13. Each of these methods refers to the private variables and functions defined earlier, so those variables and functions will stay alive as long as the object returned by the function stays alive.

The createToggleHandler is a method that returns a function. That's because it's meant to attach an event handler to the Pause/Resume toggle button. It starts by storing a reference to its this keyword in a variable named me. This value refers to the object literal that contains the createToggleHandler method.

Then, the inner function checks the private play variable. If it's true, it calls the private stopSlideShow function to stop the slide show. If it's false, it calls the startSlideShow method to start the slide show. Because startSlideShow is a method of the object literal, not a private function, the code uses the me variable that contains a reference to the object literal to call it.

Next, the inner function passes the value of the button that was clicked to the private setPlayText function. It can do that because the button is the value of the inner function's this keyword. Finally, it toggles the value of the private play variable by setting it to the opposite of its current value.

The library_slide_show.js file

```
var createSlideshow = function() {
    // private variables and functions
    var timer, play = true, speed = 2000;
    var nodes = { image: null, caption: null };
    var img = { cache: [], counter: 0 };

    var stopSlideShow = function() { clearInterval( timer ); };
    var displayNextImage = function() {
        img.counter = ++img.counter % img.cache.length;
        var image = img.cache[img.counter];
        nodes.image.src = image.src;
        nodes.caption.firstChild.nodeValue = image.title;
    };
    var setPlayText = function(btn) {
        btn.value = (play)? "Resume" : "Pause";
    };
    // public methods that have access to private variables and functions
    return {
        loadImages: function(slides) {
            var image;
            for ( var i = 0; i < slides.length; i++ ) {
                image = new Image();
                image.src = "images/" + slides[i].href;
                image.title = slides[i].title;
                img.cache.push( image );
            }
            return this;
        },
        startSlideShow: function() {
            if (arguments.length === 2) {
                nodes.image = arguments[0];
                nodes.caption = arguments[1];
            }
            timer = setInterval(displayNextImage, speed);
            return this;
        },
        createToggleHandler: function() {
            var me = this;          // store 'this', which is the object literal
            return function() {
                // 'this' is the clicked button; 'me' is the object literal
                if ( play ) { stopSlideShow(); } else { me.startSlideShow(); }
                setPlayText(this);
                play = ! play;   // toggle play flag
            };
        }
    };
};
```

Description

- This library consists of an outer function called createSlideShow that returns an object literal with three methods.
- The rest of the slideshow variables and functions are in the outer function, which means that they are available to the inner functions but not to outside code.

Figure 14-9   The slide show library for the Slide Show application

The main JavaScript file

Figure 14-10 shows the main JavaScript file for this version of the Slide Show application. It's almost the same as the one you saw in the last chapter, with one important difference. Before, the slideshow object was an object literal with global scope. This meant that the code in the main JavaScript file could use the slideshow object without declaring or creating it first.

In this case, though, the onload event handler calls the global createSlideshow function of the last figure to create the slideshow object. This function returns the object with its three methods that are needed for running the slide show.

Next, the event handler creates an array of slide objects with information about the images that will be in the slideshow. After that, the code chains two of the slideshow object's methods. First, it calls the loadImages method and passes it the array of slide objects. Second, it calls the startSlideShow method and passes it the image and span tags that will be used to display the slide show.

Finally, the event handler calls the createToggleHandler method of the slideshow object to get the function that it will use as the click event handler for the play_pause button.

Below the code in this figure is a screen shot of the slideshow object in the Watch Expressions pane of the Sources panel in Chrome's developer tools. Note that only the three public methods, plus the object's prototype object, are visible. This shows that outside code can't access variables like speed or nodes, or functions like stopSlideShow or displayNextImage. This means that the users of the slide show library can't overwrite the variables and functions in the slideshow object's private state.

The main JavaScript file

```
var $ = function(id) { return document.getElementById(id); };

window.onload = function() {
    // create the slideshow object
    var slideshow = createSlideshow();

    var slides = [
        {href:"gear.jpg", title:"Fishing Gear"},
        {href:"plane.jpg", title:"Bush Plane"},
        {href:"release.jpg", title:"Catch and Release"},
        {href:"lunch.jpg", title:"Streamside Lunch"},
        {href:"dusk.jpg", title:"Day's End"}
    ];
    slideshow.loadImages(slides).startSlideShow($("image"), $("caption"));

    $("play_pause").onclick = slideshow.createToggleHandler();
};
```

The slideshow object in the Watch Expressions pane

```
▼ Watch Expressions                        +  C
▼ slideshow: Object
  ▶ createToggleHandler: function () {
  ▶ loadImages: function (slides) {
  ▶ startSlideShow: function () {
  ▶ __proto__: Object
```

Description

- In this version of the Slide Show application, you have to create the slideshow object before you can use it. That's because it's a closure returned by an outer function, rather than a global object literal.

- You can examine the slideshow object in Chrome's developer tools to see that only the three methods returned by the createSlideshow function are available to outside. As a result, there's no way to overwrite any of the slideshow object's private state.

Figure 14-10   The main JavaScript file for the Slide Show application

How to use callbacks

When you pass a function as an argument to another function, the function you pass is a *callback function* (or just *callback*). You've already seen callback functions in native JavaScript methods like setTimeOut and the sort method of an array. Now you'll learn how callback functions work, and how you can create and use your own callback functions

How callback functions work

As you've already seen, one function can be returned by another function. That's because a function is an object just like any other object. This means that a function can also be passed as an argument to another function. A function that is passed to another function is called a *callback function*, or a *higher order function*.

The table in figure 14-11 summarizes some of the native JavaScript methods that use callback functions. It's important to note that you don't invoke the callback function when you pass it as an argument. Rather, you pass the definition of the function, and the function that receives it is in charge of invoking it.

As this figure shows, there are two main reasons to use callback functions. The first is to create *asynchronous* code, or code that will be called later. Common examples are the setTimeout, setInterval, and addEventListener functions.

The second reason is to create a general function that can be used in a lot of different situations. The array methods that accept functions are good examples of this. For instance, the sort method can be used to sort any array, no matter what it contains. You just need to pass it a callback function that tells it how the sorting should be done.

In the next figures, you'll learn how to create and use your own callback functions. But first, you should be aware of the best practices for coding callback functions. These are summarized in this figure.

All of the best practices have to do with making it so your code will still work if a callback function isn't passed. So first, you should make the callback function parameter an optional parameter. Second, you should check to make sure the callback function exists and is a function before you try to invoke it. Third, you should have some sort of default behavior that the function will do if a callback function isn't sent. For example, the array sort method treats the array elements as strings and sorts them alphabetically if it doesn't receive a callback function.

Some JavaScript methods that use callback functions

Method	Callback
`setTimeout`	The function to be called when the specified interval elapses.
`setInterval`	The function to be called when the specified interval elapses.
`addEventListener`	The function to be called when the event is triggered.
`Array.sort`	The function to be called to sort the array items.
`Array.reduce`	The function to be called to reduce the array items to a single value.

Two reasons to use callback functions

- To create *asynchronous code* in which you pass the function at one time but it won't be be called until later. Examples are the setTimeout and addEventListener functions.
- To create utility code that is flexible so it can be used in lots of situations with lots of different data types. Examples are many of the Array methods, like sort and reduce.

Some best practices for writing code that uses callback functions

- Make the callback function an optional parameter.
- Check to make sure the callback function exists and is a function before you call it.
- Do something if the optional callback function isn't received.

Description

- In JavaScript, functions are objects. That means they can be returned by other functions, and passed as arguments to other functions.
- A function that is passed to another function is a *callback function*, or a *higher order function*.
- When a function is passed as an argument, only its definition is passed. The function itself will be called later, by the function that receives it. This is similar to assigning a function as an event handler.

Figure 14-11   How callback functions work

How to create and use callback functions

Figure 14-12 shows how to create and use a utility function that accepts a callback function as one of its parameters. In the first group of examples, the calculateSalesTax function accepts parameters named amount, taxRate, and getTaxableAmount. The last parameter is a callback function that will determine how much of the value in amount is taxable.

The utility function starts by declaring a variable named taxable and setting it to the value of the amount parameter. This means that, by default, the function will treat the entire amount passed to it as taxable.

Then, this function checks to see if the getTaxableAmount parameter exists and is a function. If both are true, the utility function invokes the callback function, passing it the value in the amount parameter. It then stores the return value of the callback function in the taxable variable, replacing the value that was already there. The utility function then multiplies the value in the taxable variable by the value in the taxRate parameter, and returns the result of the calculation.

This utility function is followed by two examples that use it. Each of these examples passes an amount value of 100 and a taxRate value of 0.08. But as you can see, the utility function returns different results, depending on whether a callback function has been passed to it.

In the first example, no callback function is passed so the utility function just multiplies the amount by the tax rate. By contrast, the second example starts by coding a callback function named discount. This callback function applies a 10 percent discount to the amount passed to it. The code then passes the callback function as the third parameter. As a result, the utility function invokes the callback function, which returns a taxable amount of 90, and then sets the tax equal to 90 times 0.08, or 7.2.

The second group of examples uses a more complicated callback function named exemptFood. This function starts by setting the default taxable amount. Like the utility function, this is the entire amount passed to it. It then checks to see if it's been sent an array. It so, it loops through the array and looks for a property named type whose value is "food". If it finds it, it exempts the food item by adding zero to the total. If it doesn't, it adds the value in the total property to the total.

Next are two examples that use the exemptFood callback function with the utility function. In the first, the amount value is numeric. Since it's not an array, the callback function returns the entire amount as taxable. In the second example, though, an array provides the amount value, with one item of type "food". As a result, the callback function exempts that item from the taxable amount, so the taxable amount is 80, and the tax is 6.40.

A utility function that accepts a callback function

```
var calculateSalesTax = function(amount, taxRate, getTaxableAmount) {
    var taxable = amount;    // set default taxable amount
    // check to make sure callback exists and is a function
    if (getTaxableAmount && typeof getTaxableAmount === "function") {
        taxable = getTaxableAmount(amount);
    }
    // calculate and return tax
    var tax = taxable * taxRate;
    return (isNaN(tax))? "Invalid calculation." : tax;
};
```

Code that uses the utility function with no callback

```
var tax = calculateSalesTax(100, 0.08);                        // tax = 8
```

Code that uses the utility function with a callback

```
var discount = function(amount) {
    return amount * .90;    // 10 percent discount before tax
};
var tax = calculateSalesTax(100, 0.08, discount);              // tax = 7.2
```

An application that uses the utility function with a different callback

```
var exemptFood = function(amount) {
    var total = amount;       // set default value of total
    if (Array.isArray(amount)) {
        total = 0;
        for (var i in amount) {
            var item = (amount[i].type === "food")? 0 : amount[i].total;
            total = total + item;
        }
    }
    return total;
};
var items = [
    {type:"food", total: 35.00},
    {type:"clothing", total: 35.00},
    {type:"pet supplies", total: 45.00}
];
```

Code that uses the utility with a callback and a numeric first argument

```
var tax = calculateSalesTax(100, 0.08, exemptFood);            // tax = 8
```

Code that uses the utility with a callback and an array as the first argument

```
var itemized = calculateSalesTax(items, 0.08, exemptFood);     // tax = 6.4
```

Description

- When you use callback functions, you can write utility functions that are general-purpose. Then, when you call the utility function, you can provide the specifics required by the application in the callback function.

- In short, callbacks give you the flexibility to handle simple or complex requirements with the same utility function.

Figure 14-12   How to create and use callback functions

How to work with the this keyword in callback functions

A callback is a function within a function. That means that it has access to the scope of the function that contains it, and it has its own value for the this keyword and the arguments property. Therefore, you might need to use some of the techniques of figure 14-7 if you want to access the outer function's this keyword or arguments property.

Additionally, you might want to set the value of a callback function's this keyword when you call it inside a function or when you pass it to a function. Figure 14-13 shows two examples of doing that.

The first example shows how to set the value of the callback's this keyword at the time the callback is invoked. First is the utility function you saw in the last figure. This time, though, the utility function calls a function named getTaxableAmountTracker and stores the result in a variable named tracker. The getTaxableAmountTracker function isn't shown here, but you can assume that it has a log method that stores a value.

When the utility function invokes the callback function, it uses the callback function's call method. This lets it pass the tracker object to the callback, which sets it as the value of the this keyword. The function also passes the amount parameter the callback needs as the second parameter of the call method. Then, the exemptFood callback method checks whether its this keyword has a log method. If it does, it invokes it and passes the taxable amount to it.

This adds flexibility to your code. Since the utility function always makes the tracker object the value of the callback function's this keyword, you can decide whether or not to use it when you code your callback. If you don't want to use it, you can just ignore the this keyword. If you do want to use it, you can add code that calls its methods. Be sure, though, to check that the object and its methods exist before calling them. This is a best practice, and also makes it so you can pass your callback to functions that don't set the value of this.

The second example shows how to set the value of the callback's this keyword at the time the callback is passed. Here, the utility function is the same as in the last figure. But now, the exemptFood callback checks whether its this keyword is a span tag. If it is, it displays the value of the taxable amount in the span tag.

The code then uses the bind method of the callback function to set the value of its this keyword in the onload event handler. First, it retrieves the span tag with an id of taxable. Then, it creates a click event handler for a link. Within the click event handler, it calls the calculateSalesTax method, passing it the array of items from in the last figure, a tax rate, and the exemptFood callback function.

Crucially, the code calls the exemptFood function's bind method when it passes it to the utility function, and it passes the span tag to the bind method. This is what causes the taxable amount to be displayed in the page. If it passes the callback without calling its bind method, the taxable amount won't be displayed. This gives you the flexibility to show the taxable amount on pages where it's needed.

How to set the callback function's this keyword when calling the function

```
var calculateSalesTax = function(amount, taxRate, getTaxableAmount) {
    var tracker = getTaxableAmountTracker();
    var taxable = amount;
    if (getTaxableAmount && typeof getTaxableAmount === "function") {
        taxable = getTaxableAmount.call(tracker, amount);
    }
    var tax = taxable * taxRate;
    return (isNaN(tax))? "Invalid calculation." : tax;
};
var exemptFood = function(amount) {
    var total = amount;
    if (Array.isArray(amount)) {
        // calculate total...
    }
    // log the total if 'this' has a log method
    if (this !== undefined && this.log) { this.log(total); }
    return total;
};
```

How to set the callback function's this keyword when passing the function

```
var exemptFood = function(amount) {
    var total = amount;
    if (Array.isArray(amount)) {
        // calculate total...
    }
    // display the total if 'this' is a span tag
    if (this !== undefined && this.tagName && this.tagName === "SPAN") {
        this.firstChild.nodeValue = total;
    }
    return total;
};
window.onload = function() {
    var span = $("taxable");
    $("items").onclick = function() {
        calculateSalesTax(items, 0.08, exemptFood.bind(span));
    };
};
```

Description

- If the callback function uses the this keyword, you can use the call, apply, or bind method to set its value. This can help you create and use callback functions with optional functionality, like logging or displaying data.

- The function that receives and invokes the callback function can use the call or apply method to set the value of the callback's this keyword.

- The code that passes the callback function to the receiving function can use the bind method to set the value of the callback's this keyword. Doing this will prevent the this keyword from being set by the call or apply method in the receiving function.

Figure 14-13   How to use the this keyword in callback functions

How to use recursion

Up until now, you've used loops whenever you've needed to iterate through data or repeat an action a certain number of times. But there's another way to perform iteration, and that's with a *recursive function*.

How recursion works

A *recursive function* is one that repeatedly calls itself. With each call, the data or structure that's being processed is simplified until a *base case* is reached. That stops the recursive function and returns the result.

Most of the time, a loop is more appropriate for iteration because it's easier to read, faster, and uses fewer resources. Sometimes, though, recursion is better. For instance, recursion might be the better choice when you're dealing with a hierarchical structure, like the DOM, or when you think it will make your code easier to understand. Recursion can also be best when you're iterating through a large number of items, as you'll see in the next figure.

Figure 14-14 shows how to use both a loop and recursion to calculate a factorial. The factorial of a number is the product of all positive integers less than or equal to it. For example, the factorial of 3 is 3 * 2 * 1 = 6. The factorial of zero is 1, and negative numbers don't have factorials. To keep this simple, though, both of these factorial functions return 1 for zero and negative numbers.

To calculate a factorial using a loop, the first example starts by storing a default value of 1 in a variable named result. Then, it begins a for loop, and replaces the value of result with the value of result multiplied by the value of i, the loop counter variable. The loop stops when the counter gets to the number passed to the function.

Notice, though, that the loop counter variable, i, is initialized to 1 instead of zero. Initializing the counter to 1 makes it so the code inside the loop is skipped for negative values and zero, and the function returns 1 for those values. This is a fairly subtle variation on a normal loop, and might be missed by another programmer looking at your code. In that case, recursion might be clearer.

To calculate a factorial using recursion, the second example starts by returning 1 if the value it receives is less than one. This is the base case. Otherwise, it multiplies the value it received by the result of calling itself. When it calls itself, it passes the number it received decremented by 1.

When a function calls another function, it waits until the function it calls completes before it finishes. Thus, each function call in a recursive function waits until the base case is reached. Then, each function call that's been "on hold" uses the value returned to it by the function it called to complete its work.

The third example in this figure shows how to use a *named function expression* when you write a recursive function. First, it shows how you can break a recursive function that isn't named. Then, it shows that you can name a function expression by coding a name after the word *function* and before the parameter list. This makes it so the function will always be able to call itself, even if the variable holding it is reassigned.

How to calculate a factorial using a loop

```
var calculateFactorial = function(num) {
    var result = 1;
    for (var i = 1; i <= num; i++) {
        result = result * i;
    }
    return result;
};
calculateFactorial(4);      // 4 * 3 * 2 * 1 = 24
```

How to calculate a factorial using a function that calls itself (recursion)

```
var calculateFactorial = function(num) {
    if (num <= 1) {
        return 1;                                // base case
    } else {
        return num * calculateFactorial(num - 1);    // calls itself
    }
};
calculateFactorial(5);      // 5 * 4 * 3 * 2 * 1 = 120
```

How to improve a recursive function by using a named function expression

You can break a recursive function by reassigning its variable

```
var calculate = calculateFactorial;
calculateFactorial = undefined;
calculate(5);                 //TypeError: undefined is not a function
```

A named function expression works even if its variable is reassigned

```
var calculateFactorial = function factorial (num) {
    if (num <= 1) {
        return 1;
    } else {
        return num * factorial(num - 1);
    }
};
var calculate = calculateFactorial;
calculateFactorial = undefined;
calculate(5);                 // 120
```

Description

- *Recursion* is a form of iteration in which a function repeatedly calls itself. Each call produces smaller and smaller amounts of data until a *base case* is found and returned.

- Recursion is often used with hierarchical data, like the DOM, and extremely large arrays. You can also use recursion if you think it makes your code easier to understand.

- It's a best practice to use named function expressions with recursive functions. Then, the name of the named function doesn't change, even if the variable holding the recursive function is reassigned. This way, the recursive function will always be able to call itself.

- To name a function expression, you code the name after the word *function* and before the parameter list.

Figure 14-14   How recursion works

How to code and use a binary search recursive function

Figure 14-15 presents a recursive function that searches an array of numbers for a specific value by using a *binary search.*

To put that in perspective, a sequential search, such as a loop, starts with the first element in an array and continues in order until the value is found. So on average, the search goes through half the elements before it finds the value. If, for example, an array contains 256 elements, the search takes an average of 128 comparisons. And if the size of the array doubles, the average search time doubles.

In contrast, a binary search starts at the midpoint of a sorted array. Then, if the searched for value is higher than the value at the midpoint, the search continues at the midpoint of the upper half of the array. Or, if the value is lower, the search continues at the midpoint of the lower half of the array. The search continues by halving the number of elements until the value is found.

In this type of search, half of the array is discarded with each comparison. As a result, searching an array of 256 items takes at most 9 comparisons. And if the size of the array doubles, the search takes just one more comparison.

This figure presents a function called binarySearch that uses recursion to perform a binary search. The haystack parameter stores the array to be searched, the needle parameter stores the value to search for, the lo parameter stores the index of the lowest position that should be searched, and the hi parameter stores the index of the highest position that should be searched.

In the body of this function, the code first checks the number of arguments passed to the function. If only two arguments are passed, it initializes lo and hi to the first and last elements of the array. Next, it calculates the midpoint of the array. Then, if hi is less than lo it returns -1. This means that all the elements have been discarded and the value hasn't been found. Next, it checks to see if hi and lo are the same. If they are, there's only one element to check and it's tested to see if it's the right value. Then, either the position or -1 is returned.

Finally, the middle value is compared to the value being searched for. If they are the same, the position is returned. Otherwise, if the needle is less than the middle element, the search function is called again with a changed hi argument so the search is repeated on the lower half of the remaining part of the array. Or, if the needle is greater than the middle element, the search function is called with a changed lo argument so the search is repeated on the upper half of the array. This is where the function becomes recursive, because it's calling itself.

The last part of this figure shows the code for using the binarySearch function. To start, this code uses the getRandomNumber function from chapter 7 to create an array of 256 numbers that range from 1 through 1000. Then, this code sorts the numbers into numeric order. This sorting is required for a binary search.

Then, the code calls the binarySearch function and passes it the numbers array, which is the haystack to be searched, and the number 125, which is the needle to look for. Finally, the code logs the result of the search to the console.

A binary search recursive function

```
var binarySearch = function search (haystack, needle, lo, hi) {
    if (arguments.length === 2) {
        lo = 0;
        hi = haystack.length - 1;
    }
    var middle = Math.ceil( (hi + lo) / 2 );

    if ( hi < lo ) { return -1; }
    if ( hi === lo ) {
        if (needle === haystack[middle]) { return middle; }
        else { return -1; }
    }
    if (needle === haystack[middle]) {
        return middle;
    } else if ( needle < haystack[middle] ) {
        return search (haystack, needle, lo, middle - 1);
    } else if ( needle > haystack[middle] ) {
        return search (haystack, needle, middle + 1, hi);
    }
};
```

Code that uses the binary search function

```
// create and sort an array of 256 random numbers
var numbers = [];
for (var i = 0; i < 256; i++) {
    numbers[i] = getRandomNumber(1000);   // function from figure 7-3
}
numbers.sort(function(a, b) {
    return a - b;
});

// search the array and display the results
var index = binarySearch(numbers, 125);
if (index === -1) { console.log("Number not in array"); }
else { console.log(numbers[index] + " found at position " + index); }
```

Description

- A sequential search starts with the first element in an array and continues sequentially until the value is found. On average, a sequential search goes through half the elements before it finds the value. For extremely large arrays, this can lead to performance issues.

- A recursive *binary search* starts at the midpoint of the array, and looks for the value in either the upper or lower half of the elements. In this way, half the array is discarded with each comparison, which means that fewer searches are done. For example, searching an array of 256 items takes at most 9 comparisons.

Figure 14-15   How to code and use a binary search recursive function

The Task Manager application

This topic presents the Task Manager application that you saw implemented with functions and objects in chapters 10 and 11. Now, in this chapter, you'll see how this application can be improved by using closures and callbacks. You'll also see how you can use recursion to iterate through the hierarchical structure of the DOM.

The HTML

The Task Manager application in figure 14-16 is like the one you saw in chapter 11. It accepts and validates tasks that are entered by the user, stores the task list in local storage, and displays the tasks with a Delete Link.

What's new is that this application has a "Bold Exclamation Points" button. When the user clicks this button, the font of any task description that contains an exclamation point is changed to bold.

The Task Manager application after the Bold button is clicked

The main element of the HTML

```
<main>
    <h1>Task Manager</h1>
    <div id="tasks"></div>
    <label for="task">Task:</label><br>
    <input type="text" name="task" id="task"><br>
    <input type="button" name="add_task" id="add_task" value="Add
Task"><br>
    <input type="button" name="clear_tasks" id="clear_tasks"
        value="Clear Tasks"><br>
    <input type="button" name="bold" id="bold"
        value="Bold Exclamation Points"><br>
    <div class="clear"></div>
</main>
```

Description

- The Task Manager application for this chapter updates the Task Manager application from chapter 11. That application accepts task information from the user, stores it in local storage, and displays the tasks with a Delete link.

- This version of the Task Manager application has been rewritten to use closures and callback functions. It also has a new "Bold Exclamation Points" button, that uses recursion to find and make bold all tasks that contain an exclamation point.

- The closures make the application more stable by protecting its internal operations from being overwritten by outside code.

- The callback functions make the storage functionality more flexible.

Figure 14-16   The Task Manager application

The storage library file

The storage library file shown in figure 14-17 is a modified version of the storage library you saw in figure 11-17. In both versions of this library, there's a prototype object called localStoragePrototype whose only function is to get string values into and out of local storage.

In the chapter 11 version of the storage library, there is a second prototype object called stringArrayStoragePrototype that inherits the localStorage-Prototype object and then extends it. It does this by overriding the get method to convert a string to an array of strings, and overriding the set method to convert an array of strings to a string.

But this means that the stringArrayStoragePrototype is limited in what it can do. If, for example, you want to store and retrieve arrays of arrays, or arrays of objects, or concatenate the strings differently, you'll need to create more prototype objects.

In contrast, this new version of the storage library creates a second prototype object called storagePrototype that overrides the get and set methods by accepting callbacks. Then, inside each method, it invokes the callback function after first checking that it exists and is a function. If there's no callback function, the get method returns the string from local storage as is, and the set method stores the result of calling the toString method of whatever it receives.

As you can see, this storage library code is simpler and more generic than in previous versions. It doesn't have to know anything about what is being stored, or what form it should be transformed to. It just needs to get items into and out of storage, and call any callback functions that are sent to process them. As a result, any application that uses the library can customize it by passing callback functions to the get and set methods.

This library ends with a getStorage factory function that creates a storage object from the storage prototype. Then, it sets the key property to the key that's passed to it, and it returns the storage object.

The library_storage.js file

```
var localStoragePrototype = {
    get: function() { return localStorage.getItem(this.key); },
    set: function(str) { localStorage.setItem(this.key, str); },
    clear: function() { localStorage.setItem(this.key, ""); }
};

var storagePrototype = Object.create(localStoragePrototype);

/* get and set methods use callback functions to determine their inner
 * workings. They check to make sure a function has been passed, and
 * call it if it has. Otherwise, they just pass along whatever was in
 * storage (get) or whatever was passed in (set).
 */
storagePrototype.get = function(callback) {
    var storage = localStoragePrototype.get.call(this);
    if (callback && typeof callback === "function") {
        return callback(storage);
    } else {
        return storage;
    }
};
storagePrototype.set = function(storage, callback) {
    var storageString;
    if (callback && typeof callback === "function") {
        storageString = callback(storage);
    } else {
        storageString = storage.toString();
    }
    localStoragePrototype.set.call(this, storageString);
};

var getStorage = function(key) {
    var t = Object.create(storagePrototype);
    t.key = key;
    return t;
};
```

Description

- This library uses callback functions to create a storage library object that is more flexible. In this case, applications can pass callback functions that determine how to transform the data the library gets and sets.

- The get and set methods check to make sure that the callback functions both exist and are functions before calling them.

Figure 14-17   The storage library for the Task Manager application

The task list library file

Figure 14-18 shows the rewritten task list library that now uses closures and callback functions. If you recall, the task list library in chapter 11 was implemented as an object literal. This new version, though, starts with a function called createTaskList. This is similar to the rewritten slideshow object in figure 14-9. Like that example, the object returned by this function has access to the function's scope.

Notice that this function has two parameters named div and handler, but that it doesn't store the parameter values anywhere. That's because it doesn't have to. Since the parameter values are passed to the function, they are part of the function's scope and thus available to everything else in the function.

The createTaskList function starts by declaring a variable named tasks that holds an array, a variable named storage that holds the object returned by the getStorage factory function, and a variable named sort that holds a function for sorting the tasks array. These variables and functions have local scope, which means that they are visible to objects within the outer function but not outside it. The same is true of the div and handler parameters. That is, once those parameters have been passed to the function, they can't be changed by outside code.

After the private variables and function are two functions called getTasks and setTasks. The getTasks function accepts a string and returns an array, while the setTasks function accepts an array and returns a string. These are callback functions that specify how the items go into or out of local storage.

Next is the object that is returned by the function. It contains the public methods. The load and save methods call the get and set methods of the storage object, and pass the callback functions to them. Then, if the storage requirements ever change, the callback functions can be rewritten, but the storage library won't need to be touched.

The add, delete, clear, and display methods are the same as in chapter 11, except that they use the object's private variables and functions. Beyond that, the display method now puts the result of the Task object's toString method inside span tags. This is to help the recursive function that makes a task's font bold, as you'll see in the next figure.

All the methods in the object use the private tasks, storage, div, and handler variables and the private sort function to perform their tasks. Since these variables and tasks are private, the tasklist object is protected from outside code that could overwrite a needed variable or function and thus break the application.

The library_tasklist.js file

```
var createTaskList = function(div, handler) {
    //private variables and functions
    var tasks = [];
    var storage = getStorage("tasks_14");
    var sort = function() { tasks.sort(); };

    //private callback functions to pass to storage get and set methods
    var getTasks = function(storageString) {
        return (storageString === "")? [] : storageString.split("|");
    };
    var setTasks = function(arr) {
        return (Array.isArray(arr))? arr.join("|") : arr;
    };
    //public methods that have access to private variables and functions
    return {
        load: function() {
            if (tasks.length === 0) { tasks = storage.get(getTasks); }
            return this;
        },
        save: function() {
            storage.set(tasks, setTasks);
            return this;
        },
        add: function(task) {
            tasks.push(task);
            return this;
        },
        delete: function(i) {
            sort();
            tasks.splice(i, 1);
            return this;
        },
        clear: function() {
            tasks.length = 0;
            storage.clear();
            div.innerHTML = "";
        },
        display: function() {
            sort();
            var html = "";
            for (var i in tasks) {
                html = html.concat("<p>");
                html = html.concat("<a href='#' title='", i, "'>Delete</a>");
                html = html.concat("<span>", tasks[i].toString(), "</span>");
                html = html.concat("</p>");
            }
            div.innerHTML = html;

            var links = div.getElementsByTagName("a");
            for (var i = 0; i < links.length; i++) {
                links[i].onclick = handler;
            };
        }
    };
};
```

Figure 14-18   The task list library for the Task Manager application

The main JavaScript file

Figure 14-19 shows the main JavaScript file for the Task Manager application. It starts with the $ function, and then it declares a variable called tasklist, but it doesn't do anything with that variable yet. Next come three event handler functions named addToTaskList, deleteFromTaskList, and clearTaskList that are the same as in chapter 11. You might be wondering, though, how these functions can use the methods of the tasklist object when that variable hasn't been set to anything yet. You'll see how in a minute.

Next is a variable called boldExclamationPoint that contains a function expression named bold. This named function expression uses recursion to "walk" the DOM node in its node parameter. Yes, this could be done in other ways, but I wanted to illustrate recursion in this application, and walking the DOM is a common use of recursion.

This function starts with an if statement to see if the node has child nodes. If so, it loops the child nodes and passes each one as an argument to the bold function. In this way, it calls itself for every child node in each node it receives.

If the node doesn't have any child nodes, that is the base case that stops the recursion so the else clause is run. Within that clause, an if statement checks whether the node has a nodeValue property and whether that property contains an exclamation point. If it does, the code gets the parent node that contains the current node. This is a span tag that was added to the display method in the last figure. The code then adds an opening bold tag, the current node's value, and a closing bold tag to the span's innerHTML property. That bolds the item in the task list.

Last is the onload event handler. It starts by adding the addToTaskList function and the clearTaskList function as the handlers for the onclick events of the add_task and clear_tasks buttons. Then, it codes an event handler for the onclick event of the bold button. This handler calls the boldExclamationPoint function and passes it the DOM document object so the entire DOM is searched. However, you could start farther down the DOM tree by using the $ function to retrieve and send the tasks div to the boldExclamationPoint function.

After the event handlers are attached, the onload event handler calls the createTasklist function and stores the object it returns in the tasklist variable. It uses the $ function to get the tasks div and passes that as the first argument to the function, and it passes the deleteFromTaskList function as the second argument to the function. These values will populate the div and handler parameters you saw in the last figure.

The reason the createTasklist function is called here and not at the top of the page is because it is passing the tasks div, which is a DOM element. If the code tried to retrieve the div element at the start, it might not exist yet. Then, undefined would be passed to the function, and none of the code that uses the div parameter would work correctly. If you wait until the onload event handler, however, you can be sure the DOM elements exist. Similarly, even though the code higher in the page uses the tasklist object, those functions won't actually run until after the onload event handler runs and the tasklist object is created.

The main JavaScript file

```javascript
var $ = function(id) { return document.getElementById(id); };
var tasklist;

var addToTaskList = function() {
    var taskTextbox = $("task");
    var newTask = new Task(taskTextbox.value);
    if (newTask.isValid()) {
        tasklist.add(newTask).save().display();
        taskTextbox.value = "";
    } else { alert("Please enter a task."); }
    taskTextbox.focus();
};
var clearTaskList = function() {
    tasklist.clear();
    $("task").focus();
};
var deleteFromTaskList = function() {
    tasklist.delete(this.title).save().display(); // 'this' - clicked link
    $("task").focus();
};

var boldExclamationPoint = function bold (node) {
    //if there are child nodes, loop them and call function for each one
    if (node.childNodes && node.childNodes.length > 0) {
        for(var i in node.childNodes) {
            bold(node.childNodes[i]); //recursion - calls itself
        }
    } else { // base case: add bold tags if node has an exclamation point
        if (node.nodeValue && node.nodeValue.indexOf("!") > -1) {
            var span = node.parentNode;
            span.innerHTML = '<b>' + node.nodeValue + '</b>';
        }
    }
};

window.onload = function() {
    $("add_task").onclick = addToTaskList;
    $("clear_tasks").onclick = clearTaskList;
    $("bold").onclick = function() {
        boldExclamationPoint(document);
    };

    tasklist = createTaskList($("tasks"), deleteFromTaskList);
    tasklist.load().display();
    $("task").focus();
};
```

Description

- This application calls the createTaskList function to get the object to work with tasks, and passes it the tasks div and the deleteFromTaskList event handler function.

- The boldExclamationPoint function uses recursion to "walk" the DOM, starting with the document node, looking for nodes that have text that contains an exclamation point.

Figure 14-19   The main JavaScript file for the Task Manager application

Perspective

Now that you've completed this chapter, you should understand how closures can make your code more stable, how callbacks can make your code more flexible, and how recursion can help you do certain types of iterative tasks. You should also start to recognize when you need to use closures or set the this keyword. Much of this material, though, is conceptually difficult, so you will probably need to refer back to this chapter whenever you need to apply some of its more difficult skills.

Terms

scope chain	block scope
in scope	callback function
out of scope	higher order function
closure	asynchronous code
private state	recursion
immediately invoked function	base case
expression (IIFE)	binary search

Summary

- The *scope chain* refers to what can be seen and used by an object. An object has access to its own scope and the scope of every object that contains it, including global scope. Object visibility moves up the scope chain, not down.

- A *closure* is a function within a function that has access to the outer function's scope. As long as a reference to the inner function is alive, the outer function's variables stay *in scope*.

- Closures can be used to create *private state* that protects an object's internal functions from outside code. Closures can be used with *immediately invoked function expressions (IIFEs)* to create *block scope*. And closures can be used to solve problems that are created by using closures in loops.

- Every function has its own this keyword. An inner function can have access to an outer function's this keyword by using the bind method or storing the this keyword in a variable.

- A *callback function* is a function that's passed to another function as an argument, and then is invoked by the function that receives it. Callback functions help you create code that can be adapted to a variety of applications.

- You can use the call and bind methods of a callback function to set the value of its this keyword when it is passed to a function or when it is invoked by the function.

- A *recursive function* iterates data or a structure by repeatedly calling itself until it reaches a *base case*. Recursion is often used for iterating hierarchical structures like the DOM.

- Recursion lends itself to a *binary search*, which is a search that starts at the midpoint of an array and throws out half of the remaining array on each pass. A binary search requires fewer comparisons than a sequential search.

Exercise 14-1   Try to break the Slide Show applications

This exercise lets you compare the Slide Show applications in chapter 13 and chapter 14 by trying to break them.

Break the chapter 13 application

1. Use your text editor or IDE to open the HTML and JavaScript files for the chapter 13 version of the application in this folder:

    `c:\javascript\exercises\ch13\slide_show`

    Then, run the application to make sure it works.

2. At the end of the onload event handler in the slide_show.js file, add this line of code:

    `slideshow.nodes = null;`

3. Test this change in Chrome, and note that the slide show doesn't start when the page loads. Then, press the F12 key to bring up Chrome's developer tools, and click on Console to view the error messages. The application has been broken.

4. Delete the statement that you added in step 2.

Try to break the chapter 14 application

5. Use your text editor or IDE to open the HTML and JavaScript files for the chapter 14 version of the application in this folder:

    `c:\javascript\exercises\ch14\slide_show`

    Then, run the application to make sure it works. (Disregard the Change Speed button, which you'll deal with in exercise 14-2.)

6. At the end of the onload event handler in the slide_show.js file, add this line of code:

    `slideshow.nodes = null;`

7. Test this change in Chrome, and note that the slide show is still working correctly. This is because you can't overwrite the inner workings of the slide show object because they're in private state.

8. Delete the statement that you added in step 6.

Exercise 14-2   Add a Change Speed button to the Slide Show application

This exercise gives you a chance to work with private state and public methods by adding the code for the Change Speed button.

1. If they aren't already open, use your text editor or IDE to open the HTML and JavaScript files for the application in this folder:

    `c:\javascript\exercises\ch14\slide_show`

    Then, run the application, and note that a Change Speed button has been added to the user interface. However, this button doesn't work.

2. In the library_slide_show.js file for the application, add a method named getSpeed to the object literal that's returned by the createSlideshow function. This method should return the value of the private speed variable that's in the createSlideShow function.

3. Still in the object literal, add a method named setSpeed that accepts a parameter named newSpeed. This method should check to make sure the new speed is a number and is greater than or equal to 200 milliseconds. If it is, set the value in the private speed variable to the new number. If it isn't, don't do anything. This method should return the this keyword so it can be chained.

4. You'll need to be able to stop the slideshow before setting a new speed. So in the createSlideShow function, either make the private stopSlideShow function a public method, or call it in the startSlideShow method before calling the setInterval function.

5. In the slide_show.js file, notice that there's an event handler named changeSpeed that prompts the user for a new speed in milliseconds, and that this handler is attached to the onclick event of a button named change_speed.

6. In the changeSpeed event handler, use the new getSpeed method of the slideshow object to adjust the string in the msg variable so it shows the user the current speed of the slideshow.

7. Still in the changeSpeed event handler, chain method calls to the setSpeed and startSlideShow methods. If you've made stopSlideShow a public method, call it before calling startSlideShow. Remember to pass the milliseconds variable to setSpeed.

8. Test the application in Chrome to make sure the Change Speed button works.

Exercise 14-3   Modify a callback function in the Task Manager application

This exercise gives you a chance to work with callback functions that customize your application's code.

1. Use your text editor or IDE to open the HTML and JavaScript files for the application in this folder:

   `c:\javascript\exercises\ch14\task_manager`

   Then, run the application to see how it works.

2. In the library_tasklist.js file for the application, find the callback function named getTasks. Then, change it so it capitalizes the first word of each task.

3. Test this change to see that the tasks display the way you coded them in the last step. Next, add a new task, and notice that the change isn't applied to the new task. Then, refresh the browser, and see that the change is now applied.

4. To fix this, add a method called reload to the object literal returned by the createTaskList function. Within this method, get the tasks from storage and return the this keyword. To do this, you can copy the code from the load method, and then remove the if statement that checks the length of the tasks array.

5. In the task_list.js file, find the addToTaskList event handler. Then, chain the reload method in this handler just before the display method.

6. Test the application in Chrome to see that this fixes the problem.

15

How to work with namespaces, modules, and custom properties

In the last chapter, you learned some ways to protect your applications from outside code. Now, in this chapter, you'll learn some techniques for taking that to the next level.

How to work with namespaces

In programming, a *namespace* is a container or grouping of certain objects, usually related objects. Although many programming languages have a specific structure or keyword that allows you to create a namespace, JavaScript doesn't. But it's still easy to create your own namespaces in JavaScript.

The global namespace pollution problem

Recall from previous discussions on scope that variables, functions, or objects coded outside any other object have global scope. You can think of them as being in the *global namespace*. To illustrate, the table in figure 15-1 summarizes the many global objects that are created by the chapter 10 and chapter 11 versions of the Task Manager application.

Although global objects are convenient, they can also lead to *global namespace pollution.* This is especially true if you're working on a large project with several programmers and many third-party libraries. For example, imagine that Grace has a library file called g_library.js that contains a clearStorage function that clears local storage. Charles, meanwhile, has a library file called c_library.js that contains a clearStorage function that clears session storage.

If you include both files in your application, your application will have a *name collision*, because one object named clearStorage has two different definitions. When there's a collision, whichever file was loaded last will overwrite the previous object. So, if Grace's library file is loaded last, her version of clearStorage will overwrite Charles', but if his library is loaded last, his version of clearStorage will overwrite hers. And if you don't realize that your objects are being overwritten, your code is likely to do some unexpected things.

Another problem with adding objects to the global namespace is that it makes it harder to implement security checks. For example, if you want to run a check for global objects that shouldn't be there, you need to have a list of the global objects that are allowed. Then, every time anyone adds or removes a variable, function, or object on the list, the list needs to be updated. In contrast, if you have a policy that every variable, function, or object must be added to one of a small number of existing namespaces, the list and security checks will be manageable.

The Task Manager application

Task Manager

Task:

[   ]

[Add Task]

[Clear Tasks]

Delete Finish current project
Delete Meet with Mike
Delete Write project summary

The global objects created by previous versions of the Task Manager application

Chapter 10 functions	Chapter 11 functions and objects
$	Task
addToTaskList	$
capitalizeTask	addToTaskList
clearStorage	clearTaskList
clearTaskList	deleteFromTaskList
deleteFromTaskList	getTaskStorage
deleteTask	storagePrototype
displaySortedTaskList	tasklist
displayTaskList	
getStorage	
setStorage	
sortTaskList	
tasks	

Problems with adding functions and objects to the global namespace

- There's a possibility of *name collisions* with other libraries.
- It's harder to implement security checks that detect malware.

Description

- JavaScript variables, functions, and objects that are created outside of any other object have global scope so they're in the *global namespace*.
- When multiple libraries add variables, functions, and objects to the global namespace, it can lead to *global namespace pollution*.
- One way to reduce this pollution is to create and use your own namespaces.

Figure 15-1   The global namespace pollution problem

How to create and use namespaces

As the first example in figure 15-2 shows, it's easy to create a namespace in JavaScript. To do that, you just code an empty object literal and assign it to a variable. However, if someone else has already added that namespace, you could overwrite all their code this way.

It's safer, therefore, to use code like the second example in this figure when you create a namespace. This code will set the variable to the value of the existing namespace or, if that namespace doesn't exist, to an empty object literal.

You also need to make sure the file containing the code that creates the namespace is the first file that is loaded for a page. That way, the other files in your application will have access to the namespace.

Once a namespace is created, you can add objects to it the same way you would to any other JavaScript object. The next group of examples shows how this works. First, an object literal named events with three methods is added to the namespace. Next, a constructor function named Task is added to the namespace, followed by two methods that are added to the Task object type's prototype. Finally, a tasks variable that holds an array and an addToTaskList function are added to the namespace.

These examples are similar to code that you've already seen in this book. The main difference is that instead of using the var keyword, the variables, functions, and objects are added to the object that functions as a namespace. Thus, this code only adds one new object, myapp, to the global namespace.

The last group of examples shows that it's also easy to use the objects in a namespace. One way is to use the dot operator, as in the first statement in this group. The other way is to use brackets, as in the second statement. Most of the time, you'll probably use dot notation. But brackets can be helpful if you're creating objects dynamically, as you'll see in a moment.

If you're one of many programmers working on a project, or you're writing a third-party library that will be used by many others, you'll want to give your namespace a unique name. To that end, some companies use naming conventions that lead to names like <Department>.<Project>, while others use reverse domain names, like com.murach. Although this can lead to unwieldy names, you'll learn how to mitigate this problem in the next figure.

How to create a namespace

```
var myapp = {};
```

How to ensure you don't overwrite an existing namespace

```
var myapp = myapp || {};
```

How to add objects to a namespace

```
// an event object
myapp.events = {
    attachEvent: function() { /*code goes here*/ },
    removeEvent: function() { /*code goes here*/ },
    preventDefault: function() { /*code goes here*/ }
};

// a Task constructor function
myapp.Task - function(text) {
    this.text = text;
};
myapp.Task.prototype.isValid = function() {
    /*code goes here*/
};
myapp.Task.prototype.toString = function() {
    /*code goes here*/
};

// an array and event handler function
myapp.tasks = [];
myapp.addToTaskList = function() {
    /*code goes here*/
};
```

How to use the objects in a namespace

```
var task = new myapp.Task("go to the store");
myapp["tasks"].push(task);;
```

Description

- You create a namespace by creating an empty object and then adding objects to it. This way, you only add one object to the global namespace.

- You can use the OR operator to make sure you don't overwrite an existing namespace when you create it.

- You normally use dot notation to work with the objects that you've added to the namespace, but you can also use brackets notation.

- Some programmers use unique identifiers like reverse domain names for their namespaces. This reduces the chances of name collisions, but can make for unwieldy namespace names.

Figure 15-2   How to create and use namespaces

How to create nested namespaces and use aliases

Since a namespace is a normal object, it can be nested within other objects. In fact, nesting namespaces is a useful way to organize your code. This is illustrated by the example in figure 15-3.

Here, the main myapp namespace has sub-namespaces of products, customers, utility, and eventHandlers. This divides the code up in clearly defined sections, and helps keep the top-level namespaces at a reasonable number. Then, each sub-namespace can have its own sub-namespaces, like the utility namespace does.

A downside to nesting namespaces is that the object names can become long. For instance, the second example in this figure uses the event object and $ method of the utility namespace and the buttonClick method of the eventHandlers namespace to attach an event handler to a button. Since each object name includes all its namespaces, the code is unwieldy and hard to read.

To fix that problem, though, you can use *aliases*, as shown by the third example in this figure. Here, the utility namespace is stored in the variable u, and the eventHandlers namespace is stored in the variable eh. This shortens the line of code that attaches the event handler and makes it easier to read. Be sure, however, that you don't create aliases in the global namespace because that would defeat the purpose of having namespaces.

If you're working on a small application, you should be able to manually create the namespaces you need. But if you're working on a large application, or one with deeply nested namespaces, you can easily get confused by trying to keep the namespaces straight. For that reason, many programmers use a namespace creator function to create the namespaces.

This is illustrated by the fourth example. Here, a namespace creator function has been added to the myapp namespace. It accepts the name of a namespace or a nested namespace separated by dots. Then, it declares variables named currentName, parent, and names. The parent variable is initialized with the value of the this keyword, which is the myapp object. The names variable is initialized with an array that contains the names in the string that's passed to the function.

Next, the code loops through the namespace names. First, it stores the current name in the names array in the currentName variable. Then, it uses the currentName variable and bracket notation to create the namespace on the parent object, but it uses the OR operator to make sure it doesn't overwrite the namespace if it already exists. Last, this loop sets the parent variable to the value of the namespace it just created. This way, the next namespace will be added to the newest namespace, not the top-level namespace.

After the loop is completed, the function returns the myapp object, so it can be chained. The function ends by calling its bind method and passing it the myapp object. Although using this bind method is optional, it makes sure that the value of the this keyword is myapp no matter how the function is invoked.

The last example in this figure shows how the creator function can be used to create the namespaces in the first example. Notice that you don't need to send "utility" separately. It will be created along with the events namespace when the "utility.events" string is processed.

How to create a nested namespace

```
var myapp = {
    products: {},
    customers: {},
    utility: {
        events: {},
        storage: {}
    },
    eventHandlers: {}
};
```

How to use nested namespace objects without aliasing

```
window.onload = function() {
    myapp.utility.events.attachEvent(myapp.utility.$("button"), "click",
        myapp.eventHandlers.buttonClick);
};
```

How to use aliasing to make long namespace names easier to use

```
window.onload = function() {
    var u = myapp.utility;
    var eh = myapp.eventHandlers;
    u.events.attach(u.$("button"), "click", eh.buttonClick);
};
```

A nested namespace creator function

```
var myapp = myapp || {};
myapp.addNamespace = function(namespace) {
    var currentName;
    var parent = this;
    var names = namespace.split(".");

    for (var i in names) {
        currentName = names[i];
        parent[currentName] = parent[currentName] || {};
        parent = parent[currentName];
    }
    return this;
}.bind(myapp); // use the bind method to make sure namespaces are
               // added to the myapp namespace
```

How to use the creator function to create the namespaces above

```
myapp.addNamespace("products").addNamespace("customers")
    .addNamespace("utility.events").addNamespace("utility.storage")
    .addNamespace("eventHandlers");
```

Description

- You can use *nested namespaces* to organize your code. However, this can lead to long object names that are hard to read.

- You can create *aliases* to shorten the namespace names. However, you must make sure that you don't create the aliases in the global namespace.

- You can use a namespace creator function to create nested namespaces.

Figure 15-3   How to create nested namespaces and use aliases

How to prevent global pollution with an IIFE

When variables and functions only need to be used by the file they're in, you may not want to add them to a namespace object. But if you code them using the var keyword, they'll be in the global namespace, which you also don't want.

One way to handle this is to use an IIFE like you learned about in chapter 14. Figure 15-4 shows how this works. Here, an IIFE is created. Then, two variables are created that will act as aliases for two nested namespaces.

After that are two event handler functions. Later, you'll see the code inside these event handlers, which use the alias variables. For now, though, you should just focus on how this code is laid out. Specifically, these variables and functions are coded with the var keyword. But since they're inside the IIFE, they won't be added to the global scope.

Next is the onload event handler function. It uses the u variable, which is an alias for the utility library, to retrieve two buttons from the page. Then, it attaches the event handler functions to the onclick events of the buttons.

Last, the function is immediately invoked. As a result, the variables and functions inside the IIFE will go out of scope as soon as the IIFE completes, or as soon as the objects that refer to them, like the buttons, go out of scope. This means that nothing is added to the global scope.

How to use an IIFE to define and assign event handlers

```
(function() {
    // create aliases for nested namespaces
    var tasklist = myapp.tasklist;
    var u = myapp.utility;

    // define the event handlers
    var addToTaskList = function() {
        /* code goes here */
    }
    var clearTaskList = function() {
        /* code goes here */
    }

    // attach the event handlers in the onload event
    window.onload = function() {
        u.$("add_task").onclick = addToTaskList;
        u.$("clear_tasks").onclick - clearTaskList;
    }
})(); // invoke the IIFE
```

Description

- If variables and functions don't need to be re-used, you may not want to add them to your namespace object. But if you just code them with the var keyword, they'll pollute the global namespace.

- One way to handle this is to use an immediately invoked function expression (IIFE) so the variables and functions used by your code won't be in the global namespace.

- This works because the variables and functions that you code within an IIFE go out of scope as soon as the IIFE completes, or as soon as all objects that have references to them go out of scope.

Figure 15-4   How to prevent global pollution with an IIFE

The Task Manager application

Figure 15-1 showed the user interface for the chapter 10 Task Manager application, and it summarized the thirteen objects that the application adds to the global namespace. But now, you'll see how this application looks when it's updated by the techniques you just learned. In this version, the application adds only one object to the global namespace.

The namespace library

Figure 15-5 shows the namespace library for this version of the application. It starts by creating a namespace called myapp, which is the top-level namespace. Since it is created using the var keyword, it will be added to the global namespace. However, this is the only object that will be.

Next is the namespace creator function that you saw in figure 15-3. This function is followed by a line of code that adds namespaces named tasklist, utility, and utility.storage to the top-level myapp namespace.

For an application of this size, it may not be necessary to use a namespace creator function. But this is a convenient way to create all the namespaces you need in one spot. It's also easy to add additional namespaces as you need them, by chaining more calls to the addNamespace method.

Since this file creates all the namespaces for the application, it needs to be loaded by the first script tag in the index.html file, which isn't shown. That ensures that the namespaces are created and available to all the rest of the files in the application.

The storage library

Figure 15-5 also shows the application's updated storage library. The only change is that the get, set, and clear functions are now added to the myapp. utility.storage namespace, rather than created with the var keyword. This keeps them out of the global namespace.

The library_namespace.js file

```javascript
// create the namespace and namespace creator function
var myapp = myapp || {};

myapp.addNamespace = function(namespace) {
    var currentName;
    var parent = this;
    var names = namespace.split(".");

    for (var i in names) {
        currentName = names[i];
        parent[currentName] = parent[currentName] || {};
        parent = parent[currentName];
    }
    return this;
}.bind(myapp);

// add the namespaces the application will use
myapp.addNamespace("tasklist").addNamespace("utility.storage");
```

The library_storage.js file

```javascript
myapp.utility.storage.get = function(key) {
    var storage = localStorage.getItem(key) || "";
    if (storage === "") {
        return [];
    } else {
        return storage.split("|");
    }
};

myapp.utility.storage.set = function(key, arr) {
    if (Array.isArray(arr)) {
        var storageString = arr.join("|");
        localStorage.setItem(key, storageString);
    }
};

myapp.utility.storage.clear = function(key) {
    localStorage.setItem(key, "");
};
```

Figure 15-5   The namespace and storage libraries for the Task Manager application

The task list library

Figure 15-6 shows the application's updated task list library. Like the storage file, the main change here is that the sort, display, delete, and capitalize functions are now added to the myapp.tasklist namespace, rather than being created with the var keyword. Again, this keeps them out of the global namespace.

Notice that the display and delete functions are also changed to accommodate the new namespaces. This is because they call the tasklist's sort function. But now, that function is in a nested namespace, so the code has to use the namespace name when it calls the sort method.

You could use an alias when calling this sort method, since the name is rather long. In this case, though, there's little benefit to that, because the lines of code that contain the function calls are still pretty clear.

The library_tasklist.js file

```javascript
myapp.tasklist.sort = function(tasks) {
    var isArray = Array.isArray(tasks);
    if (isArray) {
        tasks.sort();
    }
    return isArray;
};


myapp.tasklist.display = function(tasks, div, handler) {
    var html = "";
    var isArray = myapp.tasklist.sort(tasks);

    if (isArray) {
        //create and load html string from sorted array
        for (var i in tasks) {
            html = html.concat("<p>");
            html = html.concat("<a href='#' title='", i, "'>Delete</a>");
            html = html.concat(tasks[i]);
            html = html.concat("</p>");
        }
        div.innerHTML = html;

        // get links, loop and add onclick event handler
        var links = div.getElementsByTagName("a");
        for (var i = 0; i < links.length; i++) {
            links[i].onclick = handler;
        }
    }
};


myapp.tasklist.delete = function(tasks, i) {
    var isArray = myapp.tasklist.sort(tasks);
    if (isArray) { tasks.splice(i, 1); }
};


myapp.tasklist.capitalize = function(task) {
    var first = task.substring(0,1);
    return first.toUpperCase() + task.substring(1);
};
```

Figure 15-6   The task list library for the Task Manager application

The main JavaScript file

Figure 15-7 shows the application's main JavaScript file. It starts with the $ function. This time, though, the $ function is added to the utility namespace rather than to the global namespace.

Next comes an IIFE. You can tell that's what it is because the function keyword is preceded by an opening parenthesis. The rest of the page's code is inside the IIFE because it doesn't need to be added to the myapp namespace, but it shouldn't be in the global namespace.

The code inside the IIFE is similar to the chapter 10 application's code. Like the previous version, it creates a tasks array to hold the tasks entered by the user, and a displayTaskList function that displays the tasks in the array. Then, it creates event handler functions that add a task, delete a task, and clear all tasks. And it ends with an onload event handler that attaches the add task and clear tasks functions to the onclick events of buttons named add_task and clear_tasks.

The difference is that this code, besides being in an IIFE, creates variables with aliases that store the tasklist and utility namespace objects. Then, it uses the methods of those objects inside the display and event handler functions. For example, the displayTasks function calls the get method by using u.storage to refer to the the myapp.utility.storage namespace. It also calls the display method in the myapp.tasklist namespace by using tasklist.display. The three event handlers also use the aliases to call methods in those namespaces, and also to call the $ method that was added to the utility namespace.

In the last line of code, the IIFE is invoked. Thus, all the code within the IIFE runs, and anything that doesn't have a reference to it goes out of scope. This keeps anything from being added to the global namespace.

The main JavaScript file

```javascript
myapp.utility.$ = function(id) { return document.getElementById(id); };

(function() {
    // create local variable
    var tasks = [];

    // create aliases
    var tasklist = myapp.tasklist;
    var u = myapp.utility;

    //define the display function
    var displayTasks = function() {
        if (tasks.length === 0) {
            tasks = u.storage.get("tasks_15");
        }
        tasklist.display(tasks, u.$("tasks"), deleteFromTaskList);
        u.$("task").focus();
    },

    //define the event handlers
    var addToTaskList = function() {
        var task = u.$("task");
        if (task.value === "") {
            alert("Please enter a task.");
        } else {
            tasks.push(tasklist.capitalize(task.value));
            u.storage.set("tasks_15", tasks);
            task.value = "";
            displayTasks();
        }
    };
    var deleteFromTaskList = function() {
        tasklist.delete(tasks, this.title);
        u.storage.set("tasks_15", tasks);
        displayTasks();
    };
    var clearTaskList = function() {
        tasks.length = 0;
        u.storage.clear("tasks_15");
        u.$("tasks").innerHTML = "";
        u.$("task").focus();
    };

    //onload event
    window.onload = function() {
        u.$("add_task").onclick = addToTaskList;
        u.$("clear_tasks").onclick = clearTaskList;
        displayTasks();
    };
})(); // invoke the IIFE
```

Description

- This code uses an IIFE so that local variables, aliases, and event handlers aren't added to either the global namespace or the myapp namespace.

Figure 15-7   The main JavaScript file for the Task Manager application

How to work with the module pattern

What the module pattern is

Another way to reduce global namespace pollution is to use the *module pattern*. This pattern lets you create a single instance of an object that has global scope but private state. Many third-party libraries, including jQuery, use the module pattern.

A *singleton* is a pattern in which you can have only one instance of an object. The easiest way to create a singleton in JavaScript is with an object literal. For example, the slideshow object you saw in chapter 13 is a single object that's in charge of all the operations of the Slide Show application. It's created when the file that contains it loads, and there's no way to create a second one. If you code a second slideshow object, it doesn't create a second instance of the slideshow object. Rather, it overwrites the first instance. The problem with object literals, though, is that they can't have private state.

In chapter 14, you saw the slideshow object literal replaced by a function that creates and returns a closure. This has the benefit of providing an object with private state, but now you can create multiple instances of the object by calling the function that produces it multiple times.

Sometimes having more than one instance is what you want, like with the Rollover application. But sometimes it causes problems. For example, if you had two slideshow objects that held references to different images, or had play variables that were out of sync, the Slide Show application might not work correctly.

The *module pattern* allows you to combine the pros listed in the table in figure 15-8. It uses an IIFE to create a single instance of the object returned by the closure function. This way, you get the benefits of an object literal while still having the private state of a closure.

The example in this figure shows how this works. Here, the IIFE has private state, and returns an object that refers to the private state. Since it's immediately invoked, it doesn't need to be called to create the object. Instead, the slideshow object in the myapp namespace will contain the object returned by the IIFE as soon as the file that it's in loads and the IIFE runs. Like an object literal, you can overwrite it, but you can't create a second instance of it.

The module pattern is easy to augment, too, so you can split an object up among multiple files. This is helpful when you have a large code base or when you're working among several programmers. You'll learn how to augment a module in the next figure.

Several third-party libraries use the module pattern, including jQuery. So once you understand how to create and augment modules, you'll understand how to create jQuery plugins.

The pros and cons of object literals vs closures

Type	Pros and cons
Object literal	Pros: There's only one, and it doesn't need to be created in code before it can be used.
	Cons: All properties and methods are public.
Closure	Pros: Creates private state that protects the object's inner operations.
	Cons: Must be created before it can be used, and can create more than one instance.

A module pattern that creates a single slideshow object with private state

```
myapp.slideshow = (function() {
    // private variables and functions
    var timer, play = true;
    var nodes = { image: null, caption: null };
    var img = { cache: [], counter: 0 };

    var stopSlideShow = function() { ... }
    var displayNextImage = function(){ ... }
    var setPlayText = function(btn) { ... }

    // public properties and methods
    return {
        speed: 2000,
        loadImages: function(slides) { ... },
        startSlideShow: function(){ ... },
        createToggleHandler: function(){ ... }
    }
})(); // Invoke the IIFE to create the object
```

Description

- The *module pattern* uses an immediately invoked function expression (IIFE) to create a single instance of the closure returned by the function. That way, you get the benefits of an object literal while still having the private state of a closure.

- Since a module is easy to augment, you can split an object among multiple files. This is helpful when you have a large code base or when you're working among several programmers.

- Several third-party libraries use the module pattern, including jQuery.

Figure 15-8   What the module pattern is

How to augment a module

As you learned in the last figure, you use an IIFE to create a module. As figure 15-9 shows, that's also how you *augment* a module.

The first example in this figure *imports* the the myapp.slideshow module created in the last figure and adds a method called changeSpeed to it. This code imports the module by passing it as an argument to the IIFE. Thus, the mod parameter of the IIFE contains the module that was passed to the IIFE.

To augment the module, this IIFE adds a method called changeSpeed to the mod parameter, which contains the module object. The changeSpeed method accepts a parameter named speed, creates a private variable named newSpeed, and calls the parseInt function to convert the value in the speed parameter to an integer. Then, it sets the module's speed property to either the newSpeed value or a default value, and finally it returns the this keyword so the changeSpeed method can be chained.

As in the example in the last figure, this pattern allows you to create methods with private state. Also, the new methods are added to the module as soon as the file loads and the IIFE runs. This means that files that augment an existing module should be loaded after the file that creates the module, but before any other files that might use the augmented methods.

Once a method has been added to a module, it can be used like any other method. This is illustrated by the second example in this figure. Here, the changeSpeed method is chained with the startSlideShow method.

One drawback of distributing module code across several files is that you have to make private state public if you want to be able to work with it. For example, the slideshow object in the last figure made its speed property public so it could be changed by the code in this figure.

This leads to situations where internal operations can be overwritten or changed. Later in this chapter, you'll learn a way to address this drawback.

An example that uses an IIFE to augment the slideshow object

```
(function(mod) {
    mod.changeSpeed = function(speed) {
        // private state
        var newSpeed = parseInt(speed);

        // set slideshow speed - use default speed if number not OK
        this.speed = (newSpeed < 200 || isNaN(newSpeed))? 2000 : newSpeed;

        // return 'this' so method can be chained
        return this;
    };
})(myapp.slideshow); // invoke IIFE; import the module to be augmented
```

An example that uses the slideshow object's new method

```
$("change_speed").onclick = function() {
    var ms = prompt("Enter slideshow speed in milliseconds.", "2000");
    myapp.slideshow.changeSpeed(ms).startSlideShow();
};
```

Description

- To *augment* a module object, you use an IIFE, and you *import* the module to be augmented by passing it as an argument when you invoke the IIFE.

- One drawback of distributing module code across several files is that you have to make private state public if you want to be able to work with it. Later in this chapter, you'll learn a way to address this drawback.

Figure 15-9   How to augment a module

The Slide Show application

This topic updates the Slide Show application you saw in chapter 14 by using the module pattern. With the module pattern, only one instance of the slideshow object is allowed, which makes the application more stable. But the slideshow object can still use private state to protect its internal operations.

Figure 15-10 shows the user interface of the updated Slide Show application. As you can see, this version of the application adds a button that allows a user to change the speed of the slide show. When it's clicked, a prompt showing the current interval between slides, in milliseconds, is shown, and the user is asked to enter a new interval, with a minimum value of 200 milliseconds.

The HTML

In the head section of the HTML for this application, you can see three script tags. First, the library_slide_show.js file contains the code that creates the namespace for this application as well as the module object itself, so it's loaded first. Second, the library_slide_show_enhancements.js file contains code that augments the slide show module, so it's loaded second. Third, since the main JavaScript file uses the module that's created in the first file and augmented in the second, it's loaded last.

The body of the HTML is almost identical to the HTML in chapter 14. The only difference is that this version has a second button named change_speed. This is the button that allows the user to adjust the number of seconds between slides.

The Slide Show application after the Change Speed button is clicked

The HTML

```html
<head>
    <title>Chapter 15 Slide Show</title>
    <link rel="stylesheet" type="text/css" href="slide show.css"/>
    <script src="library_slide_show.js"></script>
    <script src="library_slide_show_enhancements.js"></script>
    <script src="slide_show.js"></script>
</head>
<body>
    <main>
        <h1>Fishing Slide Show</h1>
        <p><input type="button" id="play_pause" value="Pause">
            <input type="button" id="change_speed" value="Change Speed"></p>
        <p><img src="images/gear.jpg" id="image" alt=""></p>
        <p><span id="caption">Fishing Gear</span></p>
    </main>
</body>
```

Description

- This Slide Show application adds a button that changes the slideshow's speed.
- The application uses the module pattern. This lets the application use a single slideshow object with private state. It also allows the slideshow object's code to be split among multiple files.

Figure 15-10   The Slide Show application with the module pattern

The slide show library

Figure 15-11 shows the slide show library file. This is the file that loads first and contains code for the myapp namespace and the slideshow object. It starts with a line of code that creates the namespace. This is followed by an IIFE that adds a slideshow object to the namespace.

Note here that the IIFE is assigned to the slideshow method so it doesn't have to be enclosed in parentheses. Remember, though, that this coding convention tells other programmers that this is an IIFE.

Most of the function code in the IIFE is the same as the code shown in chapter 14, so it isn't shown to save space. One exception is the startSlideShow method, which now stops any currently running slide shows before starting a new slide show. This version of the application also makes the speed property a public property, whereas before it was private. Because this property is now public, it's available to outside code. But as you'll see, this is both good and bad.

Like the closure example in chapter 14, the private state in the IIFE is available to the object that is returned by the IIFE. And like the closure example, the private state in the IIFE isn't available to outside code.

An important difference between this code and the code in chapter 14 is that the function in this code is invoked as soon as the file loads. Thus, a single instance of the slideshow object is created. What's more, it isn't possible to create a second instance of the object. Instead, loading this file again would just recreate the object, not create a new one. And coding a new value for myapp. slideshow would overwrite the object, not create a new one.

The library_slide_show.js file

```
// create the namespace used by the application
var myapp = myapp || {};

// create the slideshow module object and add it to the namespace
myapp.slideshow = (function() {
    // private variables and functions
    var timer, play = true;
    var nodes = { image: null, caption: null };
    var img = { cache: [], counter: 0 };

    var stopSlideShow = function() { clearInterval( timer ); }
    var displayNextImage = function() { ... }
    var setPlayText = function(btn) { ... }

    // public properties and methods
    return {
        speed: 2000,
        loadImages: function(slides) { ... },
        startSlideShow: function() {
            if (arguments.length === 2) {
                nodes.image = arguments[0];
                nodes.caption = arguments[1];
            }
            stopSlideShow(); // stop any currently running slideshow
            timer = setInterval(displayNextImage, this.speed);
            return this;
        },
        createToggleHandler: function(){ ... }
    }

})(); // Invoke the IIFE to create the slideshow module object
```

Description

- The slide show library creates the myapp namespace, and then it creates the slide-show object using an IIFE and the module pattern.

- As with the closure example in chapter 14, the private variables and functions in the IIFE are available to the methods of the object that it returns, but not to outside code.

- The function in this code is invoked as soon as the file loads. Thus, a single instance of the slideshow object is created.

- The speed property of the slideshow object is public and available to outside code.

Figure 15-11   The slide show library for the Slide Show application

The slide show enhancements library

Figure 15-12 shows the slide show enhancements library. This is the library that loads second, and it contains the code that augments the slideshow object created by the file that loads first.

The enhancements library consists of an IIFE. The first line of the IIFE includes a parameter named mod. This parameter receives the myapp.slideshow module when it is immediately invoked. Then, the changeSpeed method augments the slideshow module. The code in this method is the same as in figure 15-9.

The last line of the enhancements library immediately invokes the IIFE and passes the myapp.slideshow object as an argument. But notice that it doesn't need to create the myapp.slideshow object before it uses it. That's because it will be created by the IIFE in the last figure when that file is loaded.

Because the slide show module is augmented within an IIFE, the new method is available as soon as this file loads and the IIFE runs. Also, this structure allows the new method to have private state.

The main JavaScript file

Figure 15-12 shows the main JavaScript file. It contains the code for the page's onload event handler. Note that this handler creates the $ function it will use to retrieve DOM elements from the page. Of course, if other functions or objects need this function, you won't be able to code it in the onload event handler. But if you can code it there, that's another way to keep it from being in the global namespace.

Next, the code sets up and starts the slideshow, and hooks up the event handlers for the buttons. Notice that the click event handler for the Change Speed button uses the public speed property of the slideshow object to let the user know the current slideshow speed. Then, after it gets the new speed from the user, it passes it to the new changeSpeed method and chains the startSlide-Show method after that.

The library_slide_show_enhancements.js file

```javascript
// augment the slideshow object using the module pattern
(function(mod) {
    mod.changeSpeed = function(speed) {
        var newSpeed = parseInt(speed);   // private state
        this.speed = (newSpeed < 200 || isNaN(newSpeed))? 2000 : newSpeed;
        return this; // so method can be chained
    };
})(myapp.slideshow); // invoke IIFE; import module to be augmented
```

The main JavaScript file

```javascript
window.onload = function() {
    var $ = function(id) { return document.getElementById(id); };

    // create slides and start slide show
    var slides = [
        {href:"gear.jpg", title:"Fishing Gear"},
        {href:"plane.jpg", title:"Bush Plane"},
        {href:"release.jpg", title:"Catch and Release"},
        {href:"lunch.jpg", title:"Streamside Lunch"},
        {href:"dusk.jpg", title:"Day's End"}
    ];
    myapp.slideshow.loadImages(slides).startSlideShow(
        $("image"), $("caption"));

    // button event handlers
    $("play_pause").onclick = myapp.slideshow.createToggleHandler();
    $("change_speed").onclick = function() {
        var msg = "Current speed is ".concat(myapp.slideshow.speed,
            " milliseconds.\n",
            "Please enter a new speed in milliseconds (200 min).");
        var ms = prompt(msg, 2000);
        myapp.slideshow.changeSpeed(ms).startSlideShow();
    };
};
```

Description

- The slide show enhancements library adds a new method to the existing slideshow object. It does this by using an IIFE and importing the slideshow object.

- The new method changes the speed of the slide show. It can do that because the speed property is public.

- The main JavaScript file codes the $ function inside the onload event handler so it won't be in the global namespace. It then sets up and starts the slideshow, and hooks up the event handlers for the buttons.

- The click event handler for the change_speed button gets the new speed from the user, passes it to the changeSpeed method that has been added to the slideshow object, and then chains the startSlideShow method of that object.

Figure 15-12   The slide show enhancements library and main JavaScript file

How to customize properties

As you learned in the last chapter, using closures is an effective way to give an object private state, which helps protect its internal operations. But as you've also learned, if you want to work with an object's internal properties across multiple files, you need to make them public. Otherwise, a second file won't have access to the first file's private state. For example, the Slide Show application in the last topic had to make its speed property public so it could be used and augmented.

This can cause problems, though. For instance, what if outside code sets the value of the speed property to null, or deletes it? Then, the Slide Show application won't work as expected. To help with this, ECMAScript5 added the ability to protect internal operations by setting a property's attributes.

You should know, however, that these techniques are in the sham.js file of figure 1-17. That means they won't work properly in browsers that aren't ECMAScript5 compliant. So if you need to support older browsers, you may not be able to use these features.

The attributes of an object property

The table in figure 15-13 shows three attributes of a property. They all return Boolean values indicating whether or not the property meets certain criteria. *Writable* indicates whether the property can have its value set or changed. *Configurable* indicates whether the property can be deleted or have its type changed. *Enumerable* indicates whether the property will appear in code that enumerates an object's properties.

When you add a property to an object, the values of these attributes are true by default. And prior to ECMAScript5, there was no way to change them. That's why the shim.js file isn't able to make these features work for older browsers.

How to enumerate an object's properties

To enumerate an object's properties, you can use either a for-in loop or the keys method of the Object object. The first group of examples in figure 15-13 shows how this works. First, it creates an object that has three properties. (Remember that a method is a property whose value is a function definition.)

Then, it enumerates the object's properties in a for-in loop, storing the property names in an array. After that, it uses the keys method to enumerate the properties, which creates the same array of property names.

However, things are different if a property is coded on the object's prototype, rather than directly on the object. This kind of property is called an *inherited* property. In this case, the for-in loop still gets all the properties, but the keys method only gets the *direct* properties. You can see this in the second group of examples.

Three of the attributes of an object property

Attribute	Determines whether...
`writable`	the property's value can be assigned or changed.
`configurable`	the property can be deleted or its type changed.
`enumerable`	the property will appear in a for-in loop or the Object.keys method.

Two ways to enumerate an object's properties

The object to be enumerated

```
var calculate1 = {
    a: 5, b: 7,
    add: function() { return this.a + this.b; }
};
```

A for-in loop that enumerates the properties of the object

```
var names = [];
for (var propertyName in calculate1) {
    names.push(propertyName);
}                                       // names = ["a", "b", "add"]
```

An Object.keys method that enumerates the properties of the object

```
var names = Object.keys(calculate1);      // names = ["a", "b", "add"]
```

Direct vs inherited properties

- Direct properties are those that are assigned to the object directly.

- Inherited properties are those that are assigned in the object's prototype chain.

- A for-in loop returns inherited properties, but the Object.keys method doesn't.

Examples of enumerating direct and inherited properties

The object to be enumerated

```
var Calc = function(a, b) { this.a = a, this.b = b; }          // direct
Calc.prototype.add = function() { return this.a + this.b; }   // inherited
var calculate2 = new Calc (5, 7);
```

A for-in loop that enumerates the properties of the calculate2 object

```
var names = [];
for (var propertyName in calculate2) {
    names.push(propertyName);
}                                       // names = ["a", "b", "add"]
```

An Object.keys method that enumerates the properties of the calculate2 object

```
var names = Object.keys(calculate2);      // names = ["a", "b"]
```

Description

- When you assign a property or method to an object, it is *writable, configurable,* and *enumerable* by default. Prior to ECMAScript5, there was no way to change this.

- You can enumerate the properties of an object using a for-in loop or the Object.keys method. The enumerations produce different results depending on whether the properties are *direct* or *inherited*. Direct properties are also known as an object's *own* properties.

Figure 15-13   How to enumerate an object's properties

The defineProperty method of the Object object

You can use the defineProperty method of the Object object to create or modify a property and customize the property's attributes. Figure 15-14 shows the syntax of this method, and the table below it describes the three parameters that this method accepts.

The first parameter is the object on which the property will be created or modified. The second is a string that specifies the name of the property to be created or modified. And the third is a descriptor object that specifies the values of the property's attributes.

The descriptor object can be used for two types of properties, as shown in the next table in this figure. A *data property* is the location where data is read from and written to. It can be a primitive type, like a number or a string, or it can be an object, like a Date or a function definition. A property that's created by assigning it to an object or an object's prototype is a data property.

An *accessor property*, by contrast, is not the actual location of the property's value. Rather, it contains getter and setter functions that read and write the property's data. An accessor property with only a *getter function* is a *read-only property*. An accessor property with only a *setter function* is a *write-only property*.

The last table in this figure shows the attributes that can be set for the two types of properties. Here, *configurable* and *enumerable* are attributes of both data and accessor properties. *Value* and *writable* are attributes of data properties only, and *get* and *set* are attributes of accessor properties only.

Please note the default values of the attributes in the table. As you saw in the last figure, a data property that's added to an object by assignment has its writeable, configurable, and enumerable attributes set to true by default. But a data property added to an object by the defineProperty method has its writeable, configurable, and enumerable attributes set to false by default.

Similarly, an accessor property has its configurable and enumerable attributes set to false by default. This means that unless you specifically set these attributes to true, properties created with the defineProperty method are non-configurable and non-enumerable.

You should also know that if you're modifying the attributes of an existing property, you don't need to worry about accidentally overwriting attribute values. That's because only the attributes you specify in the descriptor parameter will be changed.

Last, you should know that you can create a data property or an accessor property, but you can't create a property that has the attributes of both. For instance, you can't have a property descriptor object that contains both a writable attribute and a set attribute.

The syntax of the defineProperty method of the Object object

```
Object.defineProperty(object, property, descriptor)
```

The parameters of the Object.defineProperty method

Parameter	Description
`object`	The object on which the property will be created or modified.
`property`	A string containing the name of the property to be created or modified.
`descriptor`	An object that specifies the attribute values for the property. The descriptor object sets the attributes of either a data property or an accessor property.

The two descriptor types

Type	Description
`Data property`	A property that is the location where the data is read from and written to. The data can be a primitive data type value or an object like a Date or a function.
`Accessor property`	A property that contains getter and setter functions to read and write data.

The attributes of the two descriptor types

Attribute	Type	Description
`configurable`	both	Whether the property can be deleted or have its type changed. The default value is false.
`enumerable`	both	Whether the property will be enumerated in a for-in loop or by the Object.keys method. The default value is false.
`value`	data	The value of the property. The default value is undefined.
`writable`	data	Whether the property's value can be assigned or changed. The default value is false.
`get`	accessor	The function that allows the property's value to be read. The default value is undefined.
`set`	accessor	The function that allows the property's value to be written. The default value is undefined.

Description

- You can use the defineProperty method of the Object object to create or modify a *data property* or an *accessor property* and to customize the property's attributes.

- A property added to an object by assignment is a data property, and its writeable, configurable, and enumerable attributes are true by default.

- A data property created by the defineProperty method is non-writable, non-configurable, and non-enumerable unless you specifically set those attributes to true.

- An accessor property created by the defineProperty method is non-configurable and non-enumerable unless you specifically set those attributes to true. It can be *read-only* if you only include a *getter function*, or *write-only* if you only include a *setter function*.

- When you modify an existing property, only the specified attributes will be changed.

Figure 15-14   The defineProperty method of the Object object

How to use the defineProperty method

Figure 15-15 shows how to use the defineProperty method to create data and accessor properties. Here, the first group of examples works with data properties. First, a constructor function creates an object named Calc1 that accepts two parameters named a and b. Inside this function, though, the code doesn't assign the parameter values to the properties. Instead, it calls the defineProperty method three times to create properties named a, b, and add.

The first call to the defineProperty method in this constructor passes the this keyword as the object parameter. This means the property will be a direct property created on each instance of the Calc1 object. This call also passes the string "a" as the property parameter, which will become the name of the property. And it passes an object literal as the descriptor parameter with one attribute named value that is set to the value of the a parameter that's passed to the constructor function. Thus, this first call to the defineProperty method creates a direct property named a and sets its value to the value of the a parameter.

This is similar to adding the property by assignment. What's different, though, is that a property added by assignment is writable, configurable, and enumerable by default. By contrast, the a property that's added with this defineProperty method is non-writable, non-configurable, and non-enumerable. That's because the descriptor object doesn't set those attributes to true.

The second call to the defineProperty method creates a direct property named b and sets its value. This time, however, the descriptor object contains an enumerable property that sets that attribute to true. This property is still non-writable and non-configurable, though, because those attributes aren't set to true.

The third call to the defineProperty method creates a method named add. But instead of sending the this keyword as the object, it sends Calc1.prototype. This means the method will be created on the prototype object, so it will be an inherited property. The descriptor object also contains a function definition for this property's value attribute that adds the a and b property values, and it sets the enumerable and configurable attributes to true.

After this object definition, the examples check the property attributes. This shows that the value of the a property can be retrieved, but not changed, because it's non-writable. The b property can't be deleted because it's non-configurable. The b property can be used in both a for-in loop and with the keys method, because it's a direct enumerable property. The add property only shows in the loop, because it's an inherited enumerable property. And the a property doesn't show in either because it's non-enumerable.

The next group of examples works with accessor properties. This time, a constructor function creates an object named Calc2 that accepts two parameters named a and b. Inside the function, the code stores the parameter values in private variables, and then calls the defineProperty method to create two direct properties named a and b. Then, the getter and setter functions read from and write to these private variables, and the setter functions also include logic that won't change the values unless they're passed numbers.

How to create custom data properties using the Object.defineProperty

```
var Calc1 = function(a, b) {
    Object.defineProperty(this, "a", { value: a });
    Object.defineProperty(this, "b", { value: b, enumerable: true });
    Object.defineProperty(Calc1.prototype, "add", {
        value: function() { return this.a + this.b; },
        enumerable: true, configurable: true
    });
};
var calc1 = new Calc1 (5, 7);
```

Check value, writable, and configurable attributes

```
console.log(calc1.a); // 5
calc1.a = 8;            // TypeError: Cannot assign to read only property 'a'
delete calc1.b;         // TypeError: Cannot delete property 'b'
```

Check enumerable attribute

```
var names = [];
for (var propName in calc1) { names.push(propName); }     // ["b", "add"]
var names = Object.keys(calc1);                           // ["b"]
```

How to create custom accessor properties using the Object.defineProperty

```
var Calc2 = function(a, b) {
    var aValue = a, bValue = b;   // private state
    Object.defineProperty(this, "a", {
        get: function() { return aValue; },
        set: function(val) { if (!isNaN(val)) { aValue = val; } }
    });
    Object.defineProperty(this, "b", {
        get: function() { return bValue; },
        set: function(val) { if (!isNaN(val)) { bValue = val; } }
    });
};
var calc2 = new Calc2 (5, 7);
```

Check get and set attributes

```
calc2.a = 800;
calc2.b = "b";
console.log("a = " + calc2.a + ", b = ", + calc2.b);       // a = 800, b =  7
```

Check configurable attribute

```
delete calc2.b;        // TypeError: Cannot delete property 'b'
```

Check enumerable attribute

```
var names = Object.keys(calc2);                            // []
```

Description

- The defineProperty method gives you a lot of control over the property you're defining.

- In strict mode, you'll get a TypeError if you try to write to a non-writable property or delete a non-configurable one. In non-strict mode, the attempt is ignored but there's no error.

Figure 15-15   How to use the defineProperty method of the Object object

The code that follows the creation of this object checks that the attributes work as expected. Here, the value of property a can be reset. The value of property b can't be reset with a value that isn't a number. Property b can't be deleted. And the properties of Calc2 can't be enumerated.

How to use the defineProperties and create methods of the Object object

The defineProperty method lets you create or modify one property at a time. In contrast, the defineProperties and create methods let you create several properties at once. Here again, the properties created by these methods have their configurable and enumerable attributes set to false by default. And if they're data properties, their writable attributes are also false by default.

Figure 15-16 shows the syntax of the defineProperties method and summarizes its two parameters. The first is the object on which the properties will be created or modified. The second is an object that contains one or more property descriptor objects.

The example below the table shows how this works. First, an object literal named calc1 is created with two direct properties, a and b. Because these properties are created by assignment, they are writable, configurable, and enumerable. Then, the defineProperties method is called. It is passed the calc1 object and an object literal with three property descriptor objects.

The first descriptor object modifies the a property, making it non-configurable. The second descriptor object modifies the b property, making it non-enumerable. And the third descriptor object adds a property named multiply.

Because the descriptor object's value property for the multiply property contains a function definition, the multiply property is a method. Also, because no other attributes are included in the descriptor object, the multiply property is non-writable, non-enumerable, and non-configurable.

After the call to the defineProperties method, the code attempts to delete the a and b properties of the calc1 method. Here, property b is deleted, because the value of its configurable attribute was originally true, and the call to define-Properties didn't change it. But property a isn't deleted, because its configurable attribute was changed to false.

Next, this figure presents the syntax of the create method and summarizes its parameters. The first parameter is the prototype for the object that will be created. You used this method and parameter in chapter 11. The second parameter is an object that contains one or more property descriptor objects, which you haven't used before.

The example below the table presents an object named calc2 that's created by using an IIFE and the module pattern. The IIFE starts by declaring a variable named divisor, which is the module's private state. Next, the function calls the create method with the prototype parameter and returns the object it creates. This is the same as creating an object literal. The properties parameter for the create method is a descriptor that creates a data property named a, an accessor property named b, and a data property named divide that's a method. Notice that the accessor property reads from and writes to the private divisor variable, and that it makes sure the value of b is always a number and never zero.

The syntax of the defineProperties method of the Object object

```
Object.defineProperties(object, properties)
```

The parameters of the Object.defineProperties method

Parameter	Description
object	The object on which the properties will be created or modified.
properties	An object that contains one or more descriptor objects.

How to use the Object.defineProperties method

```
var calc1 = { a: 5, b: 7 };        // writable, enumerable, and configurable
Object.defineProperties(calc1, {
    a: { configurable: false },    // modify 'a' - make it non-configurable
    b: { enumerable: false },      // modify 'b' - make it non-enumerable
    multiply: { value: function() { return this.a * this.b; } }
});
delete calc1.b          // succeeds
delete calc1.a;         // TypeError: Cannot delete property 'a'
```

The syntax of the create method of the Object object

```
Object.create(prototype, properties)
```

The parameters of the create method

Parameter	Description
prototype	The object that will be the prototype for the created object.
properties	An object that contains one or more descriptor objects.

How to use the Object.create method

```
var calc2 = (function() {  // use the module pattern to create the object
    var divisor;              // private state
    return Object.create(Object.prototype, {
        a: { writable: true },                        // data property
        b: { get: function() { return divisor; },     // accessor property
            set: function(val) {
                divisor = (isNaN(val) || val === 0)? 1 : val;
            }
        },
        divide: { value: function() { return this.a / this.b; } }
    });
})(); // Invoke IIFE
calc2.a = 5, calc2.b = 0;
var result = calc2.divide();    // result = 5
```

Description

- The defineProperties method of the Object object lets you create or modify several properties at once.

- The create method of the Object object lets you create one or more properties at the time you create an object.

- The properties parameter for both works like the descriptor parameter in figure 15-14.

Figure 15-16   How to use the defineProperties and create methods of the Object object

How to inspect property attributes

The Object object also provides several methods for checking the attributes of a property. These are sometimes useful when debugging, and they can also be used to prevent errors. If, for example, you try to delete a non-configurable property in strict mode, JavaScript will throw an error. Bu if you first check whether its configurable attribute is false, you know not to try to delete it.

The table in figure 15-17 summarizes some of these methods. The first four are static methods that are defined on the Object type directly. That means they are called directly on the Object object, not on an instance of Object. The last two are defined on the Object type's prototype. That means an instance of type Object must exist before they can be called.

For instance, the getOwnPropertyNames method accepts an object, and returns an array containing the names of all the direct, or own, properties of the object. The getOwnPropertyDescription method accepts an object and a property name string, and returns an object containing that property's attribute values. Or, if the property doesn't exist or isn't a direct property, it returns undefined.

In contrast, the hasOwnProperty method accepts a property name string and returns a Boolean value indicating whether the instance contains that direct property. And the propertyIsEnumerable method accepts a property name string and returns a Boolean value indicating whether that property is enumerable.

Below the table are examples of how these methods work. The first group of examples use the calc1 object from the last figure, which is an instance of type Calc1 and Object. It has three data properties: a and b are direct properties, and add is an inherited property. Both b and add are enumerable, but a is not. Add is also configurable, and none of the properties are writeable.

In the examples, the first two statements call the propertyIsEnumerable method. Remember that this method is on the Object type's prototype, so you have to have an instance of type Object to use it. Then, the next two statements call the keys and getOwnPropertyNames methods. Since these are static methods directly on the Object type, they're not available on an object instance. Rather, you call them directly on the Object type by coding "Object" followed by the dot operator. The two statements after that use the hasOwnProperty method to show that a is an own property but add isn't.

Next, you can see calls to the getOwnPropertyDescriptor method that get descriptions of the specified property's attributes. Since add is an inherited property, the getPrototypeOf method is used to get the prototype of the object that contains it before it passes that prototype to the getOwnPropertyDescriptor method.

The second group of examples works with the calc2 object from the last figure, which is an object of the Object type that has two accessor properties, a and b. These are direct properties, and they aren't writable, configurable, or enumerable.

As a result, the keys method returns an empty array, while the getOwnPropertyNames method returns both properties. Also, the object returned by the getOwnPropertyDescriptor method shows the get and set attributes of the accessor for the a property.

Object methods that return information about an object's properties

Method	Description
`getOwnPropertyNames(object)`	Returns an array of all properties created directly on the specified object, whether they are enumerable or not. Doesn't include properties in the prototype chain.
`getOwnPropertyDescriptor(` `object, property)`	Returns an object containing the values for the specified property's attributes if the property is created directly on the specified object.
`getPrototypeOf(object)`	Returns the prototype object of the specified object.
`keys(object)`	Returns an array of all the enumerable properties created directly on the specified object. Doesn't include properties in the prototype chain.
`prototype.hasOwnProperty(` `property)`	Returns a Boolean value indicating whether the instance of the object has the specified property created directly on it.
`prototype.propertyIsEnumerable(` `property)`	Returns a Boolean value indicating whether the specified property is enumerable.

Examples that use the objects from the last figure

Calc1 – an object with direct and inherited data properties

```
var aIsEnum = calc1.propertyIsEnumerable("a");    // false
var bIsEnum = calc1.propertyIsEnumerable("b");    // true

var names = Object.keys(calc1);                   // ["b"]
var names = Object.getOwnPropertyNames(calc1);    // ["a", "b"]

var aIsOwn = calc1.hasOwnProperty("a");           // true (a = own property)
var addIsOwn = calc1.hasOwnProperty("add");       // false (add = inherited)

var attributes = Object.getOwnPropertyDescriptor(calc1, "a");
// {value: 5, writable: false, enumerable: false, configurable: false}

var attributes = Object.getOwnPropertyDescriptor(calc1, "b");
// {value: 7, writable: false, enumerable: true, configurable: false}

// to inspect inherited properties, first get the object's prototype
var calcPrototype = Object.getPrototypeOf(calc1);
var attributes = Object.getOwnPropertyDescriptor(calcPrototype, "add");
// {value: function, writable: false, enumerable: true, configurable: true}
```

Calc2 – an object with direct accessor properties

```
var aIsEnum = calc2.propertyIsEnumerable("a");    // false
var bIsEnum = calc2.propertyIsEnumerable("b");    // false

var names = Object.keys(calc2);                   // []
var names = Object.getOwnPropertyNames(calc2);    // ["a", "b"]

var attributes = Object.getOwnPropertyDescriptor(calc2, "a");
// { enumerable: false, configurable: false, get: function, set: function }
```

Figure 15-17   How to inspect property attributes

The enhanced Slide Show application

If you recall, the Slide Show application from earlier in this chapter made the internal speed variable a public property so outside code could work with it. But this made the Slide Show application less stable, because outside code could also set the value of the speed property to null, or delete it altogether.

In the figures that follow, you'll see how to use the techniques you just learned to expose the value in the speed variable to outside code while still protecting the variable itself.

The slide show library

Figure 15-18 presents an updated version of the slide show library that you saw in figure 15-11. It still creates a namespace and it still uses an IIFE and the module pattern to create a single instance of the slideshow object. Besides that, the code in the methods is the same, which is why it isn't shown here.

In this library, though, the speed variable is private again. This means there's no way for it to be overwritten or deleted. Also, instead of returning an object literal that contains the slideshow's methods, this code loads the object in a private variable named prototype. Then, it creates another object that contains a single property descriptor object and stores it in a private variable named properties.

This descriptor object describes a property named slideShowSpeed, which is an accessor property. Its get attribute is a function that returns the value of the private speed variable. Its set attribute is a function that sets the value of the private speed variable. This function calls the parseInt function on the newSpeed parameter it accepts. Then, it only sets the value of the internal speed variable to the parameter value if it's a number and at least 200 milliseconds. Otherwise, it uses the default value of 2000 milliseconds. This allows outside code to access the internal speed variable, but protects it from being deleted or accepting a value that breaks the applications.

The descriptor object also sets the enumerable attribute of the slideShow-Speed property to true, which means that this property will show in both for-in loops and in arrays created by the keys method. However, it also sets the configurable attribute to false, which means this property can't be overwritten or deleted. Because this is an accessor function, the value and writable attributes aren't set because trying to set either one would throw an exception.

Finally, the IIFE calls the create method of the Object object with the prototype variable and the properties variable as the parameters. Then, it returns the object returned by the create method. In the last line of code, the IIFE is invoked and the slideshow object is created.

The library_slide_show.js file

```javascript
var myapp = myapp || {};

myapp.slideshow = (function() {
    // private variables and functions
    var timer, play = true, speed = 2000;   // speed is private
    var nodes = { image: null, caption: null };
    var img = { cache: [], counter: 0 };

    var stopSlideShow = function() { ... }
    var displayNextImage = function() { ... }
    var setPlayText = function(btn) { ... }

    // prototype object for public methods
    var prototype = {
        loadImages: function(slides) { ... },
        startSlideShow: function() { ... },
        createToggleHandler: function(){ ... }
    };

    // property descriptor object(s)
    var properties = {
        slideShowSpeed: { // accessor property
            get: function() { return speed; },
            set: function(newSpeed) {
                var ns = parseInt(newSpeed);
                speed = (ns < 200 || isNaN(ns))? 2000 : ns;
            },
            enumerable: true,
            configurable: false
        }
    };
    // create and return the slideshow module object
    return Object.create(prototype, properties);

})(); // Invoke the IIFE
```

Description

- In this version of the Slide Show application, the speed variable is once again private.

- This version uses the module pattern and the Object.create method to create a single slideshow object. The slideshow object has a slideShowSpeed accessor property that allows the slide show speed to be changed.

- The getter function of the accessor property simply returns the value of the speed variable. The setter function uses a default value to update the speed variable if the value it receives doesn't meet certain conditions.

- Because the speed variable is accessible only through the slideShowSpeed accessor property, it can't be directly changed by outside code. This protects the internal functioning of the object while still allowing some access to the speed variable.

Figure 15-18   The slide show library for the Slide Show application

The slide show enhancements library

Figure 15-19 shows the updated slide show enhancements library. In previous versions, the changeSpeed method did some data validation to make sure the new speed was a number and at least 200 milliseconds. But now, this data validation is done in the setter method of the slideShowSpeed property.

In fact, there's not much use for the changeSpeed method any more, unless you want to do more data validation. As a result, you could dispense with this method altogether and just use the slideShowSpeed property when you want to change the speed value.

However, this method does return the this keyword, which makes it chainable. And since chaining methods makes your code more readable, you might want to keep this method, even though it is no longer necessary.

The main JavaScript file

This figure also shows the main JavaScript file for the enhanced Slide Show application. The only difference between this file and the previous version is that this one uses the new slideShowSpeed property to get the current speed of the slide show.

This is an important difference, though. Although both of the files in this figure have access to the internal speed variable via the slideShowSpeed property, neither of them can change that variable in a way that hurts the application.

The library_slide_show_enhancements.js file

```
(function(mod) {
    mod.changeSpeed = function(newSpeed) {
        this.slideShowSpeed = newSpeed;
        return this;
    };
})(myapp.slideshow); // invoke IIFE; import module to be augmented
```

The main JavaScript file

```
window.onload = function() {
    var $ = function(id) { return document.getElementById(id); };

    var slides = [
        {href:"gear.jpg", title:"Fishing Gear"},
        {href:"plane.jpg", title:"Bush Plane"},
        {href:"release.jpg", title:"Catch and Release"},
        {href:"lunch.jpg", title:"Streamside Lunch"},
        {href:"dusk.jpg", title:"Day's End"}
    ];
    myapp.slideshow.loadImages(slides).startSlideShow(
        $("image"), $("caption"));

    $("play_pause").onclick = myapp.slideshow.createToggleHandler();
    $("change_speed").onclick = function() {
        var msg = "Current speed is ".concat(myapp.slideshow.slideShowSpeed,
            " milliseconds.\n",
            "Please enter a new speed in milliseconds (200 min).");
        var ms = prompt(msg, 2000);
        myapp.slideshow.changeSpeed(ms).startSlideShow();
    };
};
```

Description

- In this version of the Slide Show application, the new changeSpeed method just passes the new speed to the slideshow object's slideShowSpeed accessor property.

- As before, the main JavaScript file sets up and starts the slide show, and hooks up the event handlers for the buttons.

Figure 15-19   The slide show enhancements library and main JavaScript file

Perspective

Now that you've completed this chapter, you should be able to use namespaces, modules, and custom variables to add a professional level of protection to your applications. This means that they can be used by other programs and with third-party libraries with little chance of name collisions or other problems that will break your applications.

Terms

namespace	writable
global namespace pollution	direct property
name collision	own property
nested namespaces	inherited property
alias	data property
module pattern	accessor property
singleton	getter function
augment a module	setter function
import a module	read-only property
configurable	write-only property
enumerable	

Summary

- A *namespace* is a grouping of certain, usually related, objects. You can use namespaces to organize your code and prevent *global namespace pollution*.

- In JavaScript, you create a namespace by creating an empty object literal and then adding other objects to it. You can also create *nested namespaces*, and you can use *aliases* to shorten long names and keep your code readable.

- If you don't want to add an object to a namespace, you can work with it inside an immediately invoked function expression (IIFE) to keep it out of the global namespace.

- The *module pattern* lets you create a single instance of an object, or *singleton*, that has private state. It combines the benefits of object literals and closures. To create or *augment* a module object, you use an IIFE.

- Properties that are added to an object by assignment are *configurable*, *enumerable*, and *writable* by default. Properties added with the defineProperty, defineProperties, or create methods are non-configurable, non-enumerable, and non-writable by default.

- Properties added directly to an object are *direct properties*, or that object's *own properties*. Properties added to an object's prototype are *inherited properties*.

- A for-in loop or the keys method can be used to retrieve enumerable properties. Both direct and inherited properties show in a for-in loop, but only direct properties are available when you use the keys method.

- A *data property* is the location where data is read from and written to. It has these attributes: configurable, enumerable, writable, value.

- An *accessor property* uses functions to read and write the property value. A *getter function* reads the value, and a *setter function* writes the value.

- An accessor property with only a getter function is a *read-only property*. An accessor property with only a setter function is a *write-only property*. An accessor property has these attributes: configurable, enumerable, get, set.

- A property can have data attributes or accessor attributes, but it can't mix them.

- The defineProperty and defineProperties methods let you create properties with custom attributes or customize the attributes of existing properties. When modifying an existing property, only the specified attributes will be changed.

- The create method lets you create properties with custom attributes when you create an object.

- The Object object has several methods that let you inspect property attributes. Some are called directly on the Object object, and some are called on an instance of the Object type.

Exercise 15-1   Try to break the Slide Show applications

This exercise has you test the two versions of the Slide Show applications that are presented in this chapter to see whether you can break them.

Try to break the module version of the application

1. Use your text editor or IDE to open the HTML and JavaScript files for the application in this folder:

    ```
    c:\javascript\exercises\ch15\slide_show_module
    ```

    Then, run the application to see how it works.

2. In the slide_show.js file, find the onload event handler function. After the slides array and before the code that loads and displays the slides, add this line of code:

    ```
    myapp.slideshow.speed = null;
    ```

3. Test this change in Chrome, and notice the effect this change has on the application. Then, click on the Change Speed button, enter a valid speed, click OK, and notice that the application runs smoothly again.

4. Delete the statement that you added in step 2.

Try to break the version with the custom speed property

5. Use your text editor or IDE to open the HTML and JavaScript files for the application in this folder:

    ```
    c:\javascript\exercises\ch15\slide_show_properties
    ```

    Then, run the application to see how it works.

6. In the slide_show.js file, find the onload event handler function. After the slides array and before the code that loads and displays the slides, add this line of code:

    ```
    myapp.slideshow.speed = null;
    ```

7. Test this change in Chrome, and notice that it has no effect on the slide show. That's because all you've done is add a new, unused property named speed.

8. In the onload event handler function, after the code you added in step 6, add this line of code:

    ```
    myapp.slideshow.slideShowSpeed = null;
    ```

9. Test your changes in Chrome, and notice that this also has no effect on the slide show. That's because the slideShowSpeed property uses a default value if the value it receives is NaN or below 200.

10. Delete the code you added in steps 6 and 8.

Exercise 15-2   Add namespaces to a Task Manager application

This exercise has you add namespaces to the chapter 11 version of the Task Manager application.

Add namespaces to the application

1. Use your text editor or IDE to open the HTML and JavaScript files for the application in this folder:

    `c:\javascript\exercises\ch15\task_manager`

    Then, run the application to see how it works.

2. In the library_namespace.js file, note that the code creates a namespace and a namespace creator function.

3. Uncomment the line of code that calls the addNamespace method, and modify the code so it adds these namespaces to the myapp namespace: prototype, storage, tasklist, and Task. To do this, you'll need to chain more method calls.

Modify the other JavaScript files to use the namespaces

4. Modify the objects in the JavaScript files so they're added to a namespace instead of being created with the var keyword. In the library_storage.js file, for example, change localStoragePrototype so it's added to the prototype namespace rather than being created with the var keyword.

5. If necessary, use Chrome's developer tools to help you find all the code you need to change. To do that, run the application in Chrome, press F12 to open the developer tools, and go to the Console panel to see where the errors are.

6. Continue until all the code is in a namespace and the application runs with no errors.

Modify the main JavaScript file to use an IIFE instead of namespaces

7. In the task_list.js file, code an IIFE. Then, move the $ and event handler functions inside the IIFE. When you move them, remove the namespaces that you added earlier.

8. If necessary, use Chrome's developer tools to help you find all the code you need to change. To do that, run the application in Chrome, press F12 to open the developer tools, and go to the Console panel to see where the errors are.

9. Continue until all the code in the main JavaScript file is in the IIFE, and the application runs with no errors.

Exercise 15-3   Modify a Slide Show application

The Slide Show application that you'll work with in this exercise is a slightly modified version of the one for exercise 15-1. This will give you more practice with the use of custom properties and the module pattern.

Review and run this version of the application

1. Use your text editor or IDE to open the HTML and JavaScript files for the application in this folder:

    `c:\javascript\exercises\ch15\slide_show`

2. Review the JavaScript files for this application, and note that (1) the speed variable in the slide show library is private, (2) the changeSpeed method is in the slide show library, (3) the slide show library's displayNextImage function stores the array index of the current image in the span tag's title attribute, and (4) the slide show enhancements library is empty.

3. Run this application in Chrome, and note that there's a "Change Caption" button that prompts you for a caption but doesn't actually change anything. Note also that the prompt for the "Change Speed" button displays undefined as the current slide show speed.

Modify this application

4. In the library_slide_show.js file, after the slideshow object has been created, add two read-only accessor properties to the slideshow object. To do that, you can use the defineProperties method or the defineProperty method twice. The first property should be named "getSpeed" and return the private speed variable. The second should be named "getImages" and return the private img.cache array. (Remember, an accessor property with only a getter function is read-only.)

5. Test this change in Chrome by clicking on the "Change Speed" button. If you've done this right, the correct current speed should show in the prompt.

6. In the library_slide_show_enhancements.js file, add an IIFE that accepts a parameter, and populate this parameter by passing the myapp.slideshow object in the set of parentheses that invokes the IIFE.

7. Inside the IIFE, add a method called changeCaption to the slideshow object. This method should accept two parameters, one for the array index of the current slide, and one for the new caption text. This method should also (1) use the getImages property to retrieve the current slide object from the array using brackets and the index parameter, (2) change the slide object's title property to the new caption, and (3) return the slideshow object.

8. In the slide_show.js file, uncomment the line of code in the event handler for the Change Caption button. If you want the new caption to show immediately, add code that sets the caption tag's firstChild node value. Otherwise, you'll see the change when the slide cycles around again.

16

How to work with JavaScript Object Notation (JSON)

When you work with JavaScript, you'll often want to transfer or store data. In fact, you've already seen this in the Task Manager application, which stores data in local storage.

Now, in this chapter, you'll learn how to use JavaScript Object Notation, or JSON, as a data format for transferring and storing data. As you will see, JavaScript has special features for working with JSON.

An introduction to JSON

JavaScript Object Notation, or *JSON* (pronounced "jason"), is one of several data formats for transferring and storing data. But before you learn about how to use it, you should understand what it is and why it's needed.

What data serialization and deserialization are

When a user adds an order to a shopping cart or checks a "Remember Me" checkbox, the application needs to store the data. This data can be stored on the server in a database, in the web storage of the browser, or in some other data store. But before it can be stored, it must be converted to a *data format* that the data store can use. When you do this conversion, you *serialize* the data.

After the application stores this data, it must also be able to retrieve the data and work with it. This means the data must be converted from its data format back to its original structure. When you do this conversion, you *deserialize* the data.

How data formats work

Most data formats for storing serialized data are either *binary* or *textual*. A binary format uses ones and zeros to represent the data in a structure. A textual format uses text to represent the data in a structure. Besides storing the data in a structure, these formats store information about the structure itself. Then, this information is used to rebuild the structure when the data is deserialized.

Some of the most common data formats are presented in the table in figure 16-1, along with examples of each format. All four of these examples serialize the same data structure, which is an object with two properties. The first property is named first and has a value of "Grace", while the second property is named last and has a value of "Hopper".

As you can see, the three textual formats store not just the values of the properties ("Grace" and "Hopper"), but the names of the properties (first and last). This is so the objects can be correctly rebuilt when they're deserialized. Although the binary format stores this information too, you can't see it because everything is represented by ones and zeros.

It's also important to note that only an object's data is serialized. For example, if the object in this figure had a method named getFullName, the method wouldn't be stored when the object was serialized.

What happens when a data structure is serialized and deserialized

- When a data structure is *serialized*, it's converted to a *binary* or *textual data format*. This is also called *marshalling*.

- When the data in a binary or textual data format is *deserialized*, it is restored to its original data structure. This is also called *unmarshalling*.

When to serialize a data structure

- To store it, either permanently (database) or temporarily (session storage).

- To transmit it across a network connection.

Four common data formats

Format	Type	Description
Binary	Binary	A series of 0's and 1's.
CSV (Comma Separated Values)	Text	Usually used with tabular data.
XML (eXtensible Markup Language)	Text	Similar to HTML.
JSON (JavaScript Object Notation)	Text	A subset of the JavaScript object literal syntax.

Examples of the data formats

Object to be serialized
```
{ first: "Grace", last: "Hopper" }
```

Binary
```
011110110010000001100110011010010101110010011100110111010000011101000100000001
000111011100100110000101100011011100101001011000010000001101100011000010111
0011011101000011101000100000010010000110111101110000011100000110010101110010
00010000001111101
```

CSV
```
first,last
"Grace","Hopper"
```

XML
```
<person>
  <first>Grace</first>
  <last>Hopper</last>
</person>
```

JSON
```
{"first":"Grace","last":"Hopper"}
```

Description

- An object is *serialized* when it's converted to a format that can be stored or transmitted, and it's *deserialized* when it's converted back.

- Only an object's data is serialized, not its methods.

Figure 16-1   How data formats work

What JavaScript Object Notation (JSON) is

Of the four data formats presented in the last figure, JavaScript Object Notation (JSON) is the one that's preferred for JavaScript. Some of the reasons for this are listed in figure 16-2.

One of the main reasons is that it's easy to work with JSON in JavaScript because JSON is a subset of JavaScript. However, JSON isn't a programming language. Rather, it's a data format that uses some of the features of the JavaScript programming language to store data.

Because JSON is only a subset of JavaScript, not all of the JavaScript rules apply. That's why this figure presents some of the JSON rules you should know. For instance, you can't use some data types, you can't use single quotes for strings, and you must put key names in double quotes.

To illustrate the JSON rules, the example in this figure presents a variable named employee that contains some JSON. First, the JSON uses the object literal syntax that you're already familiar with. Second, all the key names are enclosed in double quotes. Third, values that aren't strings don't need to be enclosed in double quotes. Fourth, the arrays use the brackets of an array literal. Fifth, the objects use the braces of an object literal, but their property names are in double quotes.

Because JSON uses the object literal syntax, you can use the dot operator or brackets to work with it. To show how this works, the last three statements in this figure log information from the employee object to the console. The first statement uses the dot operator to get the id value, while the second statement uses bracket notation to get the name value from the region object. Then, the third statement uses dot operators to get the length of the monthlySales array.

Some of the benefits of JavaScript Object Notation (JSON)

- It can be read and understood by humans as well as computers.
- It's more flexible than CSV.
- It's less verbose than XML.
- It's easier to work with in JavaScript than binary, CSV, or XML.

Some of the JSON rules

- There are six allowed data types – strings, numbers, Booleans, arrays, objects, and null.
- The undefined data type, function definitions, and object instances aren't supported.
- All data types are represented as key/value pairs, with the key name in double quotes.
- Arrays are represented by brackets and objects are represented by braces.
- Single quotes aren't supported.

An object represented in JSON

```
var employee = {
    "id":1001,                              // number
    "startdate":"7/18/2011",                // string
    "enddate":null,                         // null
    "isActive":true,                        // boolean
    "reviewScores":[88,95,92,85],           // array
    "region":{                              // object
        "name":"Northwest",
        "joined":"5/1/2012"
    },
    "monthlySales":[                        // array of objects
        {"productid":"CS101","quantity":2},
        {"productid":"NG203","quantity":5,"returns":1}
    ]
};

console.log(employee.id);                   // 1001
console.log(employee["region"]["name"]);    // Northwest
console.log(employee.monthlySales.length);  // 2
```

Description

- JavaScript Object Notation (JSON) is more flexible than CSV and lighter weight than XML. In recent years, JSON has become the preferred data format for JavaScript, and most web services provide data in both XML and JSON formats.
- JSON uses the object literal syntax, so it allows familiar syntax like dot notation.

Figure 16-2   An introduction to JavaScript Object Notation

How to work with JSON in JavaScript

As you just learned, JSON is a subset of JavaScript, so you can work with a JavaScript object that follows the JSON rules just as you would work with any other JavaScript object. However, an object like that still isn't in a format that can be transmitted or stored. Rather, you need to serialize it by converting it to a *JSON string*. Also, if you start with a JSON string, you need to deserialize it by converting it back to a JavaScript object.

An introduction to the global JSON object

Prior to ECMAScript5, JavaScript didn't have native support for converting JavaScript objects to and from JSON strings. Instead, JavaScript programmers had to use a JSON shim like the one that's available at the URL in figure 16-3. Now, though, all the modern browsers have a *global JSON object* that makes it easier to work with JSON.

This global JSON object has two methods named stringify and parse. The *stringify method* lets you serialize a JavaScript object by converting it to a JSON string, while the *parse method* lets you deserialize a JSON string by converting it to a JavaScript object.

JSON support in JavaScript

- ECMAScript5 provides a *global JSON object* that provides methods for converting objects to and from *JSON strings*.
- Older browsers that aren't ECMAScript5 compliant can use the JSON shim for this purpose.

The URL for the JSON shim

`http://bestiejs.github.io/json3/`

The methods of the JSON object

Method	Description
stringify	Serializes a JavaScript object by converting it to a JSON string.
parse	Deserializes a JSON string by converting it to a JavaScript object.

Description

- All modern browsers have a global JSON object that provides *stringify* and *parse methods* for working with native JSON objects and JSON strings.

Figure 16-3   An introduction to the global JSON object

How to use the stringify method of the JSON object

Figure 16-4 shows the syntax of the stringify method and the three parameters it accepts. The first parameter is the object to be serialized, and the next two are optional parameters that let you customize how the object is serialized and how the JSON string looks. You'll learn about these optional parameters later in this chapter.

The stringify method converts the JavaScript object that's passed to it to a JSON string. As part of this serialization, this method adds double quotes to key names, converts single quotes to double quotes, and converts Date objects to strings that represent the date in universal time.

Beyond that, if the stringify method finds an unsupported type in an object property, it drops the property. Similarly, if the stringify method finds an unsupported object in an array, it converts that element to null.

To illustrate how the stringify method converts objects to JSON strings, this figure presents several examples. In the first example, a string is serialized, and the stringify method converts single quotes to double quotes. In the second example, an object is serialized, and the stringify method includes the key name enclosed in double quotes.

In the third example, an array of strings is serialized, and the stringify method uses brackets to indicate that the strings are in an array. In the fourth example, an array of objects is serialized. In this example, the stringify method converts single quotes to double quotes, converts Date objects to date strings, and uses brackets to indicate the arrays and braces to indicate the objects.

This example also illustrates how the stringify method handles unsupported data types. For example, the first element added to the array is an object literal with a property named t that contains a string, a property named d that contains a Date object, and a method named test. Since functions aren't supported in JSON, the object in the JSON string for this element has properties named t and d, but no property named test.

The second element added to the array is also an object literal with a property named t that contains a string and a property named d that contains an undefined value. Since undefined isn't supported in JSON, the object in the JSON string for this element has a property named t but no property named d.

The third element added to the array is an undefined value, and the fourth is a function definition. As before, these values aren't supported in JSON. This time, though, the unsupported values are array elements, not object properties. So, instead of being dropped, the final two array elements are represented by null.

The syntax of the stringify method of the JSON object

```
JSON.stringify(object, replacer, space)
```

The parameters of the stringify method

Parameter	Description
`object`	The JavaScript object to be serialized to JSON.
`replacer`	An optional function or array that controls how the object is serialized.
`space`	An optional number or string that inserts whitespace.

How to use the stringify method

To serialize a string

```
var task = 'Go to the store';
var json = JSON.stringify(task);
// "Go to the store"
```

To serialize an object

```
var task = { task: 'Go to the store' };
var json = JSON.stringify(task);
// {"task":"Go to the store"}
```

To serialize an array of strings

```
var tasks = [];
tasks.push("Go to the store");
tasks.push("Do laundry");
var json = JSON.stringify(tasks);
// ["Go to the store","Do laundry"]
```

To serialize an array of objects

```
var tasks = [];
var dt = new Date('4/15/2016');
tasks.push( {t:'Taxes', d:dt, test:function(){alert('hello');}} );
tasks.push( {t:'Laundry', d:undefined} );
tasks.push( undefined );
tasks.push( function(){alert('hello');} );
var json = JSON.stringify(tasks);
// [{"t":"Taxes","d":"2016-04-15T07:00:00.000Z"},{"t":"Laundry"},null,null]
```

Description

- The stringify method of the JSON object converts the JavaScript object that's passed to it to a JSON string.

- By default, this method adds double quotes to the key names, converts single quotes to double quotes, and converts Date objects to strings that represent the dates in universal time.

- Also by default, if this method finds unsupported items like function definitions or undefined values in an object, it drops them. If they're in an array, this method converts them to nulls.

- If necessary, you can use the optional replacer and space parameters to customize how the object is serialized (see figures 16-10 and 16-11).

Figure 16-4   How to use the stringify method of the JSON object

How to use the parse method of the JSON object

Figure 16-5 shows the syntax of the parse method and the two parameters it accepts. The first parameter is the string to be deserialized, and the second is an optional parameter that lets you customize how the string is deserialized. You'll learn about the optional parameter later in this chapter.

The parse method uses the information in the JSON string to deserialize the data structure that was serialized. For example, it creates an object from braces and an array from brackets. Similarly, it creates an object property from a key/value pair inside braces.

To illustrate how the parse method converts JSON strings to objects, this figure presents several examples. Note here that the JSON strings use the escape sequence for double quotes (\").

In the first two examples, a number and an object are deserialized. Here, the parse method in the second example recognizes the object by the braces in the JSON string. Also, note that the task key it creates isn't enclosed in double quotes, even though the task key in the JSON string is.

In the third example, the parse method deserializes an array of strings, which it recognizes by the brackets in the JSON string. In the fourth example, the parse method deserializes an array of objects, which it recognizes by the braces in the JSON string. By the way, the JSON string in this example is on two lines, but that's only because of space considerations for the book. In a real application, the string would probably be on one line.

The next group of examples shows how the parse method handles date strings. Note here that this method doesn't convert date strings back to Date objects. To illustrate, the first statement in this group just shows that the first element in an array named tasks is set to an object whose d property contains a date string. This was done by the parse method in the last example in the first group in this figure.

Then, when the second statement tries to call the toDateString method of the d property, it throws an error because the value of d isn't a Date object. To fix this, the last two statements in this group show that you need to manually convert date strings to Date objects after you deserialize data with the parse method.

One more thing to be aware of is that the parse method will throw exceptions in certain situations. One of these is when the JSON string isn't valid JSON. Another is when the JSON string has an array or object with trailing commas.

The syntax of the parse method of the JSON object

```
JSON.parse(text, reviver)
```

The parameters of the parse method

Parameter	Description
text	The JSON string to be deserialized.
reviver	An optional function that controls how the JSON string is deserialized.

How to use the parse method

To deserialize a number

```
var json = "18";
var num = JSON.parse(json);
// 18
```

To deserialize an object

```
var json = "{\"task\":\"Go to the store\"}";
var task = JSON.parse(json);
// {task: "Go to the store"}
```

To deserialize an array of strings

```
var json = "[\"Go to the store\",\"Do laundry\"]";
var tasks = JSON.parse(json);
// ["Go to the store", "Do laundry"]
```

To deserialize an array of objects

```
var json = "[{\"t\":\"Taxes\",\"d\":\"2016-04-15T07:00:00.000Z\"}";
json = json + ",{\"t\":\"Laundry\"},null,null]";
var tasks = JSON.parse(json);
// [Object, Object, null, null]
```

How the parse method handles date strings

The parse method doesn't convert a date string back to a Date object

```
tasks[0];                      // {t: "Taxes", d: "2016-04-15T07:00:00.000Z"}
tasks[0].d.toDateString();     // TypeError
```

You must manually convert the date string

```
var d = new Date(tasks[0].d);
d.toDateString();              // Fri Apr 15 2016
```

When the parse method throws a SyntaxError exception

- If the string to parse isn't valid JSON, such as property names in single quotes.

- If the string to parse has an array or object with trailing commas, such as "[1,2,3,]".

Description

- The parse method of the JSON object converts a JSON string to a JavaScript object. However, it doesn't convert date strings to Date objects, and it throws syntax exceptions.

- This method has an optional reviver parameter that lets you customize how the JSON string is deserialized (see figure 16-13).

Figure 16-5   How to use the parse method of the JSON object

The Task Manager application

The topic updates the Task Manager application of chapter 9 so it saves the tasks in web storage in the JSON data format. As a result, this application needs to serialize the data before it's stored and deserialize the data when it's retrieved.

Figure 16-6 shows the user interface for this updated version of the Task Manager application. Like the version in chapter 9, it has a text box for task entries, and it displays all the tasks in a textarea control. This version, though, also has a text box that lets the user enter a due date for each task, and it includes the due date when it displays the tasks.

The HTML

In the main element of the HTML for this application, you can see the label and input elements for the text box that gets the date. All of the other HTML is the same as in the chapter 9 version of this application.

The JSON string in local storage

This figure also shows the JSON string for the two tasks in the text area. This is the string that is stored in local storage.

This JSON string represents an array that contains two elements, and each element is an object with properties named task and date. If you look at the value in the date properties, you'll see that it looks different than the date string in universal time that you saw in the last couple of figures. That's because the application stores the result of the Date object's toDateString method, rather than the Date object itself. You'll see how this works next.

The Task Manager application

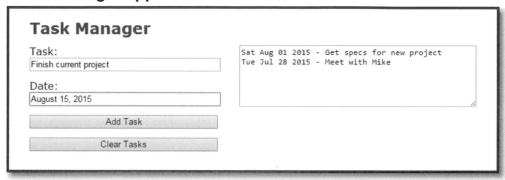

The HTML

```
<main>
    <h1>Task List Manager</h1>
    <p id="tasks"><textarea id="task_list" rows="6" cols="50"></textarea>
    </p>

    <label for="task">Task:</label><br>
    <input type="text" name="task" id="task"><br>
    <label for="task_date">Date:</label><br>
    <input type="text" name="task_date" id="task_date"><br>

    <input type="button" name="add_task" id="add_task" value="Add Task"><br>
    <input type="button" name="clear" id="clear " value="Clear Tasks">
</main>
```

The JSON string stored in local storage

```
[{"task":"get specs for next project","date":"Sat Aug 01 2015"},
{"task":"meet with Mike","date":"Tue Jul 28 2015"}]
```

Description

- This application is an updated version of the Task Manager application from chapter 9. Like the previous version, this application gets task information from the user, stores it in local storage, and displays the tasks in a textarea control.

- This version of the Task Manager application also adds a date to each task, and uses the JSON object to serialize and deserialize the task data.

- The date in the JSON string is the result of calling a Date object's toDateString method. Thus, the date is serialized as a string with the date only, rather than a string with the date in universal time.

Figure 16-6   The Task Manager application

The main JavaScript file

Figure 16-7 shows the main JavaScript file for the Task Manager application. Like the chapter 9 application, this file starts with the $ function and then creates a tasks array that will hold the tasks entered by the user. After that, it has a displayTaskList function, an addToTaskList function, a clearTaskList function, and an onload event handler.

What's different about this version of the application is how it handles the values it gets from and sends to local storage. Before, it only had to serialize and deserialize strings. It did this by using the join method of the array to serialize the array elements to a string, and the split method of the string to deserialize the string back to an array. Now, though, this application uses the JSON object to serialize and deserialize a JSON string.

Since the JSON string in local storage contains an array of objects with properties named task and date, the tasks variable now contains this array of objects. Then, the remaining code in the displayTaskList function works with these objects to capitalize the first letter of each task description and create a display string that shows the due date and the capitalized task.

The tasks are capitalized by using the map method of the tasks array to create a new array named capitalized. Within the function that's passed to the map method, the task and date properties of the current array element are used to create a new task object with a capitalized task. (To refresh your memory of how the map method works, you can refer back to figures 9-7 and 9-8.)

Next, the display string is created by using the reduce method of this capitalized array. Within the function that's passed to the reduce method, the task and date properties of the current array element are again used, this time to concatenate the due date and task description. Also, an empty string is passed as the second parameter of the reduce method, which sets the initial value of the prevValue parameter. (Here again, you can refresh your memory of how the reduce method works by referring back to figures 9-7 and 9-8.)

Conversely, the addToTaskList function uses the stringify method of the JSON object to serialize the task array and then store it in local storage. Before it calls the stringify method, though, it uses the values entered by the user to create an object literal with a task and date property, and it adds the object to the tasks array. Notice that it uses the toDateString method of the Date object when it creates the object literal. This function ends by clearing the two text boxes and calling the displayTaskList function to update the text area display.

Finally, the clearTaskList function clears the tasks array and clears local storage, and the onload event handler attaches the addToTaskList and clearTaskList functions to the add_task and clear buttons. Both of these functions end by calling the displayTaskList function to display the tasks in the text area.

The main JavaScript file

```javascript
var $ = function(id) { return document.getElementById(id); };
var tasks = [];

var displayTaskList = function() {
    // get tasks from storage and load them in tasks array
    var storage = localStorage.getItem("tasks_16_1") || null;
    tasks = JSON.parse(storage) || [];

    // create capitalized tasks
    var capitalized = tasks.map(function(value){
        var first = value.task.substring(0,1);        // get first letter
        var remaining = value.task.substring(1);       // get remaining letters
        return {task: first.toUpperCase() + remaining, date: value.date };
    });
    // display capitalized tasks, set focus on task text box
    $("task_list").value = capitalized.reduce(function(prevValue, value) {
        return prevValue.concat(value.date, " - ", value.task, "\n");
    }, ""); // pass empty string as initial value
    $("task").focus();
};
var addToTaskList = function() {
    var task = $("task");
    var taskDate = $("task_date");
    var d = new Date(taskDate.value);

    if (task.value === "" || d === "" || d.toString() === "Invalid Date"){
        alert("Please enter a task and date.");
    } else {
        // add task to array, reset storage, clear form, and display tasks
        tasks.push( {task: task.value, date: d.toDateString() } );
        localStorage.setItem("tasks_16_1", JSON.stringify(tasks));

        task.value = "";
        taskDate.value = "";
        displayTaskList();
    }
};
var clearTaskList = function() {
    tasks.length = 0;
    localStorage.setItem("tasks_16_1", "");
    displayTaskList();
};

window.onload = function() {
    $("add_task").onclick = addToTaskList;
    $("clear").onclick = clearTaskList;
    displayTaskList();
};
```

Description

- This code creates an object literal for task data, calls the stringify method to store an array of objects as a string, and calls the parse method to restore the string to an array of objects.

Figure 16-7   The main JavaScript file for the Task Manager application

How to customize the stringify method

As you've seen, the default behavior of the stringify method does an excellent job of serializing data. It not only stores an object's data, but also information about the object's structure, so the object can be deserialized.

Most of the time, this default behavior is all you need. Sometimes, though, you'll want to customize the way the stringify method serializes data. For example, you may want to omit a sensitive property like salary when you serialize the data. Or you may want to combine property values or add a new property. In topics that follow, you'll learn how to customize the way the stringify method serializes JavaScript objects.

How to use the toJSON method

One way to customize the results of the stringify method is to add a *toJSON method* to the object being serialized. The examples in figure 16-8 show how this works.

In the first example, an object literal named obj is coded with three properties named first, last, and salary. Then, the object is passed to the stringify method. As you can see, all three properties appear in the JSON string that's returned by the stringify method.

In the second example, a toJSON method is added to the object. This method concatenates the value of the last property and the value of the first property, and excludes the salary property. Then, the object is passed to the stringify method. Now, only the string returned by the toJSON method is returned by the stringify method.

In the last example, the toJSON method returns an object instead of a string. This object contains the last property from the original object, and a property named full whose value is the same concatenated string you just saw. It also excludes the salary property. Then, the object returned by the toJSON method is serialized by the stringify method.

The toJSON method is a simple way to customize individual objects. You can use it when you want to exclude sensitive properties, when you don't need to serialize every property of an object, or when you want to transform the data in an object, like combining property values or adding new properties.

How the toJSON method affects the output of the stringify method

An object without a toJSON method

```
var obj = {
    first: "Grace",
    last: "Hopper",
    salary: 90000
};
JSON.stringify(obj);      // {"first":"Grace","last":"Hopper","salary":90000}
```

An object with a toJSON method that returns a string

```
obj.toJSON = function() {
    return this.last + ", " + this.first;
};
JSON.stringify(obj);      // "Hopper, Grace"
```

An object with a toJSON method that returns an object

```
obj.toJSON - function() {
    var full - this.last + ", " + this.first;
    return { last: this.last, full: full };
};
JSON.stringify(obj);      // {"last":"Hopper","full":"Hopper, Grace"}
```

When you might use the toJSON method

- To combine two or more properties.
- To add to the serialization output.
- To keep properties from appearing in the serialization output.

Description

- You can override the default serialization of the stringify method by adding a *toJSON method* to the object being serialized.
- If a toJSON method exists on an object and contains a function definition, the value returned by calling the function is what the stringify method will serialize. This allows you to specify how objects will be transmitted and stored.

Figure 16-8   How to use the toJSON method

How to use a toJSON method to customize the Task Manager application

Now that you know how the toJSON method works, you can use it to simplify the Task Manager application you saw earlier in this chapter. As figure 16-9 shows, this can simplify the code and shorten the JSON string that's stored in local storage. Here, you can see the shorter strings that are displayed in the enhanced application and stored in local storage.

To use the toJSON method, this version of the Task Manager application adds a library_task.js file that contains a Task constructor. This constructor accepts task and date parameters, and it stores these parameter values in properties named text and date. Then, the constructor adds a toJSON method to the object that capitalizes the first letter in the task, converts the text and date properties to a single string value, and returns that string.

This means that when a Task object is passed to the stringify method, the stringify method will serialize the string returned by the toJSON method, not a string that represents an object with two properties. That in turn means that when an array of Task objects is passed to the stringify method, the returned string will represent an array of strings, not an array of objects.

This allows the rest of the application code to be simplified. For instance, the displayTaskList function of the main JavaScript file no longer needs to call the array map and reduce methods to create a display string. Instead, it can use the array join method, because the array returned by the parse method is an array of strings, not an array of objects.

In addition, the addToTask function of the main JavaScript file no longer needs to create an object literal to store the task data it gets from the user. Instead, it calls the new Task constructor and passes it the task string and the Date object.

The tasks displayed in the customized Task Manager application

```
8/1/2015 - Get specs for new project
7/28/2015 - Meet with Mike
```

The JSON string stored in local storage

```
["8/1/2015 - Get specs for new project","7/28/2015 - Meet with Mike"]
```

The library_task.js file

```javascript
var Task = function(task, date) {
    this.text = task;
    this.date = date;
};
Task.prototype.toJSON = function() {
    // get date parts
    var m = this.date.getMonth() + 1; // correct for zero-based month
    var d = this.date.getDate();
    var y = this.date.getFullYear();

    // get task parts
    var first = this.text.substring(0,1).toUpperCase();
    var remaining = this.text.substring(1);

    // return short date string and capitalized task
    return m + "/" + d + "/" + y + " - " + first + remaining;
};
```

The updated displayTaskList function of the main JavaScript file

```javascript
var displayTaskList = function() {
    var storage = localStorage.getItem("tasks_16_2") || null;
    tasks = JSON.parse(storage) || [];
    $("task_list").value = tasks.join("\n");
    $("task").focus();
};
```

The updated code in the addToTaskList function of the main JavaScript file

```javascript
// add task to array and local storage
tasks.push( new Task(task.value, d) );
localStorage.setItem("tasks_16_2", JSON.stringify(tasks));
```

Description

- This version of the Task Manager application uses a constructor function to create a new Task object with a toJSON method.

- The toJSON method converts the Task object to a string that displays the due date and task. This simplifies the application's display code because it no longer needs to use the map and reduce methods of the array of tasks returned by the parse method, and it no longer needs to create object literals to store task data from the user.

Figure 16-9   How to use a toJSON method to customize the Task Manager application

How to use the replacer parameter of the stringify method

In the last two figures, you learned to use the toJSON method to customize the way the stringify method serializes an object. But what if you want to customize all objects? For example, maybe you want to ensure that salary properties are never serialized or that strings are always capitalized. Then, you can use the *replacer parameter* of the stringify method.

Figure 16-10 shows the syntax for the replacer parameter, which can be either a function or an array. If it's a function, it's called for every property or array element, and it returns the value to be serialized. If it's an array, the values in the array indicate which object properties should be serialized. In other words, a replacer array is a "whitelist" of property names.

When the replacer parameter is a function, it accepts two parameters. The first contains the name of the object property or the index of the array element that's being serialized. The second contains the value of the property or element.

The first time a replacer function is called, the key parameter contains an empty string, the value parameter contains the object being serialized, and the value of the this keyword is the object being serialized. Usually, you'll want to handle this key/value pair differently than the individual properties or elements. The rest of the times that a replacer function is called, the key and value parameters refer to the individual property or element being serialized. Then, the value of the this keyword is the object that contains the key.

To illustrate, the first group of examples in this figure presents two objects to be serialized. The first is an object literal named employee with properties named name, start, and salary. The second is an array named regions with four string elements.

Then, the second group of examples shows how to use a function as the replacer parameter. This function first returns the value whose key is an empty string, which is the object being serialized. Next, it returns "undefined" for any key whose value is "salary". Since object properties with unsupported types are dropped, this means that any property named "salary" won't be serialized in the JSON string. Then, it capitalizes and returns any value that's a string. Last, it returns the value of any key/value pair that doesn't meet the previous criteria.

The next two statements in this group use the replacer function as the second parameter in calls to the stringify method. The first statement serializes the employee object, and the second one serializes the regions array. As you can see, the employee object is serialized with its strings capitalized and its salary property dropped. And the region array is serialized with its elements capitalized.

The third group of examples shows how to use an array as the replacer parameter. Here, the first statement passes an array that contains the strings "name" and "start", so the stringify method returns a JSON string that contains those properties. However, none of the name object's properties are in the JSON string because their names aren't in the array. To fix this, the second statement passes an array that includes the names of those properties.

The syntax of the replacer parameter of the stringify method

```
function ( key, value ) {...}          // if the parameter is a function
["name1", "name2", "name3", ...]       // if the parameter is an array
```

How a replacer function works

- The first time the function is called, the key parameter contains an empty string and the value parameter contains the object being serialized.

- After that, the key contains a string that is the name of the current object property or the index of the current array element, and the value contains the property or element value.

- The value of the this keyword is the object that contains the key.

The objects to be serialized

```
var employee = {
    name: { f: "grace", l: "hopper" },
    start: new Date("1/1/2000"),
    salary: 90000
};
var regions = ["northwest", "southwest", "central", "east"];
```

How to use a replacer parameter that's a function

```
// capitalize strings and don't return salary information
var replacer = function(key, value) {
    if (key === "") { return value; }
    if (key === "salary") { return undefined; }
    if (typeof value === "string") {
        var first = value.substring(0,1).toUpperCase();
        var remaining = value.substring(1);
        return first + remaining;
    } else { return value; }
};
JSON.stringify(employee, replacer);
// {"name":{"f":"Grace","l":"Hopper"},"start":"2000-01-01T08:00:00.000Z"}


JSON.stringify(regions, replacer);
// ["Northwest","Southwest","Central","East"]
```

How to use a replacer parameter that's an array

```
JSON.stringify(employee, ["name", "start"]);
// {"name":{},"start":"2000-01-01T08:00:00.000Z"}  // name but no properties


JSON.stringify(employee, ["name", "f", "l", "start"]);
// {"name":{"f":"grace","l":"hopper"},"start":"2000-01-01T08:00:00.000Z"}
```

Description

- If the *replacer parameter* is a function, it's called on every object property or array element, and the value returned by the function is serialized.

- If the replacer parameter is an array, only the properties that match array elements are serialized.

Figure 16-10   How to use the replacer parameter of the stringify method

How to use the space parameter of the stringify method

The JSON string returned by the stringify method has no whitespace, which makes it difficult to read. Usually, this doesn't matter, since most of the time you're using JSON for data transmission and storage. Sometimes, though, you might want to display a JSON string. In those cases, you can use the *space parameter* of the stringify method to format the way the JSON string looks.

As figure 16-11 explains, the space parameter accepts either a number or a string, and it indents the return value with either that number of white spaces or the characters in the string. However, even though you can pass any number or length of string, there's a limit on how much the space parameter will indent. Specifically, it will only use ten white spaces or the first ten characters in a string, even if you pass more than that.

When you use the space parameter, you need to make sure that it's the third parameter of the stringify method. Thus, you need to code a value for the replacer parameter. In cases where you're not using a replacer function or array, you can code null for the replacer parameter.

The examples in this figure show how to use the space parameter. Here, the first group of examples shows the creation of the object to be serialized along with a replacer function, which is the same as in the last figure. Then, the three statements in the second group call the stringify method inside alert methods, and the alert dialog boxes show the results of the serialization.

The first statement passes the employee object and the replacer function to the stringify method. Then, the dialog box displays the JSON string with no salary property, because of the replacer function, and no whitespace, because there's no space parameter.

The second statement passes the employee object and the replacer function, but this time it also includes the number 4 as the space parameter. The dialog box now displays the JSON string with whitespace, which makes it easier to read.

The third statement passes the employee object and null as the replacer parameter, along with the number 200 as the space parameter. The dialog box now displays the salary property, because the replacer parameter is null. And even though the space parameter is 200, the space parameter only adds the limit of 10 white spaces to the JSON string.

How the space parameter of the stringify method works

- The space parameter accepts either a number or a string.
- If the space parameter is a number, the return value is indented with that number of white spaces at each level, up to a limit of 10 spaces.
- If the space parameter is a string, the return value is indented with the characters in the string at each level, up to a limit of 10 characters.
- The space parameter is the third parameter, so you must also pass something for the replacer parameter. If you don't have a replacer function or array, you can pass null.

The object to be serialized

```
var employee = {
    name: { f: "grace", l: "hopper" },
    start: new Date("1/1/2000"),
    salary: 90000
};
var replacer = function(key, value) {
    /* same as last figure */
};
```

How to use a space parameter

```
alert(JSON.stringify(employee, replacer));       // no space parameter
```

```
{"name":{"f":"Grace","l":"Hopper"}
,"start":"2000-01-01T08:00:00.000Z"}
```

```
alert(JSON.stringify(employee, replacer, 4));  // 4 white spaces
```

```
{
    "name": {
        "f": "Grace",
        "l": "Hopper"
    },
    "start": "2000-01-01T08:00:00.000Z"
}
```

```
alert(JSON.stringify(employee, null, 200));    // stops at limit of 10
```

```
{
        "name": {
                "f": "grace",
                "l": "hopper"
        },
        "start": "2000-01-01T08:00:00.000Z",
        "salary": 90000
}
```

Description

- You can use the *space parameter* of the stringify method to control how a JSON string looks. This is helpful when you want to make a JSON string easier to read.
- The space parameter accepts a number or a string, with a limit of 10 white spaces or 10 string characters.

Figure 16-11   How to use the space parameter of the stringify method

The serialization order of the stringify method

When you customize the way the stringify method serializes Javascript objects, it's important that you understand the order of its steps. Otherwise, your customization might not work the way you want. That's why figure 16-12 shows the steps that the stringify method takes when it serializes an object.

In the first step, the stringify method checks for a toJSON property whose value is a function definition. If it finds one, it invokes the function, passes it the current item being serialized, and returns the value it gets back from the function. If it doesn't find a toJSON method, it applies the default serialization to the current item and returns the result.

In the second step, the stringify method looks for a replacer parameter to apply to the value returned from the first step, which is either the result of the toJSON method or the default serialization. If the replacer parameter is an array, the stringify method looks to see if the property name of the value is in the array, and returns it if it is. If the replacer parameter is a function, the stringify method invokes the function, passes it the value, and returns the value it gets back.

In the third step, the value from the second step is serialized as needed. For example, if the value returned is an object or array, the process starts again. In the fourth step, the return value is formatted if there's a space parameter.

The examples show how this works. Here, the first group creates the object to be serialized, which is an object literal named employee with three properties. The name property is an object, the start property is a string, and the salary property is a number. Initially, the employee object has no toJSON method.

The second group of examples shows how the stringify method works with this object. Here, the first example passes the employee object and no other parameters to the stringify method, which returns a JSON string that includes all three properties as an object, a string, and a number.

The second example adds a toJSON method to the employee object. This method returns an object that has only the name and start properties, and it converts the name property from an object to a string. Then, the code passes the employee object and no other parameters to the stringify method. Now, the JSON string includes only the name and start properties, and both are strings.

The third example starts with a replacer function that converts the name property to uppercase if the property value is a string. Then, it passes the employee object to the stringify method, this time with the replacer function as the second parameter. The resulting JSON string is the same as the last one, except now the name string is all capital letters. You can see here that the replacer function was applied after the toJSON method. Otherwise, the name property would be an object when the replacer function was called, so the replacer wouldn't change it.

The last example deletes the toJSON method and passes the employee object and the replacer function to the stringify method again. This time, the name property is an object, so the replacer function doesn't convert it to uppercase. Also, the salary property now appears in the JSON string because it's no longer removed by the toJSON method.

The serialization order of the stringify method

1. If the object has a toJSON property whose value is a function, that function is called and its value returned. Otherwise, the default serialization is applied. The value that's returned is either the return value of the toJSON method or the return value of the default serialization.

2. If the replacer parameter is provided, it is applied. If the replacer parameter is a function, the return value from step 1 is passed to it, and the return value of the function is returned.

3. The value from step 2 is serialized as needed. For example, if the value is an object or an array, the process starts again.

4. If the space parameter is provided, the return value is formatted accordingly.

The object to be serialized

```
var employee = {
    name: { f: "Grace", l: "Hopper" },
    start: "1/1/2000",
    salary: 90000
};
```

Stringifying the object

Call the stringify method with no toJSON method or replacer parameter

```
JSON.stringify(employee);
// {"name":{"f":"Grace","l":"Hopper"},"start":"1/1/2000","salary":90000}
```

Add a toJSON method to the object

```
employee.toJSON = function() {
    var full = this.name.l + ", " + this.name.f;
    return { name: full, start: this.start };
};
JSON.stringify(employee);
// {"name":"Hopper, Grace","start":"1/1/2000"}
```

Pass a replacer parameter to the stringify method

```
var replacer = function(key, value) {
    if (key === "") { return value; }
    if (key === "name" && typeof value === "string") {
        return value.toUpperCase();
    } else { return value; }
};
JSON.stringify(employee, replacer);
// {"name":"HOPPER, GRACE","start":"1/1/2000"}
```

Delete the toJSON method from the object but still pass the replacer parameter

```
delete employee.toJSON;
JSON.stringify(employee, replacer);
// {"name":{"f":"Grace","l":"Hopper"},"start":"1/1/2000","salary":90000}
```

Description

- When you invoke the stringify method, it looks for the toJSON method and the replacer and space parameters, and uses them in a specific order.

Figure 16-12   The serialization order of the stringify method

How to customize the parse method

As you've seen, the default behavior of the parse method does an excellent job of deserializing data. Most of the time, this default behavior is all you need. Sometimes, though, you'll want to customize how the parse method deserializes data. For example, you may want to add a new property to the data. Or you may want to convert all date strings to Date objects. In the topics that follow, you'll learn how to customize the way the parse method deserializes JSON strings.

How to use the reviver parameter of the parse method

Figure 16-13 shows the syntax for the *reviver parameter*. This parameter must be a function, and this function is called for every property or array element in the JSON string that is being parsed. The first parameter for this function contains the name of the object property or the index of the array element being deserialized. The second parameter contains the value of that property or array element. And this function returns the corresponding JavaScript object.

The last time a reviver function is called, the key parameter contains an empty string, the value parameter contains the object that was just deserialized, and the value of the this keyword is the deserialized object. The rest of the times that this function is called, the key and value parameters are for the individual property or element being deserialized, and the value of the this keyword is the object that contains the key.

The examples in this figure show how to use a reviver function with the parse method. Here, the first example creates the JSON string that will be deserialized. This string represents an object with a property named name, which is an object, and a property named start, which is a date string in universal time. The last statement in this example passes the JSON string to the parse method, and stores the value it returns in a variable named obj. This value is a JavaScript object with a name property that's an object and a start property that's a string.

The second example starts with a function named reviver. This function first returns the value whose key is an empty string, which is the deserialized object. Then, it tries to convert every value to a Date object. If it can, it returns the new Date object. Otherwise, it returns the original value. The statement after this function passes the JSON string and the reviver function to the parse method. Now, the start property in the returned object is a Date object instead of a string.

The third example changes the reviver function so it adds a new property named short to any property that it converts to a Date object. This new property is a string representation of the Date object. The statement after this function passes the JSON string and the reviver function to the parse method, which returns a Date object with the new property.

The last example replaces the reviver function with one that converts the name property from an object to a string. Then, it calls the parse method with that function as its second parameter.

The syntax of the reviver parameter of the parse method

```
function( key, value ) {...}
```

How the reviver function works

- The last time the function is called, the key parameter contains an empty string and the value parameter contains the object being returned.
- Before that, the key contains a string that is the name of the current object property or the index of the current array element, and the value contains the property or element value.
- The value of the this keyword is the object that contains the key.

The JSON string to be deserialized

```
var s = "{\"name\":{\"f\":\"grace\",\"l\":\"hopper\"},";
s = s + "\"start\":\"2000-01-01T08:00:00.000Z\"}";


var obj = JSON.parse(s);              // name is an object, start is a string
// Object {name: Object, start: "2000-01-01T08:00:00.000Z"}
```

Use a reviver parameter to convert any date string to a Date object

```
var reviver = function(key, value) {
    if (key === "") { return value; }
    var dt = new Date(value);
    return (dt.toString() === "Invalid Date")? value : dt;
};
var obj = JSON.parse(s, reviver);    // start is now a date object
// Object {name: Object, start: Sat Jan 01 2000 00:00:00 GMT-0800 (Pacific
Standard Time)}}
```

Add an additional property to any Date object

```
var reviver = function(key, value) {
    if (key === "") { return value; }
    var dt = new Date(value);
    if (dt.toString() === "Invalid Date") { return value; }
    else {
        var m = dt.getMonth() + 1;
        dt.short = m + "/" + dt.getDate() + "/" + dt.getFullYear();
        return dt;
    }
};
var obj = JSON.parse(s, reviver);
console.log(obj.start.short);        // "1/1/2000"
```

Convert the name object to a string

```
var reviver = function(key, value) {
    return (key === "name")? value.l + ", " + value.f : value;
};
var obj = JSON.parse(s, reviver);
// Object {name: "hopper, grace", start: "2000-01-01T08:00:00.000Z"}
```

Description

- The optional *reviver parameter* of the parse method is a function that's called on every object property or array element. This lets you control the deserialization.

Figure 16-13   How to use the reviver parameter of the parse method

Some problems with checking if a string is a date

One of the most common uses of a reviver function is to convert date strings to Date objects, as you saw in the last figure. Unfortunately, JavaScript doesn't have a built-in way to check whether a string is a valid date. Although there are many ways you can code this kind of check, all of them have problems.

For example, most of the examples in this book check for a date by passing the string to the Date constructor and then checking the value of the resulting object's toString method. If the toString method returns "Invalid Date", it's not a date. However, as figure 16-14 shows, the Date constructor can take values that clearly aren't dates and create Date objects with them.

The table in this figure describes some of the other techniques for checking whether a string is a valid date. For instance, you can use regular expressions to check for dates, as you learned in figure 12-5. However, a regular expression can only check that the format of a date is okay. As a result, you have to add additional code to check whether the day, month, and year values are valid and to deal with issues like leap years.

Another option is to use the instanceof operator that you learned about in figure 11-16, but it can return false negatives in some situations. A third option is to use the toString method on the Object prototype. But to do so, you need to use the toString method's call method, as this figure illustrates. This is so you can pass the toString method the value you want the this keyword to represent. Note, however, that the toString method falsely returns "object Object" instead of "object Date" in some situations.

Last, you can use string manipulation, which means using the split method to break the string into parts, and then inspecting the parts. This can be cumbersome, however, since you need to check for a date string that's separated by dashes, slashes, periods, or any other standard date format. Then, as with regular expressions, you need to check the month, day, and year values for validity, deal with leap years, and perhaps deal with international date formats.

Since each way of checking whether a string is a date has problems, you often need to combine several methods to reduce the chance of error. Or, better yet, you can use third-party libraries like the ones at the URLs in this figure.

Some values that aren't dates but convert to valid Date objects

```
var dt = new Date(null);
dt.toString();   // Wed Dec 31 1969 16:00:00 GMT-0800 (Pacific Standard Time)

var dt = new Date("Check the Russell 2000");
dt.toString();   // Sat Jan 01 2000 00:00:00 GMT-0800 (Pacific Standard Time)

var dt = new Date("Party like its 1999");
dt.toString();   // Fri Jan 01 1999 00:00:00 GMT-0800 (Pacific Standard Time)
```

Some ways to check whether a string is a date

Technique	Problem
Date object constructor	Some values that aren't dates are converted to valid Date objects.
Regular expression (fig 12-5)	Can check the format but not whether the month, day, and year values are valid.
instanceof operator (fig 11-16)	Can return false negatives in some situations.
Object toString method	Returns "[object Object]" in some situations.
String manipulation	Cumbersome, hard to cover every possibility.

Typical usage of the Object toString method for checking dates

```
if (Object.prototype.toString.call(dt) === "[object Date]"
```

Some third-party libraries for working with dates

- http://momentjs.com/
- https://code.google.com/p/datejs/

Description

- One of the most common uses of the reviver parameter is to convert JSON date strings to JavaScript Date objects. Unfortunately, JavaScript doesn't have a built-in way to check whether a string is a valid date.

- Since all of the techniques for checking a date string have problems, you often need to combine techniques so they can make up for each other's shortcomings.

- Many programmers use third-party libraries for working with dates in JavaScript.

Figure 16-14   Some problems with checking if a string is a date

The enhanced Task Manager application

So far in this chapter you've seen two versions of the Task Manager application. The first one stored and displayed the due date in the format returned by the Date object's toDateString method, while the second one used a custom toJSON method to format the due date. Both applications, though, stored the due date as a string. This means that the application can't sort the tasks by date, even though that would be a useful feature.

Now, this chapter ends by presenting a third version of the Task Manager application. It uses replacer and reviver functions to customize the stringify and parse methods. It also converts the stored date strings to Date objects, so the tasks can be sorted by date.

Figure 16-15 shows this enhanced Task Manager application. Here, the tasks are displayed in the same format as before, but with one important difference: the tasks are sorted by due date in ascending order.

The JSON string in local storage

This figure also shows the JSON string for the two tasks in the text area. This is the string that is stored in local storage. It represents an array that contains two elements, and each element is an object with properties named task and date. The value in the date property is a date string in universal time, which is the result of serializing a Date object.

If you study this JSON string, you can also see that the tasks in storage have not been sorted. However, they are sorted by date by the time they are displayed in the text area of the user interface.

The Task Manager application

Task Manager

Task:

Finish current project

Date:

August 15, 2015|

| Add Task |

| Clear Tasks |

7/28/2015 - Meet with Mike
8/1/2015 - Get specs for new project

The JSON string stored in local storage

```
[{"task":"Get specs for new project","date":"2015-08-01T07:00:00.000Z"},
{"task":"Meet with Mike","date":"2015-07-28T07:00:00.000Z"}]
```

Description

- This application is an enhanced version of the Task Manager application in figure 16-6.

- This application uses the replacer parameter of the stringify method to capitalize the task description before storing it, and the reviver parameter of the parse method to convert date strings to Date objects when retrieving tasks from storage.

- This keeps the main JavaScript code simple, while adding the ability to sort the tasks by date.

Figure 16-15   The enhanced Task Manager application

The storage library

In the first version of the Task Manager application in this chapter, the stringify and parse methods were used with no optional parameters to serialize and deserialize the data in local storage. This made the code simple enough to be in the main JavaScript file.

The enhanced application, however, includes replacer and reviver functions with some complex logic. Thus, it makes sense to move this code to a separate library so it doesn't complicate the main JavaScript code. The other benefit of a separate library is that it puts the code that serializes and deserializes data in one spot, which makes it easier to maintain. Figure 16-16 shows this library, which contains three functions named getTasks, setTasks, and clearTasks.

The getTasks function starts with a reviver function that starts by checking if the current value is the object that the parse method has built and is returning. It does this by looking for a key value of an empty string. In previous examples, this value was just returned. Now, though, the code does something with it first.

Since the JSON string being deserialized is an array of objects, when the key is an empty string, the value is that array. Then, this code calls the array's sort method and passes it a function for sorting the objects in the array by date. Next, the array's reduce method is used to convert all the task objects in the array to a single string, and this string is added to the array in a new property named display. As you can see, the reduce method uses a property of the date property named short, and you'll see where that property comes from in a moment. (To refresh your memory about the reduce method, you can refer back to figures 9-7 and 9-8.)

After the reviver function finishes processing the deserialized array, it returns it. Then, it processes the rest of the object properties and array elements. First, it attempts to convert each one to a Date object, and then checks to see if it's a valid date. As you learned earlier, this check isn't foolproof, but it's good enough for now. If the Date object isn't valid, the code returns the original value. Otherwise, the code adds a property named short to the Date object that contains a date string in the format "m/d/yyyy", and it returns the Date object.

The getTasks function ends by getting the JSON string from local storage. Or, if nothing is in local storage, this function returns an empty array. Otherwise, this function returns the result of calling the parse method with the JSON string and the reviver function as the parameters.

The setTasks function uses a replacer function that checks whether the current value being serialized is a string. If it is, the replacer function capitalizes the first letter. Otherwise, it returns the value unchanged. The setTasks function then calls the stringify method, passes it the array of task objects and the replacer function, and stores the string it returns in local storage.

The clearTasks function just sets the value in local storage to an empty string.

The library_storage.js file

```javascript
var getTasks = function() {
    var reviver = function(key, value) {
        if (key === "") { // value is the object being returned
            // sort tasks by date
            value.sort(function(a,b){ return a.date - b.date; });

            // add a display string that combines all objects in the array
            value.display = value.reduce(function(prevValue, value) {
                return prevValue.concat(value.date.short,
                " - ", value.task, "\n");
            }, ""); // pass empty string as initial value to reduce method

            return value;
        } else {
            var dt = new Date(value);
            if (dt.toString() === "Invalid Date") { return value; }
            else {
                var m = dt.getMonth() + 1; // correct for zero-based month
                dt.short = m + "/" + dt.getDate() + "/" + dt.getFullYear();
                return dt;
            }
        }
    };
    var storage = localStorage.getItem("tasks_16_3") || "";
    return (storage === "")? [] : JSON.parse(storage, reviver);
};
var setTasks = function(tasks) {
    var replacer = function(key, value) {
        if (key === "") return value;

        if (typeof value === "string") {
            // capitalize and return
            var first = value.substring(0,1).toUpperCase();
            var remaining = value.substring(1);
            return first + remaining;
        } else { return value; }
    };
    var json = JSON.stringify(tasks, replacer);
    localStorage.setItem("tasks_16_3", json);
};
var clearTasks = function() {
    localStorage.setItem("tasks_16_3", "");
};
```

Description

- The reviver function converts date strings to Date objects, adds a date string property named short to Date objects, and adds a property named display to the value returned by the parse method. This display property reduces all the task objects in the array to a single string.

- The replacer function capitalizes strings.

- Both the reviver and replacer functions treat the main object that's being serialized or deserialized (with a key value of an empty string) differently than the other objects.

Figure 16-16   The storage library for the enhanced Task Manager application

The main JavaScript file

Figure 16-17 shows the main JavaScript file for the enhanced Task Manager application. Like the earlier version in this chapter, this file starts with the $ function, creates a tasks array that will hold the tasks entered by the user, and has three other functions and an onload event handler.

What's different about this version of the main JavaScript file is that the code is the simplest yet, even though this version of the application has more functionality than before. That's because the storage library allows the data serialization code to be centralized. This also makes it so the functions in the main file no longer need to know anything about how the tasks are stored. That keeps this code clean and easy to understand.

For instance, the displayTaskList function calls the storage library's getTasks function to get an array of task objects. Then, the function uses the display property added by the reviver function to display the tasks in the application. First, though, it checks to make sure that property exists. That's because the getTasks function returns an empty array if there's nothing in local storage, and the empty array doesn't have a display property. Another way to handle this would be to change the getTasks function so it adds a display property containing an empty string to the empty array before it returns it.

The addToTaskList function retrieves the task and date information entered by the user, converts the date string to a Date object, and then checks if the user's data is valid. Again, the date check isn't foolproof, but it's good enough for now. If the data is valid, the function creates a task object and adds it to the tasks array, then passes the array to the storage library's setTasks function. After that, the code clears the text boxes and calls the displayTaskList function to display the updated tasks.

The clearTaskList function clears the tasks array and local storage. This time, though, it clears local storage by calling the storage library's clearTasks function.

Last, the onload event handler attaches the addToTaskList and clearTaskList functions to the add_task and clear buttons. Then, it calls the displayTaskList function.

The main JavaScript file

```javascript
var $ = function(id) { return document.getElementById(id); };
var tasks;

var displayTaskList = function() {
    // get tasks from storage
    tasks = getTasks();

    // display tasks, or empty string if no tasks
    $("task_list").value = (tasks.display)? tasks.display : "";

    // set focus on task text box
    $("task").focus();
};
var addToTaskList = function() {
    var task = $("task");
    var taskDate = $("task_date");
    var d = new Date(taskDate.value);

    if (task.value === "" || d === "" || d.toString() === "Invalid Date") {
        alert("Please enter a task and date.");
    } else {
        // add task to array and local storage
        tasks.push( { task: task.value, date: d } );
        setTasks(tasks);

        // clear text boxes and re-display tasks
        task.value = "";
        taskDate.value = "";
        displayTaskList();
    }
};
var clearTaskList = function() {
    tasks.length = 0;
    clearTasks();
    displayTaskList();
};
window.onload = function() {
    $("add_task").onclick = addToTaskList;
    $("clear_tasks").onclick = clearTaskList;
    displayTaskList();
};
```

Description

- This file uses the storage library functions to get, set, and clear the tasks in local storage.

Figure 16-17   The main JavaScript file for the enhanced Task Manager application

Perspective

Now that you've completed this chapter, you should be able to use JSON as a data format for transferring and storing data. As you have seen, this is an effective format that works especially well for JavaScript applications because JavaScript provides all of the features that you need for working with JSON at both simple and complex levels.

Terms

JavaScript Object Notation (JSON)	global JSON object
serialize	stringify method
marshall	parse method
deserialize	toJSON method
unmarshall	replacer parameter
binary data format	space parameter
textual data format	reviver parameter
JSON string	

Summary

- *JavaScript Object Notation (JSON)* is a data format for transferring and storing data that works especially well with JavaScript applications.

- *Serialization* is the process of converting a data structure to a data format, and *deserialization* is the process of converting serialized data back to its original structure.

- JavaScript provides a *global JSON object* that has a *stringify method* for serializing data into a *JSON string* and a *parse method* for deserializing data.

- The stringify method has an optional *replacer parameter* that lets you customize how the data structure is serialized. It accepts either a function or an array.

- The stringify method also has an optional *space parameter* that lets you format the JSON string that this method returns.

- You can also customize how the stringify method serializes an object by adding a *toJSON method* to the object.

- When you use the stringify method with a toJSON method and replacer and space parameters, you need to understand the order in which they're applied.

- The parse method has an optional *reviver parameter* that accepts a function that lets you customize how a data structure is deserialized. A common use of the reviver parameter is converting date strings to Date objects.

Exercise 16-1   Convert the chapter 11 Task Manager application to use JSON

This exercise has you change the chapter 11 version of the Task Manager application so it uses the JSON object to get tasks to and from local storage. You may remember that this version of the application has this interface:

Task Manager

Task:

[   ]

[Add Task   ]

[Clear Tasks   ]

Delete Finish current project
Delete Get specs for next project
Delete Meet with Mike

1. Use your text editor or IDE to open the HTML and JavaScript files for the application in this folder:

    `c:\javascript\exercises\ch16\task_manager`

    Then, run the application to see how it works.

2. Press F12 to open Chrome's developer tools, then view local storage. To do that, click on the Resources tab, expand the Local Storage item, click on the appropriate URL, and look for the ex_16 key.

3. Enter two or three tasks in the application, click the browser's Reload button, and note how the tasks are stored in local storage. Then, click the Clear Tasks button to clear local storage, and click the Reload button.

4. In the library_storage.js file, find the line of code that uses the String split method. Replace it with code that uses the JSON parse method.

5. Find the line of code that uses the Array join method. Replace it with code that uses the JSON stringify method.

6. Test your changes in Chrome by refreshing the page, entering two or three tasks, and clicking the browser's Reload button. Note how the tasks look now in local storage. Then, click the Clear Tasks button and the Reload button.

Exercise 16-2   Add a date field and a toJSON method

This exercise has you add a date text box to the application in exercise 16-1 and use a toJSON method that customizes the stringify method.

1. In the index.html file, uncomment the HTML that adds a Date input element.

2. In the library_task.js file, add a date parameter to the constructor function. Inside the constructor, convert the date parameter value to a Date object and store it in a new property named date.

3. Adjust the isValid method so it checks the date for validity. To do that, use one of the techniques in figure 16-14.

4. Change the toString method to a toJSON method. Within the method, add a shortDate property to the Task object. The shortDate property should be a string in the "m/d/yyyy" format. Then, replace the text property value with the result of calling the text property's capitalize method. Finally, return the value of the this keyword, which will be the amended Task object.

5. In the library_tasklist.js file, find the add method. Then, change the array push method call so it only passes the task object. In other words, remove the call to the toString method.

6. Find the sort method. Then, pass a function to the array's sort method that sorts the task objects by date.

7. Find the display method. Then, change the code that creates the display string so it concatenates the Task object's shortDate and text properties.

8. In the task_list.js file, find the addToTaskList function. Next, uncomment the code that gets the entry in the date text box and sets its value to an empty string. Then, adjust the code that creates a new Task object to pass the date value as well as the task value.

9. Test your changes in Chrome by refreshing the page and entering two or three tasks. Note how they look now in local storage. Also note that in the web page they aren't sorted by date, even though you added code to do that. That's because the value of the date property is a string, but you can fix that in the next exercise.

Exercise 16-3   Add a reviver function to change the date property to a Date object

The updated Task Manager application isn't sorting by date because the value of the date property is a string. In this exercise, though, you'll use a reviver function to convert the value of the date property from a string to a Date object. That will make the sort work correctly.

1. In the library_storage.js file, find the get method for the string array storage prototype. Then, add a function named reviver that accepts a key parameter and a value parameter.

2. In the reviver function, code an if-else statement that checks for a key with a value of "date". If the key is "date", convert the value to a Date object and return the Date object. Otherwise, return the value unchanged.

3. Pass the reviver function as the second parameter to the parse method.

4. Test your changes in Chrome by refreshing the page. Now, the application should be correctly sorting by date.

17

When and how to use jQuery

In this chapter, you'll learn how you can use jQuery instead of JavaScript for your DOM scripting. As you will see, that makes the DOM scripting in your JavaScript applications easier to code and understand.

This chapter will also introduce you to the use of a related JavaScript library called jQuery UI (User Interface) as well as to the of use jQuery plugins. Both of these can help you work more productively by using tested code. Last, since you already know how to use JavaScript, this chapter will show you how to create your own jQuery plugins.

Introduction to jQuery

The goal of this chapter is to give you a good idea of what you can do with jQuery and why you should master it. As a result, this introduction shows you how to use the common jQuery selectors, methods, and event methods. It also demonstrates how jQuery can be used to simplify JavaScript applications.

What jQuery is

jQuery is a free, open-source, JavaScript library that provides dozens of methods for common functions that make JavaScript programming easier. Beyond that, the jQuery functions are coded and tested for cross-browser compatibility, so they will work in all browsers.

As figure 17-1 shows, those are just two of the reasons why jQuery is used by more than 60% of the 1,000,000 most-visited websites today. And that's why jQuery is commonly used by professional web developers. In fact, you can think of jQuery as one of the four technologies that every web developer should know: HTML, CSS, JavaScript, and jQuery. But don't forget that jQuery is actually JavaScript.

When to use jQuery

The short answer is that you should use jQuery whenever you can. That will usually make your code shorter and easier to read, test, and debug. Besides that, your code will be cross-browser compatible.

The trouble is that jQuery is limited so it can't be used for everything. That's why you normally use jQuery in conjunction with JavaScript. And that's why professional web developers need to master both JavaScript and jQuery.

The jQuery website at www.jquery.com

What jQuery offers

- Dozens of methods and event methods that make it easier to add JavaScript features to your web pages
- Cross-browser compatibility
- Selectors that are compliant with CSS3
- A compressed library that loads quickly so it doesn't degrade performance

When to use jQuery

- You should use jQuery whenever it lets you do what you want to do. The resulting code will be shorter, easier to read, and cross-browser compatible.

When to use JavaScript

- Because jQuery is limited, you need to use JavaScript with jQuery for most applications. In general, the more complicated the applications is, the more you need JavaScript.

Description

- *jQuery* is a free, open-source, JavaScript library that provides methods that make JavaScript programming easier.
- Today, jQuery is used by more than 60% of the 1,000,000 most-visited websites.

Figure 17-1   What jQuery is and when to use it

How to include jQuery in a web page

If you go to the web page that's in figure 17-2, you'll see that it contains links that let you download various releases of the jQuery core library. The most current release at this writing is jQuery 2.1.4, and it comes in two versions. The compressed version is around 83KB. As a result, this version loads quickly into browsers, which is another reason why developers like jQuery.

The other version is uncompressed and currently about 242KB. If you download this version, you can study the JavaScript code that's used in the library. But beware, this code is extremely complicated.

Once you've downloaded the compressed version of the core library, you can include it in a web page by coding a script element like the first one in this figure. Then, if you store the file on your own computer or a local web server, you'll be able to develop jQuery applications without being connected to the Internet. For production applications, though, you'll need to deploy the file to your Internet web server.

The other way to include the jQuery library in your web applications and the one I recommend is to get the file from a *Content Delivery Network* (*CDN*). A CDN is a web server that hosts open-source software, and the Google, Microsoft, and jQuery websites are CDNs for getting the jQuery libraries. In the second example in this figure, the script element uses the jQuery CDN with a URL that gets version 2.1.4 of jQuery, and that's the way all of the applications in this chapter include the jQuery library.

One benefit to using a CDN is that you don't have to download the jQuery file. Another is that other web sites use it, so it might already be cached in a user's browser, which makes your page's load time faster. The disadvantage is that you have to be connected to the Internet to use a CDN.

Although you might think that you should always use the most current release of jQuery, that's not necessarily the case. For example, jQuery 2.1.4 doesn't provide support for IE6, IE7, or IE8. So if you think that some of your users may be using these browsers, you'll want to use jQuery 1.11.2 instead since it's the most current release that supports these browsers. Note, however, that this release doesn't support the features that were dropped in jQuery 1.9. But if you need to provide for those features, you can use the jQuery migrate plugin.

The last example in this figure illustrates how this works. Here, the jQuery CDN is used to get release 1.11.2 of the jQuery core library as well as the migrate plugin. Because of that, the jQuery will work in older IE browsers and it will provide for the jQuery features that were dropped in release 1.9.

The jQuery page for downloading the latest versions of jQuery

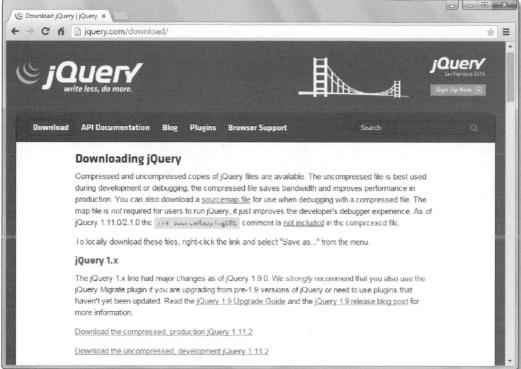

The current versions of jQuery

- jQuery 2.1.4 is the newest version of jQuery, but it no longer supports IE6, IE7, and IE8.
- jQuery 1.11.2 provides support for older browsers, but it doesn't support the features that were dropped in jQuery 1.9. To provide for those, you must include the migrate plugin.

How to include jQuery 2.1.4 after you've downloaded it to your computer

```
<script src="jquery-2.1.4.min.js"></script>
```

How to include the jQuery file from a Content Delivery Network (CDN)

```
<script src="http://code.jquery.com/jquery-2.1.4.min.js"></script>
```

How to include jQuery 1.11.2 and the migrate plugin from a CDN

```
<script src="http://code.jquery.com/jquery-1.11.2.min.js"></script>
<script src="http://code.jquery.com/jquery-migrate-1.2.1.min.js"></script>
```

Description

- Each version of jQuery comes in a compressed version (min) that is relatively small and loads fast, and an uncompressed version with all of the JavaScript code in the library.
- If you include the jQuery file from a *Content Delivery Network* (*CDN*), you don't have to provide it from your own server, but then you can't work offline.
- If you include the migrate plugin with jQuery 1.11.2, jQuery will support the features of the earlier versions that were dropped in jQuery 1.9.

Figure 17-2   How to include jQuery in a web page

How to code jQuery selectors, methods, and event methods

To give you some idea of how jQuery works, figure 17-3 introduces the selectors, methods, and event methods that you use in your jQuery code. To start, you should know that the $ sign always refers to the jQuery library. So if you're using jQuery, you *shouldn't* use the $ function you've used up until now, because it will conflict with jQuery. The good news is that jQuery makes the $ function unnecessary.

In the parentheses after the dollar sign, you code a *selector* that identifies the HTML element or elements that the jQuery will be applied to. This is similar to using the $ function, but jQuery gives you a lot more options for selecting elements.

This is illustrated by the first group of examples in this figure. Here, the first selector is a type selector that applies to all h2 elements. The second selector is an id selector that applies to the HTML element with "email_address" as its id. And the third selector is a class selector that applies to all of the elements with "warning" as their class name. This shows how closely the jQuery selectors relate to the CSS selectors, which is another reason why developers like jQuery.

After the selector, you can use the dot operator to run a jQuery *method* on the HTML element that's referred to by the selector. This is illustrated by the second group of examples. Here, the first statement uses the val method to get the value in the text box with "email_address" as its id attribute. The second statement uses the text method to set the text that's in an element with "email_address_error" as its id. And the third statement uses the next and text methods to set the text for the sibling element that follows the element with "email_address" as its id. This is much simpler than comparable JavaScript code.

The jQuery library also provides *event methods*, which let you code event handlers. These are illustrated by the third group of examples in this figure. The first example in this group uses the ready event method, which is executed when the DOM for the entire page has been built. Here, the alert method of the window object is executed when the ready event occurs.

The ready event method is important because some applications that use the DOM can't be run until the entire DOM has been built. As a result, this event method is a nice improvement over the JavaScript onload event which occurs while the page is being loaded and the DOM is being built.

The second example in this group shows how the click event method can be used to provide an event handler for the click event of all h2 elements. Here again, an alert method is executed when an h2 element is clicked. But note that the click event method is inside the ready event method. This is a common way to make sure the DOM is ready before attaching the other event handlers.

The third example in this group shows how to use the preventDefault method of the event object that's passed to the event handler to cancel the default action of the event. This jQuery method is executed in place of the preventDefault method of the browser that you learned about in chapter 13. Because this jQuery method is cross-browser compatible, it simplifies your code because you don't need to write any cross-browser compatibility code of your own.

How to code jQuery selectors
By element type
```
$("h2")
```

By id
```
$("#email_address")
```

By class attribute
```
$(".warning")
```

How to call jQuery methods
How to get the value from a text box
```
var emailAddress = $("#email_address").val();
```

How to set the text in an element
```
$("#email_address_error").text("Email address is required");
```

How to set the text for the next sibling
```
$("#email_address").next().text("Email address is required");
```

How to code jQuery event methods
How to code the ready event method
```
$(document).ready(function() {
    alert("The DOM is ready");
});
```

How to code the click event method for all h2 elements within the ready event
```
$(document).ready(function() {
    $("h2").click(function() {
        alert("This heading has been clicked");
    }); // end of click event handler
}); // end of ready event handler
```

How to code a preventDefault method that stops the default action of an event
```
$("#faqs a").click(function(evt) {   // the event object
    evt.preventDefault();            // the method is run on the event object
}); // end click
```

Description
- When you use jQuery, the dollar sign ($) is used to refer to the jQuery library. Then, you can code jQuery *selectors* by using the CSS syntax in quotation marks and parentheses.

- To call a jQuery *method*, you code a selector, the dot operator, the method name, and any parameters within parentheses. Then, that method is applied to the element or elements that are selected by the selector.

- To code a jQuery event handler, you code a selector, the dot operator, and the name of the jQuery *event method*. Then, you pass the method a function that handles the event.

- The event handler for the ready event method will run any methods that it contains as soon as the DOM is ready, even if the browser is loading images and other page content.

- The preventDefault method is executed on the event object that gets passed to an event handler when an event occurs.

Figure 17-3   How to use jQuery selectors, methods, and event methods

Some common jQuery selectors, methods, and event methods

Now that you know how jQuery selectors, methods, and event methods work, figure 17-4 presents some of the ones that you're likely to use when you work with jQuery. For instance, the selectors in the first table let you select just about any element that you need to select.

The methods in the second table are taken from several jQuery categories. For instance, the prev and next methods are DOM traversal methods. The attr, addClass, removeClass, and toggleClass methods are DOM manipulation methods. The hide and show methods are effect methods. And the each method is a miscellaneous method.

In most cases, the jQuery methods operate on all of the selected elements, but there are some exceptions. If, for example, you use the attr method to get the value of an attribute, it will get the value for only the first selected element.

The third table in this figure summarizes some useful event methods, including the ready and click methods. As you can see, an event method attaches an event handler that runs when the event occurs on the selected element. And when you select more than one element, the event method attaches the event handler to each of the selected elements. This makes it much easier to attach event handlers with jQuery than it is with JavaScript.

Some common jQuery selectors

Selector	Selects
[attribute]	All elements with the named attribute.
[attribute=value]	All elements with the named attribute and value.
:contains(text)	All elements that contain the specified text.
:first	The first element within the selected set.
:first-child	All elements that are first children of their parent elements.
:last	The last element within the selected set.
:last-child	All elements that are the last children of their parent elements.
:not(selector)	All elements that aren't selected by the selector.
:parent	All elements that are parents of other elements, including text nodes.

Some common jQuery methods

Method	Description
val([value])	Set a control's value if the parameter is coded. Else, get the value.
text([value])	Set an element's text if the parameter is coded. Else, get the text.
next([type])	Get the next sibling of each selected element or the first sibling of a specified type if the parameter is coded.
prev([type])	Get the previous sibling of each selected element or the previous sibling of a specified type if the parameter is coded.
attr(name,[value])	Set the value of the specified attribute for each selected element if the value parameter is coded. Otherwise, get the value of the first selected element.
addClass(name)	Add one or more classes to the selected elements. Separate multiple class names with spaces.
removeClass(name)	Remove one or more classes. Use spaces to separate multiple names.
toggleClass(name)	If the class is present, remove it. Otherwise, add it.
each(function)	Run the function for each element in an array.
extend(obj1,obj2)	Merge the contents of two or more objects into the first object.
hide()	Hide the selected elements.
show()	Show the selected elements.
find(selector)	Get the specified descendants of the selected elements.
focus()	Move the focus to the selected form control or link.
submit()	Submit the selected form.
evt.preventDefault()	Prevent the default action of the event.

Some common jQuery event methods

Event method	Description
ready(handler)	The handler runs when the DOM is ready.
click(handler)	The handler runs when the selected element is clicked.
mouseover(handler)	The handler runs when the pointer moves over the selected element.
mouseout(handler)	The handler runs when the pointer leaves the selected element.

Figure 17-4   Some common jQuery selectors, methods, and event methods

How to use jQuery to simplify the FAQs application

Now that you've been introduced to the jQuery selectors, methods, and event methods, figure 17-5 shows how jQuery can be used to simplify the FAQs application that you studied in figures 5-5 and 5-6 in chapter 5. You may remember that this application displays or hides the answer to a question when you click on its heading. If you're like most people, you found the JavaScript code for that application hard to follow...because it is.

In contrast, the jQuery code in this figure is easier to follow, even if you're new to jQuery. This code starts with a ready event method that runs as soon as the DOM for the page is ready.

Within this event method, the click event method is used to set up event handlers for the click event of each h2 element in the HTML element with the id attribute of "faqs". Here, the jQuery selector is:

```
$("#faqs h2")
```

and

```
#faqs h2
```

is the same as it would be in a CSS selector. This makes it easy for web developers to use the jQuery selectors.

Within the click event method, the this keyword refers to the current h2 element. Then, the toggleClass method is used to change the class attribute to and from "minus" each time the heading is clicked. In the if statement that follows, the jQuery attr selector is used to check whether the class attribute for the h2 element is "minus". If it isn't, the next and hide methods are used to hide the div element that follows. If it is, the next and show methods are used to show the div element that follows.

The last statement in the click event method uses the preventDefault method to stop the default action of the link that's clicked. And it does that in a browser-compatible way with just one line of code. (Compare that to the code in figure 13-3 of chapter 13 that was required for browser-compatibility.)

Then, the last line of code in the ready event method uses a CSS3 selector to select the first link in the element with "faqs" as its id and move the focus to it. Here again, a CSS selector is used to select that link. Even better, jQuery supports CSS3 selectors in browsers that don't support all of the CSS3 selectors, which is another reason why developers like jQuery.

In summary, using jQuery cuts the code for this application in half when compared to the JavaScript code, even though the jQuery prevents the default action of a clicked link, which the JavaScript version didn't do. Beyond that, you'll find that once you get used to the jQuery selectors, methods, and event methods, the code is easier to read, test, and debug.

Note, however, that jQuery often requires the use of one or more functions within another function. So it takes a while to get comfortable with that. It also helps to code inline comments that mark the ends of functions and methods, as shown in this figure, although that isn't required.

The FAQs application in a browser

jQuery FAQs

✛ **What is jQuery?**

─ **Why is jQuery becoming so popular?**
Three reasons:
- It's free.
- It lets you get more done in less time.
- All of its functions are cross-browser compatible.

✛ **Which is harder to learn: jQuery or JavaScript?**

The HTML

```
<main id="faqs">
    <h1>JavaScript FAQs</h1>

    <h2><a href="#">What is jQuery?</a></h2>
    <div><p><!-- the content for the panel --></p></div>

    <h2><a href="#">Why is jQuery becoming so popular?</a></h2>
    <div><p><!-- the content for the panel --></p></div>

    <h2><a href="#">Which is harder to learn: jQuery or JavaScript?</a></h2>
    <div><p><!-- the content for the panel --></p></div>
</main>
```

The critical CSS

```
h2 { background: url(images/plus.png) no-repeat left center; }
h2.minus { background: url(images/minus.png) no-repeat left center; }
div { display: none; }
```

The jQuery for the application

```
$(document).ready(function() {
    $("#faqs h2").click(function(evt) {
        $(this).toggleClass("minus");
        if ($(this).attr("class") !== "minus") {
            $(this).next().hide();
        }
        else {
            $(this).next().show();
        }
        evt.preventDefault();
    }); // end click

    $("#faqs a:first").focus(); // set focus on first link in faqs div
}); // end ready
```

Description

- This application illustrates the use of the ready event method, a jQuery selector that's just like a CSS selector, five jQuery methods, the preventDefault method of the event object, and another CSS3 selector.

- This shows how jQuery can shorten the code and make it easier to read.

Figure 17-5   How to use jQuery to simplify the FAQs application

The Email List application in jQuery

To show how jQuery works in the context of another type of application, figure 17-6 presents the Email List application. This is the jQuery version of the application that you studied in figures 4-12 and 4-13 of chapter 4.

To use the application, the user enters text into the first three text boxes and clicks on the Join our List button. Then, the JavaScript and jQuery code validates the entries and displays appropriate error messages if errors are found. If no errors are found, the data in the form is submitted to the web server for processing.

The HTML

In the HTML in this figure, note first the script element that loads jQuery. It is followed by the script element that identifies the file that holds the JavaScript for this application. That sequence is essential because the JavaScript file is going to use the jQuery library.

In the HTML for the form, note that the span elements are adjacent siblings to the input elements for the text boxes. The starting text for each of these span elements is an asterisk that indicates that the entry is required. Later, if the JavaScript and jQuery code finds errors in the entries, it displays error messages in these span elements.

Note also that the span elements don't require id attributes as they did for the JavaScript version of this application. That's because jQuery can change the text in those elements without referring to them by id. In other words, the use of jQuery has also simplified the HTML requirements for this application.

The user interface for the Email List application

Please join our email list

Email Address: `grace@yahoo.com`
Re-enter Email Address: `grace@yahoo` This entry must equal first entry.
First Name: This field is required.
[Join our List]

The HTML

```
<!DOCTYPE html>
<html>
<head>
    <meta charset="UTF-8">
    <title>Join Email List</title>
    <link rel="stylesheet" href="email_list.css">
    <script src="http://code.jquery.com/jquery-2.1.4.min.js"></script>
    <script src="email_list.js"></script>
</head>
<body>
    <main>
        <h1>Please join our email list</h1>
        <form id="email_form" name="email_form"
            action="join.html" method="get">
            <label for="email_address1">Email Address:</label>
            <input type="text" id="email_address1" name="email_address1">
            <span>*</span><br>

            <label for="email_address2">Re-enter Email Address:</label>
            <input type="text" id="email_address2" name="email_address2">
            <span>*</span><br>

            <label for="first_name">First Name:</label>
            <input type="text" id="first_name" name="first_name">
            <span>*</span><br>

            <label> </label>
            <input type="button" id="join_list" value="Join our List">
        </form>
    </main>
</body>
</html>
```

Note

* The script element for the jQuery library must come before the script element for any JavaScript file that uses it.

Figure 17-6   The HTML for the Email List application

The jQuery

Figure 17-7 presents the jQuery for this application. This is the code in the email_list.js file that's included by the HTML. Here, all of the jQuery is highlighted. The rest of the code is basic JavaScript code.

To start, you can see that an event method for the click event of the Join our List button is coded within the event method for the ready event. Within the click event method, the first two statements show how jQuery selectors and the val method can be used to get the values from text boxes.

In the first if statement, you can see how an error message is displayed if the user doesn't enter an email address in the first text box. Here, the next method gets the adjacent sibling for the text box, which is a span element, and the text method puts an error message in that span element. This changes the DOM, and as soon as it is changed, the error message is displayed in the browser. The next and text methods are used in similar ways in the next two if statements.

Finally, the fourth if statement tests to see whether the isValid variable is still true. If it is, the submit method of the form is issued, which sends the data to the web server.

If you compare this jQuery code to the JavaScript code in chapter 4, you can see that the jQuery makes the code simpler and easier to read. This example should also give you a better idea of how JavaScript and jQuery can be used in a JavaScript application. Here, jQuery is used for the DOM scripting, and JavaScript is used for everything else.

The jQuery for the Email List application (email_list.js)

```javascript
$(document).ready(function() {
    $("#join_list").click(function() {
        var emailAddress1 = $("#email_address1").val();
        var emailAddress2 = $("#email_address2").val();
        var isValid = true;

        // validate the first email address
        if (emailAddress1 == "") {
            $("#email_address1").next().text("This field is required.");
            isValid = false;
        } else {
            $("#email_address1").next().text("");
        }

        // validate the second email address
        if (emailAddress2 == "") {
            $("#email_address2").next().text("This field is required.");
            isValid = false;
        } else if (emailAddress1 != emailAddress2) {
            $("#email_address2").next().text(
                "This entry must equal first entry.");
            isValid = false;
        } else {
            $("#email_address2").next().text("");
        }

        // validate the first name entry
        if ($("#first_name").val() == "") {
            $("#first_name").next().text("This field is required.");
            isValid = false;
        }
        else {
            $("#first_name").next().text("");
        }

        // submit the form if all entries are valid
        if (isValid) {
            $("#email_form").submit();
        }
    }); // end click
}); // end ready
```

Description

- This shows how JavaScript can be used in conjunction with jQuery. Here, jQuery is used for the DOM scripting, and JavaScript drives the logic of the application.

Figure 17-7   The jQuery for the Email List application

Introduction to jQuery UI

jQuery UI (User Interface) is a free, open-source, JavaScript library that extends the use of the jQuery library by providing higher-level features that can simplify your applications even more. That's why most jQuery programmers use jQuery UI whenever it can save time and improve their applications. What follows is a quick introduction to what jQuery UI offers and how to use it.

What jQuery UI is

Figure 17-8 shows the home page and the URL for the jQuery UI website. If you scroll down the left sidebar of this page, you can see the four types of features that jQuery UI provides: widgets, themes, interactions, and effects. Of these, the most commonly used are *widgets*.

In contrast, *themes* provide the formatting for widgets, and they are implemented by a CSS style sheet. *Interactions* make it so users can do things like resize a page element or sort items in a list. And *effects* provide features like animations.

When you work with jQuery UI, you need to pick a theme and include its CSS style sheet with your application. You can do that by clicking on the Themes link on the website in this figure, which brings up the ThemeRoller page. Then, you can make your own theme or choose one of the predefined themes.

If you roll your own theme, you'll need to download the resulting CSS file and include it in your page, just like any other CSS file. By contrast, if you use a predefined theme, you can use a CDN to include the CSS file.

How to include jQuery UI in a web page

Like the core jQuery library, you can use a CDN to include jQuery UI with your web application, or you can download the library and include it that way. This is illustrated in figure 17-8. Again, the benefits to using a CDN are that you don't have to download the library file, and you can take advantage of browser caching. A disadvantage is that you have to be connected to the Internet.

Another disadvantage to using a CDN with jQuery UI is that you have to include the entire library when you may need just a few features. Since the jQuery UI library is significantly larger than the core jQuery library, this might cause performance problems.

If you would rather download just the parts of the jQuery UI library that you need, you can click on the Download link on the home page, which brings up the Download Builder page. Then, you can choose the features you want to download and include the downloaded file in your application.

Whether you're using a CDN or a downloaded file, the script tag for the jQuery UI library must come *after* the script tag for the core jQuery library. That's because jQuery UI uses jQuery. Also, since your own scripts will use the features of the jQuery and jQuery UI libraries, they should come after the tags that load those libraries.

The jQuery UI website

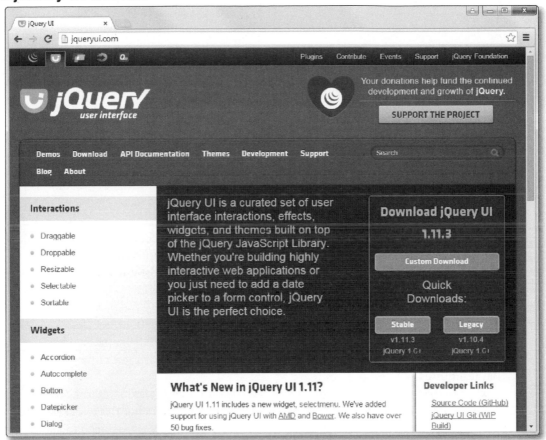

The URL for jQuery UI

```
http://jqueryui.com/
```

How to include jQuery UI in your application

```
<!-- link element for the selected jQuery UI theme -->
<link rel="stylesheet"
   href=" http://code.jquery.com/ui/1.11.4/themes/smoothness/jquery-ui.css">

<!-- the script elements for the jQuery and jQuery UI libraries -->
<script src="http://code.jquery.com/jquery-2.1.4.min.js"></script>
<script src="http://code.jquery.com/ui/1.11.4/jquery-ui.min.js"></script>

<!-- the script elements for any other JavaScript files go here -->
```

Description

- *jQuery UI* is a free, open-source, JavaScript library that extends the jQuery library by providing higher-level features.
- jQuery UI consists of four types of features: widgets, themes, interactions, and effects. Of the four, widgets are the most commonly used feature.

Figure 17-8   What jQuery UI is and how to include it in a web page

How to use any jQuery UI widget

All of the jQuery UI widgets follow a basic pattern, which is that you use a lowercase version of the widget's name to call the widget. However, the jQuery UI widgets also provide options, events, and methods that go beyond the basics. So, if you want to see how else a widget can be used, you can review the jQuery UI documentation for the widgets, which is excellent.

For instance, figure 17-9 shows how to use the documentation for the Accordion widget. A good way to start is to click on the names of the examples in the right sidebar to see how the widget can be used. Then, you can click on the View Source link to see the source code that makes the example work. After that, you can review the options, methods, and events for the widget by clicking on the API Documentation link.

After you're comfortable with the way a widget works, you're ready to implement it on a web page, which you do in three stages. First, you code the link and script elements for jQuery UI as shown in the previous figure. Second, you code any HTML required by the widget. For example, the Accordion widget requires h3 tags for the headings and divs for the content. Third, you code the jQuery for running the widget.

If you're working with a downloaded version of jQuery UI, rather than a CDN, you must also make sure that the jQuery CSS file is at the same level as the images folder. That's because that's where jQuery UI looks to get the images that it requires.

In the jQuery example in this figure, you can see the general structure for the jQuery code that's required for a widget. First, the code for using the widget is within the jQuery ready event handler. Second, a jQuery selector is used to select the HTML element that's used for the widget. Third, the method for running the widget is called, which is a lowercase version of the widget's name. Finally, any options for the widget are coded in an object literal that's passed to the method.

The accordion documentation on the jQuery UI website

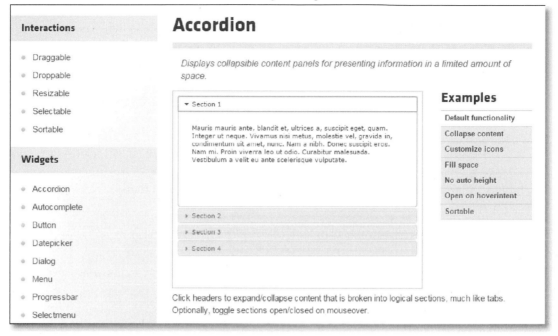

How to use the jQuery UI documentation

- In the left sidebar, click on a widget name to display its documentation.

- In the right sidebar, click on an example name to see a working example, then click on the View Source link to see the code for the example.

- Click the API Documentation link to display information about the widget's options, methods, and events.

The jQuery for using a widget

```
$(document).ready(function(){
    $("selector").widget ({
        // option settings
    });
});
```

Description

- To use a jQuery UI *widget*, you code the HTML and jQuery that's required for the widget.

- In the jQuery, you code a selector, the widget method to be used, and the options.

Figure 17-9   How to use any jQuery UI widget

How to use the Accordion widget to implement the FAQs application

Figure 17-10 shows a version of the FAQs application that uses the Accordion widget. Note here that now the HTML elements for the FAQs are in a div with an id of "accordion." Note also that the HTML in this div is just like the HTML in figure 17-5, except h3 elements are used for the question headings instead of h2 elements. That's because jQuery UI requires that h3 elements be used.

Then, to implement this widget, you need just the three lines of JavaScript code that are in the first example after the HTML. In this case, a link element gets the CSS file for the smoothness theme from a CDN, and that provides the formatting for the accordion.

You can also set options for a widget by passing it an object literal with the settings you want. For instance, the default behavior of the accordion is to always have at least one panel open. If you want something different than that, you'll need to pass the widget some options.

This is illustrated by the second example. Here, the code changes the accordion so that all its panels can be closed and all its panels are closed when the page first loads. It also sets the height of an open panel to the height of the content in the panel. You can find these and other settings in the widget documentation you learned about in the last figure.

Because jQuery UI can make JavaScript development even easier than it is when using jQuery, it makes sense to use jQuery UI whenever it provides a widget, interaction, or effect that you need. Keep in mind, though, that jQuery UI is limited, so you'll still need jQuery for most of your web applications.

The FAQs application as a jQuery UI accordion

jQuery FAQs

- ▼ What is jQuery?

  jQuery is a library of the JavaScript functions that
  you're most likely to need as you develop web sites.

- ▸ Why is jQuery becoming so popular?

- ▸ Which is harder to learn: jQuery or JavaScript?

The HTML for a jQuery UI accordion

```
<h1>JavaScript FAQs</h1>
<div id="accordion">
    <h3><a href="#">What is jQuery?</a></h3>
    <div><p><!-- the content for the panel --></p></div>

    <h3><a href="#">Why is jQuery becoming so popular?</a></h3>
    <div><p><!-- the content for the panel --></p></div>

    <h3><a href="#">Which is harder to learn: jQuery or JavaScript?</a></h3>
    <div><p><!-- the content for the panel --></p></div>
</div>
```

The jQuery code for the jQuery UI accordion

```
$(document).ready(function() {
    $("#accordion").accordion();
});
```

The jQuery UI accordion with some options set

```
$(document).ready(function() {
    $("#accordion").accordion({
        collapsible: true,        // makes it so all the panels can close
        heightStyle: "content",   // sets panel height to content height
        active: false             // closes all the panels on initial load
    });
});
```

Description

- In general, if you can find a widget or jQuery UI feature that does what you want it to do, you should use it.
- Often, though, you won't be able to find what you want so you'll need to develop the feature yourself with the core jQuery library and JavaScript.

Figure 17-10   How to use the Accordion widget to implement the FAQs application

Introduction to jQuery plugins

A *jQuery plugin* is just jQuery code that does one web task or a set of related web tasks. For instance, the Accordion widget is a plugin. Similarly, jQuery plugins can make it easy to implement features like slide shows and accordions.

As you will see, jQuery plugins make use of the jQuery library, and most plugins can be used with limited knowledge of JavaScript and jQuery. That's why most jQuery programmers use jQuery plugins whenever they can save time and improve their applications. What follows is a quick introduction to jQuery plugins and how to use them.

How to find jQuery plugins

Figure 17-11 starts with a screen capture that shows the results of a Google search for "jquery plugin rotator". Often, doing a search like this is the best way to find what you're looking for. Note, however, that the search entry includes the word *jquery* because there are other types of plugins.

Another way to find the type of plugin that you're looking for is to go to the URLs for the websites in the table in this figure. The first one is for the jQuery Plugin Repository, which is part of the jQuery website, and the second one is for a site that is only for jQuery plugins.

In contrast, the next three websites are repositories for many types of code, including jQuery plugins. As a result, you must search for jQuery plugins to find what you want on these sites.

In most cases, jQuery plugins are free or are available for a small price or donation. Besides that, jQuery plugins can often be used by non-programmers, and they can save you many hours of development time if you are a JavaScript programmer. For those reasons, it makes sense to look for a plugin whenever you need to add a common function to your website.

You'll want to be careful, though, and only use plugins from trusted sources. Often a quick Google search can help you decide if you should use a particular plugin or keep looking.

This figure also summarizes some of the most useful plugins for displaying images and running slide shows, carousels, and galleries. You'll see how to use one of these plugins in a minute.

A Google search for a jQuery plugin

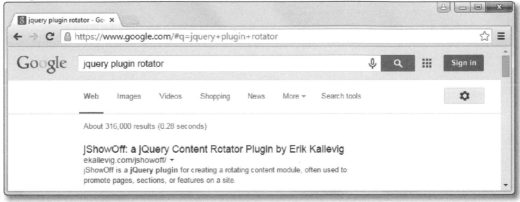

Websites for finding jQuery plugins

Site name	URL
jQuery Plugin Repository	`http://plugins.jquery.com`
jQuery Plugins	`http://www.jqueryplugins.com`
Google Code	`http://code.google.com`
GitHub	`https://github.com`
Sourceforge	`http://sourceforge.net`

Popular plugins for displaying images

Lightbox	`http://lokeshdhakar.com/projects/lightbox2/`
Fancybox	`http://fancybox.net`
ThickBox	`http://jquery.com/demo/thickbox`
Shadowbox.js	`http://www.shadowbox-js.com`

Popular plugins for slide shows, carousels, and galleries

bxSlider	`http://bxslider.com`
Malsup jQuery Cycle 2	`http://jquery.malsup.com/cycle2`
jCarousel	`http://sorgalla.com/jcarousel`
Nivo Slider	`http://nivo.dev7studios.com`
Galleria	`http://galleria.io`

Description

- *jQuery plugins* are JavaScript applications that extend the functionality of jQuery. These plugins require the use of the core jQuery library.

- Some of the websites that provide jQuery plugins are listed above. Often, though, you can find what you're looking for by searching the Internet.

- Plugins are available for dozens of web functions like slide shows, carousels, and data validation. In general, if you can find a plugin for doing what you want, that's usually better than writing the jQuery code yourself.

Figure 17-11   How to find jQuery plugins

How to use any jQuery plugin

Figure 17-12 shows how to use any plugin after you find the one you want. First, you study the documentation for the plugin so you know what HTML and CSS it requires and what methods and options it provides. Usually, you'll do this as you evaluate the plugin to see if it does what you want and if its documentation tells you everything you need to know.

Second, you usually download the files for the plugin and save them on your web server. This download is often in the form of a zip file, and it will always include at least one JavaScript file. In addition, it may include CSS or image files that are used by the plugin.

The download may also include two versions of the main JavaScript file for the plugin. If you want to review the code for the file, you can open the full version in your text editor. But the one you should use for your applications is the compressed version, which usually has a name that ends with min.js.

For some plugins, the files are also available from a Content Delivery Network (CDN). If you want to access the files that way, you can record the URLs for the files. Then, you can use those URLs in the link and script elements for the files.

Third, if a plugin requires one or more CSS files, you code the link elements for them in the head element of the HTML. Then, you code the script elements for the JavaScript files for the plugin. Usually, only one JavaScript file is required, but some plugins require more than one.

Fourth, if the download includes a folder for images, you need to make sure the folder has the right structural relationship with the CSS and JavaScript files for the plugin. Otherwise, you may have to adjust the CSS or JavaScript code so it can find the images folder (and you probably don't want to do that).

At this point, you're ready to use the plugin. So, fifth, you code the HTML and CSS for the plugin. And sixth, you code the JavaScript for using the plugin, usually in an external file.

This procedure is illustrated by the example in this figure, which uses the bxSlider plugin. Here, the script elements show that the element for the plugin must come after the element for the jQuery library. That's because all jQuery plugins use the jQuery library. As the first caution in this figure points out, not coding these script elements in this sequence is a common error.

The HTML that follows shows the elements that the plugin requires. In particular, the id attribute for the unordered list is set to "slider" so the jQuery code can select that element when it calls the bxSlider method of the plugin. Also, the title attributes for the img elements are set to the captions for the slides.

This is followed by the jQuery code for using this plugin. As you can see, it is like the code for using a jQuery UI widget. Here, the bxSlider method is called as the first statement within the function for the ready method for the document. This method name is followed by an object literal that contains the code for setting four options for this method.

Before you continue, note the second caution in this figure, which is that some plugins won't work with the latest version of jQuery. So if a plugin doesn't work, you should check to see what version of jQuery it requires.

General steps for using a plugin within your web pages

1. Study the documentation for the plugin so you know what HTML and CSS it requires as well as what methods and options it provides.

2. If the plugin file or files are available via a Content Delivery Network (CDN) and you want to access them that way, get the URLs for them. Otherwise, download the file or files for the plugin, and save them in one of the folders of your website.

3. In the head element of the HTML for a page that will use the plugin, code the link elements for any CSS files that are required. Also, code the script elements for the JavaScript files that are required. These script elements must be after the one for the jQuery library because all jQuery plugins use that library.

4. If the download for a plugin includes an images folder, make sure the folder has the right structural relationship with both the CSS and JavaScript files for the plugin.

5. Code the HTML and CSS for the page so it is appropriate for the plugin.

6. Write the jQuery code that uses the methods and options of the plugin.

The script elements for the jQuery library and the bxSlider plugin

```
<!-- the script element for the core jQuery library -->
<script src="http://code.jquery.com/jquery-2.1.4.min.js"></script>
<!-- the script element for the plugin when it has been downloaded -->
<script src="js/jquery.bxSlider.min.js"></script>
```

The HTML for the bxSlider plugin

```
<ul id="slider">
    <li><img src="images/gear.jpg" alt="" title="Fishing Gear"></li>
    <li><img src="images/plane.jpg" alt="" title="Bush Plane"></li>
    ...
</ul>
```

The jQuery for using the bxSlider plugin

```
$(document).ready(function(){
    $("#slider").bxSlider({
        minSlides: 2,
        maxSlides: 2,
        slideWidth: 260,
        slideMargin: 10
    });
});
```

Two cautions

- Make sure that you include a script element for jQuery and make sure that the script element for the plugin comes after it. Not doing one or the other is a common error.

- Some plugins won't work with the latest version of jQuery. So if you have any problems with a plugin, check its documentation to see which version of jQuery it requires.

Description

- Some plugins can be accessed via a CDN, but most must be downloaded and stored on your server.

Figure 17-12   How to use any jQuery plugin

How to use the bxSlider plugin for carousels

Figure 17-13 shows how to use the bxSlider plugin for creating carousels. In this example, this plugin displays two images at a time, it slides from one set of images to the next automatically, it provides captions in the slides, it provides controls below the carousel, and you can move to the next or previous image by clicking on the right or left icon that's displayed.

If you download the JavaScript file for this plugin, the script element can refer to it as shown in this figure. As part of this download, you also get a CSS file and an images folder that contains the images that can be used with this plugin.

One way to set up the HTML for use with this plugin is shown in this figure. Here, img elements are coded within the li elements of an unordered list. Then, the src attributes of the img elements identify the images that are displayed, and the title attributes provide the captions.

To run the bxSlider plugin, you use the jQuery code in this figure. Within the ready function, the selector selects the ul element that contains the slides and executes the bxSlider method.

Within that method, several options are set. The auto option makes the carousel run automatically, the autoControls option puts the controls below the carousel, the captions option causes the title attributes to be used for captions, the minSlides and maxSlides options set the carousel so 2 slides are always displayed, and the slideWidth and slideMargin options set the size of the slides and the space between them.

These options show just some of the capabilities of this plugin. To learn more, you can go to the website for this plugin and review its demos and option summaries.

By the way, if you try to run a page that contains a bxSlider plugin from Aptana, you'll see that the plugin doesn't work. Because of that, you'll need to run the page from outside of Aptana.

When you use this plugin, you will often want to change the location of components like the left and right icons, the captions, and the controls below the carousel. To do that, you can adjust the styles in the CSS file for this plugin.

If, for example, you want to adjust the location of the left and right icons, like moving them outside of the slider, you can modify the CSS for the bx.next and bx.prev classes. You won't find these classes in the HTML, though, because they're added to the DOM by the plugin. Usually, you'll learn a lot by studying the code in the CSS files for plugins and by making adjustments to that code.

A web page that uses the bxSlider plugin for a carousel

The URL for the bxSlider website

```
http://bxslider.com
```

The link and script elements for the bxSlider plugin

```
<link href="styles.css" rel="stylesheet">
<link href="jquery.bxslider.css" rel="stylesheet">
<script src="http://code.jquery.com/jquery-2.1.4.min.js"></script>
<script src="js/jquery.bxSlider.min.js">
```

The HTML for the bxSlider plugin

```
<ul id="slider">
    <li><img src="images/gear.jpg" alt="" title="Fishing Gear"></li>
    <li><img src="images/plane.jpg" alt="" title="Bush Plane"></li>
    ...
</ul>
```

The jQuery for using some of the bxSlider options

```
$(document).ready(function(){
    $("#slider").bxSlider({
        auto: true,
        autoControls: true,
        captions: true,
        minSlides: 2,
        maxSlides: 2,
        slideWidth: 260,
        slideMargin: 10
    });
});
```

Description

- The bxSlider plugin makes it easy to develop a carousel. The HTML is an unordered list with one list item for each slide that contains images or other HTML.

- If the slide images contain title attributes, the captions option will make them captions.

- The bxSlider download consists of a JavaScript file, a CSS file, and an images folder that contains the images that are used by the plugin.

Figure 17-13   How to use the bxSlider plugin for carousels

How to create your own plugins

One of the features of jQuery is that it provides an *API* (*Application Programming Interface*) that lets you create your own plugins. Sometimes, for example, you can't find a plugin that does what you want, or you don't trust its source, or it does far more than you need. In those cases, it makes sense to build your own plugin. And now that you have the JavaScript skills that you've learned in this book, you have all the skills for making your own jQuery plugins.

The structure of a plugin

Since the jQuery library uses the module pattern that you learned about in chapter 15, the jQuery object is available in your web pages without needing to be called or created. That's why the script tag for the core jQuery library must be included before anything that depends on it.

That also means that you can use an IIFE to create plugins that augment the jQuery object. The examples in figure 17-14 show how this works.

The first example shows how to use an IIFE to import the jQuery object so it can be modified. Here, the jQuery library is imported within parentheses at the end of the IIFE and assigned to the $ sign parameter of the function. Not only is this the standard way to work with the module pattern, it also has the benefit of preventing conflicts with other libraries and plugins that use the $ sign.

Within the IIFE, $.fn refers to the jQuery object's prototype object. This prototype object is where you should add your methods when you create a plugin. It's also a good practice to add only one method to the $.fn object for each plugin.

The second example shows how to make your plugin chainable. It does this by returning the this keyword. The third example shows how to make your plugin able to iterate all the selected elements by putting its code inside the jQuery each method. If, for example, the jQuery selector selects all <a> tags in the page, a plugin whose code is inside an each method will apply its code to each selected <a> tag. Plugins that use this technique support *implicit iteration*.

The fourth example shows how to combine the coding practices in the second and third examples to write plugins that support chaining and implicit iteration. This works because the each method also returns the this keyword, so returning the result of the each method is the same as ending your plugin code with "return this". This is the way most professionals code a plugin.

This figure also shows the naming conventions for plugin files as well as the API standards for plugins. As you've learned, you use the each method within the plugin function to support implicit iteration, and you return the this keyword to preserve chaining. Beyond that, you should be sure to end all method definitions with a semicolon, and you should provide reasonable defaults if your plugin offers options. Above all, your plugin should be well documented if it's going to be used by others.

The module pattern of a jQuery plugin

An IIFE that imports the jQuery object and adds a method to its prototype

```
(function($){
    $.fn.pluginName = function() {
        // the code for the plugin
    };
})(jQuery);
```

A method that returns the this keyword so it can be chained

```
(function($){
    $.fn.pluginName = function() {
        // the code for the plugin
        return this;
    };
})(jQuery);
```

A method that uses the each() method so it iterates all selected elements

```
(function($){
    $.fn.pluginName = function() {
        this.each(function() {
            // the code for the plugin
        });
        return this;
    };
})(jQuery);
```

The way most professionals code a plugin

```
(function($){
    $.fn.pluginName = function() {
        return this.each(function() {
            // the code for the plugin
        });
    };
})(jQuery);
```

Naming conventions for plugin files

```
jquery.pluginName.js
```

The API standards for plugins

- The plugin should support *implicit iteration*.
- The plugin should preserve chaining by returning the selected object.
- The plugin definitions should end with a semicolon.
- The plugin options should provide reasonable defaults.
- The plugin should be well documented.

Description

- The jQuery library uses the module pattern. This means that a jQuery plugin augments the jQuery object using the techniques you learned in chapter 15.
- For many plugins, most of the code will be in the function of the each() method.
- When the plugin finishes, the this object should be returned to the calling application.

Figure 17-14   The structure of a plugin

How to code a plugin that highlights the items in a menu

Now that you know the structure of a plugin, figure 17-15 shows how to create a simple plugin. This plugin highlights a menu item when the mouse enters that item, and it returns the item to its original state when the mouse leaves it.

This figure shows the HTML for the nav element that will be affected by the plugin, and the CSS rule sets for the nav element. Notice the mouseover class in the CSS. This is what will be added and removed to create the highlight effect.

The code for this plugin uses the coding practices you learned in the previous figure. Thus, it imports the jQuery object, adds the plugin method to the $.fn prototype object, puts its code inside the each method, and returns the value of the each method.

Within the each method, the first statement uses the find method to select the <a> elements that are children of the element the plugin is applied to, and it stores them in a variable named items. Then, the code provides functions for the mouseover and mouseout events of those <a> elements. The function for the mouseover event uses the jQuery addClass method to add the mousover class to the <a> tag. This changes the tag's color and background color when the mouse is over it. The function for the mouseout event uses the jQuery removeClass method to remove the mouseover class from the <a> tag. This restores the tag to its previous color and background color when the mouse leaves.

Because the plugin is stored in a file named jquery.highlightmenu.js, the script element for the plugin reflects this. Then, the jQuery to activate the plugin selects the nav by type and calls the highlightMenu method of the plugin.

A menu that is highlighted by the highlightMenu plugin

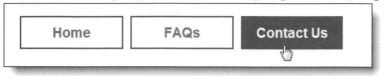

The HTML for the menu

```
<nav>
    <ul>
        <li><a href="index.html">Home</a></li>
        <li><a href="faq.html">FAQ</a></li>
        <li><a href="contact.html">Contact Us</a></li>
    </ul>
</nav>
```

The CSS for the menu

```
nav ul {
    list-style-type: none; }
nav ul li {
    border: blue solid 2px;
    float: left;
    margin-right: 10px; }
nav ul li a {
    text-decoration: none;
    text-align: center;
    display: block;
    width: 120px;
    padding: .5em;
    color: blue;
    font-weight: bold;
    font-size: 125%; }
.mouseover {
    background-color: blue;
    color: white; }
```

The highlightMenu plugin in a file named jquery.highlightmenu.js

```
(function($){
    $.fn.highlightMenu = function() {
        return this.each(function() {
            var items = $(this).find("a");
            items.mouseover(function() {
                $(this).addClass("mouseover");
            });
            items.mouseout(function() {
                $(this).removeClass("mouseover");
            });
        });
    };
})(jQuery);
```

jQuery that uses the highlightMenu plugin (jquery.highlightmenu.js)

```
$(document).ready(function() {
    $("nav").highlightMenu();
});
```

Figure 17-15   The Highlight Menu plugin

How to add options to a plugin

To make a plugin more useful, you usually provide some options for it. To do that, you can use the coding technique that is illustrated in figure 17-16.

To start, you code an options parameter in the function for the plugin method. This is highlighted in this figure. This parameter will receive all of the options that are set by the user as properties in an object literal.

As the API standards for plugins in figure 17-14 point out, a plugin should always provide defaults for the options so the users don't have to set the options if they don't want to. To do that, you can use the $.extend method to set up the defaults as shown in this example. Here, a variable named o stores the object that's created by the $.extend method.

The first parameter of the $.extend method consists of an object literal that provides the default properties for the options object. The second parameter is the parameter that's passed to the plugin, which is the object literal set by the user. Then, when this method is executed, the user options in the second parameter are merged with the default options in the first, and the user options replace any default options with the same name. The result is that the o variable contains one property for each option, and that property contains either the default value or the value that the user set to override the default value.

Then, the o variable is used in the mouseover and mouseout event handlers. For example, the code in the mouseover function passes the value of o.mouseoverClass to the addClass method. That way, if the user has passed in a different CSS class to use, the plugin will use it, but otherwise the plugin will use the default class named "mouseover".

This version of the highlight menu plugin also lets the user specify whether a mouseout class should be applied when the mouse leaves the link, and what that mouseout class should do. This allows for effects like making links that have been hovered over a different color than those that have not. The default behavior of the plugin is to apply the mouseout class, and to use the default class named "mouseout".

To show how to use the plugin with options, the last example in this figure sends in one option. In this case, the useMouseout property is changed to false from its default value of true. This means that the plugin will simply remove the default mouseover class on mouseout, rather than applying the "mouseout" class.

The highlightMenu plugin with options

```
(function($){
    $.fn.highlightMenu = function(options) {
        var o = $.extend({
            "mouseoverClass"   : "mouseover",
            "mouseoutClass"    : "mouseout",
            "useMouseout"      : true
        }, options);

        return this.each(function() {
            var items = $(this).find("a");
            items.mouseover(function() {
                $(this).addClass(o.mouseoverClass);
                if (o.useMouseout) {
                    $(this).removeClass(o.mouseoutClass);
                }
            });
            items.mouseout(function() {
                $(this).removeClass(o.mouseoverClass);
                if (o.useMouseout) {
                    $(this).addClass(o.mouseoutClass);
                }
            });
        });
    };
})(jQuery);
```

jQuery that uses the highlightMenu plugin and sets one of its options

```
$(document).ready(function() {
    $("nav").highlightMenu({
        useMouseout: false
    });
});
```

Description

- To provide options for a plugin, you code a parameter for the plugin that will receive the options that the user sets. In the example above, this parameter is named "options".

- To set the default options, you use the $.extend method, which merges the properties in its first parameter, an object literal, with the properties in its second parameter, which is the object literal that is passed to the plugin by the calling statement. This object literal is the one that contains the user's options.

Figure 17-16   The Highlight Menu plugin with options

Perspective

Now that you've completed this chapter, you should understand why jQuery, jQuery UI, and jQuery plugins are commonly used for JavaScript applications. You should also be able to start using these libraries and plugins for simple applications of your own. And you should even be able to create your own jQuery plugins.

Of course, there's a lot more that a professional web developer needs to learn about jQuery. For that, we recommend *Murach's jQuery*, which is the perfect companion to this book. It not only shows how to use all of the jQuery selectors, methods, and event methods, but also how to use all of the jQuery UI widgets, interactions, and effects. Beyond that, it shows you how to use jQuery for Ajax calls with JSON data, how to use the APIs for Flickr and Google Maps, and how to use the HTML5 APIs for Geolocation and Web Workers.

Terms

jQuery	widget
CDN (Content Delivery Network)	jQuery plugin
jQuery selector	implicit iteration
jQuery method	API (Application Programming
jQuery event method	Interface)
jQuery UI (User Interface)	

Summary

- *jQuery* is a JavaScript library that makes JavaScript programming easier. You can access jQuery through a *Content Delivery Network* (*CDN*) or a downloaded file.

- When you code statements that use jQuery, you use *selectors* that are like those for CSS. You also use jQuery *methods* and *event methods*.

- *jQuery UI (User Interface)* is a JavaScript library that extends the use of the jQuery library by providing higher-level features like widgets, themes, interactions, and effects. But *widgets* are the most-used feature of jQuery UI.

- A *jQuery plugin* is just jQuery code that does one web task or a set of related web tasks. A plugin makes use of the jQuery library, and most plugins can be used with limited knowledge of JavaScript and jQuery.

- jQuery provides an *API* that lets you create your own plugins. Since the jQuery library uses the module pattern, you can create a plugin by augmenting the jQuery object. To do that, you use the techniques you learned in chapter 15.

- A custom plugin should follow the naming conventions for plugin files as well as the API standards for plugins.

Exercise 17-1   Enhance the jQuery FAQs application

In this exercise, you'll enhance the jQuery FAQs application that's in figure 17-5.

1. Use your text editor or IDE to open the files in this folder:
   `c:\jquery\exercises\ch17\faqs\`

2. Test this application to refresh your memory about how it works. Note that none of the panels are open when the page is loaded and that all of the panels can be opened at the same time.

3. Enhance this application so the first panel is open when the page loads.

4. Enhance this application so only one panel can be open at the same time.

Exercise 17-2   Modify the jQuery UI accordion

In this exercise, you'll enhance the way the jQuery UI accordion in figure 17-10 works.

1. Use your text editor or IDE to open the files in this folder:
   `c:\jquery\exercises\ch17\accordion\`

2. Test this application to see how it works. Note that none of the panels are open when the page is loaded and only one panel can be opened at a time.

3. Modify the options for the accordion so the first panel is open when the page is loaded and so the mouseover event triggers the opening and closing of the panels.

Exercise 17-3   Use the Highlight Menu plugin

In this exercise, you'll work with the Highlight Menu plugin that's in figure 17-15.

1. Use your text editor or IDE to open the files in this folder:
   `c:\jquery\exercises\ch17\highlight_plugin_options\`

2. In the CSS file, review the rule sets for the four CSS classes.

3. Test this application to see how it works. Note that this plugin changes the formatting of a menu item whenever the mouse hovers over it, but the item is restored to the original formatting when the mouse moves out of it.

4. Modify the call to this plugin so the formatting when the mouse moves over an item is modified by the formatting in the mouseover_changes class in the CSS file. Then, test the application.

5. Modify the call to this plugin so it uses the default CSS class to provide formatting for an item after the mouse moves out of the item. Then, test the application.

6. Modify the call to this plugin so the formatting when the mouse moves out of the item is modified by the formatting in the mouseout_changes class in the CSS file. Then, test the application.

Exercise 17-4   Create a Reveal plugin

In this exercise, you'll create a plugin named Reveal. This plugin will do the work of the FAQs application. That is, it will open or close a panel on alternative clicks of a heading.

1. Use your text editor or IDE to open the files in this folder:
    `c:\jquery\exercises\ch17\reveal\`

2. In the jquery.reveal.js file, you can see the standard plugin structure with the method name set to reveal. In the faqs.js file, you can see the jQuery for the FAQs application.

3. Test this application and see that it works because it's using the faqs.js file. But for this exercise, the use of that file should be replaced by the use of the Reveal plugin.

4. Copy the code for the click event handler of the faqs h2 elements into the each method of the reveal file. Then, change the selector for the faqs h2 elements to the this keyword so this plugin will work with any elements.

5. In the HTML file, delete the script element that adds the faqs.js file. Also, note that this HTML file already contains a script element for the Reveal plugin.

6. Add a statement to the ready event method in the last script element that calls the Reveal plugin. Then, test this application. It should show and hide the answers of the FAQs application.

7. Add another statement to the ready event method that sets the focus to the first <a> element of this application.

8. Note that this Reveal plugin can be used for any application that works like this. The user just has to change the selection that's used.

Appendix A

How to set up your computer for this book

This appendix shows how to install the software that we recommend for editing and testing the web pages and applications for this book. That includes Aptana Studio 3 as the text editor for both Windows and Mac OS users, plus the Chrome and Firefox browsers for both Windows and Mac OS users. This appendix also shows you how to download and install the source code for this book.

As you read these descriptions, please remember that most websites are continually upgraded. As a result, some of the procedures in this appendix may have changed since this book was published. Nevertheless, these procedures should still be good guides to installing the software.

How to install Aptana Studio 3

If you're already comfortable with a text editor that works for editing HTML, CSS, and JavaScript, you can continue using it. But otherwise, we recommend that you use Aptana Studio 3. It is a free editor that offers many features, it runs on both Windows and Mac OS systems, and chapter 1 presents a quick tutorial on it that will get you started right.

On a Windows system

Figure A-1 shows how to download and install Aptana Studio 3 on a Windows system.

On a Mac OS system

Figure A-1 also shows how to download and install Aptana Studio 3 on a Mac OS system.

The website address for downloading Aptana Studio 3
<u>http://www.aptana.com/products/studio3/download</u>

How to install Aptana Studio 3 on a Windows system

1. Go to the website address above.
2. Click on the Download Aptana Studio 3 button near the bottom of the page.
3. If a dialog box is displayed asking if you want to run or save the exe file, click on the Save button.
4. If a Save As dialog box is displayed, identify the location where you want the exe file saved.
5. When the Download finishes, use Windows Explorer to find the exe file, and double-click on it to start it.
6. As you step through the wizard that follows, you can accept all of the default settings that are offered.
7. After Aptana Studio 3 is installed, start it. Then, if you don't have a Git application installed on your system, Aptana will ask you if you want it to install a Portable Git application. Accept that option because Aptana won't run without it.

How to install Aptana Studio 3 on a Mac OS X system

1. Go to the website address above.
2. Click on the Customize Your Download button, and select Mac OS X.
3. Click on the Download Aptana Studio 3 button, and click on the Save File button in the resulting dialog box.
4. When the Download finishes, double-click on the dmg file in the Downloads folder to display the Aptana Studio 3 window.
5. Double-click the Aptana Studio 3 Installer folder to start the installation.
6. When the installation is complete, start Aptana Studio 3. Then, if you don't have a Git application installed on your system, Aptana will ask you if you want it to install a Portable Git application. Accept that option because Aptana won't run without it.

Description

- Aptana runs on Windows, Mac, and Linux systems.
- Git is a source code management tool that Aptana requires. If necessary, Aptana will install it for you when you start Aptana for the first time.
- Chapter 1 of this book presents a tutorial that will get you off to a fast start with Aptana.

Figure A-1   How to install Aptana Studio 3 as your text editor

How to install Chrome and Firefox

When you develop JavaScript applications, you need to test them on all of the browsers that the users of the application are likely to use. For a commercial application, that usually includes Chrome, Internet Explorer, Firefox, Safari, and Opera. Then, if an application doesn't work on one of those browsers, you need to debug it.

As you do the exercises and work with the applications in this book, though, you can test your applications on just two browsers. Windows users should use Internet Explorer plus Chrome, and Mac OS users should use Safari and Chrome. Then, if you need to debug an application, you can use the Chrome's developer tools as described in chapter 6.

The first procedure in figure A-2 is for downloading and installing Chrome. As you respond to the dialog boxes for the installer, we recommend that you make Chrome your default browser. Then, you can follow the second procedure in this figure to download and install Firefox so you can use it for any additional testing you want to do. If you want to install Opera or Safari, you can use a similar procedure.

The website address for downloading Chrome

`https://www.google.com/intl/en-US/chrome/browser/`

How to install Chrome

1. Go to the website address above.
2. Click on the Download Chrome button.
3. Review the Google Chrome Terms of Service that are displayed. Then, indicate if you want Chrome to be your default browser and if you want to automatically send usage statistics and crash reports to Google.
4. Click the Accept and Install button.
5. If a dialog box is displayed with a security warning, click the Run button.
6. If you're asked if you want to allow the program to make changes to your computer, click the Yes button.
7. The installer is downloaded and Chrome is installed and started.
8. When the Welcome to Chrome dialog box is displayed asking you to set the default browser, click the Next button and then select a browser.
9. When the Set up Chrome tab is displayed, you can log in using your email address and password so your bookmarks, history, and settings are updated on all the devices where you use Chrome. Or, you can click the "Skip for now" link to skip this step.
10. A tab is displayed with the Google home page.

The website address for downloading Firefox

`http://www.mozilla.com`

How to install Firefox

1. Go to the website address above.
2. Click on the Download Firefox - Free button.
3. Save the exe file to your C drive.
4. Run the exe file and respond to the resulting dialog boxes.

Description

- Because Chrome is the most popular browser today, we suggest that you test all of the exercises that you do for this book in this browser.
- If you have a Windows system, Internet Explorer will already be on it and you should test with it as well.
- If you have a Mac, Safari will already be on it and you should test with it too. You won't be able to install Internet Explorer because it doesn't run on Macs.
- Because Firefox, Safari, and Opera are also popular browsers, you may want to install them too. To install Safari and Opera, you can use a procedure similar to the one above for installing Firefox.

Figure A-2   How to install Chrome and Firefox

How to install and use the source code for this book

The next two figures show how to install and use the source code for this book. One figure is for Windows users, the other for Mac OS users.

For Windows users

Figure A-3 shows how to install the source code for this book on a Windows system. This includes the source code for the applications in this book, the starting files for the exercises, and the solutions for the exercises.

When you finish this procedure, the book applications, exercises, and solutions will be in the three folders that are in the first group in this figure, but the exercises will also be in the next folder that's shown. So, when you do the exercises, you use the subfolders and files in this folder:

    c:\javascript\exercises

but you have backup copies of these subfolders and files in this folder:

    c:\murach\javascript\exercises

That way, you can restore the files for an exercise to their original state by copying the files from the second folder to the first.

As you do the exercises, you may want to copy code from a book application into a file that you're working with. That's easy to do because the applications are in this folder:

    c:\murach\javascript\book_apps

When you finish an exercise, you may want to compare your solution to ours, which you'll find in this folder:

    c:\murach\javascript\solutions

You may also want to look at a solution when you're having trouble with an exercise. That will help you get past the problem you're having so you can continue to make progress. Either way, the solutions are an important part of the learning process.

The Murach website

www.murach.com

The Windows folders for the applications, exercises, and solutions

```
c:\murach\javascript\book_apps
c:\murach\javascript\exercises
c:\murach\javascript\solutions
```

The Windows folder for doing the exercises

```
c:\javascript\exercises
```

How to download and install the source code on a Windows system

1. Go to www.murach.com, and go to the page for *Murach's JavaScript*.

2. Scroll down the page until you see the "FREE downloads" tab and then click on it. Then, click on the DOWNLOAD NOW button for the exe file for Windows. This will download a setup file named 2jst_allfiles.exe onto your hard drive.

3. Use Windows Explorer to find the exe file on your hard drive. Then, double-click this file. This installs the source code for the book applications, exercises, and solutions into the folders shown above. After it does this install, the exe file copies the exercises folder to c:\javascript so you have two copies of the exercises.

How to restore an exercise file

*   Copy it from its subfolder in
    ```
    c:\murach\javascript\exercises
    ```
    to the corresponding subfolder in
    ```
    c:\javascript\exercises
    ```

Description

*   The exe file that you download stores the exercises in two different folders. That way, you can do the exercises using the files that are stored in one folder, but you have a backup copy in case you want to restore the starting files for an exercise.

*   As you do the exercises that are at the ends of the chapters, you may want to copy code from a book application into the file you're working on. That's easy to do because all of the applications are available in the book_apps folder.

*   In the solutions folder, you can view the solutions for the exercises.

Figure A-3   How to install the source code for this book on a Windows system

For Mac OS users

Figure A-4 shows how to install the source code for this book on a Mac OS system. This includes the source code for the applications in this book, the starting files for the exercises, and the solutions for the exercises.

When you finish this procedure, the book applications, exercises, and solutions will be in the three folders that are listed in this figure. Then, before you start the exercises, you should copy the exercises folder from:

```
documents\murach\javascript
```

to

```
documents\javascript
```

That way, you can restore the files for an exercise to their original state by copying the files from the first folder to the second.

As you do the exercises, you may want to copy code from a book application into a file that you're working with. That's easy to do because the applications are in this folder:

```
documents\murach\javascript\book_apps
```

When you finish an exercise, you may want to compare your solution to ours, which you'll find in this folder:

```
documents\murach\javascript\solutions
```

You may also want to look at a solution when you're having trouble with an exercise. That will help you get past the problem you're having so you can continue to make progress. Either way, the solutions are an important part of the learning process.

The Murach website

www.murach.com

The Mac OS folders for the book applications and exercises

```
documents\murach\javascript\book_apps
documents\murach\javascript\exercises
documents\murach\javascript\solutions
```

The Mac OS folder for doing the exercises

```
documents\javascript\exercises
```

How to download and install the source code on a Mac OS system

1. Go to www.murach.com, and go to the page for *Murach's JavaScript*.

2. Scroll down the page until you see the "FREE downloads" tab and then click on it. Then, click on the DOWNLOAD NOW button for the zip file for any system. This will download a setup file named 2jst_allfiles.zip onto your hard drive.

3. Move this file into the Documents folder of your home folder.

4. Use Finder to go to your Documents folder.

5. Double-click the 2jst_allfiles.zip file to extract the folders for the book applications, exercises, and solutions. This will create a folder named javascript in your documents folder that will contain the book_apps, exercises, and solutions folders.

6. Create two copies of the exercises folder by copying the exercises folder from
   ```
   documents\murach\javascript
   ```
   to
   ```
   documents\javascript
   ```

How to restore an exercise file

- Copy it from its subfolder in
  ```
  documents\murach\javascript\exercises
  ```
  to the corresponding subfolder in
  ```
  documents\javascript\exercises
  ```

Description

- This procedure stores the exercises in two different folders. That way, you do the exercises using the files that are in one folder, but you also have a backup copy.

- If you want to copy code from a book application into an exercise file that you're working on, you can find all of the applications in the book_apps folder.

- In the solutions folder, you can view the solutions for the exercises at the end of each chapter.

Figure A-4   How to install the source code for this book on a Mac OS system

Appendix B

The ECMAScript5 methods in the shim.js and sham.js files

In chapter 1, you are introduced to the ECMAScript5 specification and to the shim.js and sham.js files for ensuring cross-browser compatibility. Then, throughout this book, you learn about other ECMAScript5 features whenever they are relevant.

Now, this appendix provides a single reference for the methods of the ECMAScript5 specification. Here, you can see what methods are in this specification, which of the methods are in the shim.js and sham.js files, and where you can get more information about them.

The ECMAScript5 methods

Figure B-1 presents two tables that list the EMCAScript5 methods that are in the shim.js and sham.js files. These tables also say whether each method is an instance method or a static method.

An *instance* method is one that is on the object type's prototype. This means that you have to create an instance of the object type before you can use the method, like this:

```
var arr = [3,4,2,1];
arr.sort();
```

By contrast, a *static* method is on the object type itself. This means that to use it you code the object type, followed by the dot operator, followed by the method name, like this:

```
var isArr = Array.isArray(arr);
```

This figure also provides three web addresses. The first one is to a page that hosts the shim.js and sham.js files. At this site, you can download both files in a zip file, and you can review the documentation that describes how well each method is supported. The second and third web addresses are for the CDN that hosts the shim.js and sham.js files.

The shim.js file

The first table in this figure lists the methods that are in the shim.js file. Methods in this file can be safely used with older browsers. However, there are some caveats to that. For example, the bind method of the Function object will work correctly most of the time, but there are some edge cases where it might behave unexpectedly. And the replace method of the String object might have problems with certain versions of Firefox. In cases like these, you should consult the documentation at the first URL in this figure.

The sham.js file

The second table in this figure lists the methods that are in the sham.js file. There are two important things to know about this file. First, it depends on the shim.js file, so you need to include that file in your application before you include the sham.js file.

Second, just because something is listed in the sham.js file doesn't mean you can't use it. For example, the Object.create method is in the sham.js file, but it will work just fine if you only use the first parameter that sets the prototype object. It's the second parameter that sets the object's properties that might fail, and even then it won't always fail.

So here again, you should consult the documentation at the first URL in this figure if you need to find out which methods will work some of the time and under which conditions, and which methods will always fail in browsers that don't support ECMAScript5.

The website address for the shim.js and sham.js documentation

https://github.com/es-shims/es5-shim

The URLs for the shim.js and sham.js files

https://cdnjs.cloudflare.com/ajax/libs/es5-shim/4.0.5/es5-shim.min.js
https://cdnjs.cloudflare.com/ajax/libs/es5-shim/4.0.5/es5-sham.min.js

The methods in the shim.js file

Method	Type
Array.prototype.every	Instance
Array.prototype.filter	Instance
Array.prototype.forEach	Instance
Array.prototype.indexOf	Instance
Array.prototype.lastIndexOf	Instance
Array.prototype.some	Instance
Array.prototype.reduce	Instance
Array.prototype.reduceRight	Instance
Array.isArray	Static
Date.now	Static
Date.prototype.toJSON	Instance
Function.prototype.bind	Instance
Number.prototype.toFixed	Instance
Object.keys	Static
String.prototype.split	Instance
String.prototype.trim	Instance
String.prototype.replace	Instance
Date.parse	Static
Date.prototype.toISOString	Instance

The methods in the sham.js file

Method	Type
Object.create	Static
Object.getPrototypeOf	Static
Object.getOwnPropertyNames	Static
Object.isSealed	Static
Object.isFrozen	Static
Object.isExtensible	Static
Object.getOwnPropertyDescriptor	Static
Object.defineProperty	Static
Object.defineProperties	Static
Object.seal	Static
Object.freeze	Static
Object.preventExtensions	Static

Figure B-1   The ECMAScript5 methods

Index